lonely planet

Louisiana
& the Deep South

Tom Downs
Kate Hoffman
Virginie Boone
Dani Valent
Gary Bridgman

LONELY PLANET PUBLICATIONS
Melbourne • Oakland • London • Paris

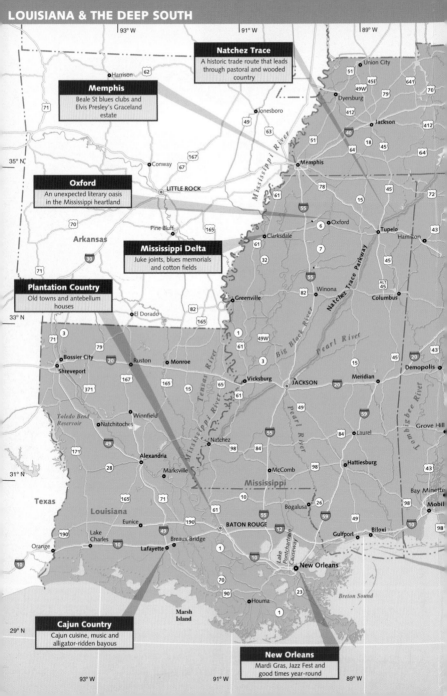

LOUISIANA & THE DEEP SOUTH

Natchez Trace
A historic trade route that leads through pastoral and wooded country

Memphis
Beale St blues clubs and Elvis Presley's Graceland estate

Oxford
An unexpected literary oasis in the Mississippi heartland

Mississippi Delta
Juke joints, blues memorials and cotton fields

Plantation Country
Old towns and antebellum houses

Cajun Country
Cajun cuisine, music and alligator-ridden bayous

New Orleans
Mardi Gras, Jazz Fest and good times year-round

ALABAMA 404

TENNESSEE 472

GLOSSARY 523

INDEX 528

MAP LEGEND 536

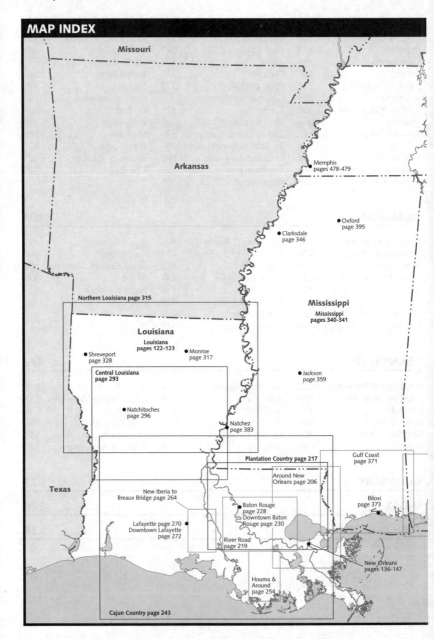

MAP INDEX

Missouri

Arkansas

● Memphis
pages 478-479

● Oxford
page 395

● Clarksdale
page 346

Mississippi

Mississippi
pages 340-341

Northern Louisiana page 315

Louisiana

Louisiana
pages 122-123

● Shreveport
page 328

● Monroe
page 317

Central Louisiana
page 293

● Jackson
page 359

● Natchitoches
page 296

● Natchez
page 383

Plantation Country page 217

Gulf Coast
page 371

Around New
Orleans page 206

Texas

New Iberia to
Breaux Bridge page 264

Biloxi
page 373

● Baton Rouge
page 228
Downtown Baton
Rouge page 230

Lafayette page 270 ●
Downtown Lafayette
page 272

River Road
page 219

New Orleans
pages 136-147

Houma &
Around
page 254

Cajun Country page 243

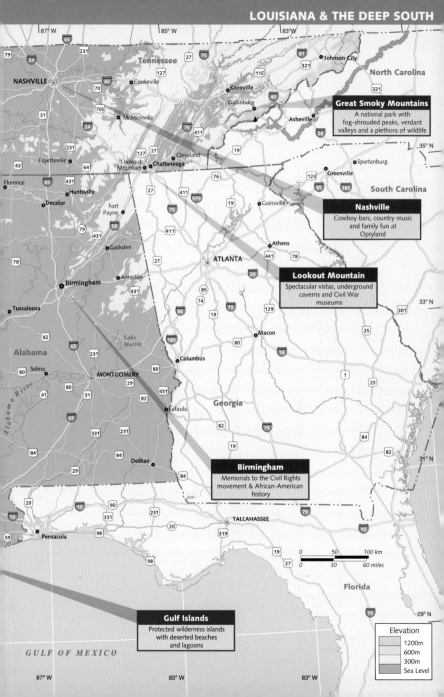

Great Smoky Mountains
A national park with fog-shrouded peaks, verdant valleys and a plethora of wildlife

Nashville
Cowboy bars, country music and family fun at Opryland

Lookout Mountain
Spectacular vistas, underground caverns and Civil War museums

Birmingham
Memorials to the Civil Rights movement & African-American history

Gulf Islands
Protected wilderness islands with deserted beaches and lagoons

Tennessee

North Carolina

Johnson City

NASHVILLE
Cookeville
Knoxville
Gatlinburg
Asheville
McMinnville

Fayetteville
Cleveland
Chattanooga
Lookout Mountain
Spartanburg
Greenville

Florence
Huntsville
Decatur
Fort Payne
Gainsville
South Carolina

Gadsden
ATLANTA
Athens

Tuscaloosa
Birmingham
Anniston

Alabama
Lake Martin
Macon

Selma
MONTGOMERY
Columbus

Georgia
Eufaula

Dothan

Pensacola
TALLAHASSEE

Florida

GULF OF MEXICO

0   50   100 km
0   30   60 miles

Elevation
1200m
600m
300m
Sea Level

87° W
85° W
83° W

35° N
33° N
31° N
29° N

Alabama River

Louisiana & the Deep South
1st edition – March 2001

Published by
Lonely Planet Publications Pty Ltd   ABN 36 005 607 983
90 Maribyrnong St, Footscray, Victoria 3011, Australia

Lonely Planet Offices
Australia Locked Bag 1, Footscray, Victoria 3011
USA 150 Linden St, Oakland, CA 94607
UK 10a Spring Place, London NW5 3BH
France 1 rue du Dahomey, 75011 Paris

Photographs
Many of the images in this guide are available for licensing from
Lonely Planet Images.
W www.lonelyplanetimages.com

Historic photos courtesy of Library of Congress

Front cover photograph
Bayou, Louisiana (Olivier Cirendini)

Title page photographs
Courtesy of the Library of Congress
Louisiana (Dorothea Lange)
Mississippi (Marion Post Wolcott)
Alabama (Ben Shahn)
Tennessee (Marion Post Wolcott)

ISBN 1 86450 216 9

text & maps © Lonely Planet Publications Pty Ltd 2001
photos © photographers as indicated 2001

Printed by The Bookmaker International Ltd
Printed in China

Contents

Gary Bridgman

Although he is technically an army brat who simultaneously learned English and Turkish as a toddler in Izmir, Gary has lived in the South almost all of his life, including Virginia, Arkansas and Mississippi, but mostly Memphis, Tennessee. His magazine articles have appeared in *Utne Reader, Gadfly,* and *Nightclub & Bar Magazine,* and he served as editor of the trucking magazine *Southern Motor Cargo.* He has worked as a limousine driver, a bartender, a tour guide at the FedEx SuperHub and a headwaiter in a three-star restaurant. In 1998, during a stint as a swamp guide for western Tennessee's Wolf River Conservancy, he and a friend were the first people on record to travel (hiking and canoeing) the entire length of that river. With the exception of some whiskey-soaked road trips in his forgotten (until now) fraternity-boy phase, Gary didn't travel to any Alabama destinations before working on this book. He was pleasantly surprised by his adventures in the 'Heart of Dixie.' He and his wife, Melissa, live in Rossville, Tennessee, near Memphis.

FROM THE AUTHORS

Tom Downs I'd like to dedicate my portion of this book to Fawn, for her support and understanding.

Thanks to all my pals in the South, who provided essential information and made working down there such a joy: Bob Girault, Robert Florence, Helene Florence (for the *pain perdu),* Matt Goldstein of Jazz Fest and Bev Gianna of the NOTCB. Thanks also to Kate Hoffman, Dani Valent, Gary Bridgman and Virginie Boone – pleasure working with y'all. And, of course, thanks to editors China Williams and Rebecca Northen for making us look good.

Kate Hoffman First and foremost, I want to thank my partner Tim Kingston, who kept me sane throughout this project, reminding me gently when I had misplaced my sense of humor. Thanks also to Mariah Bear, Brigitte Barta, and the senior editors at Lonely Planet, who covered for me while I was lost on Louisiana's backroads. Tom Downs was a helluva coach and friend throughout, too. Editors China Williams and Rebecca Northen did a great job of teasing my text and maps into shape, and cartographer Guphy made huge improvements to the maps. I'd also like to acknowledge John and Mike and Friends in Lafayette for telling me all about the music and food scene there while plying me with Miller beer, and the folks at Juban's in Baton Rouge, who set me straight on that city's restaurant scene.

Virginie Boone Thanks to Lawrence West and crew at Jim's Westside Bar-b-q in Alexandria; Betty Metoyer, one of the Metoyer descendants, at Melrose Plantation; Kent Gresham, owner-chef of The Landing in Natchitoches; and the Winn Ranger Office.

Dani Valent Thanks to all the Mississippi and Tennessee CVB and tourism folk, Tad Pierson for the pink umbrella, the Hopson gang and Nan from Clarksdale, Tommy Polk for having his birthday party while I was in Nashville, Gary Bridgman for hospitality and a cheap rental car, and Josh Haynes for emergency takeout and a ride to Memphis. Thanks also to Matt Pirrie, Braden King, Brigitte Barta, John T Edge and Tom Downs.

Gary Bridgman I would like to thank my wife, Melissa, for her encouragement and support, and for marrying me last summer. I also owe big ones to John T Edge, Dani Valent, Susan Speir, Vickie Ashford, Patty Tucker, Heather Green, Albert Robinson, some guy at the Blue Monkey with that … that hat, and Georgia Turner and Hank MacCann for their salvations on the road. Thanks also go to Joey and Donna Benton for help in the early stages and to Diane Marshall.

This Book

The first version of this book was researched and written by Kap Stann, Diane Marshall and John T Edge. For this edition, Tom Downs served as coordinating author. He updated the introductory chapters and wrote the New Orleans chapter, Kate Hoffman covered Plantation Country and Cajun Country, Virginie Boone handled Central Louisiana and Northern Louisiana, Dani Valent wrote Mississippi and Tennessee, and Gary Bridgman covered Alabama.

FROM THE PUBLISHER

Louisiana & the Deep South was produced in Lonely Planet's Oakland office by a number of Moon Pie and meat-and-three lovers. China Williams, a native Southerner, and Rebecca Northen, a former Memphian, edited the book with senior editor Michele Posner's expert advice. Senior editor Brigitte Barta oversaw the project in its beginning stages. Paul Sheridan, Vivek Waglé (who also jumped in to help at layout), Erin Corrigan, Rachel Bernstein, China and Rebecca, and Elaine Merrill proofed the book, and super-indexer Ken DellaPenta did his thing.

Lead cartographer and country & western expert Guphy and cartographer Connie Lock created the maps, with mapping wisdom provided by senior cartographer Monica Lepe. Ed Turley, Kat Smith, Dion Good, Patrick Phelan, Tessa Rottiers, Matthew DeMartini and Chris Howard also lended their cartographic skills. All was done so under the guidance of Alex Guilbert.

Stellar designer Margaret Livingston handled layout, and Jenn Steffey designed the cover and the sumptuous color pages. Illustrations were coordinated by Beca Lafore and drawn by Justin Marler, Hannah Reineck (lover of Elvis, though not one of Elvis' lovers as far as we know), Beca, Mark Butler, Hugh D'Andrade, Shelley Firth, Hayden Foell, Rini Keagy, Lisa Summers, Jim Swanson and Wendy Yanagihara. Efforts were overseen by design manager Susan Rimerman.

Special thanks to authors Tom Downs and Kate Hoffman, who, since they also work in-house, got tapped for extra information along the way.

THANKS

This book was improved by the letters and helpful advice of readers Emma Chippendale and Mike & Susan Lacy.

Foreword

ABOUT LONELY PLANET GUIDEBOOKS

The story begins with a classic travel adventure: Tony and Maureen Wheeler's 1972 journey across Europe and Asia to Australia. Useful information about the overland trail did not exist at that time, so Tony and Maureen published the first Lonely Planet guidebook to meet a growing need.

From a kitchen table, then from a tiny office in Melbourne (Australia), Lonely Planet has become the largest independent travel publisher in the world, an international company with offices in Melbourne, Oakland (USA), London (UK) and Paris (France).

Today Lonely Planet guidebooks cover the globe. There is an ever-growing list of books, and there's information in a variety of forms and media. Some things haven't changed. The main aim is still to help make it possible for adventurous travelers to get out there – to explore and better understand the world.

At Lonely Planet we believe travelers can make a positive contribution to the countries they visit – if they respect their host communities and spend their money wisely. Since 1986 a percentage of the income from each book has been donated to aid projects and human-rights campaigns.

Updates Lonely Planet thoroughly updates each guidebook as often as possible. This usually means there are around two years between editions, although for more unusual or more stable destinations the gap can be longer. Check the imprint page (following the color map at the beginning of the book) for publication dates.

Between editions, up-to-date information is available in two free newsletters – the paper *Planet Talk* and email *Comet* (to subscribe, contact any Lonely Planet office) – and on our website at www.lonelyplanet.com. The *Upgrades* section of the website covers a number of important and volatile destinations and is regularly updated by Lonely Planet authors. *Scoop* covers news and current affairs relevant to travelers. And, lastly, the *Thorn Tree* bulletin board and *Postcards* section of the site carry unverified, but fascinating, reports from travelers.

Correspondence The process of creating new editions begins with the letters, postcards and emails received from travelers. This correspondence often includes suggestions, criticisms and comments about the current editions. Interesting excerpts are immediately passed on via newsletters and the website, and everything goes to our authors to be verified when they're researching on the road. We're keen to get more feedback from organizations or individuals who represent communities visited by travelers.

Lonely Planet gathers information for everyone who's curious about the planet – and especially for those who explore it firsthand. Through guidebooks, phrasebooks, activity guides, maps, literature, newsletters, image library, TV series and website, we act as an information exchange for a worldwide community of travelers.

Research Authors aim to gather sufficient practical information to enable travelers to make informed choices and to make the mechanics of a journey run smoothly. They also research historical and cultural background to help enrich the travel experience and allow travelers to understand and respond appropriately to cultural and environmental issues.

Authors don't stay in every hotel because that would mean spending a couple of months in each medium-size city and, no, they don't eat at every restaurant because that would mean stretching belts beyond capacity. They do visit hotels and restaurants to check standards and prices, but feedback based on readers' direct experiences can be very helpful.

Many of our authors work undercover; others aren't so secretive. None of them accept freebies in exchange for positive write-ups. And none of our guidebooks contain any advertising.

Production Authors submit their raw manuscripts and maps to offices in Australia, the USA, the UK or France. Editors and cartographers – all experienced travelers themselves – then begin the process of assembling the pieces. When the book finally hits the shops, some things are already out of date, we start getting feedback from readers and the process begins again....

WARNING & REQUEST

Things change – prices go up, schedules change, good places go bad and bad places go bankrupt – nothing stays the same. So, if you find things better or worse, recently opened or long since closed, please tell us and help make the next edition even more accurate and useful. We genuinely value all the feedback we receive. A well-traveled team reads and acknowledges every letter, postcard and email and ensures that every morsel of information finds its way to the appropriate authors, editors and cartographers for verification.

Everyone who writes to us will find their name listed in the next edition of the appropriate guidebook. They will also receive the latest issue of *Planet Talk*, our quarterly printed newsletter, or *Comet*, our monthly email newsletter. Subscriptions to both newsletters are free. The very best contributions will be rewarded with a free guidebook.

We may edit, reproduce and incorporate your comments in all Lonely Planet products, such as guidebooks, Web sites and digital products, so let us know if you don't want your comments reproduced or your name acknowledged.

Send all correspondence to the Lonely Planet office closest to you:

Australia: Locked Bag 1, Footscray, Victoria 3011
USA: 150 Linden St, Oakland, CA 94607
UK: 10a Spring Place, London NW5 3BH
France: 1 rue du Dahomey, 75011 Paris

Or email us at: talk2us@lonelyplanet.com.au

For news, views and updates, see our Web site: www.lonelyplanet.com

HOW TO USE A LONELY PLANET GUIDEBOOK

The best way to use a Lonely Planet guidebook is any way you choose. At Lonely Planet, we believe the most memorable travel experiences are often those that are unexpected, and the finest discoveries are those you make yourself. Guidebooks are not intended to be used as if they provided a detailed set of infallible instructions!

Contents All Lonely Planet guidebooks follow the same format. The Facts about the Country chapters or sections give background information ranging from history to weather. Facts for the Visitor gives practical information on issues like visas and health. Getting There & Away gives a brief starting point for researching travel to and from the destination. Getting Around gives an overview of the transport options available when you arrive.

The peculiar demands of each destination determine how subsequent chapters are broken up, but some things remain constant. We always start with background, then proceed to sights, places to stay, places to eat, entertainment, getting there and away, and getting around information – in that order.

Heading Hierarchy Lonely Planet headings are used in a strict hierarchical structure that can be visualized as a set of Russian dolls. Each heading (and its following text) is encompassed by any preceding heading that is higher on the hierarchical ladder.

Entry Points We do not assume guidebooks will be read from beginning to end, but that people will dip into them. The traditional entry points are the list of contents and the index. In addition, however, some books have a complete list of maps and an index map illustrating map coverage.

There may also be a color map that shows highlights. These highlights are dealt with in greater detail later in the book, along with planning questions and suggested itineraries. Each chapter covering a geographical region usually begins with a locator map and another list of highlights. Once you find something of interest in a list of highlights, turn to the index.

Maps Maps play a crucial role in Lonely Planet guidebooks and include a huge amount of information. A legend is printed on the back page. We seek to have complete consistency between maps and text, and to have every important place in the text captured on a map. Map key numbers usually start in the top left corner.

Although inclusion in a guidebook usually implies a recommendation, we cannot list every good place. Exclusion does not necessarily imply criticism. In fact, there are a number of reasons why we might exclude a place – sometimes it is simply inappropriate to encourage an influx of travelers.

Introduction

In North America, where it's business and progress as usual, the Deep South is that unexpected snarl of handkerchiefs hidden up a magician's sleeve. It's the doomed cat that clawed out of the bag. It's a tangled dream, an exotic nightmare, a cardiac citizen's arrest induced by a sizzling saucepan and an invigorating jolt of hot sauce.

In North America, that industrious, full-steam-ahead continent, the Deep South is where steam never seems to go anywhere. It hangs over everything, impervious to movement. It purifies and stupefies and mesmerizes. It diffuses light, creating torpid, ethereal days and lurid sunset evenings. It carries the night's strange and glorious sounds.

It transmits the guttural cries of a human voice delivering a religious sermon, a Cajun wail, or the Delta blues. It upholds the sonorous and muted timbres of a jazz trumpet, the sliding blue notes of a bottle-neck guitar, the shuffled rhythms of brushes on a snare drum, and oily, inebriated notes on an old, dented trombone that no longer shines like brass. Through the second-line parades, jazz funerals, Mississippi juke joints, Cajun dance halls, Nashville hootenannies and Sunday church services wends America's great artery, the Mississippi River, mainlining so much melted snow from Minnesota to the Gulf of Mexico and pumping so much lively music back upstream. The pulsing heart at the river's end, the jammed little juke joint bursting with vibrant sound – that's the Deep South.

It's a big-hearted place where folks seem genuinely glad to see you. Food is piled high on plates, the beer is cold, and an elderly

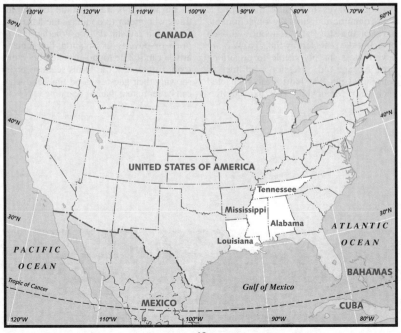

13

gent inquires, in a curious French accent, if you wouldn't mind his dancing with your girl. Life seems simplified, and time seems to have slowed down. Down here, time chooses the back roads over the interstate.

Indeed, the region is a little at odds with time. A swamp is a trip into the primordial past. In fact, a swamp is probably about as *different* a place a modern city-dweller can ever hope to visit. The king of the swamp – the toothy *Alligator mississippiensis* – appears to have crawled out of the Jurassic age. It's a large, grotesque creature with a stomach engineered to digest pretty much anything. If one appears genuinely glad to see you, don't wait to find out what's for dinner. Later, alligator!

Along an ancient Native American footpath, the Natchez Trace is frozen in a different era. The old road's tony Greek Revival homes hearken to the Old South, when a charmed way of life for a privileged few whites was built on the backs of African-American slaves. To be sure, this period is over-romanticized, and the objectionable parts of the story are frequently glossed over, but the scars left by the Civil War are nevertheless sharply visible to discerning eyes. An age-old obsession continues as countless Civil War battles are reenacted each year. Meanwhile, the many battles fought in the name of Civil Rights are solemnly remembered as well. In the modern South, blacks and whites have struck a somewhat discordant harmony – like it or not, it's as distinct a part of the American grain as a raw country blues or the flavor of bourbon whiskey.

But make no mistake, this is the 21st century, and culture is now more a commodity than ever before. Shrewd operators continue to demonstrate a willingness to monkey with anything for the tourist dollar. It certainly makes things easier on a visitor when culture is neatly packaged into festivals and historic districts. For many people, a jazz festival, a blues festival, a crawfish festival, a Cajun or zydeco festival, a gospel jubilee, or a country music songwriters festival might be the best way to cut to the quick and get exactly what they came for. New Orleans' French Quarter, Memphis' Beale St, Nashville's Opryland, and Natchez' antebellum homes all offer 80%-proof distillations of what most tourists want, and all of these events and sights are worth the trip. But for those who prefer to do things the hard way, the region can still deliver. Whether due to pride or poverty or isolation, the genuine article can still be found at the end of a dirt road. Either way, the locals seem to enjoy showing their guests a good time, and what can be more real than a good time?

Facts about the Deep South

HISTORY

More than any other region in the US, the American South lives intimately with its unusual past. Southerners have a highly personal sense of this history that is closely connected to the land. Where a visitor might see a mound of earth, the Choctaw see remnants of an ancestral civilization. Heirs to the Lost Cause might come across a quiet river bluff and see the setting of a painful siege. Miles of cotton fields in the Mississippi Delta are more than cropland; to African-Americans they are the setting of a wrenching oppression lamented in the blues. As William Faulkner explained, 'The past is never dead. It's not even past.'

Original Peoples

The history of the Western Hemisphere begins with the stretch of land connecting Asia and Alaska. As the rising and falling waters of each successive ice age alternately submerged and exposed this land bridge, waves of immigrants from Siberia crossed over to North America. These nomadic people migrated throughout the Americas. How long ago the earliest migration occurred is a matter of scientific debate: conservative estimates place it at around 15,000 years ago, while other estimates speculate it was at least twice that long ago.

Some of the earliest evidence of human habitation has been found in northern Alabama's cave country. Crude stone tools found alongside projectile points are attributed to the oldest Paleo-Indian period, at least 11,000 years ago. During the following Archaic period (9000–1000 BC), Russell Cave (now a national park in northeastern Alabama) was inhabited. During this period, the first evidence of crop cultivation appears with the earliest settlements.

Adaptation to warmer climates marks the end of the Pleistocene era. Evidence of this transition has been found on the lower Tennessee River in shell-and-earth middens (prehistoric garbage heaps). Refuse indicates reliance on freshwater mussels, fish and game (primarily deer). Ready access to a greater variety of food sources gave early inhabitants the time for other pursuits; pottery and personal adornments such as beads and pendants first appeared. Burial techniques reveal the beginnings of mortuary practices and traditions that would grow increasingly elaborate in time.

In the Woodland period (1000 BC–900 AD), an increasingly sophisticated civilization established fully realized villages and croplands. Pottery was stylized with stamped patterns. The widespread distribution of shells from the Gulf of Mexico and ocean, and mica from the Great Lakes, reveals an extensive trade network. But most distinctive among the Woodland traditions was the first appearance of laboriously constructed earthen mounds. One of the most archaeologically rich sites from this period can be seen today in northeastern Louisiana at Poverty Point, a site so vast its full extent was not recognized until aerial observation became possible. Though mounds had become commonplace across the South by this time, mound construction reached a refined state of development in the subsequent Mississippian period.

Mississippian Civilization

The culture that developed along the lower Mississippi River around 700 AD – dubbed 'Mississippian' – spread throughout the southeast, reaching its height around 1200 AD. This Mississippian civilization represents the highest state of cultural development in the pre-Columbian southeast, or even, as some anthropologists argue, in all of aboriginal North America.

The Mississippian culture is most noted for refining mound construction and making mounds the centerpiece of village life and religious traditions. Typically, Mississippian mounds had steep-sided walls like a pyramid, but they were rectangular and the top was flattened. These flat tops were used as temple grounds for religious ceremonies and also held the houses of tribal leaders. Once a tribal leader died, his house was destroyed and he was buried under a fresh layer of soil. The new leader then built a house on top and the cycle would repeat itself.

At the Chucalissa site above the Mississippi River in Memphis, Tennessee, a cutaway trench reveals this layering technique. The cropland surrounding this 15th-century village was planted with corn, beans and squash (often referred to as the 'three sisters'), which remain staples of Southern cuisine to this day.

The 300-acre Moundville site in Alabama (south of Tuscaloosa) preserves 20 square and oval platform mounds. Decorative artifacts excavated here help to shed light on the belief system of the Mississippian inhabitants.

Mounds throughout the South are today so integrated with the landscape that they can easily be mistaken for natural features of an uncommonly geometric shape. Many examples have been preserved as historical sites, and some mounds are still considered sacred in the mythology of today's southeastern Indian nations. One such site is Nanih Waiya in eastern Mississippi, the legendary birthplace of the Choctaw Nation.

Amer-Indian Nations The decline of the Mississippian civilization accelerated after European contact in the mid-15th century. Europeans brought diseases that decimated whole tribes. Survivors were dominated by the groups that became known as the Five Civilized Tribes – the Cherokee, Choctaw, Chickasaw, Creek and Seminole – so named by Europeans for their sophisticated agriculture and political organization.

The Cherokee Nation was centered in the Appalachian Mountains, extending to northeastern Alabama's foothills and plateau. The antagonistic but culturally similar Choctaw and Chickasaw occupied the Mississippi region north into Tennessee. The Creek Confederacy stretched from around the Tombigbee River in western Alabama to the Atlantic Coast. The Semi-noles broke away from the Creek ('seminole' is Creek for 'runaway' or 'separatist') and settled in southern Alabama and Georgia along the Chattahoochee River before they were pushed farther south into Florida.

In Louisiana, the Caddo Nation predominated. Smaller groups along the Gulf of Mexico, such as the Biloxi, had coastal cultures that were distinct from inland cultures.

Over the three hundred years following European contact, the southeastern nations were conquered by Europeans with an insatiable desire for new land on which many hoped to grow cotton. The means by which Europeans acquired this land varied. Some groups were conquered by military might, among them the Natchez of the lower Mississippi River, who were vanquished after a thorough assault by the French in 1729. But most were defrauded by economic pressure. The US government's strategy (originally devised by Thomas Jefferson) was to establish trading posts among the Indians, to encourage a dependence on European goods, to allow the Indians to fall into debt and then to force them to cede lands as repayment. Treaties sealed the deal.

The Choctaw experience was typical. In 1805, the Choctaw surrendered more than four million acres in southern Mississippi to forgive a $48,000 trading debt. More treaties in 1820 and 1826 further eroded Choctaw territory until in 1830 the Treaty of Dancing Creek surrendered most of the remaining Choctaw Indian land. Greenwood LeFlore was among the handful of Indian leaders bribed by President Andrew Jackson into signing. In exchange for signing away the homeland of his kin, LeFlore was enriched with a large estate. Hundreds of such forced or fraudulent treaties appropriated Indian land throughout the southeast.

The final assault on the remaining tribes came in the 1830s. Jackson issued an ultimatum to move voluntarily to Indian Territory out west or be 'removed' by force. Of all the southeastern Indians, the Cherokee fought the most determined legal battle against removal. In 1827, they formalized their own sovereignty as the Cherokee Nation by adopting a constitution based on the US model. In 1829, the state of Georgia passed legislation annexing a large portion of Cherokee territory and declaring Cherokee law null and void. The Cherokee appealed all the way to the Supreme Court. In *Worcester* v *the State of Georgia*, Chief Justice John Marshall found these Georgia laws unconstitutional. Nonetheless, in contempt of the authority of the Supreme Court, President Jackson is reported to have said 'John Marshall has rendered his decision, now let him enforce it.' In 1838, the US Army along with local militias forced 18,000 Cherokee off their land and sent them west with little more than the clothes on their backs; 4000 Cherokee died en route.

Besides the Choctaw and Cherokee, other southeastern nations were similarly banished and forced along a route that has come to be remembered as the Trail of Tears. Survivors established communities in what is now Oklahoma, and their descendants remain there still.

Isolated Native American communities managed to remain in the southeast; some were eventually granted trust land. Today, the 6000-member Mississippi Band of the Choctaw Indians in central Mississippi and the Chitimacha of southern Louisiana's Bayou Teche have built thriving reservations on portions of their ancestral lands (thanks largely to casino dollars). Other Amer-Indian communities remain sprinkled throughout the region without trust land. Native American traditions and powwows are celebrated on reservations and at historic sites throughout the region.

Ironically, though the US government stopped only one step short of outright genocide in its attempt to rid the region of Native Americans, it readily adopted Indian names for the territories it claimed, among them Mississippi and Alabama.

European Exploration

In 1540, Spanish explorer Hernando de Soto led an army of 900 soldiers and hundreds of horses through the southeast in search of gold to rival the looting of Peru's Inca empire. His route led from the Atlantic Coast through Alabama, across northern Mississippi, through Louisiana, then down the Mississippi River and across the Gulf of Mexico back to Florida. Though he charged through the southeast on the attack, the greatest damage he wrought was affected not by brutal encounters but by exposing the Amer-Indian populations to devastating diseases.

A major battle fought in southern Alabama signaled a turning point in the expedition. Although the Indian foot soldiers were superior warriors, they were no match for the Spanish Cavalry, and after great numbers of Indian casualties, the Spanish were victorious. Yet the Spanish were convinced that these inhabitants were unlike the native peoples de Soto had encountered in Mexico and Peru.

According to historian Edward G Bourne, the Spanish became convinced that it was 'impossible to dominate such bellicose people or to subjugate men who were so free, and that because of what they had seen up until that time, they felt they could never make the Indians come under their yoke either by force or trickery, for rather than do so these people would all permit themselves to be slain.'

As de Soto stepped up his attacks, the Choctaw and Chickasaw in Mississippi were becoming more effective opponents and continued harassing raids against the Spanish. After burning several towns in a densely populated area of eastern Louisiana, de Soto fell ill and died in May 1542. His body was laid afloat down the Mississippi River. His successor led about 300 survivors down the river to the Gulf and back to Spanish Florida.

La Louisiane

It was more than a century before Europeans returned to the Mississippi River. In 1673, the team of Father Marquette and trader Joliet sailed downriver from French outposts on the Great Lakes to the lower Mississippi before heeding warnings about hostile tribes and turning back. Nine years later, René Robert Cavelier La Salle headed an expedition of 23 French and 18

Native Americans that pushed through to the Gulf of Mexico. Upon reaching the Gulf, La Salle staged a ceremony to claim the Mississippi River and all its tributaries for France, naming it *La Louisiane* in honor of reigning King Louis XIV.

La Salle was not the only European to lay claim to the region. The lower portion of the land La Salle declared Louisiana was considered by the British to be part of a vaguely mapped 1629 Carolina Grant that essentially claimed everything west of Charleston as British territory. Furthermore, Spanish outposts scattered from Florida to Texas established an equally broad Spanish claim to dominion over the Gulf Coast. The three powers would continue to exercise power within the region for nearly two centuries (and the newly formed US would enter the fray after 1776).

France knew it needed to occupy its new colony to strengthen its claim. In 1699, two Quebecois brothers – Pierre le Moyne, Sieur d'Iberville and Jean Baptiste le Moyne, Sieur de Bienville – were sent to found France's first permanent settlement in the South. They founded Fort de Maurepas at what is now Ocean Springs, Mississippi. The brothers set up trading operations with the Biloxi Indians, and peopled the settlement with 200 colonists, mostly male. The fort soon became the seat of government for the new colony. (Ocean Springs remains the second-oldest European settlement to endure in the US after St Augustine, Florida.)

In 1702, England declared war on France, leading the French king to order the new colony moved to the Mobile River to be closer to allies at Fort Pensacola in Spanish Florida. Though the Fort de Maurepas settlement was not completely abandoned, the seat of Louisiana government moved to this new fort, named Louis de la Mobile.

In 1704, the French government sponsored the transport of 20 young women as prospective brides for the colonists. Dubbed 'cassette girls,' these orphans and peasants were 'stationed' on Ship Island (off the Mississippi coast) with their suitcases *(cassettes)* bearing their state-issued trousseaux. This was the first of several such boatloads of French women.

The le Moyne brothers continued westward to explore the Mississippi River Delta, which had previously eluded European explorers on the Gulf. With a Native American guide, the brothers sailed up the Mississippi, taking note of the spit of land between the river and a huge lake, linked by a narrow portage route – the future site of New Orleans. Upriver, they established Fort Rosalie in 1716 at the future site of Natchez, Mississippi.

In 1718, Bienville laid out the city of New Orleans. The original colonists included 30 convicts, six carpenters and four Canadians who struggled against the floods and yellow-fever epidemics endemic to the region. But promoters omitted these harsher details of colonial life, and French, Canadian and a few German immigrants were drawn to the new colony. The capital of La Louisiane was moved from Mobile to New Orleans in 1722. At this time, New Orleans had a population of 370 – 147 male and 65 female colonists, 38 children, 73 slaves and 21 Indians. Over the next 20 years, New Orleans grew to a population of around 5000, more than half of whom were enslaved Africans. Offspring of free foreign immigrants born in the colony were called Creoles.

Not all blacks were slaves. Once manumitted (released from slavery), blacks joined free black communities the French called *les gens de couleur libre*, the free people of color. Louisiana's Code Noir (Black Code), adopted in 1724, regulated the treatment and rights of slaves and 'freemen of color' (see the boxed text 'Les Gens de Couleur Libre'). Free black men and women still had to carry passes to identify their status and were restricted from voting, holding public office or marrying outside their race.

Louisiana soon became a drain on the French treasury, which was already strapped with the expenses of waging war against England, so French officials negotiated a secret pact with Spanish King Charles III – the 1762 Treaty of Fountainbleu. In return for ceding to Spain the remote and unprofitable Louisiana territory west of the Mississippi along with the 'Isle of Orleans,' France gained an ally in its war against England. Louisiana provided a buffer between Spain's possessions in New Spain and English colonies along the Atlantic Coast.

In 1763 under the Peace of Paris, Britain acquired France's Louisiana territory east of the Mississippi and north of New Orleans. Spain ceded to Britain its territories of East and West Florida. In 1779, war broke out between Spain and Britain; the Spanish captured the British outpost in Baton Rouge, Louisiana. As a result of this victory, portions of West Florida were returned to Spain.

Two important events in the Americas brought tremendous changes to Louisiana's population. Around the onset of Spanish control, French refugees from L'Acadie (now Nova Scotia) began arriving after the British seizure of French Canada. The British banished thousands of Acadians in 1755. In 1765, France began transporting the forlorn Acadians to New Orleans, hoping to advance French interests in Louisiana. The Acadians (or 'Cajuns' as they came to be called) settled in south Louisiana west of the Mississippi River (the region that remains 'Cajun Country' today). Then in 1791, the slave revolt in St Domingue (Haiti) and ensuing turmoil led thousands of former black slaves to seek refuge in Louisiana as freemen.

Louisiana Purchase

By the late 18th century, Louisiana was proving as troublesome and costly to the Spanish as it had previously been to the French. Spain also feared that it would have to fight the upstart Americans to retain control. So when Napoleon Bonaparte offered to retake control in 1800, Spain jumped at the chance and ceded territory in another secret pact. (France did not actually resume control until November 1803.)

Meanwhile, President Thomas Jefferson recognized that seizing the river capital

Les Gens de Couleur Libre

Throughout the 18th and 19th centuries, it was not altogether uncommon for slaves to be granted their freedom after years of loyal service. Sometimes the mixed offspring of slaves and owners unions were granted their freedom. Still others, by working jobs on the side after fulfilling their duties on their home plantation, were able to earn enough money to buy their freedom.

Before the Civil War, French-speaking New Orleans had the South's largest population of free blacks, called *les gens de couleur libre*, and as this community grew an increasing number of blacks were born free. The subtle gradations of mixed color led to a complex class structure in which those with the least African blood (octoroons, for instance, who were in theory one-eighth black) tended to enjoy the greatest privileges. The city's elite class of French-minded blacks was well educated, cultured, owned land, and in some cases even owned slaves. Affairs between the races were socially accepted, but interracial marriages were not. The *plaçage* was a cultural institution – in such an arrangement, white Creole men 'kept' octoroon women, providing them with a handsome wardrobe and a cottage in the Vieux Carré, and supporting any resulting children.

Most free blacks worked in trades, like bricklaying, cigarmaking, and carpentry, and a few accumulated funds to buy the freedom of enslaved relatives. In general, the free blacks of New Orleans probably had a better life than blacks anywhere else in the US. Still, they were not entitled to vote or serve in juries, and marriage between the races was illegal. In public, blacks could be asked to show identification in order to prove that they were at liberty to go about their own business.

New Orleans would promote US western expansion. Bonaparte needed to raise funds, feared losing New Orleans to the British and preferred to see the territory in American hands, so he offered the Louisiana territory to the US for a price of $15 million, a purchase that would double the young country's national domain. On the final day of November 1803 in the Place d'Armes in New Orleans, the Spanish flag was quietly replaced by the French flag, which in turn was replaced by the American flag on December 20.

In 1812, Louisiana joined the Union as the 18th state. In the same year, the US declared war against England. With the British navy approaching from the Gulf of Mexico, General Andrew Jackson assembled a ragtag band of pirates, Indians and volunteer militia. These troops fought the British at the Battle of New Orleans in 1815 and won (the war had actually been declared over before the battle, but neither side had been alerted).

Though Spain had relinquished its lands west of the Mississippi, it held onto West Florida, its lands east of the river. The US contested this assertion, claiming it was all US territory as a result of the French concession. Americans within this region began to rebel against Spanish rule; residents of the eastern Louisiana region still known today as 'the Florida Parishes' briefly declared themselves an independent republic in 1810. With the US Army on active duty during the War of 1812, the US took the opportunity to seize control of the disputed territory. Mobile, an isolated European outpost, finally came under American control in 1812.

With US dominion firmly in place, the government began to plot state lines. Boundaries were contested by various factions for years, but the new states of Mississippi and Alabama joined the Union in 1817 and 1819, respectively, with borders close to those in effect today. Indian removal in the 1830s opened up free and easily cultivated land. Speculators and settlers from the Piedmont region of the southern Atlantic seaboard populated the region and expanded cotton cultivation. In southern Louisiana, sugar cane dominated the economy, and rice and indigo flourished on Alabama's Gulf Coast.

The Mississippi River served as a primary transportation corridor. Goods from as far away as Pittsburgh and St Louis passed through New Orleans on their way abroad. Steamboats plied the navigable waters of the river's entire Mississippi drainage basin. At first riverboats were welcomed in river towns with calliope steam-organ music announcing their arrival, but soon they transported as many shady characters as freight and became an unwelcome nuisance (see the boxed text 'Steamboats: Floating Palaces & Crop Couriers'). Many trading boatsmen found it easier to sell the boat lumber than to fight their way back upstream; they returned north on foot via the Natchez Trace. (As early as 1801, the US government had secured a right-of-way treaty along this ancient buffalo trail through Chickasaw territory.)

Cotton Was King

Long after the cities of the North were transformed by the Industrial Revolution, the Deep South maintained its old agricultural way of life. The majority of the South's farms were small, owner-operated properties growing mostly subsistence crops, but large-scale plantations dominated the economy and politics of the region. In southern Louisiana, sugar cane was a common plantation crop. But almost everywhere else, the sole crop was cotton.

So predominant was cotton, that it was matter-of-factly referred to as 'King Cotton.' The Southern climate and soil, enriched by thousands of years of the meandering Mississippi River flooding over it, were ideally suited for growing cotton, and in the 18th and 19th centuries textile factories in Europe could not get enough of it. Stretching across hundreds of acres of dark fertile soil, Southern plantations were the domain of a privileged class of planters with immense political clout, which they used to uphold the system that had served them so

Steamboats: Floating Palaces & Crop Couriers

Rafts, flatboats and keelboats floated down the Mississippi River from early colonial days onward, carrying goods to market. Most traffic remained downstream until 1811, when the steamboat *New Orleans* departed her namesake city by way of the Mississippi River for points north. With her maiden voyage, river transportation was changed forever.

The Mississippi River remained the primary waterway throughout the late 1800s. However, the South abounded with navigable rivers plied by steamboats both large and small during the golden age of riverboat transportation.

Whether serving as floating palaces bedecked with chandeliers and skylights or as de facto barges loaded down with cotton en route to market, the steamboat's familiar bells, whistles and billowing smoke symbolized modernity for the farmers and townspeople who gathered at the river whenever the boats arrived. Though as many boats provided crop transport as luxury passenger service, the most fondly remembered of these great vessels were the luxury boats. Foremost among these was the *Robert E Lee*.

Built in 1866 for the then astronomical sum of $200,000, the *Lee* boasted an opulent main cabin outfitted with crystal chandeliers, stained-glass skylights, rosewood furniture and Egyptian marble sills. Its opulent appointments were emblematic of an elegance that historian Louis C Hunter dubbed 'steamboat gothic.'

For its time, the *Lee* was an exceedingly fast craft, able to reach neck-wrenching speeds of close to 20mph. Its closest competitor in opulence and power was the *Natchez*. In 1870, the two steamboats raced from New Orleans to St Louis for bragging rights to the title of the best boat on the

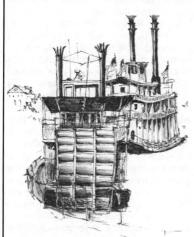

river. On June 30, the *Lee* steamed into St Louis after traveling 1218 miles in 80 hours and 30 minutes. It was six hours ahead of the *Natchez*.

Despite the popularity of steamboat travel, by the late 1800s another form of steam transportation began overshadowing it. As railroads became the more economical and practical means of moving people and goods, the once grand steamboats were either taken out of service or relegated to lesser routes.

Today, steamboats are enjoying something of a renaissance. Refurbished treasures like the *Delta Queen* offer luxury cruises and have achieved the status of national landmarks, but most of today's steamboats are nothing more than floating facades, outfitted with slot machines and the like to take advantage of newly enacted laws that allow water-based gambling.

– John T Edge

well. It was a system – and a way of life – that would prove resistant to change.

Toward the end of the 18th century, cotton profits began to lag – its production might have waned if not for the invention of the cotton gin in 1793. Gins mechanized the laborious task of separating seeds and hulls from cotton fibers, thus making production much more efficient, and soon they were installed on plantations all over the South.

Even with the new technology, cotton was labor-intensive and not particularly profitable if those who labored over it were paid a fair wage. But, of course, the Southern planters didn't have that problem. Historian Ulrich B Phillips described the plantation economy as a 'kind of agribusiness whose machines were human beings.' These 'machines' were slaves.

The Slaves

Most Southern planters failed to recognize the inhumanity of slavery. Exhibiting an impressive faculty for self-deception, slave owners shared a common perception that their slaves were merely a docile lot, content to remain in servitude for their entire lives. Planters frequently boasted that their slaves were the 'happiest people on earth' – and seemingly believed it. Satisfied that their slaves were being treated fairly, slave owners typically felt betrayed when one ran away or deceived them in other manners.

The unhappy reality was that, in addition to being denied the most basic human liberties, slaves were not allowed to maintain African cultural practices, many were prohibited from learning to read, some masters sexually exploited female slaves, and all too often slaves experienced painful separations as family members were sold to other plantations. And though it would have been in a planter's best economic interest to ensure adequate food and health care for slaves, brutality and generally dehumanizing conditions served to underscore a master's authority. While some slaves rose in stature by learning trades or becoming house servants, the great majority were field workers whose legal status was hardly greater than that of domestic animals.

The runaway slave's chance of achieving freedom was slim. Punishment, if a runaway was caught, was always severe – sometimes it was death – and slave hunters and their hounds were not so easily eluded. But many slaves were willing to take these risks. Some escapees hoped to find refuge in self-sufficient runaway colonies in remote corners of the South's dense, watery wilderness. Many more slaves headed to the North via the Underground Railroad.

Meanwhile, many planters enjoyed a comfortable lifestyle modeled on the traditions of European aristocracy. The wealthiest planters inhabited impressive Greek Revival mansions with household servants attending to domestic needs, including cooking, craftwork, child-raising and even wet-nursing. In this rarified atmosphere, an elitist code of ethics was maintained, upholding values like chivalry and honor that by that time might well have seemed old-fashioned to most Northerners.

Approaching Conflict

By 1850, slavery was illegal in half of the states that then formed the US. As a political issue, it was clearly at the center of a maelstrom that threatened to divide the nation. A figurative line had already been drawn between the 'slave states' and 'free states.' Put simply, south of the line, the prevailing argument was for preserving the balance of power as the nation grew – for each new free state admitted to the rapidly expanding Union, Southern lawmakers wanted a new slave state admitted. In the North, however, there was a growing movement to abolish slavery altogether.

The conflict came to a head in the election of 1860, with the Republican candidate Abraham Lincoln running against two Democratic candidates, one favored by the North, the other representing Southern interests. Lincoln was an unlikely front runner, being a softspoken, ungainly man who frequently dared to be candid about controversial subjects. He'd made public his feelings that slavery was morally wrong, and he boldly summarized the state of the Union: 'I believe this government cannot endure permanently half slave and half free.' But with the Democrats divided, Lincoln won the election.

The Confederacy

Making good on Lincoln's own prophecy, seven Southern states seceded from the Union before he took office in January 1861. From their perspective, the political influence of the slave states had diminished in Washington, and secession was their only recourse. Southerners also considered it the *right* of their states to leave the Union. The Union had, after all, been entered into voluntarily – it followed that these states were free to remove themselves from it. Soon after, at a convention in Montgomery, Alabama, delegates from Alabama, Mississippi, Georgia, South Carolina, Florida, and Louisiana (Texas' representatives were late) created the provisional government of the Confederate States of America. Their choice for president was Jefferson Davis of Mississippi.

Davis, a US senator and former Secretary of War, had established himself as pro-secessionist a decade earlier. Like Lincoln, he was born in a log cabin, but during his lifetime his family rose to be one of the wealthiest and most influential in the state of Mississippi. He was avowedly pro-slavery and devoted to his home state. On the eve of Lincoln's election, Jefferson made a fiery speech expressing sentiments that many Southerners shared: '…before I would see [Mississippi] dishonored I would tear it from its place, to be set on the perilous ridge of battle as a sign around which her bravest and best shall meet the harvest home of death.'

It was Davis' private hope that the question of states' rights would be resolved in the US Supreme Court, but even as he and many others prayed for a peaceful solution, both sides began to arm themselves. And the Confederacy quickly grew, as Tennessee, Arkansas, North Carolina and Virginia joined. Four peripheral slave states (including West Virginia, which broke from the state of Virginia) chose to remain with the Union.

Southern Loyalists

It was not easy for many states – Louisiana and Tennessee included – to make the decision to secede, and divisions within the Confederate borders would last until the Civil War (also known as the War between the States in some parts of the South) was over. Regional pride, rather than economics,

pushed Louisiana into the Confederacy. The state's sugar planters, though slave owners, benefited from US tariff laws, and New Orleans, a port city with deep commercial ties to the North, had a lot to lose with secession. In eastern Tennessee and in the hilly northern counties of Alabama, few farmers owned slaves or cared to leave the Union over this issue. They had even less desire to die fighting for that cause. Throughout the South, members of the non-planter class opposed secession, regarding the approaching conflict a 'rich man's war and a poor man's fight.' In some Southern counties, popular movements leaned toward seceding from their states, in order to rejoin the Union. This might have happened in Eastern Tennessee (as in West Virginia) if the Union hadn't occupied that state before the war's end. Andrew Johnson, a Tennessee senator, made a bold gesture when he chose to remain in the US Senate even though his state had left the Union. A number of men from the lower classes made the comparable decision to fight with the Union army.

Civil War – Western Theater

Fighting began April 12, 1861. Provoked by Lincoln's decision to resupply troops at Fort Sumter in South Carolina, Jefferson Davis sent orders to fire the first shot of what

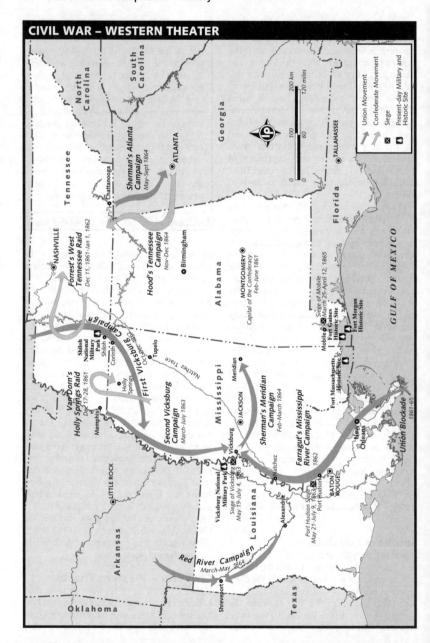

CIVIL WAR – WESTERN THEATER

would prove the bloodiest war in US history. Many of the Civil War's early battles were likewise fights for control of coastal forts along the Atlantic Ocean and Gulf of Mexico. Among these battles was one at Fort Massachusetts on Ship Island off the Mississippi coast, which was occupied by Union troops on December 3, 1861.

A key Union objective from the outset was to control the Mississippi, which would cut an important lifeline for Southern states and divide the Confederacy in two. The Union blockade at the mouth of the Mississippi began in 1861. Later that year, major campaigns were launched simultaneously upriver from the Gulf and downriver along the Mississippi and its tributaries from the Union position in Kentucky.

In the spring of 1862, Union troops took Nashville – a Cumberland River port, railroad hub and Confederate supply depot and arsenal – opening a pathway for a Union invasion of the Deep South. Continuing their advance, Union troops met the Confederate army in Shiloh, Tennessee, on April 6, 1862. Two days of battle resulted in a Union victory at a cost of 23,746 lives on both sides, making it one of the bloodiest battles of the war. Crossing into Mississippi, the Federals besieged Corinth from April 29 to May 30 until the Confederates evacuated. To the west, Union forces seized Memphis on June 6.

Meanwhile, US admiral David Farragut and the US Navy secured the surrender of New Orleans, Baton Rouge and Natchez by the middle of 1862. They tried to take Vicksburg but failed and withdrew in July. Perched on a high bluff above one of the river's most treacherous curves, Vicksburg presented a real challenge to the invading army. As the strongest Confederate holdout between Union-occupied Memphis and Natchez, the 'Gibraltar of the West' became the primary target of the Union's Western Theater operations. 'Vicksburg is the key,' said Lincoln. 'The war can never be brought to a close until that key is in our pocket.'

Union general Ulysses S Grant launched his first campaign toward Vicksburg in October 1862, but a series of daring Con-

If Not for the Flux

It took more than Northern artillery to bring down the Confederacy. Dysentery and other diseases, caught while fighting in swamps and spread through unsanitary conditions that followed infantries from battle to battle, took a huge toll. As one modern pharmacist mused in Tony Horwitz' book *Confederates in the Attic*, 'The South could have won the war if it had found a cure for the flux.'

federate raids against his supply lines led Grant to abandon it. These raids included one by Nathan Bedford Forrest in West Tennessee and another by Earl Van Dorn in Holly Springs.

Grant began a second offensive the following spring. His 45,000 troops failed to take Vicksburg by storm, so instead they encircled it and imposed a siege that lasted 48 days before the city surrendered 31,000 Confederate soldiers on July 4, 1863. When Port Hudson, the last Confederate stronghold on the Mississippi, fell five days later, Lincoln declared 'The Father of Waters again goes unvexed to the sea.'

Union general Tecumseh Sherman headed east to Meridian, Mississippi, testing his 'total war' technique (remembered as an unprecedented assault on nonmilitary targets). Later in the year, he perfected the technique in his Atlanta campaign (also known as the 'March to the Sea').

In Louisiana, a Union offensive headed up the Red River, but despite reinforcements on the way from the north, they were forced to withdraw. In the summer of 1864, the fall of forts guarding Mobile Bay enabled Union forces to threaten the city of Mobile.

Confederate general John B Hood, licking his wounds after his defeat to Sherman in Atlanta in September 1864, regrouped and launched a major offensive through Alabama to Tennessee in the hopes of retaking Nashville, but after several engagements his army was largely destroyed.

After Sherman captured the Confederate capital of Richmond, Virginia, on April 3, 1865, the war was all but over. Confederate general Robert E Lee surrendered to General Grant in Appomattox, Virginia, on April 7, 1865. Five days later Mobile surrendered to the Union siege. Two days after that, President Lincoln was assassinated in Washington, DC, by John Wilkes Booth, an avowed white supremacist.

More struggles lay ahead.

Reconstruction

The prolonged war destroyed the Southern economy and spent an entire generation of Southern white men. Huge tracts of Southern soil had been laid to waste by advancing and retreating armies. Homes had been looted and torched, fields had been plundered and left to fallow, and families had been decimated. Southern blacks – now free – faced a decidedly uncertain future. Lincoln had not arrived at a coherent plan for bringing the South back into the fold, and after his death, his successor, Andrew Johnson, fumbled with the issues of Reconstruction.

Establishing pro-Union governments in the South proved tricky, particularly as the radical movement gained momentum in Washington, DC. With voting restricted to loyalists, the way was paved for opportunists from the North, who headed South and assumed an influential political role. Known as 'carpetbaggers' – many had arrived with their clothes packed in traveling bags made of carpet, which were popular at the time – these outsiders represented a bitter pill for the defeated South to swallow. Southern Unionists who took political posts were derogatorily known as 'scalawags.'

Emancipation – and everything that it implied – proved not so easy to sort through, either. Blacks amounted to about 40% of the South's population, and in some areas they constituted a majority. Yet the argument over whether the right to vote necessarily followed emancipation ran on for years. Meanwhile, many former slaves continued to work plantations as they had before the war. Only now, as paid laborers, they were required to pay rent and for supplies and food. A share-cropper system gradually developed, in which field hands relied on the landowners for supplies and were constantly in debt. One recourse blacks had was that when living conditions

The Emancipation Proclamation

At the outset of the war, the North's chief objective was to preserve the Union. Abolishing slavery remained on the back burner while the Union hoped to retain the loyalty of the border slave states. But after nearly a year and a half of fighting it became clear that this war would have to decide the slavery debate once and for all. In January 1893, Lincoln made his Emancipation Proclamation, a step which officially made freeing the slaves a condition of surrender. Although the proclamation exempted the four slave states still in the Union, it nevertheless spelled the end of the 'peculiar institution.'

The most immediate effect of the Emancipation Proclamation was that it paved the way for blacks to take up arms for the Union cause. The war had lasted longer than either side had foreseen, and the North, which had strongly resisted the idea of allowing blacks to fight, now saw the advantages of having additional – and highly motivated – reinforcements. The presence of black Union soldiers in the South brought home the news that slavery was nearly dead – hundreds of slaves left their plantations during this period, some to join the Union army. Though blacks accounted for less than 1% of the population in the North, by the war's end they constituted 10% of the Union Army. A small number of blacks fought on the side of the Confederacy, largely Creole landowners from Louisiana.

were unbearable they were free to pack up and move to a new plantation. A large number of blacks soon became part of a migrant workforce with a limited range of opportunities before them.

As the Reconstruction period continued, the wounds of war seemed to open wider. By the time Reconstruction ended in 1877, Southern fury had been well stoked. The region would burn and smolder a long, long time.

Post-War Backlash

To be sure, white supremacy was at the core of slavery, but it had generally been masked by the paternalism many slave owners demonstrated toward their slaves. With emancipation, the pretense of paternalism was gone, and deep-seeded hatreds rose to the surface. Emancipation was followed by white resistance to black suffrage; blacks gaining the right to vote led to efforts to limit eligibility and intimidate black voters. 'Jim Crow' restrictions, which maintained segregation of transportation modes, waiting rooms, hotels, restaurants, theaters, were enforced. Separate public institutions were created, including schools and hospitals, with blacks getting facilities of inferior quality. 'White' and 'colored' signs began to appear over doorways and drinking fountains throughout the region. For many blacks, such as the black Creoles of New Orleans, who'd been free before the war, this actually represented a severe drop in social status.

In 1896, a Supreme Court decision solidified institutionalized racism. Earlier that year, Homer Plessy, a biracial man from Louisiana, bought a train ticket from New Orleans to Covington. He took a seat in the whites-only car and refused to move to the 'colored' car when directed by the conductor. He was arrested for violating segregation laws. Plessy sued the railroad, arguing that segregation was illegal under the 14th Amendment. The *Plessy* v *Ferguson* case came before the US Supreme Court, which decided that separation of the races was within the bounds of the Constitution as long as equal accommodations were made

for blacks, underpinning the 'separate-but-equal' doctrine for decades.

Meanwhile, whites frequently acted outside the law in order to reinforce discriminatory standards. In Tennessee, the Ku Klux Klan (KKK) was formed almost immediately after the war ended, and it quickly grew in other states. Its first imperial wizard was Nathan Bedford Forrest, the Confederate War hero who had uttered the famous words 'War means fightin', and fightin' means killin'.' The Klan's primary motive at the time was to oppose the excesses of the Reconstruction. It disbanded in 1870, when ugly racist overtones led to a federal crackdown. But it returned in 1915 after the release of the film *Birth of a Nation*, based on Thomas Dixon's novel *The Clansman*. By this time, the KKK's unambiguous mission was to keep blacks down. (The Klan also targeted Jews, Catholics and foreigners.)

The Klan, a terrifying force, reached peak membership in the 1920s. Riding horseback at night, wearing hoods to obscure their identity (many of whom were

Who Was Jim Crow?

At one time, 'Jim Crow' was used to describe African-Americans, much as 'Mick' described Irish Americans, and its sense was either derogatory or patronizing. It later came to refer to the legal separation of the races, as in 'Jim Crow laws.'

The origins of the term are hazy and we are left with unlikely stories. But it is known that the term was popularized by a white minstrel entertainer, Thomas 'Daddy' Rice, who performed a black-face routine under the name Jim Crow. Rice said he'd met a slave named Jim whose master's surname was Crow, but this explanation is generally discredited. It's more probable that whimsical wordplay brought together 'Jim' (being, like 'Joe' and 'Mac,' a name used when a man's given name wasn't known) and 'Crow' (referring to the color black).

prominent citizens), clansmen harassed targeted individuals and groups without legal consequence. Arson and bombing became common strategies – and fightin' continued to mean killin'. Rampant violence led the Klan to lose public favor, and membership fell drastically in the 1930s. But the KKK would rear its ugly head again during the Civil Rights era.

Enter the King Fish

In 1914, the boll-weevil infestation ravaged cotton crops across the South and revealed the folly of dependence on a single crop. Blacks, finding their rights had been strangled and even fewer opportunities to raise out of poverty, began to leave the South by the thousands to look for work in factories booming in such northern cities as Detroit and Chicago. It was the beginning of the 'Great Migration,' which would continue unabated into the 1950s. To make matters worse for Southerners, the Great Depression struck in 1929 and the crippled Southern economy sank even further.

From all this pain and poverty arose some great Southern contributions to American culture. The early 20th century saw the birth of jazz and the blues. Likewise, the literary arts flourished; Mississippians William Faulkner and Thomas 'Tennessee' Williams, and Tennessee's Agrarian Poets gave rise to a Southern literature drawn from the everyday struggles and dramas of rural society (see Music and Literature under the Arts section, later in this chapter). But locally, people weren't so interested in the works of Faulkner. In fact, many resented his indelicate treatment of sensitive issues. Increasingly, what people wanted was political solutions to concrete problems. In Louisiana, many voters believed that a solution had already arrived – in the form of the 'King Fish,' Huey Long.

Long, a man of humble origins from northern Louisiana, was elected governor of the state in 1928. His populist campaign made no small promises. In the face of a still-powerful planter class and emerging oil interests, he championed the common man and proposed progressive reforms. Education and public health were top priorities, and public works on a grand scale would create jobs and benefit the people. This was a bit ahead of its time, considering it would be another four years before Franklin D Roosevelt was elected US president, ushering in the era of sweeping New Deal programs across the nation. However Long quickly constructed a powerful political machine and he assumed unprecedented powers for himself. He soon came to be regarded – with justifiable suspicion – as a demagogue.

After serving a four-year term as governor, he won a seat in the US Senate. From Washington, DC, Long continued to dominate Louisiana politics, as members of his political machine held key offices in the state. All that came to a crashing halt in 1935 – as he prepared to make a bid for the White House, Long was assassinated by a Baton Rouge physician. Despite resorting to questionable means to his ends, many of Long's actions genuinely benefited the state of Louisiana, and he left behind a truly colorful legacy.

After Long's death, New Deal programs continued to bring some respite to the entire region and addressed environmental destruction caused by soil erosion and clear-cut forestry. The parks and recreation areas constructed by skilled WPA laborers and craftsworkers remain in constant use today.

The Heart of Darkness

There's no arguing that US history is dark and disturbing, and if you've been reading this section you've already cottoned to the idea that Southern history is a particularly dense brier patch to crawl through. However, a balanced overview reveals that more than a few roses have managed to bloom amid the thorns. See Arts, later in this chapter, for some of the more positive – and indeed significant – events in the region's history.

During the two World Wars, countless Southerners joined the military. Many Cajun soldiers played an important role as translators in France. Black soldiers experienced less racist societies in the North and in Europe. In general, WWII helped unify the US as had nothing before, with people of all races, from North and South, joining in a single cause. Mississippians observed Independence Day, July 4, for the first time since the fall of Vicksburg. Of course, this unprecedented patriotism merely overshadowed the looming racial disharmony that awaited in the South. The post-war period would hold another series of grueling trials for the region.

Civil Rights Movement

For most Americans, the Civil Rights movement began on May 17, 1954, when the Supreme Court handed down its decision in the *Brown* v *Board of Education* case outlawing segregation in public schools. Since the rise of Jim Crow segregation, schooling in the South was separate but not equal; it was common for Southern states to spend five times more money educating white children than black children.

From this decision until the passage of the Voting Rights Act in 1965, the US experienced more social change, court decisions and legislation in the name of civil rights than in any other decade of US history, and many of these pivotal events occurred in the Deep South. Though the period is remembered for its violent clashes, many advocates for change were committed to nonviolence. This strategy enabled such dramatic social change to occur without the massive bloodshed that often accompanies revolution. But make no mistake, blood *was* spilt.

School Desegregation The *Brown* decision did not automatically lead to school desegregation. In the decade that followed, some schools defied the court order, necessitating the arrival of federal troops to guarantee that black students could register. In 1954, Mississippi voters approved a constitutional amendment allowing the legislature to abolish public schools rather

Thurgood Marshall (center) and fellow attorneys celebrating the ruling on *Brown* v *Board of Education*, 1954

than integrate them. President Eisenhower dispatched the 101st Airborne Division for the 'Little Rock Nine' to integrate Central High School in Little Rock, Arkansas.

In Alabama, Governor George Wallace personally stood in the doorway at the University of Alabama to block the entrance of James Hood and Vivian Malone. (In 1996, George Wallace would attend a 'reconciliation' ceremony with the former Miss Malone.) At the bastion of the Old South, the 'Ole Miss' campus of the University of Mississippi in Oxford, it took thousands of state and federal guardsmen to quell the riots that broke out when James Meredith attempted to register in 1962; the price of opposition to Meredith's admission was 160 injured marshals and two deaths.

Emergence of MLK Throughout the South, laws mandated that blacks had to board buses up front to pay their fare and then reboard through the rear door to take seats in the back; laws also specified that black riders had to yield their seats to whites. In 1953, bus riders in Baton Rouge, Louisiana, petitioned the government for first-come, first-served seating, and by leading a boycott of the buses, they were able to reach a compromise.

On December 1, 1955, in Montgomery, Alabama, 42-year-old seamstress Rosa Parks refused to surrender her seat to a white passenger and was arrested for violating the segregation laws. This incident spurred the African-American community to mobilize a citywide boycott galvanized by the leadership of Dr Martin Luther King Jr. The boycott that few expected to last a week continued 13 months before the Supreme Court affirmed a lower court's ruling outlawing segregation.

Despite a violent backlash that included the bombing of King's home, the Montgomery boycott inspired blacks in neighboring Birmingham and Mobile to boycott for change in their cities. Birmingham was later the scene of mass demonstrations calling for wider desegregation. In 1963, King was among nearly 15,000 protesters arrested in Birmingham; as a prisoner he wrote the inspirational civil rights manifesto known as 'Letter from a Birmingham Jail.'

Freedom Riders Though the federal government outlawed segregation in interstate travel in 1955, Southern states routinely ignored federal policy and continued to separate white and colored waiting rooms, bathrooms and water fountains. In 1961, Civil Rights activists organized a 'Freedom Ride,' intending to ride buses from Washington, DC, to New Orleans to challenge segregation laws in public facilities. Riders were beaten in South Carolina. When they crossed into Alabama, the bus was firebombed; they were again stopped by a violent attack in Birmingham. More Freedom Riders volunteered to continue the route, and flank upon flank the volunteers were met by mob violence. When they reached Jackson, Mississippi, the riders were followed by police through the whites-only waiting room and then jailed for violating state segregation laws.

More than 300 Freedom Riders traveled through the Deep South, but the ensuing violence led the movement to shift the strategy to voter registration, which was thought to be a less confrontational avenue for activism.

Mississippi Burning In the 1950s, the population of Mississippi was 45% black, the highest of any state in the nation, yet only 5% of voting-age blacks were registered, the lowest of any state. With majorities in many counties, blacks might well have controlled local politics through the ballot box, a fact not lost on local segregationists who did whatever it took to suppress black voter registration. Blacks attempting to register to vote were frequently subjected to economic or violent retribution against them or their families. Churches, the mainstay of the black community, were often targets of firebombings designed to suppress the pursuit of civil rights.

Several murders in Mississippi made national news during the early 1960s. On June 12, 1963, Medgar Evers, field secretary of the NAACP, was shot to death in the driveway of his home outside Jackson. It took 30 years and two trials for his murderer to be brought to justice (see the boxed text 'And Justice Shall Prevail' in the Mississippi chapter). On June 21, 1964, the disappearance of three Civil Rights workers on a voter-registration drive through Mississippi prompted an FBI investigation. Kennedy had been assassinated the previous November, and Vice President Lyndon B Johnson (LBJ) had assumed the job of bringing civil rights to the South. Thanks to help sent in by Johnson, the bodies of the three were pulled from an earthen dam outside Meridian on August 4. Though murder charges were dropped in the state court, six of the accused white men were found guilty of violating federal Civil Rights laws and were sentenced to jail.

Selma-to-Montgomery March Though the Civil Rights Act of 1964 was intended to protect equal voting rights, Southern states continued to put up barriers specifically designed to restrict the black vote. To protest such practices and gain full enfranchisement, grassroots organizers planned a march from Selma, Alabama, to the state capitol in Montgomery, 58 miles east. On March 7, 1965, 500 marchers – mostly black, but many white as well – started out from the Brown Chapel AME Church. They got no farther than six blocks. At the Edmund Pettus Bridge over the Alabama River, state troopers standing three-deep and on horseback blocked Hwy 80. They descended on the marchers with nightsticks, bullwhips and tear gas. Three marchers died (including a white man, which drew increased media attention) and 87 were injured. The sight of the battered band bleeding and limping in retreat memorialized the event as 'Bloody Sunday.'

As the scene was broadcast around a shocked nation, President Johnson, in one of the most stirring speeches of his presidency, was moved to proclaim: 'At times, history and fate meet in a single place to shape a turning point in man's unending search for freedom. So it was at Lexington and Concord. So it was a century ago at Appomattox. So it was last week in Selma, Alabama.'

Two weeks after Bloody Sunday, Dr Martin Luther King Jr returned from Norway after accepting the Nobel Peace Prize and in Selma joined 4000 black and white demonstrators to renew the march – their numbers swelled to 25,000 as they proceeded up the Jefferson Davis Hwy to Montgomery. They climbed the steps of the State Capitol, with its Confederate battle flag waving outside, but their request to see Governor Wallace was refused.

Voting Rights Act of 1965 Four months after Bloody Sunday, LBJ signed into law the Voting Rights Act of 1965, which banned literacy tests as a prerequisite to voting and other obstacles designed to block the black franchise. Significantly, the act shifted 'the burden of proof' to state governments, meaning it was now up to the states to prove they hadn't intended to discriminate. The act required all or part of seven states – Alabama, Georgia, Louisiana, Mississippi, Virginia and the Carolinas – to have every change in local or state election laws approved by the US Justice Department or federal courts in Washington, DC.

Enforcement of the act led to sweeping changes in the nature of the American political process. In Louisiana, black registered voters rose from 32% of those eligible in 1964 to 47% in 1966. In Alabama during that same period, the gain was from 23% to 51% of eligible blacks. In Mississippi, the percentage of registered eligible black voters skyrocketed from 7% in 1964 to 33% just two years later. By 1984 it would rise to 86% of the state's black voting-age population, a higher proportion of registration among eligible blacks than eligible whites.

When LBJ declared the new act 'one of the most monumental laws in the entire history of American freedom,' there were only 300 black elected officials in the nation. Twenty years later, there were more than 2300 in the seven states first covered by the Voting Rights Act alone. Sixty percent of the increase in black officials nationwide had occurred in the South. These officials included mayors in New Orleans, Birmingham, Atlanta and many smaller cities and towns throughout the Deep South.

However, the act was no panacea. Stalwart segregationists derided its enforcement as a 'second Reconstruction' and found ingenious ways to continue to impede the black vote. In 1985, a Justice Department official reflecting on the number of federal observers still dispatched to enforce the act said, 'We're far from going out of business.' Intimidation also continued, and a segregationist backlash intensified in the decade following the 1965 legislation. Economically, gaining the vote could only begin to reverse centuries of oppression; blacks in the region (as well as in the nation) continued to trail far behind whites in every economic measure.

Nonetheless, much change was swift and visible. When the Selma-to-Montgomery march was reenacted in 1985, the Alabama state troopers – including black officers formerly barred from the force – served as guardians to the marchers. At the capitol, the group was welcomed by Governor

Wallace, whose reelection now depended on black voters.

King's Assassination On April 4, 1968, Dr Martin Luther King Jr was assassinated on the 2nd-story balcony of the Lorraine Motel in downtown Memphis, Tennessee. King's assassination dealt a tremendous blow to the movement and the cause of civil rights in general. His absence from the national stage left a vacuum that remains unfilled three decades later.

The 'New' South

The concept of a 'New' South has been around since the end of Reconstruction, but it never seemed so much a reality until recently. Cotton is still grown region-wide, but since WWII machines have been doing the picking. WWII also brought US military bases to the region, and other industries have come and gone.

The biggest economic development has been the discovery of oil in Louisiana. In many ways, oil has been much less a boon than a detriment to the region. Outside oil interests soaked up most of the profits while locals gave up traditional lifestyles to work in the new industry. The environmental damage caused by oil refineries is already proving to outlast the short-term gains. When the oil industry went belly-up in the 1980s, the working class was left high and dry. The oil industry may never fully recover, as geologists have noted the region's oil reserves are rapidly depleting. In New Orleans, many of the high rises that define the Central Business District – as well as the mammoth, noticeably aging Louisiana Superdome – are oil boom cathedrals. It certainly qualifies as one of the less attractive symbols of the New South.

Race relations are not nearly so volatile as in the past, and blacks and whites are probably more familiar with each other in this part of the country than they are in cities to the north and on the West Coast. And while most Southerners today espouse positive but complex views on race relations, deep-seated animosities exist on both sides of the white-black divide.

Continuously lagging economies do not make things easier for people of any color. Increasingly, the region has turned to tourism as the answer. New Orleans has spiffed up its French Quarter in an effort to make tourists feel more welcome, and the Superdome and other convention facilities have ensured a rather full calendar of tradeshows and conventions. Meanwhile, gambling casinos have shot up like termite nests up and down the Mississippi River and along the Gulf Coast. Many of the companies behind the new gaming industry are national corporations that rely on the tried and true formulas of Las Vegas and Atlantic City. It doesn't take a mathematician to figure out that, while locals get jobs, it's also primarily locals who lose at the slot machines – and out-of-state interests make most of the profits. But a great number of casinos are operated by Native Americans. In fact, for many Indian tribes, the gaming industry has sparked the first economic boom since their near demise over a century ago.

GEOGRAPHY

From the Appalachian heights in northeast Alabama to Louisiana's low-lying coastal wetlands (much of New Orleans is actually below sea level), the Deep South slopes slowly downhill in a fan shape. (Definitions of 'Deep South' sometimes include the states of Georgia and South Carolina.) The primary geographical feature of the Deep South is the great Mississippi River, which meanders along the borders of Mississippi, Louisiana and western Tennessee.

In Alabama, the geographical features of the Atlantic Seaboard meet those of the Gulf states. Three provinces related to the Appalachian Mountain range extend into eastern Alabama: the Cumberland Plateau (reaching a maximum height of 2407 feet), the Ridge-and-Valley region in the north and the central Piedmont Plateau. In southern Alabama, the wide Atlantic Coastal Plain meets the Gulf Coastal Plain, which stretches west through lower Mississippi and Louisiana. In upper Mississippi, the Central Plateau rises to a maximum elevation of 780 feet in the northeast corner and drops to 535 feet in northern Louisiana.

The Mississippi River has a unique geography and ecology that dominates the central US. Left to its own devices, the Mississippi would naturally flood and change course periodically, replenishing the fields of the alluvial basin; if not for human intervention, it would today be emptying into the Atchafalaya River. For centuries humans have worked to control the river's flow to maintain a single shipping channel and to protect cities, industries and farmland along the riverbanks. An impressive arsenal of artificial levees, reservoirs, pumping stations and dredging fleets has – so far – proven successful. This technology has altered the topography of the region, diverting waters that would naturally flow elsewhere and carrying silt deposits down a stream-lined shipping channel to build up at the river's mouth in the Gulf of Mexico (an estimated two million tons of sediment per day).

Most of the other major rivers in the region – the Tennessee River in Tennessee and Alabama, the Yazoo River in Mississippi and Louisiana's Red and Ouachita Rivers – are part of the Mississippi River navigation system. The Mobile drainage basin consists of the Black Warrior and Alabama Rivers in Alabama and the Tombigbee River in Mississippi; these rivers meet the Gulf in Mobile Bay. (A note on the regional lexicon: though the Mississippi River disperses through a delta at Louisiana's Gulf shore, the leaf-shaped alluvial

Reining in the Mighty Mississippi

Geologists know it's just a matter of time before the Mississippi River shifts its course again, as it has done many times over the last millennia. In *The Control of Nature* (1989), author John McPhee describes such an event:

> Southern Louisiana exists in its present form because the Mississippi River has jumped here and there within an arc about two hundred miles wide, like a pianist playing with one hand – frequently and radically changing course, surging over the right or left bank to go off in utterly new directions. Always it is the river's purpose to get to the Gulf by the shortest and steepest gradient.

Currently, a direct path to the Gulf is being followed by the Red and Atchafalaya Rivers, which curve dangerously close to the Mississippi about 200 miles upriver from New Orleans. If the Mississippi were to jump its banks here, it would in all likelihood change course and join with the Atchafalaya. As though instinctively, the river is inclined to do this. But the US Army Corps of Engineers, determined not to let that happen, maintains a navigation lock called the Old River Control Auxiliary Structure, which operates as a 'safety valve' by diverting excess water flow from the Mississippi to the Atchafalaya. The idea is to prevent an uncontrollable flood. However, the river has already indicated that, in the end, there may be no controlling it. In 1973, the force of the river at flood stage partially undermined the Old River Control. A rebuilt and reinforced structure repelled repeated floods in 1983 and 1993; yet none of these events matched the flow of the '100-Year Flood' of 1927. Most observers agree that the structures will not withstand another cataclysmic flood.

The consequences of such a change in course would be monumental. New Orleans and the River Road communities all the way north to Baton Rouge would be left with a mere stream. The region would lose its primary fresh water source, its port and many of its industries. Near the foot of the Atchafalaya, Morgan City could conceivably be washed away by the massive force of so much water coursing past it.

basin from Memphis to Vicksburg is known locally as the 'Mississippi Delta,' or just 'the Delta.')

Barrier islands in the Gulf of Mexico are also distinctive. Sandbars that evolved to support maritime forests, the Gulf Islands (now preserved as the Gulf Islands National Seashore) off the southern coast are forever shifting. Petit Bois Island, for example, was partially in Alabama as late as 1950; now it's entirely in Mississippi. Hurricanes, common to the coast, can also influence geography – Ship Island was split in two by Hurricane Camille in 1965; now it's known as West and East Ship.

The wetlands of southwestern Louisiana represent another unique environment comprising swamps, marshes and bayous. The region's only natural areas of solid ground are the indigenous river levees. Swamps are permanently waterlogged areas that often exhibit tree growth. Marshes tend to be poorly drained areas that may be only periodically inundated. Bayous are the sluggish freshwater tributaries of the main river channel, often becoming cut-off and abandoned bodies of water. The combination of elevated land (however slight), a rich freshwater environment and removal from the threat of over-bank river flooding makes bayous relatively attractive settlement areas – at least when compared with other wetland environments.

GEOLOGY

Alabama is the most geologically diverse state in the region. In its northeastern Appalachian corner, numerous caves are hidden among limestone deposits; some, such as Russell Cave, hold tremendous archaeological significance. Natural bridges, springs and waterfalls make this limestone-and-shale landscape dramatic, particularly so at De Soto State Park. South of the Tennessee River, a mineral belt contains vast deposits of coal, iron, ore and other minerals, and the soils of the Piedmont region consist of sandy loam and red clay.

Southern Alabama's geology holds much in common with the other states in the region. The 'Black Belt' – so-called for its

sticky, black calcareous clay soil – stretches from Georgia to Texas and, along with the rich alluvial soils of the Mississippi River basin, supports the fertile fields that are responsible for the region's cotton industry. A sandy-soiled pine belt, stretching nearly as wide, is the source of the region's lumbering and pulp-and-paper industries.

In Mississippi, loess bluffs shoulder the eastern boundary of the alluvial basin. Many antebellum houses remain on these 'Bluff Hills' of brown loam, which are underlain by a yellowish calcareous silt.

The region's Gulf shore holds oil deposits in submerged salt domes, particularly at the neck of the Mississippi River. While offshore drilling for oil and gas in the region is concentrated off the Louisiana coast, you'll also see rigs offshore in Mississippi and Alabama. This is often a source of local controversy; see the Ecology & Environment section, later in this chapter.

CLIMATE

The low-lying subtropical coastal plain in the lower half of the region is hot, wet and sticky most of the year – other times it's just wet, receiving around 60 inches of precipitation annually. The climate is cooler and drier at the higher elevations in the upper half of the region. Spring is the most colorful season, with wildflowers and gardens in bloom, and fall is the driest season.

In New Orleans and across the coastal plain, summer is extremely humid, with temperatures reaching 100°F in the shade during the dog days of July and August. The high humidity is broken daily by afternoon thundershowers. City folk head to Gulf Coast beaches to find a breeze, or they head north. Summer nights are languidly hot.

The mountainous region of northeastern Alabama has the coolest temperatures, and the most varied forest colors in fall, though you can find fall colors on trees throughout the upper half of the region. Alabama's mountains get some snow each winter and the occasional odd storm will also bring frost and even snow to the coastal plain. A freak storm in the winter of 1996 coated coastal palmettos with snow. But it rarely

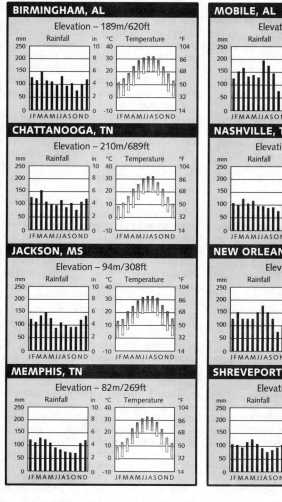

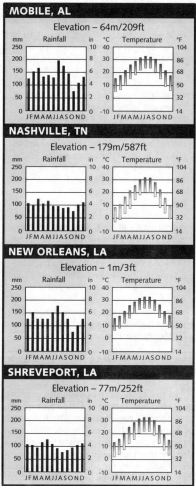

drops below 50°F even in mid-winter at the lower elevations.

Hurricane season, which brings severe periodic storms that last a day or two, begins in June and usually ends in October, but can continue through November. If you plan to travel the Gulf region during this time, pay particular attention to Gulf and Caribbean storm forecasts.

ECOLOGY & ENVIRONMENT

The ravaging of the South's many natural riches is legendary. Exploitation of the region has continued almost unabated since colonial times. Even today, vestiges of a near-feudal mentality among politicians and industrialists remain, encouraging predominant industries to carry on business with little oversight from local authorities.

Hurricane Season

As it passes through New Orleans, I-10 is flanked by signs informing motorists that the interstate serves as a hurricane evacuation route. Local officials estimate that a full-scale evacuation of the low-lying flood-prone city would take three days. Motorists caught in the typical rush-hour gridlock can imagine that such an evacuation might even be impossible. Just remember that the average elevation here is 2 feet below sea level and all evacuation routes cross open water.

Hurricanes in the Gulf of Mexico occur from the beginning of June to the end of November, with the greatest frequency in late summer and early autumn. Hurricanes are sighted well in advance. There are two distinct stages of alert: a Hurricane Watch, issued when a hurricane may strike in the area within the next 36 to 48 hours, and a Hurricane Warning, issued when a hurricane is likely to strike the area. This is when you should consider canceling your visit or evacuating. Hotels generally follow evacuation orders and ask guests to leave. Ask at your hotel or hostel for more information as to the logistics of evacuation.

By the early part of the 20th century, poor land management of the singly important cotton crop had exhausted the soil, perhaps the costliest environmental degradation in the South. Artificial levees restricting the rejuvenating cycles of river flow were also hurting the soil and sending silt to clog the coastal delta. Vital wetlands were being drained or filled for agricultural development.

During this same period, timber companies swooped in and cleared whole regions of forest, destroying habitats and further eroding the soil in their wake. In the 1930s, the Civilian Conservation Corps – called 'Roosevelt's Tree Army' in these parts – performed restorative work by replanting trees and establishing erosion controls, in addition to building recreation areas.

This did little to stop the destruction. As the 20th century progressed, the Army Corps of Engineers dammed rivers for reservoirs, giant paper mills replaced varied forests with biologically sterile pine plantations and more wetlands disappeared. In fact, of all wetlands destruction in the nation – saltwater and fresh – the southeast has been hardest hit.

Today, industrial toxins add insult to injury – according to the Institute for Southern Studies Green Index, the region leads the nation in per-capita exposure to industrial toxins in the air and water, yet when it comes to state spending on waste management, the Deep South states are at the bottom of the list. Not surprisingly, the worst dumps and hazards are located near poor communities, especially those with minority residents.

Environmental advocates have now begun to speak out and defend the region's natural resources more vigorously, though state governments continue to accommodate polluting industries. In Alabama, state officials often look the other way when influential, job-providing, land-owning, pulp-and-paper companies release dioxin into state waters exceeding EPA standards. In Louisiana, giant polluting corporations are given tax breaks instead of getting slapped with fines.

Though current offshore oil and gas drilling in the Gulf remains a potentially serious threat, companies in the region have so far maintained standards for environmental protection and records free of major accidents. Nevertheless, coastal residents view drilling as visual pollution; in Mississippi, for example, coastal residents are mounting a drive to keep oil drilling out of sight of the nationally protected Horn Island wilderness.

The container ships that pass the shoreline as they travel the Intracoastal Waterway may represent a greater threat of spills – with their loads of chemicals and who knows what all – but again, so far there have been no major accidents.

Of course, natural disasters such as hurricanes have always wreaked enormous havoc on the coast. The last occurred when Hurricane Betsy crashed ashore in early September 1965, taking 74 lives throughout coastal Mississippi and Louisiana. The hurricane cycle is in itself an argument for keeping coastal development of housing and industry to a minimum, but this logic routinely goes unheeded.

There are few silver linings in this cloud, except that environmental organizations are now on guard and have teamed up with local advocates vocal in their opposition to any offense to their land. Properties that have become protected, and habitats that have been restored, if only on a small scale, represent major miracles.

FLORA & FAUNA

The South's lush flora and abundant wildlife are what draw many people to visit and live in the region. The incredibly varied woodlands, the moody swamps and bayous, and the sounds of katydids and whippoorwills have been memorialized and romanticized in Southern literature for generations.

Flora

At the Davis Bayou on the Mississippi Gulf Coast, the back deck of the ranger station overlooks the water's edge. A short boardwalk leads down to the reedy marshland through a forest of chinquapin, pawpaw, sassafras, holly, cypress and several species of pine and oak, for starters. Along this 30-foot path, a naturalist could spend half a day cataloging and enjoying the fascinating variety of trees, understory plants and aquatic vegetation.

This is the richness of the Southern landscape – incredible diversity within a compact area. Residents quickly fall in love with their particular parcel of countryside, from the colorful Southern Appalachian Forest of northern Alabama's Cumberland Plateau down to Louisiana's cypress-filled bayous. Locals become attuned to nuances in a forest's mood and subtleties in animal behavior. Whether you immerse yourself in one region or visit several, you'll find each landscape unique, intricate and evocative.

The South is well known for many flowering species of trees, shrubs and flowers – 1500 varieties in all. From the blooming of the first white serviceberry in early March until the last yellow witch hazel petal drops in December, Southern blossoms can be seen throughout most of the year. Some of the common flowering species include southern magnolia (Mississippi is the Magnolia State), azalea, rhododendron, mountain laurel, dogwood, redbud, chinaberry, crepe myrtle, wisteria and a variety of wildflowers, such as violets, goldenrod and the Cherokee rose. Southern gardeners make the most of this natural abundance, beauty and fragrance.

Perhaps the most evocative image of the South is of wispy tendrils of Spanish moss draped from the broad limbs of a live oak. However, despite its name, Spanish moss is neither moss nor Spanish. Related to the pineapple, the flowering plant is an epiphyte: it takes all the nutrients its needs from the air. The plant's name was supposedly derived from its resemblance to a Spaniard's beard. It clings to live oaks because the craggy bark gives seeds a secure hold, and long limbs that never lose their leaves provide protection from the wind and sun. Between 1900 and 1940, Spanish moss was 'ginned' in Louisiana and neighboring states, and used to stuff upholstery and repair fishing nets.

Varied Southern habitats harbor distinct plant communities, such as cordgrass-lined bayous, cypress swamps, canebrakes, piney woods and maritime forests of palmetto, pine and oak. The Southern Appalachian Forest – vestiges of which can be found in northeastern Alabama – contains more tree types than can be found in all of Europe (130 compared to 85), including towering hardwoods and softwoods and deciduous and evergreen varieties. There's even a 'petrified forest' outside the town of Flora in central Mississippi, said to be the only one of its kind in the eastern US.

Another common sight – and common blight – of Southern landscapes is the unstoppable kudzu (KUD-zoo) vine, which shrouds whole forests along interstate byways, choking growth and killing native species. Originally imported from Japan in the early 19th century for erosion control, kudzu exploded without any natural controls in the American South.

Fauna

Amphibians & Reptiles The American alligator (or 'gator') lives in the Deep South's bayous, creeks and lowland marshes. Once hunted to dwindling numbers for its valuable hide, the alligator has made a comeback due to the protection provided by the Endangered Species Act. However, Louisiana has reinstated a legal cull, and today visitors will see lacquered alligator heads for sale at the French Market in New Orleans and elsewhere.

A rare, blind, lungless salamander native to the cave region in northeastern Alabama is one of many species of lizards, skinks and newts found in the South. Freshwater turtles are abundant (the soft-shelled variety is considered the most tasty and is marketed commercially), but sea turtles, some of which are endangered, are seen only rarely. Oak toads are one of the distinctly Southern varieties of the many common toads and bullfrogs in the region. (Leland, Mississippi, claims Kermit the Frog, one of the world's most famous amphibians, as a native son.)

Poisonous snakes are present but are encountered rarely. Water moccasins – called 'cottonmouths' for the white lining they reveal when extending their jaw – live in the coastal plain, but because the common Southern water snake so closely resembles a cottonmouth, alleged sightings far outnumber actual encounters. Copperheads are found at the region's higher elevations.

Birds The naturalist John James Audubon (1785–1851) painted over 80 of his beautiful folios for the monumental *Birds of America*, while staying in New Orleans and near St Francisville, Louisiana, during 1821 and 1822.

The Mississippi Flyway is one of the four flyways across the North American continent. Migratory birds stop over at wetlands up and down the Mississippi River basin. Many of these wetlands are protected as national wildlife refuges for wintering waterfowl, mostly ducks. In April and May, over 70 species of thrushes, warblers, buntings, vireos, grosbeaks and tanagers arrive from South America. Many fly the 600- to 800-mile journey over the Gulf of Mexico in a single night.

Year-round you'll find all manner of herons, egrets, ibis and anhingas roosting in the region's wetlands. In the woodlands you'll hear many songbird varieties, including warblers, sparrows, mockingbirds and thrashers. Gulf shorebirds include gulls, terns, brown pelicans in addition to several dozen species of sandpiper and plover. Southern gardens attract ruby-throated hummingbirds.

The wild turkey is one of the most popular native game birds, along with the quail and dove.

Fish Mississippi leads the nation in farm-raised catfish, capitalizing on the native species named for the long whiskerlike barbels extending from its lower jaw. (Belzoni, Mississippi, calls itself the 'Catfish

JERRY ALEXANDER

Has anyone seen my turtle?

Capital of the World' and crowns a Catfish Queen at its annual catfish festival.) On the coast, mullet was such an important food source during the beefless days of WWII that it earned the nickname 'Biloxi Bacon,' and it's commemorated at the annual Mullet Festival. Bass, speckled trout, white perch and the Gulf Coast redfish are also prime Southern catches.

Also lurking in the Mississippi River are ancient species such as the paddlefish, a Paleozoic monster that grows up to 6 feet long and shares characteristics of both bony fish and cartilaginous sharks. Now protected, its numbers were reduced by commercial fishing for its roe. The alligator gar – which grows up to 9 feet with platelike scales reputed to turn an ax – inhabits shallow water, where it captures fish in its ferocious-looking jaws. You can see some of these exotic species at the Aquarium of the Americas in New Orleans.

Insects The South has many varieties of huge and colorful butterflies, which are drawn to the region's abundant flowering plants; indeed, some gardens are specially designed to attract butterflies. Dragonflies inhabit the wetlands, and katydids and crickets chirp through the night.

Mosquitoes – the vampire of the marsh – are the most feared wildlife in the region; listen for the soft drone in the still air of early evening that signals their emergence. You'll also make the acquaintance of nuisance gnats so small they're frequently called 'no-see-ums.'

Huge, brown, winged cockroaches are another pest; they grow up to three inches long, can fly, and live both indoors and out.

Mammals White-tailed deer are by far the most significant large mammal of the Southern forest. The primary food source for generations of Native American inhabitants, deer is still prized game for Southern hunters. But what you will see most frequently are the smaller mammals, primarily raccoon, opossums (called 'possum'), rabbits, squirrels, bats and strange creatures called armadillos.

The armadillo has an interesting history in these parts. As the story goes, a pair of native South American armadillos escaped from a circus truck in Florida in the early 1900s and their offspring spread like wildfire throughout the South. They've proliferated so much, in fact, that they are now called 'weed' wildlife (another nickname is 'possum-on-the-half-shell'). They're slow-moving creatures, and sadly you'll see them most often littered alongside Southern roads. (They're inspiration for the local joke: 'Why did the possum cross the road? To show the armadillo it could be done!')

The short-haired Catahoula leopard dog is a breed native to Louisiana. The hound is a cross between a domestic dog raised by Indians of the Catahoula Lake region and a Spanish 'war dog' that came through the area in the early 1500s.

Nutria, a large rodent, thrives in Louisiana bayous and swamps. It goes by the name *coypu* in its native South America and is sometimes called a mouse beaver. The nutria was imported to the South for its fur. An accident during a storm in 1938 allowed nutrias to escape from cages kept by the McIlhenny family on Avery Island, after which it proliferated in the wild.

In the Gulf, bottle-nosed dolphins can often be seen accompanying boats out to the Gulf Islands.

Other Marine Life The crawfish is the best-known regional crustacean (also known as crayfish or crawdad). Found in swamps and marshes, the Louisiana crawfish is a sought-after and much-celebrated delicacy. Freshwater and saltwater shellfish include mussels and clams, and the Gulf of Mexico provides an abundance of local oysters and shrimp.

Jellyfish and Portuguese man-of-war are common in Gulf waters and should be avoided when swimming (applying meat tenderizer is said to be effective treatment for stings).

Endangered Species

Before European settlement, the continent's southern wilderness was full of bison, bear, wildcat, wolf and cougar; beaver, muskrat, mink and otter were also plentiful. Indiscriminate trappers annihilated these species, though recent efforts have been aimed at saving the remaining species and reintroducing lost species.

In Louisiana, about a hundred black bears remain, and habitat preservation has been dedicated to their survival. The preserved wilderness of several Gulf Islands provides ideal habitats for the reintroduction of diminishing or disappeared species. A pair of red wolves was reintroduced to the Horn Island wilderness, for example. Bald eagles have also returned to the islands as a result of coastal conservation efforts.

A local variety of sandhill crane neither migrates nor interbreeds with other varieties; the crane's survival is dependent on the preservation of its favored water-logged savanna habitat. The Sandhill Crane National Wildlife Refuge near the coastal Mississippi-Alabama border is devoted to this cause.

Native to the Southern woods, the red-cockaded woodpecker – with its distinctive 'Woody the Woodpecker' cry – is now endangered. Many programs throughout the region are dedicated to its preservation.

According to Elizabeth Rooks, executive director of the Mississippi Wildlife Federation, 'the greatest threat to wildlife in Mississippi today is loss of habitat due to changes in land use, plain and simple.'

The same could be said for the rest of the Deep South.

National Parks

Federal sites in the Deep South overseen by the National Park Service (NPS) in Mississippi include the Gulf Islands National Seashore, Vicksburg National Military Park and the Natchez Historic District. In Louisiana, the Jean Lafitte National Historic Park and Preserve encompasses five sites in southern Louisiana. In Alabama, NPS maintains a national military park at Horseshoe Bend, and another branch of the Gulf Islands National Seashore is found near Mobile. Within our coverage of

western Tennessee, visitors will find the Shiloh National Military Park.

The Natchez Trace Parkway is an NPS-maintained scenic highway that traverses Nashville to Natchez through parts of Tennessee, Alabama and Mississippi.

For state parks and other protected areas, see individual state chapters.

GOVERNMENT & POLITICS

Each US state is a separate governing entity that sends representatives and senators to Congress in Washington, DC. Each state is headed by a governor. In keeping with the nature of complex Southern history, Southern states like to operate as independently as the federal government will allow, while the legacy of a feudal plantation culture favors state control over individual liberties. State identification is a tremendous source of local pride and loyalty.

In its political organization, as in so many other ways, Louisiana is an American anomaly due to its founding as a French colony. While other states are based on the Common Law of England, Louisiana's political foundation is drawn from the Napoleonic Code of France. While other states in the region are subdivided into political units called counties, Louisiana retains the Catholic designation of 'parishes.' While political corruption elsewhere is generally regarded as a sinister and a serious offense, Louisiana has historically been led by a string of colorful characters who have artfully managed to turn corruption into political theater.

The entire South has undergone a radical political shift in the last decade. After the Civil War, Southern whites shunned the Republican party of Abraham Lincoln, even though as the 20th century progressed the Democratic party became more closely aligned with Lincolnian principles. This created a region of 'Dixiecrats' – whites on the Democratic rolls whose conservative voting records departed from the liberalism of the rest of the party. In the last 10 years, even the old-line Dixiecrats have changed camps and 'come out' as Republicans, joining the party that, today, is more consistent with their beliefs and values.

African-Americans in the South historically aligned with the Republican party of Reconstruction, but the civil rights efforts of Kennedy's Democratic administration caused many to register as Democrats.

The voting rights struggles of the 1960s continue in more subtle campaigns today. One of the most significant and controversial is redistricting. How district lines are drawn – the degree to which they highlight or diminish minority population areas – can mean the difference in the election of minority or majority candidates.

The South's conservative agenda has historically set the region apart, but recently the entire US has moved to the right, and now the South appears less isolated – a Southern platform that appeared extremely conservative 20 years ago now seems more mainstream. The Christian Right, a national lobbying movement that promotes a staunch conservative 'Christian' political agenda, has strong support in the 'Bible Belt,' and regional politicians largely support prayer in schools, support capital punishment and oppose abortion rights. But there are exceptions. New Orleans represents one comparatively liberal pocket.

ECONOMY

Agriculture and other industries based on natural resources continue to dominate the economies of the region. The South's historical reliance on cotton has been diversified and supplemented with soybeans and sugar cane. Lumbering and pulp-and-paper mills continue to be mainstays of many local economies. The coastal seafood industry peaked a few decades back, but it continues to make its contribution. Mississippi raises more catfish on fish farms than does any other state.

Louisiana's oil and gas industry was an important economic force until the region's oil boom went bust in the mid-1980s, when oil prices plummeted and oil production

Aquaculture – Crawfish & Catfish Farming

Though generations of Southerners have made crawfish and catfish staples of their diet, until recently these bottom-dwelling creatures were dismissed by many as 'mudbugs' or 'trash fish.' Thought to be inferior to other crustaceans and fish, they were consumed mainly by poorer Southerners, who were accustomed to eking out a living from the lands and waters of the region.

But with the advent of commercial aquaculture in the 1970s, what was once the province of folks with cane poles and croaker sacks is now big, big business. It turns out that the flat lands of the Mississippi Delta are ideally suited for catfish ponds, while the equally flat Louisiana rice fields are well suited for raising crawfish.

Thanks to aggressive marketing campaigns and concerted efforts to maintain high quality and high prices, crawfish and, to an even greater degree, catfish farmers are enjoying great returns on their watery investments. Today, more than 100,000 acres of Mississippi are devoted to catfish ponds, with more being added yearly. And, though crawfish lags far behind in number of acres under cultivation, the future looks bright, as the nation's curiosity about all things Cajun shows no sign of ending.

But all is not good news, especially for the catfish industry. Many of the people who work for minimum wage in catfish processing plants scattered about the region will tell you that chopping catfish is not very different from picking cotton like their ancestors did before them. Driven by quotas and afflicted by carpal tunnel syndrome, these workers are seeing none of the profits and feeling much of the pain. But, in a region where unemployment can reach 25%, these jobs are still sought after.

– John T Edge

dropped by more than half. Production has declined seriously since with little hope for recovery to previous levels. The oil industry is also active in coastal Mississippi (the Chevron refinery there is reportedly the state's single largest employer) and in Alabama. The river and Gulf ports of the region, which include those in New Orleans, Mobile and Memphis, drive local economies, and the shipping business is on the rise.

In recent decades, tourism has become a major industry in exotic New Orleans and the surrounding area and is also important in Memphis and Nashville. But it's had little impact in the rest of the economically depressed Deep South.

As for manufacturing, Mississippi is the largest manufacturer of upholstered furniture in the country.

The South was formerly the center of textile manufacture (related to its cotton production), but this industry has declined considerably over the last decade. For many years the anti-union South was a haven for manufacturing businesses eager to relocate from the pro-union North. The 1996 passage of the North American Free Trade Agreement (NAFTA) caused many businesses to look to foreign countries as a cheaper alternative to the South. Many of these businesses have begun to leave the US entirely, stranding thousands of textile workers with skills not readily adaptable to other industries.

In 1994, the three states with the lowest per-capita wages in the US were Mississippi, Arkansas and Louisiana. The Deep South states also have the highest poverty rates nationally – 24% of the population in Mississippi, 22% in Louisiana and 19% in Alabama (the national average is 14%).

Lackluster local economies have resulted in the explosive expansion of gaming casinos in the region. While riverboat gambling is a long-romanticized Southern tradition, it bears little resemblance to the huge Vegas-style casinos dropped onto small waterfront communities in rural Mississippi in recent years. Unfortunately, many of these casinos are a drain on the local economy

rather than a boon – more locals find employment, but many are tempted to spend their service salaries at gambling tables, which siphon money from local economies to out-of-state casino operators.

POPULATION & PEOPLE

Approximate state populations are as follows: Louisiana 4.3 million, Mississippi 2.7 million, Alabama 4.3 million and Tennessee 5.4 million. While these populations break down into distinct racial demographic groups, it should be noted that there has also been much cultural and racial intermixing over the past 200 years, and that racial categories and definitions are often not as sharp as they appear. The following descriptions are in order of prevalence in the population.

Describing racial intermixing, former Louisiana governor Huey Long said that all the 'pure whites' in Louisiana could be fed 'with a nickel's worth of red beans and a dime's worth of rice.' But white people are still the majority in the Deep South, and there's a big cultural difference between the heritages of whites in inland areas and those in New Orleans and along the coast. The city and coast were settled early in the colonial period by Europeans, largely French and Spanish Catholics. The inland areas were settled almost a century later by Anglo-Saxon Protestants from the Piedmont areas of the Atlantic Coast states (principally Virginia). While these white populations may appear homogeneous compared to other racial groups, they come from historically distinct cultures that can still be distinguished today.

The majority of blacks in the Deep South today are descended from African slaves who were brought to the Americas to work on plantations, and the majority of blacks in the US continue to live in the South. In 1900, 35 years after the Civil War, over 90% of African-Americans in the US lived in the states that had made up the Confederacy. Beginning around WWI and continuing into the 1950s, millions of African-Americans migrated north to escape economic hardship and entrenched racism. And yet today, the Deep South states still have the greatest proportion of blacks: 26% in Alabama, 30% in Louisiana and 36% in Mississippi (the only state in the nation whose population is over one-third African-American). Significantly, African-Americans are now relocating back to the South in record numbers. Between 1990 and 1995, a net total of 369,000 people have relocated to 15 Southern states at a rate 92% higher than in the 1980s.

Cajuns are descendants of 17th-century French settlers from Nova Scotia (called L'Acadie), many of whom were deported by the British beginning in 1755 after Britain wrested control of Canadian territories from France. After nearly a decade of exile, the majority of the dispersed Acadians (later shortened to Cajuns) migrated to south Louisiana, where they reestablished themselves in the wetlands and prairie regions west of New Orleans. Today, the 22-parish (or county) region is dubbed 'Acadiana.' The Cajun dialect mixes French, Southern and English pronunciations and terms. Cajun cuisine, folkways and music are also distinctive. See the Cajun Country chapter.

As is true everywhere in the US, the Deep South has been home to Native Americans from prehistory to the present, and the indigenous Mississippian culture of 700 to 1200 AD is considered one of the greatest in North America. However, disease, war and forcible removal wiped out many of the local Native American tribes in the 18th and 19th centuries. Several Native American communities live on state and federal reservations in the Deep South, though their current lands and numbers are small compared to others in the United States.

In Mississippi, the thriving Choctaw federal reservation, northwest of Meridian, has 6000 residents, and the smaller Chickasaw reservation is outside Tupelo. In Alabama, there's a Creek community northeast of Mobile. In Louisiana, a federal Chitimacha reservation is in the heart of Cajun Country; the state is also home to

Choctaw, Tunica, Coushatta and Houma communities without trust land.

As a result of widespread racial intermixing in the Deep South, many individuals of mixed race claim some Indian blood.

Perhaps no ethnic definition has caused more confusion than the term Creole. This is because in New Orleans the meaning of the term has evolved over the centuries. From the Spanish *criollo* (person native to a locality), the term was first coined in the early 18th century to describe children born of European immigrants in the New World – in Louisiana, this meant the children of the French. As New Orleans slowly transformed into an American city after the Louisiana Purchase in 1803, the term came to refer to native New Orleanians (as opposed to the large influx of English-speaking Americans, who moved to the bustling port in the 19th century). Thus, a 19th-century Creole could have been French, German, black (a 'Creole of Color'), or of mixed ancestry. Today, relatively few Louisianans identify themselves as Creole, and of those who do most are black.

The region has a smattering of many different ethnic and racial minorities. For example, Chinese and Lebanese laborers and tradespeople emigrated to the agribusiness zone of the Mississippi Delta earlier this century, and their descendants remain. Sicilian fishermen and their families moved to the Gulf Coast during the early part of the 20th century. A US government resettlement program in the 1970s and '80s brought Vietnamese families to the Gulf Coast because they were skilled at fishing; today you can find Vietnamese cuisine and Buddhist temples in New Orleans and in remote towns in Louisiana.

EDUCATION

Southern schools were the battlegrounds of integration during the Civil Rights era after the Supreme Court outlawed segregation in its *Brown* v *Board of Education* ruling in 1954. Many white politicians fought segregation in the following decade, but none more vocally than George Wallace, who vowed to defy federal law ordering integration of Alabama public schools.

As integration of the schools became reality in the 1960s, many white families enrolled their children in somewhat hastily established private academies, leading many public schools to become predominantly black, especially in the cities. In the last decade or so, however, the private academies have lost some of their allure, due mostly to cost, and more white families are enrolling in public schools, making the schools more representative of their communities. It can vary dramatically from district to district – for example, a school district with a good academic record and reputation can draw a more equitable racial mix than a neighboring district with lower achievement test scores.

Overall today, education in the Deep South suffers from neglect and apathy. In national educational achievement rankings, Louisiana, Mississippi and Alabama fall among the lowest seven states (and below national averages) for per capita government expenditures on education and for percentages of the population completing high school or earning a bachelor degree. Frequently, those with higher degrees find little economic opportunity in the region, and so they leave, creating a downward spiral for educational spending.

These statistics are not the whole story, of course, and in the extremely stratified Deep South there's an upper section of highly educated folks and a number of fine institutions, both public and private.

Distinguished universities in Louisiana include Tulane and Loyola, both well-known institutions in New Orleans that attract students from all over the country. The bastion of the Old South, the University of Mississippi (called 'Ole Miss'), is in Oxford. Mississippi's Alcorn State University was the nation's first land-grant university for African-Americans in 1875. In Alabama, Tuskegee University was founded by Booker T Washington in 1881. Tuskegee's graduates include Rosa Parks and the 'Tuskegee Airmen' (members of the Army's first all-black aviation unit in the 1940s); its professors included agronomist George Washington Carver. In Nashville, Tennessee, Fisk and Vanderbilt Universities are both historic and distinguished.

ARTS

One of the best reasons to visit the South is to experience the distinctive cultural arts the region has produced – arts that are intimately linked with the history, the land and the Southern experience.

Literature

Sahara of the Bozarts In a column for the *New York Evening Mail* published in 1917, cultural critic HL Mencken dubbed and damned the South the 'Sahara of the Bozarts,' charging that the region was 'almost as sterile, artistically, intellectually, culturally as the Sahara Desert.' As was to be expected, Mencken's words irked not a few chauvinistic Southerners. However, by the artistic standards of Mencken's day, the hyperbole was true.

Today, Southern artistic expression is celebrated around the world. The fictional works of Richard Wright, Eudora Welty and William Faulkner are recognized as among the most original and important of the 20th century. Yet there was a time when the Deep South was indeed almost bereft of 'great art.'

While South Carolina and Virginia claim a long and storied literary legacy, the states of Alabama, Louisiana, Mississippi and Tennessee are comparative latecomers to literary enterprise. Settled much later than the Upland South, the Deep South was considered a frontier area through much of the late 19th century. Ironically enough, this frontier mystique gave rise to the area's first literary movement.

19th-Century Humorists The most influential Southern writers of the antebellum years were not writers at all but doctors, lawyers, salesmen and other professionals whose work required travel and whose comparative wealth and education afforded the perspective and ability to translate the region's rich oral culture into written dispatches from the American hinterlands.

Often first published in Northern newspapers, the tales told were bawdy, vulgar, violent and often hilarious. Among the most accomplished of the Southwestern humorists was a Tennessean, George Washington Harris (1814–69). Best remembered for his 1867 publication *Sut Lovingood: Yarns Spun by a 'Nat'ral Born Durn'd Fool,'* Harris created protagonists 'full of fun, foolery and mean whisky' who displayed a rough-hewn, subversive humor.

By reading and studying Harris and other humorists of the old southwest, Missouri-born Samuel Clemens (pseudonym Mark Twain, 1835–1910) learned the writing trade. His first sketches bear the unmistakable imprint of those, such as Harris, who went before him. Twain, who worked as a Mississippi River steamboat pilot from 1857 to 1861, immortalized life along the river in his masterwork *The Adventures of Huckleberry Finn*, a poignant satire of Southern race relations and attitudes that tells of the unlikely friendship between Huck, a white boy, and Jim, a black man.

Local Color While the humorists of the old southwest were writers by circumstance or default, the next breed of writers from the Deep South were more purposeful. Though still concerned with the eccentricity and vagaries of Southern life, this postwar movement sold a romanticized Southern lifestyle to Northern editors intent on depicting the South as a 'land out of time,' where simplicity, honor and insularity prevailed. Two Louisiana authors, Kate Chopin (1851–1904) and George Washington Cable (1844–1925), were among the foremost practitioners of this 'local-color' style.

Though a native of St Louis, Missouri, Kate Chopin is identified most closely with Louisiana, where much of her work is set and where she once lived. During her lifetime, *Bayou Folk* (1894), a collection of local-color sketches, was regarded as her best work, but lately her second novel has risen to the forefront. In *The Awakening*

(1899), a tormented woman embraces adultery and later suicide along the path to enlightenment. In its day, the novel was scandalous; today it is revered as a prototype of feminist literature.

George Washington Cable is remembered both for his courageous stand in favor of civil rights in *The Negro Question* (1890) and for his writings about Creole life in New Orleans as depicted in *The Grandissimes* (1880) and *Old Creole Days* (1879). Balancing criticism and understanding of Southern culture, his work is a link to the modernist styles that followed.

Southern Renaissance As the rest of the US grew into 20th-century prosperity, the South lagged far behind in terms of education, race relations and nutrition – not to mention high art and literature. Yet, sometime in the early century, this region of storytellers, steeped in the oral tradition, came alive with great literature, their skills honed on the front porches of African-American homes, suffused with Native American myths and adapted from European balladeers.

Perhaps the phenomenon was a result of a long period of regional self-analysis brought about by military defeat and Reconstruction. Perhaps it was a result of lingering guilt over the treatment of African-Americans. In any case, the generation of Southern writers who emerged in the early and mid-20th century remains among the most well regarded in world literature.

An exhaustive accounting of the Deep South's primary renaissance writers and accompanying themes would be an encyclopedic undertaking; what follows is only a short overview.

Faulkner It doesn't all start and end with William Faulkner, but it might as well. As the Georgia-native Flannery O'Connor (perhaps the greatest short story writer of the 20th century) commented: 'The presence alone of Faulkner in our midst makes a great difference in what the writer can and cannot permit himself to do. Nobody wants his mule and wagon stalled on the same tracks the Dixie Limited is roaring down.'

Faulkner won the Nobel Prize in 1949, and in 1955 he won both the Pulitzer Prize and the National Book Award. Ironically, he received this acclaim after breaking almost all the rules of literature. In a style inspired by James Joyce, Faulkner wrote stream-of-consciousness accounts of his 'own native postage stamp of soil,' thinly disguised as Yoknapatawpha County with its county seat of Jefferson. In so doing, he grappled with the universality of man's inhumanity to man, and changed the way people of all nations will read and write for generations to come.

Born William Cuthbert Falkner (he added the u in later life) on September 25, 1897, this slight, intensely private man is best remembered for his Yoknapatawpha County novels: *The Sound and the Fury* (1929), a multigenerational account of the Compson family, and *Absalom, Absalom!* (1936). Also of note are the novels *As I Lay Dying* (1930) and *Light in August* (1932).

Faulkner spent stretches of time in Hollywood, Paris and New Orleans, but he always returned to live and write in the hills of northern Mississippi and the town of Oxford, for it was from those hills and from its people that he drew his inspiration.

He was often derided by local townspeople, who thought his work unreadable and his habits uncouth, and Faulkner struggled throughout his life to make ends meet. Despite their critical acclaim, all of his earlier novels were out of print by the mid-1940s. It was not until the 1946 publication of *The Portable Faulkner* that his work began to reach a wider audience.

Faulkner died on July 6, 1962. Today, his home, Rowan Oak, is maintained by the University of Mississippi as a literary landmark and is open to the public (see Oxford in the Mississippi chapter).

Faulkner's Contemporaries Among the few influential writers on the cusp of the Renaissance was William Alexander Percy (1885–1942). The scion of a wealthy Greenville, Mississippi, family, Percy was a poet, novelist, farmer and lawyer. (His nephew, novelist Walker Percy, spent much of his childhood in Uncle Will's care.) His autobiographical novel *Lanterns on the Levee* (1941) is a paean for a way of life on the wane, which, when read today, is seductive in its use of language if not its sentiment.

In 1922, a group of young Vanderbilt professors including John Crowe Ransom and Donald Davidson and their students, including Robert Penn Warren and Allen Tate, began publication of a small literary magazine called *The Fugitive*, which was dedicated to poetic expression. The title referred to the authors as fugitives from Victorian sentimentalism. Though the Nashville-based magazine lasted but three years, the literary group gave birth to one of the South's most enduring (and some would say cantankerous) documents. The group members, along with eight others, published *I'll Take My Stand* (1930), a collection of essays that was an agrarian manifesto, pointing to the virtues of the agrarian South in the face of America's creeping industrialism. The Agrarian movement, which emerged around 1928, died around 1935.

Though all were of great intellect and influence throughout American literature, today only Warren is still widely read. In collaboration with Cleanth Brooks (one of Ransom's students and a prominent Faulkner biographer), Warren developed a new formalist approach to literature called the New Criticism, which eschewed context for text. But Warren (1905–89) will be best remembered for his Pulitzer Prize–winning novel *All the King's Men* (1946). Inspired by the life of Louisiana politician Huey Long, the novel is a meditation on history and self-determination.

Tennessean Peter Taylor (b 1917), a master of the short story, was influenced by New Criticism; his collections include *A Long Fourth* (1948). His novel *A Summons to Memphis* was published in 1987, for which he won the Pulitzer Prize.

Like Faulkner, Richard Wright (1908–60) was a native of Mississippi. In both his nonfiction (*Black Boy*, 1945) and fiction (*Native Son*, 1940), Wright wrote of the suffocating despair and poverty that defined black life in America. His works are now appreciated as among the first and most enduring of black protest novels.

Along the Same Path Though her age makes her a contemporary of Wright's, Eudora Welty's (b 1909) style and subject matter stand in stark contrast to the works of her fellow Mississippian. Best known for her short stories ('Why I Live at the PO' and 'A Worn Path'), Welty, in a style some describe as sentimental, masterfully evokes the Southern attachment to place and family. Both stories can be found in *The Collected Stories of Eudora Welty* (1980).

From the town of Monroeville, Alabama, came two of the South's most original voices: Harper Lee (b 1926) and Truman Capote (1924–84). Lee is the author of but one work of fiction. Yet, her Pulitzer Prize–winning meditation on race and the guilelessness of youth, *To Kill a Mockingbird* (1960), places her in the upper tier of Southern writers. Truman Capote, who grew up with Lee in the same small Alabama town, is perhaps best known for *Breakfast at Tiffany's* (1958), the tale of a lovely but sad Southern girl who comes to New York to escape her past, and the genre-bending *In Cold Blood* (1965), a 'nonfiction novel' of the mass murder of a Kansas family.

Tennessee Williams (1911–83), a native of Mississippi who lived much of his life in New Orleans, was America's preeminent playwright during his lifetime. His works explore the Southern penchant for romanticizing the past while denying the reality of the present. Among his best works are *The Glass Menagerie* (1945) and *Cat on a Hot Tin Roof* (1955). *A Streetcar Named Desire* (1947) introduced two of the most enduring characters in American letters – Stanley Kowalski, the brutish interloper, and Blanche Dubois, the myopic fallen woman.

Walker Percy (1916–90), a native of Alabama, lived much of his life in Mississippi and Louisiana. After contracting tuberculosis, Percy abandoned a medical career to work as a novelist and thinker. His first novel, *The Moviegoer* (1961), as well as

subsequent works such as *Lancelot* (1977), portray humanity as alienated and adrift. Percy's boyhood friend, Mississippian Shelby Foote (b 1916), is best known for his three-volume history *The Civil War: A Narrative*, completed in 1974.

Contemporary Southern Fiction Despite popular perceptions, contemporary Southern literature is more than the sum of John Grisham's predictable plots and Anne Rice's horror-stoked gothic romances.

John Kennedy Toole was the author of the comedic tour de force *A Confederacy of Dunces* (1980). Toole's portrait of the pompous, flatulent, over-educated Ignatius Reilly is rivaled only by his perfect rendition of the wretched excesses of New Orleans. Unfortunately, the book was not released until long after Toole's suicide in 1969, when his mother sought Walker Percy's help in getting the manuscript published.

Raised in Henning, Tennessee, Alex Haley (1921–92) is known for coauthoring the *Autobiography of Malcolm X* (1965) as well as writing *Roots* (1976), a combination of history and fiction. An account of Haley's own journey to find his ancestors, *Roots* quickly rose to the top of the bestseller list, won the Pulitzer Prize in 1977, and inspired the TV miniseries that remains one of the most-watched shows in history.

Tennessee Williams

Other influential works included Margaret Walker Alexander's *Jubilee* (1966), a classic work in the African-American tradition. Ernest Gaines' *The Autobiography of Miss Jane Pittman* (1971) is a black history beginning with the Civil War. Will Campbell, a Mississippian by birth, is the author of *Brother to a Dragonfly*, one of the most poignant memoirs of family fidelity ever published. And Nobel Prize–winner Dr Martin Luther King Jr wrote perhaps the most evocative appeal for human understanding ever in his 'Letter from a Birmingham Jail' (1963).

A promising new generation of writers are honing their craft in the Deep South. One of the best working today is Pulitzer Prize–winning novelist Richard Ford, a native of Mississippi now living in Louisiana. His most acclaimed works are *The Sportswriter* (1986) and *Independence Day* (1995), both of which track the inner turmoil of everyman Frank Bascomb. According to some literary critics, he is a perfect example of the postmodern Southern writer, and his New Jersey landscapes are emblematic of a suburban new South.

Larry Brown, also of Mississippi, writes about the Mississippi backwoods as if he owns them outright. Recent novels like *Father and Son* (1996) and short story collections like *Big Bad Love* (1990) have ensured Brown's stature in the world of contemporary Southern letters.

Of the themes most prevalent in today's Southern fiction, most obvious and affecting is the South's struggle to come to terms with its troubled past. For the writers of the Southern Renaissance, that troubled past was a legacy of slavery and racial suppression that was to have culminated with the Civil War, and yet it lived on. For the writers of this newer generation, racism is still a haunting legacy.

Some authors, like Alabama's Mark Childress, deal with the horror in a lighthearted way. His *Crazy in Alabama* (1993) sets a boy's coming of age against the backdrop of the Civil Rights movement. Vicki Covington, also of Alabama, looks at the same period in her novel *The Last Hotel for Women* (1996), while Mississippi native Lewis Nordan uses magical realism in a fictionalized account of the 1955 murder of young Emmett Till in *Wolf Whistle* (1993).

Architecture The architecture most commonly associated with the South is the neoclassical antebellum plantation house. The plantation regions along the lower Mississippi River where Mississippi and Louisiana come together, and Alabama's Black Belt region, hold the highest concentrations of these homes. The small city of Natchez boasts an exceptional collection. ('That's because *they* surrendered,' explained one envious Vicksburg neighbor.)

Throughout the Deep South, many antebellum mansions are open to public tours. Houses are carefully restored and decorated, both by local historical societies and by individuals, with elaborate interior furnishings in period style; many display the furnishings of the original residents. On guided tours, you'll find that each piece has a story to tell, and the history of the family is at least as important as the house (if not more so). Often, the original architectural craftwork was done by slaves, and a few antebellum houses retain their original slave cabins.

Distinctive architecture is also a major draw for visitors to New Orleans. Historic homes in the French Quarter reflect the Spanish influence – nearly all of the French buildings were destroyed in the late 18th century by a succession of fires – as well as some Caribbean styles. including the Creole style of verandas, overhanging balconies (called 'galleries'), colorful palettes, lacy iron railings and ornamenture. Of later origin, many Greek revival mansions remain visible in the city's Garden District. The ultimate in Grecian architecture, however, is found in Nashville, Tennessee, where you'll find a full-size reproduction of the Greek Parthenon, built in 1897, including a 42-foot statue of the goddess Athena.

The humble houses of the working class also make a striking impression. A block and a half from Mississippi's grand capitol in Jackson, for example, there's a juxtaposing neighborhood of shotgun shacks shaded by palmettos. You see these narrow, often unpainted shacks all over the South. Their rooms are lined up one after another – behind the small porch there's a living room, then a bedroom, and then a kitchen – affording little privacy for whole families. The term shotgun stems from the ability to stand at the front porch and shoot straight through the back door. The single-wall construction is 'insulated' with layers of newspaper, posters or sometimes wallpaper in an effort to keep out the draft.

You'll also notice that many families in poorer communities live out of trailers and keep a 'swept lawn' in the dirt apron out front.

Pioneer architecture, common to the hill regions of Mississippi and Alabama, is exemplified by 'dogtrot' cabins, so-called for the central breezeway constructed between the living quarters and the kitchen. Only isolated examples of early colonial architecture remain, such as the Old Spanish fort in Pascagoula, Mississippi, constructed from 'tabby' – an adobe-like mixture of ground oyster shells, clay and Spanish moss.

Ideal places to see examples of the South's architecture are recreated towns, such as Montgomery's Old Alabama Town and Huntsville's Constitution Village, where historic buildings – from simple dogtrots to antebellum mansions – have been relocated to give a view of how people lived and worked in the state. In Mississippi, the premier reconstructed village is at the Agriculture and Forestry Museum in Jackson. In Louisiana, the Folklife Center in Baton Rouge contains pioneer restorations, and plantation houses are seen along River Rd north of New Orleans.

Perhaps the most distinctive modern architectural skyline is found in Memphis, where the recent addition of a mirrored pyramid, housing a convention center, creates a striking impression.

Gardens Elaborate Southern gardens feature exquisite landscaping and are often meticulously designed, accompanied by statuary, sculpture, fountains and monuments. A prime example of a Southern garden is Bellingrath, outside Mobile, Alabama, with its profusion of azaleas, dogwoods and rhododendrons. It was originally a swampside fishing camp, and part of it has been left that way to show just how much work has been done. New Orleans' house and garden tours take visitors to inviting gardens with dramatic secluded courtyards.

Visual Arts There are fine art museums in New Orleans, Nashville, Memphis, Jackson, Birmingham, Montgomery and Tuscaloosa, all of which have excellent permanent collections of classical and/or contemporary works. Many emphasize American paintings, though there's a strong regional appetite for European impressionism.

Locally produced artwork is very distinctive and worth seeing in its native context. Folk arts, for example, express the self-taught artistry of Southerners and reflect their connection to the landscape. Many works explore Southern themes and rural scenes in self-styled media – quilts, recycled scrap wood and other found objects. Fascinating environmental works include Earl's Art Gallery in Bovina, Mississippi, where proprietor/artist Earl Simmons has made his house into a colorful living sculpture. In Lucedale, Mississippi, the late Reverend Harvell Jackson was inspired to build a miniature version of the Holy Land he called Palestinian Gardens. In Memphis, the First Church of the Elvis Impersonator exhibits an artful kinetic shrine of Elvisabilia that operates when you drop in a quarter.

The region is also famous for its crafts, especially pottery and woodwork made from native materials; traditions range from the fluid styles of Mississippian George E Ohr ('the Mad Potter of Biloxi') to handmade accordions for sale in Cajun Country.

Performing Arts Social dancing is a highly valued traditional pastime, especially in Cajun Country, where the Cajun two-step and waltz take over the dance floor. Jackson, Mississippi, is regarded as a regional center for ballet, and there is an international ballet competition hosted there every four years.

The Alabama Shakespeare Festival in Montgomery, Alabama, has one of the world's best Shakespeare companies. Also, once a year the festival stages a production of a play by a Southern writer under its Southern Writers Project.

As for film, the South is not known for independent filmmaking, yet many independent and Hollywood filmmakers are drawn to the region to evoke the mystery, drama and landscape of the Deep South. For a list of titles, see Film in the Facts for the Visitor chapter.

Music

Jazz Music historians no longer call New Orleans the 'birthplace of jazz,' as any notion that the music was born here – or in any one place – has been decisively shot down. However, in its infancy jazz was certainly rocked and burped here, which has led recent jazz writers to describe New Orleans as the 'cradle of jazz.' Jelly Roll Morton, King Oliver, Louis Armstrong, Sidney Bechet and many others strengthened their chops while suckling on the Crescent City's ample bosom.

It's also not uncommon to hear New Orleans referred to as the most musical city in America – which may well be a valid claim. The French and their Creole descendants were mad about ballroom dancing and opera; New Orleans boasted two opera companies before any other US city had even one, and slaves and free persons of color preserved African music and dance at public markets like Congo Square. French-speaking black Creoles, who prided themselves on their versatile musicianship and training, played formal ballrooms for the whites, and music livened up with African rhythms for their black audiences. The atmosphere was ripe for sophisticated hybrid music forms.

A proliferation of brass instruments after the Civil War led to a brass-band craze that spread throughout the South and the Midwest, and many musicians of that generation learned how to play without learning to read sheet music. These musicians 'faked' their way through a tune, playing by ear and by memory, often deviating from the written melody. Soon, improvisation became another way to breathe extra life into musical arrangements. The stage was set for jazz.

To consider all of the great musicians who played jazz early on in New Orleans is to regard a rare and wonderful ensemble of talent. Many musicians left New Orleans, but they carried the imprint of the city with them. According to some, New Orleans jazz began with Charles 'Buddy' Bolden (1877–1931). One of the most problematic figures in jazz history, for little is known about his life and no recordings survive, Bolden was New Orleans' first 'King of Jazz.' For roughly a decade, between 1895 to 1906, he dominated the music scene in a town loaded with stellar musicians. Unfortunately, Bolden, at the top of his game, rapidly lost his mind. He was institutionalized for 25 years, oblivious to the fact that jazz was becoming popular worldwide and evolving into swing. When Bolden died, he was already long forgotten. He is buried in an unmarked grave in Holt Cemetery.

After Bolden, New Orleans coronated a series of cornet-playing kings, including Freddie Keppard, Bunk Johnson and Joe Oliver. Oliver is best known for taking New Orleans jazz to Chicago, where it reached a national audience, and for introducing Louis Armstrong to the world in 1922.

Armstrong (1901–71) made his greatest contributions to music during the 1920s, when he began to modify the New Orleans sound. New Orleans jazz had always emphasized ensemble playing, but to better

Gershwin on Jazz

Jazz I regard as an American folk music; not the only one but a very powerful one which is probably in the blood and feeling of the American people more than any other style.
– George Gershwin

showcase his own gifts for improvisation, Armstrong assembled his Hot Five (including Kid Ory on trombone and Johnny Dodds on clarinet) and shaped his arrangements specifically to support his own driving improvised solos. With his cornet riding above the ensemble, songs like 'Muskrat Ramble' and 'Yes! I'm in the Barrel' had an intensity not heard before. If the music sounds all too familiar today, it's because Armstrong's influence was so far-reaching.

Pianist Jelly Roll Morton was a controversial character – he claimed to have 'invented' jazz while performing in a Storyville bordello in 1902 – but he had uncommon talents in composition and arrangement. Kid Ory, who hailed from nearby La Place, Louisiana, was also important in the development of jazz. His expressive 'tailgate' style on the trombone accompanied many of the first jazz stars, including Louis Armstrong, and when Ory moved his band to Los Angeles in 1919, he introduced jazz to the West Coast. Sidney Bechet was the first jazz musician to make his mark on the soprano saxophone, an instrument he played with vibrato and deep, often moody feeling. Louis Prima, the Italian American trumpet maestro (and composer of the standards 'Sing Sing Sing' and 'Just a Gigolo'), also hailed from New Orleans.

In recent years, young talent has continued to flow out of the Crescent City. When Wynton Marsalis released his first album in 1982, he was only 19 years old – and yet music critics proclaimed him a genius. Not since Louis Armstrong had a New Orleans musician been so well received on the national scene. Soon, Wynton's older brother Branford Marsalis was also making waves, and other young musicians who were studying with Wynton and Branford's father, Ellis Marsalis, at the New Orleans Center for the Creative Arts, formed the nucleus of a New Orleans jazz revival. These included pianist Harry Connick Jr and trumpeter Roy Hargrove. This wasn't another resuscitation of 'trad jazz,' though. The young turks of the '80s were clearly coming out of the post-Miles Davis and John Coltrane world. Since

their beginnings in New Orleans, they have all relocated to other parts of the country, where media exposure and greater amounts of money tend to be available.

But a number of talented musicians have stayed home. Henry Butler, a blind pianist with extraordinarily quick hands, moved to California but then returned to New Orleans, where he plays several nights a week in local clubs. Trumpeter Nicholas Payton began his career recording classic New Orleans standards with a modern musical approach.

Trumpeter Kermit Ruffins is one of the hardest-working men in show business, and a major talent as well. Another trumpet player to watch is Irvin Mayfield, whose popular outfit, Los Hombres Calientes, includes yet another Marsalis brother, drummer Jason Marsalis, and the relatively elder statesman, the legendary percussionist Bill Sumners. They've got a good thing going, an intense cocktail of wildly expressive and percussive Latin jazz, and they put on a great live show.

Another trumpet player, James Andrews, has been gaining notice since the release of his album 'Satchmo of the Ghetto,' on which Dr John (tinkling the ivories) and Allan Toussaint (producing) lend support. Additional musicians to check out include Davell Crawford (grandson of Sugarboy Crawford, of 'Jockamo' fame), a funk-driven tour de force on piano and Hammond B-3, and Donald Harrison Jr (namesake son of the late Mardi Gras Indian chief), an inspired contemporary jazz innovator.

Delta Blues Out of the hardship endured by generations of Mississippi cotton-pickers and the rough and tumble – and often violent – world of the Delta juke joints, emerged some of the most expressive, beautiful and influential music of the 20th century. Alabama orchestra leader and composer WC Handy, an enormously popular entertainer, reportedly 'discovered' the blues in 1903 while passing through Tutwiler, in the heart of the Mississippi Delta. As described in Robert Palmer's

Rebirth of Brass

It could reasonably be argued that modern New Orleans music began with marching brass bands. Mobile brass outfits parading through the city's back streets for funerals and benevolent society 'second-line' parades during the late 19th century pretty much set the tone for things to come – Buddy Bolden, Freddie Keppard and even Louis Armstrong grew up idolizing the horn players who frequently played along the streets where these future jazz innovators lived. While early-20th-century ensembles like the Excelsior, Onward and Olympia brass bands never became nationally recognized, their tradition did not die. Many brass bands today, including the current generation of the Onward, Olympia and the Tremé brass bands, still play very traditional New Orleans music, though surely they're jazzier than pre-20th-century bands were.

The brass band scene received a welcome infusion of new blood in the late 1970s with the emergence of the Dirty Dozen Brass Band. The Dirty Dozen were anything but traditional, fusing diverse styles of music from 'trad jazz' to funk to R&B to modern jazz, much as jazz bassist and composer Charles Mingus had been doing since the 1950s. No longer a marching band, the Dirty Dozen continue to perform in clubs around town and tour frequently. They paved the way for the much funkier and streetwise Rebirth Brass Band, formed in 1983. Original members of Rebirth, including trumpeter Kermit Ruffins, have moved on, but a younger crew of musicians has kept the band alive, and it remains one of the most popular groups in New Orleans, where Rebirth performs regular club gigs. In recent years, brass music has continued to evolve in New Orleans, sometimes fusing with reggae music and even hip-hop. Rappin' trombone player Coolbone is at the forefront of what he terms the 'brasshop' movement.

book *Deep Blues*, Handy found the music 'primitive' and 'the weirdest music I'd ever heard.' Nevertheless he was intrigued by it, and began incorporating blues into popular dancehall music.

What Handy had heard was a solo musician performing intricate guitar patterns – simultaneously playing the melodic and bass lines – in a heavily rhythmic style. He slid a metallic object, possibly a table knife, over the strings to make his guitar 'sing.' The unknown musician also sang a plaintive tune, and his voice and his guitar seemed to interact, or 'talk' to each other. This was Mississippi Delta blues. It would be more than 20 years before music like this was recorded by anyone.

The Delta blues drew heavily on African traditions, chiefly call-and-response vocal motifs that had survived slave times in the form of church spirituals and field hollers. Guitars became popular in the region after Sears & Roebuck introduced its inexpensive Stella model, which could be purchased

by anyone for a few dollars and delivered to just about anywhere. The innovation of slide guitar traces back to a traditional African instrument, the diddley bow, which was often fastened to front porches across the Delta and was played with a bottleneck as a slide. The even more affordable – and portable – harmonica (or 'harp,' in blues parlance) soon also became a standard blues instrument.

Most early blues musicians worked the farms by day and played house parties and juke joints at night. They also played in town, on street corners and by railroad stations, where large crowds of black folks tended to congregate on Saturday afternoon. As the music grew more popular, many musicians began to travel the region, hitching rides and riding the rails between towns and plantations where parties and bars might offer work. The first artist to enjoy widespread fame and influence was Charlie Patton, a powerful singer and performer who hailed from Will Dockery's plantation, in the vicinity of Tutwiler. Patton's reign as King of the Delta blues ran the length of the 1920s, but he didn't record until 1929. By that time, a new generation of highly sophisticated musicians, including Skip James and Son House, was also beginning to record.

In the mid-1930s, Delta blues reached probably its finest level in the person of Robert Johnson. Johnson combined precision and ferociousness in his guitar playing, and his singing is intense and deeply expressive. But he's remembered as much for the intriguing details and myths of his life as he is for his musicianship. See the boxed text 'Robert Johnson at the Crossroads' in the Mississippi chapter for more on Johnson.

In the early 1940s, Tutwiler native Sonnyboy Williamson (Rice Miller) began his famous 'King Biscuit Time' radio program, out of Helena, Arkansas – it was the first radio program dedicated to blues music, and its success inspired a slew of copycat programs, making it suddenly possible for blues artists to reach large audiences. Radio encouraged greater exchanges in styles, and the music began to change. But change was perhaps inevitable, since many musicians were beginning to leave the Delta.

After Johnson, many blues artists chose to improve their prospects by relocating to Memphis or Chicago, where they amplified their instruments and made blues more popular nationally. These musicians include Muddy Waters (McKinley Morganfield), from the Clarksdale area, and Howlin' Wolf (Chester Burnett), who spent a few years working on the Dockery Plantation, where he learned many of Charlie Patton's tricks of the trade, before moving to Memphis and then on to Chicago. It was Waters who popularized the electric Chicago blues sound when he pulled together his legendary band with Little Walter Jacobs (a Louisiana native) on the harp. Wolf, who would be Waters' biggest rival in Chicago, first recorded at Sam Phillips' Sun Studios in Memphis. Though Phillips is now best known for introducing Elvis Presley to the world, he has repeatedly stated that the greatest talent he's ever known was Howlin' Wolf. BB King followed a path similar to Wolf's. A native of Indianola, Mississippi, he moved to Memphis, where he hosted a radio program and made his first recordings at Sun Studio.

Country & Bluegrass Nashville is indisputably the Country Music Capital of the World. For over 60 years, Nashville's Grand Ole Opry and recording studios have popularized what's been called the 'white man's soul music.'

Country music descended from the folk music of Elizabethan England, Scotland and Ireland, yet American pioneers made those traditions their own – in fact, some historical musical traditions were still practiced here in the Appalachian South long after they had died out in the British Isles. Elizabethan-esque ballads can still be heard in the Deep South (largely in the uplands), sometimes accompanied by the dulcimer. Bluegrass, still heard largely in the hill regions, carries on this tradition with music made from violins (called fiddles), guitars, mandolins, five-string banjo, bass and dobro guitar.

Country first became distinguished for its fast fiddlin', and it was carried through the hinterlands by traveling minstrels and snake-oil salesmen (seriously). Fiddle music swept through the rural southeast. In time, the guitar displaced it as the symbol of country music. Classic performers include Jimmie Rodgers (1897–1933), the 'Singing Brakeman,' who combined country blues with yodeling in the 1920s. Rodgers was the first country music star to attract a national audience with his recordings. His hometown of Meridian, Mississippi, maintains a museum in his honor.

After Rodgers, a long series of country & western stars emerged from the South. In the 1930s, Roy Acuff released several big hits, including 'Wabash Cannonball.' Acuff even ran for governor of Tennessee, but lost. In Louisiana, another singing politician, Jimmie Davis, actually succeeded in singing his way to the governor's office. Davis is best known for his pop tune 'You

MUSIC HIGHLIGHTS

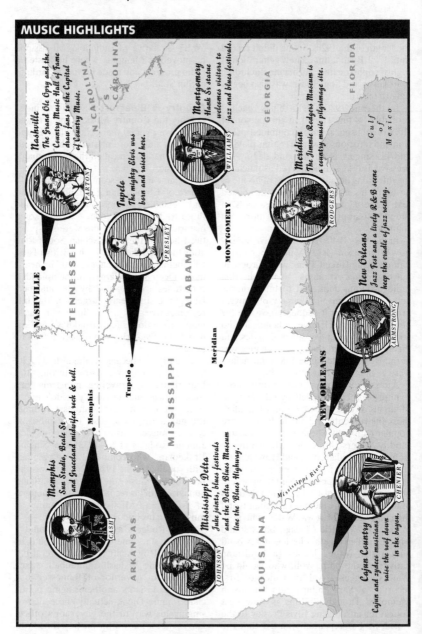

Nashville
The Grand Ole Opry and the Country Music Hall of Fame draw fans to the Capital of Country Music.

PARTON

Tupelo
The mighty Elvis was born and raised here.

PRESLEY

Montgomery
Hank Sr statue welcomes visitors to jazz and blues festivals.

WILLIAMS

Meridian
The Jimmie Rodgers Museum is a country music pilgrimage site.

RODGERS

Memphis
Sun Studio, Beale St and Graceland midwifed rock & roll.

CASH

Mississippi Delta
Juke joints, blues festivals and the Delta Blues Museum line the 'Blues Highway.'

JOHNSON

New Orleans
Jazz Fest and a lively R&B scene keep the cradle of jazz rocking.

ARMSTRONG

Cajun Country
Cajun and zydeco musicians raise the roof down in the bayou.

CHENIER

N CAROLINA
S CAROLINA
GEORGIA
FLORIDA
Gulf of Mexico
WILLIAMS
MONTGOMERY
ALABAMA
TENNESSEE
NASHVILLE
Tupelo
Meridian
MISSISSIPPI
Memphis
ARKANSAS
LOUISIANA
Mississippi River
NEW ORLEANS

Are My Sunshine,' which nearly every school kid in America is taught at some point.

The late '40s and early '50s belonged to honky-tonkin' Hank Williams of Montgomery, Alabama. Williams elevated country & western songwriting to unforeseen heights with lyrics that were by turns witty and deeply felt. He rolled out an extraordinary collection of hit songs before he died at the age of 29. 'Your Cheatin' Heart,' 'Kaw-liga,' 'So Lonesome I Could Cry' and 'Hey Good Lookin'' are all Williams compositions, and he wrote many more all-too familiar tunes.

Country music has largely been the sole province of Southerners until recently. While individual performers such as Johnny Cash have broken out (or 'crossed over') to become widely popular with increasing frequency, over the last five years or so country music has exploded wildly, with performers from farflung parts of the continent (like *Canada...*) attracting a national audience. Country is currently the nation's largest radio format, with 2600 radio stations – 1400 more than the nearest competing radio format. You can't get away from that old twang.

Cajun & Zydeco The traditional music of southern Louisiana, the music of the Cajuns and black Creoles who settled there, began with dances – waltzes, quadrilles and two-steps that were carried over from Europe. The 20th century brought innovations that led to two separate types of music, Cajun and zydeco.

The traditional Cajun dance party is a family affair called a *fais-do-do*, which translates to 'make sleep'; the custom at these events was to rock the children to sleep, letting them curl up with a blanket on the floor, so that the parents could get back out on the dance floor. In the old days, musical ensembles at these events typically comprised of fiddle, accordion, guitar and triangle (a ringing percussive instrument also referred to as a 'little iron'). Eventually, string bass was added to the mix, as were amplified instruments.

Early on, the diatonic button accordion was the driving force behind the Cajun sound. The first Cajun music recordings, from the late 1920s, feature the accordionist Joseph Falcon with his wife Cleoma Breaux on guitar. The record 'Allons á Lafayette' made Falcon a star in South Louisiana, enabling him to quit his job as a farmer.

The accordion fell from favor during the 1930s and '40s, as 'hillbilly' music and western swing began to exert an influence in Acadiana. Popular bands from this period, including the Hackberry Ramblers (who continue to play today, though they're getting up in years), featured the fiddle and guitar. Drawing on the popularity of Bob Wills from Texas and even blues chanteuse Bessie Smith, the Ramblers became the first Cajun band to appeal to wider audiences beyond southern Louisiana.

At the same time, Cajun music began to influence musical styles outside the state – most famously in Hank Williams' huge hit 'Jambalaya (On the Bayou),' which was inspired by the Cajun song 'Big Texas' by Papa Cairo (who remained bitter about the 'stolen' song for the rest of his life).

During this time, black Creoles like Amadé Ardoin (who first recorded soon after Joe Falcon, in the late '20s) and Adam Fontenot maintained very similar musical traditions, with the accordion the chief melodic instrument in simple waltzes at country dances. Ardoin's haunting, often plaintive Creole music was initially called 'la la.' An old one-step Creole number, 'Les Haricot Sont Pas Salés' ('the snap beans aren't salted') yielded a new name for the evolving music: 'les haricot,' in the local dialect, was pronounced (and soon spelled) 'zodeco' or 'zydeco.' But whereas changes to Cajun music were introduced by country & western, zydeco turned to the sounds of the Caribbean and blues for new ideas. Zydeco soon differed greatly from Cajun – the louder, more versatile piano accordion gained favor over the smaller button-box, and the fiddle all but disappeared. More importantly, syncopated rhythms began to drive the music. Even after drums were widely used, zydeco's primary percussion instrument was the *frottoir*, a metal washboard-like instrument that's worn like armor and played with spoons.

Zydeco began to take off in the 1950s, when Clarence Garlow released one of Louisiana's enduring standards, 'Bon Ton Roula' (also known as 'Bon Ton Roulé'), which made the national R&B charts. That smash hit was followed by Boozoo Chavis' infectious 'Paper in My Shoe,' and, soon afterwards, by the emergence of the 'King of Zydeco,' Clifton Chenier. Chenier gave the music a decidedly R&B feel, and in the 1960s he popularized zydeco well beyond the Louisiana state line.

By the 1960s, rock & roll and rhythm & blues were more popular among younger Louisianans, leading to a new regional pop music now known as 'swamp pop.' Bobby Charles' 'See You Later Alligator,' and Phil Phillips' 'Sea of Love' put local recording stars in the national limelight at a time when national radio and TV were turning musicians into major stars. Meanwhile, a Cajun revival began with the Balfa Brothers and Marc Savoy, who stripped the music down to its essential elements, revealing its traditional beauty to a wide national audience. Perhaps the biggest Cajun success story is Beausoleil, who continue to regularly play folk festivals and music events around the world. The music has changed as artists like Wayne Toups try to reach larger, younger audiences. Zydeco stars Queen Ida, Rockin' Dopsie, Buckwheat Zydeco, and Rosie Ledet also ensure that the locals, young and old, stay light on their feet.

Rhythm & Blues Although New Orleans is still widely regarded as a jazz city, it is as much an R&B and soul city. Since the 1950s and '60s, the city has been churning out singers, drummers and piano players in truly mind-boggling numbers.

New Orleans owes its solid reputation as a breeding ground for piano players to a man named Henry Roeland Byrd – also known as Professor Longhair. His rhythmic rhumba and boogie-woogie style of playing propelled him to local success with tunes like 'Tipitina' (for which the legendary

nightclub is named) and 'Go to the Mardi Gras.'

Some very unforgettable tunes came out of the Crescent City to rock the nation. In collaboration with Dave Bartholomew, Fats Domino became one of the city's most successful musicians, recording a string of hit singles including 'I'm Walkin',' 'Blueberry Hill,' 'My Blue Heaven' and 'Ain't that a Shame.' Also in the '50s, Johnny Adams wooed the city with smooth, gut-wrenching ballads.

The 1960s were greatly influenced by the guiding hand of Allan Toussaint, a talented producer, songwriter and musician whose legion of hits is mind-boggling. Artists who worked with Toussaint include Ernie K-Doe, who hit pay dirt with 'Mother-in-Law,' a chart-topper in 1961. Irma Thomas also frequently collaborated with Toussaint. The former waitress was discovered in a talent show and was soon recording hits like her touching, autobiographical 'Wish Someone Would Care.' A number of Toussaint-penned ballads, including 'It's Raining' and 'Ruler of My Heart,' lent definition to her body of work.

Toussaint's most enduring and successful partnership was with the Neville Brothers, who have reigned as the first family of New Orleans music for four decades. Aaron Neville, whose soulful falsetto and inflections are hallmarks of one of the most instantly recognizable voices in pop music, began working with Toussaint in 1960. Art Neville, a piano player, formed the group Art Neville and the New Orleans Sound with guitarist Leo Nocentelli, bassist George Porter and drummer Zigaboo Modeliste, a group that would soon change its name to the Meters and define 1970s funk music. The Meters and the Neville Brothers later joined forces with George Landry, who as Big Chief Jolly was head of the Wild Tchoupitoulas Mardi Gras Indian gang; Landry also happened to be uncle of the Nevilles. When Wild Tchoupitoulas began performing funk- and reggae-based Indian anthems ('Meet de Boys on de Battlefront') in the mid-'70s, it marked the first time the four Neville brothers performed together –

Charles and Cyrille rounded out the quartet. The original Meters disbanded and Landry passed away, but the brothers continue to perform together to this day, as do Cyrille Neville & the Uptown Allstars.

The Meters and Allan Toussaint also contributed to the success of Dr John (Mac Rebennack), who recorded his best-selling album 'Right Place Wrong Time' with their support in 1973.

Gospel Traditional African-American gospel music can best be heard in churches throughout the Deep South, though gospel radio programs and all-night gospel 'sings' (concerts featuring many performers) also feature this sacred music. The easiest way to get a gospel fix is to hang out in the Gospel Tent at the New Orleans Jazz & Heritage Festival – it's a truly uplifting experience.

Many spirituals originated in slavery, and their Biblical themes of freedom and return to the promised land were significant anthems of emancipation. The spirituals were later resurrected as protest songs during the Civil Rights movement of the 1960s. Many preachers, choirs and vocal groups have recorded over the years, with notable successes being New Orleans native Mahalia Jackson and the Five Blind Boys of Alabama.

White gospel music, though still celebrated in Southern churches, has been popularly eclipsed by 'Christian music.' Even in the smallest markets around the South, there's usually at least one radio station broadcasting a Christian music format.

Rockabilly Elvis Presley played a significant role in the incredible evolution of the hybrid sounds of rock & roll. In his 'Sun Sessions,' recorded in 1954 by Sam Phillips, Elvis and his band (including Scotty Moore on guitar and Bill Black on bass) added a rocking rhythm to the hillbilly standard 'Blue Moon of Kentucky,' and mixed in a little country feel to the blues number 'That's Alright Mama.' They experimented with other styles like a thumping, clacking string bass and jazz-influenced guitar licks, and in the process created something en-

tirely new, undeniably danceable and – by 1950s standards – *dangerous*. The formula would be copied for years, long after 'the King' had begun performing more mainstream pop tunes and starring in films like *Clambake*. See the boxed text 'Elvis the Pelvis' in the Tennessee chapter for more on the King of Rock & Roll.

Sun soon had a stable of talented performers playing this style of music, among them Johnny Cash (who dared to introduce rhythm to the Grand Ole Opry with 'I Walk the Line'), Carl Perkins (who penned 'Blue Suede Shoes'), Jerry Lee Lewis ('Great Balls of Fire') and Sonny Burgess, Roy Orbison and Conway Twitty.

The style seems to perpetually be undergoing a revival. Chances are a rockabilly band will be playing in a bar in Nashville or Memphis during your stay.

SOCIETY & CONDUCT

Southern hospitality is legendary, and most folks are friendly, accessible, hospitable and courteous, though they can be a bit xenophobic regarding outsiders perhaps due in part to the stereotypical and generally negative image of Southerners broadcast by the mainstream media.

Female travelers from less chivalrous parts of the world may be somewhat surprised to find that many Southern men continue to uphold traditional manners, like holding doors open for women. Male travelers, on the other hand, may risk offending local women by *not* holding doors open. However, Southerners are by and large a reasonable lot who know a non-Southerner when they meet one, and won't necessarily expect the same standards of politeness in others.

African-American culture has developed alongside of but distinct from white Southern culture. One of the most interesting things about traveling in the South is learning about these separate heritages, discovering where they intersect in addition to how they differ.

Locals may get edgy discussing Southern racial dynamics. Be cautious about initiating such a discussion until you've established a good rapport with someone. Simple politeness will keep your curiosity from inadvertently causing offense.

Southerners have a well-earned reputation for storytelling that springs from an extensive oral tradition, so once you get someone started, make yourself comfortable to enjoy a long tale. You'll notice, too, that time moves more slowly in the subtropical South than in other regions of the country. Travelers who can adopt the local pace will avoid frustrations and get the most out of their visit.

Be aware that being clean and tidy is important in the class-conscious South, and visitors who appear unkempt (wearing cutoffs, flip-flops or anything too revealing) will draw negative attention.

Dos & Don'ts

Southern rules of courtesy demand that locals use formal rules of address – no sir, yes ma'am – but they don't necessarily expect outsiders to be so polite. However, such small courtesies will certainly be noticed and appreciated; being extraordinarily polite and not coming on too strong will ease social interaction tremendously. Being sincerely curious, nonjudgmental, patient and deferential will also stand you in good stead for a trip through the South.

RELIGION

Religious conviction plays a large role in Southern culture. In the words of Victorian rationalist Sir William Archer:

The South is by a long way the most simply and sincerely religious country I ever was in. It is not, like Ireland, a priest-ridden country; it is not, like England, a country in which the strength of religion lies in its social prestige; it is not, like Scotland, a country steeped in theology. But it is a very large factor in life, and God is very real and personal.

More recently in the US, the South has been labeled the 'Bible Belt' to describe its commonly conservative, fundamentalist stance, which is dominated by Southern Baptists. In the past, the South has been nearly as divided over religion as it has been over race. Protestants did not tend to associate with Catholics or Jews, and intermarriage between faiths, even among different Protestant branches, was scandalous. The Klan persecuted Catholics and Jews along with blacks. Today it's still common for whites and blacks to attend their own churches.

Any sincere visitor with an open heart will be welcome at churches in the region. Learning about different faiths can be a very powerful experience, and it's a fascinating window into the local culture and community. Some tips: Arrive early, dress well, be generous with your contributions and be prepared to sit through a long service. Sunday services in Southern churches typically last from 11 am to 1 or 2 pm. Note also that since everyone – at least in the rural areas – is expected to be attending church, most businesses will be closed and few people will be out at this time.

In a typical Sunday service, dress is semiformal and modest. Even in the humblest communities, men wear jackets and ties and women wear dresses, though visitors not meeting this criteria are easily forgiven if they've made some effort to be presentable. Visitors are commonly announced (the preacher may even ask visitors to stand up to be recognized during the service) and greeted by church elders and members of the congregation. Note also that some churches assemble the children up front for a short separate sermon during the service, and visiting children would most likely be expected to join.

Southerners are very up-front about their religious beliefs, and you might be asked about yours. A question like 'Do you accept Jesus Christ into your life?' may be merely a conversation starter and not an evangelical query.

In Catholic churches, only baptized and indoctrinated Catholics are invited to participate in the Communion ritual of bread and wine. Protestant churches are more liberal in sharing their rituals.

Many visitors are attracted to the Full Gospel Tabernacle in Memphis, Tennessee, presided over by the Reverend Al Green. The Reverend Green was formerly a popular rhythm & blues singer when, at the height of his recording career, he got the calling to leave his secular profession and begin preaching. He preaches now with the accompaniment of bass and lead guitarists, a drummer and a keyboardist, who also back up the soulful gospel choir (see the boxed text 'Rev Green's Gospel' in the Tennessee chapter).

Protestantism

Fire-and-brimstone sermons, creekside baptisms, vacation bible school and strict blue laws are all part of a standard Bible Belt experience today. The Southern Baptists who now prevail in the South are a product of a split in the Baptist Church in antebellum times. During the 1840s, debates occurred over the interpretation of the religious constitution concerning slavery, resulting in the establishment of the pro-slavery Southern Baptist Convention in 1845. Other mainstream Protestant sects represented in the region include Methodists, Lutherans, Presbyterians and Episcopalians.

African-American Christianity

During slavery, all expressions of African or Haitian religious traditions were prohibited and repressed, and they had to be carried out in secrecy. Slaves were allowed (many were obligated) to attend Sunday services at their white slave-owner's church; some early black communities even founded their own churches during slavery. After emancipation, missionaries from Northern churches successfully set up congregations in black communities; the African-Methodist Episcopal church helped found many of the AME churches now prolific throughout the South.

Black poet James Weldon Johnson, writing in the early 1900s, found it remarkable that Christianity should have been so earnestly embraced by slaves, in view of 'the vast gulf between the Christianity that was preached and the Christianity that was practiced by those who preached.' Johnson ascribed the sustaining influence to the Old Testament chronicle of the Jews: 'This story at once caught and fired the imagination of the Negro bards, and they sang their hungry listeners into a firm faith that as God saved Daniel in the lion's den, so would He save them; as God delivered Israel out of bondage in Egypt, so would He deliver them.'

The church has always been a powerful unifying force in African-American communities. Early civil rights leaders, such as Dr Martin Luther King Jr, came from the preacher's ranks. Black churches have been the target of numerous racially motivated attacks, both historically (most well remembered during the Civil Rights era) and in a rash of arson across the South in 1995 that prompted a federal investigation.

Roman Catholicism

Roman Catholics predominate in southern Louisiana, creating an anachronism amid the Protestant 'Bible Belt' that shapes much of the South. French and Spanish heritages, along with a later Irish influx among others, account for the Catholic preeminence. Slaveholders were required by Bienville's 1724 Code Noir to baptize and instruct their slaves in the Catholic faith – an edict not rigidly followed – and black Catholicism abounds today.

New Orleans' signature celebration – Mardi Gras – is rooted in Catholic beliefs. Carnival begins on 'Twelfth Night,' January 6 (the twelfth night following Christmas), and continues to Mardi Gras, or 'Fat Tuesday.' Catholics traditionally feast (hence in 'carnival' the Latin root *carne* or meat) before Ash Wednesday, the beginning of Lent and a period of fasting and penitence that continues through Easter. Celebrations also take place in Lafayette and across Cajun Country, and along the Gulf Coast in Biloxi and Mobile, Mississippi.

Judaism

While Judaism is not often associated with the South, a significant Jewish community took up early residence here, particularly in river cities. Scattered temples attest to its presence, as does the Museum of the Southern Jewish Experience in Utica, Mississippi.

Voodoo

African slaves transported to Haiti (a New World clearinghouse port for the slave trade) brought an Afro-Haitian amalgamated voodoo (also called hoodoo) tradition to the Mississippi Valley. Much conjecture about voodoo focuses on its mystery and on ceremonies where worshipers enter a trance. As these colonized peoples had Christianity imposed on them, Catholic saints and Christian beliefs began to mingle with the pagan idols of African voodoo traditions. In New Orleans, the Voodoo Spiritual Temple is a local center for followers. The black-dominated Mississippi Delta region in northwestern Mississippi also has many voodoo believers and practitioners – many blues musicians carry talismans of traditional voodoo charms, such as a root called 'High John the Conqueror' held in red flannel 'mojo' bags worn around the neck or tacked to corners of rooms.

LANGUAGE
Southern Dialect

Southern variations on standard English are well known and rampant – in fact, you're not likely to hear any standard English except in some cities and along the Gulf. Southern dialects vary widely in pronunciation, pace, delivery and, often, lexicon. They vary not only by geography – accents in New Orleans differ from those in the Mississippi Delta, which differ from those in Northern Alabama and so on – but also by race and social class.

For general reference, Louisiana is pronounced 'LOO-si-AN-a,' New Orleans is 'New OR-lins,' and Tupelo is 'TOO-pill-oh.' The distinction between second person singular and second person plural is not made in standard English, but is found in the Southern speech of both whites and blacks as *y'all*.

Cajun French

Louisiana's Cajun population speaks its own dialect of French, which is widely spoken in Cajun Country, though mostly among old people and schoolchildren, as the language is enjoying a revival after many years of repression. New Orleans and lower Louisiana retains its historically French-speaking roots in its lexicon, but an outside French-speaker will likely have trouble comprehending the local dialect, mostly because of pronunciation.

Facts for the Visitor

HIGHLIGHTS
Since you haven't yet experienced any highlights of your own, we'll get you started with our own highly subjective list!

Southern Backroads – It doesn't take long to get off the beaten track, and when you do, you inevitably encounter the region's dense, unruly wilderness, or Americana straight out of Walker Evans' 1930s photographs. Be sure to bring along good music for the tape deck.

Getting Brassed in New Orleans – At Jazz Fest stages, bars and nightclubs, check out the local brass talent.

Eat Your Way Through New Orleans – Dive into a plate of trout muddy waters or slurp down a half dozen oysters on the half shell at Uglesich, or do a little daydreaming with a café au lait and beignets in the French Quarter.

Civil Rights Sights – The region is dotted with battlegrounds from the Civil Rights movement; the historic Selma-Montgomery march is reenacted every year.

Mardi Gras Parades – It can be as traditional as a Cajun Country horseback procession or as glitzy as a New Orleans 'super krewe' extravaganza, but either way (or somewhere in between), going to a Mardi Gras parade is an unreal experience.

Crawfish in Southern Louisiana – As they say down in these parts: 'Pinch da tail, suck da head' – and then clean yourself up.

Cajun Accents – Even if you aren't lost, stop to ask directions from an oldtimer in Cajun Country.

Weekend Lounging – Fred's Lounge in Mamou, Louisiana, on Saturday morning for a good dose of Cajun music.

Juking in the Mississippi Delta – Thought the blues was dead? Go back to the source.

Natchez Trace Parkway – There isn't even so much as a gas station to spoil the illusion that the Old South is still alive on this scenic drive.

Barbecue Pork in Memphis – If you know what we're talking about, you're already salivating.

Graceland – Elvis' estate welcomes the public over to the house – don't blow the opportunity.

Club-hopping on Beale St – The Memphis strip, once the Main Street of urban blues, still comes alive at night, albeit in a retro-touristy fashion.

An acquired taste

Country Music in Nashville – You may not care for Garth Brooks, and line dancing mightn't be your thing, but you'll have to admit Nashville is purty darn entertaining.

Smoky Mountains – Become a hillbilly in one of the country's most popular national parks.

Alligators – Seeing these grinning reptiles up close is a trip back to the Dinosaur Age.

Ice Cold Beer – After driving for hours with bugs splattered on your windshield, pull off the highway at an unassuming roadhouse that doubles as a bait-and-tackle retailer, and discover that Bud in a bottle, chilled nearly to the freezing point, ain't so bad after all.

'Nuff said. Have a great trip.

SUGGESTED ITINERARIES
A travel itinerary of the region covered in this book would almost certainly include New Orleans or Memphis, the two airline hubs, although one could also fly into Atlanta (not covered in this book) and from there easily explore eastern Tennessee or northern Alabama.

A three-day trip would be best spent in either New Orleans or Memphis, or someplace nearby, to cut down on time spent on the road. No matter where you stay, you'll wish you had more time. But from either city, you'd have your choice of exciting day trips (or overnight stays). From Memphis, home to Elvis and countless other historic American music figures, the Mississippi Delta town of Clarksdale is just an hour and change away, as is the college town of Oxford, where William Faulkner made his home. One might also arrive into Memphis, see some of the sights there, then move on over to Nashville, the capital of country & western music, in just a few short days.

Visitors to New Orleans with a spare day can make forays up the River Road into Plantation Country, where opulent antebellum mansions have been lovingly maintained. Cajun Country is just 60 to 90 minutes from New Orleans, and during carnival, one could easily see a rural Cajun Mardi Gras parade during the day and be back in New Orleans hours later, in time to see an urban night parade. In the last weekend of April, many visitors spend one day at the New Orleans Jazz & Heritage Festival, and make the drive up to Lafayette the following morning to take in a day of that city's more down-home Festival International de Louisiane. A two-night trip would allow you to sleep in a Creole cottage in the French quarter one night and in a Cajun trapper's shack near Houma on the second night, and be back in New Orleans the following day.

Similarly, one could fly into Atlanta, rent a car and spend three days or so exploring the Smoky Mountains, home to one of America's most popular national parks.

Of course, many travelers enter the region by car, bus or train, and bypass the major cities altogether. One could spend several days exploring the highways that frame the Mississippi Delta by car, but this would most certainly require a die-hard devotion to the blues. To see live music in a Delta juke joint, plan a weekend trip.

But ideally you'd have more time to explore the region, letting your interests determine which towns and cities you visit. Any one of the above itineraries could be stretched out over a longer period. In five to 10 days, one could do a thematic tour that would knit together all of the states covered in this book. Of course, if you don't have a one-track mind and are interested in all of the following themes, you'll need even more time for your trip.

Musical Heritage Tour

The section of the Mississippi River between New Orleans and Memphis (and onward, to Chicago) forms the backbone of American music, particularly African-American music. The various highways connecting these two cities via the Mississippi Delta, especially Hwy 61 (the 'Blues Highway'), are well traveled by musicians and music lovers. One could travel this route between these two cities in three to five days and be somewhat satisfied, but a 10-day trip, with a few days of jazz clubs in New Orleans, a bit of time juking in the Delta, and a few days club hopping on Beale St and visiting Sun Studio and Graceland in Memphis, is the way to go. If returning to New Orleans, you can always hightail it back down I-55 in about seven hours.

A two-week trip would allow tacking on a few days in the country & western mecca of Nashville, returning to New Orleans via Montgomery (where Hank Williams is buried) and perhaps routing through Meridian, Mississippi, to see the Jimmie Rogers Museum. Other detours on the music tour are Mamou (Cajun music capital), Opelousas (zydeco capital), Shreveport (where Leadbelly came from and where the Louisiana Hayride took place) and Muscle Shoals (where the WC Handy museum stands, and where soul music history was made). Any one of these towns would add at least half a day to your trip, and many really warrant an overnight stay on the weekend, when live music can be seen.

Civil Rights Sights

This is an emotional tour, by turns inspirational and bone chilling, and the road is stained with the blood of many who died for the cause. A tour of important Civil Rights sights might begin in Memphis and end in New Orleans, taking about five days; add a day if making a complete loop.

In Memphis, the motel where Dr Martin Luther King Jr was assassinated has been turned into a moving Civil Rights museum. Half a day's drive down Hwy 78 takes you down to Birmingham and the soul-stirring Civil Rights Institute. To the south, Montgomery has several significant sights, including the Civil Rights Memorial and the State Capitol, where Dr King and Governor George Wallace each gave speeches on the topic of segregation. In nearby Selma, voting rights marches began, and 'Bloody Sunday' happened here in 1965. (In fact, by driving Hwy 80 from Montgomery to Selma you can see the march route in reverse.) From Selma, head on to the Mississippi town of Philadelphia, where a memorial commemorates the murder of activists James Earl Chaney, Andrew Goodman and Michael Schwerner. From here, head to Jackson, where Medgar Evers was murdered, then south to New Orleans, where Homer Plessy is buried.

Wilderness Tour

Obviously, getting lost in the wilderness can be time consuming. In this region, the highlights are the Cajun wetlands and the Smoky Mountains, each of which merits several days of exploration. The long drive between the two regions warrants an overnight stop or two – perhaps to visit the Moundville Archaeological Park, where nature trails wind past ancient Native American mounds. Such a trip might be done in a week, but stretch it to 10 days – you'll be glad you did. An excursion to the Alabama Gulf Coast's wetlands and beaches would add two days. There are also beaches in Mississippi. In a two-week trip, you could also go spelunking in northern Alabama, take a rural bike tour of the midlands, or go on a sea-kayak trip out to wilderness of the Gulf islands.

A word of advice: don't pet the gators.

Antebellum House Calls

Architecture and antique furnishings are the primary ingredients on this tour – read up on your history to fill in the gaps. The River Road, through Louisiana's Plantation Country, and the Natchez Trace Parkway, which runs all the way from Natchez, Mis-

sissippi, to Nashville, Tennessee – a drive that can be done rather leisurely in four or five days (with stops to tour, and even sleep in, some of the houses) – will easily exhaust anybody's interest in glorious antebellum mansions. Be creative; break this tour up. Civil War sights are a nice complement.

Civil War Tour of Duty

All of the states covered in this book were part of the Confederacy during the War Between the States (1861–65), and all were profoundly affected by the events of that war. Begin in New Orleans, a town that was occupied by Union forces for most of the war, and visit the surprisingly charming Museum of the Confederacy. Vicksburg's National Military Park & Cemetery is just a few hours' drive away. From there, head north along the Natchez Trace Parkway to western Tennessee, where Shiloh was the sight of the bloodiest battle in the war. Heading southward again, stop in Montgomery to visit the first White House of the Confederacy, and end up back in New Orleans. This is a four- or five-day loop, perhaps more if you are also mansion hopping.

Scenic Routes

Many roads are destinations in themselves rather than mere routes between point A and point B. These routes aren't always 'scenic' in the classic, nature-loving sense, but they're older and slower than the more direct interstates, and tend to wend their way past sights of interest. In many of the above tours, we've already recommended scenic roads such as Hwy 61 or the Natchez Trace Parkway through Mississippi. Other interesting routes are Lookout Mountain Parkway in Alabama, which follows the high plateau along the western rim of Little River Canyon in DeSoto State Park. Motorcyclists can take the Trail of Tears corridor, which stretches 200 miles from Ross Landing in Chattanooga, Tennessee, to Waterloo, Alabama, tracing a route followed by Native Americans who were forced off their lands by the US government's official Native American Removal

Act of 1830. By car, you can approximate the route along the parallel Hwy 72. In Louisiana, the only way to get to little towns such as Mamou is to drive down the two-lane highway past rice and sugarcane fields, slowing as the road cuts right through other small towns on the way. Smaller highways link all of the towns in southern Louisiana.

Food Tour
You gotta eat, right? Don't just fill your belly with fast food, though. No matter what your itinerary, save your tummy for fine Creole food, po' boys and red beans and rice in New Orleans; some o' dem crawfish, fried shrimp and spicy Cajun fare in Cajun Country; and in the Mississippi Delta and Memphis, barbecue like you never even dreamed of.

PLANNING
Most destinations in the Deep South can be visited without a whole lot of planning beyond looking for bargain airfare. During special events (and you may want to plan your trip to coincide with a festival), planning is more important, particularly during Mardi Gras, when the most desirable hotel rooms may be booked up a year in advance. Reservations are necessary during Mardi Gras and for Jazz Fest in New Orleans. Popular festivals in smaller towns, such as blues festivals in the Mississippi Delta, can exhaust the limited local motel room supply quickly; here, too, reservations would be a good idea. Cities on busy interstate highways – such as Memphis, Nashville and Lafayette – rarely exhaust their abundance of motel rooms.

When to Go
Spring and fall are the most temperate seasons for travel in the Deep South, and many regional festivals are scheduled to coincide with the agreeable climate. These are also the most scenic seasons – spring is beautifully lush with fresh blooms and high rivers, and colorful fall foliage covers upland woodlands in October.

New Orleans celebrates Mardi Gras in February or March. Tamer celebrations can be found in Cajun Country and along the Gulf Coast (such as in Biloxi or Mobile).

The summer months of July and August are the least comfortable season in the Deep South. Heat and humidity can reach insufferable extremes. Anyone unaccustomed to a tropical climate will probably want to seek refuge in air-conditioning until the sun goes down. On the bright side, nocturnal travelers can enjoy sultry Southern nights languidly sipping a Dixie beer and listening to soulful music. And despite the weather, since most schools are not in session, summers are when most people travel through the region.

In winter, you'll find special holiday events and off-peak discounts on lodging. Although temperatures are chilly for the region, they're balmy in comparison to most of the US.

What Kind of Trip
Rural destinations can most readily be visited (and sometimes can only be visited) by private car. Travelers without a car are limited to large cities if they journey by plane or train, or large and small cities if they go by bus.

Outdoor adventuring – say, camping, backpacking or bike touring – is good most of the temperate months, though rain is frequent. Fall is the most predictably dry for long stretches.

Maps
As for most of the US, you can find good state and city maps for the Deep South. New Orleans and major cities will of course have the greatest selection of maps. Regional and backroad maps, however, can be difficult to come by. But considering how many places are unmarked or unnamed and known only by local landmarks, maps serve only a limited use in the Deep South anyway. In smaller towns, chambers of commerce usually distribute county and city maps, though these are not designed with tourists in mind. Outdoor stores are a good source for backwoods maps.

The American Automobile Association (AAA) issues the most comprehensive and dependable highway maps, which are free with AAA membership (see the Useful Organizations section, later in this chapter) and available for a price to nonmembers. These range from national, regional and state maps to very detailed maps of cities, counties and even relatively small towns.

The US Geological Survey (USGS), a federal agency, publishes very detailed topographic maps of the entire country, at different scales up to 1:250,000. Maps at 1:62,500, or approximately 1 inch=1 mile, are ideal for backcountry hiking and backpacking. Specialty bookstores and outdoor equipment specialists may carry topographic maps.

What to Bring

Casual clothing is largely fine, though it's good to pack a more formal outfit for certain social, business or church functions. Summer travelers should expect their feet to swell in the heat; pack only shoes with room to expand. Sunscreen, insect repellent and a hat are also wise additions to your luggage.

For outdoor adventuring, only light hiking boots are ever necessary; an old pair of sneakers will often suit for river floats or exploring muddy bayous. In winter, a light overcoat and gloves are comfortable.

Outside the major cities there are few bookstores, so bring the paperbacks and periodicals you want to read.

TOURIST OFFICES

The following tourist offices distribute statewide guides, maps, events calendars and often specialized guides such as B&B listings, African-American heritage sites or Civil War sites – all free of charge.

Each state also operates welcome centers at its borders, usually at major interstate highways. Some welcome centers can arrange lodging or distribute coupons for discounts at local motels – for example, if driving south from Mississippi to New Orleans, you might cut down your hotel expense by checking for coupons at the Louisiana welcome center. City welcome centers are often in the heart of tourist districts and are a good source for maps and brochures.

Alabama Bureau of Tourism & Travel, PO Box 4927, Montgomery, AL 36103 (☎ 800-252-2262)

Louisiana Office of Tourism, PO Box 94291, Baton Rouge, LA 70804 (☎ 504-342-8119, 800-414-8626)

Mississippi Division of Tourist Development, PO Box 1705, Ocean Springs, MS 39566-1705 (☎ 800-927-6378)

Tennessee Department of Tourist Development, 320 6th Ave N, Nashville, TN 37243 (☎ 615-741-8299, 800-836-6200, TDD/TTY 615-741-0691)

The US does not have a well-developed overseas tourist-office system. However, some states have information hotlines in the UK (there is no walk-in service). These include Louisiana (☎ 020-8760-0337), Mississippi (☎ 01462-440784) and Tennessee (☎ 01462-440784). Contact your local US diplomatic office for information from the US Travel & Tourism Administration.

VISAS & DOCUMENTS

In addition to required documents (see below), visitors should bring their driver's license and any health insurance or travel insurance cards. You'll need a picture ID to show that you are over 21 to buy alcohol or to gain admission to bars or clubs (make sure your driver's license has a photo, or else get some other form of photo ID).

Passports & Visas

With the exception of Canadians, who need only proper proof of Canadian citizenship, all foreign visitors to the US must have a valid passport and most are also required to have a US visa. It's a good idea to keep photocopies of these documents; in case of theft, they'll be a lot easier to replace.

Your passport should be valid for at least six months longer than your intended stay in the US, and you'll need to submit a recent 1½-inch square photo (37 x 37mm) with the application. Documents of financial stability and/or guarantees from a US resident are sometimes required, particularly for those from Third World countries.

Most foreign visitors need to obtain a visa from a US consulate or embassy. In most countries the process can be done by mail or through a travel agent. Canadians and those entering under the Visa Waiver Pilot Program may enter the country without a US visa, for stays of 90 days or less. Currently these countries are Andorra, Argentina, Australia, Austria, Belgium, Brunei, Denmark, Finland, France, Germany, Iceland, Ireland, Italy, Japan, Liechtenstein, Luxembourg, Monaco, the Netherlands, New Zealand, Norway, San Marino, Spain, Sweden, Switzerland and the UK. Under this program you must have a roundtrip ticket that is nonrefundable in the US, and you will not be allowed to extend your stay beyond 90 days. Check with the US embassy in your home country for any other requirements.

Visa applicants may be required to 'demonstrate binding obligations' that will ensure their return back home. Because of this requirement, those who are planning to travel through other countries before arriving in the US are generally better off applying for their US visa while they are still in their home country – rather than while on the road.

A Non-Immigrant Visitors Visa is the most common visa (B1 for business purposes, B2 for tourism or visiting friends and relatives). A visitors visa is good for one or five years with multiple entries, and it specifically prohibits the visitor from taking paid employment in the US. The validity period depends on what country you're from. The length of time you'll be allowed to stay in the US is ultimately determined by US immigration authorities at the port of entry. If you're coming to the US to work or study, you will probably need a different type of visa, and the company or institution you're connected with should make the arrangements. Allow six months in advance for processing the application.

For further information on work visas, see Work, later in this chapter.

Entering the US If you have a non-US passport, you must complete an Arrival/Departure Record (form I-94) before you go to the immigration desk. It's usually handed out on the plane, along with the customs declaration. It's a rather badly designed form, and lots of people take more than one attempt to get it right. Some airlines suggest you start at the last question and work upwards. For question 12, 'Address While in the United States,' give the address of the location where you will spend the first night. Complete the Departure Record, too (the lower part of the form), giving exactly the same answers for questions 14 to 17 as for questions 1 to 4.

The staff of the Immigration & Naturalization Service (INS) can be less than welcoming. Their main concern is to exclude those who are likely to work illegally or overstay, so visitors will be asked about their plans, and perhaps about whether they have sufficient funds for their stay. If they think you're OK, a six-month entry is usually approved.

It's a good idea to be able to list an itinerary that will account for the period for which you ask to be admitted, and to be able to show you have $300 or $400 for every week of your intended stay. These days, a couple of major credit cards will go a long way toward establishing 'sufficient funds.' Don't make too much of having friends, relatives or business contacts in the US – the INS official may decide that this will make you more likely to overstay.

Visa Extensions & Re-Entry If you want, need or hope to stay in the US longer than the date stamped on your passport, go to the local INS office (or call ☎ 800-755-0777, or look in the local white pages telephone directory under US Government) *before* the stamped date to apply for an extension. A visit anytime after that will usually lead to an unamusing conversation with an INS official who will assume you want to work illegally. If you find yourself in that situation, it's a good idea to bring a US citizen with you to vouch for your character. It's also a good idea to have some verification that you have enough money to support yourself.

Alternatively, cross the border into Mexico and apply for another period of entry when you come back. US officials don't usually collect the Departure Record cards from your passport when you leave at a land border, so they may not notice if you've overstayed by a couple of days.

Returning to the US, you go through the same procedure as when you entered

HIV & Entering the USA

Everyone entering the USA who isn't a US citizen is subject to the authority of the Immigration & Naturalization Service (INS), regardless of whether that person has legal immigration documents. The INS can keep someone from entering or staying in the USA by excluding or deporting them. This is especially relevant to travelers with the HIV virus. Though being HIV-positive is not a ground for deportation, it is a 'ground of exclusion' and the INS can invoke it to refuse admission.

Although the INS doesn't test people for HIV at customs, it may try to exclude anyone who answers yes to this question on the non-immigrant visa application form: 'Have you ever been afflicted with a communicable disease of public health significance?' INS officials may also stop people if they seem sick, are carrying AIDS/HIV medicine or, sadly, if the officer happens to think the person looks gay, though sexual orientation is not legally a ground of exclusion.

It's imperative that visitors know and assert their rights. Immigrants and visitors should avoid contact with the INS until they discuss their rights and options with a trained immigration advocate. For legal immigration information and referrals to immigration advocates, contact the National Immigration Project of the National Lawyers Guild (☎ 617-227-9727), 14 Beacon St, Suite 506, Boston, MA 02108; or Immigrant HIV Assistance Project, Bar Association of San Francisco (☎ 415-267-0795), 685 Market St, Suite 700, San Francisco, CA 94105.

the US for the first time, so be ready with your proposed itinerary and evidence of sufficient funds. If you try this border hopping more than once, to get a third six-month period of entry, you may find the INS very strict. Generally it seems that they are reluctant to let you stay more than a year.

International Driving Permit

An International Driving Permit is a useful accessory for foreign visitors in the US. Local traffic police are more likely to accept it as valid identification than an unfamiliar document from another country. Your national automobile association can provide one for a small fee. They're usually valid for one year.

Copies

Before you leave home, you should photocopy all important documents (passport data page and visa page, credit cards, travel insurance policy, air/bus/train tickets, driving license, etc). Leave one copy with someone at home and keep another with you, separate from the originals.

It's also a good idea to store details of your vital travel documents in Lonely Planet's free online Travel Vault in case you lose the photocopies or can't be bothered with them. Your password-protected Travel Vault is accessible online anywhere in the world; visit www.ekno.lonelyplanet.com for more information.

EMBASSIES & CONSULATES
US Embassies Abroad

US diplomatic offices abroad include the following:

Australia
21 Moonah Place, Yarralumla ACT 2600 (☎ 2-6270-5900)
Level 59 MLC Center 19-29 Martin Place, Sydney NSW 2000 (☎ 2-9373-9200)
553 St Kilda Rd, Melbourne, Victoria (☎ 3-9526-5900)

Austria
Boltzmanngasse 16, A-1090, Vienna (☎ 1-313-39)

Belgium
Blvd du Regent 27, B-1000, Brussels
(☎ 2-508-2111)

Canada
490 Sussex Dr, Ottawa, Ontario K1N 1G8
(☎ 613-238-5335)
1095 W Pender St, Vancouver, BC V6E 2M6
(☎ 604-685-4311)
1155 rue St-Alexandre, Montreal, Quebec H2Z
1Z2 (☎ 514-398-9695)

Denmark
Dag Hammarskjolds Allé 24, 2100 Copenhagen
(☎ 35-55-31-44)

Finland
Itäinen Puistotie 14B, Helsinki (☎ 9-171-931)

France
2 rue Saint Florentin, 75001 Paris
(☎ 01 43 12 48 76)

Germany
Neustädtische Kirchstr. 4-5, 10117 Berlin
(☎ 30-8305-0)

Ireland
42 Elgin Rd, Ballsbridge, Dublin 4
(☎ 1-668-8777)

Israel
71 Hayarkon St, Tel Aviv 63903 (☎ 3-519-7575)

Italy
Via Vittorio Veneto 119a-121, Rome 00187
(☎ 39-6-46-741)

Japan
1-10-5 Akasaka Chome, Minato-ku, Tokyo 107-
8420 (☎ 3-224-5000)

Mexico
Paseo de la Reforma 305, Colonia Cuauhtémoc,
06500 Mexico City (☎ 5-209-9100)

Netherlands
Lange Voorhout 102, 2514 EJ The Hague
(☎ 70-310-9209)
Museumplein 19, 1071 DJ Amsterdam
(☎ 20-575-5309)

New Zealand
29 Fitzherbert Terrace, Thorndon, Wellington
(☎ 644-472-2068)

Norway
Drammensveien 18, Oslo (☎ 22-44-85-50)

Russia
Novinskiy Bulivar 19/21, Moscow 121099
(☎ 095-728-5000)

South Africa
877 Pretorius St, Box 9536, Pretoria 0001
(☎ 12-342-1048)

Spain
Calle Serrano 75, 28006 Madrid (☎ 91-587-2200)

Sweden
Dag Hammarskjölds Väg 31, SE-115 89 Stock-
holm (☎ 8-783-5300)

Switzerland
Jubiläumsstrasse 93, 3001 Berne
(☎ 31-357-70 11)

UK
24 Grosvenor Square, London W1A 1AE
(☎ 20-7499-9000)
3 Regent Terrace, Edinburgh EH7 5BW
(☎ 31-556-8315)
Queens House, 14 Queen St, Belfast BT1 6EQ
(☎ 28-9032-8239)

Foreign Consulates in New Orleans

Many countries do not have diplomatic representation in the Deep South; what consulates exist are located in New Orleans. Most countries have representation in Washington, DC; call that city's directory assistance (☎ 202-555-1212) for information. The closest Canadian consulate is in Miami, Florida.

It's important to realize what your own embassy – the embassy of the country of which you are a citizen – can and can't do to help you if you get into trouble. Generally speaking, it won't be much help to you if the trouble you're in is remotely your own fault. Remember that you are bound by the laws of the country you are in. Your embassy will not be sympathetic if you end up in jail after committing a crime locally, even if such actions are legal in your own country.

In genuine emergencies, you might get some assistance, but only if other channels have been exhausted. If you need to get home urgently, a free ticket home is exceedingly unlikely – the embassy would expect you to have insurance. If all your money and documents are stolen, it might assist you with getting a new passport, but a loan for onward travel is out of the question. Consulates in New Orleans include:

Austria
Consulate of Austria, 755 Magazine St
(☎ 504-581-5141)

Denmark
Consulate of Denmark, 321 St Charles Ave
(☎ 504-586-8300)

Finland
    Consulate of Finland, 1100 Poydras Ave
    (☎ 504-523-6451)

France
    Consulate-General of France, 300 Poydras Ave
    (☎ 504-523-5772)

Germany
    Honorary Consulate of FRG, 639 Loyola Ave
    (☎ 504-576-4289)

Italy
    Consulate of Italy, 630 Camp St (☎ 504-524-2271)

Japan
    Consulate-General of Japan, 639 Loyola Ave
    (☎ 504-529-2101)

Mexico
    Consulate-General of Mexico, 2 Canal St
    (☎ 504-522-3596)

Netherlands
    Consulate of the Netherlands, 643 Magazine St
    (☎ 504-596-2838)

Spain
    Consulate-General of Spain, 2 Canal St
    (☎ 504-525-4951)

Sweden
    Consul of Sweden, 2640 Canal St (☎ 504-827-8600)

UK
    Honorary Consulate of Great Britain, 321 St
    Charles Ave (☎ 504-524-4180)

CUSTOMS

US Customs allows each person older than the age of 21 to bring one liter of liquor and 200 cigarettes duty free into the US. US citizens are allowed to import, duty free, $400 worth of gifts from abroad, while non-US citizens are allowed to bring in a maximum of $100 worth.

MONEY
Currency

The US dollar is divided into 100 cents (¢). Coins come in denominations of 1¢ (penny), 5¢ (nickel), 10¢ (dime), 25¢ (quarter) and the seldom seen 50¢ (half-dollar; larger in size than a quarter with a profile of John F Kennedy) and $1 (the silver colored Susan B Anthony coin and the new gold colored Sacajawea coin). Quarters are the most commonly used coins in vending machines and parking meters, so

it's handy to have a stash of them. You are unlikely to see either the half-dollar or dollar coins, unless you go gambling and play the slots, or get them as change from ticket and stamp machines. Be aware that they look similar to quarters. Notes, commonly called bills, come in $1, $2, $5, $10, $20, $50 and $100 denominations – $2 bills are rare, but perfectly legal.

US law permits you to bring in, or take out, as much as US$10,000 in US or foreign currency, traveler's checks or letters of credit without formality. Larger amounts of any or all of the above – there are no limits – must be declared to customs.

Exchange Rates

At press time, exchange rates were:

country	units		dollars
Australia	A$1	=	$0.54
Canada	C$1	=	$0.67
Euro	€1	=	$0.87
France	FF1	=	$0.13
Germany	DM1	=	$0.45
Hong Kong	HK$10	=	$1.28
Japan	¥100	=	$0.92
New Zealand	NZ$1	=	$0.40
United Kingdom	UK£1	=	$1.46

Exchanging Money

Most banks in major cities will exchange cash or traveler's checks in major foreign currencies, though banks in smaller cities and outlying areas don't do so very often, and it may take them some time. It's probably less of a hassle to exchange foreign currency in larger cities. Although you will get a better rate at a bank, Thomas Cook, American Express and exchange windows in airports also offer exchange.

Cash & Traveler's Checks Though carrying cash is more risky, it's still a good idea to travel with some for the convenience; it's useful to help pay for all those tips, and some smaller, more remote places might not accept credit cards or traveler's checks.

Traveler's checks offer greater protection from theft or loss and in many places can be

Whistling 10

Prior to the Civil War, the Citizen's Bank of New Orleans minted $10 bank notes. On the back of these bills appeared the French word *dix* (10). Southerners handling these bills came to refer to them as 'dixies.' Eventually, a popular tune called 'Dixie' was the theme commonly whistled by Confederate soldiers on the march – hence, 'whistling Dixie' has come to mean pursuing a lost cause. And, of course, in this roundabout way, Dixie (or Dixieland) became the nickname for the American South.

used as cash. American Express and Thomas Cook are widely accepted and have efficient replacement policies.

Keeping a record of the check numbers and the checks you have used is vital when it comes to replacing lost checks. Keep this record separate from the checks themselves.

You'll save yourself trouble and expense if you buy traveler's checks in US dollars. The savings you *might* make on exchange rates by carrying traveler's checks in a foreign currency don't make up for the hassle of exchanging them at banks and other facilities. Restaurants, hotels and most stores accept US-dollar traveler's checks as if they were cash, so if you're carrying traveler's checks in US dollars, the odds are you'll rarely have to use a bank or pay an exchange fee.

Take most of the checks in large denominations. It's only toward the end of a stay that you may want to change a small denomination check to make sure you aren't left with too much local currency.

ATMs Automated teller machines (ATMs) are a convenient way of obtaining cash from a bank account within the US or abroad. Most banks charge a $1 to $4 fee for using their ATM with a card not issued by them – it's federal law that you must be warned in advance of how much your account will be charged.

However, their convenience can't be beat: small-town banks in the middle of nowhere and shopping centers have ATMs, and they often operate 24 hours a day. There are various ATM networks (Exchange, Accel, Plus and Cirrus are widespread throughout the US) and most banks are affiliated with several.

Using a credit, debit or charge card, you can withdraw money from an ATM with a 2% fee ($2 minimum) plus the non-issuing bank service charge. Check with your bank or credit card company for exact information.

Credit & Debit Cards Major credit cards are accepted at hotels, restaurants, gas stations, shops and car-rental agencies throughout the US. In fact, without one you'll find it hard to perform certain transactions, such as renting a car or purchasing tickets to performances.

Even if you prefer to rely on traveler's checks and ATMs, it's a good idea to carry a credit card for emergencies. If you're planning to rely primarily upon credit cards, it would be wise to have a Visa or MasterCard in your deck, since other cards aren't as widely accepted.

Carry copies of your credit card numbers separately from the cards. If you lose your credit cards or they get stolen, contact the company immediately. Following are toll-free numbers for the main credit card companies.

Visa	☎ 800-336-8472
MasterCard	☎ 800-826-2181
American Express	☎ 800-528-4800
Discover	☎ 800-347-2683
Diners Club	☎ 800-234-6377

International Transfers You can instruct your bank back home to send you a draft. Specify the city, bank and branch to which you want your money directed, or ask your home bank to tell you where a suitable one is, and make sure you get the details right. The procedure is easier if you've authorized someone back home to access your account.

Money sent by telegraphic transfer should reach you within a week; by mail allow at least two weeks. When it arrives it will most likely be converted into local currency – you can take it as cash or buy traveler's checks.

You can also transfer money by American Express, Thomas Cook or Western Union, though the latter has fewer international offices.

Security

Carry your money (and only the money you'll need for that day) somewhere inside your clothing (in a money belt, a bra or socks) rather than in a handbag or an outside pocket. Put the money in several places. Most hotels and hostels provide safekeeping, so you can leave your money and other valuables with them. Hide or don't wear any valuable jewelry. A safety pin or key ring to hold the zipper tags of a daypack together can help deter theft.

Costs

Costs for accommodations vary widely, depending on the season, what city or town you are staying in, whether or not festivals are happening, and the type of accommodations you choose. Going against the grain, in many areas near the Gulf Coast (including New Orleans), room rates drop significantly during summer and rise in the spring and fall. Generally, rates are highest in cities, with New Orleans having the highest median rate in the region. On the whole, hotels in southern Louisiana tend to charge more than comparable lodgings elsewhere.

Compounding that, New Orleans' calendar is filled with festivals and conventions, which drive rates up even more: during Jazz Fest and Mardi Gras, rates double or even triple, so an affordable $40 room suddenly costs $120 for the night. In Mississippi and Alabama, the cheapest motel rates usually be in the $30 to $40 range. In Louisiana and Tennessee, you might have to raise that minimum by $10 to $20. For B&B's, unique cabins, and luxury hotels, expect to pay $80 to $120 or even more. Rustic camping is inexpensive – about $8 or so per night – but only costlier sites have amenities such as hot showers.

Food is very reasonable. The occasional splurge at a first-rate restaurant will cost anywhere between $25 and $50 per person depending on where you are, but good restaurant meals can be found for $10 – or even half that for lunch. If you purchase food at markets, you may get by even more cheaply.

In all, the US is probably the most promotion-oriented society on Earth. Though the bargaining common in many other countries is not generally accepted in the US, you can work angles to cut costs. For example, at hotels in the off-season, casually and respectfully mentioning a competitor's rate may prompt a manager to lower the quoted rate. Discount coupons are widely available – check circulars in Sunday papers and at supermarkets, tourist offices, chambers of commerce and welcome centers.

Intracity public transportation is relatively inexpensive; buses or streetcars cost from 80¢ to $1.50 depending on distance and the system. Owning or renting a car is much less expensive than in other parts of the world. In some areas a car is the only way of getting around; rentals are fairly inexpensive in large cities, and gasoline costs a fraction of what it does in Europe and most of the rest of the world. Promotional deals are published every Sunday in the travel sections of US Sunday papers, and some deals are available only on rental agency Web sites. Shop carefully. For more information on purchasing and operating a car, see the Getting Around chapter.

Tipping

Tipping is expected in restaurants and better hotels, and by taxi drivers, hairdressers and baggage carriers. In restaurants, wait staff are paid minimal wages and rely upon tips for their livelihoods. Tip 15% unless the service is terrible (in which case a complaint to the manager is warranted) or up to 20% if the service is great. Never tip in fast-food or take-out restaurants. At Southern cafeterias or buffet-style restaurants with drink waiters, it's customary to leave $1 or $2, depending on the size of your party or your requests.

Taxi drivers expect 10% and hairdressers get 15% if their service is satisfactory. Baggage carriers (skycaps in airports, attendants in hotels) get $1 for the first bag and 50¢ for each additional bag.

Taxes & Refunds

Almost everything you pay for in the US is taxed. Occasionally, the tax is included in the advertised price (eg plane tickets, gas, drinks in a bar and entrance tickets for museums or theaters). Restaurant meals and drinks, accommodations and most other purchases are taxed, and this is added on top of the advertised cost. Unless otherwise stated, the prices given in this book don't reflect local taxes. International visitors should inquire about sales tax refunds, especially in Louisiana.

When inquiring about hotel or motel rates, be sure to ask about tax amounts, which can exceed 10%.

POST & COMMUNICATIONS
Postal Rates

Postage rates increase every few years. Currently, rates for 1st-class mail within the US are 33¢ for letters up to 1oz (23¢ for each additional ounce) and 20¢ for postcards.

International airmail rates (except to Canada and Mexico) are 60¢ for a half-ounce letter and 40¢ for each additional half-ounce. International postcard rates are 55¢. Letters to Canada are 48¢ for a half-ounce letter and 45¢ for a postcard. Letters to Mexico are 40¢ for a half-ounce letter, 40¢ for a postcard. Aerogrammes are 60¢.

The cost for parcels airmailed anywhere within the US is $3.20 for 2lbs or less, increasing up to $6.50 for 5lbs. For heavier items, rates differ according to the distance mailed.

Sending Mail

If you have the correct postage, you can drop your mail into any blue mailbox. However, to send a package 16oz (1lb) or larger, you must bring it to a post office. If you need to buy stamps or weigh your mail, go to the nearest post office. The address of each town's main post office is given in the

text. In addition, larger towns have branch post offices and post office centers in some supermarkets and drug stores. For the address of the nearest, check the telephone directory.

Usually, post offices are open from 8 am to 5 pm weekdays and 8 am to 3 pm on Saturday, but it all depends on the branch.

Receiving Mail

You can have mail sent to you care of General Delivery at any post office that has its own zip (postal) code. Mail is usually held for 10 days before it's returned to sender; you might request your correspondents to write 'hold for arrival' on their letters. Mail should be addressed like this:

Name
c/o General Delivery
New Orleans, LA 70112
USA

You can also rent a post office box at US post offices or at businesses such as Mail Boxes Etc if you're staying a month or more. Alternatively, have mail sent to the local representative of American Express or Thomas Cook, which provide mail service for their customers.

Telephone

All phone numbers within the US consist of a three-digit area code followed by a seven-digit local number. If you are calling locally, just dial the seven-digit number. If you are calling long distance, dial 1 + the three-digit area code + the seven-digit number. If you're calling from abroad, note that the international country code for the US is 1.

For local directory assistance, dial ☎ 411. For directory assistance outside your area code, dial ☎ 1 + the three-digit area code of the place you want to call + 555-1212. For example, to obtain directory assistance for New Orleans, dial ☎ 1-504-555-1212.

A local and national area code map is in the telephone directory. Be aware that metropolitan areas are being divided into multiple new area codes. These changes are not reflected in older phone books. When in doubt, ask the operator.

The 800, 888, and 877 area codes are designated for toll-free numbers within the US and sometimes Canada. Calling areas can be restricted to outside the local area or within the US. For toll-free directory assistance, call ☎ 800-555-1212.

Local calls usually cost 35¢ at pay phones. Long-distance rates vary depending on the destination and which telephone company you use – call the operator for rate information. Don't ask the operator to put your call through, however, because operator-assisted calls are much more expensive than direct-dial calls. Generally, nights (11 pm to 8 am), all day Saturday, and from 8 am to 5 pm Sunday are the cheapest times to call. Day calls (8 am to 5 pm, Monday to Friday) are generally full-price within the USA.

In an attempt to make their phone numbers snappy and memorable, many businesses use words, which translate to numbers on the phone keypad. To translate: 1 is unassigned, 2 – ABC, 3 – DEF, 4 – GHI, 5 – JKL, 6 – MNO, 7 – PRS, 8 – TUV, 9 – WXY. Sorry, no Qs or Zs.

International Calls To make a direct international call, dial 011, then the country code, followed by the area code and the phone number. You may need to wait as long as 45 seconds for the ringing to start. International rates vary depending on the time of day and the destination. Call the operator (☎ 0) for rates. The first minute is always more expensive than extra minutes.

Hotel & Pay Phones Many hotels (especially the more expensive ones) add a service charge of 50¢ to $1 for each local call made from a room phone, and they also have hefty surcharges for long-distance calls. Public pay phones, which can be found in most lobbies, are always cheaper. You can pump change into, use a credit or phone card with, or make collect calls from pay phones.

Phone Debit Cards There's a wide range of local and international phonecards. Lonely Planet's eKno Communication Card is aimed specifically at independent travelers and provides budget international calls, a range of messaging services, free email and travel information – for local calls, you're usually better off with a local card.

You can join on the Web at www .ekno.lonelyplanet.com or by phone from the Southern US by dialing ☎ 800-707-0031. To use eKno from the Southern US once you have joined, dial ☎ 800-706-1333.

Check the eKno Web site for joining and access numbers from other countries and updates on super budget local access numbers and new features.

Other phonecards are widely available in airports, US post offices, Western Union and other sources.

Fax
You can typically find fax machines at shipping companies such as Mail Boxes Etc, photocopy services and hotel business service centers, but be prepared to pay high prices (more than $1 a page).

Email & Internet Access
In recent years, it's become very easy to get online. Campus or public libraries may provide connections, as well as hotel business service centers. Trendy cafes in major cities sometimes offer Internet service.

Through Yahoo! or Hotmail you can set up an absolutely free email address that you can access from any Web-connected computer anywhere in the world. Email services are complete (attachments, address book, copying multiple recipients).

INTERNET RESOURCES
The World Wide Web is a rich resource for travelers. You can research your trip, hunt down bargain airfares, book hotels, check on weather conditions and chat with locals and other travelers about the best places to visit (or avoid).

There's no better place to start your Web explorations than the Lonely Planet Web site (www.lonelyplanet.com). Here you'll find succinct summaries on traveling to most places on earth, postcards from other travelers, and the Thorn Tree bulletin board, where you can ask questions before you go or dispense advice when you get back. You can also find travel news and updates for many of our most popular guidebooks, and the subWWWay section links you to the most useful travel resources elsewhere on the Web.

BOOKS

Beyond the wealth of evocative Southern literature that you might wish to read before a trip to the Deep South (see the Literature section in the Facts about the Deep South chapter), nonfiction books can also enhance your visit tremendously. Visitors should note, however, that outside of major cities and university towns there are few high-quality bookstores in the region. Bookstores with exceptional collections of works on Southern subjects and themes can be found most easily in New Orleans, Oxford and Memphis. Major chains such as Barnes & Noble are found in major cities throughout the region. Select titles can be mail ordered from Square Books (☎ 601-236-2262, 800-648-4001) in Oxford, Mississippi.

Most books are published in different editions by different publishers in different countries. As a result, a book might be a hardcover rarity in one country but readily available in paperback in another. Fortunately, bookstores and libraries can search by title or author, so your local bookstore or library is the best placed to advise you on the availability of the following recommendations.

Lonely Planet

The Lonely Planet *New Orleans* city guide is essential for visitors planning on spending a lot of time in the Crescent City, particularly if you will be visiting during Mardi Gras or just want to learn more about the culture of the city. If sightseeing is what you do between meals, then check out Lonely Planet's *World Food New Orleans* guide. *Hiking in the USA* covers hiking trails and gateway cities in Tennessee's Great Smoky Mountains. Once you've conquered the Deep South, set your sights on the Lone Star State with Lonely Planet's *Texas* guide.

Guidebooks

The Sierra Club's *Trail Guide to the Delta Country*, edited by John P Sevenair, explores the natural world of the lower Mississippi River and around. It describes hikes, backpacking and canoeing trips, and bike routes from the Delta region to the Gulf of Mexico. It may be hard to find. *Hiking Mississippi*, by Helen McGinnis, is a comprehensive guide to state trails.

The *Smithsonian Guide to Historic America: Deep South* emphasizes historic architecture and design in landmark buildings throughout the region.

The *Jazz & Blues Lover's Guide to the US*, by Christiane Bird, covers music sights in the entire country. (Its club listing is in need of an update, but its chapters dealing with the states covered in this book are very informative.)

Members of the American Automobile Association may want to carry AAA's free *TourBook* covering Alabama, Louisiana and Mississippi (another edition covers Tennessee along with Kentucky), which contains listings for most chain motels and hotels in the region.

History & Culture

Charles Hudson's *The Southeastern Indians* is considered the seminal work on that region's archaeological and Native American history. The heritage of northeastern Alabama's Cherokee Indians is explored in adult and children's books in a range of works on history, folklore and spirituality distributed by the Eastern Band of the Cherokee; write for their catalog (PO Box 256, Cherokee, NC 28719).

The fascinating development of Afro-Creole culture is documented in *Africans in Colonial Louisiana*, by Gwendolyn Midlo Hall, and *The Free People of Color of New Orleans*, by Mary Gehman.

Of the tomes written on the Civil War, one considered a major sourcebook is the three-volume *The Civil War: A Narrative*, written by Mississippi historian Shelby Foote (whose wry and poignant observations appeared throughout the PBS *Civil War* TV series). The *Civil War Almanac*, edited by John S Bowman and introduced by noted historian Henry Steele Commager, is an authoritative single-volume book with a detailed chronology and biographies of key players.

Been in the Storm So Long, by Leon Litwak, explores the aftermath of slavery in the South through moving and revealing personal accounts of ex-slaves and former slaveholders. (The book takes its title from a 19th-century black spiritual.)

Let Us Now Praise Famous Men, by James Agee and Walker Evans, is a stark portrait of poor white tenant farmers in Alabama in the 1930s. *Coming of Age in Mississippi*, the autobiography of Ann Moody, describes the harsh life of a black share-cropping family in the Mississippi Delta in the 1950s. Stetson Kennedy's 1959 *Jim Crow Guide: The Way It Was* is an eye-opening survey of the Jim Crow South. The Civil Rights era from 1954 to 1965 is chronicled in Juan William's *Eyes on the Prize* (also a PBS documentary series by the same name). *Free at Last*, by Margaret Edds, covers the behind-the-scenes struggles for Civil Rights in several Southern cities.

Anthony Walton's *Mississippi* is the autobiographical story of a black man who grew up in Illinois after his family left Mississippi. The story of his return south makes for a sad and wonderful book. *Mississippi Backroads*, by Elmo Howell, is a collection of eclectica with a literary bent. *Baptized in Blood*, by Charles Reagan Wilson, helps the visitor understand why, for many Southerners, the War between the States isn't over.

Tony Horowitz' *Confederates in the Attic: Dispatches from the Unfinished Civil War* has some Alabama, Tennessee and Mississippi chapters on the Neo-Confederate movement and the Civil War reenactment phenomenon. It takes another stab at the perennial topic of the South's 'rising again.' Highlights include an interview with Shelby Foote in his home and visits to Selma, Alabama; Shiloh battlefield in Tennessee; and Vicksburg, Mississippi.

The Louisiana folktales and oral histories compiled in Lyle Saxton's *Gumbo Ya Ya* are a rich source of cultural entertainment. Hailed as one of the best collections of black American folklore is Zora Neale Hurston's *Mules and Men*, which was written in the Southern vernacular. It recounts tales of conjure men and hoodoo cures and is based on stories she collected while traveling from Florida to New Orleans and eventually to the Caribbean.

Robert Palmer's *Deep Blues*, a musical and cultural history of the Delta, is essential and engrossing for anybody seriously into the music of this region. Another good read is *Elvis, Hank, and Me: Making Musical History on the Louisiana Hayride*, by Horace Logan and Bill Sloan, about the Municipal Auditorium in Shreveport and its role in the early careers of Hank Williams, Elvis Presley, Johnny Cash and many others.

VS Naipaul, an East Indian who grew up on a Caribbean island, shares his observations on the modern South, particularly as it relates to race, in *A Turn in the South*.

Dixie Rising, by Yankee observer and *New York Times* reporter Peter Applebome, is the most recent contribution to sociopolitical observations on the Southern region. Other scholars and historians who have authored dissections of Southern culture as it relates to politics include C Vann Woodward, John Hope Franklin, George Tindall and Dan Carter.

The gargantuan *Encyclopedia of Southern Culture*, edited by Charles Reagan Wilson and William Ferris, covers everything from agriculture to 'women's life.' The section on Southern politics draws from the authoritative work of Merle and Earl Black of Emory and Rice Universities.

Cookbooks

Celebrity New Orleans chefs such as Emeril Lagasse and Paul Prudhomme are always coming out with self-promoting cookbooks containing their versions of regional recipes. These books are not necessarily the best way to go if you're planning to try Southern cooking at home, particularly since they tend to leave out the basics, such as grits, pulled pork, and banana-and-peanut-butter sandwiches.

A Gracious Plenty: Recipes and Recollections from the American South, by John T Edge, et al, spices its recipes with stories and myths of Southern culinary culture. *Best of the Best from Alabama: Selected Recipes from Alabama's Favorite Cookbooks*, by Gwen McKee, and the similarly constructed *Best of the Best of Louisiana* cull the knowledge of hundreds of regional chefs. *Soul Food: Classic Cuisine from the Deep South*, by Sheila Ferguson, is a popular guide on the fixing of soul staples such as pulled pork and turnip greens.

And, of course, no wannabe Southern kitchen is without *Are You Hungry Tonight? Elvis' Favorite Recipes*, by Brenda A Butler.

FILMS

Many films set in the Deep South give a flavor for the region, especially films made from books listed under Literature in Facts about the Deep South. Apart from this, the PBS-produced *Civil War* series, available on home video, sheds a drawn-out light on Southern history. *Eyes on the Prize* is a good film that details civil rights history.

Some of the music of the region has been documented on film, whether it be to illustrate a storyline or for its own sake. Anything starring Elvis is haute-Hollywood (*Jailhouse Rock* and *King Creole*), but it gives viewers an idea of the man, his music and his appeal. New Orleans' own Louis Armstrong is immortalized in a number of films, including *New Orleans* (1947) and *Hello Dolly!* (1969), a very popular musical. In the cult favorite *Down by Law*, John Lurie (noted jazzman of the group the Lounge Lizards), Tom Waits (noted cult figure and songwriter) and Roberto Benigni (crowned prince of Italian slapstick) do their best to break out of Orleans Parish prison. It's a 1986 B&W film with songs by Waits and background music by Lurie. The little-known film *Crossroads* is set in the Mississippi Delta and tries to evoke the legend of Robert Johnson. Robert Altman's *Nashville* is more about the people who live there rather than about the place or music.

Louisiana is often in the movies. In 1996, the state's (and US) death penalty legislation came under scrutiny in the affecting *Dead Man Walking*, a true story about the work of Sister Helen Prejean. Former governor Earl Long is memorialized by Paul Newman in the comedic *Blaze*. Former governor Huey Long is fictionalized in *All the King's Men* and *A Lion Is in the Streets*. Academy Award-winning performances enhance Tennessee Williams' play *A Streetcar Named Desire*. Louis Malle filmed a cheeky 16-year-old Brooke Shields in *Pretty Baby* at the Columns Hotel in New Orleans. *Steel Magnolias*, filmed entirely in Natchitoches, is a bittersweet story of the friendship between a group of women in a small town, with some classic southern lines. The 1945 semi-documentary film *The Louisiana Story* is about a Cajun boy who scouted the swamps for oil drillers – it's an interesting insight into the region, but it's a somewhat skewed vision as the production was partially funded by Standard Oil.

Films set in Mississippi include *Mississippi Masala*, a biracial romance filmed partially in Biloxi. *Biloxi Blues* is the Neil Simon comedy in which a character from New York remarks on the heat of the Gulf South: 'It's not just hot; it's Africa-hot.' Dramatizations of civil rights struggles include *Mississippi Burning*, an intense account of events in the rural town of Philadelphia. *Ghosts of Mississippi* dramatizes the trial for the murderer of Medgar Evers. Both of the latter films were somewhat criticized for enlarging the role of whites as 'rescuers.' Set in Holly Springs, Mississippi, *Cookie's Fortune* is a Robert Altman-directed comedy about keeping up appearances in a small town with few secrets.

Everything from Alabama's racism *(To Kill a Mockingbird)* to its space industry *(Space Camp)* has been the fodder for filmmakers. Eccentric or exceptional characters have proved equally worthy of footage: the fictional *Forrest Gump* and the women of *Fried Green Tomatoes*, and the biographical films *The Miracle Worker* (about Helen

Keller), *Buffalo Soldiers* and *Your Cheatin'
Heart.*

NEWSPAPERS & MAGAZINES
No single paper speaks for the region;
dailies in New Orleans, Memphis, Nashville,
Jackson and Montgomery cover local news
the best, but also attempt to cover the state,
region and beyond. The *Atlanta Constitution* purports to speak for the region, but its
coverage of neighboring Alabama is more
thorough than other Southern states farther
afield. Newspapers from outside the region,
such as the *New York Times* or the *Wall
Street Journal* can be found in major cities
only, and often not readily.

The *Oxford American* is a provocative
monthly literary magazine that also covers
regional issues. The bimonthly *Southern Exposure* carries on the muckraking tradition
of Stetson Kennedy's 1946 book by the
same name.

RADIO & TV
All rental cars have car radios and travelers
can choose among hundreds of stations.
Most radio stations have a range of less
than 100 miles, and in and near major cities
scores of stations crowd the airwaves with a
wide variety of music and entertainment.
You can hear wonderful music programs –
especially jazz, blues, country & western
and gospel – on radio stations throughout
the region, though a regional format called
'Southern rock' and Top 40 pop tunes are
predominant. In some regions, all you may
be able to pick up is the local Christian
broadcasting station featuring 'Christian
music' and commentary. Local PBS radio
stations usually air nationally syndicated
news and feature programs.

Almost all hotel rooms have TVs (most
with cable) although many B&Bs do not.
Television sets in all but the smallest towns
will usually receive the major American TV
networks (ABC, CBS, NBC and FOX) and
PBS, the Public Broadcasting System. Cable
TV guarantees clear reception and will
include CNN and TBS – two cable channels
originating out of Atlanta.

PHOTOGRAPHY & VIDEO
Traveling photographers will want to have
cameras and bags hand-checked when
passing through airport security. Summertime travelers need to be aware that the
South's extreme heat can damage film. For
purchasing film, only stores in major cities
will offer a wide selection of specialty film
(black & white, professional slide, etc);
check expiration dates on film. Inexpensive,
quick film processing is widely available; if
you care about the quality of your photos,
it's best to wait until you are back home and
can have your processing done at a place
you already know does good work.

Tips for the best photography and
videography: avoid midday, when light and
shadows are too contrasting and the sun's
glare causes washed out images. The magic
hours around dawn and dusk offer the
most dramatic lighting. Always protect
camera lenses with a haze or ultraviolet
(UV) filter.

Some poorer communities may make riv-
eting subjects for photography, yet locals
may be understandably sensitive about
being the subject of such a portrait. Be sure
to ask before photographing people, and be
prepared for a possible refusal.

Overseas visitors considering buying
videotapes should note that the US uses the
National Television System Committee
(NTSC) color TV standard, which is incom-
patible with other standards, such as Phase
Alternative Line (PAL).

TIME
The region covered in this guide falls under
Central Standard Time, six hours behind
Greenwich Mean Time. Alabama commu-
nities on the Georgia border, such as Phenix
City, observe Georgia time (Eastern Stan-
dard Time, which is one hour earlier). All
Deep South states observe daylight saving
time (comparable to Summer Time in
Britain).

ELECTRICITY
Electric current is 110-120 volts, 60-cycle.
Appliances that take 220-240 volt, 50-cycle

current (as in Europe and Asia) will need a converter (transformer) and a US-style plug adapter with two flat pins.

WEIGHTS & MEASURES

The US uses a modified version of the traditional English measuring system of feet, yards, miles, ounces, pounds and gallons. Three feet equals one yard (0.914 meters); 1760 yards or 5280 feet equal one mile. Dry weights are in ounces (oz), pounds (lbs) and tons (16 oz equal 1 lb; 2000 lbs equal 1 ton), but liquid measures differ from dry measures. One pint equals 16 fluid ounces; 2 pints equal 1 quart, a common measure for liquids such as milk, which is also sold in half gallons (2 quarts) and gallons (4 quarts). Gasoline is dispensed by the US gallon, which is about 20% less than the Imperial gallon. See the back of this book for a conversion chart.

LAUNDRY

Pricier hotels and motels usually provide laundry service, and many budget motels provide coin-operated washers and dryers. You can also find either self-service laundries (called 'washaterias' or 'washerettes') or wash-and-fold service in most towns. Laundries usually have machines to dis-

pense change and to sell single-serving supplies of detergent. A wash typically costs around $1, a dry another $1. You can find laundry and dry-cleaning services under 'Laundries' or 'Cleaners' in the yellow pages telephone directory.

TOILETS

You will find relatively clean toilets (most often marked 'restrooms') in airports, attractions, restaurants, hotels, visitor information centers and more upscale bars and clubs. Restrooms in small restaurants and bars, bus and train stations, highway rest areas or fuel stations may or may not be as well maintained, but are generally usable (they commonly run low on toilet tissue, soap and towels). The quality of public facilities in parks and off the street, if available, may vary considerably.

Only the most enlightened establishments, most often catering to upscale families, provide diaper-changing tables in women's restrooms (write if you find one in a men's restroom in the Deep South). Many women's restrooms provide tampon vending machines. In some bars and clubs, restroom vending machines dispense condoms.

HEALTH

For most foreign visitors no immunizations are required for entry, though cholera and yellow fever vaccinations may be required of travelers from areas with a history of those diseases. There are no unexpected health dangers, excellent medical attention is readily available, and the only real health concern is that a collision with the medical system can cause severe injuries to your financial state.

Hospitals and medical centers, walk-in clinics and referral services are easily found throughout the region.

In a serious emergency, call ☎ 911 for an ambulance to take you to the nearest hospital's emergency room. But note that charges for this service in the US are incredibly high.

Predeparture Preparations

Make sure you're healthy before you start traveling. If you are embarking on a long

Fashion and function

MARION POST WOLCOTT/LIBRARY OF CONGRESS

trip, make sure your teeth are in good shape. If you wear glasses, take a spare pair and your prescription. You can get new spectacles made up quickly and competently for well under $100, depending on the prescription and frame you choose. If you require a particular medication, take an adequate supply and bring a prescription in case you lose it.

Health Insurance A travel insurance policy to cover theft, lost tickets and medical problems is a good idea, especially in the US, where some hospitals will refuse care without evidence of insurance. There are a wide variety of policies and your travel agent will have recommendations. International student travel policies handled by STA Travel and other student travel organizations are usually a good value. Some policies offer lower and higher medical expenses options, and the higher one is chiefly for countries such as the US with extremely high medical costs.

Some policies specifically exclude 'dangerous activities' such as scuba diving, motorcycling and even trekking. If these activities are on your agenda, avoid this sort of policy. Check the fine print.

You may prefer a policy that pays doctors or hospitals directly, rather than one where you pay first and claim later. If you have to claim later, keep *all* documentation. Some policies ask you to call back (reverse charges) to a center in your home country for an immediate assessment of your problem.

Check whether the policy covers ambulance fees or an emergency flight home. If you need two seats, somebody has to pay for it!

Travel & Climate-Related Problems

Motion Sickness Eating lightly before and during a trip will reduce the chances of motion sickness. If you are prone to motion sickness, try to find a place that minimizes disturbance – for example, near the wing on aircraft or near the center on buses. Fresh air usually helps. Commercial anti-motion

Medical Kit Check List

Following is a list of items you should consider including in your medical kit – consult your pharmacist for brands available in your country.

❑ **Aspirin or paracetamol** (acetaminophen in the USA) – for pain or fever

❑ **Antihistamine** – for allergies, eg, hay fever; to ease the itch from insect bites or stings; and to prevent motion sickness

❑ **Cold and flu tablets, throat lozenges and nasal decongestant**

❑ **Multivitamins** – consider taking for long trips, when dietary vitamin intake may be inadequate

❑ **Antibiotics** – consider including these if you're traveling well off the beaten track; see your doctor, as they must be prescribed, and carry the prescription with you

❑ **Loperamide or diphenoxylate** – 'blockers' for diarrhea

❑ **Prochlorperazine or metaclopramide** – for nausea and vomiting

❑ **Rehydration mixture** – to prevent dehydration, which may occur, for example, during bouts of diarrhea; particularly important when traveling with children

❑ **Insect repellent, sunscreen, lip balm and eye drops**

❑ **Calamine lotion, sting relief spray or aloe vera** – to ease irritation from sunburn and insect bites or stings

❑ **Antifungal cream or powder** – for fungal skin infections and thrush

❑ **Antiseptic (such as povidone-iodine)** – for cuts and grazes

❑ **Bandages, Band-Aids (plasters) and other wound dressings**

❑ **Water purification tablets or iodine**

❑ **Scissors, tweezers and a thermometer** – note that mercury thermometers are prohibited by airlines

sickness preparations, which can cause drowsiness, have to be taken before the trip commences; once you feel sick, it's too late. Ginger, a natural preventative, is available in capsule form from health food stores.

Jet Lag The phenomenon of jet lag arises when a person travels by air across more than three time zones (each zone represents a one-hour time difference). It occurs because many of the functions of the human body are regulated by internal 24-hour cycles called circadian rhythms. When we travel long distances rapidly, our bodies take time to adjust to the 'new time' of our destination, and we may experience fatigue, disorientation, insomnia, anxiety, impaired concentration and loss of appetite. These effects will usually be gone within three days of arrival, but there are ways of minimizing the impact of jet lag:

• Rest for a couple of days prior to departure; try to avoid late nights and last-minute dashes for traveler's checks or passports.

• Try to select flight schedules that minimize sleep deprivation; arriving in the early evening means you can go to sleep soon after you arrive. For very long flights, try to organize a stopover.

• Avoid excessive eating (which bloats the stomach) and alcohol (which causes dehydration) during the flight. Instead, drink plenty of noncarbonated, nonalcoholic drinks such as fruit juice or water.

• Make yourself comfortable by wearing loose-fitting clothes and perhaps bringing an eye mask and ear plugs to help you sleep.

• Avoid smoking as this reduces the amount of oxygen in the airplane cabin even further and causes greater fatigue.

Heat Exhaustion Without heeding certain precautions, visitors not acclimated to a sub-tropical climate may experience discomfort from extreme summertime heat, humidity and overexposure to the sun. Avoid exposure to the midday sun and heat – have a plan to be indoors – and confine strenuous activity to early morning and late afternoon (locals have made a sport of 'mall-walking' to get exercise within an air-conditioned

environment). Wear sunscreen and a hat, and even carry an umbrella to shield more sensitive types from the sun. Rent a car with air-conditioning and light-colored interiors. Drinking lots of water is also good.

Note also that many establishments over-compensate for the heat by overchilling their interiors – brace yourself for the bodily shock of alternating between the 100°F exterior and 70°F interiors. Carry a cover-up.

Heatstroke This serious, occasionally fatal, condition can occur if the body's heat-regulating mechanism breaks down and the body temperature rises to dangerous levels. Long, continuous periods of exposure to high temperatures and insufficient fluids can leave you vulnerable to heatstroke.

The symptoms are feeling unwell, not sweating very much (or at all) and a high body temperature (39°C to 41°C or 102°F to 106°F). Where sweating has ceased the skin becomes flushed and red. Severe, throbbing headaches and lack of coordination will also occur, and the sufferer may be confused or aggressive. Eventually the victim will become delirious or convulse. Hospitalization is essential, but in the interim get victims out of the sun, remove their clothing, cover them with a wet sheet or towel and then fan continually. Give fluids if they are conscious.

Fungal Infections These infections, which occur with greater frequency in hot weather, are most likely to occur on the scalp, between the toes or fingers (athlete's foot), in the groin (jock itch or crotch rot) and on the body (ringworm). You get ringworm (which is a fungal infection, not a worm) from infected animals or by walking on damp areas, such as shower floors.

To prevent fungal infections, wear loose, comfortable clothes, avoid artificial fibers, wash frequently and dry carefully. If you do get an infection, wash the infected area daily with a disinfectant or medicated soap and water, and rinse and dry well. Apply an antifungal powder and try to expose the infected area to air or sunlight as much as possible. Change underwear and towels frequently and wash them often in hot water.

Infectious Diseases

Diarrhea A change of water, food or climate can all cause the runs; diarrhea caused by contaminated food or water is more serious, but it's unlikely in the US. Despite all your precautions, you may still have a mild bout of traveler's diarrhea from exotic food or drink. Dehydration is the main danger with any diarrhea, particularly for children, for whom dehydration can occur quite quickly. Fluid replacement remains the mainstay of management. Weak black tea with a little sugar, soda water or soft drinks diluted 50% with water are all good. With severe diarrhea, a re-hydrating solution is necessary to replace minerals and salts. Such solutions, such as Pedialyte, are available at pharmacies throughout the region.

Hepatitis The general term 'hepatitis' refers to inflammation of the liver. There are many causes of this condition: poor sanitation, contact with infected blood products, drugs, alcohol and contact with an infected person are but a few. The symptoms are fever, chills, headache, fatigue, and feelings of weakness and aches and pains, followed by loss of appetite, nausea, vomiting, abdominal pain, dark urine, light-colored feces and jaundiced skin. The whites of the eyes may also turn yellow. Viral hepatitis is an infection of the liver, which can have several unpleasant symptoms, or no symptoms at all, with the infected person not knowing that they have the disease. The discovery of new strains has led to a virtual alphabet soup, with hepatitis A, B, C, D and E. Hepatitis C, D and E are fairly rare.

Tetanus Difficult to treat, tetanus is preventable with immunization. Tetanus occurs when a wound becomes infected by a germ that lives in the feces of animals or people, so clean all cuts, punctures or animal bites.

HIV/AIDS Exposure to blood, blood products or bodily fluids may put an individual at risk for getting HIV/AIDS. Infection can come from unprotected sex or sharing contaminated needles. Apart from abstinence, the most effective preventative is always to practice safe sex using condoms. It is impossible to detect a person's HIV status without a blood test.

HIV/AIDS can also be spread through infected blood transfusions, though the blood supply in the US is now well screened. It can also be spread if needles are reused for acupuncture, tattooing or body piercing.

A good resource for help and information is the Centers for Disease Control and Prevention (check the local phone book). The US AIDS hot line (☎ 800-342-2437, 800-344-7432 in Spanish) offers advice and support.

Cuts, Bites & Stings

Cuts & Scratches Skin punctures can easily become infected in hot climates and heal slowly. Treat any cut with an antiseptic such as Betadine. Where possible avoid bandages and Band-Aids, which can keep wounds wet.

Bites & Stings Bee and wasp stings and nonpoisonous spider bites are usually more painful than dangerous. Calamine lotion will give relief, and ice packs will reduce the pain and swelling. More common are mosquito bites. Mosquitoes usually appear at dusk, and can be found around stagnant water. Use insect repellent: *Consumer Reports* rates a product called 'Ultra Muskol' the highest, though locals use Avon's 'Skin So Soft' hand lotion for everyday repelling. You might want to carry an insect bite cream, such as Benadryl. Clothing that covers your limbs is a good deterrent to insects.

Ticks Ticks are a parasitic arachnid that may be present in brush, forest and grasslands, where hikers may get them on their legs or in their boots. The adults suck blood from hosts by burying their head into skin, but they are often found unattached and can simply be brushed off. However, if one has attached itself to you, pulling it off and leaving the head in the skin increases the likelihood of infection or disease, such as Lyme disease.

Always check your body for ticks after walking through a high-grass or thickly forested area. If you do find a tick on you, induce it to let go by rubbing on oil, alcohol or petroleum jelly, or press it with a very hot object like a match or a cigarette. The tick should back out and can then be disposed of. If you feel ill in the next couple of weeks, consult a doctor.

AFRICAN-AMERICAN TRAVELERS

African-Americans are as much a part of the South as blues, jazz, plantations and the Mississippi River. Their heritage is a major reason why visitors from around the globe come to the region.

The stereotype of redneck Southern whites lynching blacks is drawn from a bygone era and does not truly reflect today's South. True, there are occasional racial incidents, but they are more a reflection of individual bigotry than widespread attitudes. Except for in a few isolated pockets – and certainly at all tourist attractions – black visitors will feel welcome. In those rare areas where blacks may find themselves uncomfortable, outsiders of any color or culture are generally spurned.

Although most blacks and whites comfortably coexist in the Deep South, centuries of discrimination and segregation have resulted in many communities, churches and institutions – at almost every socioeconomic level – that remain predominantly black or white. Churches may have a sprinkling of other races in their congregations, but, in general, they are attended by one race. While casual attire is acceptable in Northern churches, in black churches in the South, the dress code is much more formal. Southern colleges and universities are open to all races, but there are numerous highly regarded learning institutions that are his-

torically black, including Alabama's Tuskegee University and Alabama A&M in Huntsville, Tennessee's Fisk University in Nashville, Xavier University in New Orleans and Southern University in Baton Rouge, and Mississippi's Alcorn State University in Lorman. These institutions host many African-American related lectures, exhibitions and cultural events that both blacks and whites attend. Some also operate radio stations that broadcast soul, rhythm & blues and jazz programs.

The region's nightlife ranges from dance clubs and bars to theaters and performance centers. Black visitors can enjoy nightlife in traditionally African-American neighborhoods as well as other parts of town. However, outsiders of any color should avoid bars with parking lots full of pickup trucks bearing bumper stickers reading, 'The South Will Rise Again,' 'Keep the Confederate Flag Flying' or related slogans.

At golf courses, tennis courts, stables, parks, pools, beaches and sporting events blacks are welcome. With that said, keep in mind that there are still private clubs with white-only membership policies. It wasn't until 1990 that Birmingham's Shoal Creek Country Club offered admission to blacks and that was only after the club's racist policy drew public outcry as the club prepared to host a Professional Golf Association championship.

Resources & Organizations

If you find your rights jeopardized, call the police or one of the following agencies. The National Association for the Advancement of Colored People (NAACP) (☎ 202-638-2269, www.naacp.org) is the largest civil rights organization in the US and has branches throughout the country. Its Legal Affairs Department (☎ 410-358-8900) can refer you to a local branch where you can get guidance. The Southern Poverty Law Center (☎ 334-264-0286, www.splcenter .org) handles extreme cases of civil rights violations; its office is in Montgomery, Alabama. If you need an attorney, contact the National Legal Aid & Defender's Association (☎ 202-452-0620, www.nlada.org), which provides low-cost legal assistance and has offices in major cities around the country. Call the main number or check with local directory information under Legal Aid Society or Legal Services for an office near you. You can also contact the American Bar Association's (☎ 312-988-5522) state referral services for a directory of attorneys practicing in Louisiana (☎ 504-561-8828), Mississippi (☎ 601-948-5488), Alabama (☎ 334-269-1515) and Tennessee (☎ 615-383-7421).

The Greater New Orleans Black Tourism Network (☎ 504-523-5652), in the Superdome at 1520 Sugar Bowl Dr, New Orleans, LA 70112, provides guides to heritage sites and directories to minority-owned businesses. The Heritage Tourism Program (☎ 601-446-6345, 800-647-6724) administered by the Natchez Visitors Bureau, 422 Main St, Natchez, MS 39120, offers a similar service.

The state of Tennessee produces the *African American Guide to Cultural & Historical Sites*, available from the Tennessee Department of Tourist Development (☎ 615-741-2159), at the Rachel Jackson Bldg, 5th floor, 320 6th Ave N, Nashville, TN 37243.

Alabama's Black Heritage is a 56-page guide to more than 300 African-American historical and cultural sites. It's produced by the Bureau of Tourism & Travel (☎ 334-242-4169, 800-252-2262), PO Box 4927, Montgomery, AL 36103. Special-interest groups can contact the black heritage coordinator (☎ 334-242-4493). Birmingham's convention and visitors bureau (☎ 205-458-8000, 800-458-8085), 2200 9th Ave N, maintains a list of tour operators providing individual and group tours. The Historical 4th Ave Visitors & Information Center (☎ 205-328-1850), 319 17th St N, in Birmingham, provides information and guided walking tours of the city's historic black business district.

Roots & Wings (☎ 334-262-1700), 1345 Carter Hill Rd, Montgomery, champions African-American culture through fiction, nonfiction, children's books, cards, calendars, magazines, recordings, art exhibitions and readings, lectures and storytelling sessions. Two Birmingham bookstores specialize in African-American fiction and nonfiction: Yamini's Books (☎ 205-322-0037), 1417 4th Ave N, and the Civil Rights Institute Book Shop (☎ 205-328-9696), 520 16th St N. The weekly *Birmingham World* has served the black community since 1930.

WOMEN TRAVELERS

If you are a woman traveler, especially a woman traveling alone, it's not a bad idea to get in the habit of traveling with a little extra awareness of your surroundings. Conducting yourself in a common-sense manner will help you to avoid most problems. For example, you're more vulnerable if you've been drinking or using drugs than if you're sober, you're more vulnerable alone than if you're with company, and you're more vulnerable in a high-crime urban area than in a 'better' district.

In general, exercise more vigilance in large cities than in rural areas. Try to avoid the 'bad' or unsafe neighborhoods or districts; if you must go into or through these areas, it's best to go in a car or taxi. Nighttime is more dangerous, but in the worst areas crime can occur even in the daytime. If you are unsure which areas are considered unsafe, ask at your hotel or telephone the tourist office for advice. Tourist maps can sometimes be deceiving, compressing areas and making distances look shorter than they are.

While there is less to watch out for in rural areas, women may still be subject to unwelcome attention by men unaccustomed to seeing women traveling independently. Try to avoid hiking or camping alone, especially in unfamiliar places. Hikers all over the world use the 'buddy system,' not only for protection from other humans, but also for aid in case of unexpected falls or other injuries.

In an emergency, call the police (☎ 911). In rural areas where ☎ 911 is not active, just dial '0' for the operator and ask for the police. Cities and larger towns have crisis centers and women's shelters that will provide help and support; they are listed in the telephone directory, or the police can refer you to them.

Men may interpret a woman drinking alone in a bar as a bid for male company, whether you intend it that way or not. If you don't want the company, most men will respect a firm but polite 'no thank you.'

At night, avoid straying from your car to flag down help; turn on your hazard lights, put up the hood and wait for the police to arrive. If you're planning extensive solo driving, consider renting a cellular phone (available from major car-rental agencies) as an all-around extra precaution. Be extra careful at night on public transit, and remember to check the times of the last bus or train before you go out.

To deal with potential dangers, many women protect themselves with a whistle, mace, cayenne pepper spray or some self-defense training. Laws regarding sprays vary, so be informed based on your destination. On board an airplane, it is a federal felony to carry pepper spray, owing to its combustible design.

Resources & Organizations

Women's bookstores are good places to find out about gatherings, readings and meetings, and they often have bulletin boards where you can find or place travel and short-term housing notices.

National resources with regional affiliates include:

National Organization for Women
An advocacy organization, NOW is a good resource for political and women's rights issues. The national center can refer you to state and local chapters. 733 15th St NW, 2nd floor, Washington, DC 20005 (☎ 202-331-0066, now@now.org, www.now.org)

Planned Parenthood
This organization operates clinics throughout the country and offers advice on medical issues such as women's health, birth control and sexually transmitted diseases. 810 Seventh Ave, New York, NY 10019 (☎ 212-541-7800)

Several well-established women's resources in Memphis may serve as regional resources as well:

Center for Research on Women
A resource center and clearinghouse for information for and about Southern women and women of color. University of Memphis, TN 38152 (☎ 901-678-2770)

Memphis Center for Reproductive Health
Women's health clinic that also offers counseling and referrals. 1462 Poplar Ave, Memphis, TN 38104 (☎ 901-274-3550, outside Tennessee 800-843-9895)

Meristem Bookstore
Books and other resources for women and their friends. 930 S Cooper, Memphis, TN 38104 (☎ 901-276-0282)

GAY & LESBIAN TRAVELERS

There are gay people everywhere in the US, but by far the most visible are in the major cities. In the cities and on both coasts it is easier for gay men and women to live their lives with a certain amount of openness. As you travel into the middle of the country it is much harder to be open. Gay travelers should be careful, *especially* in the rural areas where holding hands might invite harassment.

New Orleans has a large gay community centered in the lower French Quarter. People around greater New Orleans and the Gulf Coast generally hold more open views of gays and lesbians.

In most of the Bible Belt, however, you might expect a reception ranging narrowly from intolerant to hostile. But it's hard to say; the South is full of contradictions. While the women at Camp Sister Spirit in Mississippi came under attack by locals when starting up, after years of maintaining a local food bank and clothes closet they're a welcome part of the community. Fellow tourists on one recent Natchez tour included a gay couple from California; the two men reported nothing but the most welcoming hospitality. Nashville, a fundamentalist Christian Shangri-la, seems to be surprisingly tolerant of the local gay and lesbian population.

As is true for all travelers to the Deep South, a respectful attitude and a modest decorum are important, yet there's always the chance that you will come across a few reactionaries.

See the New Orleans chapter for local periodicals and resources for the gay and lesbian community.

Resources & Organizations

The Women's Traveller, which lists lesbian resources, and *Damron's Address Book* for men are both published by Damron Company (☎ 415-255-0404, 800-462-6654), PO Box 422458, San Francisco, CA 94142-2458. Also helpful are *Men's Travel In Your Pocket* and *Women's Travel In Your Pocket*, which are both published by Ferrari Publications (☎ 602-863-2408, fax 602-439-3952, www.ferrariguides.com), PO Box 37887, Phoenix, AZ 85069. Neil Miller's *In Search of Gay America*, a book about gay and lesbian life across America in the 1980s, is a bit dated but gives a good view of life outside major cities.

The Gay Yellow Pages (☎ 212-674-0120), PO Box 533, Village Station, NY 10014-0533, has good national and regional editions.

Useful national resources include: National AIDS/HIV Hotline (☎ 800-342-2437), National Gay/Lesbian Task Force (☎ 202-332-6483 in Washington, DC) and Lambda Legal Defense Fund (☎ 212-995-8585 in New York City, 213-937-2728 in Los Angeles).

Regional resources include: Camp Sister Spirit (☎ 601-344-2005), PO Box 12, Ovett, MS 39462, a feminist educational retreat center in southeastern Mississippi (camping and dorm beds available for $15 to $20 a night including communal meals). The South's oldest gay bookstore is the Faubourg Marigny Book Store in New Orleans (☎ 504-942-9875), 600 Frenchman St. *The Pink Pages of Greater New Orleans* is a free bimonthly guide to gay and lesbian businesses, entertainment, hotels and guesthouses. The New Orleans AIDS task force hot line is ☎ 504-944-2437, 800-992-4379.

DISABLED TRAVELERS

Travel within the US is becoming easier for people with disabilities. Public buildings are now required by law to be wheelchair accessible and have accommodating restrooms, and transportation must be made accessible to all. Telephone companies are required to provide relay operators for the hearing impaired.

The most compliance is found in federal facilities and in modern and newly renovated properties in larger cities. Look to chain motels for the most modern accessible rooms and fully equipped suites. Many banks now provide ATM instructions in Braille. Major car-rental agencies in larger cities offer hand-controlled models at no extra charge.

All major airlines, Greyhound buses and Amtrak trains allow service animals to accompany passengers and frequently sell two-for-one packages when attendants of seriously disabled passengers are required. Airlines will also provide assistance for connecting, boarding and deplaning the flight – just ask for assistance when making your reservation. (Note: airlines must accept wheelchairs as checked baggage and have an onboard chair available, though some advance notice may be required on smaller aircraft.)

Of course, the more populous the area, the greater the likelihood of facilities for the disabled. But the South has few big, modern cities, so it's important to call ahead to see what is available. Some of the best attractions in the South are historic buildings including house museums and B&B lodging, and these are not generally handicap accessible, or may have only select accessible rooms.

Resources & Organizations

A number of organizations and tour providers specialize in the needs of disabled travelers:

Access-Able Travel Source
This travel resource has an excellent Web site with links to international disability sites, travel newsletters, guidebooks and travel tips to popular US destinations. PO Box 1796, Wheat Ridge, CO 80034 (☎ 303-232-2979, fax 239-8486, www.access-able.com)

Mobility International USA
This organization advises disabled travelers on mobility. It primarily runs an educational

exchange program. PO Box 10767, Eugene, OR 97440 (☎ 541-343-1284, fax 541-343-6812, www.miusa.org)

Moss Rehabilitation Hospital's Travel Information Service
This rehabilitation center can provide hospital and doctor referrals for disabled travelers. 1200 W Tabor Rd, Philadelphia, PA 19141-3099 (☎ 215-456-9600, TTY 456-9602)

SATH (Society for the Advancement of Travel for the Handicapped)
This society provides information for disabled travelers and publishes a quarterly magazine. 347 Fifth Ave, No 610, New York, NY 10016 (☎ 212-447-7284)

Helen Keller's hometown of Tuscumbia (near Florence, Alabama) opens her home to public tours and sponsors a festival in honor of Annie Sullivan's famous student every June. You can reach the Alabama Institute for the Deaf and Blind by calling ☎ 205-761-3206.

SENIOR TRAVELERS
Culturally, elders are more venerated in the South than in many other regions of the US, and consequently many seniors particularly enjoy the respectful and welcoming reception they generally receive. The usually mild climate, low prices, golf courses and extensive camping opportunities for RVs also appeal to many seniors. A 1995 tourism study revealed that one third of the visitors to Mississippi, for example, were over the age of 50.

Senior travelers can find many discounts at hotels, campgrounds, restaurants, parks, museums and other attractions. The age at which senior discounts apply generally starts at 50, though it more commonly applies to those 65 or older. Be sure to inquire about discount rates when you make your reservation.

Visitors to national parks and campgrounds can cut costs greatly by using the Golden Age Passport (see this section under Useful Organizations later in this chapter).

Resources & Organizations
National advocacy groups that can help in planning your travels include the following:

American Association of Retired Persons
AARP is an advocacy group for Americans 50 years and older and is a good resource for travel bargains. US residents can get one-year/three-year memberships for $8/20. Citizens of other countries can get the same memberships for $10/24. 601 E St NW, Washington, DC 20049 (☎ 800-424-3410)

Elderhostel
This organization is a nonprofit that encourages travel through scholarship. The programs, which are conducted throughout the Deep South, last one to three weeks and include meals and accommodations; they are open to people 55 years and older and their companions. The cost is extremely reasonable. The organization also has service programs in association with Habitat for Humanity. Address correspondence to 75 Federal St, Boston, MA 02110-1941 (☎ 617-426-8056, www.elderhostel.org)

Grand Circle Travel
This group offers escorted tours and travel information in a variety of formats. 347 Congress St, Boston, MA 02210 (☎ 617-350-7500, fax 617-350-6206)

National Council of Senior Citizens
Membership in this group (you needn't be a US citizen) gives access to added Medicare insurance, a mail-order prescription service and a variety of discount information and travel-related advice. Fees are $13/30/150 for one year/three years/lifetime. 1331 F St NW, Washington DC, 20004 (☎ 202-347-8800)

TRAVEL WITH CHILDREN
The Deep South is an exceptionally family-friendly destination with many discounts, services, facilities and attractions designed to entertain kids, including such considerate touches as high chairs on wheels at cafeterias. Attitudes toward children and parents are generally welcoming and understanding. Southerners like to offer candy to children; some may pat children on the head.

Though New Orleans is typically considered an adult playground, many city attractions are designed for kids and families, including the zoo and children's museum. B&Bs often have age restrictions (children under 12 are not typically allowed); a motel room – or a cabin in the Cajun wetlands – would be much more comfortable for families anyway.

For advice and reassurance, see Lonely Planet's *Travel With Children*, by Maureen Wheeler.

USEFUL ORGANIZATIONS
American Automobile Association

For its members, AAA provides great travel information, distributes free road maps and guidebooks and sells American Express traveler's checks without commission. The AAA membership card will often get you discounts for accommodations, car rental and admission charges. If you plan to do a lot of driving – even in a rental car – it is usually worthwhile joining AAA. It costs $56 for the first year and $39 for subsequent years.

Members of other auto clubs, such as the Automobile Association in the UK, are entitled to the same services if they bring their membership cards and/or a letter of introduction.

AAA also provides emergency roadside service to members in the event of an accident or breakdown or if you lock your keys in the car. Service is free within a given radius of the nearest service center, and service providers will tow your car to a mechanic if they can't fix it. The nationwide toll-free roadside assistance number is ☎ 800-222-4357 (800-AAA-HELP). All major cities and many smaller towns have a AAA office where you can become a member.

National Park Service & US Forest Service

The federal government controls public lands through at least two groups. The National Park Service (NPS) administers the use of designated national parks. The US Forest Service (USFS), part of the US Department of Agriculture, administers the use of designated national forests. National forests are less protected than parks, allowing commercial use (including logging and mining) of some areas.

For more information, write to NPS Southeast Region, 100 Alabama St SW, 1924 Bldg, Atlanta, GA 30303, or USFS Southern Region, 1720 Peachtree Rd NW, Atlanta, GA 30309.

For camping information, see the Accommodations section, later in this chapter. General information about other publicly owned land is available from each state's Fish and Wildlife Service.

Golden Passports You can apply in person for any of the following Golden Passports at any national park or regional office of the USFS or NPS.

Golden Eagle Passports cost $50 annually and offer one-year entry into national parks to the holder and accompanying guests.

Golden Age Passports are free and allow US residents 62 years and older unlimited entry to all sites in the national park system, with discounts on camping and other fees.

Golden Access Passports offer the same to US residents who are medically blind or permanently disabled.

DANGERS & ANNOYANCES

Although street crime is a serious issue in large urban areas, most notably New Orleans, visitors need not be obsessed with security.

Always lock cars and put valuables out of sight, whether leaving the car for a few minutes or longer, and whether you are in a town or in the remote backcountry. Rent a car with a lockable trunk. If your car is bumped from behind in a remote area, it's best to keep going to a well-lit area or service station.

Be aware of your surroundings and who may be watching you. Avoid walking on dimly lit streets at night, particularly when alone. Walk purposefully. Avoid unnecessary displays of money or jewelry. Try to use ATMs in well-trafficked areas.

In hotels, don't leave valuables lying around your room. Use safety-deposit boxes or at least place valuables in a locked bag. Don't open your door to strangers – check the peephole or call the front desk if unexpected guests try to enter.

Visitors to New Orleans should be aware of the city's reputation for high crime. As in cities throughout the world, the majority of crimes occur in the poorest neighborhoods among local residents.

The US has a widespread reputation, partly true but also propagated and exaggerated by the media, as a dangerous place because of the availability of firearms. Guns do play a significant role in the lives of a hunting and self-protecting rural culture throughout the Deep South. Many people own guns, and some people may carry guns.

When walking in the woods during hunting seasons (generally fall and winter; inquire locally), rangers recommend hikers wear 'blaze' orange vests.

EMERGENCIES

Throughout most of the US, dial ☎ 911 for emergency service of any sort. This is a free call from any phone. Rural phones might not have this service, in which case dial ☎ 0 for the operator and ask for emergency assistance – it's still free. Each state also maintains toll-free phone numbers for traffic information and emergencies.

Lost or Stolen Documents

Carry a photocopy of your passport separately from your passport. Copy the pages with your photo and personal details, passport number and US visa. If it is lost or stolen, this will make replacing it easier. In this event, you should call your embassy. Similarly, carry copies of your traveler's check numbers and credit card numbers.

LEGAL MATTERS

If you are stopped by the police for any reason, bear in mind that there is no system of paying fines on the spot. For traffic offenses, the police officer will explain your options to you. Attempting to pay the fine to the officer is frowned upon at best and may compound your troubles by resulting in a charge of bribery. Should the officer decide that you should pay up front, the officer can exercise his or her authority and take you directly to the magistrate instead of allowing you the usual 30-day period to pay the fine.

If you are arrested for more serious offenses, you are allowed to remain silent. There is no legal reason to speak to a police officer if you don't wish, but never walk away from an officer until given permission. All persons who are arrested are legally allowed (and given) the right to make one phone call. If you don't have a lawyer or family member to help you, call your embassy. The police will give you the number upon request.

The minimum age for gambling is 21.

Drinking & Driving Laws

The drinking age is 21 and you need an ID (identification with your photograph on it) to prove your age. Drinking and driving is a serious offense; you could incur stiff fines, jail time and penalties if caught driving under the influence of alcohol (called 'DUI' or 'DWI'). It is illegal even to carry an open container of alcohol in a car. In Tennessee, a driver found to be DUI with a child under 12 in the car could be charged with felony for child endangerment. During some holidays and special events, road blocks are sometimes set up to deter drunk drivers.

Each state has its own laws, and what is legal in one state may be illegal in others. Some general rules are that you must be at least 16 years of age to drive (younger with certain restrictions in some states). Seat belts and motorcycle and bicycle helmets must be worn in most states.

Speed limits are 65 mph on interstates and freeways unless otherwise posted. Speed limits on other highways are 55 mph or less. In cities, limits vary from 25 to 45 mph. In small towns, driving over the posted speed by any amount may attract attention. Watch for school zones, which can be as low as 15 mph during school hours – these limits are strictly enforced and can result in very costly tickets.

BUSINESS HOURS

While in New Orleans business hours may be seasonal or casual and a few establishments operate around the clock, in the rest of the region standard US business hours prevail. Public and private office hours are normally 9 am to 5 pm weekdays (Monday through Friday). Most stores are open Monday through Saturday, from 10 am to around 6 pm, or later in big cities or shopping malls. Some convenience stores or fuel stations may be open 24 hours, usually in the larger cities or at interstate freeway exits.

In the South, most businesses are closed Sunday. Even tourist-oriented businesses and attractions are usually closed Sunday morning. Many tourist-oriented restaurants and shops may stay open weekends but then close Monday or Tuesday.

Businesses, especially banks and federal and state offices, typically close on major holidays; in some instances, they might close on the nearest Monday instead, creating a three-day weekend.

PUBLIC HOLIDAYS & SPECIAL EVENTS

On major holidays expect celebrations, parades or observances, and be prepared for the closure of local businesses. The region also celebrates many events geared around the life of the Deep South. For a taste of the region's folk culture, don't bypass an opportunity to attend a local turkey-calling contest, barbecue cookoff, rattlesnake rodeo, mullet toss, catfish-eating contest or county or state fair.

Elvis fans will note a surge of activity at Elvis shrines in Tupelo and Memphis around the King's January 8 birthday and the anniversary of his death on August 16.

House and garden 'pilgrimages' – extended house tours led by guides in period costume – are best seen in full bloom in spring, though fall is also nice.

Jubilee is a rare phenomenon in which crabs, fish, shrimp and other sea life swim to the shallow waters along the eastern shore of Mobile Bay, Alabama. Local residents put out the call for Jubilee! and run to the shore to gather buckets full of fresh seafood. The exact date is not predictable, but it generally occurs two to five times a year between June and September.

See the destination chapters for more events and complete information on those mentioned below.

January

New Year's Day – January 1 is a national holiday.

Elvis' Birthday – Around January 8, the 'King's' birthday is celebrated at Graceland with dramatic tributes near the grave.

Martin Luther King Jr Day – In honor of the Civil Rights leader, the third Monday in January is a public holiday.

Robert E Lee's Birthday – On January 19, more than a few Southerners remember the Confederate general.

February

Mardi Gras – In New Orleans, 'Fat Tuesday' marks the pinnacle of the city's holiday calendar. Occurring sometime in February or March (47 days before Easter), Mardi Gras is preceded by a festive carnival season of parades, balls and social events. Mardi Gras is also celebrated throughout southern Louisiana, most notably in Cajun Country. In Mississippi, it's celebrated along the coast, principally in Biloxi. Mobile, AL, has the country's oldest Mardi Gras celebration, with smaller parades than in New Orleans.

Presidents' Day – The third Monday in February is a public holiday.

March

The Azalea Trail – The colorful azalea is ablaze, and numerous events celebrate it in Mobile, AL.

Bridge Crossing Jubilee – On the first weekend, Selma recalls the Civil Rights era with a reenactment of the Selma-Montgomery march.

Future Mardi Gras Dates

Mardi Gras can occur on any Tuesday between February 3 and March 9, depending on the date of Easter. Here are the dates for the next several years:

2001	February 27
2002	February 12
2003	March 4
2004	February 24
2005	February 8

Tennessee Williams Literary Festival – In New Orleans, panels, plays and walking tours celebrate the work of the playwright during the last weekend of the month.

Easter – The first Sunday after a full moon in March or April marks the most important day on the Christian calendar.

April

World Catfish Festival – On the first Saturday of the month, Belzoni, MS, has a big fish fry.

MLK Memorial March – In Memphis, the anniversary of the assassination of Dr Martin Luther King Jr is remembered with a march on April 4.

French Quarter Festival – In New Orleans, the Vieux Carré features bands on 12 stages during the second weekend of the month.

Tin Pan South – This mid-month tribute to songwriters is a major musical event in Nashville.

Festival International de Louisiane – At the end of the month, six days of music and performing arts shows are held to celebrate French-speaking cultures in Lafayette, LA.

New Orleans Jazz & Heritage Festival – New Orleans' second-largest draw, Jazz Fest is held over two weekends in late April and early May.

Confederate Memorial Day – Fallen Southern heroes are remembered April 26.

May

Memphis in May – The city celebrates its premier festival in proper fashion: with music and barbecue all month long.

Crawfish Festival – Breaux Bridge, LA, comes alive with Cajun music, crawfish-eating contests and mudbug races during the first weekend of the month.

Mississippi Crossroads Blues Festival – Bluesmen and blues lovers converge on Rosedale, MS, the last Saturday of the month.

Siege of Vicksburg – Reenactments are held in late May in Mississippi.

Gospel Jubilee – On Memorial Day weekend, gospel singing groups and choirs raise the roof at Opryland in Nashville.

Memorial Day – The last Monday in May is a national holiday in remembrance of war dead.

June

International Country Music Fan Fair – In midmonth in Nashville musicians and their fans descend on the country-music capital.

Helen Keller Festival – Occurring during the last weekend of June, this festival opens a two-month seasonal production of *The Miracle Worker* at Ivy Green, AL.

BB King's Homecoming – The blues legend returns on the first weekend to perform and party in his hometown, Indianola, MS.

July

Choctaw Indian Fair – Traditional dances and costumes uphold cultural pride in late July in Philadelphia, MS.

Faulkner Conference – This literary event is held in late July/early August in Oxford, MS.

Independence Day – July 4 is a national holiday.

August

Sunflower River Blues Festival – The Northern Delta comes alive during the first weekend in August in Clarksdale, MS.

Elvis Tribute – The anniversary of Elvis' death on August 16 inspires weeklong events, including all-night candlelight vigils at the grave at Graceland in Memphis.

Louisiana Shrimp & Petroleum Festival – Fuels for people and cars are celebrated in Morgan City, LA, near the end of the month.

September

Labor Day – The first Monday in September is a national holiday.

Gospel Jubilee – The soul stirrers return to Opryland over Labor Day weekend in Nashville.

Southwest Louisiana Zydeco Festival – The premier zydeco event in the world features a 13-hour concert in Plaisance, LA, during Labor Day weekend.

Festivals Acadiens – The foremost Cajun festival celebrates with music, food and traditional Acadian crafts in Lafayette, LA, during mid-month.

Mississippi Delta Blues Festival – If Clarksdale in August was too hot for you, perhaps the third weekend of the month in Greenville, MS, will be more comfortable.

Louisiana Sugarcane Festival – At the end of September, New Iberia, LA, celebrates the sweet crop.

Tennessee State Fair – Livestock and midway rides draw huge crowds to Nashville in the second and third weeks of the month.

Alligator Festival – On the third weekend of the month, a healthy respect for the toothy reptiles is shown (but, alas, no human sacrifices are made) in Boutte, LA.

October

Moundville Native American Festival – Native American heritage is celebrated with dancing, crafts demonstrations and traditional foods. It's held the first week of the month at the University of Alabama's Moundville Archaeological Park, near Tuscaloosa.

Louisiana Folklife Festival – The state's finest musicians are showcased in this fest held the second week of the month in Monroe, LA.

King Biscuit Blues Festival – Blues fans cross the river to Helena, Arkansas (not far from Clarksdale, MS), during the second weekend of the month.

Tennessee Williams Festival – Mid-month, the late playwright is honored with readings and performances in his hometown, Clarksdale, MS.

Rice Festival – Another Louisiana staple crop is celebrated mid-month in Crowley, LA.

Columbus Day – The Italian-born explorer is remembered on the second Monday of the month.

National Shrimp Festival – Nearly 200,000 visitors flock to eat shrimp in Gulf Shores, AL.

Kentuck Festival – One of the South's biggest arts and crafts festivals, with everything from storytelling and jazz to blacksmithing and quilting, is held the third weekend of the month in Northport/Tuscaloosa, AL.

Tale Tellin' Festival – Storytellers from around the South gather in the 'Tale Tellin' Capital of Alabama,' Selma, on Friday and Saturday nights throughout the month.

Mid-South Fair – Amusement park rides and a carnival atmosphere come to Memphis' fairgrounds for 10 days in late September.

Halloween – In New Orleans, where the people are famous for their love of masks and costumes, the night of October 31 is spooky indeed.

November

Celebration of the Giant Omelet – More than 5000 eggs are cracked and cooked on a giant skillet in Abbeville, LA, around the beginning of the month.

Country Christmas – Opryland in Nashville holds events and is specially decorated from November 1 through Christmas.

Veterans' Day – November 11 is a national holiday.

Thanksgiving – On the fourth Thursday in November, Americans give thanks before stuffing themselves with turkey, mashed potatoes and cranberries.

December

Christmas – In many parts of the South, this is a month-long celebration with bonfires along the Mississippi River levees that light the way through Louisiana's Plantation Country. There's a Christmas boat parade in Biloxi, MS. Graceland is specially lit for Christmas in Memphis. The actual holiday, of course, is December 25.

ACTIVITIES

The most common mainstream outdoor activities in the Deep South are fishing, hunting and golfing, followed by RV camping and boating. This leaves less-common pursuits, such as sea kayaking, river running, mountain biking and backpacking, uncrowded. While recreational equipment and supplies for these activities can be found in the larger cities, rentals elsewhere are scarce.

Beach swimming, sunbathing, boating and saltwater fishing are popular along the Gulf Coast in Mississippi and Alabama. The most pristine and deserted beaches are found on Mississippi's Gulf Islands, which require a 12-mile sea-kayak ride through the relatively calm Mississippi Sound to get there. Primitive camping is allowed on the protected islands. There is no scuba or surfing activity to speak of along the coast.

Bicyclists, as well as pedestrians, will find that this region is largely car-dependent and inaccessible. That said, the Natchez Trace Scenic Parkway, 440-mile corridor between Natchez, Mississippi, and Nashville, Tennessee, is a wonderful exception. The parkway preserves portions of the original trace as a footpath. In addition, the Bartram Trail near Tuskegee, Alabama, traces a route explored by 18th-century naturalist William Bartram through what is now the Tuskegee National Forest.

For Louisiana outdoor adventures, Pack & Paddle (☎ 318-232-5854, 800-458-4560), in Lafayette, organizes biking, kayaking, canoeing and hiking trips. They also rent equipment, distribute maps and guides, and host classes in kayaking, backpacking and in-line skating.

Off-road biking trails can be found in the region's national forests, but forest service roads themselves are also well suited for mountain or dirt biking. Contact the USFS (see Useful Organizations, earlier in this chapter) or see national forest listings in state chapters.

Backpacking opportunities are scattered but available. In Louisiana, Chicot State Park maintains a backpacking loop around a lake in Cajun Country, while the Kisatchie National Forest has many areas around the state with forested terrain. In Mississippi, the Black Creek Trail runs along a designated wild and scenic river corridor. In Alabama, the 102-mile Pinhoti Trail is the state's longest and most popular trail.

Hiking trails throughout the region offer a variety of terrain, from bayou and beach to woodlands and canyons. National forests, along with state parks, feature some of the most developed trails in each state. National wildlife refuges offer the best chance to see local wildlife (particularly birds along the Mississippi flyway) in a variety of peaceful settings – from the coastal marshes of the Sabine refuge in southwestern Louisiana and Sandhill Crane on the Mississippi Gulf Coast to the wooded Noxubee in northeastern Mississippi or the Bon Secour in Alabama's Gulf Coast.

Boating is particularly popular through the wetlands in the southern part of the region. While independent travelers might enjoy wandering around the area's swamps and bayous on their own, everyone should take a guided tour as a window into the local culture. See the Cajun Country chapter for more information.

The Pearl River, near Bogalusa in Louisiana, offers a chance to canoe through a protected wildlife management area of cypress and tupelo swamp and hardwood forest. In Mississippi, local outfitters run trips down the wild and scenic Black Creek River in the Mississippi Gulf Coast region.

The cave region in TAG country (at the intersection of Tennessee, Alabama and Georgia) is a nationally known destination for spelunkers. (It's always a pleasure to make use of that word.) The National Speleological Society (☎ 205-852-1300), 2813 Cave Ave, Huntsville, AL 35810, can provide detailed information. (See Fort Payne in the Alabama chapter for local outfitters.)

WORK

The USFS puts volunteers to work as campground hosts and forest hands. Each state has its own USFS headquarters; the regional Southern USFS Information Center is in Atlanta (☎ 404-347-2384), 1720 Peachtree Rd NW, Atlanta, GA 30367.

In New Orleans, many bars and restaurants hire seasonal labor – several get desperate for reliable help during Mardi Gras and Jazz Fest. Year-round, you can push a mobile hot dog cart for Lucky Dogs (☎ 504-523-9260), 517 Gravier St.

If you're not a US citizen, you'll need to apply for a work visa from the US embassy in your home country before you leave. The type of visa varies depending on how long you're staying and the kind of work you plan to do. Generally, you'll need either a J-1 visa, which you can obtain by joining a visitor-exchange program, or an H-2B visa, which you get when being sponsored by a US employer. The latter is not easy to obtain (since the employer has to prove that no US citizen or permanent resident can do the job); the former is issued mostly to students for work in summer camps.

ACCOMMODATIONS

Of the many types of overnight accommodations available in the Deep South – from a state park cabin in the woods to a luxurious suite overlooking the French Quarter – perhaps the most distinctive lodging of the region has to offer is in historic homes transformed into B&Bs and inns.

Budget travelers can find plenty of roadside chain motels for comfortably predictable accommodations.

It's a general rule of thumb that visiting cities on the weekends and the country during the week helps keep costs down, but many other factors (festivals and seasonal appeal are two) also come into play. In some towns with casinos, an influx of gamblers on the weekend can drive hotel rates up.

During peak seasons or festivals, it's wise to reserve well in advance to get your first choice. For many festivals – including Mardi Gras and Jazz Fest – waiting might mean you'll have to stay somewhere out of town. Many towns in Mississippi simply do not have enough hotel rooms for the thousands who come to a blues festival held there; it is likely that you will end up staying in a nearby town unless you reserve several months ahead. Also, since hotels in these towns depend on having full occupancy during festivals, it isn't uncommon that you be asked to pay a deposit (sometimes a personal check) when reserving the room. It's the hotel's way of ensuring advance notice from you if you decide not to take the room after all.

Prices in this guide can only be an approximate guideline at best. Also, be prepared to add room tax. Children often stay free with their parents, but rules for this vary; inquire if traveling with a family. You can often find discounts from the so-called 'rack rate' quoted to guests who arrive without a reservation. Discounts of 10% or more are commonly granted to members of the American Automobile Association (AAA), as well as senior citizens, students, military personnel, government employees and those with some corporate affiliations. Even someone walking in off the street without a reservation can often negotiate a discount if armed with knowledge that occupancy is down. Conversely, don't expect a discount at a hotel that is booked for a convention.

Another note: the 800 numbers of the chains are not your best bet for getting a good deal or checking on room availability. These hotlines also can't guarantee a particular room (say, one with a balcony or a view or one that's been remodeled). Lower rates are often quoted at the local numbers.

Camping

Camping is the cheapest, and can be the most enjoyable, approach to a vacation. Visitors can take advantage of hundreds of private and public campgrounds at prices of $10 per night or even less.

National wilderness areas offer the most natural and rugged camping adventures in the Deep South. If you can get a boat (or sea kayak), you can camp on the Gulf Islands off the Mississippi coast.

National parks maintain impressive campgrounds often in beautiful areas. The campground in Davis Bayou near Ocean Springs, Mississippi, the mainland component of the Gulf Islands National Seashore, is a particularly nice spot. Wooded campgrounds along the Natchez Trace Parkway are also scenic and well maintained. For reservations or information for national park campgrounds, call ☎ 800-365-2267 or write to National Park Service Public Inquiry, Dept of Interior, PO Box 37127, Washington, DC 20013-7127.

National forests in all Deep South states provide primitive campsites – tables, grills, drinking water, vault toilets, some cold

The deet, Spot! Fetch the deet!

showers – for around $6 a night. These are first-come, first-served, and the maximum stay is 14 nights. You may also camp anywhere in the national forest unless posted otherwise; no fee or permit is required. Current information about national forests can be obtained from ranger stations, which are listed in the text. National forest campground and reservation information can be obtained by calling ☎ 800-280-2267.

State park campgrounds are more developed, often with flush toilets and hot showers. Most are first-come, first-served. Of the Deep South states, Louisiana and Alabama maintain the nicest state park facilities. Mississippi's facilities are humble by comparison (with office trailers where the other states have fancy visitor centers), but will likely appeal to those who like their natural areas only lightly touched and not overdeveloped or interpreted.

County parks or recreational areas may also offer camping; facilities vary considerably but are likely not plush.

Private campgrounds may run the gamut, but are most often on the 'camping resort' side of things and include developed sites, RV hookups and other amenities, such as a swimming pool, stocked trout pond or even hayrides. These can climb to around $20. Kampgrounds of America (KOA) is a national network of private campgrounds with sites usually ranging from $12 to $15. You can get the annual directory of KOA sites by calling or writing: KOA (☎ 406-248-7444), PO Box 30558, Billings, MT 59114-0558.

To make reservations at national, state and local parks, you must pay with Visa, MasterCard or Discover. If you know what state park or national forest campground you'd like to stay at, call ☎ 800-280-2267 for reservations. For sites in national parks, call Destinet at ☎ 800-365-2267.

A Note on Camping When camping in an undeveloped area, choose a campsite at least 200 feet (approximately 70 adult steps) from water and wash up at camp, not in the stream, using biodegradable soap. Dig a 6-inch-deep hole to use as a latrine and cover

and camouflage it well when leaving the site. Burn toilet paper, unless fires are prohibited. Carry out all trash. Use a portable charcoal grill or camping stove; don't build new fires. If there already is a fire ring, use only dead and downed wood or wood you have carried in yourself. Make sure to leave the campsite as you found it.

Even though developed areas usually have toilets and drinking water, it is always a good idea to have a few gallons of water when venturing out to the boonies.

Cabins

Renting a cabin for a week or two is popular for families in the Deep South, but not particularly easy for those who do not live in the region, except at state park cabins. Most state parks offer cabin rentals that can accommodate eight to 12 people; prices are extremely reasonable. These are not shacks – they usually have central heating and air-conditioning, and they supply all the necessary dishware, cookware and linens. Some were built by the Civilian Conservation Corps (CCC) in the 1930s; these CCC-built stone-and-wood cabins are the most desirable picks today. But because of their popularity and low rates, cabins may be booked up months in advance.

For private cabins, local chambers of commerce generally maintain listings of properties available for short-term rental. Note that since many cabins are outfitted to accommodate families, some bedrooms are likely outfitted with twin beds and may not be suitable for several couples traveling together.

Hostels

The 'official' youth hostels in the US are affiliated with Hostelling International (HI), which is a member of the International Youth Hostel Federation. Regrettably, hostels are few and far between in the region covered in this book. In New Orleans there is one hostel affiliated with HI, and there are two independent hostels. An independent hostel operates in Memphis. Expect decent beds in rooms that sleep four to eight people. Rates vary from $10 to $20 a night. A party atmosphere often prevails, which means you are likely to meet people but may have a hard time getting a good night's rest. Most hostels have a few private rooms for $30 to $45 a night. You can get information at www.hostels.com.

Motels

The all-American motel is usually a roadside lodging with parking and rooms that can be accessed from the parking lot. Security is not as tight as at a hotel (where one must pass the front desk before going to the rooms), but rates are generally cheaper. In the South, motels with $30 rates can be found, especially in small towns on major highways and in the motel strips of larger towns. At this price the beds may sag, the decor and furnishings may be worn, heat or air-con may be uneven, and the odor of disinfectant or incense may be powerful, but rooms come with private bath and the sheets and towels should be clean. Housecleaning tends to improve as the rates increase. Also, rooms are often priced according to the number of beds they have. Rooms with two double beds may be ideal for families.

The cheapest bottom-end hotels and motels may not accept reservations, but at least phone from the road to see what's available; even if they don't take reservations, they'll often hold a room for an hour or two.

Some of even the cheapest motels may advertise kitchenettes. These may cost a few dollars more but give you the chance to cook a simple meal for yourself. Kitchenettes vary from a two-ring burner to a spiffy little mini-kitchen and may or may not have utensils.

Chain Motels While chains are not too exciting, they are reliably clean and come with dependable air-conditioning units. (The downside to this is that often there's no way to open the windows – you have no choice but to crank the air-con.) The consistently cheapest national chain is Motel 6. Rooms start below $40 for a single in smaller towns,

in the $50s in larger towns. They usually charge a flat $6 for each extra person. Super 8, Days Inn and Econo Lodge are a little more expensive. These provide basic clean rooms with TVs, phone and private bath; most have pools.

Stepping up to chains with rates in the $45 to $80 range (depending on location), you'll find nicer rooms; cafes, restaurants or bars may be on the premises; and the swimming pool may be indoors with a spa or exercise room also available. Best Western, La Quinta, Comfort Inn and Sleep Inn are in this category.

Normally, you have to give a credit card number to make a room reservation. If you don't show and don't call to cancel, you will be charged the first night's rental. Cancellation policies vary, so find out when you book. Make sure to let the place know if you plan on a late arrival – many will give your room away if you haven't arrived or called by 6 pm.

The reservation operators at toll-free numbers might not be aware of local special discounts and availability. The reservation numbers of some of the best-known chains are as follows:

Best Western	☎ 800-528-1234
Comfort Inn, Sleep Inn	☎ 800-221-2222
Days Inn	☎ 800-329-7466
E-Z 8 Motels	☎ 800-326-6835
Econo Lodge, Rodeway Inn	☎ 800-424-4777
Howard Johnson	☎ 800-446-4656
Motel 6	☎ 800-466-8356
Super 8 Motel	☎ 800-800-8000
Travelodge	☎ 800-578-7878

Hotels

City hotels in the region are often geared to business travelers and their rates sometimes drop on weekends. Such chains as Marriott and Sheraton provide rooms from $80 a night; in larger cities prices are higher. These may include health clubs with sauna and hot tub, room service, and restaurants and taverns on the premises.

Inns & B&Bs

European visitors should be aware that North American B&Bs are not the casual, inexpensive sort of accommodations found on the continent or in Britain. Many wonderfully preserved historic homes in the Deep South now serve as inns or B&Bs, offering visitors a personal up-close look at the architectural and cultural heritage of the South. These accommodations can vary widely, from a hotel-like inn with many guests and little personal contact to a home-like experience where your hosts live in the property and treat you as their personal guests. Particularly in the South, with its reputation for hospitality, hosts are often eager to lavish attention on their guests, and they will regale them with stories if offered the opportunity.

The nature of the rooms may also vary widely – some inns have all the modern conveniences (private baths, TV, phones, heat and air-conditioning), others maintain a historic authenticity (shared baths, no TV or phone, ceiling fans, quirky plumbing and the like). They may be furnished with period reproductions or antiques. Rates range widely, from $50 for a weeknight stay at a small place to $200 for an all-out historic plantation house.

Be aware that B&B conditions may vary considerably. Some welcome small children, while others have an age minimum, usually around 12 years. Most B&Bs prohibit smoking, if not entirely, at least in rooms. A continental or full Southern breakfast is almost always included, but other meals may be provided as well. Check whether a certain room (view, private bath) can be reserved, or if room choice is on a first-come, first-served basis. Finally, find out whether credit cards, personal checks or traveler's checks are accepted, or if payment is by cash only.

FOOD

Southern-style American cuisine is inexpensive – fine dining in New Orleans being the exception – and typically served up in heaps. Southerners take their time preparing and serving meals, and the local preference seems to be for food that is served less than piping hot.

When you eat at a restaurant, expect the final bill to be inflated by about 25% above prices quoted in the menu because of the addition of 8% or so sales tax and a 15% or so tip. (Tipping is not expected in fast-food take-out restaurants.)

The style of service may differ from other regions. Luncheon and dinner buffets are common in the South (cafeterias are very popular), and many restaurants serve 'family-style,' seating unrelated groups at the same table to pass plates around and serve yourself. Note that many Southern families say a prayer before eating; restaurant patrons would not necessarily be expected to join in (guests at a family's home *would* be expected to do so), but it would be respectful to wait silently until they're done before serving or eating.

Server tips are slightly lower at buffet- and family-style restaurants (usually around 10%); at cafeterias, it's considered kind to leave a small tip for the table-clearer (around $1 or $2).

Most restaurants offer the choice of non-smoking and smoking areas; some prohibit smoking altogether. Many restaurants are air-conditioned to the point of refrigeration; even if it's 100°F outside, you might want to have a sweater handy for lunch.

Breakfast

Restaurants serve breakfast from around 6 to 11 am; some budget motels put out a simple complimentary breakfast bar (juice, pastries, cold cereals) from around 7 to 9 am, which can be a good way to save time as well as money. Otherwise, standard breakfast choices range from a Danish and coffee for under $2 to a full Southern breakfast of eggs, breakfast meat (bacon, ham or beef), 'grits' (a hot cereal of ground hominy seasoned with butter and salt) and biscuits-and-gravy, all for around $6 with juice and coffee. A meal that size isn't necessarily conducive to an active day, but may be just the thing after an action-filled night. Some coffeeshop chains offer breakfast around the clock. In coffeeshops, free coffee refills

Breakfast plantation style: eggs, sausage, grits, biscuits, java & ojay – hungry yet? Natchez, MS

Rabbit stew made in Eunice, LA

WHEN LIGHT
IS FLASHING
STOP FOR
HOT BREAD

#1 cause of traffic accidents in New Orleans

Crescent City Farmer's Market, New Orleans

SWEET SEEDLESS LOUISIANA SATSUMAS

YELLOW-RIPE BANANAS   CREOLE TOMATOES

Old farmers know their fruits. New Orleans

Something cold & sweet to beat the heat, LA

Mr Lasyone & his meat pies, Natchitoches, LA

Uglesich's restaurant, New Orleans

are offered by attentive waitstaff ('Top that off for ya, hon?').

Lunch

This meal is served from around 11:30 am to 2 or 3 pm; sandwiches, salads, hamburgers and other short orders for around $4 to $5 are common choices. At better restaurants, many lunch entrées are identical to their dinner choices but nearly half the cost (a $12 dinner plate might go for $7).

Dinner

The largest meal of the day, dinner starts around 6 pm (in New Orleans, the rush comes later, around 8 pm, which gives early eaters a jump on things). Traditional Sunday dinner is eaten earlier, as early as noon, and throughout the region many restaurants close early that day, around 2, 3, or 4 pm; visitors whose timing is off may be stranded. Some city hotels and restaurants offer elaborate Sunday brunch buffets, but many restaurants are closed until midday.

Budget travelers will want to seek out farmers markets for the freshest produce at the lowest prices. Grocery stores and deli counters commonly offer prepared foods for take-out bargains. Restaurants offer discounts on meals for children and seniors, sometimes also for military and clergy in uniform.

Regional chain restaurants offer a healthier and more regionally distinctive alternative to standard American fast food; cafeterias in particular are often just as cheap and quick (and you can see what looks good before ordering). Two that are good and reliable are Morrison's Cafeterias and Piccadilly Cafeterias; you can generally find them near shopping malls off freeway exits. For table service, there's the hick-themed Po' Folks and Cracker Barrel and the more upscale newcomer Black-eyed Pea.

Southern Cuisine

Classic Southern country-cooking is often described as 'hearty' – no doubt because it tastes wonderful, is satisfying, makes you feel relaxed and, if enjoyed in great quantities, eventually produces a nice, cushy coat of fat around your arteries. In culinary terms, 'Southern' is frequently followed by 'fried' – as in Southern fried chicken. Of course, some things are merely 'country-fried,' such as that tough piece of steak that granny pounded down and breaded, thus converting it into country-fried steak. Catfish, shrimp and oysters also get the fried treatment.

A 'meat-and-three' plate means you pick an entree and three well-cooked vegetables from a list of choices – typically okra, corn, black-eyed peas, collard greens, mustard greens or turnip greens. However, if you have a heart condition or if you are a strict vegetarian, you'll need to talk to your server before ordering vegetables. Ever wonder why red beans cooked in New Orleans taste so much better than anywhere else? The answer: LARD. Other beans and greens might well be stewed in lard as well. Of course, if you have no health issues, all of this tastes terrific.

Other side items might include your choice of a flaky biscuit or cornbread (called 'hushpuppies' when fried in small balls, or 'corn pone' if it's cylindrical or triangular).

Barbecue A particularly revered Southern cuisine, barbecue can be made with smoked or marinated meat, which is grilled and then smothered in a tangy, spicy sauce. Pork is the meat of choice (offered chopped, sliced, 'pulled,' or in ribs), but barbecued chicken and beef are also widely available. 'BBQ' sauces can be mustard, vinegar or tomato-based (or a combination of all three; recipes are often closely guarded family secrets), and meats are usually served with a slice of white bread and a side of coleslaw, baked beans or macaroni. The classic venue is a no-frills roadside stand with long picnic tables out front and a hickory-scented smoking chimney out back. In some areas, bars will have a barbecue on the sidewalk.

Soul Food Much of the Southern diet could be described as 'soul' food – the brand of cooking favored by many African-Americans – since blacks and whites eat many of the same foods prepared similarly.

However, in serious black soul food joints, you have the additional choice of exotic meats that were considered castoffs in slavery days, such as chitterlings (fried tripe, called 'chitlins'), pigs' feet and turkey necks.

Seafood Specialties The Gulf Coast is famous for its fleet-fresh fish and shellfish. Oysters, shrimp and mullet are commonly served either on a you-crack-'em plate or prepared in a variety of dishes. Mullet was so popular as a substitute for scarce meat during WWII that it earned the name 'Biloxi Bacon,' and still today an annual mullet festival honors the local mascot and features a mullet toss competition. Catfish, another flavorful item once dismissed by 'discriminating' diners, has always been a staple in the Deep South.

Creole & Cajun Cuisine

Put very simply, Creole food is urban cooking and Cajun food is country cooking. Just the same, New Orleans' indifference to this type of definition may drive visitors bats if they're trying to figure out the difference between the two cuisines. Restaurants ad-vertising Creole cuisine often have similar menus to those calling themselves Cajun. Then there are the growing number of Cajun-Creole restaurants.

Gumbo, the region's signature soup, doesn't shed much light on the subject of broad distinctions. Not only is it a mainstay of both Creole and Cajun food, but no two gumbos are alike. As a rule, Creoles use okra as a thickener – 'gombo' is, after all, an African term for okra – while the Cajuns are more likely to use filé (ground sassafras leaves). Ultimately, after tasting a variety of gumbos, you'll have to agree with the locals that the difference between Creole and Cajun cuisines isn't important, as long as it's delicious.

The origins of both Creole and Cajun food are quite similar, as both result from adaptations made by European settlers in the difficult environment of southern Louisiana. Both the Creoles and the Cajuns began with a basic understanding of French cuisine, and both incorporated Native American knowledge of local ingredients. And, of course, they learned from each other. Consequently, the basic elements of

RUSSELL LEE/LIBRARY OF CONGRESS

Enjoying a crab boil, LA, 1938

Creole and Cajun cuisine are the same: distinctive *roux* (flour browned with butter), the backbone of so many of the region's dishes; substitutes for wheat flour, such as okra or filé, used as thickening agents; and all the meats, fish, crustaceans and shellfish that are so abundant in southern Louisiana and along the Gulf Coast.

But traditionally there are some significant differences. If it comes from the swamp – alligator meat, frog legs, crawfish – it's probably Cajun in origin. The use of cayenne and other peppers also makes Cajun food hotter and spicier – Cajun country is, in fact, where that ubiquitous American condiment, Tabasco sauce, comes from. And over the years, Cajuns developed a reputation for experimentation, the result being versatile dishes like jambalaya that can accommodate just about any added ingredients. It's on the whole an earthier and, some say, livelier cuisine. Creole cooking is usually described as more refined, milder and more subtle. It has also benefited more from the contributions of African cooks.

Desserts

Southerners have more of a sweet tooth than other Americans, so you will find such wonderful desserts as pecan pie, banana and bread pudding, and peach cobbler. Even meats and vegetables are sometimes laced with sugar, such as honey-roasted ham and sweet potato soufflé, for example.

DRINKS
Nonalcoholic Drinks

Most Americans start the day with a cup of coffee. On the whole, Americans prefer weaker roasts than Europeans, but in New Orleans and other major cities you can find espresso and its varieties. Another Crescent City twist is coffee brewed with ground chickory. Brewed decaffeinated coffee is widely available. In New Orleans, where café au lait (served with milk) is the norm, you'll have to specify 'black' when you don't want milk.

Iced tea, sweetened or unsweetened with a slice of lemon, is considered the 'house wine' of the South. This is what they'll bring if you ask for 'tea.' If you want hot tea, you'll have to be specific. Coca-Cola, 7-Up, root beer and the like are also common choices; lemonade is a popular summer drink. Restaurants serve iced tap water (safe to drink) on request at no charge with a meal.

Alcoholic Drinks

If you've been reading the food section, you've already deduced that wine doesn't always go with dinner. In finer restaurants, where the food is less regional, wine is likely to be available. Microbrewed beer is increasingly popular, and you'll find cozy brewpubs in most cities. Hard liquor is widely available.

Beverage laws vary from state to state, and liquor sales in stores and restaurants throughout the region may be restricted on Sunday. 'Dry counties,' counties in which the sale of alcohol is illegal, are scattered throughout the region, but proliferate in Alabama. It's illegal to drive with open containers of alcohol in the car; drunk driving is a serious felony offense. Drinking alcohol outdoors is generally prohibited, but it's tolerated at festivals, on Bourbon St in New Orleans and on Beale St in Memphis.

The minimum drinking age is 21 throughout the region, and photo identification (driver's license or passport) is often requested at stores and restaurants as proof of age (this ritual is called being 'carded'). Persons under 21 (minors) are not allowed in bars and pubs, even to order nonalcoholic beverages. Unfortunately, this means that most dance clubs are also off-limits to minors. Minors are, however, welcome in the dining areas of restaurants where alcohol may be served.

ENTERTAINMENT
Music & Clubs

From the bluesy homespun 'juke joints' of the Mississippi Delta to the barn dance atmosphere at the Grand Ole Opry to the outdoor New Orleans Jazz & Heritage Festival, you will find wonderful live music performed in a variety of inviting venues throughout the region – music is a primary draw for visitors.

Discos and nightclubs without live music often feature DJs (disc jockeys) spinning records. Bars and pubs sometimes feature jukeboxes and often set up pool tables or dartboards. However, take every opportunity to hear live music – it's widely available, diverse, regionally distinctive and usually inexpensive.

Performing Arts

New Orleans is the region's hub for cultural arts (see the city chapter) – but it often falls short of international standards. In New Orleans as well as throughout the region, folk arts are the highlight. A few exceptions are worth noting.

Jackson hosts an international ballet competition every four years. This international affair, which brings famous dance companies from as far as Russia and Asia, lends renown to the local Jackson Ballet. In Montgomery, the Alabama Shakespeare Festival is nationally recognized. They perform repertory theater year-round and host an annual festival.

Performing arts troupes are organized in nearly every major city; colleges and universities also host performing arts events open to the public.

Gambling

Casinos in the region can be found in New Orleans, Shreveport, along the Mississippi Gulf Coast and up the Mississippi River (in Natchez, Vicksburg and Tunica County just south of Memphis). The casinos are open 24 hours a day, and only to people age 21 or over. They're heralded by local promoters for bringing in employment, sales taxes and frequently other services as well (expanded transportation options, for example). Some casinos offer promotional deals, with discounted lodging and car rental.

SPECTATOR SPORTS

Sports are a way of life in the South. Folks root for their local team – whether it's major league, minor league, college or high school – with fierce loyalty. One of the best

ways to experience local culture is to sit elbow to elbow with cheering fans of all ages at a local sporting event.

Some of Alabama's best local attractions pay homage to sports heroes, notably in the sports halls of fame in Birmingham and Jackson. In Tuscaloosa, a museum dedicated to the career of 'Bear' Bryant attests to the popularity of the former University of Alabama (U of A) football coach, who led the school to national notoriety.

Football

The Tennessee Titans, who played in the Super Bowl in 2000, play in Nashville's Adelphia Coliseum. The New Orleans Saints play professional NFL football at the Superdome.

Grambling University, a historically black school in Louisiana, was home to Eddie Robinson, the winningest college football coach in the US, until he retired in 1997. The current head coach is Doug Williams, the first black quarterback to lead his team (the Washington Redskins) to the Super Bowl. Other college teams in the state include Louisiana State University (LSU), Tulane and Southwestern Louisiana State University. Ole Miss has a competitive team. The U of A also attracts loyal crowds to games. The Sugar Bowl, an NCAA championship game, is played at the Superdome in New Orleans on New Year's Day.

Baseball

The region is not host to a major league team – but this makes attending a less prestigious game all the more fun. Minor league and college games are cheap and fun and a good way to experience a community.

Minor league baseball teams in the region include the Jackson Generals, the Memphis Chicks, the New Orleans Zephyrs, the Shreveport Captains, the Mobile Bay Bears, the Birmingham Barons and the Greenville Braves. Inquire at local chambers of commerce for schedules and game details.

As for college teams, the Bulldogs of Mississippi State University at Starkville are well known in the region. LSU, Tulane, Ole Miss and U of A also field respectable teams. In late February, college teams from Mississippi pair off against those from Louisiana in the Winn-Dixie Showdown, a three-day series of doubleheaders in the Superdome.

Basketball

There are no professional basketball teams in the region.

Highly ranked women's collegiate basketball teams include the University of Tennessee, Ole Miss and Mississippi State University. Tulane, LSU and U of A have good teams also.

In men's college basketball, LSU is consistently highly ranked and notable as the former team of pro player Shaquille O'Neal. Other outstanding NCAA Division I men's teams include Ole Miss, Mississippi State University, Memphis State University and Tulane.

SHOPPING

Handmade quilts, pottery and baskets made from native materials, and woodworking from rough to fine are just a few of the traditional Southern crafts available throughout the region.

Historic house museums often have nice little gift shops with a dainty collection of souvenirs, such as cotton boll wreaths and anything with a magnolia on it. Packages of gift-wrapped Southern food specialties available throughout the region make inexpensive souvenirs – it's easy to find fancy stone-ground grits in small canvas sacks, jars of local fruit preserves and syrups daintily topped with calico-print fabric, and colorful pickled relishes made of corn, cucumber and red pepper.

African-influenced crafts – masks and wooden figurines, as well as a variety of fine and folk arts – are produced by local African-American artists.

Textile companies in the region retain some outlet stores, but the low quality of goods makes them not worth going out of the way for.

Every city has its shopping mall, where you can find all the necessities – clothing, traveling supplies, recreational and sporting equipment, you name it.

Throughout the region you can sift through antique stores and flea markets for one-of-a-kind souvenirs – refined crystal and china to dusty old washboards and hand-cranked coffee grinders. Prices may be negotiable for antiques; can't hurt to try.

Music recordings of bands you've heard are great souvenirs; tapes and CDs can be cheaper if bought at the venue than in stores.

New Orleans has wonderfully weird things to buy: voodoo charms, amulets, beads, feathered Mardi Gras masks, Cajun spices and cookbooks, street art, handmade accordions, alligator skulls – stuff you can't imagine.

Getting There & Away

The two most common ways to reach the southern states covered in this book are by air and by car, but you can also get there by train and by bus. Travelers coming from the Midwest and the mid-Atlantic and Great Plains states don't have far to go if they want to drive, and in general, excellent highways connect the region to every part of the US and neighboring countries.

Travelers from farther afield usually fly in, then rent a car. The region's two main gateways, New Orleans (MSY) and Memphis (MEM), are international airports that serve very few direct international flights. International travelers almost always have to change planes in another US gateway.

AIR

US domestic airfares vary tremendously depending on the season you travel, the day of the week you fly, the length of your stay and the flexibility the ticket allows for flight changes and refunds. Fares also vary depending on which airport you are flying into – at a given time, your cheapest option could be flying into New Orleans, Memphis or Atlanta, while smaller airports in Nashville and Birmingham might offer even cheaper fares at other times. It's also worth asking about fares to Little Rock, Arkansas, which is not so far from the westernmost areas covered in this book. No single airport in the region has a lock on the best deals.

Nothing determines fares more than demand, and when things are slow, regardless of the season, airlines will lower their fares to fill empty seats. There's a lot of competition, and at any given time any one of the airlines could have the cheapest fare. In general, high season for nationwide airline travel rates in the US is mid-June to mid-September (summer) and the weeks before and after Christmas. However, Americans generally avoid the stultifying heat of the South during the summer months, so deals from other parts of the country may still be available then. See Buying Tickets, later in this section, for advice on getting the best deals.

Airports

There are very few direct international flights to Southern hubs; international travelers often arrive on connecting flights from such traditional ports of entry as New York, Los Angeles and Miami. Expanded international service to the Hartsfield Atlanta International Airport (☎ 404-530-6834) may provide additional direct service to the South.

The following list of major airports runs roughly from largest on down. The Memphis International Airport (☎ 901-922-8000) is a major hub for Northwest Airlines, which is closely affiliated with KLM Royal Dutch Airlines, which provides direct flights from Amsterdam with connections from other European countries.

Warning

The information in this chapter is particularly vulnerable to change: Prices for international travel are volatile, routes are introduced and canceled, schedules change, special deals come and go, and rules and visa requirements are amended. Airlines and governments seem to take a perverse pleasure in making price structures and regulations as complicated as possible. You should check directly with the airline or a travel agent to make sure you understand how a fare (and ticket you may buy) works. In addition, the travel industry is highly competitive and there are many lurks and perks.

The upshot of this is that you should get opinions, quotes and advice from as many airlines and travel agents as possible before you part with your hard-earned cash. The details given in this chapter should be regarded as pointers and are not a substitute for your own careful, up-to-date research.

New Orleans International Airport (☎ 504-464-3547) is served by major carriers, including Aeroméxico and Lacsa.

Nashville International Airport (☎ 615-275-1600) is served by major carriers, but is more expensive to fly into than Memphis or New Orleans.

Jackson International Airport (☎ 601-939-5631) in Mississippi is a minor airport, though it's the state's largest. Travelers should consider using the airports in New Orleans or Memphis.

Like Jackson, Birmingham International Airport (☎ 205-595-0533) is Alabama's largest airport, but it's still a minor airport for the region. Travelers considering flying into Birmingham should check fares for Atlanta's Hartsfield airport (see above).

Airlines

The following are the major international airlines that serve the region:

Air Canada	☎ 888-247-2262
Air France	☎ 800-237-2747
Air New Zealand	☎ 800-262-1234
American Airlines	☎ 800-433-7300
British Airways	☎ 800-247-9297
Canadian Airlines	☎ 800-426-7000
Continental Airlines	☎ 800-231-0856
Japan Air Lines	☎ 800-525-3663
KLM	☎ 800-374-7747
Northwest Airlines	☎ 800-447-4747
Qantas Airways	☎ 800-227-4500
TWA	☎ 800-221-2000
United Airlines	☎ 800-538-2929
US Airways	☎ 800-428-4322
Virgin Atlantic	☎ 800-862-8621

The following are the major domestic airlines that serve the region:

AirTran Airways	☎ 800-247-8726
Alaska Airlines	☎ 800-426-0333
America West	☎ 800-235-9292
American Airlines	☎ 800-433-7300
Continental Airlines	☎ 800-525-0280
Delta Air Lines	☎ 800-221-1212
Hawaiian Airlines	☎ 800-367-5320
Northwest Airlines	☎ 800-225-2525
Southwest	☎ 800-435-9792
TWA	☎ 800-892-4141
United Airlines	☎ 800-241-6522

Buying Tickets

The plane ticket will probably be the single most expensive item in your budget, and buying it can be intimidating. So rather than just walking into the nearest travel agent or airline office, you should do a bit of research and shop around first. It's always worth putting aside a few hours to check into the current state of the market. Start shopping for a ticket early. Low advertised fares are often available on a limited basis and sell out quickly. Some of the cheapest tickets must be bought months in advance, and popular flights often sell out early. Talk to recent travelers – they may offer more specific cost-saving advice. Look at the ads in newspapers and magazines and consult the Internet.

If you are buying tickets within the US, the *New York Times*, *Los Angeles Times*, *Chicago Tribune*, *San Francisco Examiner* and other major newspapers all produce weekly travel sections with numerous travel agents' ads. Council Travel (☎ 800-226-8624, www.ciee.org) and STA (☎ 800-777-0112, www.statravel.com) have offices in major cities nationwide. The magazine *Travel Unlimited*, PO Box 1058, Allston, MA 02134, publishes details of the cheapest airfares and courier possibilities.

Those coming from outside the US might start by perusing travel sections of magazines like *Time Out* and *TNT* in the UK, or the Saturday editions of newspapers like the *Sydney Morning Herald* and *The Age* in Australia. Ads in these publications offer cheap fares, but don't be surprised if they happen to be sold out when you contact the agents: they're usually low-season fares on obscure airlines with conditions attached.

Increasingly, travelers are turning to Internet travel services for cheap airline deals. Travelocity (www.travelocity.com), Cheap Tickets (www.cheaptickets.com), Expedia

Air Travel Glossary

Cancellation Penalties If you have to cancel or change a discounted ticket, there are often heavy penalties involved; insurance can sometimes be taken out against these penalties. Some airlines impose penalties on regular tickets as well, particularly against 'no-show' passengers.

Courier Fares Businesses often need to send urgent documents or freight securely. Courier companies hire people to accompany the package through customs and, in return, offer a discount ticket, which is sometimes a phenomenal bargain. However, you may have to surrender all your baggage allowance and take only carry-on luggage.

Full Fares Airlines traditionally offer 1st class (coded F), business class (coded J) and economy class (coded Y) tickets. These days there are so many promotional and discounted fares available that few passengers pay full economy fare.

Lost Tickets If you lose your airline ticket an airline will usually treat it like a traveler's check and, after inquiries, issue you with another one. Legally, however, an airline is entitled to treat it like cash and if you lose it then it's gone forever. Take good care of your tickets.

Onward Tickets An entry requirement for many countries is that you have a ticket out of the country. If you're unsure of your next move, the easiest solution is to buy the cheapest onward ticket to a neighbouring country or a ticket from a reliable airline that can later be refunded if you do not use it.

Open-Jaw Tickets These are return tickets where you fly out to one place but return from another. If available, this can save you backtracking to your arrival point.

Overbooking Since every flight has some passengers who fail to show up, airlines often book more passengers than they have seats. Usually excess passengers make up for the no-shows, but occasionally somebody gets 'bumped' onto the next available flight. Guess who it is most likely to be? The passengers who check in late.

Promotional Fares These are officially discounted fares, available from travel agencies or direct from the airline.

Reconfirmation If you don't reconfirm your flight at least 72 hours prior to departure, the airline may delete your name from the passenger list. Ring to find out if your airline requires reconfirmation.

Restrictions Discounted tickets often have various restrictions on them – such as needing to be paid for in advance and incurring a penalty to be altered. Others are restrictions on the minimum and maximum period you must be away.

Round-the-World Tickets RTW tickets give you a limited period (usually a year) in which to circumnavigate the globe. You can go anywhere the carrying airlines go, as long as you don't backtrack. The number of stopovers or total number of separate flights is decided before you set off and they usually cost a bit more than a basic return flight.

Transferred Tickets Airline tickets cannot be transferred from one person to another. Travelers sometimes try to sell the return half of their ticket, but officials can ask you to prove that you are the person named on the ticket. On an international flight tickets are compared with passports.

Travel Periods Ticket prices vary with the time of year. There is a low (off-peak) season and a high (peak) season, and often a low-shoulder season and a high-shoulder season as well. Usually the fare depends on your outward flight – if you depart in the high season and return in the low season, you pay the high-season fare.

(http://expedia.msn.com) and Flifo (www .flifo.com) are just four popular sites on the Web. Sometimes contacting an airline directly is the best way to find cheap deals. Although the Web is certainly one way to get good deals, it doesn't always produce the lowest fares. Shopping carefully, using a variety of information sources, continues to make the most sense.

Airlines themselves can supply information on routes and timetables, but except during fare wars, they do not supply the cheapest tickets. Airlines do, however, often have competitive low-season, student and senior citizens' fares. Find out the fare, the route, the duration of the journey and any restrictions on the ticket.

Once you have your ticket, write down its number, together with the flight number and other details, and keep the information separate from the ticket. If the ticket is lost or stolen this information will help you get a replacement.

Remember to purchase travel insurance as early as possible (see Travel Insurance under Visas & Documents in the Facts for the Visitor chapter).

Use the fares quoted in this book as a guide only. They are approximate and based on the rates advertised by travel agents and airlines at press time. Quoted airfares do not necessarily constitute a recommendation for the carrier.

Discount Tickets Airline deals can be learned about in a variety of ways. You can find out about advance purchase fares simply by calling the airline a week ahead of time, or in some cases even earlier. Other airline specials might require a certain number of days between arrival and return, or staying in your destination on Saturday night, or flying on specific days. Some special fares are released through selected travel agents.

The cheapest tickets are often non-refundable and require an extra fee for changing your flight. Many insurance policies will cover this loss if you have to change your flight for an emergency. Return (roundtrip) tickets usually work out cheaper – often

much cheaper – than two one-way fares. However, the recent emergence of smaller airlines specializing in one-way fares is making it easy to avoid buying roundtrip tickets. America West and Southwest, from the western US, and AirTran Airways, from the eastern US, sell one-way fares that are half the cost of a regular roundtrip fare. These airlines also connect major airports with smaller, regional airports.

If traveling from the UK, you will probably find that the cheapest flights are advertised by obscure bucket shops whose names haven't yet reached the telephone directory. Many such firms are honest and solvent, but there are a few rogues who will take your money and disappear, to reopen elsewhere a month or two later under a new name. If you feel suspicious about a firm, don't give them all the money at once – leave a deposit of 20% or so and pay the balance on receiving the ticket. If they insist on cash in advance, go elsewhere. And once you have the ticket, call the airline to confirm that you are booked on the flight.

You may decide to pay more than the rock-bottom fare by opting for the safety of a better known travel agent. Established firms like STA Travel, which has offices worldwide, Council Travel in the US and Travel CUTS in Canada are valid alternatives, and they offer good prices to most destinations.

Visit USA Passes Almost all domestic carriers offer Visit USA passes to non-US citizens. The passes are actually a book of coupons that you buy – each coupon equals a flight. The following airlines are the most representative, but it's a good idea to ask your travel agent about other airlines that offer the service. These must be booked outside the US, and you must be a non-US resident and have a return ticket to a destination outside the US.

Continental Airlines' Visit USA pass can be purchased in countries on both the Atlantic and Pacific sides. You must have your trip planned out in order to purchase the coupons. If you decide to change destinations once in the US, you will be fined

US$50. Prices are US$479 for three flight coupons (minimum purchase) and US$769 for eight (maximum purchase). Northwest offers a similar deal.

American Airlines uses a similar coupon structure but passengers must reserve flights at least one day in advance.

Delta has two different systems for travelers coming across the Atlantic: Visit USA grants discounts on fully planned itineraries; Discover America allows travelers to buy coupons good for standby travel anywhere in the continental US. The minimum purchase is three coupons, the maximum is 10. The price depends on where you start from, but averages about $125 per coupon. Children's coupons are less.

When flying standby, call the airline a day or two before the flight and make a 'standby reservation.' This way you get priority over all the others who just appear and hope to get on the flight the same day.

Round-the-World Tickets Special Round-the-World (RTW) tickets can be a great deal if you want to visit other regions as well as the US. Often they work out to be no more expensive or even cheaper than an ordinary roundtrip ticket.

The official airline RTW tickets are usually put together by a combination of two airlines, and permit you to fly anywhere you want on their route systems as long as you do not backtrack. Other restrictions are that you must usually book the first sector in advance and cancellation penalties apply. There may be restrictions on the number of stops permitted, and tickets are usually valid for between 90 days and a year. An alternative type of RTW ticket is put together by a travel agent using a combination of discounted tickets.

Most airlines restrict the number of sectors that can be flown within the US and Canada to three or four, and some airlines black out a few heavily traveled routes (like Honolulu to Tokyo). In most cases a 14-day advance purchase is required. After the ticket is purchased, dates can be changed without penalty and tickets can be rewritten to add or delete stops for $50 each.

Travelers with Special Needs

If you have special needs of any sort – a broken leg, dietary restrictions, dependence on a wheelchair, responsibility for a baby, fear of flying – you should let the airline know as soon as possible so that they can make arrangements accordingly. You should remind them when you reconfirm your booking (at least 72 hours before departure) and again when you check in at the airport. It may also be worth calling a number of airlines before you make your booking to find out how they can handle your particular needs.

Airports and airlines can be surprisingly helpful, but they do need advance warning. Most international airports can provide escorts, when needed, from check-in desk to plane, and there should be ramps, elevators, accessible toilets and reachable phones. Aircraft toilets, on the other hand, are likely to present a problem; travelers should discuss this with the airline at an early stage and, if necessary, with their doctor.

Guide dogs will likely have to travel in a specially pressurized baggage compartment with other animals, away from their owner, though smaller guide dogs may be admitted to the cabin. Guide dogs are not subject to quarantine as long as they have proof of being vaccinated against rabies.

Deaf travelers can ask for airport and in-flight announcements to be written down for them.

Children under two travel for 10% of the standard fare (or free, on some airlines), as long as they don't occupy a seat. (They don't get a baggage allowance either, however.) 'Skycots' should be provided by the airline if requested in advance; these will hold a child weighing up to 22lb. Children between two and 12 can usually occupy a seat for half to two-thirds of the full fare, and do get a baggage allowance. Strollers can often be taken on as hand luggage.

Baggage & Other Restrictions

On most domestic and international flights you are limited to two checked bags, or three if you don't have a carry-on. There could be a charge if you bring more or if the size or weight of the bags exceeds the airline's limits. It's best to check with the individual airline if you are worried about this.

If your luggage is delayed upon arrival (which is rare), some airlines will give a cash advance to purchase necessities. If sporting equipment is misplaced, the airline may pay for rentals. Should the luggage be lost, it is important to submit a claim. The airline doesn't have to pay the full amount of the claim, rather they can estimate the value of your lost items. It may take them anywhere from six weeks to three months to process the claim and pay you.

Smoking All types of smoking are prohibited on all US domestic flights. Many international flights are following suit, so be sure to call and find out. Incidentally, the restriction applies to the passenger cabin and the lavatories but not the cockpit. Many airports in the US also restrict smoking, but they compensate by having 'smoking rooms.'

Illegal Items Some items that are illegal to take on a plane, either checked or as carry-on, include aerosols of polishes, waxes, etc; tear gas and pepper spray; camp stoves with fuel; and divers' tanks that are full. Matches should also not be checked.

Arriving in the US
Even if you are continuing immediately to another city, the first airport that you land in is where you must carry out immigration and customs formalities. Even if your luggage is checked from, say, London to Denver, you will still have to take it through customs if you first land in New York.

If you have a non-US passport, with a visa, you must complete an Arrival/Departure Record (form I-94) before going to the immigration desk. See Visas & Documents in the Facts for the Visitor chapter for advice on filling out this form and for information on what to expect from immigration officials.

Departure Tax
Airport departure taxes are normally included in the cost of tickets bought in the US, while tickets purchased abroad may or may not have this included. There's also a $6 airport departure tax charged to all passengers bound for a foreign destination. However, this fee, as well as an additional $6.50 North American Free Trade Agreement (NAFTA) tax charged to passengers entering the US from a foreign country, are hidden taxes added to the purchase price of your airline ticket.

Within the US
During the months leading up to press time roundtrip airfares from New York to Memphis or New Orleans or Atlanta ranged from $195 to $250.

From Boston, the fares to the three regional hubs ranged from $180 to $240. From Washington, DC, fares were $150 to $200.

From Chicago, ticket fares ranged rather widely from $150 to $300.

From San Francisco, airfares hovered between $220 and $300, with New Orleans fares consistently dipping to the lower end of this range, while rates to Atlanta tended to occasionally jump over $300. Flights to Memphis sometimes topped $400.

From Southern California, sometimes the best fares are for flights out of Orange County or Ontario. Rates fluctuate from $240 to $320.

Canada
Travel CUTS has offices in all major cities. The Toronto *Globe & Mail* and *Vancouver Sun* carry travel agents' ads. Typically, to reach the Deep South, you'll have to fly into another US gateway and change planes. US–Canadian airline partnerships do offer 'through ticketing.' This is when you check in at one airport with one airline, and later change airlines at another airport but don't have to check in again because the two airlines' boarding systems are connected. This procedure allows the first airline to assign you boarding passes for all connections, even though you are actually flying on another airline on a subsequent leg.

Low-season roundtrip airfares from Vancouver to this region are approximately C$550. Fares from Toronto are C$275 to

C\$340, while from Montreal it'll cost from C\$380 to C\$430.

The UK

Check the ads in magazines like *Time Out*, plus the *Evening Standard* and *TNT*. Also check the free magazines widely available in London in places like outside the main railway stations.

Most British travel agents are registered with the ABTA (Association of British Travel Agents). Some agents are bonded under agreements such as the Air Transport Operators License (ATOL); if you buy a ticket from such an agent and it then goes out of business, ATOL guarantees a refund or an alternative. Unregistered or un-bonded bucket shops are riskier but some-times cheaper.

London is arguably the world's head-quarters for bucket shops, which are well advertised and can usually beat published airline fares. Three good, reliable agents for cheap tickets in the UK are Trailfinders (☎ 020-7938-3939, www.trailfinder.com), 194 Kensington High St, London, W8 7RG; Council Travel (☎ 020-7437-7767, www.counciltravel.com), 28a Poland St, London, W1; and STA Travel (☎ 020-7581-4132, www.statravel.com), 86 Old Brompton Rd, London SW7 3LQ.

Direct flights from London to New York connect to flights to Deep South cities for around UK£300. Nonstop flights to Atlanta are sometimes the cheapest way to the region, and tickets can be as low as UK£200.

Continental Europe

In Amsterdam, NBBS (☎ 020-624-09-89) is a popular travel agency with several branches. Fares range from f600 to f900. There's an additional tax on all flights.

In Paris, Council Travel is at 22, rue des Pyramides, 75001 Paris (☎ 01-44-55-55-44). Or try FUAJ (Fédération unie des auberges de jeunesse) at 10, rue Notre-Dame-de-Lorette, 75009 Paris (☎ 01-42-85-55-40), or at 9, rue Brantôme, 75003 Paris (☎ 01-48-04-70-40). For great student fares, contact usit CONNECT at 6, rue de Vaugirard, 75006

Paris (☎ 01-42-34-56-90). Paris flight fares cost 2700FF to 3150FF.

Council Travel has only two offices in Germany: in Düsseldorf at Fraf-Adolf Strasse 18 (☎ 211-36-30-30) and in Munich at Aldalbertsrasse 32 (☎ 089-39-50-22). STA Travel has several offices in Germany, in-cluding one in Frankfurt at Bergerstrasse 118 (☎ 069-43-01-91) and two in Berlin at Dorotheenstrasse 300 (☎ 030-20-16-50-63) and at Goethestrasse 73 (☎ 030-311-09-50). Frankfurt flight fares cost about DM875 to DM980.

Australia & New Zealand

In Australia and New Zealand, STA Travel and Flight Centres International are major dealers in cheap airfares; check the travel agents' ads in the yellow pages and call around. Qantas flies to Los Angeles from Sydney, Melbourne (via Sydney or Auck-land) and Cairns. United flies to San Fran-cisco from Sydney and Melbourne (via Sydney), and to Los Angeles. From these cities connections can be made to US do-mestic flights.

The cheapest tickets have a 21-day advance-purchase requirement, a minimum stay of seven days and a maximum stay of 60 days. Fares to/from Sydney cost about A\$1200, to/from Aukland about NZ\$1800.

Flying with Air New Zealand is usually slightly cheaper than with Qantas, and both airlines offer tickets with longer stays or stopovers, but you pay more.

Asia

Hong Kong is the discount plane ticket capital of the region, but its bucket shops can be unreliable. Ask the advice of other travelers before buying a ticket. STA Travel (www.statravel.com), which is dependable, has branches in Guangzhou, Tokyo, Osaka, Singapore, Bangkok and Kuala Lumpur. Many if not most flights to the continental US go via Honolulu, Hawaii.

United Airlines has three flights a day to Honolulu from Tokyo with connections to West Coast cities. Northwest and Japan Air Lines also have daily flights to the West Coast from Tokyo; Japan Air Lines also flies to Honolulu from Osaka, Nagoya, Fukuoka and Sapporo.

Central & South America

Most flights from Central and South America go via Miami, Houston or Los Angeles, though some fly via New York. Most countries' international flag carriers (like Aerolíneas Argentinas and LanChile), as well as US airlines like United and American, serve these destinations, with onward connections. Continental has flights from about 20 cities in Mexico and Central America, including San José, Guatemala City, Cancún and Mérida.

BUS
Greyhound

The only nationwide bus company with thorough coverage to Deep South cities and towns is Greyhound (☎ 800-231-2222). Buses are air-conditioned, and most are decently maintained. However, dealing with Greyhound on the telephone is often a major investment in time and patience. Visit its Web site at www.greyhound.com.

Fares are not necessarily cheap, and depend on the distance, day of the week and how far in advance the ticket is bought. The best deals ($50 to $110) are 'plan-ahead' specials that require ticket purchase two weeks prior to your departure date.

Some Greyhound specials are not so special, particularly if you are not traveling alone. For instance, the Ameripass is not such a bargain at $209 for unlimited stops within a seven-day period. For that price, you can rent a car (which allows you to double or triple your savings if two or more people travel together and split the costs). Admittedly, though, Ameripass offers a unique way to travel the US, particularly if you opt for the 60-day package.

Green Tortoise

An alternative, if traveling from the West Coast, is Green Tortoise (☎ 415-956-7500, 800-867-8647, www.greentortoise.com), 494 Broadway, San Francisco, CA 94133. A throwback to Ken Kesey's Merry Pranksters of the 1960s, the Tortoise makes an annual trip from San Francisco to New Orleans for Mardi Gras ($400, plus $130 for food), and makes infrequent cross-country runs (April, May, August and September) from Frisco to Boston via New Orleans. Fares for the 11-day journey to New Orleans start at $389 (plus $121 for meals).

TRAIN

Amtrak (☎ 800-872-7245, www.amtrak .com) is the only railroad in the US that provides cross-country passenger service, with lines running between Los Angeles and Florida, via New Orleans, and from Chicago to New Orleans, via Memphis.

From Chicago, Amtrak's *City of New Orleans* rides the same rails upon which blues music first traveled to Chicago. The route runs through Memphis, the Mississippi Delta and Jackson before arriving in New Orleans.

From New York City, Amtrak's *Crescent* runs through Washington, DC, and Atlanta with stops in Birmingham and Meridian, Mississippi, before arriving in New Orleans.

From Los Angeles, Amtrak's *Sunset Limited* takes 45 hours to New Orleans (via Houston). From New Orleans, the route continues east along the Gulf Coast through Mississippi and Alabama to Orlando, Florida.

Rail travel in the US is not cheap, but you can cut costs by purchasing special fares in advance. Fares vary according to type of seating; you can travel in coach seats or in various types of sleeping compartments. The child fare is half the adult fare (children must be traveling with an adult paying full fare). Anyone over age 62 qualifies for a 15% discount. Special fares are also available for disabled travelers.

The best overall value is the Explore America Pass, available to foreigners and US citizens alike, that permits three stops within 45 days of travel. This pass divides the country into three zones, with travel in one zone (western, central or eastern) costing $239/209 peak/off-peak season. Two adjacent zones cost $339/279; all zones cost $399/339. You must book your itinerary in advance, however, specifying traveling dates and destinations.

Non-US citizens also have the option of the USA Rail Pass, which must be purchased from a travel agent outside the US or from an Amtrak office within the country (you must show a foreign passport). While valid, the pass allows you to get on and off wherever you wish. Comfort seats or sleeping accommodations are extra. Prices vary from high to low season from about $200 to $435. Advance booking is recommended.

Note that most small train stations don't sell tickets. You must book them with a travel agent or Amtrak directly. Trains may only stop at certain small stations if you have bought a ticket in advance.

CAR & MOTORCYCLE

Foreign drivers of cars and riders of motorcycles will need their vehicle's registration papers, liability insurance and an international driver's permit, in addition to their domestic driver's license. Canadian and Mexican driver's licenses are accepted.

See Getting Around for more information on driving in the region.

Drive-Aways

Drive-aways are cars that belong to owners who can't drive them to a specific destination but are willing to allow someone else to drive it for them. For example, if somebody moves from New Orleans to Washington, DC, they may elect to fly and leave the car with a drive-away agency. The agency will find a driver and take care of all necessary insurance and permits. If you happen to want to drive from New Orleans to DC, and have a valid driver's license and a clean driving record, you can apply to drive the car. Normally, you have to pay a small refundable deposit. You pay for the gas (though sometimes a gas allowance is given). You are allowed a set number of days to deliver the car – usually based on driving eight hours a day. You are also allowed a limited number of miles, based on the best route and allowing for reasonable side trips, so you can't just zigzag all over the country. However, this is a cheap way to

get around if you like long-distance driving and meet eligibility requirements.

Drive-away companies often advertise in the classified sections of newspapers under 'Travel.' They are also listed in the yellow pages under 'Automobile Transporters & Drive-Away Companies.' You need to be flexible about dates and destinations when you call. If you are going to a popular area, you may be able to leave within two days or less, or you may have to wait over a week before a car becomes available. The routes most easily available are coast to coast, although intermediate trips are certainly possible.

ORGANIZED TOURS

In getting to and from the Deep South, package tours can be an efficient and relatively inexpensive way to go, especially for those interested in seeing the whole country. However, many tours do not focus on the Deep South and instead give travelers only one or two days in either New Orleans or Memphis and Nashville.

TrekAmerica (☎ 201-983-1144, 800-221-0596, fax 201-983-8551, www.trekamerica .com), PO Box 189, Rockaway, NJ 07866, offers roundtrip camping tours to different areas of the country. In England, they are at 4 Water Perry Court, Banbury, Oxon OX16 8QG (☎ 01295-256777, fax 01295-257399), and in Australia contact Adventure World (☎ 9956-7766, 800-221-931, fax 4956-7707), 75 Walker St, North Sydney, NSW 2060. These tours are designed for small, young international groups. Tour prices vary with season, with July to September being the highest, and don't include airfare. Some excursions and cultural events are included in the price, and participants help with cooking and camping chores.

AmeriCan Adventures (☎ 800-873-5872, fax 310-324-3562, amadlax@aol.com, www .americanadventures.com), PO Box 1155, Gardena, CA 90249, offers seven- to 21-day camping trips to different parts of the US. They also have offices in the UK (☎ 01892-512700, fax 01892-522066, amadsales@ twins.co.uk), 64 Mount Pleasant Ave, Tunbridge Wells, Kent TN1 1QY.

Road Runner USA/Canada (☎ 800-873-5872), a big Massachusetts-based company, leads small group tours in conjunction with Hostelling International to regions of the US and across the country. The Confederate Trail tour begins in New York and ends in Florida, but spends a bit of time in the Deep South; prices start at around $720.

Green Tortoise (☎ 415-956-7500, 800-867-8647, www.greentortoise.com), 494 Broadway, San Francisco, CA 94133, offers alternative cross-country bus transportation with stops at places like hot springs and national parks. Meals are cooked cooperatively and you sleep on bunks on the bus or you camp. New Orleans is the only Deep South stop on the cross-country routes – see Bus, earlier in this chapter.

For tours within, rather than to, the region, see the Getting Around chapter.

Getting Around

If you want to see the dispersed rural attractions that are so closely associated with a trip to the South, the best way is by car. The highways are good, and public transportation is not as frequent or as widespread as in some other countries. A more focused trip – say a music tour – could be accomplished by air, train or bus transit between major destinations.

AIR

Very few tourists fly between small regional airports in this region, as it's expensive and service is primarily geared toward business passengers. However, one can travel between the major hubs in New Orleans, Memphis and Atlanta (see the Getting There & Away chapter) in order to quickly get from one end of the region to the other.

Contact these airlines for regional flight information:

AirTran Airways	☎ 800-247-8726
American Eagle	☎ 800-433-7300
Continental Express	☎ 800-525-0280
TWExpress	☎ 800-221-2000
US Airways Express	☎ 800-428-4322

BUS

Bus transit, mainly by Greyhound (☎ 800-231-2222 for reservations), efficiently links the dispersed smaller cities of the Deep South. The quality of the neighborhoods in which bus stations are located, and the facilities offered there, may vary widely, but generally are well-maintained and staffed stations in OK areas. See destination chapters for specific information. The Web site is www.greyhound.com.

One well-served bus route is the Memphis-Jackson-New Orleans corridor. The Memphis-Jackson leg takes four to five hours and costs around $30 one-way; there are discounts for roundtrip tickets. The Jackson-New Orleans leg takes from four to five hours and costs the same.

Other popular corridors are between Birmingham and Atlanta (three hours, $22 one-way) and between Mobile and New Orleans (2½ to three hours, $23 one-way).

Buying Tickets

Tickets can be bought over the phone or Internet with a credit card (MasterCard, Visa or Discover) and then received by mail if purchased 10 days in advance, or else picked up at the terminal with proper identification. Greyhound terminals also accept American Express, traveler's checks and cash. Note that all buses are nonsmoking, and reservations are made with ticket purchases only.

Greyhound occasionally introduces a mileage-based discount-fare program that can be a bargain, especially for very long distances, but it's a good idea to check the regular fare anyway. As with regular fares, promotional fares are subject to change.

Ameripass Greyhound's Ameripass is potentially useful, depending on how much you plan to travel, but the relatively high prices may impel you to travel more than you normally would simply to get your money's worth. There are no restrictions on who can buy an Ameripass; it costs $209 for seven days of unlimited travel year-round, $319 for 15 days of travel and $429 for 30 days of travel. Children under 11 travel for half price. You can get on and off at any Greyhound stop or terminal, and the Ameripass is available at every Greyhound terminal.

International Ameripass This can be purchased only by foreign tourists and foreign students and lecturers (and their families) staying less than one year. These prices are $179 for a seven-day pass, $269 for a 15-day pass and $369 for a 30-day pass. The International Ameripass is usually bought abroad at a travel agency, or online. It can also be bought at the Greyhound International depot in New York City (☎ 212-971-0492) at 625 8th Ave at the Port Authority Subway level; it's open 9 am to 4:30 pm weekdays.

To contact Greyhound International to inquire about regular fares and routes, call ☎ 800-246-8572. Those buying an International Ameripass must complete an affidavit and present a passport or visa (or waiver) to the appropriate Greyhound officials.

There are also special passes for travel in Canada that can be bought only through the New York City office or abroad.

TRAIN

Amtrak (☎ 800-872-7255) can be an efficient way to travel through popular corridors, such as the Memphis-Jackson-New Orleans route. Routes covered in the Getting There & Away chapter serve destinations within the region.

As with bus transit, the quality of the neighborhoods in which train stations are located, and the facilities offered there, may vary widely. See destination chapters for more information.

CAR & MOTORCYCLE

Driving a car or motorcycle offers visitors the most flexibility at a reasonable cost. For visitors traveling alone, cars are convenient but isolating and possibly expensive; bus and train fares become more competitive with car-rental costs for single travelers. However, since distances are great and buses can be infrequent, car transportation is worth considering despite the expense.

Rental

Major international rental agencies like Hertz, Avis, Budget and A-1 have offices throughout the region, but there are also local agencies. To rent a car, you must have a valid driver's license, be at least 25 years of age and present a major credit card, like MasterCard or Visa, or else a large cash deposit.

Many rental agencies have bargain rates for weekend or week-long rentals, especially outside the peak summer season or in conjunction with airline tickets. Prices vary greatly in relation to region, season and type or size of car you'd like to rent.

Some agencies tack on a fee for each additional driver in the car. Be aware that some major rental agencies may no longer offer unlimited mileage in less competitive markets – be sure to calculate the cost of your estimated mileage before you rent.

Here is a list of some of the major car-rental agencies:

Alamo	☎ 800-327-9633
Avis	☎ 800-831-2847
Budget	☎ 800-527-0700
Dollar	☎ 800-800-4000
Enterprise	☎ 800-325-8007
Hertz	☎ 800-654-3131
Thrifty	☎ 800-367-2277

Purchase

If you're spending several months in the US, purchasing a car is worth considering; a car is more flexible than public transportation and buying one is likely to be cheaper than renting one; however, it can also be very complicated and require research.

It's possible to purchase a viable car in the US for about $2000, but you can't expect to go too far before you'll need some repair work that could cost several hundred dollars or more. It doesn't hurt to spend more to get a quality vehicle. It's also worth spending $75 or so to have a mechanic check it for defects before you buy it. (Some AAA offices have diagnostic

Driving Distances (in miles)

	Birmingham, AL	Jackson, MS	Memphis, TN	Montgomery, AL	Nashville, TN
Jackson, MS	237				
Memphis, TN	236	208			
Montgomery, AL	93	249	326		
Nashville, TN	189	414	214	279	
New Orleans, LA	339	189	394	310	526

centers where they'll do this on the spot for members and those of foreign affiliates.) You can check out the official valuation of a used car by looking it up in the *Blue Book*, a listing of cars by make, model and year issued and the average resale price. Local public libraries have copies of the *Blue Book*, as well as back issues of *Consumer Reports*, a magazine that annually tallies the repair records of common makes of cars.

If you want to purchase a car, the first thing to do is contact AAA (☎ 800-477-1222) for some general information. Then contact the Department of Motor Vehicles to find out about registration fees and insurance, which can be very confusing and

expensive. As an example, say you are a 30-year-old non-US citizen and you want to buy a 1984 Honda. If this is the first time you have registered a car in the US, you may have to fork over about $300 first and then about $100 to $200 more for general registration.

Inspect the title carefully before purchasing the car; the name of the owner on the title must match the identification of the person selling you the car. If you're a foreigner, you may find it very useful to obtain a notarized document authorizing your use of the car, since the motor vehicle bureau in the state where you buy the car may take several weeks or more to process the change in title.

Two-Way Talk Radio: Ask a Trucker

One way to get up-to-date travel information while driving in the South is to install a citizens band, or CB, radio into your car. Truck drivers all over the US use them to communicate with each other (over distances less than 2 miles) about road conditions and the location of police speed traps or to keep each other alert with mindless, yet amusing, chatter.

During the mid- to late-1970s, millions of non-truckers across the country purchased CB radios for their cars and joined in the Southern-flavored trucker subculture. This gave rise to popular trucker movies such as *Smokey and the Bandit* and top 40 hits such as CW McCall's 'Convoy' (the first record this author ever bought). CB radios fell out of vogue with the public long before they were replaced in a practical sense by cellular phones and in a cultural sense by the Internet, but truckers and other savvy wanderers still use them.

Before the rise of this fad, long-haul truck drivers had been using CB radios for several years in relative isolation. During this time, the truckers devised their own radio dialect based on jargon filtered down from military, aviation and law enforcement radio protocols. A basic understanding of on-air etiquette and terminology is essential for those wishing to join in the conversations.

The best known element of the truckers' CB language is their '10-codes.' The term '10-4' means 'I hear (and understand) you clearly.' Other 10-code terms include 10-1, transmitting poorly; 10-7, goodbye; 10-9, repeat what you said; and 10-20, what is your location?

A typical CB conversation might include an exchange like this (with translations):

'Break one-nine' ('Please, gentlemen or ladies, might I break in on this conversation on channel 19?')

'Go ahead, breaker.' ('Oh, by all means.')

'Hey JB, you got your ears on?' ('You, sir, driving the JB Hunt truck, are you listening to your CB radio?')

'10-4.' ('Yes.')

'Can I get a bear report?' ('Are there any police behind you?')

'That town up ahead of you is crawling with local yokels.' ('The town I just left has a number of municipal police looking for speeders.')

Insurance

While insurance is not obligatory in every state, all states have financial responsibility laws and insurance is highly desirable; otherwise, a serious accident could easily dry up your funds. In order for you to get insurance, some states require you to have had a US driver's license for at least 18 months. If you meet this qualification, you may still have to pay anywhere from $300 to $1200 a year for insurance, depending on where the car is registered.

Collision coverage has become very expensive, with high deductibles, and unless the car is somewhat valuable, you may want to consider passing on this portion of the policy. Regulations vary from state to state but are generally becoming stringent throughout the US.

Rental vehicles come with liability insurance so that if you hit another person or property, the damage will be paid for. What is not covered is damage to the rental vehicle itself. The so-called Collision Damage Waiver (CDW) or Loss Damage Waiver on a rental car may cost between $10 and $16 or more per day, significantly increasing the cost of the overall rental. Though it would be foolish to rent without insuring the vehicle in some way, you do not necessarily have to buy the rental company's inflated CDW.

If you own a car registered in the US, your own auto insurance may cover damage

---

Two-Way Talk Radio: Ask a Trucker

The term 'bear' comes from Smokey the Bear and refers to state police, who sometimes wear wide-brimmed hats similar to the one worn by the anti–forest fire mascot.

Aside from its unique terminology, CB radio speech is also typified by a Southern accent. Truckers from all over America will commonly use Southern speech inflections and syntax, described as a cross between an Arkansas and a West Texas dialect. When they are not speaking on their radios, the non-Southern truck drivers will revert to their native accents.

American truckers also picked up Southern tastes in music, food, manners, clothing, religion, and, most tellingly, reading habits. 'If you look at the paperbacks for sale in truck stops, they're almost all westerns,' explains pop-culture expert James Thomas. 'Truckers read a lot of cowboy novels, and most cowboy themes emerged from the Southern plantation myths. In the movies, cowboys and gunslingers were often ex-Confederates in exile.' This also led to the adoption of the Confederate flag as a symbol of the free-spirited trucker.

For an average motorist, tuning a CB radio to channel 19 for the first time is like being cured of lifelong deafness – provided there are truckers nearby. The big rigs that loomed large and soulless suddenly have personalities emanating from them. Truckers with similar destinations will keep each other awake for hundreds of miles at a stretch, chatting about politics, religion, sex, sports and working conditions. This provides hours of entertainment for those listeners who can penetrate the jargon and rich accents and endure the ranting of the occasional extremist. There are Christian alternative channels that vary from region to region for truckers who don't like all the trash-talk and even gay channels (channel 23 in some areas).

Good-quality CB radios may be purchased as cheaply as $40 from online radio stores. Stick to dependable brands such as Uniden, Cobra or Midland, and consider extra features like weather channels. Truck stops sell them as well, but for higher prices. Handheld CB radios are available, but they require magnet-mount, external antennae because car bodies will impede their already weak transmission power.

– Gary Bridgman (former editor of *Southern Motor Cargo*,
a trucking industry magazine covering the South)

to a rental car; check with your insurance agent to be sure. Some major credit card companies may provide coverage for any vehicle rented with their cards; check your credit card agreement to see what coverage is provided. Note that in case of damage, rental companies may require that you not only pay for repairs, but also that you pay normal rental fees for all the time that the rental car is off the road for repairs. Your policy should cover this loss as well.

Safety

To avert theft, do not leave items such as cell phones, purses, compact discs, cameras, baggage or even sunglasses visible inside the car. Tuck items under the seat, or even better, put them in the trunk and make sure your car does not have trunk entry through the back seat; if it does, make sure this is locked. Don't leave anything in the car overnight.

BICYCLE

Hurricanes and floods notwithstanding, conditions are generally amenable to bike touring in the Deep South. The topography throughout the region is largely flat, and motorists are generally courteous. Some cities require helmets, others don't, but as a safety precaution helmets should always be worn. Also as a safety measure, cyclists should carry at least two full water bottles and refill them at every opportunity. The availability of spare parts and repair shops vary from plentiful in New Orleans and south Louisiana, to adequate along the Natchez Trace, to unheard-of in more remote parts. It's important to be able to do basic mechanical work, like fixing a flat, yourself.

In south Louisiana, Pack & Paddle (☎ 337-232-5854, 800-458-4560), 601 E Pinhook Rd, Lafayette, can get you oriented and outfitted for an extended adventure. See Organized Tours, later in this chapter, for more bike-touring information.

The harsh summer temperatures should be generally avoided, and frequent rains may dampen bicyclists. Fall is the most con-sistently dry season, and many outfitters schedule group tours during that time.

For independent bicyclists, rentals are extremely limited in the region, so you may want to bring your bike with you. Bicycles can be transported by air. You can disassemble them and put them in a bike bag or box, but it's much easier simply to wheel your bike to the check-in desk, where it should be treated as a piece of baggage. You may have to remove the pedals and front tire so that it takes up less space in the aircraft's hold; check with the airline for details well in advance, preferably before you pay for your ticket. Be aware that some airlines welcome bicycles, while others treat them as an undesirable nuisance and do everything possible to discourage them.

HITCHHIKING

It is never entirely safe to hitchhike in any country in the world, and we don't recommend it. Travelers who decide to hitch should understand that they are taking a small but potentially life-threatening risk. You may not be able to identify the local rapist, murderer, thief, or even a driver who's just had too much to drink, before you get into the vehicle. People who nevertheless choose to hitch will be safer if they travel in pairs, let someone know where they are planning to go, keep their luggage light and with them at all times, and sit by a door.

RIVERBOAT

This once common mode of travel continues to be offered by a few paddle wheel riverboats and ocean-going cruise ships. Costs are high compared to other modes of travel. River travel is now typically offered as a package tour or excursion that includes top-end food and lodging.

Headquartered in New Orleans, the Delta Queen Steamboat Company (☎ 800-543-1949, www.deltaqueen.com) offers occasional paddle wheel riverboat travel to and from ports on the Mississippi River, including St Paul (14 nights), St Louis (seven nights) and Memphis (five nights). It also connects New Orleans with riverboat ports on Mississippi River tributaries such as Little Rock (10 nights), Pittsburgh (12 nights), Nashville (nine nights) and Chattanooga (10 nights); all times are for downriver travel – add at least one day for each five days to head upriver. In addition, voyages on the *Delta Queen* occasionally ply the Intracoastal Waterway between New Orleans and Galveston (six nights).

Riverboat fares typically start at $495 per person for the first three nights for a simple double occupancy berth and include all meals, entertainment, and port and departure taxes. Of the three paddle wheel riverboats operated by the company, two are modern diesel-engine vessels, while the handsomely restored *Delta Queen* – first launched in 1927 – follows the steam-powered tradition.

LOCAL TRANSPORTATION

Cities and metropolitan areas operate local bus transit, but coverage and service is extremely limited compared to cities of comparable size in other parts of the country. Historically, public transit has been largely the domain of poorer and generally underserved residents, and it's not uncommon for municipal transit systems in the Deep South to exist largely to transport domestic workers from poor neighborhoods to places of employment in rich neighborhoods – routes incompatible with the needs of travelers. Often harsh temperatures may also discourage travelers.

In historic towns or resort areas (such as the Gulf Coast), local 'trolleys' (buses resembling trolley cars) may provide localized transportation to major sites, along with commentary. In casino areas (principally along the Mississippi River and along the Gulf Coast), casinos sponsor shuttles to and from area motels/hotels.

Taxis are common in downtown New Orleans and Memphis and can easily be flagged for a fare there. Outside of this, you generally must phone for taxi service, and since distances are longer, taxis will be more expensive, especially if you're traveling alone. Average fare for taxis is $2 for the first mile, $1 for each additional mile, with an added 10% tip (possibly more in cities).

Shuttle

Coastline Transportation (☎ 601-432-2649, 800-647-3957) runs nine shuttles each way between the New Orleans airport and the Mississippi Gulf Coast. The shuttle will drop you wherever you need to go, be it a hotel or car-rental office. Reservations are suggested.

ORGANIZED TOURS

For adventure excursions or specialized tours – such as swamp exploring or African-American heritage sites – an organized tour might be your best bet.

For outdoor activities, operators provide all equipment and provisions, and guides know the territory best. Most of these are localized (see destination chapters), but a few will traverse the region.

Bicyclists might request a packet of bike-touring information from Natchez Trace Parkway headquarters (☎ 601-842-1572), Rural Route 1, NT-143, Tupelo, MS 38801. In Nashville, Tally Ho (☎ 615-354-1037), 6501 Hardin Rd No B-26, organizes overnight bike tours of the trace.

Backroads (☎ 510-527-1555, 800-462-2848, www.backroads.com), 801 Cedar St, Berkeley, CA 94710 has two bicycling tours of the region that have multiple starting dates in the spring and a couple in the fall. The Cajun & Plantation Country tour is five nights for $1700; the Natchez Trace tour is five days for $1800 (prices include meals, but not lodging).

For a unique way to tour the region, see Riverboat, earlier.

Louisiana

Facts about Louisiana

Among the 50 states that compose the USA, Louisiana stands apart. Its unique joie de vivre is reflected in its zesty cuisine, its uplifting music, and in the state's highly spirited festivals. Although the South has always been generally praised for its hospitality, travelers of the region will quickly note that Louisiana turns it up a notch in this department too. A traveler can have an unforgettable visit to this state and enjoy the kinds of varied experiences one usually only encounters by touring the far corners of an entire country.

For around-the-clock culture and entertainment, there's New Orleans, with its jazz clubs, Creole restaurants and historic neighborhoods. The 'Big Easy,' as it's often known, also hosts two of the nation's biggest parties, Mardi Gras and Jazz Fest, each of which distills all that is great about the local way of life into overwhelmingly potent cocktails.

The traveler can easily decompress from the New Orleans bacchanalia by going back in time to Plantation Country, where the mansions of the antebellum South still stand. Many guides in these mansions offer incomplete, or even inaccurate, renderings of the local history, focusing on the lifestyle of privileged plantation owners and neglecting to delve into the more somber side of the story. But others make an effort to tell it like it really was.

Or one can go back to nature. The Cajun wetlands are very accessible – visitors can even see alligators from the comfort and safety of their cars. Birders will be amazed by the tremendous variety of species, which is seen in no other part of the USA. You can even rent a shack or a houseboat and lie awake at night listening to the multitudinous chorus of frogs, crickets and cicadas that insistently reminds you, even as you sleep, that you are in the middle of a vast swampland. For a less intense experience, there's the Cajun prairie, where people still two-step to the sonorous strains of a tradi-

tional country waltz or to the more syncopated rhythms of zydeco music. And of course meeting the offbeat and friendly Cajun people is reason enough to come to Louisiana.

In the narrow waist of Central Louisiana, the landscape of swamps and prairies gives way to forested midlands, a quiet neutral ground between the historically French Catholic communities below and the Anglo-Protestants above. The state is dotted with the various districts of the Kisatchie National Forest, which are favorites for hiking and canoeing. Other area attractions include the Native American ruins at Marksville and the home of the South's best-known demagogue, Huey Long. (See the Government & Politics section, later in this chapter, for more on the King Fish).

Frosty Treats for Young & Old

Visitors to Louisiana may well wonder where all the snow in the state comes from. Along four-lane highways and tiny back roads, signs advertise enough 'snowballs' to supply a Civil War–scale fight. But what Louisianans call a snowball is elsewhere known as a snow cone or shaved ice, and whether you're melting along the bayou or on the white sands of Waikiki, a cone of these ice crystals topped with a garish 'fruit' syrup can quickly cool brows and tempers.

But fellas in fancy pickups might feel a little silly with a snowball in hand. So what to do when temperatures soar? Head for a drive-thru daiquiri stand. Almost as ubiquitous as snowball stands, daiquiri drive-thrus provide grown-ups with a mature method for cooling off. Of course, drinking and driving, as well as driving with an open container of alcohol, is illegal. Daiquiri dealers pop a lid on top, and voilà, packaged liquor. Straws provide easy access.

North Louisiana is most often seen off the shoulder of the I-20 thoroughfare, but even through-travelers will find local diversions – including Poverty Point, one of the most significant Native American sites in North America. In mid-September, the region's highlight is the Louisiana Folklife Festival, held each year in Monroe.

HISTORY

The European history of Louisiana and the Mississippi River valley starts with the expedition of Hernando de Soto in 1541. Nearly a century and a half later, in 1682, Robert Cavelier, Sieur de La Salle, came down the river and liberally claimed the entire Mississippi basin for France. The town of Natchitoches was settled in 1714, and New Orleans was founded four years after that.

Following the Seven Years War, in which France lost Canada to the British, French officials quietly negotiated to pass off the territory to Spain in 1762. Louisiana, which had yielded disappointing profits, had become a drain on the French treasury, and rather than risk losing still more territory to England, the French opted instead to sell. Spain initially had little interest in assuming control of the colony, and the colony's French inhabitants were even less enthusiastic about becoming Spanish subjects. In 1769, General Alexander O'Reilly, an Irishman employed by the Spanish army, was sent to New Orleans to quell a mounting rebellion. O'Reilly's troops nearly outnumbered the population of New Orleans at that time, and the rebellion was easily put to an end.

By 1779, Spain found itself in a costly war with Britain, and Napoleon was advancing French interests in the New World. In a secret treaty with Napoleon in 1800, the Spanish ceded the Louisiana Territory back to France. However, Napoleon also was at war with the British and needed funds.

It had become apparent to US president Thomas Jefferson that whoever controlled the port at New Orleans would also control the Mississippi River, US western expansion and midwestern trade. After the disclosure of Napoleon's secret acquisition, James Monroe and Robert Livingston, the US ambassador to France, were authorized to make an offer for New Orleans. The French countered with a deal that would cede all of Louisiana to the US. The two parties ultimately settled on a price of $15 million. This became the Louisiana Purchase, and in December 1803 Louisiana was officially handed over to the young nation. The Louisiana Purchase effectively doubled the domain of the USA.

When Louisiana became the 18th state in 1812, Americans were already descending upon the new state in great numbers. By the time of the Civil War, the transition was nearly complete: although Cajun and Creole communities had maintained their distinct cultures, Louisiana had lost much of its 'Frenchness.' Louisiana was for a brief time an independent republic before it joined the Confederate States of America in 1861. At the end of the war, after enduring a long Yankee occupation, Louisiana rejoined the Union.

In 1901, the state's first oil well was struck, ushering in Louisiana's modern economy. Since then, mineral resources have become an important factor in the state's economy, and lax environmental laws have attracted chemical manufacturers. Pollution has led to serious health epidemics in the state, leading some to refer to the stretch of the Mississippi River connecting Baton Rouge and New Orleans as 'Cancer Alley.'

GEOGRAPHY

The boot-shaped state of Louisiana is bounded on the north by Arkansas, on the east by Mississippi, on the west by Texas and on the south by the Gulf of Mexico. Slightly larger than New York state, Louisiana encompasses 48,114 sq miles, of which nearly 4000 sq miles are water. The state's elevation slopes downward from the 400-foot uplands of north Louisiana to two feet below sea level in New Orleans.

The Mississippi River and the Atchafalaya River dominate the geography (and history, and culture, and economy...)

LOUISIANA

LOUISIANA

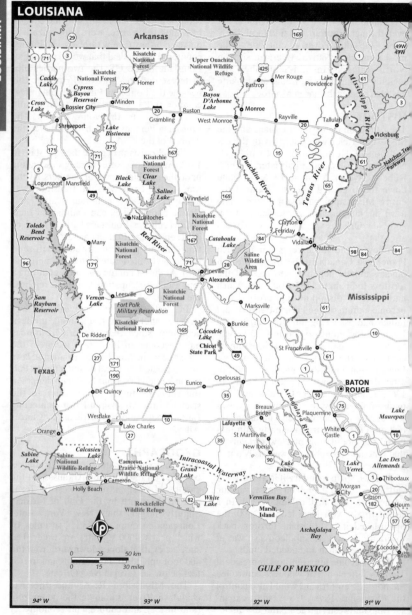

of southern Louisiana. Second only to these natural wetlands are the levees, basins, dams and channels built to control and constrain the river system. Both the historic capital of New Orleans and the modern capital of Baton Rouge are on the Mississippi's banks. Other significant waterways include the Sabine River at the Texas border, the Pearl River at the southeastern border with the state of Mississippi, and the Red River, which flows diagonally through the center of the state.

The forested midlands and uplands of central and northern Louisiana provide a sharp contrast with the lowland swamps and prairies – a contrast also manifested in the divergent cultures of northern and southern Louisiana.

One more geographic note: Louisiana is divided into 'parishes' rather than counties as in other states.

GOVERNMENT & POLITICS

Ever since 1682 when La Salle extravagantly laid claim to the bulk of the continent with a wave of his hand, Louisiana's promoters have been well-known for theatrical excess.

The most legendary modern actor in Louisiana political theater was the irrepressible Huey Long (1893–1935). The charismatic Long was first elected governor in 1928, and over the course of his growing regime he dominated state politics with a nearly despotic ruthlessness, which he threatened to carry onto the national political scene.

As a populist demagogue, Long frequently sidestepped the democratic process to achieve his goals, which included building a modern infrastructure that brought Louisiana out of post-Reconstruction antiquity. Graft, corruption, intimidation and bribery characterized his administration, and he'd positioned himself to make a run for the US presidency when he was struck down in the state capitol by an assassin.

The winking, good-ole-boy style of state politics was given a brief respite in 1943 with the gubernatorial election of country music singer Jimmie Davis, a Baptist from northern Louisiana. He is still (not surprisingly) the only governor also elected to the Country Music Hall of Fame, the Nashville Songwriters Hall of Fame and the Gospel Music Hall of Fame, and his hit song 'You Are My Sunshine' has since been adopted as the state anthem. Despite an optimistic start, Davis' reputation was in time corrupted by handlers who sought to maintain the governor's power through racist appeals.

Then, in 1959, the Longs returned to center stage when Huey's brother Earl was elected governor. The 'Earl of Louisiana' never quite lived up (or down) to Huey's nefarious reputation, but he steadfastly maintained the low standards expected of Louisiana's politicians with a series of embarrassing personal scandals. (For more on the Longs, see the 'Louisiana Politics – The Long Way' boxed text in the Central Louisiana chapter.)

More disturbing political weirdness took place in 1988, when voters from the New Orleans suburb of Metairie sent David Duke – an acknowledged former Grand Wizard of the Ku Klux Klan – to the state capital as their representative. Three years later, Duke's race for governor gave voters the unenviable choice of either him or former governor Edwin Edwards, who had already established himself as a corrupt politician. During the campaign Edwards quipped, 'The only way I won't get re-elected is if I get caught in bed with a live boy or a dead woman.' Despite these odds, Edwards only managed a narrow victory, claiming 34% of the vote (compared to Duke's 32%). After serving four terms as governor, in early 2000 Edwards was tried and convicted of extortion.

Current governor Mike Foster has neither lived up to Long's standards for drinking, nor Edwards' glib quips, but so far he has not disappointed political cynics. In 1996, the Republican Foster said he, like 'any good Christian person,' would support David Duke for US Senate if the race was to come down to a runoff against a Democrat.

As for the governmental nuts and bolts, Louisiana's state legislature is composed of a Senate of 39 members and a House of Representatives of 105 members; members of both houses are elected for four-year terms.

ECONOMY

Louisiana's economy is dominated by manufacturing, which includes its petroleum and chemical industries along with smaller outfits such as the Tabasco empire. Agricultural products account for nearly a third of the gross state product, with soybean, rice and sugar cane the biggest crops. The ports at New Orleans and Baton Rouge are among the five busiest in the US.

POPULATION & PEOPLE

The population of Louisiana is 4.3 million. More than half of the people define themselves as Caucasian, more than a third identify themselves as black. Slightly less than a quarter are Hispanic, and only a small fraction are Asian. The Caucasian population is divided evenly between urban and rural areas; the remaining ethnic groups are found predominantly in urban areas.

While the southern portion of the state was settled by French Catholics, northern Louisiana was settled by Appalachian immigrants of largely Scottish and Irish descent who adopted the Southern Baptist faith.

Other significant ethnic groups are the Cajuns and Creoles, terms that can be confusing to outsiders. Cajun describes residents of Acadian heritage, and it applies largely to white people. Creole, while first used to describe Louisiana-born offspring of the French colonists, is now largely used to describe a predominantly black population whose heritage may include European, Native American and Caribbean roots.

INFORMATION
Tourist Offices

The Louisiana Department of Culture, Recreation & Tourism (☎ 504-342-8119, 800-633-6970, www.louisianatravel.com), PO Box 94291, Baton Rouge, LA 70804-9291, oversees historic preservation and the tourist bureaus, state museums and state parks (for more information on parks, see below).

Louisiana maintains 10 state welcome centers at state borders on major freeways, in Baton Rouge and in New Orleans. All centers are open daily (excluding major holidays), and are good resources for maps, events calendars, sightseeing information and coupons for discounted lodging. They also have public restrooms and can serve as convenient pit stops.

Taxes
In Louisiana, sales tax is 4% statewide plus additional local levies. New Orleans sales tax totals 9%, and the city also levies an additional 5% on food and beverage sales, a 5% tax on amusements and a total accommodations tax of 11% plus $1 per person. At New Orleans International Airport, taxes total 12% on all retail purchases – try to avoid buying anything there.

Driving & Liquor Laws
The minimum driving age is 16. Motorcycle helmets are required throughout the state.

The minimum drinking age is 21 years (not strictly enforced in New Orleans). Unlike in some other locales, liquor sales are permitted around the clock in New Orleans.

State Parks & Protected Areas
The parks department can be reached at ☎ 504-342-8111 or ☎ 888-677-1400.

The Louisiana Department of Wildlife & Fisheries in Baton Rouge (☎ 504-765-2800) issues fishing licenses and additional information. To use any Louisiana Wildlife Management Area, visitors between 16 and 59 years old must possess one of the following Louisiana licenses: a valid wildlife

---

Tax-Free Shopping

International visitors to Louisiana can receive refunds of up to 10% on sales tax on items purchased from more than a thousand Louisiana Tax Free Shopping (LTFS) stores. Look for the 'Tax Free' sign in store windows. Foreign visitors must show participating LTFS merchants a valid passport (Canadians may substitute a birth certificate or driver's license) to receive a tax-refund voucher. At the LTFS refund center at New Orleans International Airport (in the main lobby next to entry door 3; ☎ 504-467-0723), visitors must present the following: voucher(s) with associated sales receipts, passport, and roundtrip international ticket for less than a 90-day stay. Refunds for less than $500 are made in cash; otherwise, a check will be mailed to the visitor's home address. Visitors can also mail in receipts (Louisiana Tax-Free Shopping, Airport Refund Center, PO Box 20125, New Orleans, 70141).

To get a complete listing of LTFS merchants, call ☎ 504-568-5323 or ask for one via email (ltfs@bellsouth.net). For more information about the program, check this Web site: www.louisianataxfree.com.

---

stamp, a fishing license or a hunting license. You can purchase them at sheriff's departments, the Department of Wildlife and Fisheries, fishing outfitters and some stores around the state.

A multitude of other national, state and local authorities oversees other natural areas in Louisiana; see specific destination chapters for detailed information.

New Orleans

New Orleans seduces its visitors. It casts its spell Uptown in the spotted shade of a live oak tree and again downtown within the worn stucco confines of a Creole courtyard, slipping voodoo potions into sweet-tasting cocktails, casually dropping anecdotes about its past. It subdues defenseless hearts with a sultry heat that makes the French Quarter's lacy iron galleries and peeling rusted balustrades sag. A moist gust of wind makes fan-like palmettos slap into each other, dime-sized raindrops pelt the leaves of banana trees, and Caribbean colors intensify.

New Orleans – lazily pronounced 'new OR-luns' by some, more liltingly articulated as 'new OR-lee-uns' by others – is a psychologically complex city, unlike any other in North America, with an impractical, romantic heart and a defiant, artistic nature. Its very setting, on a waterlogged patch of earth beside a particularly sensuous and ominous curve of the Mississippi River, defies logic. Its tragic flaws only endear the city to those who love it.

Despite, or perhaps because of, its impracticalities, this enigmatic municipality has become a major tourist draw, and its decadence has become something of a commodity. Just as sailors once salaciously anticipated shore leaves spent lolling about in Storyville parlors, today's enthused travelers and conventioneers come to hedonistic New Orleans with thoughts of stepping out of the routines of their lives. They flood Creole restaurants, Bourbon St bars and French Quarter jazz clubs, they lose themselves for a little while, go a little crazy…and in the morning civic workers come out to hose away the previous night's sins.

Although New Orleans remains somewhat secretive and mysterious, it is sincere in welcoming visitors. The city graciously hosts two of the nation's most spectacular cultural events each year: Mardi Gras and Jazz Fest. And, of course, few cities can treat its guests to a fine, unforgettable and fattening meal the way New Orleans can.

HISTORY

A few days in New Orleans is enough time to see for yourself that this city has been profoundly influenced by the waves of cultural groups who have either passed through or settled permanently. Being a major capital of the American South has determined many events in the city's history

and continues to contribute to its character today.

French New Orleans

New Orleans was founded in 1718 by the Canadian-born explorer Jean-Baptiste Le Moyne, Sieur de Bienville, who chose the site for its narrow portage between the Mississippi River and Lake Pontchartrain, which offered a more direct access to the Gulf of Mexico. Bienville and his party of settlers struggled to make a city out of the soggy landscape, suffering floods and yellow fever epidemics. But within four years the outpost had a street plan (which would outline what is today the French Quarter), and an aggressive promoter in the shrewd Scotsman named John Law. Law, who possessed a vivid imagination and had larceny in his soul, busily portrayed the swampy burg as heaven on earth to unsuspecting French, Germans and Swiss, and soon the first wave of immigrants began arriving in New Orleans by the shipload. To augment these numbers, convicts and prostitutes were freed from French jails if they agreed to relocate in Louisiana.

The young colony's population soon included African slaves, hundreds of whom the French landed during New Orleans' first decade. Whites born in New Orleans, mostly of French descent, came to be known as Creoles, and their French-derived culture quickly evolved into one that was unique to New Orleans. German immigrants gallicized their names, began to speak French and blended in. Black and white unions, although legally forbidden, were not uncommon, and several new castes emerged based on the amount of African blood people had – quadroons were one-fourth black, octoroons one-eighth black, and so on. These people, too, spoke French and in time also became known as Creoles.

Colonial mercantilism was an economic failure, and the harsh realities of life in New Orleans inhibited willful civilian immigration – especially by women. As a result, the colonists created an exchange economy based on smuggling and local trade, and, to address the paucity of womenfolk, the Ursuline nuns brought young, marriageable women over from France. But, as the nuns surely realized, rough and tumble New Orleans was hardly an ideal place for innocent mademoiselles. One of the nuns, upon disembarking in New Orleans, famously commented that 'the devil here has a very large empire.'

Antebellum New Orleans

When the Louisiana Purchase suddenly put New Orleans in the United States, little cheer arose from the Creole community over the transfer. The Creoles, who had cultivated a culture that was morally and industrially relaxed, dreaded the arrival of Americans, with their unappealing puritanical work ethic. In 1808 the territorial legislature sought to preserve Creole culture by adopting elements of Spanish and French laws – especially the Napoleonic Code as it relates to equity, succession and family. Elements of the code persist in Louisiana to the present.

The War of 1812, between the US and British, barely registered with New Orleans residents until a British force assembled in Jamaica. General Andrew Jackson arrived in Louisiana in November 1814, but New Orleanians were suspicious of his intentions when he imposed martial law. Much of the locals' distrust of Jackson changed when word spread that the British intended to free slaves willing to fight against the Americans. Meanwhile, Jackson convinced the pirate Jean Lafitte to side with the American forces in exchange for amnesty, thereby gaining the help of the pirate's band of sharpshooters and his considerable arsenal of weapons. Jackson also shocked many whites when he enlisted free black battalions and Choctaws. The Battle of New Orleans at Chalmette, just 4 miles from the French Quarter, was a one-sided victory for the Americans – around 300 British losses versus only 13 US losses. Unfortunately, these soldiers died for naught, as the war had ended earlier – news was slow reaching New Orleans.

The city's populace began spilling beyond the borders of the French Quarter as Americans moved into New Orleans and formed their own district on the other side of Canal St. American developers further transformed upriver plantations into posh Uptown neighborhoods. By 1835, the New Orleans & Carrollton Railroad had laid streetcar tracks along St Charles Ave to serve the growing community of Lafayette (not to be confused with the present Louisiana city) and beyond.

In spite of the Napoleonic Code's mandate for Jewish expulsion, and an anti-Semitic Southern Christian culture, trade practicalities led to tolerance of Jewish merchants. In particular, Alsatian immigrants augmented the small Jewish community in New Orleans, and they established a synagogue. Judah Touro, whose estate was valued at $4 million upon his death in 1854, funded orphanages and hospitals that would serve Jews and Christians alike.

Americans finally took control of the municipal government in 1852, illustrating that the Creole influence in New Orleans had eroded. American commerce had turned New Orleans into one of the world's wealthiest cities, but a political maelstrom had already appeared on the national horizon and would soon bring the city's prosperity to a crashing halt.

Civil War

At the dawn of the Civil War, New Orleans was by far the most prosperous city south of the Mason-Dixon line, and the city wavered on the issue of secession. Merchants and bankers argued that New Orleans was economically tied to the North, but the tide shifted as the election of 1860 neared. Firebrand politicians warned that 'tame submission' to the North would lead to 'widespread ruin.' Following Abraham Lincoln's victory, Louisiana seceded from the Union, joined the Confederacy, and took New Orleans with it.

The Union quickly gained control of the lower Mississippi River and New Orleans' port, taking the city in April 1862. Captain David G Farragut led a US Naval fleet up the Mississippi, bombarding Fort Jackson and Fort St Philip, which flanked the river

south of New Orleans. The battle that took place there was brief but dramatic – likened to the 'breaking of the universe with the moon' by one particularly rhapsodic eyewitness – and Farragut's ships reached New Orleans a day later. It was the first Confederate city to be captured, and it would be occupied until the war's end, in 1865.

New Orleanians, otherwise famous for their hospitality, didn't take too kindly to the occupation forces, who were led by the notorious Major General Benjamin Butler. 'Beast' Butler, as the locals called him, was not exactly intent on winning the hearts of the city's populace, and his presence unified the city in its hatred of him. Soon after the US flag went up in front of the US Mint, a local named William Mumford cut it down. Butler's swift response was to have the man hanged from the very same flagpole. The women of New Orleans repeatedly insulted Butler's troops by spitting on them and yelling insults.

Under Butler's rule, property was confiscated from citizens who refused to pledge loyalty to the Union. On a more positive note, Butler was also credited with giving the French Quarter a much-needed cleanup, building orphanages, improving the school system and putting thousands of unemployed – both whites and blacks – to work. But he didn't stay in New Orleans long enough to implement Lincoln's plans for 'reconstructing' the city. Those plans, preliminaries to the Reconstruction of the South that followed the war, went into effect in December 1863, a year after Butler returned to the North.

Reconstruction & Racial Fallout

During the Reconstruction period that followed the war, attempts to extend suffrage to all black men resulted in a bloody riot that led to the deaths of 34 blacks and two whites. It was a grim beginning for the Reconstruction period, foreshadowing an endless series of race-related struggles that would leave the people of New Orleans hardened, embittered and battered.

Causing no small amount of resentment among white Southerners, Louisiana's state

Mardi Gras Indians, New Orleans

Orpheus krewe, Mardi Gras

Jazz funeral procession for voodoo priest 'Chicken Man,' New Orleans

When clowns dream, Mardi Gras

A romantic spot for you & your honey, New Orleans

RICHARD CUMMINS

French Quarter window finery, New Orleans

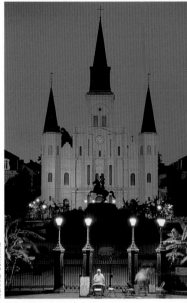

RICHARD CUMMINS

St Louis Cathedral, Jackson Square

DAVID ZINGARELLI

Vampire Lestat's eye view of the Quarter

RICHARD CUMMINS

Sans bra at the Casbah, French Quarter

constitution was redrawn to include full suffrage to black men but not to former Confederate soldiers and rebel sympathizers. Blacks, attempting to gain further rights, began challenging discrimination laws forbidding them from riding 'white' streetcars, and racial skirmishes regularly flared up around town.

White supremacist groups initiated a reign of terror that targeted blacks and claimed several hundred lives during a particularly bloody few weeks. In the 1870s, the White League was formed, with the twin purposes of ousting what it considered an 'Africanized' government (elected in part by newly enfranchised black voters) and of ridding the state of 'carpetbaggers' and 'scalawags,' popular terms for the Northerners and Reconstructionists then in government. They actually succeeded in ousting the state's scalawag governor for five days in 1874, prompting federal troops to enter the city to restore order. Although Reconstruction ended in 1877, in New Orleans the dark cloud that had hung over the city since the beginning of the Civil War wouldn't lift for many decades.

As the 20th century neared, New Orleans got back to business, staging the World's Industrial and Cotton Centennial Exposition of 1884–85 to herald the city's return to life. Although the expo was, by most accounts, a disappointing spectacle with lackluster exhibits (the awkward name was emblematic

Storyville

Hard as New Orleans has always tried to keep its mind on business, it has consistently shown a tendency to succumb to every vice known to humankind. As the song goes:

> There is a house in New Orleans
> They call the Rising Sun
> It's been the ruin of many a poor gal
> And me, I know I'm one …

As the 20th century began, many such houses – live-work spaces for thousands of plump gals from every corner of the globe – were open for business all over town, catering to the natural and unnatural needs of men. At the end of the 19th century, prostitution was such a flourishing business that it began to invade even the city's finer neighborhoods, and politicians, having little hope of ending the trade, sought at least a way to contain and control it. A district where prostitution would remain legal was created to the lakeside of the French Quarter, and it quickly gained renown as a modern Gomorrah – a domain of whores, pimps, madams, drug peddlers and a tragic number of wanton street urchins; a district whose very existence rested on its ability to foster and nurture any form of depravity.

Some of the district's houses were sordid cribs enlivened by barrelhouse piano players like Jellyroll Morton, a jazz pioneer who was also a journeyman card cheat and pimp, while other houses of prostitution, capped with Moorish turrets, were genuinely posh. This district was proposed in 1897 by a city official named Sidney Story, and although Story reputedly lived a squeaky-clean life, he will always be remembered as the man for whom Storyville was unofficially named. Its residents simply called it 'the District.'

WWI spelled the end for Storyville. In 1917, Secretary of the Navy Joseph Daniels ordered the District officially closed, expressing the Navy's fears that legalized prostitution would cause the spread of social disease among servicemen based at a New Orleans training camp. However, prostitution continued illegally along the same streets until the entire district was razed in the 1940s. A housing project now stands on the site and only a few of the original buildings survive.

of muddled planning), it did serve notice to the rest of the world that the city was making a comeback. Manufacturing, shipping, trade and banking all resumed, and soon the city was again bustling with all the vigor and passions of a major port.

20th-Century Adjustments

New Orleans snapped out of the Great Depression as WWII industries created jobs, and continued prosperity in the 1950s led to suburban growth around the city. Many middle-class whites fled the city to live in the suburbs as the number of poor blacks increased. Eventually, the population of New Orleans would be 70% black.

In the mid-1970s, the Louisiana Superdome opened. The home of the city's National Football League (NFL) team, the Saints, it also has hosted Super Bowls and presidential conventions and sparked a major revenue-earner for New Orleans: trade shows. All around the Superdome, new skyscrapers rose in the Central Business District, as oil and chemical companies were drawn to New Orleans by low taxes and lenient environmental restrictions, as well as oil, of course. By the end of the 1980s, however, the local oil boom went bust, throwing New Orleans into yet another economic tailspin.

Meanwhile, the French Quarter, which had become a dowdy working-class enclave during the first part of the 20th century, was treated to long overdue restoration efforts, and it emerged primed for mass tourism, which was already one of the city's most lucrative industries.

In 1978, New Orleans elected its first black mayor, Ernest 'Dutch' Morial, marking a major shift in the city's political history. Morial, a Democrat, appointed blacks and women to many city posts during his two terms. During that time, the city once again hosted a world expo, and once again the event was an utter economic failure. However, the 1984 exposition did help to revive a long-neglected warehouse district, which soon became a hub for art galleries and studios. Morial's tenure ended in 1986, and in 1994 his son, Marc Morial,

was elected mayor and subsequently re-elected in 1998.

Like most US cities, New Orleans has benefited from trends toward urban revival at the end of the millennium, and crime has dropped in recent years. Although New Orleans remains largely a poor city with a small tax base to support public schools and social programs, the city retains its unique and indomitable spirit.

ORIENTATION

New Orleans is wedged between the meandering Mississippi River to the south and Lake Pontchartrain to the north. The Mississippi River is the 'main street' and historical focal point for New Orleans. Directions, up- or downriver, are relative to the water flow, which bends to all points of the compass: 'The Convention Center is upriver from (or above) the French Quarter,' even though a compass would show that the Convention Center is south-southwest.

In addition, the river and Lake Pontchartrain serve as landmarks in 'river side' or 'lake side' directions: 'You'll find Louis Armstrong Park on the lake side of the French Quarter – head toward the lake and you'll find it,' and 'Preservation Hall is on St Peter St toward the river from Bourbon St.'

The broad Canal St divides Uptown from Downtown. However, as added confusion, a large part of the city, from the Garden District to the Riverbend, is commonly referred to as Uptown.

People of different wealth, race and ethnicity create a checkerboard of neighborhoods in the compact city. It's often only a few steps from a ghetto to endowed estates. Note that the following overview is best accompanied by a look at a map.

The French Quarter (often shortened to 'the Quarter' and also known as the Vieux Carré) originally consisted of 44 blocks (it's now 80 blocks) centered on Place d'Armes (now Jackson Square) next to the river levee. The touristy 'upper Quarter' is bounded by Canal St, where one finds most large convention-style hotels; Canal St separates the lower Quarter and the CBD (Central Business District). The lower

Quarter, at the French Quarter's downriver boundary, meets the Faubourg Marigny at Esplanade Ave, and both of these areas harbor the gay district. Below the Faubourg Marigny is the transitional Bywater, fast becoming a burgeoning artists' neighborhood.

Beyond the Quarter's lakeside boundary at N Rampart St (named for the historic fortification that once surrounded the city) begins the African-American Tremé District. Away from the Quarter, the Fair Grounds (site of the Jazz Fest) and the lakefront City Park are reached by taking Esplanade Ave.

On the river-side periphery of the CBD is the Warehouse District, a zone from Poydras Ave to Howard Ave, bounded by the river and St Charles Ave. The city encourages upscale galleries and developers to reuse the old warehouse spaces. On the river-side boundary of the Warehouse District, you'll find the Convention Center and Riverwalk Mall. Downriver past the Canal St Ferry are Woldenberg Park, the Aquarium of the Americas and the Moonwalk (a boardwalk area on the river). This general area is known as the Riverfront, and the Riverfront Streetcar Line traverses it before skirting the Quarter.

St Charles Ave, the main Uptown corridor and streetcar route from Canal St, travels upriver past the Lower Garden District and the Garden District to S Carrollton Ave in the Riverbend area.

It's worth noting that 'avenues' are generally four-lane major thoroughfares and 'streets' are one or two lanes. Street numbering between the river and lake typically starts at the river. On routes that parallel the river, street numbers begin at Canal St. Due to the vagaries of the river, Uptown streets are labeled 'south' and downtown streets are 'north.'

Maps

Good-quality maps of New Orleans are available from most bookstores, but free maps from a variety of sources are generally adequate for most visitors. The detailed *New Orleans Street Map & Visitor Guide* depicts Regional Transit Authority (RTA) bus routes, includes a street index and is available from tourist offices. Rental-car agencies also provide maps. Rand McNally's *New Orleans City Map* is more detailed than AAA's *New Orleans & Vicinity Map*, but the latter is free for AAA members.

INFORMATION
Tourist Offices

On Jackson Square in the heart of the French Quarter, the New Orleans Welcome Center (Map 2; ☎ 504-566-5031), 529 St Ann St, in the lower Pontalba Building, offers maps, up-to-date pocket guidebooks, listings of upcoming events, a variety of brochures and discount RTA passes. The friendly staff can help you find accommodations in a pinch, answer questions and offer advice about New Orleans. You can call ahead and have information sent to your home. However, relatively little information is available for the non-English speaker. The office is open 9 am to 5 pm daily. The Welcome Center has many information kiosks in the French Quarter, particularly the upper end of the Quarter towards the river, and these offer most of the same brochures.

Jean Lafitte National Historical Park and Preserve, which has six units in various parts of southern Louisiana, maintains a visitor center (Map 2; ☎ 504-589-2636), 419 Decatur St, in the French Quarter. The National Park Service's (NPS's) mission here is to interpret the history of the Mississippi Delta and New Orleans (the French Quarter and the Garden District are National Historic Districts), and it offers a variety of ranger-led programs, including talks and walks. The NPS also recently launched the New Orleans Jazz National Historic Park (☎ 504-589-4806), 365 Canal St, Suite 2400. It's not a physical 'park,' but the NPS is organizing public concerts and cultural events such as second line parades. Ultimately, the park will set up headquarters in Perseverance Hall No 4, in Louis Armstrong Park.

The New Orleans Metropolitan Convention & Visitors Bureau (☎ 504-566-5011, www.neworleanscvb.com) as well as the Greater New Orleans Multicultural Tourism Network (☎ 504-523-5652) are only open on weekdays and share an address near the Superdome at 1520 Sugar Bowl Drive, New Orleans, LA 70112. The Multicultural Tourism Network publishes a free visitor guide, *The Soul of New Orleans*, geared toward African-Americans; its Web site is at www.soulofneworleans.com. French visitors should contact Martine Espardet of France Louisiane Franco Américanie (☎ 01-45-88-02-10, 17 avenue Reille, 75014 Paris).

Money

Most major currencies and leading brands of traveler's checks are easily exchanged in New Orleans. You will also find various independent exchange bureaus. When you first arrive at the airport terminal, you can change money at Travelex (☎ 504-465-9647), which charges a sliding scale fee and is open daily from 6 am to 7 pm; or at Whitney National Bank (☎ 504-838-6492), which will charge a $5 service fee and closes by 4:30 pm most days. Since the exchanges are only feet apart, get quotes from both.

Better exchange rates are generally available at banks in the CBD, typically open 10 am to 5 pm Monday to Thursday, 10 am to 6 pm Friday and 10 am to 1 pm Saturday. American Express (Map 3; ☎ 504-586-8201), 201 St Charles Ave, buys and sells foreign currency, and card holders can obtain cash advances.

Whitney National Bank's main office (☎ 504-586-7272) is at 228 St Charles Ave, and there's a Vieux Carré branch (☎ 504-586-7502) at 430 Chartres St.

ATMs are easy to come by in the French Quarter and the CBD. Bank One contributed to producing the free *New Orleans Street Map*, which indicates the locations of the bank's branches and ATMs.

New Orleans' 9% sales tax is tacked onto virtually everything, including meals, groceries and car rentals. For accommodations, room and occupancy taxes, add 11% to your bill plus $1 per person.

Post

The main post office (Map 3; ☎ 800-275-8777), 701 Loyola Ave, is near Union Passenger Terminal. General delivery mail (poste restante) can be received here; it should be marked c/o General Delivery, New Orleans, LA 70112. There are smaller branches throughout the city, including the Airport Mail Center, in the passenger terminal; the World Trade Center, 2 Canal St (Map 3); the Vieux Carré, 1022 Iberville St (Map 2); and in the CBD at Lafayette Square, 610 S Maestri Place (Map 3). Post offices are generally open weekdays 8:30 am to 4:30 pm and Saturday 8:30 am to noon.

In the French Quarter, there are independent postal shops, including Royal Mail Service (Map 2; ☎ 504-522-8523), 828 Royal St, and the French Quarter Postal Emporium (☎ 504-525-6651), 1000 Bourbon St. These shops will send letters and packages at the same rates as the post office.

Telephone & Fax

The New Orleans area code is ☎ 504. Bell-South pay phones, charging 35¢ for a local call, are not difficult to find. Some independently owned phone booths charge more. Be aware that some guesthouses do not provide phones in the rooms – if it's important, be sure to ask when reserving your room.

In the French Quarter fax services are available at French Quarter Postal Emporium (Map 2; ☎ 504-525-6651, fax 525-6652), 1000 Bourbon St. In the CBD, Kinko's (Map 3; ☎ 504-581-2541, fax 525-6272), 762 St Charles Ave, is open 24 hours a day.

Email & Internet Access

If you are carrying your own laptop to log on or send email, ask if your room is equipped with a modem line when making hotel reservations. Even if it doesn't, some Internet service providers will actually allow you to dial up on a hotel phone line.

Free access for Internet browsing and sending and receiving email is available in the New Orleans Public Library (Map 3; ☎ 504-529-7323), 219 Loyola Ave, and at NewOrleans.net (Map 3; ☎ 504-523-0990).

900 Camp St, a cybercafe at the Contemporary Arts Center. In the French Quarter, Royal Access (Map 2; ☎ 504-525-0401), 621 Royal St, and Bastille Computer Café (☎ 504-581-1150), 605 Toulouse St, both charge for services.

Internet Resources

Useful Web sites, many of which serve as gateways to an infinite number of interesting links, include the following:

General

New Orleans Online
http://neworleansonline.com

Times-Picayune
www.neworleans.net

Entertainment

Offbeat Magazine
www.offbeat.com

WWOZ Radio (great links)
www.wwoz.org

Music

Jazz Festival
www.insideneworleans.com/entertainment/
nojazzfest

Louisiana Music Factory
www.louisianamusicfactory.com

Dr John (official site)
www.drjohn.com

Neville Brothers (official site)
www.nevilles.com

Mardi Gras

Mardi Gras Links
www.mardigrasneworleans.com

Mardi Gras Indians
www.mardigrasindians.com

Travel Agencies

The Sunday Travel section of the *Times-Picayune* is a good place to search for discount travel deals. Student and budget travelers can pick up tickets from Council Travel (Map 5; ☎ 504-866-1767), 6363 St Charles Ave, at the Loyola University Student Center.

AAA Travel Agency (☎ 504-838-7500, 800-452-7198), 3445 N Causeway Blvd, Metairie, offers complete travel planning for nonmembers and free maps and assistance for members. American Express (Map 3, ☎ 504-586-8201), 201 St Charles Ave, operates a full-service travel office and currency exchange.

Bookstores

In the French Quarter, Faulkner House Books (Map 2; ☎ 504-524-2940), 624 Pirate's Alley, is both a bookstore and a literary attraction. It offers a good selection of new titles and first editions, with a particularly strong collection of books by local and Southern authors. Of course, William Faulkner is a staple.

Among mostly new titles, the Garden District Bookshop (Map 4; ☎ 504-895-2266), 2727 Prytania St in The Rink, offers a select collection of first editions and books on the region.

For books by African-American writers, head to the Community Book Center & Neighborhood Gallery (Map 6; ☎ 504-822-2665), 217 N Broad St. Voodoo and occult works are available from Starling Books (Map 2; ☎ 504-595-6777), 1022 Royal St.

There's no dearth of second-hand bookstores. Arcadian Books & Art Prints (Map 2; ☎ 504-523-4138), 714 Orleans St, is a well-stocked and cramped store that's worth getting lost in. Beckham's Book Store (☎ 504-522-9875), 228 Decatur St, has two floors worth of used books, as does Crescent City Books (Map 2; ☎ 504-524-4997), 204 Chartres St. In the far reaches of the lower Quarter, Kaboom Books (Map 2; ☎ 504-529-5780), 915 Barracks St, has a large and varied collection.

Other bookstores include Beaucoup Books (☎ 504-895-2663), 5414 Magazine St; DeVille Books & Prints (☎ 504-525-1846), 344 Carondelet St; and Maple Street Book Shop (☎ 504-866-7059), 7523 Maple St. In the suburb of Metairie, check out Maple Street Books (☎ 504-832-8937), at 200 Metairie Rd.

Libraries

The Louisiana Room (☎ 504-596-2610), which is on the 3rd floor of the main branch of the New Orleans Public Library (Map 3;

☎ 504-529-7323, www.nutrias.org), 219 Loyola Ave, is an excellent resource for books, newspapers and maps. The library is closed Friday and Sunday and is open 10 am to 6 pm the rest of the week.

Universities

New Orleans' most prestigious private universities are Tulane and Loyola, nestled next to each other Uptown on St Charles Ave opposite Audubon Park. Founded in 1834, Tulane University (Map 5; ☎ 504-865-5000), 6823 St Charles Ave, boasts 12,000 students in 11 colleges and schools, including a law school and school of medicine. Operated by the Jesuits since 1917, Loyola University (Map 5; ☎ 504-865-2011), 6363 St Charles Ave, is best known for its College of Music, School of Business and Department of Communications.

The historically black, private schools, Dillard University and Xavier University, are well known for excellence. Founded in 1869, Dillard University (☎ 504-283-8822), 2601 Gentilly Blvd, was an important meeting site for Civil Rights leaders. Established in 1915, Xavier University (☎ 504-486-7411), 7325 Palmetto St, is the only historically black Roman Catholic university in the US.

The public Southern University at New Orleans (SUNO; ☎ 504-286-5000), 6400 Press Drive, is a relative newcomer, founded in 1959. Its Center for African and African-American Studies and Fine Arts boasts a large collection of African art. SUNO is the first major college in the US to be headed by a black woman, Chancellor Dr Dolores Spikes.

The largest public campus in New Orleans is the University of New Orleans (Map 1; UNO; ☎ 504-280-6000), on the lakefront, where 16,000 students study on a site that formerly housed a coast guard station. The history department is gaining a reputation for its cutting-edge approach to Louisiana history.

Cultural Centers

The University of New Orleans offers assistance through the Council for International Visitors (☎ 504-280-7266). Local social organizations include the following:

American Italian Museum	☎ 504-891-1904
Asocación de Guatemala en Louisiana	☎ 504-733-5070
Club Social Nicaragüense	☎ 504-524-1329
Deutsches Haus	☎ 504-522-8014
Honduran Association of Louisiana	☎ 504-456-0900
Irish Cultural Society	☎ 504-861-3746
Japan Club	☎ 504-589-6893
Japan Society	☎ 504-283-4890
Jewish Community Center	☎ 504-897-0143

Laundry

Hula Mae's Laundry (Map 2; ☎ 504-522-1336), 840 N Rampart St, is in the former J&M recording studios, where R&B history was made many times over. Countless oldies but goodies were recorded right there where your neighbor is folding his slacks, including Lloyd Price's 'Lawdy Miss Clawdy.' Peruse the building's exhibit while your socks tumble in the dryer.

Drinkers and pool players will appreciate the proliferation of New Orleans bars that offer self-service laundry facilities. Most of these are operated by the Igor's chain – with locations Uptown along St Charles Ave and Magazine St and downtown on Esplanade Ave. See the Entertainment section for more information.

Toilets

A recording by Benny Grunch, 'Ain't No Place to Pee on Mardi Gras Day,' summarizes the situation in the French Quarter. Public toilets can be found in the Jackson Brewery mall on Decatur St and in the French Market. Otherwise, relieving yourself will cost you the price of a beer or a cup of coffee, which of course feeds into an endless cycle… .

Left Luggage

There are luggage lockers in each concourse at New Orleans International Airport. You can also store your bags at Union Passenger Terminal.

Medical & Emergency Services

For immediate medical attention, you can get an ambulance by calling ☎ 911, or have someone take you to the emergency room at a major hospital with a well-staffed trauma center. Charity Hospital (Map 3; ☎ 504-568-2311), 1532 Tulane Ave, offers free services to those who qualify and assesses fees on a sliding scale for others.

Nonprescription medications, as well as certain types of contraceptives, can be purchased 24 hours a day at Walgreens (Map 6; ☎ 504-822-8073), 3311 Canal St at Jefferson Davis Parkway. Closer to the French Quarter, but not open 24 hours a day, is another Walgreens (Map 4; ☎ 504-568-9544), 900 Canal St. In the Quarter, Royal Pharmacy (Map 2; ☎ 504-523-5401), 1101 Royal St, keeps nine-to-five hours and is closed on Sunday.

The headquarters for the New Orleans Police Department (☎ 911 for emergencies, ☎ 504-821-2222 for non-emergencies) is at 715 S Broad St. The French Quarter office (Map 2; ☎ 504-565-7530) is at 334 Royal St.

Dangers & Annoyances

Many areas in New Orleans suffer from high crime rates. For the tourist, getting mugged is a very real threat, even in areas you'd think are safe (eg the Garden District). Naturally, solo pedestrians are targeted more often than people walking in groups, and daytime is a better time to be out on foot than night. If you must travel alone, avoid entering secluded areas such as the cemeteries and Louis Armstrong Park. For instance, plenty of group tours go to St Louis Cemetery No 1, and even if you don't care to join the tours, it might be a good idea to wait for them and thereby avoid walking alone on the grounds. Avoid wandering into the Quarter's unfrequented residential areas late at night or straying across N Rampart St toward the lake.

Large crowds typically make the French Quarter a secure around-the-clock realm for the visitor. However, if your hotel or vehicle is on the margins of the Quarter, you should take a taxi back at night. The CBD has plenty of activity during weekdays, but it's relatively deserted at night and on weekends. On Canal St the throngs of visitors, local shoppers and transit patrons do not generally represent a threat. The seedy rescue missions in the Warehouse District should not deter a visit to the neighborhood's galleries unless you don't like being asked for spare change. The Sunday parking enforcement in the area is a more bothersome problem for motorists.

You can feel somewhat secure at Audubon Park, but at night stay out of the dimly lit park and the nearby campuses. Ditto for City Park and the lakeshore. The clubs near S Carrollton Ave in the Riverbend are generally problem free. Not so for the Fair Grounds neighborhood, where you can enjoy Jazz Fest without problems, but you should not stray from the activity centers after the crowds disperse. Esplanade Ave represents a brave attempt at historic preservation and renewal that cuts through some dangerous areas.

Until you are familiar with the terrain, you should confine your Uptown wanderings to the corridor between St Charles Ave and Magazine St that includes the Garden District. Even this area is not entirely safe. Unless you are surveying urban blight, don't get off the St Charles streetcar below Louisiana Ave and go strolling in the lakeside direction. With a few exceptions, the Irish Channel area river-side from Magazine St is not recommended for the visitor.

In the Quarter, street hustlers frequently approach tourists. You can simply walk away – no hard feelings. Also be aware that just about anywhere, especially in bars, cashiers might have a tendency to 'assume' a tip by short-changing their customers. Keep tabs on prices and the amount of the bills you hand over, then count your change!

Pedestrians crossing the street do not have the right of way and motorists (unless they are from out of state) will not yield. The fact that so many pedestrians (and drivers) in the French Quarter are intoxicated does not help matters. Whether on foot or in a car, be wary before entering an intersection, as New Orleans drivers are notorious for running yellow and even red lights.

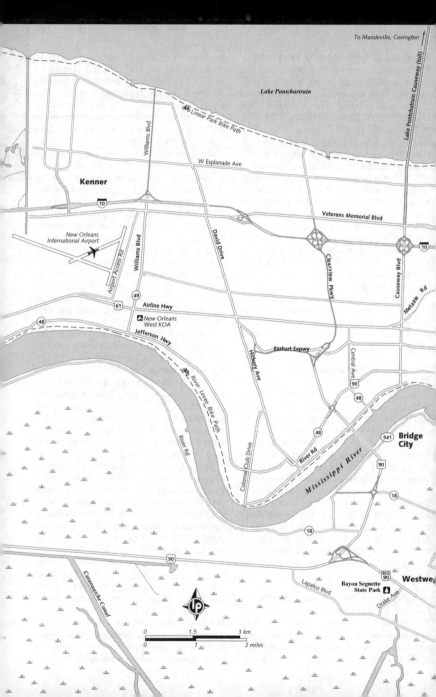

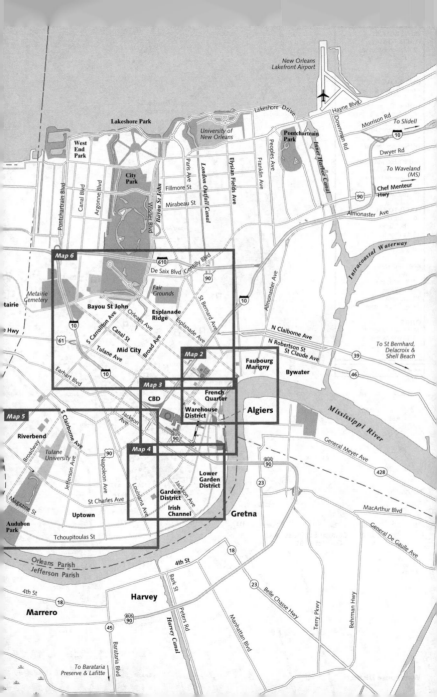

MAP 2 FRENCH QUARTER, TREME DISTRICT & FAUBOURG MARIGNY

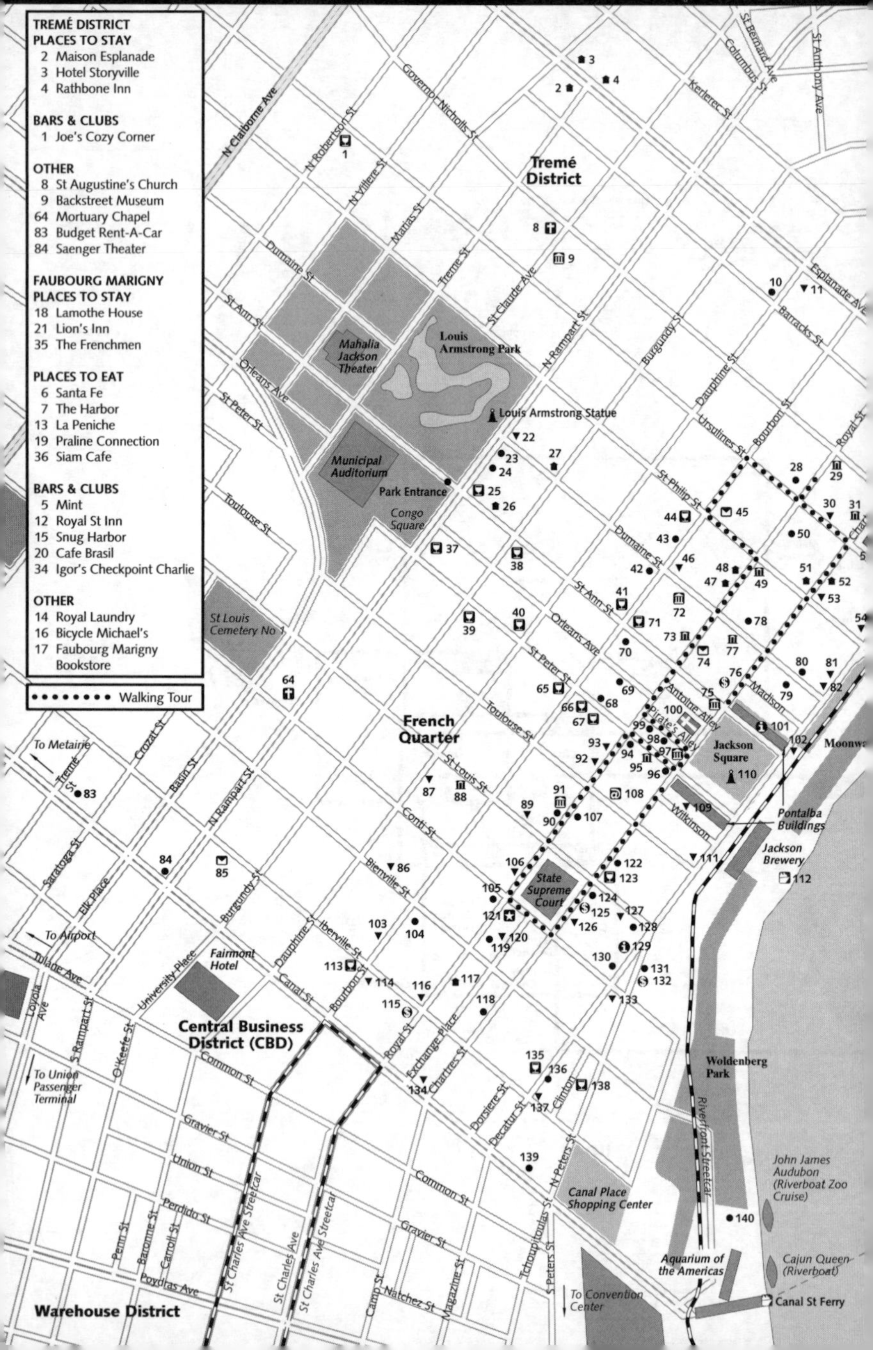

TREMÉ DISTRICT
PLACES TO STAY
2 Maison Esplanade
3 Hotel Storyville
4 Rathbone Inn

BARS & CLUBS
1 Joe's Cozy Corner

OTHER
8 St Augustine's Church
9 Backstreet Museum
64 Mortuary Chapel
83 Budget Rent-A-Car
84 Saenger Theater

FAUBOURG MARIGNY
PLACES TO STAY
18 Lamothe House
21 Lion's Inn
35 The Frenchmen

PLACES TO EAT
6 Santa Fe
7 The Harbor
13 La Peniche
19 Praline Connection
36 Siam Cafe

BARS & CLUBS
5 Mint
12 Royal St Inn
15 Snug Harbor
20 Cafe Brasil
34 Igor's Checkpoint Charlie

OTHER
14 Royal Laundry
16 Bicycle Michael's
17 Faubourg Marigny
     Bookstore

•••••••• Walking Tour

Tremé
District

Mahalia
Jackson
Theater

Louis
Armstrong
Park

Louis Armstrong Statue

Municipal
Auditorium

Park Entrance

Congo
Square

St Louis
Cemetery No 1

French
Quarter

Jackson
Square

Moonw

Pontalba
Buildings

Jackson
Brewery

To Metairie

To Airport

Fairmont
Hotel

Central Business
District (CBD)

To Union
Passenger
Terminal

Woldenberg
Park

Canal Place
Shopping Center

John James
Audubon
(Riverboat Zoo
Cruise)

Cajun Queen
(Riverboat)

To Convention
Center

Aquarium of
the Americas

Canal St Ferry

Warehouse District

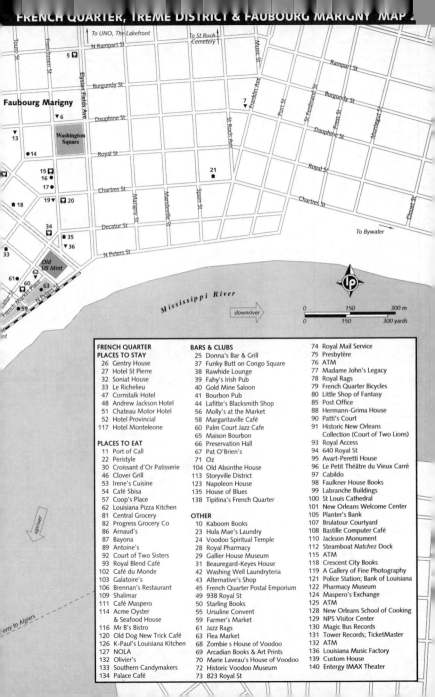

To UNO, The Lakefront
To St Roch Cemetery
To St Roch

Faubourg Marigny

Washington Square

Old US Mint

Mississippi River

downriver

To Bywater

downriver

upriver

0   150   300 m
0   150   300 yards

erry to Algiers

FRENCH QUARTER
PLACES TO STAY
26 Gentry House
27 Hotel St Pierre
32 Soniat House
33 Le Richelieu
47 Cornstalk Hotel
48 Andrew Jackson Hotel
51 Chateau Motor Hotel
52 Hotel Provincial
117 Hotel Monteleone

PLACES TO EAT
11 Port of Call
22 Peristyle
30 Croissant d'Or Patisserie
46 Clover Grill
53 Irene's Cuisine
54 Café Sbisa
57 Coop's Place
62 Louisiana Pizza Kitchen
81 Central Grocery
82 Progress Grocery Co
86 Arnaud's
87 Bayona
89 Antoine's
92 Court of Two Sisters
93 Royal Blend Café
102 Café du Monde
103 Galatoire's
106 Brennan's Restaurant
109 Shalimar
111 Café Maspero
114 Acme Oyster
     & Seafood House
116 Mr B's Bistro
120 Old Dog New Trick Café
126 K-Paul's Louisiana Kitchen
127 NOLA
132 Olivier's
133 Southern Candymakers
134 Palace Café

BARS & CLUBS
25 Donna's Bar & Grill
37 Funky Butt on Congo Square
38 Rawhide Lounge
39 Fahy's Irish Pub
40 Gold Mine Saloon
41 Bourbon Pub
44 Lafitte's Blacksmith Shop
56 Molly's at the Market
58 Margaritaville Café
60 Palm Court Jazz Cafe
65 Maison Bourbon
66 Preservation Hall
67 Pat O'Brien's
71 Oz
104 Old Absinthe House
113 Storyville District
123 Napoleon House
135 House of Blues
138 Tipitina's French Quarter

OTHER
10 Kaboom Books
23 Hula Mae's Laundry
24 Voodoo Spiritual Temple
28 Royal Pharmacy
29 Gallier House Museum
31 Beauregard-Keyes House
42 Washing Well Laundryteria
43 Alternative's Shop
45 French Quarter Postal Emporium
49 938 Royal St
50 Starling Books
55 Ursuline Convent
59 Farmer's Market
61 Jazz Rags
63 Flea Market
68 Zombie s House of Voodoo
69 Arcadian Books & Art Prints
70 Marie Laveau's House of Voodoo
72 Historic Voodoo Museum
73 823 Royal St

74 Royal Mail Service
75 Presbytère
76 ATM
77 Madame John's Legacy
78 Royal Rags
79 French Quarter Bicycles
80 Little Shop of Fantasy
85 Post Office
88 Hermann-Grima House
90 Patti's Court
91 Historic New Orleans
     Collection (Court of Two Lions)
93 Royal Access
94 640 Royal St
95 Avart-Peretti House
96 Le Petit Théâtre du Vieux Carré
97 Cabildo
98 Faulkner House Books
99 Labranche Buildings
100 St Louis Cathedral
101 New Orleans Welcome Center
105 Planter's Bank
107 Brulatour Courtyard
108 Bastille Computer Café
110 Jackson Monument
112 Steamboat *Natchez* Dock
115 ATM
118 Crescent City Books
119 A Gallery of Fine Photography
121 Police Station; Bank of Louisiana
122 Pharmacy Museum
124 Maspero's Exchange
125 ATM
128 New Orleans School of Cooking
129 NPS Visitor Center
130 Magic Bus Records
131 Tower Records; TicketMaster
132 ATM
136 Louisiana Music Factory
139 Custom House
140 Entergy IMAX Theater

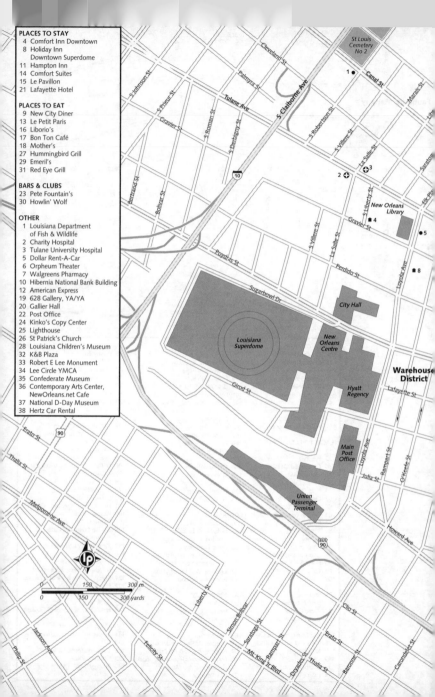

PLACES TO STAY
- 4 Comfort Inn Downtown
- 8 Holiday Inn Downtown Superdome
- 11 Hampton Inn
- 14 Comfort Suites
- 15 Le Pavillon
- 21 Lafayette Hotel

PLACES TO EAT
- 9 New City Diner
- 13 Le Petit Paris
- 16 Liborio's
- 17 Bon Ton Café
- 18 Mother's
- 27 Hummingbird Grill
- 29 Emeril's
- 31 Red Eye Grill

BARS & CLUBS
- 23 Pete Fountain's
- 30 Howlin' Wolf

OTHER
- 1 Louisiana Department of Fish & Wildlife
- 2 Charity Hospital
- 3 Tulane University Hospital
- 5 Dollar Rent-A-Car
- 6 Orpheum Theater
- 7 Walgreens Pharmacy
- 10 Hibernia National Bank Building
- 12 American Express
- 19 628 Gallery, YA/YA
- 20 Gallier Hall
- 22 Post Office
- 24 Kinko's Copy Center
- 25 Lighthouse
- 26 St Patrick's Church
- 28 Louisiana Children's Museum
- 32 K&B Plaza
- 33 Robert E Lee Monument
- 34 Lee Circle YMCA
- 35 Confederate Museum
- 36 Contemporary Arts Center, NewOrleans.net Cafe
- 37 National D-Day Museum
- 38 Hertz Car Rental

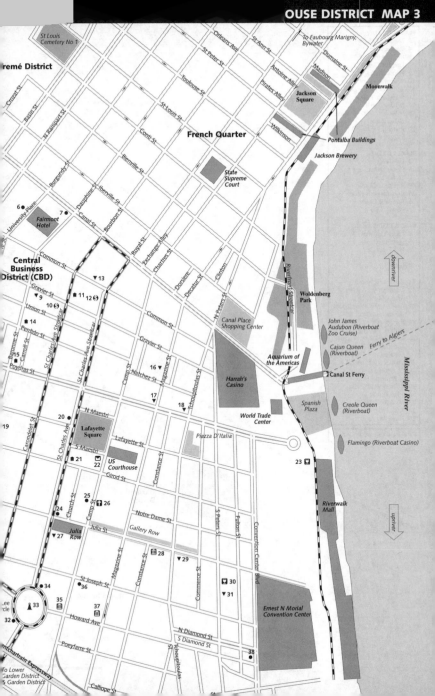

St Louis Cemetery No 1

remé District

Crozat St
Basin St
N Rampart St
Burgundy St
Dauphine St
Bourbon St
Royal St
Chartres St
Decatur St
N Peters St

Orleans Ave
St Ann St
St Peter St
Toulouse St
St Louis St
Conti St
Bienville St
Iberville St
Canal St

To Faubourg Marigny;
Bywater
Dumaine St
Antoine Alley
Pirates Alley
Madison
Wilkinson

Moonwalk

Jackson
Square

French Quarter

Pontalba Buildings
Jackson Brewery

State
Supreme
Court

6 •
University Place
7 •

Fairmont
Hotel

**Central
Business
District (CBD)**

Common St
Gravier St
Union St
Perdido St
Poydras St
St Charles Ave Streetcar
Carondelet St
Bayonne St
Carroll St

Exchange Alley
Doriene St
Clinton

Riverfront Streetcar

downriver

▼ 13
▼ 9
■ 11 12 ⊗
10 ⊗
■ 14
■ 15
■

Common St
Gravier St

Canal Place
Shopping Center

Woldenberg
Park

John James
Audubon (Riverboat
Zoo Cruise)

Cajun Queen
(Riverboat)

Ferry to Algiers

16 ▼
17 ▼
18 ▼

Magazine St
Tchoupitoulas St
Natchez St

Aquarium of
the Americas

Harrah's
Casino

Canal St Ferry

Mississippi River

19

20 •

N Maestri

**Lafayette
Square**

Lafayette St

S Maestri

21 ■
22 ▥

US
Courthouse
Girod St

Piazza D'Italia

World Trade
Center

Spanish
Plaza

Creole Queen
(Riverboat)

23 ▯

Flamingo (Riverboat Casino)

St Charles Ave

25 •
24 •
Camp St
26

Church St

Notre Dame St

S Peters St
Fulton St

Julia
Row
▼ 27

Julia St

Gallery Row

▥ 28
▼ 29

▯ 30
▼ 31

Riverwalk
Mall

upriver

34 •
35 ▥
• 36

St Joseph St

33 ⚓

37 ▥

32 •

Howard Ave

N Diamond St
S Diamond St

Ernest N Morial
Convention Center

Convention Center Blvd

ee
rcle

Poeyfarre St

38 ▯

chartrain Expressway

To Lower
arden District
& Garden District

Calliope St

Tchoupitoulas St

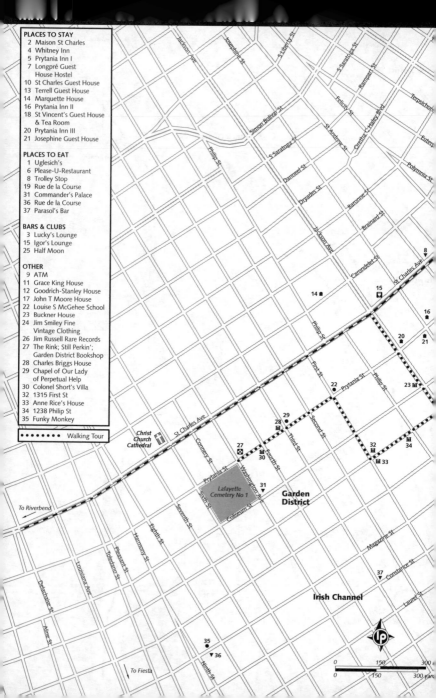

PLACES TO STAY
2   Maison St Charles
4   Whitney Inn
5   Prytania Inn I
7   Longpré Guest House Hostel
10 St Charles Guest House
13 Terrell Guest House
14 Marquette House
16 Prytania Inn II
18 St Vincent's Guest House & Tea Room
20 Prytania Inn III
21 Josephine Guest House

PLACES TO EAT
1   Uglesich's
6   Please-U-Restaurant
8   Trolley Stop
19 Rue de la Course
31 Commander's Palace
36 Rue de la Course
37 Parasol's Bar

BARS & CLUBS
3   Lucky's Lounge
15 Igor's Lounge
25 Half Moon

OTHER
9   ATM
11 Grace King House
12 Goodrich-Stanley House
17 John T Moore House
22 Louise S McGehee School
23 Buckner House
24 Jim Smiley Fine Vintage Clothing
26 Jim Russell Rare Records
27 The Rink; Still Perkin'; Garden District Bookshop
28 Charles Briggs House
29 Chapel of Our Lady of Perpetual Help
30 Colonel Short's Villa
32 1315 First St
33 Anne Rice's House
34 1238 Philip St
35 Funky Monkey

••••••••• Walking Tour

Christ Church Cathedral

St Charles Ave

Lafayette Cemetery No 1

Garden District

To Riverbend

Irish Channel

To Fiesta

0   150   300 m
0   150   300 yards

MAP 9 UPTOWN & RIVERBEND

Mississippi River

upriver

downriver

Bike Trail

Riverbend

Levee Park

Park

Newcomb College

Tulane University

Loyola University

Ursuline College & Conver

Audubon Park

Golf Course

Uptown

Audubon Zoological Gardens

| 0 | 250 | 500 m |
| 0 | 250 | 500 yards |

33

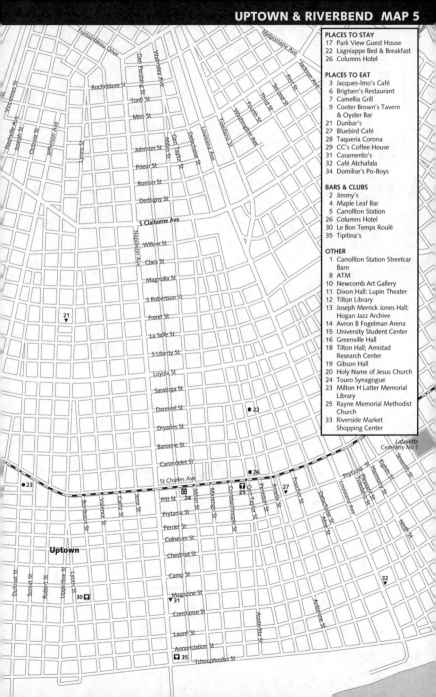

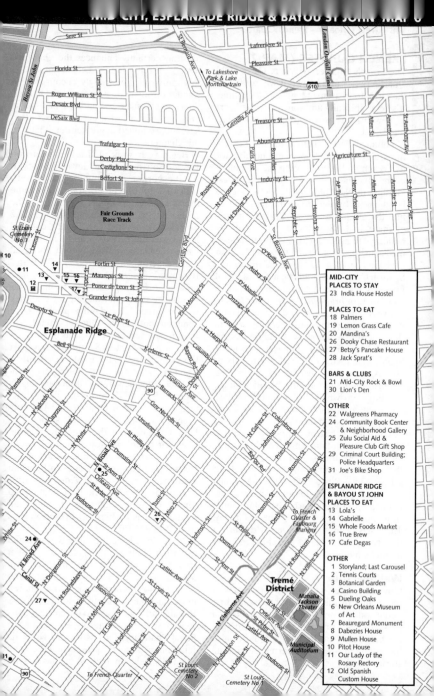

MID-CITY

PLACES TO STAY
23 India House Hostel

PLACES TO EAT
18 Palmers
19 Lemon Grass Cafe
20 Mandina's
26 Dooky Chase Restaurant
27 Betsy's Pancake House
28 Jack Sprat's

BARS & CLUBS
21 Mid-City Rock & Bowl
30 Lion's Den

OTHER
22 Walgreens Pharmacy
24 Community Book Center & Neighborhood Gallery
25 Zulu Social Aid & Pleasure Club Gift Shop
29 Criminal Court Building; Police Headquarters
31 Joe's Bike Shop

ESPLANADE RIDGE & BAYOU ST JOHN
PLACES TO EAT
13 Lola's
14 Gabrielle
15 Whole Foods Market
16 True Brew
17 Cafe Degas

OTHER
1 Storyland; Last Carousel
2 Tennis Courts
3 Botanical Garden
4 Casino Building
5 Dueling Oaks
6 New Orleans Museum of Art
7 Beauregard Monument
8 Dabezies House
9 Mullen House
10 Pitot House
11 Our Lady of the Rosary Rectory
12 Old Spanish Custom House

FRENCH QUARTER (MAP 2)

The French Quarter, or Vieux Carré (Old Quarter) as it's also known, is where 90% of the city's tourists spend 90% of their time. It's geographically and spiritually the heart of New Orleans, as well as its oldest, quaintest district.

Founded by and named for the French, the Quarter is surprisingly not notable for its French architecture. With the exception of the Ursuline Convent (1745), the oldest building in New Orleans, French-designed buildings all burned down during a pair of fires that swept through the district. The first of these, in 1788, reduced more than 800 buildings to ashes, including all businesses, mansions, the Cabildo and the church. After a second fire in 1794, the Cabildo (or Spanish Council chamber) mandated use of fire-resistant materials for multistory buildings. Brick, or *briquette entre poteaux* (bricks between posts), covered with plaster became the signature architectural style in the Quarter. While a few building designs retained some French influences, a distinctly Spanish character emerged in the rebuilt city. Among the most readily identified Spanish elements are the broad window openings crowned by graceful arches. Above many entrances, you will note handsome, fan-shaped transoms.

During the last 50 years, preservation edicts have maintained much of the historic building stock throughout the Quarter, but the preservationists also brought about social change. Since 1937, when the French Quarter acquired historic-district status, the population in the Quarter has plummeted from more than 12,000 to about 5000 today. There has been an even greater decline in the proportion of blacks and children in the population mix.

Walking Tour

Obviously, architecture has a lot to do with the beauty of the French Quarter, and an initial walk through its narrow streets and passageways is primarily an appreciation of the buildings. But the French Quarter also has more mysterious charms. Intriguing stories can be sensed, if not always seen,

and this certainly enhances the Quarter's lure. After following the course outlined in this tour, you are strongly encouraged to wander through other areas of the Quarter. Some sights, such as buildings that house museums, given just a cursory description here are examined in greater detail later in this chapter.

Begin your walk at the Presbytère on Jackson Square and head down Chartres St. At the corner of Dumaine St, go left. Halfway up the block stands **Madame John's Legacy**, 632 Dumaine St, run by the Louisiana State Museum (admission is $3/2 for adults/children). This French colonial house was built in 1788 and acquired its name when George Washington Cable used it as the setting in his story 'Tite Poullette.' Its raised basement of briquette entre poteaux offered protection from floods. Across the street, an iron gate set in a brick wall is graced by **devil's pitchforks**, a common motif in the Quarter intended to keep trespassers and evil spirits at bay.

Return to Chartres St and take a left. At the corner of Ursulines St, the **Ursuline Convent**, 1114 Chartres St, is partly obstructed from view by a wall surrounding its grounds. Built 1745–50, it's the oldest structure in the French Quarter and the only French colonial building still standing in New Orleans (see the separate section, later, for more on the convent). Directly across Chartres St, the **Beauregard-Keyes House**, 1113 Chartres St, dates to 1826 and combines Creole- and American-style design. Civil War General PGT Beauregard rented rooms here after his wife died, and author Francis Parkinson Keyes lived here from 1944 to 1970.

Walk along Ursulines St to Royal St and turn right. Halfway up the block, the **Gallier House**, 1118 Royal St, is a Greek Revival townhouse built in 1857 by architect James Gallier Jr for his family. The house is now a museum (see separate heading). Cross Royal St and backtrack to the corner of Ursulines St to take a quick peek inside the **Royal Pharmacy**, 1101 Royal St. The soda fountain, a perfectly preserved relic from the US's halcyon malt shop days, is no longer in use. The owners of the pharmacy feel it's just too beautiful to pull out.

Turn right on Ursulines St and then left on Bourbon St. The ramshackle one-story structure on the corner of St Philip St is a great little tavern called **Lafitte's Blacksmith Shop**, 941 Bourbon St. This is a National Historic Landmark, and although stories connecting it with the pirate Jean Lafitte are probably not true (legend has it he ran a blacksmith shop here with his brother), the little cottage stands out for its exposed brick-between-post construction. It is believed that the building dates to the end of the 18th century. Have a drink and then walk down St Philip to Royal St.

When it comes to classic New Orleans postcard images, Royal St takes the cake. What makes the street so picturesque is that many of its structures are graced by beautiful cast-iron galleries. As you walk along Royal St, keep an eye on the second- and third-floor balconies, where a variety of lush plants hang from the ornate cast-iron.

At the corner of Royal and St Philip Sts, the rusty cast-iron galleries at **938 Royal St** were added in 1858 to the three-story brick apartments. This attractive building stands out among its neighbors, as it has yet to be restored in the quaint manner of many French Quarter structures. Half a century ago, most buildings in the French Quarter had a similar weathered, if not dilapidated, look. Half a block up, on the other side of the street, stands the **Cornstalk Hotel**, 915 Royal St. It's one of the most frequently photographed structures in New Orleans – or at least the cornstalk-decorated cast-iron fence in front is (see the Places to Stay section for details on staying here).

The house at **823 Royal St** belonged to Daniel Clark, an Irish-born merchant who aided Thomas Jefferson in negotiating the Louisiana Purchase. His lasting notoriety came when he wounded Governor Claiborne in a duel brought about by charges that he was involved in the Aaron Burr conspiracy. Continue on Royal St to Orleans St, where lush tropical plants fill **St Anthony's Garden**, behind **St Louis Cathedral**. Vistas of the cathedral's steeple are available from anywhere along Orleans Ave.

Alongside the garden, **Pirate's Alley** is an inviting, shaded walkway that calls for a little detour. The name is a purely romantic one, as the little alleyway never harbored pirate activity – Jean Lafitte and his gang were long gone when the passageway was first opened in 1831. On the Pirate Alley side of the Labranche buildings, 622–624 Pirate's Alley, note the original wrought-iron balconies – these survived the cast-iron craze that replaced much of the Quarter's wrought-iron detail, and they date to the 1840s. In 1925, William Faulkner lived at **624 Pirate's Alley** (then called Orleans Alley). The small but charming Faulkner House bookstore opened here in 1990 and very quickly became a focal point in New Orleans literary circles.

Continue down Pirate's Alley, skirting the cathedral and circumventing the **Cabildo**. (These sights require more time than a walking tour allows, and they're covered in detail with other Jackson Square sights later.) Head up St Peter St back toward Royal St. At 632 St Peter St, the **Avart-Peretti House** is where Tennessee Williams lived 1946–47, when he was writing his most famous play, *A Streetcar Named Desire*. On the opposite side of the street there are more of the impressive **Labranche Buildings**, at 621–639 St Peter and 700–712 Royal Sts.

At the intersection of Royal and St Peter Sts, also take note of the city's first 'skyscraper,' at **640 Royal St**. Begun in 1795, the structure grew to three stories tall by 1811 (a fourth floor was added in 1876). The building's 1811 owner, Dr Yves LeMonnier, left his initials in the wrought-iron balcony that overlooks the street corner. Until that time, building in New Orleans was generally limited to two floors, for fear that taller buildings could not be supported on 'swampy' soil.

Continue on Royal St. From the solid line of façades built to the sidewalk, or *banquette*, it's hard to imagine that this block offers significant open space to merchants and residents. However, there are large interior courtyards hidden behind entryways. The Creole custom was to orient a home toward the rear, with more personal style accorded to interiors where families spent most of their time; by contrast, facades were relatively unostentatious and deliberately unrevealing. During business hours, the Old Town Praline Shop, 627 Royal St, affords entry to **Patti's Court** for a behind-the-scenes peek. Some courtyards are now poster shops, but you can go in without buying anything. You can also enjoy a pleasant coffee or a meal in an alfresco courtyard setting at the Royal Blend Café or the Court of Two Sisters restaurant (see the Places to Eat section).

At the corner of Toulouse St, the **Court of Two Lions**, 541 Royal St, was built by Jean François Merieult in 1798. The Toulouse St side is flanked by marble lions atop the entry posts. Merieult built the neighboring house at 527–533 Royal St in 1792 – it is a rare survivor of the 1794 fire. Now it's home to the **Historic New Orleans Collection**. Organized tours of the house and adjacent structures

RICHARD CUMMINS

Fountain sculpture, French Quarter

are available. You can also enter the distinctive **Brulatour Courtyard**, 520 Royal St, which was built by Bordeaux native François Seignouret after he fought in the Battle of New Orleans. The space served his wine-importing and fine-furniture-manufacturing businesses. The courtyard's name came from merchant Pierre Brulatour, who purchased the house in 1870.

Many scenes from the movie *JFK* were filmed at the massive **State Supreme Court Building**. Opened in 1909, the white marble and terra-cotta façade is out of character with the rest of the Quarter's design and scale. Across the street, the famed **Brennan's Restaurant**, 417 Royal St, has occupied this spot since 1955. Vincent Rillieux, the great-grandfather of artist Edgar Degas, owned the property and may have commissioned its 1802 construction. The building housed the Banque de la Louisiane, the first bank established after the Louisiana Purchase. At Royal and Conti Sts, **Louisiana State Bank**, 401 Royal St, was designed by nationally acclaimed architect Benjamin Henry Latrobe in 1820, shortly before his death from yellow fever.

Directly across Conti St, the **Planters Bank**, 343 Royal St, is another former bank built by Rillieux shortly after the great fire of 1794. Its wrought-iron balconies and knee braces are notable examples of Spanish colonial design. The Waldorn antique shop has been on the premises since 1881. Across the street, take a peek at the interior of the Greek Revival **Bank of Louisiana**, 332 Royal St, built in 1826. The building has served in many capacities since the bank was liquidated in 1867, including a stint as the state capitol. Now it houses a police station and a visitor center.

Head down Conti St to Chartres St and turn left. **Maspero's Exchange**, 440 Chartres St, is a restaurant formerly known as La Bourse de Maspero, the slave-trading house and coffeeshop of Pierre Maspero (see separate heading). Across St Louis St, **Napoleon House**, 500 Chartres St, is an ancient bar whose crumbling stucco walls would have some intriguing stories to tell – despite their silence, one great story about the building has become part of French Quarter lore. At the beginning of the 19th century, the building's owner, former Mayor Nicholas Girod, plotted to rescue Napoleon Bonaparte from his prison on St Helena and to keep the deposed emperor in an apartment above the bar. The emperor unfortunately died before the plan was carried out.

Another half block up Chartres St, you'll see a sign for La Pharmacie Francaise, which in 1823 was run by the USA's first licensed pharmacist. The shop is now the **Pharmacy Museum**, 514 Chartres St (see separate heading).

From here it's just a block or so back to Jackson Square, where you can find a bench and watch free entertainment almost any time of day.

Jackson Square

Jackson Square stands out as one of the loveliest public spaces in the US. The park itself is well-groomed and pleasant enough, but the surrounding architecture is what makes Jackson Square visually spectacular. A striking symmetry is created by the two Pontalba Buildings flanking the square and the nearly identical Cabildo and Presbytère structures on either side of St Louis Cathedral, which makes a perfect centerpiece.

Jackson Square thrives as the central, and most important, gathering place for visitors to the French Quarter, as it was meant to when the French laid out the city nearly 300 years ago. A host of street musicians (many of them true talents from the city's jazz and brass band scene), artists, tarot card readers and mimes compete for the attention of tourists milling about the banquette. It is a kinetic cultural scene that is almost always interesting.

Originally a muddy parade grounds called Place d'Armes, the square was transformed by Madame Micaëla Pontalba, who also commissioned the two Pontalba buildings. Her father, Don Andrés Almonaster y Roxas, was responsible for St Louis Cathedral, the Cabildo and the Presbytère. Madame Pontalba also commissioned the **Jackson Monument**, which was sculpted by

Clark Mills. The centerpiece equestrian statue honors General Andrew Jackson, hero of the Battle of New Orleans and US president from 1829 to 1837. Citizens unveiled the 10-ton bronze statue in 1856, and replicas later appeared in Washington, DC, and Nashville, Tennessee. The inscription, 'The Union Must and Shall be Preserved,' was an added – and locally unwelcome – sentiment from General Benjamin Butler, the Yankee commander of occupying forces in 1862.

St Louis Cathedral

During the Christmas midnight mass, the Cathedral of St Louis, King of France, is the most popular spot in the city. In 1722, a hurricane destroyed the first of three churches built here by the St Louis Parish. Architect Gilberto Guillemard dedicated the present cathedral on Christmas Eve in 1794, only weeks after it was saved from a devastating fire by a combination of shifting winds and the firebreak provided by the empty lot where the Cabildo had yet to be built. Extensive remodeling from 1849 to 1851 was designed by French-trained architect JNB DePouilly. In 1850, the cathedral was designated as the metropolitan church of the Archdiocese of New Orleans. Pope Paul VI awarded to the cathedral the rank of minor basilica in 1964.

Buried in the cathedral is its Spanish benefactor, Don Andrés Almonaster y Roxas, who also financed the Cabildo and the initial construction of the Presbytère – not bad for a minor official who arrived in New Orleans as a poor Spanish notary. He gained his wealth from rents on real estate facing the square.

For information about daily masses, contact the Oblates of Mary Immaculate (☎ 504-525-9585), 615 Père Antoine Alley. The cathedral is open for tours 9 am to 5 pm daily, 1 to 5 pm Sunday. Donations are accepted.

Louisiana State Museum

The centerpieces of this collection of historic buildings are the Cabildo, the Presbytère, and the lower Pontalba Building, all overlooking Jackson Square. The museum also comprises the Old US Mint and Madam John's Legacy, as well as some sights outside the city of New Orleans.

You can pay separate admission to each Louisiana State Museum, or buy a discount combination ticket to two or more of the buildings. Students, active military and AAA members will save a dollar on the adult price. Children under 12 years old are admitted free.

Cabildo The first Cabildo was a single-story structure destroyed by fire in 1788. Tenants in the rebuilt Cabildo, designed by Gilberto Guillemard and dedicated in 1799, included the Spanish Council (for which the building is named), the City Hall government from 1803 to 1853, the Louisiana Supreme Court from 1853 to 1910 and the Louisiana State Museum from 1911 to present.

Three floors of exhibits emphasize the significance of New Orleans in a regional, national and even international context. It is a challenge to see it all in part of a day. You might try to quickly survey the lower floor, paying attention to the pre-Columbian Indian artifacts and the colonial exhibits that most interest you. You can look out over Jackson Square from the Sala Capitular (Spanish Council room) on the 2nd floor. This is where the Louisiana Purchase documents were signed, transferring the extensive territory from Napoleonic France to the US. Other displays depict the Battle of New Orleans, including the role of free blacks and members of the Choctaw tribe in General Andrew Jackson's force, which decisively defeated General Packenham's British troops in 1814. The 3rd-floor exhibits of racial and ethnic groups from the American period are among the most interesting, with artifacts and shocking depictions of African slaves next to Civil War military displays that show free people of color in support of the Confederacy.

The Cabildo (☎ 504-568-6968), 701 Chartres St, is open Tuesday through Sunday from 9 am to 5 pm. Admission is $5/4 for adults/seniors and students. Children under 12 years old are admitted free.

Presbytère Although architect Gilberto Guillemard originally designed the Presbytère to be a rectory for the St Louis Cathedral in 1791, the building was never directly used by the church after it was completed in 1813. Instead, the cathedral administrators rented the building to the city for use as a courthouse before selling it to them in 1853. Ownership was finally transferred to the Louisiana State Museum in 1911.

The Presbytère's exhibit, 'Mardi Gras: It's Carnival Time in Louisiana,' is essential viewing for visitors intent on learning about Louisiana culture, whether or not you've arrived in time to experience Mardi Gras for yourself. The exhibit delves into all of the major topics, with vibrant displays of masks and costumes, parade floats, Mardi Gras Indian suits and historic photos. Documentary videos and detailed signage help convey the depth of meaning behind many of carnival's complex traditions.

The Presbytère (☎ 504-568-6968), 751 Chartres St, is open Tuesday through Sunday from 9 am until 5 pm. Admission is $5/4 for adults/seniors and students. Children under 12 years old are admitted free.

1850 House The 1850 House is one of the apartments in the lower Pontalba Building. Madame Micaëla Pontalba, daughter of Don Andrés Almonaster y Roxas, continued her father's improvements around Jackson Square by building the long rows of red-brick apartments flanking the upper and lower portions of the square. She was also responsible for renaming the once barren parade grounds, the Place d'Armes, after her friend Andrew Jackson. Initial plans for the apartments were drawn by the noted architect James Gallier Sr (see the Gallier House Museum section, later in this chapter). In 1927, the lower Pontalba Building was bequeathed to the Louisiana State Museum. (In 1930, the city acquired the upper Pontalba Building, where Micaëla once lived.)

Now, knowledgeable volunteers from the Friends of the Cabildo give tours of the apartment, which includes a central court and servants' quarters with period furnishings throughout.

The 1850 House (☎ 504-568-6968), 523 St Ann St, is open for self-guided tours Tuesday to Sunday from 9 am to 5 pm. Guides are available. Admission is $3/2 for adults/seniors and students. Children under 12 years old are admitted free.

Ursuline Convent

After a five-month voyage from Rouen, France, 12 Ursuline nuns arrived in New Orleans to care for the French garrison's miserable little hospital and to educate the young girls of the colony. They were the first nuns in the New World. The French Colonial Army built the existing convent and girls' school between 1745 and 1752, making it the oldest structure in the French Quarter and the Mississippi Valley. It is also one of the few surviving examples of French colonial architecture in New Orleans. Don't expect to see any nuns, however, as they packed up their habits and moved Uptown in 1824.

Guided tours of the fully restored convent include a visit to the Chapel of Archbishops, built in 1845. The chapel's stained-glass windows pay tribute to the Battle of New Orleans (Andrew Jackson credited his victory to the Ursulines' prayers for divine intervention) and to the Sisters of the Holy Family, an order of black Creole nuns established in 1842 by Henriette Delille. Tours of the Ursuline Convent (☎ 504-529-3040), 1114 Chartres St, are offered Tuesday to Friday at 10 and 11 am and 1, 2 and 3 pm; and Saturday and Sunday at 11:15 am and 1 and 2 pm. Admission is $5/4/2 for adults/seniors/children.

Beauregard-Keyes House

Greek Revival structures such as this house, built in 1826, with slave quarters and a rear courtyard, are uncommon in the French Quarter. After the war, it was the home of Confederate General PGT Beauregard, who made his mark on US history when he gave the order to Confederate forces to fire upon Fort Sumter in Charleston, South Carolina, thus beginning the Civil War.

The house's other illustrious resident was the author Francis Parkinson Keyes, who lived here from 1944 until her death in 1970. Beginning in 1926, she became well known for her serialized travel correspondence in *Good Housekeeping* – much of her success came from her incredible ability with foreign languages. She published 51 novels, including many that were set locally, such as *Crescent Carnival* (1942), the best-seller *Dinner at Antoine's* (1948) and *Steamboat Gothic* (1952). Her novel *Madame Castel's Lodger* (1962) is set in this house during General Beauregard's time.

Tours of the Beauregard-Keyes House (☎ 504-523-7257), 1113 Chartres St, are not as interesting as the individuals who lived there. A gift shop offers most of Francis Parkinson Keyes' books. The house is open Monday to Saturday 10 am to 3 pm, and tours begin on the hour every hour, but it's recommended that you show up five minutes early. Admission is $5/4/2.50 for adults/seniors/children.

Gallier House Museum

New Orleans owes much of its architectural heritage to James Gallier Sr and James Gallier Jr. They are both renowned for their Greek Revival designs. In 1857 Gallier Jr began work on this impressive French Quarter townhouse, incorporating numerous innovations – such as interior plumbing, skylights and ceiling vents – into the design. A cistern provided fresh water to the kitchen, which, in turn, provided hot water to the upstairs bath. It is carefully furnished with period pieces. Access to the cast-iron gallery overlooking Royal St and other handsome homes is an added highlight of the worthwhile tour.

The Gallier House Museum (☎ 504-525-5661), 1118 Royal St, is open weekdays 10 am to 3:30 pm. Admission is $6/5 for adults/seniors and children; combination tickets for both the Gallier House and the Hermann-Grima House cost $10/9.

Hermann-Grima House

Samuel Hermann, a Jewish merchant, introduced the unique Federal design to the

Quarter in 1831. Hermann sold the house in 1844 to Judge Grima after reportedly losing $2 million during the national financial panic of 1837. Cooking demonstrations in the authentic open-hearth kitchen are a special treat on Thursday from October through May.

Tours of the Hermann-Grima House (☎ 504-525-5661), 820 St Louis St, are offered Monday to Saturday 10 am to 3:30 pm. Admission is $6/5 for adults/seniors and children; see the Gallier House section for combination tickets to these two sights.

Historic New Orleans Collection

The Historic New Orleans Collection (☎ 504-523-4662, www.hnoc.org), 533 Royal St, is housed in a complex of historic buildings, anchored by the Merieult House. Beginning in 1970, it has displayed private collections of art and historical documents that attract visitors, local researchers and foreign scholars. The exhibits may be a bit dry and academic for some tastes. A gift shop offers historical postcards, new and used books and collectibles.

Williams Gallery These rotating exhibits provide visitors with an opportunity to gain an understanding of different aspects of local history. For example, one past exhibit featured historical photographs, videos and oral histories to document the changes that mechanization brought to southern Louisiana's rural sugar cane-growing areas. It's open Tuesday through Saturday 10 am to 4:30 pm. Admission is free.

Merieult History Tour Unlike the undocumented anecdotes fed to tourists by the French Quarter's ubiquitous carriage guides, the Historic New Orleans Collection of Louisiana's past is meticulously researched. The many handsome gallery displays are housed in the landmark Merieult House, built in 1792. Showcased are the original transfer documents of the 1803 Louisiana Purchase. If the guide leaves something out, you can pick up a handy listing of each room's contents to find out more on your own. It's a bit fast paced,

especially if you want to inspect the many early maps showing the city's evolution or such things as an 1849 broadside advertising '24 Head of Slaves' (individual children for $500 or entire families for $2400). Nevertheless, no better short introduction to the history of the city is available.

The Merieult House, a rare survivor of the 1794 fire, is an almost overlooked part of the tour. It was extensively remodeled in 1832, reflecting the American influence of the period. In one room, sections of plaster are removed to expose the traditional brick-and-post construction, and another room is sheathed with barge boards from river barges dismantled at the end of a downriver trip.

Tours are given Tuesday through Saturday at 10 and 11 am and 2 and 3 pm. The cost is $4.

Williams Research Center In 1996, the Historic New Orleans Collection moved its research facilities (☎ 504-523-4662) to a beautifully refurbished police station at 410 Chartres St. It really isn't of interest to the casual visitor, but if you have specific queries about almost any building in New Orleans the staff at this research center can help. The archives contain more than 300,000 images and a comprehensive block-by-block survey of the French Quarter. Ink pens are not permitted inside. It's open Tuesday through Saturday 10 am to 4:30 pm.

Maspero's Exchange

Pierre Maspero operated La Bourse de Maspero, a coffeehouse and one of many slave-trading houses in New Orleans. He was a tenant in the building that now houses the restaurant Maspero's Exchange, at 440 Chartres St (not to be confused with Café Maspero on Decatur St). Regular markets for the unfortunate trade of humans occurred two blocks away on Exchange Alley (now Exchange Place), between Conti and Canal Sts, and at the market beyond the Quarter's wall, now Louis Armstrong Park across Rampart St. Following the Good Friday fire of 1788,

Don Juan Paillet built this structure, later to become the scene of slave trading, with an *entresol* (a mezzanine floor with a low ceiling that was visible from the exterior through arched windows). This cramped room, then only reached by a ceiling door from the bottom floor, is where the African slaves are said to have been imprisoned. It is now a dining room – a rather discomfiting and tasteless use of the space.

There's one other historical note about Maspero's worth mentioning: with British troops approaching in 1814, this building served as the headquarters for the local Committee of Public Safety, charged with marshaling citizens to fight under General Andrew Jackson.

Pharmacy Museum
The Pharmacy Museum (☎ 504-565-8027), 514 Chartres St, occupies a shop established in 1823 by the nation's first licensed pharmacist, Louis J Dufilho Jr. Dufilho dispensed gold-coated pills to the rich and opium, alcohol and cannabis to those who really needed to feel better. It's open Tuesday through Sunday 10 am to 5 pm. Admission costs $2.

Old US Mint
This unremarkable Greek Revival building appears out of place among the Quarter's Creole buildings. From 1838 to 1861 and again from 1879 to 1910, the New Orleans Mint struck US coinage bearing the 'O' mint mark. The Confederate States of America briefly produced coins after seizing the mint in 1861. The current meager exhibits about the Old US Mint are likely to disappoint coin enthusiasts. It's more worthwhile if regarded as an archeological site from the Industrial Age.

After serving as a US Mint, federal prison and US Coast Guard office, the building was transferred to the Louisiana State Museum, which opened its doors to the public in the 1980s.

The Old US Mint (☎ 504-568-6968), 400 Esplanade Ave, is open Tuesday through Sunday from 9 am to 5 pm. Admission costs $5/4 for adults/seniors. Two gift shops offer a good selection of jazz recordings and an array of coins and Confederate currency minted in New Orleans.

New Orleans Jazz Exhibit Even if you wouldn't give a nickel to see where coins were once minted, the Old US Mint's exhibit on New Orleans jazz ought to lure you in. The exhibit is an intelligent assemblage of memorabilia and photographs, as well as the dented horns, busted snare drums, and homemade gut-stringed bass fiddles played by of some of the Crescent City's most cherished artists. All artifacts are organized chronologically with historical notes, and as you peruse the exhibit, the museum's piped-in music comes alive.

Houma Indian Arts Museum You might not think jazz and Houma art go together, but in Louisiana, everything goes together. The Old US Mint's exhibit of contemporary folk art by Houma Indians is an impressive collection of colorful wood carvings depicting men and animals – many of them life sized. A room dedicated to model fishing boats and pirogues, the dugout canoes traditionally used by Native Americans and Cajuns to navigate Louisiana swamps, is also worth lingering in.

French Market
For more than 200 years, New Orleans trade has focused on the high ground beside the levee. Native Americans conducted the earliest commerce by offering hides to Europeans, and French colonials followed with an open-air market. The Spanish built the first structure in 1791 to house butchers and regulate the often abused sale of food, but it was destroyed by hurricane and fire. (The site is now a parking lot between Café du Monde and the levee.) In 1813, the city surveyor, Jacques Tanesse, designed a replacement, the Halle des Boucheries (Butcher's Market).

In the 1930s the WPA (Works Progress – later Works Project – Administration) extensively renovated the city-managed French Market, on French Market Place from St Ann to Barracks Sts.

Cafes have occupied the Butcher's Market building since 1860. Café du Monde, the market's oldest tenant, sells loads of its packaged chicory blend coffee and boxed beignet mix to visitors (see the Places to Eat section, later in this chapter). It never closes.

Voodoo Spiritual Temple

A visit to Priestess Miriam Williams' Voodoo Spiritual Temple will convince you that voodoo is alive and well in the modern world. The sageness and integrity of Priestess Miriam suggests that voodoo, with its reputation for trickery and dishonesty, has gotten a bum rap.

She founded the Voodoo Spiritual Temple, in a converted storefront two doors from Lula Mae's laundry, in 1990. The site she chose is just a few blocks from Congo Square, where Marie Laveau is said to have performed her theatrical public rituals. In Miriam's dimly lit temple, altars to many deities are endowed with such worldly

Hoodoo that Voodoo

Voodoo has in no small way contributed to New Orleans' reputation as the 'least American city in America.' It is perceived as both a colorful spectacle and a frightening glimpse of the supernatural, and this has proved to be an irresistible combination. Scores of shops selling voodoo dolls, gris-gris and other exotic items attest to the fact that visitors to New Orleans can't help but buy into the mystique of voodoo. But all the hype aside, voodoo has remained a vital form of spiritual expression for thousands of practitioners.

It came to the New World via Haiti, aboard slave ships from West Africa. A hybrid American form of voodoo developed as people from many different tribal communities contributed various spiritual practices – including animism, snake worship, ancestor worship and making sacrifices to deities, called loas.

In Haiti, voodoo played an integral role in the slave rebellions that led to Haitian independence at the end of the 18th century. (Haiti is, in fact, the second-oldest nation in the Americas, having gained its independence just 28 years after the US.) Haitian vodoun cults became military units as vodoun priests urged their followers to fight for freedom, and the bravery of the rebels was probably abetted by vodoun charms carried for protection. Haitian landowners fled the island, many settling with their slaves in New Orleans. Liberated black Haitians also migrated to New Orleans, and this influx hastened the spread of voodoo.

In New Orleans, voodoo fused with Catholic beliefs as saints and deities became interchangeable for followers of both religions. And it grew extremely popular as more people turned to voodoo conjurers for advice, fortune telling, herbal medicine, love charms, and revenge against their enemies. These conjurers became increasingly influential in the community, and some of the more successful were wealthy and often controversial. Little is known about the famous 19th-century diviners with spectacular names like Dr John, Dr Yah Yah and Sanité Dédé. Even the known facts about the life of Marie Laveau, the most famous voodoo queen, baffle historians.

Voodoo shop in the Quarter

offerings as cigarettes, liquor, money, candles, toys, photographs and statuettes, and the walls are covered with colorfully patterned cloths. In a back room, a snake relaxes in its vivarium, and on occasion, with a transfixed countenance, Priestess Miriam will take it out and lift it up, the snake appearing to move its body according to her will. In an adjacent shop she does a modest trade in books, postcards, votive candles and other voodoo artifacts.

To neophyte eyes (all are welcome to visit the Voodoo Spiritual Temple), the temple is exotic and thrilling. Miriam, herself, is an impressive presence with her face beaming proudly and her hair radiating upward. But Miriam is unconcerned that her shop or the dramatic handling of the snake might conform to prevailing misconceptions about voodoo. She often seems dismissive of literal perceptions.

'It's okay that people should have a false opinion of voodoo, because all conceptions are initially false. Ideas progress toward the truth. Every thought is a misconception until something in it touches the thinker in some way. That's what voodoo is like. It is silent. It is an energy that vibrates into our minds.'

The Voodoo Spiritual Temple (☎ 504-522-9627), 828 N Rampart St, is usually open 9 am to 5 pm weekdays and sometimes on Saturday. Donations are accepted.

Historic Voodoo Museum

This fascinating museum has an intricately arrayed collection of voodoo artifacts and is worth visiting, even if it lacks an electrifying personality like Priestess Miriam (see the preceding section). It is recommended that groups of people call ahead and arrange for a guided tour, which will help shed light on the exhibited arcana. Individuals can come in with no prior arrangement, but guides will not be available.

The voodoo museum (☎ 504-523-7685), 724 Dumaine St, is open daily from 10 am to 8 pm. Admission costs $7.

Faulkner House

Considered by many the greatest American novelist, William Faulkner (1897–1962)

briefly rented an apartment in a townhouse on Pirate's Alley at the onset of his career. (At the time, the narrow passageway was called Orleans Alley.) In 1925, he moved to New Orleans from Mississippi, worked as a journalist at the *Times-Picayune* and met Sherwood Anderson, who helped him publish his first novel, *Soldier's Pay* (1926). He also contributed to the *Double Dealer*, a literary magazine published in New Orleans. The site of Faulkner's New Orleans stay is now home to Joe DeSalvo, who runs a bookstore, Faulkner House Books (☎ 504-524-2940), 624 Pirate's Alley, in the front rooms. It is open daily 10 am to 6 pm.

Custom House

The fortresslike US Custom House, at 423 Canal St, covers a square block. Construction on it was started in 1849 and supervised by Lieutenant PGT Beauregard, who later commanded Confederate forces. During the Reconstruction period after the Civil War, it served as the headquarters for African-Americans in the Republican party. During this period, blacks held a majority in the Louisiana legislature, and two African-Americans, Oscar J Dunn and Pickney Benton Stewart Pinchback, filled the office of lieutenant governor. Meetings took place in the enormous Marble Hall on the 2nd floor.

The building's construction is also interesting. A cofferdam surrounded the excavation while the foundation was under construction; cotton bales used to seal the dam gave rise to stories that the building was founded on bales of cotton. Despite a mat of cypress timbers, the foundation has settled about 3 feet under the weight of the brick-and-granite structure. All four sides of the building are identical.

St Louis Cemetery No 1

New Orleans' oldest cemetery (it dates to 1789), St Louis Cemetery No 1 has a rare beauty, enhanced by natural decay wrought by time, and if you visit just one cemetery, this one near the French Quarter is certainly a good choice. Time and a willingness to explore the grounds are key – wandering

And Now for the Boneyards

The best way to become intimate with the Crescent City's past is to visit one of its splendid boneyards.

As local historian Rob Florence notes in his book *New Orleans Cemeteries*, the city's necropoli exhibit all the diversity and style of the surrounding city. In death, as in life, the wealthy mingle with the poor, with just enough elbow room for all to express some – or, in many cases, ample – personal style. Ornate marble tombs rise to the sky like Gothic churches amid rows of inner-city apartments for the dearly departed (in fact, it is possible to rent!). Some neglected sections – postmortem ghettoes, if you will – have attracted the attention of preservationists (like Florence) who hope to restore these important emblems of a unique culture.

The vast majority of the graves in New Orleans are aboveground, and while no small amount of grandiosity inspired the more extravagant high-rise tombs, this practice of building up rather than down originated out of necessity. As early New Orleanians discovered, the region's high water table makes for wet digging; getting a buoyant wood coffin 6 feet underground meant first scuttling it to ensure that it would sink. Even then, a heavy rain could easily draw it back up to the surface again, and the dreadful sight of cadavers washing down flooded streets in the young city was not uncommon. So aboveground tombs constructed of brick and surfaced with plaster became the norm – and grandpa stayed put.

There are several distinct styles of tomb. The wall vaults that surround many cemeteries are often called 'ovens' because in the summer months they are known to get hot enough to slowly incinerate the bodies within. Once a body is decomposed – after a year and a day, according to a rule of thumb – these vaults can be reopened for the interment of a newly deceased person. Family tombs are the most common type of tomb. The cemetery equivalent of two-story, single-family homes, they are privately owned and typically house the remains of several generations. Stepped tombs, marked by steps on all sides, lack stable foundations and have a tendency to sink below ground. The stepped tomb is the only one of these five styles that is designed to contain just one body – all the others are intended for multiple burials. You are most likely to see these in St Louis Cemetery No 1, as they were no longer in use when later cemeteries were established. The grandest tombs are the society tombs, so called because they were funded by benevolent associations to ensure proper burial for members of a particular community. Many of these majestic monuments

at your leisure, you can appreciate the statuary and ornate ironwork and stumble on many historic tombs.

Voodoo queen **Marie Laveau** purportedly rests here. Fittingly, mystery surrounds her crypt. A family tomb not far from the entrance has the names Glapion, Laveau and Paris – all branches of Laveau's family – etched in its marble front, and a commemorative plaque identifies it as Laveau's 'reputed' resting site. Debates concerning *which* Marie Laveau – mother or daughter, if either – was actually buried here will never be resolved, but popular consensus has designated this as Laveau's memorial

(see the boxed text 'Hoodoo that Voodoo'). People come to scratch an 'x' in the tomb's plaster, presumably to pay their 'respects' to the voodoo queen. However, living members of the Glapion family consider this practice vandalism – there is no spiritual significance to these chicken scratches, and visitors are strongly discouraged from desecrating this or any other tomb.

In the adjacent family tomb rests **Ernest 'Dutch' Morial**, New Orleans' first black mayor. Morial was mayor from 1978 to 1986, and he died in 1989.

Civil Rights figure **Homer Plessy** also rests here, as do real-estate speculator

And Now for the Boneyards

are dedicated to particular 19th-century immigrant groups, who pooled funds to take care of their dead. Professions, religious denominations and branches of the military are also commonly represented. The larger society tombs have more than 20 vaults, and as these are reused over time, the population within these monuments can reach staggering numbers.

What really makes New Orleans' cemeteries visually enthralling is the incredible array of expressive, creative and often strange statuary and ornamentation that adorns many of the crypts. Angels praying with slumped wings and shoulders, grieving mothers tenderly cradling lethargic (perhaps dead) babies, wrought-iron crosses and gates, and stained-glass mosaics all play on light and shadow to create glorious surroundings for the dead. Some cemeteries are rapidly decaying, with broken tablets and loose plaster falling about the tombs, making them decidedly eerie.

Sadly, over the years many statues have been vandalized and even stolen. Some of the more elaborate pieces can fetch thousands of dollars on an underground market. New Orleans police recently exposed a ring of grave robbers, implicating Royal St antique dealers. Through this kind of thoughtless profiteering, the city is being drained of an attribute that should be preserved, treasured and protected.

There are more than 40 cemeteries in New Orleans. This book highlights just a few of them: St Louis Cemetery No 1, just outside the French Quarter; Lafayette Cemetery No 1, in the Garden District; Metairie Cemetery, just west of City Park; and St Roch Cemetery, a few blocks toward the lake from the Faubourg Marigny. See the appropriate neighborhood sections for more information on each of these sections, and see Organized Tours in the Getting Around chapter to find out about informative cemetery tours.

TOM DOWNS
Lavish tomb, Metairie Cemetery

Bernard de Marigny, architect **Henry Latrobe** and countless others.

The **Italian Mutual Benevolent Society Tomb** is the tallest monument in the cemetery. Like a lot of immigrant groups in New Orleans, the Italians formed a benevolent association to pool funds and assist in covering burial costs. The tomb is large enough to hold the remains of thousands. In 1969, to the obvious shock of families who own tombs here, a demented rape scene in the movie *Easy Rider* was filmed in St Louis Cemetery No 1. Note the headless statue called 'Charity' on the Italian Society tomb – urban myth maintains that actor

Dennis Hopper was responsible for tearing the head off.

The cemetery gates are open from 8 am to 3 pm, and you are free to wander around on your own. It can be hard to find all of the noteworthy sights, and a good walking tour will help you see all of them (see Walking Tours in the Organized Tours section, later in this chapter). Even if you aren't interested in a tour, it's a good idea to coincide your visit with one in order to ensure that you are not alone within the cemetery walls. Vandalism and statuary theft are the most common crimes here, but visitors ought to be mindful of their own safety as well.

LOUISIANA

TREMÉ DISTRICT (MAP 2)

Immediately to the lakeside of the French Quarter's early walls (now N Rampart St) grew New Orleans' first suburb, the Tremé District, an area traditionally populated by black Creoles. The celebrated architect who virtually rebuilt the St Louis Cathedral in 1849–51, JNB DePouilly, designed **St Augustine's Church** (☎ 504-525-5934), 1210 Governor Nicholls St. It opened in 1842 and is the second oldest African-American Catholic church in the country. One of its stained-glass panels depicts the Sisters of the Holy Family, the order of black Creole nuns founded in 1842 by Henriette Delille. Today, the small congregation works to provide food for the needy and to maintain the Tomb of the Unknown Slave.

Louis Armstrong Park

Most of the time the park that commemorates legendary jazz cornetist Louis Armstrong is quiet and considered unsafe to wander into alone, especially at night. The park is surrounded by fences that project an

Louis 'Satchmo' Armstrong

unwelcoming atmosphere. That's too bad, because a public space with a jazzy name on this particular spot makes sense.

In the mid-19th century, the area was just outside the city's walls (Rampart St, as the name suggests, was the town limit), and slaves and free persons of color met in a market here called Congo Square. African music and dances were permitted here, while in the rest of the US people of African descent were forced to repress their traditional culture. In the early 20th century, **Storyville**, a hotbed of early jazz music among other things (see the 'Storyville' boxed text), occupied the adjacent neighborhood, to the lake side of Basin St. Ironically, most of this area's historic architecture was razed in the 1950s to clear space for the park and for housing projects.

The park's **arched entrance**, on the corner of Rampart and St Anne Sts, is picturesque in a dated sort of way when the bare bulbs that spell 'Louis Armstrong Park' are lit up. (When the bulbs burn out, funds are not always available to replace them.) **Congo Square**, located on roughly the same spot as the 19th century market, is a quiet corner of the park where musicians sometimes play.

Seeing the **statue of Louis Armstrong** is the most popular reason to go inside the park, and while you're here, also check out the **bust of Sidney Bechet**, a tribute to the jazz clarinetist. Other structures here include the Mahalia Jackson Theater and the Municipal Auditorium, where music and other cultural events take place. The radio station WWOZ airs out of Armstrong park.

In the near future, the **New Orleans Jazz National Historic Park** (☎ 504 589-4806) will be based at Perseverance Hall in the Park. Tune in to WWOZ and other cultural media to learn about concerts and parades sponsored by the National Park Service.

Backstreet Museum

The term 'backstreet' refers to New Orleans' African-American traditions that have flourished independently from mainstream white culture since the city's early days. Despite prevailing poverty and the lack of official sanction and funding, many of the city's most distinctive traditions, such as jazz funerals, second line parades and the Mardi Gras Indians, have emerged in African-American neighborhoods like the Tremé District, the 9th ward and Back o' Town. (In fact, Back o' Town, a black neighborhood that formerly occupied the area around the current City Hall, yielded one of the city's greatest cultural icons, Louis Armstrong.) The backstreets are the routes that parades followed without permission of the police. No official permits were required to block traffic along thoroughfares in these neighborhoods.

Things have changed over the years. Today, most large parades must have a police escort and follow predetermined routes. Also, for many traditionalists jazz funerals have lost some of their cachet as drug dealers and gangsters have been honored with a jazz band accompanied by pistol-packing youths firing bullets into the sky. At the same time, funding has become less of a problem as some of these traditions have benefited from foundations created by Jazz Fest and the new Jazz National Historic Park.

Suitably, the former Blandin's Funeral Home, where many a jazz funeral started off, has been converted into this charming little museum, run by documentarian Sylvester Francis. The front parlors house exhibits of New Orleans' vital backstreet

Mardi Gras Indians

New Orleans' Black Indian gangs, otherwise known as the Mardi Gras Indians, are a dazzling example of authentic, unsanctioned inner-city artistry.

Indian gangs began appearing in Mardi Gras parades in the 1880s, when a group calling itself the Creole Wild West came masked in the feathered finery of Plains Indians. Since then, many gangs have come and gone, including the Wild Tchoupitoulas, Yellow Pocahontas and Wild Magnolias, led by now-legendary 'big chiefs' like Big Chief Jolly, Tootie Montana and Bo Dollis.

Masking Indian was from the beginning a serious proposition. Tribes became organized fighting units headed by a big chief, with spy boys, flag boys and wild men carrying out carefully defined roles. When two gangs crossed paths an intense confrontation would ensue as members of each tribe sized each other up. Often violence would break out. As is the case with many of Mardi Gras' strongest traditions, this was no mere game.

Over the years, Black Indian suits seem to have grown more extravagant. Although the Indians generally hail from the poorest, most crime-ridden parts of town, they devote extraordinary amounts of time and money toward the creation of their suits. Sewing, a point of pride among Indians, is done by hand, and it is an interesting sight to see tough, streetwise young men perusing the aisles in stores dealing in sewing supplies, sequins and brightly colored feathers. Layers of meaningful mosaics are designed and created in patterns of neatly stitched sequins. Multilayered feathered headdresses – particularly those of the big chiefs – are more elaborate and flamboyant than the headgear worn by Las Vegas show performers. The making of a new suit can take the better part of a year, and in the course of this arduous work, trickles of blood frequently seep into the suit's fabric as needles prick the sewer's nimble fingers.

On Mardi Gras, many suits are still unfinished. They are closer to completion by the time Indian gangs march the city's backstreets again weeks later, on St Joseph's night (roughly midway through the Lenten season), and have usually reached their full splendor by Super Sunday (which usually takes place sometime in April), when the gangs reappear to show off to crowds of admirers. On these occasions, visitors are not advised to go looking for Indians unless they are comfortable with venturing into the backstreets of this often violent city. For most people, the easiest way to see the Indians is to see them perform at Jazz Fest or at nightclubs.

culture with Indian suits, social aid and pleasure club banners, and some extraordinary, raw video footage. Francis, a photographer and filmmaker who has documented parades and backstreet events since 1980, is just the man to head up such a project. He's about as knowledgeable as anybody on these subjects, and his stated mission – to 'maintain the culture' – is the right spirit. His guided tours sometimes gloss over the fascinating details and history – there's really too much to say on any of these subjects in a short tour – but be sure to ask him lots of questions as he guides you from room to room. Occasionally, special events are held with stellar entertainment.

The Backstreet Museum (☎ 504-525-1733), 1116 St Claude Ave, is open odd hours (usually between 11 am and 3 pm, but call ahead to arrange a visit). This is a nonprofit organization and, as yet, not supported by cultural foundations – donations are strongly encouraged.

Mortuary Chapel

An unfounded fear of yellow fever contagion led the city to forbid funerals for fever victims at the St Louis Cathedral. Built in 1826 near St Louis Cemetery No 1, the Mortuary Chapel, 401 N Rampart St, offered hasty services to victims. Its bell tolled constantly during epidemics. In 1931, it was renamed Our Lady of Guadeloupe Church. Inside the chapel, you'll see a statue of St Jude, patron saint of impossible cases, and a curious statue of St Expedite, a saint who probably never existed – on the plaque there are quotation marks around his name.

FAUBOURG MARIGNY (MAP 2)

If you're heading downriver out of the French Quarter, by crossing Esplanade Ave you enter the Faubourg Marigny, which was developed by the colorful plantation owner Bernard Xavier Philippe de Marigny de Mandeville in the mid-19th century. Originally a Creole suburb, the Marigny today is one of New Orleans' gay hubs, and the neighborhood supports a vibrant bohemian scene as well. Some of the city's hottest

music clubs line Frenchmen St (see the Entertainment section for listings).

The Marigny is certainly worthy of an afternoon stroll to observe the rustic elegance of its buildings, most of which are private residences. **Washington Square**, at the heart of the neighborhood, is a peaceful and well-shaded park where you can escape the touristy French Quarter and rest your boots in peace.

St Roch Cemetery

Just a few blocks from the Faubourg Marigny (driving is recommended), St Roch cemetery qualifies as one of New Orleans' most intriguing resting places. That's no small feat! It is named after an obscure saint, a French native, whose prayers are said to have protected Rome from the Black Plague. During New Orleans' bouts with yellow fever, Catholics who prayed to St Roch (pronounced 'St Rock') are believed to have been spared, and the small chapel within the cemetery grounds was raised in his honor.

Entering this walled necropolis, you pass through an elegant wrought-iron fence, and the grounds' paved paths are lined with family and society tombs, some magnificent, some decrepit. But the real fascination here is within the chapel itself.

The small gated chamber to the right is filled with ex-votos, testaments to the healing power of St Roch. It is a strange collection of ceramic body parts (healed ankles, heads, breasts), prosthetics, leg braces and crutches, even false teeth. Marble floor tiles are inscribed with the words 'thanks' and 'merci.'

St Roch Cemetery is on St Roch Ave at N Roman St. It is open daily 9 am to 4 pm.

CBD & WAREHOUSE DISTRICT (MAP 3)

On the other side of Canal St from the French Quarter, the CBD (Central Business District) and the Warehouse District comprise the American commercial sector that was established after the Louisiana Purchase in 1803. Merchants, brokers and manufacturers from New England descended on

New Orleans and industriously began making it into a bustling port. Then called the Faubourg St Mary, the American sector developed into a nexus of offices, banks, warehouses and government buildings, with Lafayette Square at its core.

Canal St was the division between the French and American parts of town, and it still represents the boundary between Uptown and Downtown. That's no hollow distinction, as some citizens of New Orleans, set in their Uptown or Downtown ways, never seem to find any reason to cross Canal St. The wide median down the middle of Canal St was part of neither the French nor American sector and was therefore called the 'neutral ground' – in time, all medians in New Orleans would be referred to by that idiosyncratic term. Lee Circle marks the area's downtown boundary.

Toward the lake is the modern civic center, the **Louisiana Superdome** and new office buildings. This area was formerly part of the African-American district known as Back o' Town. It was in some ways an extension of Storyville, to the other side of Canal St, with Perdido St serving as a red-light district catering chiefly to a black clientele. Of course, Perdido St was immortalized by Juan Tizol's seductive composition (performed by the Duke Ellington Orchestra) that took its name.

The Warehouse District faded in its importance as the port shrank in size, but the 1984 Louisiana World Exposition focused attention on the area, as former warehouses were converted into live/work lofts and exhibit spaces for artists. A number of shops, restaurants and music clubs now make it an exciting part of town. The district is defined by Poydras St, Magazine St, Howard Ave, and the ri er. The riverfront has in recent decades been redeveloped with a convention center and a shopping mall.

Most of the sights in the CBD and Warehouse District are a good walk from the French Quarter, and with the exceptions of both streetcar lines and the No 11 Magazine bus, public transportation here isn't the best. Wear good walking shoes if you plan to explore thoroughly.

Historic Buildings

Across from Lafayette Square, the focal point of the old American sector, stands the monumental Greek Revival **Gallier Hall**, 545 St Charles Ave. Gallier Hall served as City Hall from its completion in 1853 until 1957. At the corner of Carondelet and Gravier Sts the lighted colonnade of the **Hibernia National Bank Building**, built in 1920, once rose above all of New Orleans. Its neighbor, the **New Orleans Cotton Exchange**, and the cornucopia of tropical produce gracing the entrance to the **United Fruit Company** building at 321 St Charles Ave hint at the industries upon which New Orleans was built. **Factors Row**, on Perdido St at Carondelet St, was the site where Degas painted *The Cotton Market in New Orleans* while visiting his uncle's office in 1873. South of Lafayette Square, the 13 identical red-brick houses lining **Julia Row**, between Camp and St Charles Sts, were built in 1832. The fan transoms above the doorways are indicative of the Row's aristocratic appeal – also note the servant's wings that project from the rear. The **lighthouse** at 743 Camp St was built in 1922 to house the Lighthouse for the Blind, and is now home to a glass store. Across the street, **St Patrick's Church**, 724 Camp St, was built during the 1830s by Irish immigrants making a break from the French-speaking Catholic parishes of New Orleans.

Canal St Ferry

A short ferry ride from the foot of Canal St to Algiers is the best way to get out on the water and admire New Orleans from a traditional river approach. Ride on the lower deck next to the water, and you're likely to see the state bird, the brown pelican. The state-run ferry is free and runs between 6 am and midnight, leaving Canal St on the hour and half-hour, returning from Algiers on the quarter-hour.

Woldenberg Park

Upriver from the Riverwalk along the riverfront, Woldenberg Park offers a promenade with seating and a grassy strip, where civic events and concerts are occasionally staged.

It's a comfortable place to eat a muffuletta while watching passersby and river traffic. The park ends at the aquarium and the Spanish Plaza, which continues to the entrance for the Riverwalk Mall.

Aquarium of the Americas

At the Aquarium of the Americas, operated by the Audubon Institute, you can go eye-to-eye with giant tropical creatures like the Amazon's arapaima *(Arapaima gigas)*, get a look at spotted moray eels *(Gymnothorax moringa)* and hawksbill turtles *(Etetmochelys imbricata)* in a walk-through Caribbean reef tube, or watch incredible specimens of gulf species through 14-foot-high windows. Mr Bill, the 40-year-old sawfish, shares the giant gulf tank with an oil platform that doesn't leak. Of course, the Mississippi River and Delta wetlands environments are also displayed.

The air-conditioned aquarium (☎ 504-581-4629) is at the foot of Canal St, adjacent to Woldenberg Park and next to the Canal St Ferry. Use the Riverfront streetcar if you don't want to walk from the French Quarter. Be sure to pick up a program listing times for special presentations such as the penguin feed and diver shows. The gift shop is a good place to pick up books on Louisiana's natural history.

It's open daily at 9:30 am; closing hours vary from 5 to 7 pm. Admission costs $13/10/6.50 for adults/seniors/children ages two to 12. Discounts on admission are offered in tourist magazines such as *Where*. You can get a variety of combination tickets that include the zoo, the aquarium and the Zoo Cruise aboard the *John James Audubon* riverboat, which docks here. (See Audubon Zoological Gardens in the Uptown section, later in this chapter, for more information on the Zoo Cruise.) For the best prices, double-check coupon offers against such combinations. Other combination tickets good for the aquarium and adjacent IMAX theater offer a savings of about 15%.

Harrah's Casino

The national casino chain has finally landed in New Orleans, and while one would think all manner of vice would be welcome in the Big Easy, Harrah's has had a hard go of it thus far. Within a year of opening, the casino was already reporting disappointing attendance and complaining about its enormous state tax burden. In spite of its best efforts to fit in, with a stately new brick home and a nightly Mardi Gras parade and the like, Harrah's still manages to make its guests feel like they're in Sparks, Nevada – not exactly what tourists to New Orleans had in mind. Nevertheless, people do trickle in for the casino gambling, buffet dining, free parking and hotel discounts. (Harrah's has no hotel of its own, but has agreements with some local hotels.)

Harrahs (☎ 800-427-7247) is near the foot of Canal St, at the corner of Canal and St Peters Sts. It's open 24 hours a day.

Top of the Mart

The World Trade Center, 2 Canal St, formerly known as the Trade Mart, was briefly the tallest building in New Orleans when its 33rd floor was completed in 1968. Special pumping and foundation technology had to be developed to keep such high-rises from sinking into the mud. Top of the Mart is also a member of the revolving observation deck club, which consists of some 87 buildings in North America. The slowly revolving Top of the Mart Lounge (☎ 504-522-9795) offers spectacular views for the price of a mixed drink (about $6).

Another option for a more limited high-rise view of the city is to ride the glass elevator, open 9 am to 5 pm, for $2/1 for adults/children.

Contemporary Arts Center

This tremendous exhibition and performance space occupies a renovated warehouse. Exhibits feature local and international artists. To give an idea of what the museum has to offer, the moving sculptures of Alexander Calder were featured recently. Dozens of multimedia exhibits appear each year in the gallery spaces. Also featured on the two stages are performances of plays, performance art, dance programs, musical concerts and video screenings.

Admission to the Contemporary Arts Center (☎ 504-528-3800), 900 Camp St, is $5/3/free for adults/seniors and students/children under 12, and it is free on Thursday. It's open Tuesday to Saturday 10 am to 5 pm and Sunday 11 am to 5 pm.

Louisiana Children's Museum

This educational museum is like a high-tech kindergarten. Generous corporate sponsors have helped create hands-on exhibits like a pint-sized supermarket, complete with stocked shelves and check-out registers, and a TV news studio, where young anchors can see themselves on monitors. Overall, the nonprofit museum and volunteers have done a good job in providing attractions for everyone from toddlers to 12-year-olds.

The children's museum (☎ 504-523-1357), 420 Julia St, is open Tuesday to Saturday 9:30 am to 4:30 pm and Sunday noon to 4:30 pm (also on Monday during the summer months). Children under 16 must be accompanied by an adult. Admission for anyone who is over the age of one year costs $5.

National D-Day Museum

The monumental D-Day Museum opened its doors June 2000 to extraordinary fanfare – the museum's founder, best-selling WWII historian Stephen Ambrose, was on hand, as were filmmaker Stephen Spielberg, actor Tom Hanks and the usual gaggle of network newsanchors. The museum is being touted as the only one of its kind, a 70,500-sq-foot structure presenting WWII with boats, planes, weapons, and uniforms used in the Allied effort. A special feature is the Higgins boat, the landing craft that enabled the Allies to invade Normandy by sea. The boats were designed and produced by New Orleans entrepreneur Andrew Higgins. According to Ambrose, General Dwight D Eisenhower said Higgins 'won the war for us.' The exhibits are enriched by detailed accounts and interpretations of what happened on the ground at Normandy and Iwo Jima and elsewhere during WWII. Oral history stations, with recorded first-hand accounts, and the Academy Award–winning

Just a few New Orleans cuties

film 'D-Day Remembered' (which will screen daily) add context and help to make this a worthwhile stop.

The National D-Day Museum (☎ 504-527-6012, www.ddaymuseum.org), 923 Magazine St, is open daily 9 am to 5 pm. Tickets cost $7/6/5 for adults/seniors/children.

Lee Circle

Called Place du Tivoli until it was renamed to honor Confederate General Robert E Lee after the Civil War, Lee Circle has lost some of its earlier cachet. Just a few dozen paces away, an elevated freeway structure disturbs some of the traffic circle's symmetry, and gas stations occupy two of its corners. Nevertheless, the **Robert E Lee monument** at its center, dedicated in 1884, still defiantly faces north. Also on Lee Circle, **K&B Plaza** is a modish office tower dating to 1963 with an indoor/outdoor sculpture gallery. The outdoor sculptures, featuring Isamu Noguchi's *The Mississippi*, can be viewed anytime; the indoor sections are open weekdays 8:30 am to 4:30 pm.

Confederate Museum

Dedicated to presenting Louisiana life during the Civil War, this museum is housed in gorgeous Memorial Hall, designed by Thomas Sully. Opened to the public in 1891, it's the oldest operating museum in the state. Entering the hall, with its exposed cypress ceiling beams and exhibition cases, is worth the price of admission, but the exhibit itself may also exceed expectations.

The museum focuses primarily on details, rather than on larger issues, but in so doing it humanizes the war to a greater degree than a broader historical study would. There doesn't seem to be a political objective here, apart from a few harsh words (mostly quoting federal officials in Washington, DC) about General Benjamin 'Beast' Butler, the locally reviled head of the Union forces that occupied New Orleans during the war.

Of course, there are rifles and pistols from the war, many of which are strangely beautiful artifacts of the industrial age. But what really makes this museum worth a visit is the endless collection of personal effects that belonged not only to officers and soldiers but to their families back home as well. Knapsacks, playing cards, tobacco pouches and undergarments are fastidiously arranged within the display cabinets. Curious items like Jefferson Davis' slippers and an impressive array of oddly styled hats help to shed light on life during the Civil War.

The Confederate Museum (☎ 504-523-4522), 929 Camp St, a block from Lee Circle, is open Monday to Saturday 10 am to 4 pm. Admission is $5/4/2 for adults/seniors and children two to 12/children two and under.

LOWER GARDEN DISTRICT (MAP 4)

While it might be said that this is the Garden District's bedraggled older brother, at one time the Lower Garden District was one of the country's poshest and most elegant suburbs. Developed in the early 19th century, the neighborhood reflected classical mindedness of the time. The city's elite built their mansions here, paying homage to the Greeks with columned galleries looking out over cultivated gardens burgeoning with pecan trees, banana trees, and fish ponds, and the district's streets were named to honor Greek gods, nymphs and muses. New Orleans' craze for cast-iron struck the mid-century denizens of the Lower Garden District, who adorned and fenced in their homes with ornate metallic designs, which today lend the area a rustic grace.

However, the neighborhood's glory was short-lived. The wealthy soon moved farther uptown to the newer, more fashionable Garden District, and many of the larger residences of the Lower Garden District were divided into smaller rental units so as to accommodate immigrants from Germany and Ireland, many of whom were employed on the docks. With the introduction of housing projects and a ramp to the Mississippi River bridge, the neighborhood rapidly deteriorated. The bridge ramp has since been demolished, reducing the traffic that once marred the neighborhood, and many boutique shops have moved to Magazine St. Similarly, an influx of professionals, artists and hipsters seeking fixer-uppers and cheap rents has breathed new life into the area. The block's surrounding Coliseum Square are rapidly being restored to their former splendor.

The neighborhood's well-shaded streets are well worth a daytime stroll, and a few houses deserve particular attention. At 1729 Coliseum St stands the **Goodrich-Stanley House**, built in 1837 by jeweler William M Goodrich. Goodrich sold the house to the British-born cotton factor Henry Hope Stanley, whose adopted son, Henry Morton Stanley, went on to become famous for finding the missing Scottish missionary, Dr David Livingstone. It was Stanley who first uttered the famous question, 'Dr Livingstone, I presume?' He was subsequently knighted and founded the Congo Free States.

Down the street, behind a handsome wrought-iron fence, is the papaya-hued **Grace King House**, 1749 Coliseum St, named for the Louisiana historian and author who lived there from 1905 to 1932. It was built in 1847 by banker Frederick Rodewald and features both Greek Ionic columns on the lower floor and Corinthian columns above.

Until 1852, the uppermost part of New Orleans ended at Felicity St, which is still paved with well-preserved cobblestones. The tastefully preserved **John T Moore House**, 1309 Felicity St, combines Victorian and Italianate styles and features sweeping balconies with elaborate cast-iron railings. It was built in 1880 by architect James Freret for his family; Moore, whose name the house bears, was Freret's father-in-law and originally owned the property. Opposite, at 1328 Felicity St, is a gorgeous entry door of beveled glass worth inspection (don't stare too hard – it might make the residents uneasy). Near the corner of Camp St, note the scars left in the cobblestones, evidence of uprooted streetcar tracks that once delivered wealthy residents to their front doors.

On the old **St Vincent's Infant Asylum**, 1507 Magazine St at Race St, a sign from the orphanage days still hangs from the finely styled cast-iron gallery in front. The orphanage was built in 1864 with assistance from federal troops occupying the city. It helped relieve the overcrowded orphanages filled with youngsters of all races who lost their parents to epidemics and war. The orphanage is now a guesthouse which offers afternoon teas (see St Vincent's Guesthouse & Tea Room in the Places to Stay and Places to Eat sections).

GARDEN DISTRICT (MAP 4)

Americans began settling farther beyond Canal St as development followed the streetcar tracks through the towns of Lafayette, Jefferson and Carrollton, virtually leaving the Lower Garden District in the dust. These upriver towns, laid out on expansive plantations, were populated almost exclusively by Americans, and the area reflects their wealth and taste for Greek Revival architecture. Commodious street plans allowed for larger, more ostentatious houses and lush gardens. Gradually, all of these towns became part of the city of New Orleans: Lafayette was annexed in 1852; Jefferson followed in 1870, and Carrollton in 1874.

Garden District Walking Tour

Like the French Quarter, the Garden District is a National Historic District, where there are architectural preservation ordinances that attempt to maintain the character of the area. Its boundaries are roughly those of the former city of Lafayette: St Charles Ave to Magazine St, between Jackson and Louisiana Aves. The area of greatest architectural interest is the lower half, below Washington Ave. Ironically, this premier enclave is not particularly safe to walk in at night. Plan to explore the neighborhood during daylight hours.

Begin your walk at Jackson Ave and St Charles Ave, and follow Jackson Ave toward the river. On the corner of Coliseum St is the **Buckner House**, 1410 Jackson St, built in 1856 for cotton merchant Henry S Buckner. The architect was Lewis E Reynolds. With wide galleries on four sides, it is the largest home in the Garden District. If it isn't feeding time, you'll notice that a finely conditioned Dalmatian watchdog complements the mansion's stateliness. Continue to the corner of Chestnut St and turn right.

At the corner of Philip and Chestnut Sts, the house at **1238 Philip St** was built in 1853 for merchant John Rodenberg. Semioctagonal bay windows rise above a brick wall covered with tropical mandevilla vine on the Chestnut St side of the house, contributing an interesting effect to the Greek Revival structure. This side wing with the bays was added in 1869.

Halfway down the same block of Chestnut St, a rustic **garage** benefits from an elegant decay rarely seen in the Garden District, as crumbling plaster is permitted to expose the underlying brick. The garage is your first view of the estate at **1315 First St**, a glorious Italianate-style house laced with cast-iron ornamentation. The house was designed by architect Samuel Jamison for cotton factor Joseph Carroll.

Before you stray from the corner of Chestnut and First Sts, backtrack a bit to **Anne Rice's house**, at 1239 First St. This attractive home, named Rosegate for the rose motif on the cast-iron fence, doesn't appear in any outward way to be haunted, although it does project some of the renowned occult author's eccentricity. An enormous porcelain dog – reportedly a gift from Anne to her husband, poet Stan Rice – stares whimsically from the 2nd-floor gallery. The Rices, who own several Uptown properties, graciously open their home to visitors on Monday from 1 to 3 pm; there is no charge

LOUISIANA

Anne Rice

for admission, but show up an hour ahead of time and wait in line even if it's raining.

Turn right on First St toward Prytania St. At 2343 Prytania St, the **Louise S McGehee School** occupies one of the Garden District's most impressive mansions. Built in 1872 – later than other grand mansions in the district – the house combines decorative French Second Empire and classic styles. The architect is unknown, but stylistic clues suggest it may have been James Freret. The building has been home to the all-girls academy since 1929.

Continue on Prytania St, heading toward Washington Ave. Past Second St, the **Chapel of Our Lady of Perpetual Help**, at No 2521, was designed in 1856 by Henry Howard. It was originally the home of Henry Lonsdale, a merchant who made fortunes in gunny-sacks and coffee. A block farther down Prytania St, the lovely **Charles Briggs House**, at No 2605, certainly stands out. Designed by James Gallier in 1849, the house's Gothic-style pointed-arch windows and Eliza-bethan chimneys are completely unique in the neighborhood.

On the corner of Fourth and Prytania Sts, **Colonel Short's Villa**, 1448 Fourth St, was home to a Confederate officer. The house was seized by federal authorities during the Civil War, but was returned at war's end to

Short, who lived there until his death in 1890. It is an impressive home, designed by architect Henry Howard, and it is distin-guished by a cornstalk cast-iron fence that outclasses the more famous cornstalk fence in the French Quarter (fewer layers of paint).

From Colonel Short's Villa, continue to Washington Ave, where you have several choices: You can explore Lafayette Ceme-tery No 1, walk a block on Washington Ave toward a rewarding lunch at Commander's Palace (see the Places to Eat section, later in this chapter) or turn right toward St Charles Ave and the streetcar.

Lafayette Cemetery No 1

Established in 1833 by the former City of Lafayette, this cemetery is divided by two intersecting paths that form a cross. You'll notice many German and Irish names on the aboveground graves, testifying that im-migrants were devastated by 19th-century yellow fever epidemics. Not far from the en-trance is a low tomb containing the remains of an entire family that died of yellow fever. Fraternal organizations and groups like the Jefferson Fire Company No 22 took care of their members and their families in large shared crypts. Some of the wealthier family tombs were built of marble, with elaborate detail rivaling the finest architecture in the district. But most tombs were constructed simply of inexpensive plastered brick. The cemetery filled within decades of opening, before the surrounding neighborhood reached its greatest affluence. By 1872, the prestigious Metairie Cemetery appealed to those with truly extravagant tastes.

An unusual event occurred at Lafayette Cemetery in July 1995, when author Anne Rice, who lives just a few blocks away, staged her own funeral here. She hired a horse-drawn hearse and a brass band to play dirges, and she wore an antique wedding dress as she laid down in a coffin – because, she said, she wanted to experience her funeral *before* she was dead. (The newsworthy stunt coincided with the release of one of Rice's novels, so it wasn't pure frivolity.)

The cemetery is on the corner of Prytania St and Washington Ave. The gates are closed at 2:30 pm – don't get locked in!

UPTOWN (MAP 5)

With St Charles Ave as its primary spine, Uptown New Orleans is a living – and splendid – architectural museum that contrasts sharply with the more crowded, Old World French Quarter. Block upon block of glorious mansions stand as symbols of the bustling trade and enterprise that made New Orleans one of the world's wealthiest cities in the mid-19th century.

Audubon Zoological Gardens

Once noted as one of the country's worst zoos, at a time when animals were housed in a rectangle of stately brick buildings near the present entrance, the Audubon Zoo is now among the country's best. This is the heart of the Audubon Institute, which also maintains Woldenberg Park and the Aquarium of the Americas.

The zoo is divided into distinct sections. **Louisiana Swamp** displays the flora and fauna amid a Cajun cultural setting, which shows how the Cajuns harvested Spanish moss for use as furniture stuffing, among other details. The authentic fishing camp is replete with shrimp trawls, crawfish traps and an oyster dredge. Alligators laze on the muddy bank of the bayou when they're not hibernating during the winter. Year-round in the exhibit, you'll see bobcats, red foxes, endangered Louisiana black bear and the alligator snapping turtle, a 200-pound giant that wiggles its pink tongue as bait. Human intrusions into the swamp environment are poignantly represented with a *traänasee* cutter, used by fish and game trappers to create access across shallow swamps.

The **Audubon Flight Exhibit** is best on quiet days, when you can enter the giant cage to sit and observe the bird species portrayed by ornithologist-artist John James Audubon in *Birds of America*. Of course, there are ducks galore, but you will be mesmerized by the brilliant plumage of species like the scarlet ibis and glossy ibis.

Most visitors are awed by the 'magnificent seven' in the **Reptile Encounter**, which displays representatives of the largest snakes in the world – from the king cobra that grows to over 18 feet in length to the green anaconda that reaches 38 feet.

At **Butterflies in Flight**, you enter a humid greenhouse that is home to thousands of fluttering exotic butterflies, as well as tropical birds and plants. It's worth the additional $2 admission cost, but shed any unnecessary clothes before entering.

The Audubon Zoo (☎ 504-861-2537), on the river-side of Magazine St and Audubon Park, is accessible from the French Quarter via the Zoo Cruise and the No 11 Magazine bus, or you can take the St Charles Ave streetcar and walk 1½ miles through shady Audubon Park. The zoo is open weekdays from 10 am to 5 pm and until 6 pm on weekends. Zoo admission costs $8.75 for adults, $4.75 for seniors and $4.50 for children. Look for discount coupons in tourist magazines such as *Where*.

Zoo Cruise The Audubon Zoo Cruise offers a unique way to see the zoo and the Aquarium of the Americas (see the CBD & Warehouse District section for information on the aquarium). Combined discount tickets for the riverboat cruise, zoo and aquarium are available.

The most basic combination packages are the cruise-zoo-aquarium-IMAX combination ($35/19 for adults/children) and the cruise-zoo-aquarium combination ($28/14).

The boat departs from the zoo at 10 am, noon, 2 and 4 pm. It leaves for the zoo at 11 am, 1, 3 and 5 pm, departing from the Audubon Landing near the Australian Outback exhibit.

Tulane University

Tulane University (☎ 504-865-4000) was founded in 1834 as the Medical College of Louisiana in an attempt to control the repeated cholera and yellow fever epidemics. In 1847, the University of Louisiana merged with the school. Paul Tulane's $1 million donation in 1883 initiated significant expansion – plus it immortalized his name. The highly regarded medical school has since moved downtown to Tulane Ave. Tulane's law program is also well respected.

Newt Gingrich, former speaker of the US House of Representatives, received his PhD in history from Tulane in 1971. The conservative politician has admitted to smoking pot while at Tulane – a response to President Clinton's 'didn't inhale' confession – adding that 'it was the wrong thing to do.' Other distinguished alumni include Amy Carter, daughter of former US president Jimmy Carter, who enrolled at Tulane for graduate art-history studies.

The **University Center**, across Freret St on McAlister Drive, features a bookstore, ATM and a box office (☎ 504-861-9283) that sells tickets for sporting and special events. Downstairs there's a bulletin board for information on apartment-rentals, sublets and ride shares. The *Hullabaloo*, the campus newspaper published during the school year, is a good source for campus happenings, such as free Friday open-air concerts and work opportunities.

Amistad Research Center The Amistad Research Center is one of the nation's largest repositories specializing in African-American history. It's rotating exhibits offer insight on ethnic heritage you're not likely to get from any other source.

Even the story behind the research center itself gives pause for thought. In 1839 *La Amistad* sailed from Havana with 53 illegally abducted West Africans. Three days from port, the Africans revolted and ordered the Cubans to sail into the rising sun toward Africa, but the Cubans reversed direction every night. After two months of aimless oscillations, *La Amistad* arrived at Long Island and the Africans were jailed and charged with piracy and murder. Their legal defense, the Amistad Committee, was aided by Lewis Tappan and former US President John Quincy Adams. The case went to the US Supreme Court, which ruled that the Africans were free. The Amistad Committee evolved into the American Missionary Association, which founded a Race Relations department at Fisk University in

Nashville, Tennessee. The Amistad Research Center developed from this enterprise, and moved to New Orleans in 1969.

At the center, a video of the Amistad adventure is shown for free. The displayed works of art from the Aaron Douglas Collection are another reason to drop by – a few of the works are copied for sale.

The archive (☎ 504-865-5535) is in Tilton Hall, 6823 St Charles Ave, and it's open weekdays 8:30 am to 5 pm.

Hogan Jazz Archive This specialized research library is worth visiting if you're seriously into jazz history, although most of its great wealth of material is not on exhibit. The Storyville Room is fascinating, with its emphasis on Jelly Roll Morton, who played piano in the district's bordellos during the early 20th century. The collection includes stacks of 78rpm recordings, including early sides recorded by the Original Dixieland Jazz Band in 1917, and you can ask to listen to rare tracks if you like. There's also a wealth of oral histories, photos and early concert posters. Curator Bruce Raeburn is a great man to talk to if you come with serious questions about jazz.

The jazz archive (☎ 504-865-5688), 304 Joseph Merrick Jones Hall, 3rd floor, on Freret St, is open weekdays 8:30 am to 5 pm.

Newcomb Art Gallery H Sophie Newcomb College (☎ 504-865-5565) was founded in 1886 through a gift of Josephine Louise Newcomb in memory of her daughter. It was the first degree-granting women's college in the US to be established as a coordinate division of a men's university. It has its own campus of red-brick buildings facing Broadway, adjacent to the main Tulane campus.

The Newcomb Art Gallery is a highlight of any tour of the Tulane campus. It features a permanent exhibit of the college's collection, including Newcomb Pottery, rotating exhibits from the university's art collection, nationally recognized traveling exhibits and contemporary student and faculty exhibits. Flanking the gallery entrance are two important Tiffany stained-glass triptychs depicting figurative scenes, The Resurrection and The Supper at Emmaus. The gallery is open weekdays 9 am to 4 pm. Admission is free.

ESPLANADE RIDGE & BAYOU ST JOHN (MAP 6)

Graced with a variety of residential architectural styles, the placid Bayou St John is a pleasant place to stroll. It's actually the oldest part of the city – French Canadians began settling the area before New Orleans was actually founded. Long before that, Native Americans used the waterway to reach a ridge along what is now Esplanade Ave, and this portage was the shortest link between Lake Pontchartrain and the Mississippi River. When the explorers Iberville and Bienville learned of this path, they decided it was the ideal place to settle. A canal built by Governor Carondelet later extended the bayou to the edge of the French Quarter, nearly connecting the lake and the river. Despite the waterway's commercial use, the area remained somewhat removed from the city, a place where mysterious nocturnal voodoo rituals were held well into the 19th century. Navigation ended with the filling of the canal in 1927.

Like Uptown, the Esplanade Ridge neighborhood and the area around nearby Bayou St John were prestigious addresses in the mid-19th century (but while Uptown was the domain of transplanted Americans, Esplanade Ave was home to wealthy Creoles). This part of town was hit hard by the urban decay of the mid-20th century. In recent years, residents have restored their district to its former grandeur. Upscale restaurants and shops are now clustered near the corner of Esplanade Ave and Ponce de Leon St.

This part of town is not heavily touristed for most of the year, but in late May, when the New Orleans Jazz and Heritage Festival takes over the Fair Grounds, music lovers suddenly flock in by the thousands. See the boxed text 'New Orleans Jazz & Heritage Festival,' later in this chapter, for more information on Jazz Fest.

The neighborhood is conducive to casual strolling, with its sidewalks shaded by live oaks, stately old homes, the bayou and one of New Orleans' best maintained cemeteries. A regular stop here is the **Pitot House**, 1440 Moss St, a French colonial plantation-style house built in 1799. James Pitot, the first mayor of the incorporated city of New Orleans, acquired it in 1810. The Pitot House (☎ 504-482-0312) is open to the public Wednesday to Saturday from 10 am to 3 pm; admission is $3/2/1 for adults/seniors/children.

A walk along the bayou will surely tempt you to cross **Magnolia Bridge**, a restored iron span built around the turn of the 20th century. It is now a pedestrian and bicycle crossing. Keep your eyes peeled for turtles along the water's edge. In early morning, you can often see at least one old-timer working his crab trap in the bayou.

On the same side of the waterway and just a block down from the Pitot House, **Our Lady of the Rosary Rectory**, 1342 Moss St, was built as the home of Evariste Blanc, probably in 1834. It exhibits a combination of styles characteristic of the region. The high-hipped roof and wraparound gallery, reminiscent of West Indies houses, were actually the preferred styles of the early French Canadians who settled Bayou St John. Classic details indicate this building is of a later period. At the intersection with Grand Route St John, the **Old Spanish Custom House**, 1300 Moss St, occupies a site that was the plantation of Jean Francois Huchet de Kernion from 1736 to 1771. The present French colonial plantation-style house was probably built after 1807 for Captain Elie Beauregard.

On the opposite side of the bayou, creation of the whimsical arch supports of the **Mullen House**, 1415 Moss St, is attributed to the ship carpenters employed by Thomas Mullen, who was a partner in the Mullen & Kennedy Shipyard near the Esplanade Bridge in the 1850s. Among the airy California bungalows in the Arts & Crafts style is the notable **Dabezies House**, at 1455 Moss St. Its cobblestones once paved Decatur St.

At the Esplanade Bridge, you can see the entrance to City Park, on the left, and **Beauregard Monument**, dedicated to the French Creole confederate general. Just a block away, **St Louis Cemetery No 3** was established in 1854 at the site of the old Bayou Cemetery and is worth strolling through for at least a few minutes (longer if you're a cemetery enthusiast). Inside its gates, James Gallier Jr designed a striking monument to his mother and father, who were lost at sea.

CITY PARK (MAP 6)

At 1500 acres, City Park is the nation's fifth largest urban park – but relatively little of the area has a true park-like quality. The city acquired the property in 1850 and began improvements in 1896. It is well known for its great live oaks draped with Spanish moss and its bayou lagoons, especially along the narrow strip fronting City Park Ave. Unfortunately, I-610 slices through the park, ruining the solitude and habitat of the central area. The larger, lakeside portion has been reduced to four golf courses plus a riding stable. Most visitors just explore the remaining one-third on the river-side of I-610 where there are restaurants, kiddie rides and tennis courts as well as the large New Orleans Museum of Art. Even here, nature is almost lost to the accumulation of 'improvements' like redundant stadiums, roads and parking lots. For information about outdoor activities in the park, see the Activities section, later in this chapter.

From the French Quarter, City Park (☎ 504-482-4888) is easily reached aboard the No 48 Esplanade bus. Esplanade Ave ends at the park entrance. The park is closed to bicyclists in the evening, but the issue is moot as cyclists will not find that City Park offers a convenient route to the lakeshore.

New Orleans Museum of Art

Founded in 1910, the original gift from philanthropist Isaac Delgado continues to grow as the collection of fine art is now valued at more than $200 million and covers three large floors. On the 1st floor are major traveling exhibits, which typically attract crowds and feature associated lectures, films

and workshops. A sampler of recent exhibitions included Fabergé in America, Sacred Arts of Haitian Voodoo and Andrew Wyeth: the Helga Pictures.

If you're not here for a special exhibit, you might consider starting with the 3rd-floor permanent exhibits, where pre-Columbian, Native American and African art set the stage for European influences, shown on the 2nd floor.

The New Orleans Museum of Art (☎ 504-488-2631) is reached from the French Quarter by the No 48 Esplanade bus. You can also get there from the Riverbend area aboard the No 90 Carrollton bus. The Courtyard Cafe offers lunch and snacks from 10:30 am to 4:30 pm. Admission is $6 for adults, $5 for seniors and $3 for children age three to 17. The museum is open Tuesday to Sunday 10 am to 5 pm.

Botanical Garden

This 7-acre garden was built by the WPA and features a showpiece art deco pool and fountain. Both native and exotic plant specimens from tropical and semitropical environments stimulate the sight and smell. Admission to the botanical garden (☎ 504-482-4888) is $3/1 for adults/children. It's open Tuesday through Sunday 10 am to 4:30 pm.

Carousel Gardens & Storyland

For children, the main attractions to City Park are these charmingly outdated theme parks on Victory Ave.

The centerpiece of Carousel Gardens is a restored antique carousel, housed in a 1906 structure with a stained glass cupola. In the 1980s, residents raised $1.2 million to restore the broken animals, fix the squeaky merry-go-round and replace the Wurlitzer organ. Other rides on the grounds include a small roller coaster, a tilt-a-whirl and bumper cars. The City Park Rail Road is also boarded here. Admission to Carousel Gardens is $1 (children under two are free). Rides cost an additional $1 each, and an $8 pass will allow unlimited rides for the day.

Storyland (☎ 504-483-9382) has no rides, but the park's fairytale statuary is plenty of fuel for young imaginations. Children can play amongst – and climb upon – such larger-than-life figures as the Jabberwocky from *Alice in Wonderland*, or enter the mouth of the whale from *Pinocchio*. If these characters seem strangely similar to Mardi Gras floats, it's because they were created by master float-builder Blaine Kern. Storyland is open Wednesday through Sunday, usually from 11 am to 2:30 pm (later on weekends). Admission costs $2 ($3 during the Christmas season, when it's lit up during the evening).

Dueling Oaks

Hot-headed violence is not new to New Orleans. During the 19th century, challenges to Creole honor often led to a meeting behind St Louis Cathedral or at the great oaks on the Allard Plantation near Bayou St John, where both parties could settle the offense with guns. The famous duel between a Baton Rouge newspaper editor who offended Alcée La Branche refutes the notion that the pen is mightier than the sword. After three attempts in which the combatants missed each other from 40 yards away, the fourth duel felled the editor. Despite the name, only one of the famous trees still stands near the Museum of Art.

LAKESHORE PARK

Locals cool off, bike, skate or just check each other out for nearly 10 miles along a narrow shoreline strip fronting Lake Pontchartrain. The park extends from the Southern Yacht Club, marked by the lighthouse, to the Inner Harbor Canal. You shouldn't enter the polluted water, but the park beats driving across the mind-numbing Pontchartrain Causeway to see the lake. Near the yacht club are numerous restaurants suitable for lunch.

METAIRIE CEMETERY

Having visited other New Orleans cemeteries doesn't quite prepare you for the over-the-top extravagance and stunning architectural splendor of Metairie Cemetery. Established in 1872 on a former race-

track (the grounds, you'll notice, still follow the oval around which racehorses once galloped), Metairie Cemetery is the most American of New Orleans' cities of the dead, and, like the houses of the Garden District, its tombs appear to be attempts at one-upmanship.

Obviously, this is the final resting place of many of New Orleans' most prominent citizens. William Charles Cole Claiborne, Louisiana's first American governor, is here, as is Confederate General PGT Beauregard. Jefferson Davis was laid to rest here, only to be moved to Richmond, Virginia, two years later. Trumpet player Louis Prima occupies a family tomb inscribed with the refrain from his signature song, 'Just a Gigolo' – 'When the end comes they'll know/I was just a gigolo/Life goes on without me.'

But the real highlight here is the architecture. Many of the family tombs and monuments gracing Metairie Cemetery's concentric ovals are stunning, bringing together stone, bronze and stained glass. The statuary here is often elegant, touchingly sad, even sensual. Highlights include the **Brunswig mausoleum**, a pyramid guarded by a sphinx statue, the **Estelle Theleman Hyams monument**, with its stained glass casting a somber blue light over a slumped, despondent angel statue, and the **Moriarty monument**, the reputed 'tallest privately owned monument' in the entire country.

Visitors can drop by the Lakelawn Funeral Home (☎ 504-486-6331), 5100 Pontchartrain Blvd, and select either the Soldier, Statesmen, Patriots, Rebels or Great Families and Captains of Commerce self-guided tours. You will be given a map and loaned a recorded cassette and tape player (no charge).

Seeing everything on the 150-acre grounds is most easily accomplished by car. The cemetery is on Pontchartrain Blvd at its intersection with Metairie Rd. Admission is free. Tape tours take about an hour, but stretching this out by getting out of your car for a closer look at the tombs is highly recommended.

ACTIVITIES

New Orleans is a great city to **bicycle** in – it's flat and compact. Just watch out for those mammoth potholes, which can swallow skinny tires. Fat-tire mountain bikes are recommended. For casual bicycling, pedal through City Park and around the lakefront, or loop around Audubon Park and up the riverside Levee Park. See the Getting Around section, later in this chapter, for the skinny on tours and rentals.

City Park Riding Stables (☎ 504-483-9398), 1001 Filmore Ave, offers English-style **horseback rides** accompanied by an instructor. The cost is $20 per hour if you're with a group or $25 per half hour if you want private lessons. No unaccompanied riders are allowed. Riders must be over six years old and have hard-soled boots. The stables are open 9 am to 7 pm weekdays and close at 5 pm on weekends. In Audubon Park, Cascade Stables (☎ 504-891-2246), 6500 Magazine St, offers **pony rides** for the kids.

For **tennis** enthusiasts, the City Park Tennis Center (Map 6; ☎ 504-483-9382) offers 36 lighted courts. Both hard and soft courts are available along with locker rooms, racquet rental, a pro shop and lessons from USPTA pros. It's open Monday to Thursday 7 am to 10 pm, and Friday to Sunday 7 am to 7 pm.

City Park offers four 18-hole **golf** courses. Call Bayou Oaks Clubhouse & Restaurant (☎ 504-483-9396), 1040 Filmore Ave, for information. Only a streetcar ride from downtown, the 18-hole Audubon Park golf course is open to the public.

Audubon Park and Levee Park are ideal for **in-line skating** and **jogging**. Blade Action Sports (☎ 504-891-7055), 6108 Magazine St, rents skates near the levee. Lakeshore Park is also a great place to rollerblade, because of its long, paved trails.

The Lee Circle YMCA (Map 3; ☎ 504-568-9622), 920 St Charles Ave, has complete and reasonably priced **fitness** facilities, in-

---

What's Free

Nearly every day, some of the same musicians who perform in New Orleans clubs at night also play in front of the Cabildo on Jackson Square during the afternoon. Street performers can range from solo saxophonists bouncing mournful notes off the front of the St Louis Cathedral to complete brass bands. Some may be youths that get together to jam away from the marching bands, while others are between jobs. Mimes, tarot card readers, artists and other street performers are also part of the passing show. Musicians also perform on Royal St when the street is closed to traffic. You'll run into more buskers in front of Cafe du Monde and elsewhere in the French Quarter. The price of admission is whatever you decide to drop into the hat.

Street festivals, such as the French Quarter Festival, are free and always feature good music. Second line parades, if you can catch one, are a unique New Orleans tradition that happens nearly every Sunday around town, usually in the 'back o' town,' a land of housing projects and ghettoes where tourists rarely venture. However, second lines do from time to time cross major thoroughfares like St Charles Ave, or run right by the Marriott Hotel near the Civic Center, and if you happen to be standing on the corner as one passes by, stop your standing and join the masses. A good second line will have thousands of people, one or two marching bands, and dozens of beer and food vendors, and are a helluva good time.

The NPS Jazz Historic Park also sponsors second line parades that tend to pass near the French Quarter, and these may well be more suitable for visitors. The park also puts on free concerts and jazz-related events. NPS walking tours of the French Quarter are free, but you have to show up early to get a coveted pass. For more information about NPS-related events, see Tourist Offices in the Information section and Walking Tours in the Organized Tours section.

cluding a swimming pool appropriate for laps. Day use is $8.

COOKING CLASSES

You are not likely to learn how to make complex French sauces in a short, introductory cooking demonstration, but you can learn how to make a simple one-dish Cajun or Creole meal, like jambalaya.

The **New Orleans School of Cooking** (Map 2; ☎ 504-525-2665, 800-237-4841), 524 St Louis St, offers two courses a day. A three-hour demonstration, from 10 am to 1 pm ($25) includes a meal consisting of gumbo, jambalaya, bread pudding and pralines served with a Dixie beer. A two-hour course, from 2 to 4 pm ($20), dispenses with the eating. Both courses emphasize everyday Creole and Cajun cooking and give students a basic introduction to the area's geography and history, to better explain how Creole cuisine evolved. Call ahead to make reservations.

Cookin' Cajun (Map 3; ☎ 504-586-8832), in the Creole Delicacies Gourmet Shop at the Riverwalk Mall, is a two-hour demonstration (it leaves out the geography and history lesson), and the menu typically features either gumbo or jambalaya. The cost is $18. Morning courses (10 am) are usually filled by reservations. Walk-in classes are held every day at different hours; call for times and to reserve a spot.

In the CBD, there is the **Crescent City Farmer's Market** (Map 3; ☎ 504-861-5898, www.loyno.edu/ccfm), 700 Magazine St at Girod, which has cooking demonstrations by one of New Orleans' celebrated chefs (a different chef featured each week) every Saturday at 10 am. The instructors teach you local cooking techniques using local produce and seafood, with samples. It's absolutely free. Check it out.

ORGANIZED TOURS

Although independent travelers sometimes scoff at being herded about, group tours can be an entertaining crash course on local history and architecture and can serve to orient new visitors to potentially unsafe areas.

Walking Tours

Jean Lafitte National Historical Park and Preserve (Map 2; ☎ 504-589-2636), 419 Decatur St, offers free daily 90-minute walking tours of the French Quarter. Tours, which begin at 10:30 am, are limited to 30 people, and it is advisable to show up soon after the NPS visitor center opens at 9 am to pick up a pass – the policy is that one person gets just one pass, so if you plan to sleep in, you can't send your loyal friend to pick up both of your passes. The rangers are fairly fastidious when it comes to this rule.

Knowledgeable volunteers affiliated with the nonprofit Friends of the Cabildo (☎ 504-523-3939) lead daily two-hour French Quarter walks emphasizing history, architecture and folklore. Tours cost $10/8 for adults/seniors and children over 13. As a bonus, the price includes admission to two of the four Louisiana State Museums: the Cabildo, the Presbytère, the Old US Mint or the 1850 House. Tours start at the 1850 House museum store, 523 St Ann St, at 10 am and 1:30 pm Tuesday to Sunday and at 1:30 pm Monday.

Historic New Orleans Walking Tours (☎ 504-947-2120) has a variety of tours that are dense with information. The company was founded by author Robert Florence, one of the city's leading authorities on cemeteries. His two-hour cemetery-voodoo tour ($15/13), which includes a visit to St Louis Cemetery No 1 and Miriam Williams' Voodoo Spiritual Temple, is highly recommended. The company also offers a Garden District tour ($14/12), including Lafayette Cemetery No 1, and a French Quarter Mystique tour ($12/10) that delves into the facts and myths of the Vieux Carré.

Robert Batson's well-regarded Gay Heritage Tour (☎ 504-945-6789) gets high marks for its humor and historical insight. The 2½-hour walk through the French Quarter is chock-full of colorful anecdotes about local characters, including Tennessee Williams, Ellen DeGeneres and Clay Shaw. All are more than welcome to come along, regardless of sexual orientation. Tours depart from the Alternatives shop (909 Bourbon St) on

Saturday at 2 pm and the cost is $15 per person.

Carriage Rides

Tour guides offering mule-drawn carriage rides through the French Quarter are certified by the city – which means that they have at least a modest understanding of the Quarter's history. However, you should be aware that Mark Twain's admonition, 'Get your facts first, then you can distort them all you please,' certainly applies to the carriage-guide business. Historical embellishment is commonplace.

Carriages depart day and night, until midnight, from Jackson Square. You will not be disappointed if you consider the tours to be fun orientation rides. Half-hour tours for up to four people cost $40.

African-American Heritage Tours

This company (☎ 504-288-3478) offers three-hour city-wide van tours that explore the African-American heritage of New Orleans. The company also gives van tours of a French-speaking Cajun village, with an emphasis on zydeco music, and plantation tours. The van will swing by to pick you up at your hotel. Tickets cost $30 for the city tour, $45 for the Cajun tour and $50 for the plantation tour ($75 with lunch included).

Riverboat Cruises

Take a paddle wheel cruise downriver aboard the *Creole Queen* and visit the 1815 Battle of New Orleans site at Chalmette, a unit of Jean Lafitte National Historical Park and Preserve (☎ 504-589-4430). A brief walking tour of the battlegrounds and Beauregard House is included in the 2½-hour excursion. Cruises leave daily at 10:30 am and 2 pm from the Spanish Plaza at the foot of Canal St. Tours cost $15 for adults and $8 for children ages three to 12 (all pay an additional $6 to throw a lunch into the bargain). Another, more mundane boat, the *Cajun Queen*, offers four daily one-hour sightseeing cruises downriver, departing from the Aquarium Dock at 11:30 am, 1, 2:30, and 4 pm. Tickets cost $10 for adults and $5 for children. Reservations

and information about either cruise are available from New Orleans Paddlewheels (☎ 504-529-4567, 524-0814). Tickets may be purchased at the Aquarium Dock and the Spanish Plaza Dock.

If sightseeing isn't your thing, you can dine and dance ($45/22 for adults/children) or just dance ($22/13) to live jazz aboard the *Creole Queen* (☎ 504-524-0814, 800-445-4109) as she cruises the Mississippi River. You should board at the Canal St Wharf at 7 pm for the boat's 8 pm departure.

Discordant calliope sounds announce the boarding of the *Natchez*, a 1975 steam-powered paddle wheeler, which departs for two-hour harbor cruises from a dock behind the Jackson Brewery at 11:30 am and 2:30 pm daily. Tickets cost $14.75 for adults and $7.25 for children between six and 12 years old. Tickets are sold at the dock by the New Orleans Steamboat Company (☎ 504-586-8777).

SPECIAL EVENTS
January

Sugar Bowl – This NCAA football game between two of the nation's top-ranked college teams takes place on or around New Year's Day. It originated in 1935 and fills the Superdome to capacity; call ☎ 504-525-8573 for information.

Battle of New Orleans Celebration – On the weekend closest to January 8, volunteers stage a re-creation of the decisive victory over the British in the War of 1812 at the original battleground in Chalmette National Historical Park (☎ 504-589-4430). A noontime commemoration on Sunday in Jackson Square features a military color guard in period dress.

Martin Luther King Jr Day – On the third Monday in January, a charming midday parade, replete with brass bands, makes its way from the Bywater to the Tremé District down St Claude Ave to commemorate King's birthday.

February

Mardi Gras Parades – The greatest free show on earth really heats up during the three weeks before Mardi Gras, culminating with multiple parades each day. Routes vary, but the largest krewes stage massive parades with elaborate floats and marching bands that run along portions of St Charles Ave and Canal St. None enter the French Quarter.

Mardi Gras Day – In February or early March, the outrageous activity reaches a crescendo as the French Quarter nearly bursts with costumed celebrants. It all ends at midnight with the beginning of Lenten penitence.

March

Black Heritage Festival – On the second weekend in March, the city celebrates African-American contributions to food, music and the arts at the Audubon Zoo (☎ 504-861-2537).

St Patrick's Day – Just when you thought the city would calm down, the festivities pick up again on March 17. On the actual day, a major Irish pub crawl through the French Quarter follows a parade through the Irish Channel, starting at Race and Annunciation Sts (☎ 504-565-7080). The prior weekend (if the 17th falls on a weekday) also features a motley parade, beginning at Molly's at the Market (☎ 504-525-5169), where a boisterous group tosses cabbages to the lasses in exchange for kisses.

Tennessee Williams Literary Festival – The end of March features five days dedicated to the great American playwright, with plays (by Williams and others), lectures (on such subjects as humor and the art of storytelling), literary and gay heritage walking tours, nostalgic panels starring Williams' surviving chums and – natch! – a cocktail party. The festival runs through the last weekend of the month, with events held at Le Petit Théâtre du Vieux Carré and elsewhere in the French Quarter. For more information, call ☎ 504-486-7096.

Isleños Arts & Crafts – The Canary Islanders who settled in St Bernard Parish celebrate their folklife (a culture based on natural resources) during the last week of March. They stage demonstrations and host a crawfish-eating contest at the Los Isleños Museum (☎ 504-682-0862), 7 miles south of Chalmette and 1½ miles east of Poydras on Hwy 46.

April

Spring Fiesta – Since 1935, locals have donned antebellum outfits to host visitors in historic homes that are normally closed to the public. Tours are given over a five-day period in April or May beginning on the first Friday after Easter. Fees vary, but you can find out the details by contacting the Spring Festival Association (☎ 504-581-1367), 826 St Ann St, New Orleans, LA 70116.

Crescent City Classic – Runners from all over the globe compete in a 10km race from the Jackson Brewery to Audubon Park on the first Saturday of the month. Contact the *Times-Picayune* (☎ 504-861-8686) for details.

French Quarter Festival – In this underrated festival, 12 stages throughout the French Quarter showcase New Orleans music, plus the local lifestyles, during the second weekend of April.

Jazz Fest – The Fair Grounds Race Track (and, at night, the whole town) reverberates with good sounds, plus food and crafts, through two weekends in the latter part of April and early May. See the boxed text 'New Orleans Jazz & Heritage Festival' for details.

May

Tomato Festival – In Chalmette, Our Lady of Prompt Succor Church (☎ 504-271-3441), 2320 Paris Rd, features a pre-Miss Louisiana beauty pageant along with musical performances on the first weekend of the month. Some serious Southern business.

June

French Market Tomato Festival – During the first weekend of the month, you'll find food and entertainment in the French Market (☎ 504-522-2621).

Grand Prix du New Orleans – If you thought crossing the street in New Orleans was dangerous before, check out what happens when it becomes a racetrack on the second weekend of June.

Carnival Latino – On the last weekend in June, the Riverfront comes alive with the sounds and flavors of Latin America. For information, contact the New Orleans Hispanic Heritage Foundation (☎ 504-522-9927).

July

Independence Day – Since the Civil War, folks in these parts have regarded July 4, with evident disdain, as a 'Yankee' holiday. Nevertheless, New Orleanians are not known to pass up a good time. Food stalls and entertainment stages are set up on the Riverfront and fireworks light up the night sky.

Essence Festival – On Independence Day weekend, *Essence Magazine* sponsors star-studded musical performances at the Superdome. Started in 1995, the event has featured Stevie Wonder and other renowned black recording artists. Call ☎ 504-941-5100 for details.

Wine & Food Experience – Find out what wine to drink with your catfish during a four-day foodie event in July. Sometimes the event takes place in late June; call ☎ 504-529-9463 for exact dates.

Mardi Gras

Carnival is New Orleans' leviathan holiday, a beautiful, undulating, snakelike festival that first rears its head on January 6 (Epiphany) and, weeks later, unfolds in all its startling, fire-breathing glory – to terrify and delight the millions who worship it.

Mardi Gras can be traced all the way back to the ancient Greeks and Romans, whose annual spring rights were celebrated in an atmosphere of characteristic debauchery. In Baroque Venice, carnival evolved into a theatrical masquerade in which citizens transformed themselves into characters of the commedia dell'arte. From France, it spread to New Orleans, where Creoles would emerge from their homes wearing grotesque, sometimes diabolical, disguises and masks and the citizenry tended to blend into an unruly, desegregated mob.

In the mid-19th century, New Orleans' Mardi Gras reached its so-called 'Golden Age,' when 'krewes' began parading. The Mystick Krewe of Comus, which first appeared in 1857, originated carnival parades and balls. Soon, several krewes were putting on elegant night parades that delighted audiences with torchlit floats fashioned from horse-drawn carriages. Meanwhile, African-Americans in New Orleans developed vaunted traditions like the Mardi Gras Indians, which first appeared in 1885. The all-black krewe Zulu debuted in 1909. The superkrewes that dominate Mardi Gras today began to appear in the late 1960s.

Carnival begins slowly, with parties and parades becoming more frequent as Mardi Gras nears. (Mardi Gras, translating as 'Fat Tuesday,' is used here specifically to refer to the actual day, rather than to the entire season; carnival refers to the season from January 6 to Fat Tuesday.) During the final five days, particularly on Monday (Lundi Gras) and Tuesday (Mardi Gras), many things occur simultaneously. Preplanning is definitely in order, as getting around town grows more difficult with each passing day (renting a bicycle will grant you the greatest mobility). It often pays to improvise.

Parades The parade season is a 12-day period beginning two Fridays before Fat Tuesday. Most of the early parades are charming, almost neighborly processions that whet your appetite for the later parades, which increase in size and grandeur each day, until the awesome spectacles of the superkrewes emerge during the final weekend.

There are two primary carnival parade routes in New Orleans. The Uptown route typically follows St Charles Ave from Napoleon St to Canal St. (The Zulu parade departs from this course by rolling down Jackson Ave until it reaches St Charles Ave, at which point it follows the standard Uptown route.) The Mid-City parade route begins near City Park and follows Orleans Ave to Carrollton Ave to Canal St, down toward the French Quarter.

These lengthy routes obviously afford many vantage points from which to see the parades. But your choice is fairly straightforward: Either head away from the crowded Quarter to get a more 'neighborhood' feel, or stick close to the corner of Canal St and St Charles Ave, where the crowds of tourists are denser and a raucous, sometimes vulgar party atmosphere prevails. Grandstands (with paid admission) are set up along St Charles Ave from Lee Circle to Gallier Hall.

A popular preseason night procession, usually held three Saturdays before Fat Tuesday, is that of the notoriously bawdy and satirical **Krewe du Vieux**. A lovely night parade presented by the predominantly black krewe of **Oshun** (named for a West African goddess) has been rolling very early in the season on the Mid-City route. In some years, parades are held every night of the subsequent week. Krewes to look for are the relatively traditional **Knights of Babylon** and **Hermes** and the more antiestablishment **Le Krewe d'Etat**.

Mardi Gras weekend is lit up by the entrance of the superkrewes, with their monstrous floats and endless processions of celebrities, marching bands, Shriner buggies, military units and police

Mardi Gras

officers. On Saturday night, the megakrewe **Endymion** stages its spectacular parade, with 1900 riders on nearly 30 floats rolling down Canal St from Mid-City. In 1999, the krewe debuted its massive, 240-foot steamboat float – by far the biggest float in the history of Mardi Gras. Sunday is a full day of parade-watching that culminates at night with **Bacchus**.

Monday night is parade night for **Orpheus**, a spirited superkrewe founded by singer-pianist Harry Connick Jr. For contrast, traditionalist **Proteus** also parades on this night.

On Mardi Gras morning, **Zulu** rolls down Jackson Ave, where the atmosphere is very different from the standard parade routes. Folks set up their barbecues on the sidewalk. Zulu is followed by the King of carnival, **Rex**, which puts on a traditional and elegant parade.

Parading carnival krewes don't just aim to entertain – they also give things to people. Creative throws, like Zulu's famous painted coconuts, are more prized than the basic string of plastic beads. Medallion beads bearing the emblem of the krewe seem to get bigger with each carnival season, as krewes strive to satisfy their fans' increasing hunger for bigger, better and badder booty. Other things you may acquire range from doubloons to plastic cups to bags of potato chips.

A valuable tip: When a throw lands on the street, claim it by stepping on it, then pick it up. If you try to pick it up without first stepping on it, someone else will surely step on your fingers – and then insist that the object is by rights theirs!

Walking Clubs & Foot Parades On Mardi Gras morning there are many 'unofficial' walking parades worth seeking out and, in some cases, even joining.

Jazzman Pete Fountain's **Half-Fast Walking Club** makes the Uptown barhopping rounds, starting from Commander's Palace at around 8 am. Downtown, beginning around 10 am, the arty **Society of St Anne** marches through the Bywater, Faubourg Marigny and French Quarter.

Krewe of Cosmic Debris convenes at around noon on Frenchmen St in the Faubourg Marigny. Masked walk-ins are welcome to join the Krewe. The krewe's wandering musical voyage through the French Quarter is largely determined by which bars it elects to patronize along the way.

Costume Contests On Fat Tuesday, an uncoordinated pageant unfolds as exquisitely – often bawdily – attired maskers, human beasts and exhibitionists congregate in the French Quarter. At noon, the notorious **Bourbon St Awards**, attracting a large number of gay contestants, takes place in front of the Rawhide Bar at Burgundy and St Anne Sts. The cleaner, for-the-family **Mardi Gras Maskathon** is held in front of the Meridien Hotel on Canal St, after the Rex parade concludes.

Balls You can buy your way into a party put on by one of the less exclusive krewes, including Orpheus (☎ 504-822-7211), Tucks (☎ 504-288-2481), Bacchus and Endymion. Gay krewes include Petronius (☎ 504-525-4498) and the Lords of Leather (☎ 504-347-0659).

RICHARD CUMMINS

Information Arthur Hardy's Mardi Gras Guide is an indispensable source of information. It details parade schedules and includes parade route maps. Similar information is offered by the Gambit Weekly's carnival edition. Both are widely available in New Orleans.

Costume at the Mardi Gras exhibit at the Presbytère

August

Blessing of the Shrimp Fleet – It's an Isleño tradition to parade decorated boats, then party. Festivities annually alternate between the fishing villages at Delacroix Island or Yscloskey in St Bernard Parish. Contact the Los Isleños Museum (☎ 504-682-0862) for information.

October

Swamp Festival – For four days in early October, the Audubon Institute (☎ 504-861-2537) releases swamp critters into the hands of visitors at both the Audubon Zoo and Woldenberg Riverfront Park. Both locations feature Cajun food, music and crafts.

Halloween – On October 31, Halloween is not taken lightly in New Orleans. Most of the fun is the giant costume party throughout the French Quarter. In addition, the New Orleans Metropolitan Convention and Visitors Bureau (☎ 504-566-5055) coordinates a parade, plus a monster bash and Anne Rice Vampire Lestat Extravaganza at the convention center.

November

All Saints Day – On November 1, residents honor the dead by sprucing up the local cemeteries.

Mirliton Festival – The first weekend marks the celebration of the pear-shaped edible fruit at the Mickey Markey Playground in the historic Bywater neighborhood. Call ☎ 504-948-7330 for more information.

Celebration in the Oaks – If unnatural holiday decorations turn you on, you might check out the colorful constellations of light at City Park (☎ 504-482-4888). It's a uniquely New Orleanian take on the spirit of Christmas in America – a little bit Vegas, a little bit Disneyland, right in the middle of the oak trees (ah, of course). As a clincher, you can view it in its entirety while driving your car (turn off the headlights, please); bicyclists are not allowed, and pedestrians will gain only limited access to the displays by sneaking past the checkpoints. The huge power cord (imagine Dad reaching for it beneath the Christmas tree) is plugged into the socket every night after dark, from the last week of November through the first week in January. Admission for motor vehicles is $7.

December

New Orleans Christmas – During the month of December, St Charles Ave is a festival of light, as many of New Orleans' poshest homes are lavishly decorated and illuminated for the holidays. This is also a great time to tour historic homes.

The lobby of the Fairmont Hotel in the CBD is transformed into a gaudy but charming Christmas grotto, its walls and ceiling concealed by shredded cotton. And of course, the Celebration in the Oaks continues all through the month (see November). On Christmas Eve, St Louis Cathedral attracts a tremendous crowd for its midnight choral mass. Many restaurants offer *réveillon* dinners on Christmas Eve. Contact French Quarter Festivals (☎ 504-522-5730), 100 Conti St, New Orleans, LA 70130, for a complete schedule of events, open homes and réveillon menus.

New Year's Eve – Revelers (mostly drunk tourists) pack the French Quarter, especially around Jackson Brewery, where the Baby New Year is dropped from the roof at midnight. Adding to the frenzy are thousands of college football fans, in town for the annual Sugar Bowl, which takes place on New Year's Day.

PLACES TO STAY

Most visitors to New Orleans stay within easy reach of the French Quarter or inside the Quarter itself. In the upper Quarter and along Canal St, there is a concentration of large hotels with all the conveniences you'd expect from top-end tourist accommodations; the CBD (Central Business District) is where you'll find most convention-oriented hotels. For more traditional Creole charm, consider staying in the lower Quarter or even in the Faubourg Marigny; here, numerous small hotels and guesthouses have been fashioned from old Creole cottages and houses. Many of these have secluded courtyards, where you can escape the heat and the tourist rush. Staying in or near the Quarter generally comes at a price, though some surprising deals can be found. Budget travelers looking for inexpensive accommodations should check out the guesthouses in the Lower Garden District or in the Bywater. From these areas, it can be a long walk to and from the Quarter (not advisable at night), but don't worry: public transit is available and cab rides are not too expensive.

Room rates also vary, depending on the time of year, with peaks during Mardi Gras and Jazz Fest – and to a lesser degree around New Year's Eve. Advance reservations are recommended well ahead of time during these periods, whether you plan to bunk at a hostel or stretch out at a classy hotel, where you can expect the rates to be double the norm. Off-season discounts kick in when occupancy rates drop. During the hot, wet and sticky summer months, desperate innkeepers drastically reduce rates at the most costly properties, so you should consider the comfort value of a modern air-conditioned room during those times.

Additional charges include the 11% room tax plus a $1 per person occupancy tax. You can also add about $14 a day if you choose to park a car at most of the lodgings in the French Quarter or CBD.

If you arrive in town without reservations, the New Orleans Metropolitan Convention & Visitors Bureau (☎ 504-566-5011) offers a free accommodations guide, with a list of member businesses, their price ranges and a map. The bureau has an office on Jackson Square in the French Quarter.

If you're economizing, you'll find the hostels are a good deal. If you've been to New Orleans before and got a cheap room at the YMCA, we have bad news this time: they've closed the hotel. That said, there are safe, comfortable guesthouses and hotels charging $40 to $70 for a double room. Mid-range hotels run $70 to $150, and once you get over $150 a night, you're in the 'top end.'

Camping

The best camping is outside the city of New Orleans. The most convenient campground is about 13 miles southeast at **St Bernard Parish State Park** (☎ 504-682-2101). It's near the Mississippi River and features wooded lagoons, short nature trails and a swimming pool. Take Hwy 46 along the east bank of the Mississippi to Bayou Rd and turn right on Hwy 39. The park entrance is within a mile on your left. Campsites are on a first-come, first-served basis and include water and electricity for $12. For more choices on decent campgrounds in the area, see the Around New Orleans section, later in this chapter.

In New Orleans, a few privately operated RV parks and campgrounds are along the Chef Menteur Hwy (Hwy 90) in eastern New Orleans (east of the Inner Harbor Navigation Canal). One of these offers tent sites. It isn't outdoorsy, or even attractive, but if you're hard up, head out to the **Mardi Gras Campground** (☎ 504-243-0085, 6050 Chef Menteur Hwy), near I-10 exit 240A, which offers tent sites for $18, more during Mardi Gras and Jazz Fest. It's hidden behind a gas station.

Upriver from town, almost all the way to the New Orleans International Airport, the **New Orleans West KOA** (☎ 504-467-1792, 11129 Jefferson Hwy), in River Ridge, offers tent sites for $22, more during holidays. From New Orleans, take I-10 exit 223A; it's 3 miles down Williams Blvd to Jefferson Hwy, where you take a left. There's shuttle service to and from the French Quarter.

Reserve Early for Festivals

Much as you are encouraged to join in the fun and frivolity of Mardi Gras, Jazz Fest or New Year's, you will first need to make some very businesslike telephone calls.

Get your accommodations squared away well in advance – at least two or three months ahead of time; otherwise, you may be left out in the cold (and it can be cold during Mardi Gras). After staying at the perfect place while attending a festival, many folks make their reservations for the next year as they check out; some plan even further in advance.

Also, during Mardi Gras, room rates are typically double or even *triple* the published rack rates. During Jazz Fest, room rates rise nearly as much. Most of the prices listed in this book are rack rates, so a little math will be required to figure out what a given hotel might charge during Mardi Gras.

Other holidays that are big in New Orleans, making preplanning and a bigger budget necessary, are New Year's (when the Sugar Bowl adds to an already festive atmosphere) and Halloween.

Hostels

Three hostels can be reached from the French Quarter on public transit: two are a block from the St Charles Ave streetcar, and one is in Mid-City near Canal St. Overly extended stays are discouraged. They all offer a kitchen, baggage storage, heat or air-conditioning depending on the season, and communal areas, where it's easy to make friends. The no-curfew policies will no doubt be appreciated by guests intent on making the most of New Orleans' round-the-clock action.

One of Hostelling International's, *Marquette House (Map 4; 504-523-3014, hineworleans@aol.com, 2253 Carondelet St)* is a 162-bed facility on the margins of the Garden District. A dorm bed (in rooms that sleep four) costs $15/18 for members/non-members, including tax. Private rooms cost $43/$66 for doubles; larger, four-person rooms cost $66. Sheet rental is an additional $2. Internet access is available in the lobby. To get there take the streetcar heading uptown to Jackson Ave and walk northwest one block to Carondelet St; the hostel is half a block to the left.

In the Lower Garden District, the *Longpré Guest House Hostel (Map 4; 504-581-4540, 1726 Prytania St)* offers 24 dorm beds in an 1850s Italianate-style house. Though it's no museum showpiece, the Longpré is a comfortable place, with a front porch that is perfect for hanging out. A large kitchen and rear patio are available for eating. The only real complaint comes from nonsmokers, as smoking is permitted in the communal TV room (drinking is also allowed). Bunks come with linens for $12, including tax. Cramped private rooms with loft beds start at $35. All rates go up during special events, doubling during Mardi Gras. To get to the hostel from the downtown area, take the St Charles Ave streetcar to Euterpe St and walk one block toward the river to Prytania St.

A free-spirit, party atmosphere flourishes at the *India House Hostel (Map 6; 504-821-1904, indiahse@cwix.com, 124 S Lopez St)*, off Canal St in Mid-City. The large aboveground swimming pool and cabaña-like decor behind the three well-used old houses that serve as dorms definitely add to the ambience. Bunk beds cost $14, including linen and tax. For a unique experience, ask about the private Cajun shacks out back, which come with pet alligators ($30 to $35). Guests can use the washer and dryer and log onto the Internet. The hostel also maintains a Web site at www.indiahousehostel.com. To get there from the French Quarter, take any Canal St bus heading toward the lake. Cross Canal St after you get off at Lopez St.

B&Bs

For something perhaps a little more romantic than the chain hotels you see along the highway, B&Bs typically offer a small number of rooms with antique furnishings and full breakfasts at rates that range from $70 to $150 and up.

Two organizations will help you find what you're looking for and help you make reservations. The Louisiana B&B Association (504-346-1857), PO Box 4003, Baton Rouge, LA 70821-4003, offers a free illustrated guide to member B&Bs throughout the state. Bed & Breakfast, Inc (504-488-4639), PO Box 52257, New Orleans, LA 70152-2257, makes free reservations at selected B&Bs to suit everyone from backpacking students looking for a romantic mini-splurge to the most discriminating travelers. Owner Hazel Boyce will promptly send or fax an illustrated description of the range of available properties.

New Orleans offers a couple of budget B&B options. Both welcome gay and lesbian travelers. In Faubourg Marigny, the *Lion's Inn B&B (504-945-2339, 2517 Chartres St)* has four nice rooms in a renovated house. One sleeps four for $100; the others range from $45 to $85. The *Bywater B&B (504-944-8438, 1026 Clouet St)* is a popular lesbian artist hangout housing a folk art collection. Three rooms with shared bath cost about $60.

French Quarter (Map 2)

Mid-Range In a quiet part of the lower Quarter is the *Chateau Motor Hotel*

(☎ 504-524-9636, cmhnola@aol
.com, 1001 Chartres St). Singles
range from $79 to $104 and
doubles range from $99 to
$124. Those prices include a
continental breakfast as well as
parking. A few blocks away and
a step up in quality is **Le Richelieu** (☎ 504-529-2492, 800-535-9653,
lericheliuhotel@inetmail.att.net, 1234
Chartres St), where handsomely decorated
rooms start at $85 to $170, including
parking.

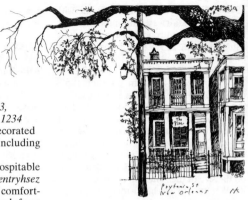

Pontalba St
New Orleans   rk

Sadie Gentry's charming and hospitable
Gentry House (☎ 504-525-4433, gentryhsez
@aol.com, 1031 St Ann St) is in a comfortable Creole cottage just half a block from
the Rampart St music clubs. It's quiet
shaded courtyard is the perfect getaway
from the noise of the Quarter. The house
has five rooms that can accommodate two
to five people and come with a coffeemaker and refrigerator. Costs range from
$70 to $115.

The **Cornstalk Hotel** (☎ 504-523-1515,
fax 522-5558, 915 Royal St) is famous for the
fence out front, which is possibly the most
photographed fence in the US. The colorful
cornstalks were cast in 1859 and attract a
steady stream of admirers. The rooms inside
are also attractive, with high ceilings and
antique furnishings. Rooms with private
bathroom range from $75 (at off-peak
times) to $185.

Hotel St Pierre (☎ 504-524-4401, 800-225-
4040, 911 Burgundy St) is a group of historic
Creole cottages with interior courtyards
and modern furnishings. Room rates are
$110 to $170, and suites cost more. The same
people operate the **Andrew Jackson Hotel**
(☎ 504-561-5881, 800-654-0224, 919 Royal
St), with the same rates and a more central
location.

The **Hotel Provincial** (☎ 504-581-4995,
800-535-7922, info@hotelprovincial.com,
1024 Chartres St) has finely restored buildings that contain around 100 high-ceilinged
rooms and suites, which open onto interior
courtyards. Standard room rates are $79 to
$225 (including parking) and suites cost
$139 and up.

Top End   For Creole-style elegance, historic **Soniat House** (☎ 504-522-0570, 800-
544-8808, 1133 Chartres St), in the lower
Quarter, has no equal. It's in a meticulously
restored 1830 townhouse with lacy ironwork, beautiful antique furnishings and a
romantic courtyard in which breakfast
($8.50) is served. Children under 12 are not
permitted to stay here. Rooms cost $195 to
$285; suites cost $325 and up. Valet parking
is $16. To get a reservation form, go to
www.soniathouse.com.

When the venerable **Hotel Monteleone**
(☎ 504-523-3341, 800-535-9595, 214 Royal
St) opened in 1907, it was the largest hotel
in the French Quarter – and it still is! The
narrow street hardly allows one to stand
back to admire its handsome white terra-
cotta exterior. All rooms were renovated in
the early 1990s, and rates typically start at
$150/170 singles/doubles, except during the
summer, when all rooms cost $95 (yes, it is
air-conditioned). A curious highlight here,
even if you're not staying in the hotel, is the
Carousel Bar off the main lobby – it actually revolves, but not fast enough to cause
your drinks to fly off the bar.

Tremé District (Map 2)

On Esplanade Ave, along the edge of the
Tremé, are a couple of reasonably priced
places worth considering for their proximity to the Quarter. One of them is **Maison
Esplanade** (☎ 504-523-8080, 800-892-5529,

1244 Esplanade Ave), a historic home with an exterior stairway and nine modest, antique-furnished rooms with private bath usually starting at $79 (but dropping to $50 or so in summer). Also inquire at the *Rathbone Inn* (☎ 504-947-2100, 800-947-2101, *1227 Esplanade Ave)*, in another 1850s mansion. Rates range from $160 to $190 in the low season to $255 to $300 in the high season. Another nice old property on the same block is *Hotel Storyville* (☎ 504-548-4800, 1261 Esplanade Ave)*, which has a variety of suites to sleep two to six people. Rates range from $80 to $300, depending on the size of the suite and the season. Visit its Web site at www.hotelstoryville.com for more information.

Faubourg Marigny (Map 2) & Bywater

Near the French Quarter, the small *Lamothe House* (☎ 504-947-1161, 800-367-5858, 621 Esplanade Ave)* offers 11 antique-crowded rooms at $79 to $175; suites, $130 to $275. For more information visit its Web site at www.new-orleans.org. Published rates for standard doubles start at $84 at *The Frenchmen* (☎ 504-948-2166, 800-831-1781, 417 Frenchmen St)*, a small, refurbished 1850s Creole house with an interior court and spa. Rates for balcony rooms cost almost $50 more, but you might negotiate an off-peak discount on any of the rooms. The Frenchmen also offers a surly 24-hour concierge.

In the lower Bywater, *Mazant Guest House* (☎ 504-944-2662, 906 Mazant St)*, at Burgundy St, is an attractive, two-story former plantation house with kitchen facilities and 11 guest rooms. Furnishings are mostly antiques, but not fussily so. The Mazant's selling points are its warm, homey charm, extremely reasonable rates and manager Bob Girault's undying enthusiasm for the local music scene (he'll steer you in the right direction). It attracts European guests who often make use of the kitchen and parlor, making this a fairly social place to stay. Most rooms (with shared bath) cost between $30 and $40; ask about rooms that afford more privacy. Free off-street parking

is available, and there are bicycles available for guests' use.

CBD & Warehouse District (Map 3)

Mid-Range Near City Hall, *Comfort Inn Downtown* (☎ 504-586-0100, 800-228-5150, *1315 Gravier St)* has basic rooms in a high-rise starting at $59 during the slow season and going up from there. *Comfort Suites* (☎ 504-524-1140, comfortno@aol.com, 346 Baronne St)* has modern rooms ranging from $89 to $189 depending on the season. A step up and only two blocks from the Quarter is the *Hampton Inn* (☎ 504-529-9990, 800-426-7866, 226 Carondelet St)*, offering free local calls and continental breakfast in modern rooms for $79 to $129, dropping as low as $59 in summer. Its Web site at www.neworleans.com/hampton/ has more information.

The *Holiday Inn Downtown Superdome* (☎ 504-581-1600, 800-535-7830, 330 Loyola Ave)* is easily recognized by the 18-story-high clarinet painted on the side of the building. Basic rooms start at $99 during nonholiday seasons, and executive accommodations are available for $129.

Top End A few hotels in this area rise above the typically overpriced convention-eers' accommodations. In particular, elegant *Le Pavillon* (☎ 504-581-3111, 800-535-9095, *833 Poydras Ave)*, opened in 1907, is a large full-service hotel offering plenty of lovely marble in the lobby and plush updated rooms, which range from $105 to $230 depending on the season. A smaller hotel that also gets high marks is the *Lafayette Hotel* (☎ 504-524-4441, 800-733-4754, 600 St Charles Ave)*, at Girod St. Rooms with a king-size bed start at $165, suites at $295.

The *Fairmont Hotel* (☎ 504-529-7111, 800-527-4727, 123 Baronne St)* was the city's elite establishment when it opened in the 1920s as the Roosevelt Hotel. It has undergone substantial remodeling, and the rooms vary tremendously in size and furnishings; look at a room before agreeing to take it. Rates start around $229 for one or two people but can drop to as low as $119 during slow summer periods; check its Web site (www.fairmont.com) for more details. The Fairmont is famous for it's still-swanky Sazerac bar, where Huey Long used to drink and where a trigger happy gangster once plugged a bullet into the wall – the bartender will point out the hole for you.

Lower Garden & Garden Districts (Map 4)
Budget The *Prytania Inn I* (☎ 504-566-1515, fax 566-1518, 1415 Prytania St) has rooms with private baths and furnishings that have seen better days. Some rooms have kitchens. Be sure to see the unit before you accept it, because the comfort level can vary greatly. Rates range from $29/39 to $55/79 singles/doubles. Add $5 for a full breakfast in the pleasant parlor downstairs. The same hotel is headquarters for two other properties down the street, *Prytania Inn II* (2041 Prytania St), in a building that looks more impressive from the outside but houses similar rooms at the same rates as Prytania I, and *Prytania Inn III* (2127 Prytania St), at the corner of Jackson St, on the edge of the Garden District. P-III's rooms cost the same, but considering the atmosphere – the building is a stunning Greek Revival 'raised villa,' built in 1857, it's one of the bargains of the city. There's a catch: none of these places is famous for stellar housecleaning, which might not be obvious from the pictures on their Web site at www.prytaniainns.com.

The large *St Vincent's Guest House* (☎ 504-523-3411, 1507 Magazine St) is in a former orphanage built during the Civil War. A courtyard swimming pool offers a welcome respite from New Orleans' all-too-frequent tortuously hot days. Charmless but clean remodeled rooms cost $59 to $79.

Greater comfort can be enjoyed at the antique-filled rooms at the *St Charles Guest House* (☎ 504-523-6556, 1748 Prytania St). Longtime owner Dennis Hilton offers a few small rooms with movie-set-like furnishings and continental breakfast for $65 to $95. If you are on a budget and roll into town with no reservations, ask Hilton about his 'backpacker' rooms, a few of which he keeps

available on a first-come, first-served basis. These are small, basic rooms with shared bath. They will cost you $30 to $45. For more information, visit its Web site at www.stcharlesguesthouse.com.

Mid-Range The *Whitney Inn* (☎ 504-521-8000, 800-379-5322, whitney.inn@worldnet.att.net, 1509 St Charles Ave) is a refurbished 19th-century guesthouse offering antique-furnished rooms, with rates ranging from $79 to $159, including a continental breakfast. Suites are also available, ranging from $149 to $179.

The *Maison St Charles* (☎ 504-522-0187, 800-831-1783, reservations@maisonstcharles.com, 1319 St Charles Ave) is a Quality Inn property with modern rooms costing $69 to $119. It offers shuttle service to the French Quarter.

The *Josephine Guest House* (☎ 504-524-6361, 800-779-6361, 1450 Josephine St), at Prytania St, is an immaculately restored mansion just a couple of blocks from the Garden District. Rooms cost $100 to $145 and include breakfast on Wedgwood china.

The 1858 Georgian Revival *Terrell Guest House* (☎ 504-524-9859, 1441 Magazine St), at Euterpe St, offers impressive antique furnishings and marble fireplaces in the main bedrooms for $150. The 3rd-floor dormer rooms and rear servants' quarters cost $100 to $125. All rooms have private bath and include a full breakfast and cocktails.

Uptown & Riverbend (Map 5)
The *Columns Hotel* (☎ 504-899-9308, 3811 St Charles Ave), at General Taylor, is a historic establishment (built 1883). The downstairs bar and patio is one of the city's most festive gathering spots. On the 2nd and 3rd floors, 20 rooms of various size range from $100/135 for a smallish double to $175/210 for the two-room 'Pretty Baby Suite' (named for the Louis Malle film shot here in the 1970s). Room No 16 ($170), with a balcony overlooking the front entry and St Charles Ave, might be noisy at night.

Just three blocks from the Columns, *Lagniappe Bed & Breakfast* (☎ 800-317-2120, 1925 Peniston St) has very quaint and comfortable rooms, all with private bath and antiques. Rates of $110 to $150 include full breakfast, off-street parking and – true to the name – numerous extras ranging from fresh flowers and fruit to complimentary beer, wine and soft drinks. Visit the B&B's Web site (www.bbonline.com/la/lagniappe) for a virtual tour.

Near Audubon Park, the **Parkview Guest House** (☎ 504-861-7564, 888-533-0746, 7004 St Charles Ave) was built in 1884 to impress visitors to the World Cotton Exchange Exposition the following year. Antique furnishings abound in the lounge and rooms. Rooms (some with shared bath) range from $85 to $130. Check the guest house's Web site (www.parkviewguesthouse.com) for more information.

PLACES TO EAT

Don't start a new diet before coming to New Orleans. Why torture yourself? Some people come to this city for the sole purpose of eating. They plan their entire itinerary around their meals, squeezing in a few museums and so on in between, and accepting the reality that they'll be a few pounds heavier when they get home.

New Orleans has rich and unique culinary traditions. Beginning with the traditions of French cuisine, the chefs and household cooks of New Orleans created and gradually elevated their own style of cooking. Creole cuisine, one of the USA's most distinctive regional cuisines, originated here, and the practices of Cajun cooks have also had a profound impact on the city's culinary scene.

In recent decades, Asian, Mexican, Indian and European influences are creeping in, sometimes in surprising combinations.

French Quarter (Map 2)

The French Quarter offers the greatest number and variety of restaurants in town, and some establishments are among the country's most famous eateries. But the Quarter is also the most expensive part of New Orleans in which to dine, and during peak seasons reservations at some of the more popular places can be difficult to get.

Budget In the French Market, *Café du Monde* (☎ 504-581-2914, 800 Decatur St) is a 24-hour New Orleans institution that's famous for café au lait and beignets (light, square-shaped doughnuts dusted with powdered sugar). This tasty snack costs just $2.

Royal Blend (☎ 504-523-2716, 621 Royal St) has a pleasant garden courtyard in which to sip coffee – an inexpensive opportunity for tourists to venture 'behind the scenes' in the French Quarter. You can log on in the upstairs cybercafe.

Croissant d'Or Patisserie (☎ 504-524-4663, 617 Ursulines Ave) is another great old place. A fluffy individual quiche and one of the extraordinary filled croissants served with juice and coffee costs about $6. Sandwiches, soups and pastries round out the selection. As you enter, notice that tile letters in the sidewalk designate one entrance for ladies – that's how old this joint is!

For pralines, drop by *Southern Candymakers* (☎ 504-523-5544, 334 Decatur St).

The *Clover Grill* (☎ 504-598-1010, 900 Bourbon St) is a 24-hour diner that has that familiar fake-'50s diner look and serves that familiar kind of food. But the nostalgia stops there. The Clover's disco-caliber sound system booms out dance music, and the boys serving the food are reputed to get pretty frisky at times. But the burgers are seriously good and attract a mixed clientele. (As is so often the case in this part of the Quarter, the later it is, the gayer the Clover gets.)

It's usually crowded with tourists, but *Café Maspero* (☎ 504-523-6250, 601 Decatur St) offers huge sandwiches or red beans and rice for about $5 and cold Abita on tap. Without trying very hard, Maspero's has atmosphere, endowed mainly by smoky brick arches, which make its street-level eating rooms feel underground.

For a muffuletta you have two choices, which are almost side by side on Decatur St between Dumaine and Philip Sts. The *Central Grocery* (☎ 504-523-1620, 923 Decatur St) is the mother church for the muffuletta. The crazy sandwich was invented here in 1906. The grocery is authentic, but swarms of tourists crowd into its narrow aisles on weekends. A whole muffuletta and a Barq's root beer ($9) is a meal for two. Two doors down, *Progress Grocery Co Inc* (☎ 504-525-6627, 915 Decatur St) serves up its own variety of muffuletta, smarmily entitled the 'mo' betta muffuletta,' which is less oily than those at Central Grocery.

Opposite the Old US Mint, *Louisiana Pizza Kitchen* (☎ 504-522-9500, 95 French Market Place) is a popular chain offering wood-fired individual pizzas ($6 to $9).

An exclusively vegetarian lunch and dinner spot, *Old Dog New Trick Café* (☎ 504-522-4569, 307 Exchange Alley) offers dinner entrees like polenta stuffed with black beans and feta ($10) and grilled tofu with peanut-ginger sauce ($9), both served with grilled vegetables. The tasty soups make an inexpensive meal.

Coop's Place (☎ 504-525-9053, 1109 Decatur St) is as much a neighborhood bar as it is a restaurant, and that's a virtue that sets it apart from so many of its tourist-trap neighbors. The darkly lit cavern has a full menu, with jambalaya, fried alligator and burgers. It's also a good place to grab a plate of red beans and rice for around $5.

Acme Oyster and Seafood House (☎ 504-522-5973, 724 Iberville St) is a neighborhood standby that's revered by locals and out-of-towners alike. It first opened in 1910, and it retains some of the atmosphere of the old Quarter, but it stands on its reputation for shucking out some of the city's best oysters, along with decent red beans and rice. Be warned – the line of people waiting for a table often spills out onto the sidewalk.

Mid-Range *Irene's Cuisine* (☎ 504-529-8811, 539 St Philip St) has small, cozy dining rooms that are perfect for quiet conversation. The food straddles the Italian-French border and includes offerings like finely seasoned roasted rosemary chicken ($15), pan-seared rack of lamb with an exquisite port-wine glaze ($18) and flavorful 'duck St Philip' ($18), served with fresh spinach, French mustard and berries. Irene's is open daily from 6 to 10 pm, and reservations are not accepted; the wait can be long.

Olivier's (☎ 504-525-7734, 204 Decatur St) often goes unnoticed because of its quiet location at the upper reaches of Decatur St. But it serves authentic, inexpensive and excellent Creole food. Start with the gumbo sampler ($9), then choose from entrees like shrimp Creole, Creole rabbit, crab cakes, and pork medallions. Main dishes range from $13 to $18; lunch is $7 to $11. Save room for bourbon pecan pie.

At *NOLA* (☎ 504-522-6652, 534 St Louis St), an exciting, but not especially relaxing, dining experience can be had at lower prices than at chef Emeril Lagasse's other restaurants. Lagasse's kitchen crew deftly culls local, Asian and Californian traditions for natural, subtle combinations. Fresh fish parts neatly under your fork, and roasted filet mignon, cooked rare, is so tender you can almost chew it with your eyebrows. The wood-fired pizzas make a good starter for a group. Lunches range from $17 to $20, and dinner entrees cost between $24 and $35.

For Indian cuisine amid splendid furnishings, try *Shalimar* (☎ 504-523-0099, 535 Wilkenson Row), where dinners cost $13 to $20 for mostly traditional tandoori and a few of the more exotic dishes from southern India. Vegetarians can choose from a variety of specialties.

Many local beef eaters agree that *Port of Call* (☎ 504-523-0120, 838 Esplanade Ave) is the place to go for a burger with a baked potato ($7). This basic bar and grill also serves good steaks ($20).

Top End New Orleans has several venerable dining establishments dating back well into the 19th century. These places maintain traditions such as requiring jackets and frowning on denim. But not all the restaurants listed in this price category are so traditional.

Antoine's (☎ 504-581-4422, 713 St Louis St) is New Orleans' oldest restaurant, having been open for business since 1840. The dated charm of its dining rooms (a brightly lit room for nonsmokers and a more ambient smoking room) is well suited for family functions, particularly if older folks are involved. The menu hasn't changed much over the last century. As is so often the case in New Orleans, rumor has it that the regulars are treated to better food than first-timers. As a visitor, you're better off with more straightforward chicken and lamb entrees. A full dinner with wine typically costs $30 to $50 per person.

Arnaud's *(☎ 504-523-5433, 813 Bienville St)*, an agglomeration of buildings that take up nearly an entire city block, is another place to go for traditional haute Creole cuisine. While the food doesn't make for the most scintillating dining experience, the kitchen expertly handles its specialties, which appear in red type on the menu and include shrimp Arnaud, oysters Bienville (an original dish) and speckled trout meunière. À la carte entrees run $17 to $29. Arnaud's is open daily for dinner, weekdays for lunch and Sunday for brunch.

Another New Orleans institution, the ***Court of Two Sisters*** *(☎ 504-522-7261, 613 Royal St)* has wonderful ambience but disappointing food. The courtyard of this historic building, with a canopy created by a sprawling, 200-year-old wisteria, is a very pleasant setting for alfresco dining, but you would expect to eat better for $30 to $50 a head.

Galatoire's *(☎ 504-525-2021, 209 Bourbon St)* is a clubby sort of place where the regulars are treated regally and tourists are sometimes dished out surprisingly average food. Local devotees so love this classic New Orleans establishment that to literally die here over a plate of, say, grilled pompano with almonds is considered a *belle mort*, or good death. (Fortunately, this doesn't happen very often.) Oysters Rockefeller, asparagus salad, chicken *clemenceau* and the to-die-for pompano are good bets off the menu (entrees run $15 to $22). It's open every day but Monday from 11:30 to 9 pm. Expect a long wait outside before being seated, unless you're into afternoon lunches.

At ***Brennan's Restaurant*** *(☎ 504-525-9711, 417 Royal St)* breakfasts is no mere *petit déjeuner*: It's a virtual gastronomic extravaganza that could start with an 'eye-opener' (if you can imagine downing a

Sazerac cocktail before breakfast), followed by turtle soup, any of about 20 egg dishes, and then dessert (bananas Foster is a Brennan's original). This will set you back about $40. Traditional Creole dinners are served nightly.

Though some complain that ***K-Paul's Louisiana Kitchen*** *(☎ 504-596-2530, 416 Chartres St)* has lost its edge, Paul Prudhomme's world-famous Cajun eatery remains a major tourist draw. The kitchen continues to eschew shortcuts. The blackened twin beef tenders ($30), a signature dish, come with an incredibly rich 'debris' – an elaborate gravy, slowly cooked for two days. You can also get gumbo ($5 a cup) and turtle soup ($5.50), which has a nice flavorful snap to it. K-Paul's takes reservations, but they're not essential unless you don't want to wait in line. For weekday lunches, you might be seated on arrival.

Bayona *(☎ 504-525-4455, 430 Dauphine St)*, in a charming converted Creole cottage, is one of the city's best all-around dining experiences. Chef Susan Spicer's menu is always inventive but rarely shocking. The grilled shrimp with black-bean cake and coriander sauce and the goat-cheese crouton with mushrooms in Madeira cream are elegant starters ($5 to $8). Representative entrees ($9 to $13 for lunch, $17 to $25 for dinner) include a grilled pork chop with savory semolina pudding and sage *jus* and a salmon with *choucroute* and Gewürztraminer sauce. Bayona is open weekdays for lunch and dinner, Saturday for dinner only.

Owned by Cindy Brennan, ***Mr B's Bistro*** *(☎ 504-523-2078, 201 Royal St)* appeals to a variety of tastes. Creole overtones predominate. The 'gumbo Ya-Ya' with chicken and andouille is excellent, and the barbecued shrimp, sautéed in a delicious buttery sauce rather than grilled, is a fun and messy dish served with a paper bib to protect your shirt. Lunch is decidedly less expensive than dinner, with main dishes running $11 to $17. It's open for lunch every day but Sunday, when brunch is served; dinner (entrees $16 and up) is served nightly.

The ***Palace Café*** *(☎ 504-523-1661, 605 Canal St)*, with a gorgeous corkscrew staircase and traditional tile floors, seems to have been claimed by businesspeople, conventioneers and office workers. The food follows through with modern, nonexperimental approaches to classic Creole standards like catfish pecan meunière ($18). Occasional surprises, such as a starter of herbed gnocchi with wild mushrooms ($6), add nice twists to the menu. The Palace is open nightly for dinner, weekdays for lunch, weekends for brunch.

Café Sbisa (☎ *504-522-5565, 1011 Decatur St*) is a Vieux Carré institution (since 1899) that has a reputation for innovative Creole cuisine. It features one of New Orleans' most atmospheric dining rooms, with exposed brick and decadent art above the long bar. New American touches spruce up a solid menu, which includes blackened redfish ($19), garlic-and-honey roasted chicken ($15) and pasta jambalaya ($17). Café Sbisa is open nightly for dinner, and Sunday for a nice brunch with a roving 'trad' jazz unit.

Peristyle (☎ *504-593-9535, 1041 Dumaine St*), at Rampart St, is one of the city's more romantic spots for dinner. Chef Anne Kearney treats diners to simple yet refined creations. Her menu plays on American tastes and French Provençal methods of preparation – it's traditional but sophisticated. It's open Tuesday to Saturday for dinner and for lunch on Friday.

Faubourg Marigny (Map 2) & Bywater

Restaurants in the Faubourg Marigny neighborhood tend to be a bargain compared to their French Quarter counterparts. They also provide a wide range of cuisine, from budget meat-and-potato dishes and spicy Thai to soul food and fine dining.

Budget Actually more of an appendage to a bar, *The Harbor* (☎ *504-947-1819, 2529 Dauphine St*) is a soul food restaurant that's uncharacteristically close to the French Quarter. You won't meet many tourists here, though. It's the real deal, with fried chicken and pork chops, mustard greens and white bread dished out unceremoni-

ously over a counter at outrageously low prices. It's open for lunch only, but you'll eat like a king for $4.

The quiet, 24-hour *La Péniche* (☎ *504-943-1460, 1940 Dauphine St*), at Touro St, comes alive as it gets late. Gays, strippers and see-and-be-seen types fill the tables on into the morning. But the food, from red beans and rice for under $5 to shrimp and oyster dinners for $13, is unremarkable. It is closed Tuesday night and Wednesday.

Hand-painted signs nailed to telephone poles along Chartres St in the Bywater subliminally direct your stomach to *Elizabeth's* (☎ *504-944-9272, 601 Gallier St*), at Chartres St. It's open for breakfast and lunch (for around $5), and no matter what you order from the unassuming menu (hearty American and New Orleans fare), it will exceed expectations in quality and quantity. It is closed Sunday and Monday.

Mid-Range *Siam Café* (☎ *504-949-1750, 435 Esplanade Ave*) serves all the Thai standards, including pad Thai ($8). But it rises to greater heights with specialties that include a royal hunter's grill ($13) and a selection of spicy curries ($7 to $13).

The popular *Santa Fe* (☎ *504-944-6854, 801 Frenchmen St*) is a rare Southwestern restaurant in New Orleans, where a *chile rellenos* dinner costs $10 and grilled tuna goes for $15.

At the original *Praline Connection* (☎ *504-943-3934, 542 Frenchmen St*), some righteous (but atypically pricey) soul food makes its way to the table: fried chicken, Creole gumbo, beans and greens ($9 to $14).

In the heart of the Bywater, *Bywater Barbeque* (☎ *504-944-4445, 3162 Dauphine St*), at Louisa St, dishes out good barbecue spare ribs, chicken and pulled pork in heaping quantities for $11 or less. But if you've already experienced Memphis barbecue, where the real shit can be found, don't bother with this snooty little joint.

CBD & Warehouse District (Map 3)

New Orleans' business district is home to some highly acclaimed and expensive power-lunch (and dinner) establishments, but the CBD and the nearby Warehouse District also have some decent eat-and-run spots as well as a pair of noteworthy greasy spoons.

Budget *Mother's* (☎ 504-523-9656, 401 Poydras St), at Tchoupitoulas St, is famous for its hearty down-home breakfasts, including biscuits, grits, debris (shredded beef) and strong coffee for about $7. Although service is over the counter, everything is cooked to order. Some justifiably complain that prices are a wee bit too high and weekend lines are too long.

The *Hummingbird Grill* (☎ 504-561-9229, 804 St Charles Ave), near Julia St, is a 24-hour greasy spoon that's surprisingly good, considering it's downstairs from a rather dicey transient hotel. Be sure to get here early for fresh biscuits and grits. Standard lunch fare won't fail you either.

Inviting aromas fill the small *Le Petit Paris* (☎ 504-524-7660, 731 Common St), which offers omelets, soups, and hot lunches for under $6. It's only open for breakfast and lunch on weekdays.

In the heart of the CBD, the cafeteria-style *New City Diner* (☎ 504-522-8198, 828 Gravier St) dishes up full breakfasts for $3 and hot lunch specials for $6. The *Red Eye Grill* (☎ 504-593-9393, 852 S Peters St) stays open late and is a place to get a greasy burger and fries.

Mid-Range & Top End At *Liborio's* (☎ 504-581-9680, 321 Magazine St), Cuban lunch specials, such as Wednesday's roast pork with black beans, get high marks and are sure to please garlic fans. Also try the grilled tuna with sweet plantains for $9. The prices are a bit high, but the business crowd doesn't seem to mind.

At *Emeril's* (☎ 504-528-9393, 800 Tchoupitoulas St), the noise level can be deafening and the service aloof and Chef Emeril Lagasse is rarely in residence. And yet this remains one of New Orleans' signature dining establishments. The kitchen's strengths are best appreciated by ordering the daily specials, though menu mainstays

like shrimp-and-andouille cheesecake with Creole mustard-tomato coulis or crawfish-stuffed filet mignon with sauce bordelaise are also worth a look. Dinner costs around $40 per person without wine.

The *Bon Ton Café* (☎ 504-524-3386, 401 Magazine St), at Poydras St, is an old-style Cajun restaurant (with a few Creole dishes). Although the dining room looks a little like a pizza parlor, folks show up dressed to the nines, and at $15 to $25 per person, meals don't come cheap. But this is a consistently good throwback to the days before Cajun food was revolutionized by chefs like Paul Prudhomme. Spices are used in tasteful moderation. Rich gumbo, red fish, shrimp étouffée and a rum-soaked bread pudding are sure to satisfy.

Lower Garden & Garden Districts (Map 4)

Some places along St Charles Ave are particularly esteemed for their 24-hour breakfasts and late-night fixings.

Budget The *Rue de la Course* (☎ 504-529-1455, 1500 Magazine St), at Race St, is a small but comfortable coffeehouse where you can buy a paper and while away the time over a variety of coffee drinks and baked goods. (There are other branches in the French Quarter and Uptown.) Across the street, *St Vincent's Guesthouse & Tea Room* (☎ 504-523-2318, 1507 Magazine St) has a daily set tea from noon to 4 pm.

Across from Lafayette Cemetery No 1, The Rink shopping center houses *Still Perkin'* (☎ 504-899-0335, 2727 Prytania St). The front deck is a good place to have a cup of coffee before or after exploring the Garden District.

The 24-hour *Trolley Stop* (☎ 504-523-0090, 1923 St Charles Ave) is a former gas station that draws a mixed crowd for basic diner fare.

The *Please-U-Restaurant* (☎ 504-525-9131, 1751 St Charles Ave) is a run-down counter-and-booths establishment that serves up cheap, satisfying meals. Whether you order steak and eggs, a soft-shell crab sandwich or a po-boy, you won't spend much more than $5. It's open weekdays till 7 pm and Saturday till 2 pm.

Parasol's Bar (☎ 504-897-5413, 2533 Constance St) is an old Irish Channel institution, hence it's as much a bar as an eatery. However, locals have long insisted that this is one of the best places to get a po-boy sandwich ($5.50 to $7). No arguments here. The roast beef is superb. Non-barflies (and juniors) can enter a side door into a casual dining room.

Busy *Uglesich's* (☎ 504-523-8571, 1238 Baronne St) is justifiably one of New Orleans' cherished institutions (since 1924), drawing suits and blue collars alike to its divey, overcrowded dining room. The food, with its strong seaward leanings, never fails to amaze. The menus tacked to the walls don't really indicate what a dish will end up like (some favorites aren't on the menu at all). When you order from the counter, engaging your server in conversation will usually result in your ordering the right thing. There's also a raw oyster bar. You'll probably wait half an hour or so for a table. Most items are under $10. Uglesich is open for lunch weekdays and every other Saturday (call ahead).

Top End In the heart of the Garden District, *Commander's Palace* (☎ 504-899-8221, 1403 Washington Ave) is frequently touted as one of the country's best restaurants, and this is one place that lives up to the hype. The service is impeccable and friendly and the food coming out of the kitchen is uniformly splendorous. Surprisingly, the dining rooms, with the exception of the upstairs Garden Room, are a little dated and stale in their decor (the shag carpet waits to be yanked out). Entrees (from $22 to $37) are where Commander's really shines. The Colorado roast rack of lamb is prepared with a Creole mustard crust and an exquisite muscadine lamb sauce. Lunch prices are mercifully reduced ($14 to $25). A reservation and a coat are required.

Uptown (Map 5)

Despite Uptown's upscale reputation, it is home to several really great dives.

Locals and medical students from nearby hospitals pack the *Bluebird Café* (☎ 504-895-7166, 3625 Prytania St), near Antonine St, for satisfying breakfasts that tend to go beyond the traditional eggs and grits; the 'powerhouse eggs' dish contains nutritional yeast, tamari and cheese. This place is also known for its malted pancakes and Belgian waffles. For lunch, sandwiches (burgers, veggie melts and BLTs) are available. You often have to wait to be seated at this popular little place.

On a residential block near the river, *Domilise's Po-Boys* (☎ 504-899-9126, 5240 Annunciation St), at Bellecastle St, is yet another of those bustling little shacks that churns out some of the city's best-loved sandwiches. Order a large fried-shrimp po-boy ($7), prepared by the bustling staff (the place is always busy) and sit at the bar, where a friendly old gent draws frosty mugs of draught Dixie. All in all, a most gratifying experience. It's open 10 am to 7 pm; closed Sunday.

Since 1949, hard-core Uptown oyster fiends go to *Casamento's* (☎ 504-895-9761, 4330 Magazine St), near Napoleon St, for their fix. The oysters are always the freshest and come raw on the half-shell at just $7.50 a dozen. The Italian-inflected gumbo ($7) also has a faithful following. It's open every day but Monday for lunch and dinner; it's closed in summer. Credit cards are not accepted.

Taqueria Corona (☎ 504-897-3974, 5932 Magazine St), near Eleonore St, draws a regular crowd of hungry people who appreciate inexpensive Mexican fare made up of fresh ingredients and zesty sauces. Meat and fish tacos cost around $2 apiece, though you'll probably want to order two. A burrito makes a filling meal for $6.

Café Atchafalaya (☎ 504-891-5271, 901 Louisiana Ave) is the kind of place where Southern hospitality and cornbread aren't on the menu, because you get them automatically. Visitors and locals flock here for fair-priced Deep South stalwarts, such as fried green tomatoes, crab cakes, fried fish and chicken, plus some original specials. It's open for lunch and dinner Monday to Saturday.

Dunbar's (☎ *504-899-0734, 4927 Freret St)*, at Upperline St, will set you up with a mess of fried chicken and red beans and rice, plus a slab of cornbread, for $5. The pork chop plate costs $6, the oyster plate $9.50. These are clean and basic soul food digs in a sketchy part of town. Drive or take a cab.

Riverbend (Map 5)

The Riverbend usually draws visitors for its nightclubs, but among its restaurants there are some real standouts.

Budget A destination in itself, the ***Camellia Grill*** (☎ *504-866-9573, 626 S Carrollton Ave)* has enjoyed increasing popularity ever since it opened in 1946. Its secret? It refuses to change with the times. Well-made American short-order fare (the burgers and omelettes stand out) is served by the city's snazziest and most entertaining waiters. The Camellia's addictive pecan waffles and pecan pies have made regulars out of people you'd never expect to see in a diner. It's is open until 3 am on Friday and Saturday nights.

Cooter Brown's Tavern & Oyster Bar (☎ *504-866-9104, 509 S Carrollton Ave)* is a popular place to stop in for oysters on the half shell ($6.50 for six, $9 for a dozen) and sandwiches (delicate fried catfish for $6.50) that far exceed bar-food standards. After 8 pm, the place turns into a rowdy college hangout.

Mid-Range You will almost certainly have to wait for a table at popular ***Jacques-Imo's Café*** (☎ *504-861-0886, 8324 Oak St)*, but it's worth it. Once inside you're led through a kitchen, which bustles with all the energy of a steamship engine room, before being seated in a comfortable closed-in patio dining room. The fried chicken ($10 with sides) is legendary, and there's genuine creativity in nightly specials ($15), like fried trout smothered with jalapeño, pecans and shrimp. It's open for dinner only, and reservations are not accepted (expect a wait).

Brigtsen's Restaurant (☎ *504-861-7610, 723 Dante St)* is a critically acclaimed place

that remains homey and inviting. Those in search of haute Cajun cuisine will not find a better restaurant in the city. Look for the roast duck with dirty rice and honey-pecan gravy or rabbit tenderloin on a tasso parmesan grits cake with Creole mustard sauce. Dinner (Tuesday to Saturday) will run about $25 per person not including wine.

Mid-City (Map 6)

Mid-City is known for its down-to-earth neighborhood eateries, and a number of good restaurants are within a block of the intersection of N Carrollton Ave and Canal St.

Budget ***Betsy's Pancake House*** (☎ *504-822-0213, 2542 Canal St)* is a busy spot offering breakfasts for about $2.50 and lunch specials for $5. ***Mandina's*** (☎ *504-482-9179, 3800 Canal St)* is a popular local Cajun and Italian restaurant with lunch and dinner for under $12, including the seafood platter. It's a good choice for guests at the nearby hostel.

Vegan diners will appreciate ***Jack Sprats*** (☎ *504-486-2200, 3240 S Carrollton Ave)*, where it's the spices that make the dish. Lunch and dinner plates cost between $5 and $8 and include a salad and bread.

Mid-Range At ***Lemon Grass Cafe*** (☎ *504-488-8335, 216 N Carrollton Ave)*, chef Minh Bui borrows freely from French cuisine as well as the cooking of his own native Vietnam. Entrees ($16 to $20) change fre-

---

Po-boys

The classic po-boy is the oyster po-boy. The name, local parlance for 'poor boy,' refers to the cheapness of oysters during the Great Depression. An oyster sandwich cost just 20¢ in those days.

These days, po-boys can come with fried catfish, roast beef, and a variety of other meats.

quently, but may include mirliton (chayote) with shrimp and a buttery French sauce, or ginger chicken and stir-fried vegetables couched in a deep-fried, cracker-like 'bird's nest.' Desserts are also exceptional.

Near Canal St, *Palmers* (☎ 504-482-3658, 135 N Carrollton Ave) is a basic Caribbean joint with nonexistent decor. Start with a bowl of Jamaican pepperpot ($3), and then move on to a plate of piquant jerk fish ($11) or West Indian–style curry chicken with plantains ($8.50).

Opposite the Lafitte housing project, *Dooky Chase Restaurant* (☎ 504-821-0600, 2301 Orleans Ave), at Miro, is a historic gathering place where civil rights activists and touring jazz artists frequently gathered. If you want to soak in the historic vibe, request a table in the convivial original Gold Room. Entrees run between $10 to $25. In the same building, but through a different entrance, Dook's down-home take-out counter and bar offers fried chicken and gumbo at considerably lower prices (call ahead and your food will be ready when you get there). The restaurant is open daily for lunch and dinner.

Esplanade Ridge (Map 6)

Restaurants in the vicinity of the Fair Grounds naturally attract huge crowds for dinner during Jazz Fest. But several places out this way are worth coming to no matter what time of year it is – you can easily combine a meal along Esplanade Ave with a trip to City Park or a stroll along Bayou St John.

Whole Foods Market (☎ 504-943-1626, 3135 Esplanade Ave), just a block from the Fair Grounds, has quality meats, fresh baked goods and salads. *True Brew* (☎ 504-947-3948, 3133 Ponce de Leon) is a nouveau coffee hangout – no chicory here.

Lola's (☎ 504-488-6946, 3312 Esplanade Ave) is an energetic little place serving good, inexpensive Spanish food. Cool, soothing gazpacho ($3) is a good way to start. Elaborate paellas and *fideuas* (an angel-hair pasta variation on the rice-based paella; $10 to $14) are specialties here – they're feasts for the eyes as well as the

stomach, and great for sharing. Lola's takes no reservations, and lines are almost inevitable. It's open for dinner only.

Cafe Degas (☎ 504-945-5635, 3127 Esplanade Ave) is a congenial and romantic little spot that warms the heart with great French bistro fare and a mildly eccentric waitstaff. Savory meat dishes are Degas' forté, but you can also order a healthy lunch, such as salad niçoise with grilled tuna ($8). Lamb shanks ($18), cooked to perfection with a delicate but assertive Dijon sauce, are arranged beautifully on the plate. It's open daily for lunch and dinner.

At *Gabrielle* (☎ 504-948-6233, 3201 Esplanade Ave), chef Greg Sonnier cooks up his innovative mixture of Creole and Cajun dishes served in modest surroundings. Dinner entrees cost between $15 and $25.

ENTERTAINMENT

No matter what, you will be entertained in New Orleans.

Your best sources for upcoming performances and reviews are the free monthly entertainment guide *Offbeat* and the weekly *Gambit*. Tune into radio station WWOZ (90.7 FM) for around-the-clock education on southern Louisiana music, or call the station's events hotline, the Second Line (☎ 504-840-4040), for a daily listing of shows. Listings for gay and lesbian bars and dance clubs appear in the biweekly *Impact* and *Ambush* magazines, which also provide an entertainment calendar and list other current events.

TicketMaster (Map 2; ☎ 504-522-5555) has information on, and sells tickets to, just about any major event in the city. You can reserve tickets over the phone with a credit card and pick them up at the venue or at Tower Records on Decatur St.

Live-Music Clubs

One way to take in live music around town and not have to do the driving is to join the folks who run the *Magic Bus* (☎ 504-314-0710 day, 504-481-9551 night). The bus operates as a club-to-club shuttle service, costing $10 per person.

French Quarter (Map 2) The arrival of *House of Blues* (☎ *504-529-2583, 255 Decatur St)* has sparked a music revival in the French Quarter. Some locals grumbled when Dan Akroyd and a pack of out-of-town investors opened the club, but the full calendar of headliner acts (from the hottest local talent to touring bands) and the congenial space have won most of them over. After hours the club turns into a popular disco. On Sunday morning, HOB's Gospel Brunch will fortify your soul. Tickets for nightly shows cost between $7 (House of Blues All Stars) to $25 (Dr John). Upstairs, *The Parish* is HOB's small show venue, where local artists with less pull tend to perform.

Tipitina's French Quarter (☎ *504-895-8477, 233 N Peters St)* doesn't live up to the reputation of the original Uptown 'Tips,' and locals who feel that following House of Blues to the Quarter was beneath the famous nightclub have taken to calling it 'House of Tips.' But having Tipitina's in the Quarter means more great music in the heart of town. (See the Uptown section, later in this chapter, for more on the original Tipitina's.)

Quint Davis' *Storyville District* (☎ *504-410-1000, 125 Bourbon St)* is the best thing to happen on Bourbon St in a long time. The club features outstanding local music and good New Orleans bar food (po-boys, etc) by none other than Ralph Brennan. The clincher: the club rarely charges a cover. Drinks are, of course, a little on the expensive side.

Those are the big clubs, but not necessarily the best. Out on Rampart St, the smaller, genuinely swanky *Funky Butt on Congo Square* (☎ *504-558-0872, 225 N Rampart St)* is a bi-level club with a sexy, Jazz Age atmosphere. There's almost always something interesting going on here – usually jazz, though on occasion a Mardi Gras Indian gang will set the joint on fire. Named to honor Buddy Bolden's raunchy 'Funky Butt' theme song, the club stands opposite Congo Square, the throbbing heart of African culture during the mid-19th century.

Nearby, *Donna's Bar & Grill* (☎ *504-596-6914, 800 N Rampart St)* is still the premier brass band club in the city, although the scene here isn't as electrifying as it was a few years ago. You can still count on seeing brass bands here every night of the week. The cover hovers around $5.

The Blathering Boozeoisie

You don't need a guidebook to tell you about Bourbon St, the main stem of New Orleans' around-the-clock tourist bacchanalia. The street's reputation as a haven of delirium precedes itself.

Bourbon St is undeniably unique. Where else in America can you find eight historic blocks closed to traffic so tourists and conventioneers can get loaded, spill beer on each other, flash their breasts from cast-iron balconies, yell their heads off, leave trash all over the place and even vomit on the buildings and streets?

New Orleans relies on the tourist dollar, and judging by the nightly scene on Bourbon St, the city effortlessly succeeds in showing visitors a good time. It isn't a bad arrangement between the city and tourists hell-bent on waking up with a major hangover. To New Orleans' credit, Bourbon St has a certain 'Big Easy' panache that's rare among tourist traps. But if you're looking for genuine local color, Bourbon St will only disappoint. Locals rarely go to Bourbon St unless they're regulars at Galatoire's or have jobs in its bars and shops.

Picturesque *Preservation Hall* (☎ *504-522-2841, 726 St Peter St)* always pleases large crowds (mostly tourists) with 'trad jazz.' A New Orleans institution, it seems to have maintained a perfect state of elegant decay, and the bands are typically made up of talented grandpas. When it's warm enough to leave the window shutters open, you can join the crowd on the sidewalk to listen to the sets. Admission is $5; line up before 8 or 10 pm.

The *Palm Court Jazz Cafe* (☎ *504-525-0200, 1204 Decatur St)* also features traditional jazz. It lacks the rustic patina of Preservation Hall, but it is roomier and has a bar, and guests can expect chairs and a table. Palm Court has an excellent calendar, too, with local legends performing here regularly. Admission prices vary depending on the featured performers.

Many visitors are given the mistaken impression from the 'Dedicated to the Preservation of Jazz' banner that *Maison Bourbon* (☎ *504-522-8818, 641 Bourbon St)* is Preservation Hall. You can almost always find a seat to enjoy a Dixieland set for the price of a drink.

Opposite the Farmer's Market, Jimmy Buffett's *Margaritaville Café* (☎ *504-592-2565, 1104 Decatur St)* may bank primarily on its cheesy Parrothead image, but it also stands on its consistent policy of booking as many as three performers each day and not charging a cover.

Tremé District (Map 2) At *Joe's Cozy Corner* (no ☎, *1030 N Robertson St)*, at Ursulines Ave, there's a regular show on Sunday night, featuring Kermit Ruffins & the Barbecue Swingers and the Rebirth Brass Band. The small neighborhood hangout gets extremely crowded, with a mix of older folks, slick inner-city operators and, of late, a greater number of Uptown college students who cab to the Tremé. Because this is a neighborhood gig, musicians from around town are always likely to drop by and sit in.

A few blocks down Claiborne Ave stands a remarkable monument to the alive and kicking, soul-singing legend Ernie K-Doe. K-Doe recorded one smash hit after another during the 1960s, topping the national charts for several weeks in 1961 with the tune 'Mother In Law.' Today, K-Doe and his wife Antoinette run a nice little bar, *Ernie K-Doe's Mother-in-Law Lounge* (☎ *504-947-1078, 1500 N Claiborne Ave)*, at Columbus. It's not for everybody. (A *New York Times* writer was once booted out of the place for allegedly trying to record an informal K-Doe performance.) You really have to be a fan of the singer to appreciate so intimate an audience with someone who bills himself as the 'Emperor of the Universe.' Call before coming, because K-Doe might be performing elsewhere. Take a cab, as this stretch of Claiborne Ave isn't good for public transportation or walking.

Faubourg Marigny (Map 2) & Bywater The premier contemporary jazz venue in New Orleans, *Snug Harbor* (☎ *504-949-0696, 626 Frenchmen St)* regularly books headliner talent. There really isn't a bad seat in the place, upstairs or down, and the room's acoustics are unparalleled in town. Performers who regularly appear here include pianist Ellis Marsalis and R&B singer Charmaine Neville. Many shows sell out in advance, particularly when artists who rarely perform here are billed; it's a good idea to call ahead, just in case.

Cafe Brasil (☎ *504-947-9386, 2100 Chartres St)*, at Frenchmen St, is a very hip, bohemian space with a colorful Caribbean vibe. The club often features the city's best jazz and brass artists. When there's no live music, the space seems too expansive for the smattering of locals sitting at the bar.

Don't expect to hear any headliners among the loud rock and R&B groups performing at *Igor's Checkpoint Charlie* (☎ *504-947-0979, 501 Esplanade Ave)*, where you can also do your laundry and play pool 24 hours a day. There's no cover – just feed the kitty.

Vaughan's (☎ *504-947-5562, 800 Lesseps St)*, at Dauphine St, on a Thursday night is as good as New Orleans gets. That's the night trumpeter Kermit Ruffins raises the roof. The weekly gig regularly features Ruffins' band, the Barbecue Swingers, and drummer

Shannon Powell, an amazing performer. Anyone might show up to sit in – Wynton Marsalis has dropped by, and when pianist Henry Butler shows up, the bar's poor little upright piano darn near explodes. The crowds spill out onto the street, and between sets Kerm often dishes out barbecue from the smoker on the back of his pickup truck. The rest of the week, Vaughan's quietly serves the neighborhood well.

CBD & Warehouse District (Map 3)

Blues are naturally part of the tradition at *Howlin' Wolf* (☎ 504-522-9653, *828 S Peters St*), but rock bands and other local acts also appear at this first-rate club. Revered blues artist Snooks Eaglin might play here one night, followed by a touring band like Southern Culture on the Skids the next.

In the Hilton Riverside Hotel, *Pete Fountain's* (☎ 504-523-4374, *2 Poydras St*) features the famed clarinet player, who has been around since the late 1950s.

A bit off the beaten track, the *Lion's Den* (☎ 504-822-4693, *2655 Gravier St*) is a neighborhood bar that happens to be owned by Irma Thomas, the 'Soul Queen' of New Orleans. Call to find out if Irma's performing anytime soon. Seeing her sing here before a small crowd is an intimate, unforgettable experience.

Uptown (Map 5) The legendary *Tipitina's* (☎ 504-895-8477, *504-897-3943 for the*

New Orleans Jazz & Heritage Festival

Jazz Fest, as New Orleans' second-biggest festival is more commonly known, began in 1968, attracting jazz musicians Louis Armstrong, Dave Brubeck, Duke Ellington, Woody Herman, Ramsey Lewis and Pete Fountain. After struggling with poor attendance, Jazz Fest moved to the Fair Grounds in 1972 and expanded to two weekends in late April and early May. The organizers also began to showcase a variety of musical forms besides jazz.

In fact, the name is now a bit of a misnomer, unless 'jazz' is understood to loosely encompass all musical forms (which would be a very New Orleanian view). The festival has a single jazz tent among its many stages. There's the always rocking gospel tent, the Fais-Do-Do stage featuring Cajun and zydeco music, Congo Square featuring African and African-American music, the House of Blues Stage featuring blues and R&B artists, and a pair of big stages where big-time international stars perform (some of the major attractions – like Sting, who performed in 2000 – seem to have little connection to New Orleans, but what the hell…). There is also a children's stage, a Native American stage and other, smaller stages where just about anything might be going on.

Gospel singers at Jazz Fest

TOM DOWNS

The 'heritage' part of the festival refers to Louisiana and local arts, crafts and food. This continues downtown at Armstrong Park's Congo Square, where African food and crafts are emphasized.

It's highly recommended to arrive at the Fair Grounds hungry – the plethora of eating options is staggering, and prices are reasonable. But you'll have to decide what you're hungry for: a plate of boiled crawfish (it's peak season!), shrimp étouffée, catfish or oyster po-boys, a heaping helping of jambalaya or red beans and rice, soft-shell crab (also

concert line, 501 Napoleon Ave), at Tchoupi-toulas St, is recovering from changes wrought by the arrival of House of Blues in the French Quarter. 'Tips,' as locals refer to it, has responded by opening a venue in the French Quarter, and some feel the Uptown location has suffered as the emphasis has been on booking name acts at the newer site. Nevertheless, Uptown Tips is still the 'real' Tips, and it remains a shrine to the great Professor Longhair, whose 1953 hit 'Tipitina' inspired the club's name. And out-standing music from the local talent pool still packs 'em in. Cover charges start at $8.

Most of the time, *Le Bon Temps Roulé* (☎ 504-895-8117, 4801 Magazine St), at Bordeaux St, is just a neighborhood bar – and a

good one – with a mostly college and post-college crowd drawn in by two pool tables and a commendable beer selection. But late at night, blues, zydeco or jazz rocks the joint's little back room. Any time you can catch an extraordinary talent like Henry Butler in such close quarters, don't miss it.

Riverbend (Map 5) The *Maple Leaf Bar* (☎ 504-866-9359, 8316 Oak St) has a solid musical calendar, and its dimly lit, pressed-tin caverns are the kind of environs you'd expect from a New Orleans club. You can regularly catch performances by local stars such as Walter 'Wolfman' Washington, Rockin' Dopsie Jr & the Zydeco Twisters or the Rebirth Brass Band.

New Orleans Jazz & Heritage Festival

in season), crawfish pie, zesty gumbo, crawfish Monica, barbecued anything, crab-stuffed mush-rooms, cherry 'snowballs' and strawberry shortcake, plus cuisine from other cultures (gyros, Cuban sandwiches, fried plantains), and the list goes on and on, with over 60 vendors to choose from. This is an excellent place to get your culinary bearings. And for some reason everything at Jazz Fest tastes more delicious than it might elsewhere! Just one word of advice: it's a long day at the Fair Grounds. Pace yourself. Don't load up on carbohydrates early in the day, as they'll just make you tired.

In addition, plan for heat and sun at the Fair Grounds – bring sunscreen and a brimmed hat and wear light-colored clothing. Keep yourself well hydrated – and though it may be the perfect thirst-quencher, not with beer! Only a few tents at Jazz Fest are ventilated (hardly air-conditioned, but at least shaded). Most stages are open-air, and you'll end up standing for long periods of time. It's a good idea to bring a blanket or ground cover for resting between concerts and a rain poncho.

You can check the schedules as early as January (they're not available earlier) and should make reservations as soon as possible to save money and assure that you get your favored weekend dates. Daily passes cost $18 in advance or $20 at the gate (prices go up each year, so expect an increase). The Fair Grounds are open daily from 11 am to 7 pm, and there are many nightly performances at other sites in New Orleans. Call or write the New Orleans Jazz & Heritage Festival (☎ 504-522-4786, 2200 Royal St, New Orleans, LA 70117). Tickets are available through Ticket-Master (☎ 504-522-5555). Visit www.insideneworleans.com/entertainment/nojazzfest.

Getting There & Away

Ditch your car, as you cannot count on getting one of the few paid parking spaces ($10 and up) near the Fair Grounds. The RTA (☎ 504-569-2700) operates their regularly scheduled No 82 Esplanade bus from the French Quarter. Special shuttles are available from the New Orleans Jazz & Heritage Festival at an additional cost. Air-conditioned shuttle buses run back and forth from major hotels on Canal St. Cabs are not difficult to get in the morning, but there's a long line of people waiting for taxis out of the Fair Grounds at night.

Carrollton Station (☎ 504-865-9190, 8140 Willow St) is only a block from the streetcar line on S Carrollton Ave, opposite the historic streetcar barn with the same name. It features live R&B music on weekends. Just down the street from Carrollton Station, *Jimmy's (☎ 504-861-8200, 8200 Willow St)* is a worthwhile addition to any Uptown pub crawl, with live music just about every night.

Mid-City (Map 6) One of the more incredible music venues in town is *Mid-City Rock & Bowl (☎ 504-482-3133, 4133 S Carrollton Ave)*. What we have here is a gimmick – live music in an already bustling bowling alley – taken about as far as it can possibly go. The clincher is that owner John Blancher consistently books artists straight out of the American musical book of legends. Watching the likes of blind blues man Snooks Eaglin, soul-singing Ernie K-Doe (self-anointed 'Emperor of the Universe') or zydeco squeeze-box king Boozoo Chavis – all of whom can still rock the house – becomes an unreal experience when you hear the crash of bowling pins

Professor Longhair

between songs. Add to this a perky teenage bar staff and unusual side acts, like a lip-synching black Elvis impersonator, and you begin to get the idea that Blancher (who *looks* fairly normal) is a genius of the absurd. He claims he was on the road to visit a religious shrine when he had an epiphany to buy the bowling alley. With two stages (upstairs and down) and a cast of musical characters you'd never expect to see in this type of setting, Rock & Bowl is a rockin' good time.

Large Music Venues

Big shows, like the Rolling Stones, fill the *Louisiana Superdome (☎ 504-587-3810, 1500 Poydras St)*, while artists with slightly less pull, such as Bruce Springsteen, are likely to perform at the more intimate *Saenger Performing Arts Center Theatre (☎ 504-522-5555, 143 N Rampart St)*. Headliners like Bob Dylan have performed at the *Kiefer University of New Orleans Lakefront Arena (☎ 504-286-7222, 6801 Franklin Ave)*.

The city's *Mahalia Jackson Theater of the Performing Arts (☎ 504-565-7470)*, in Louis Armstrong Park, is dedicated to the powerful late gospel singer, who was born in New Orleans in 1911 and in 1927 moved to Chicago, where her career blossomed. The theater holds many Mardi Gras masquerade balls and other performances.

Bars

Yeah, there are a few bars in this town, most of 'em tourist traps. Here are some of the good ones. ...

French Quarter (Map 2) Moody *Lafitte's Blacksmith Shop (☎ 504-523-0066, 941 Bourbon St)* is a dark and atmospheric haunt with a back room piano bar. Observe the impressionistic images created by table-top candles – little dabs of light brighten patrons' cheeks and eyes, transforming them into figures in a Toulouse-Lautrec oil painting. As for the lore of the place, there are plenty of unconfirmed stories about Jean Lafitte and his brother Pierre, New Orleans' legendary pirates. No one knows if they really ran a blacksmith shop as a cover for their illegal trade in slaves, but it makes a good story.

Another ancient bar, *Napoleon House* (☎ 504-524-9752, 500 Chartres St) dates to 1797. In fact, it's a particularly attractive example of what Walker Percy termed 'vital decay.' By all appearances, its stuccoed walls haven't received so much as a paint job in over two centuries, and the diffuse glow pouring through the open doors and windows in the afternoon illuminates the room's gorgeous patina. But would Napoleon himself have appreciated these surroundings? When the deposed emperor was banished to St Helena, a band of loyal New Orleanians, including former mayor Nicholas Girod and the pirate Jean Lafitte, reputedly plotted to snatch him and set him up in this building's 3rd-floor digs. But Napoleon died before the alleged plan was carried out.

The *Old Absinthe House* (☎ 504-523-3181, 240 Bourbon St) is one of many bars that served absinthe, the notorious wormwood potion, until it was outlawed in 1914. This is a historic spot, having opened in 1806, and its attractive bar is graced by an old marble water fountain topped by a bronze statuette of Napoleon Bonaparte. But if you want absinthe today, you'll have to smuggle it into the country – Pernod is the 90-proof stand-in of choice.

Jim Monaghan's *Molly's at the Market* (☎ 504-525-5169, 1107 Decatur St) is the Irish cultural center of the French Quarter. Monaghan inaugurated the wild St Patrick's Day Parade that starts at Molly's. Molly's attracts a diverse mix of New Orleans characters. *Fahy's Irish Pub* (☎ 504-586-9806, 540 Burgundy St) attracts a neighborhood crowd with pool, darts and Guinness.

You haven't completed the tourist rounds until you've had a 'Hurricane' or mint julep in the courtyard at *Pat O'Brien's* (☎ 504-525-4823, 800-597-4823, 718 St Peter St). A trademark of the bar, the Hurricane is a 29oz concoction of rum, orange juice, pineapple juice and grenadine ($5 plus $2 refundable deposit on the souvenir glass).

Something to Ponder

It probably comes as no surprise that New Orleans claims to have invented the whole concept of having a drink for the hell of it – that is, having a cocktail. As always, the Crescent City backs up that claim with a good story that may well explain the origin of the word 'cocktail.'

It all begins with a man named Peychaud, who settled in New Orleans after fleeing the 18th-century slave uprisings in Hispaniola. He opened an apothecary on Royal St, where, we are told, he developed a penchant for drinking brandy in an eggcup. The concept appealed to the people of New Orleans, and Peychaud began serving drinks in this fashion at his shop. (One might wonder why people were so willing to drink from an eggcup, but read on… .)

The eggcup, of course, was not called an eggcup in French-speaking New Orleans. It was called a *coquetier*. It was called that until Peychaud's inebriated patrons began mispronouncing it. The term evolved – much as Acadian turned into Cajun – from 'coquetier' to 'cock-tay' to 'cocktail.' In time, the eggcup was disposed of in favor of a regular glass, and other liquors came to be more popular than brandy, but the name stuck.

On another booze-related historical note: in the mid-19th century, a French brandy manufacturer, Sazerac-du-Forge, lent its name to a brandy cocktail, called the Sazerac, that evolved into an absinthe-based drink, which eventually featured whiskey instead of brandy. And today, the Sazerac cocktail includes no absinthe, either, because too many 19th-century enthusiasts of the wormwood-based liquor went out of their minds, and the beverage was outlawed in many countries, including the US. You can still order a Sazerac (with Pernod as a substitute) in just about any New Orleans bar, but don't expect great things from the syrupy beverage.

The **Rawhide Lounge** (☎ 504-525-8106, 740 Burgundy St) is – surprise! – a gay leather bar.

Faubourg Marigny (Map 2) & Bywater

The **Royal St Inn** (☎ 504-948-7499, 1431 Royal St) is a popular Marigny bar that attracts a mixed gay and straight crowd that never seems to lose the Mardi Gras spirit.

In the Bywater, the **Saturn Bar** (☎ 504-949-7532, 3067 St Claude Ave) is like an old junk store or garage that happens to have a bar in it. (Be careful not to bump into that Frigidaire on your way in.) Light comes only from two saturnine neon lamps, and there doesn't seem to be a comfortable seat in the place. The mummy hanging from the ceiling looks like somebody actually dug it up – and some of the characters who spend time here look like they might have done it. All in all, a great bar.

Lower Garden & Garden Districts (Map 4)

Barhopping trendsetters typically drop in at the **Half Moon** (☎ 504-522-7313, 1125 St Mary St), at Sophie Wright Place, but you might stay and play at the best pool tables in the area. **Igor's Lounge** (☎ 504-522-2145, 2133 St Charles Ave) is a 24-hour dive bar with a greasy grill, pool tables and washing machines. Another laundry bar, **Lucky's Lounge** (☎ 504-523-6538, 1625 St Charles Ave) offers happy hour draft beers for $1.25 from 5 to 7 pm and from midnight to 4 am.

Uptown (Map 5)

Suits and gowns abound at the lively **Columns Hotel** (☎ 504-899-9308, 3811 St Charles Ave), where the Uptown elite gather to celebrate and be seen. Ordinary out-of-town folk won't feel unwelcome, though men might want to don a jacket. Over the clinking glasses filled with mint juleps and gin fizzes, the burbling of the crowd grows louder as the night grows older.

Dance Clubs

A key to nearly two centuries of successful entertainment in New Orleans has been live music plus booze. Credit for breaking the mold must go to the large gay nightclubs on lower Bourbon St; these spots rely strictly on DJs for entertainment. Foremost are the twin sentinels of pulsing sounds: **Oz** (Map 2; ☎ 504-593-9491, 800 Bourbon St) and the **Bourbon Pub** (Map 2; ☎ 504-529-2107, 801 Bourbon St). Both are open to straights who want to dance nonstop and don't have a problem with guys in G-strings on stage.

A young mixed crowd that is predominantly heterosexual packs the dance floor at the **Gold Mine Saloon** (Map 2; ☎ 504-586-0745, 705 Dauphine St). Check the free weeklies and the gay 'zines for current information.

The **Mint** (☎ 504-944-4888, 940 Elysian Fields Blvd), in Faubourg Marigny, is a gay bar with DJs and dancing on Saturday night.

Theaters & Cinemas

Major touring troupes typically perform at the **Saenger Theatre** (☎ 504-522-5555, 143 N Rampart St) in the Tremé District, where it's worth the admission just to see the fine restoration of the ornate 1927 theater. Also check to see what's playing at the **Contemporary Arts Center** (Map 2; ☎ 504-523-1216, 900 Camp St).

Le Petit Théâtre du Vieux Carré (Map 2; ☎ 504-522-2081, 616 St Peter St) is one of the oldest theater groups in the country. The troupe offers particularly Southern fare like Steel Magnolias, as well as special children's programming such as classics from Rudyard Kipling and others.

Founded in 1986, **Southern Repertory Theatre** (Map 3; ☎ 504-861-8163, 333 Canal Place), on the 3rd floor, performs classically Southern plays that deal with relationships, crisis and humor in a 150-seat theater.

IMAX films are shown on a 74-foot by 54-foot screen at the **Entergy IMAX Theatre** (☎ 504-581-4629), at the foot of Canal St near the Aquarium of the Americas. Shows begin on the hour between 10 am and 8 pm. Admission costs $7.75 for adults, $5 for children.

For first-run art and mainstream movies, try the **Canal Place Cinemas** (☎ 504-581-5400, 333 Canal Place), on the 3rd floor. The

Uptown *Prytania Theatre* (☎ 504-895-4518, 5339 Prytania St) is a similar venue.

Classical Music Performances

New Orleans' concertgoers are justifiably proud of the *Louisiana Philharmonic Orchestra* (☎ 504-523-6530), led by music director Klaus Peter Seibel. When the New Orleans Symphony financially collapsed in 1990, the musicians invested their own money to create one of only two musician-owned symphonies in the world. From September through May, they perform at the richly ornamented *Orpheum Theater (Map 3; ☎ 504-524-3285, 129 University Place)*, downtown. Tickets cost between $11 and $36. A special concert series at nearby plantations is extremely popular and costs only $7.

SPECTATOR SPORTS

The 60,000-seat Louisiana Superdome (Map 3; ☎ 504-733-0255), 1500 Poydras St, is home to the National Football League's New Orleans Saints. The Saints play eight home games from August through December. Tickets cost $22 to $50. Seats are generally available through TicketMaster (☎ 504-522-5555).

Opened in 1872, the Fair Grounds Race Track (Map 6; ☎ 504-944-5515), 1751 Gentilly Blvd, is the third-oldest track in the nation. The racing season runs November to March on Wednesday through Sunday, with a 1:30 pm post time.

With 72 home games from April to September, you can catch the minor league New Orleans Zephyrs baseball team on almost any week of the summer season. Zephyr Field (☎ 504-734-5155), 6000 Airline Hwy, at the junction with Dickory Ave, opened in 1997. General admission costs $5, or you can splurge for reserved seats at $7 for adults, $6 for seniors and $5 for children.

SHOPPING

Because New Orleans has a culture and traditions all its own, many shops are devoted to selling items that have no market anywhere else.

Music

For new and used CDs head to the Louisiana Music Factory (Map 2; ☎ 504-523-1094), 210 Decatur St, a great shop specializing in regional music. Upstairs is a small collection of used LPs, and there's also a nice selection of T-shirts that you won't find elsewhere. Nearby, at Magic Bus (Map 2; ☎ 504-522-0530), 527 Conti St, the used CD bins are worth a look.

Jim Russell Rare Records (Map 4; ☎ 504-522-2602, 1837 Magazine St) is the best shop in New Orleans for used 45s and LPs, with several rooms that may make you seek some guidance to find what you're looking for. That old Ernie K-Doe single from 1965? It's probably in there somewhere (at a price !$!$!).

Art

Royal St anchors the local art trade, and although nothing comes cheap here it's certainly worth browsing. A Gallery of Fine Photography (Map 2; ☎ 504-568-1313, 313 Royal St) offers historical prints such as William Henry Jackson's early-20th-century views of New Orleans and regularly features the work of Herman Leonard, the great photographer of jazz artists.

In the Warehouse District, check out the 628 Gallery (Map 3; ☎ 504-529-3306), 628 Baronne St, where Young Artists/Young Aspirations (YA/YA), founded by painter Jana Napoli, is an exemplary arts program that works with at-risk teens. It's an impressive program – in 1995, the United Nations bought tapestries from YA/YA. It's open 10 am to 5 pm, and students can be seen working in the afternoon.

In Mid-City, African-American art and literature are featured at the Community Book Center & Neighborhood Gallery (Map 6; ☎ 504-822-2665), 217 N Broad Ave. In addition to exhibition space dedicated to local artists, the gallery also includes an area for performing arts events such as storytelling, African dancing, music and poetry.

Antiques & Interesting Junk

You'll find antique shops and art galleries scattered all along Magazine St, but a few clusters really stand out. The blocks between St Andrew and Jackson, and between 8th and 9th Sts, are especially busy with the secondhand trade.

In the French Quarter, head to the lower end of Decatur St, where a number of shops sell old stuff.

Mardi Gras Accoutrements

Since New Orleans is host to the USA's biggest masquerade party, there's naturally a huge market for this kind of thing. You can find inexpensive masks and beads in the flea market stalls at the French Market and in most of the tourist gimcrack shops in the Quarter. Little Shop of Fantasy (Map 2; ☎ 504-529-4243), 523 Dumaine St, and Royal Rags (Map 2; ☎ 504-566-7247), 627 Dumaine, are two places you can go for arty masks and costumes, as well as an assortment of unusual toys and creative items. The Presbytère gift shop sells cheap masks and accessories, along with hefty Zulu medallion beads. The Zulu Social Aid &

RICHARD CUMMINS

Store windows come to life at Mardi Gras.

Pleasure Club operates its own gift shop (Map 6; ☎ 504-822-1559), 7220 N Broad Ave, where Zulu T-shirts and curios can be bought straight from the source.

Vintage Clothing

When it comes to used clothing, this town ain't too shabby. However, if you're looking for outrageous stuff around Mardi Gras, you're likely to find that the stores have been picked clean.

In the French Quarter, head to lower Decatur St, where Jazz Rags (Map 2; ☎ 504-523-2942), 1215 Decatur St, aims to get you looking like Fred and Ethel from the 'I Love Lucy Show.'

In the Lower Garden District, Jim Smiley Fine Vintage Clothing (☎ 504-528-9449), 2001 Magazine St, is a great little shop dealing in very well-preserved garments, as well as laces, linens and textiles. Farther uptown, Funky Monkey (☎ 504-899-5587), 3127 Magazine St, and Fiesta (Map 4; ☎ 504-895-7877), 3322 Magazine St near Louisiana Ave, can usually be counted on for sporty duds.

Voodoo Supplies

Maybe you're not feeling well – some gris-gris worn in a sachet will make you feel better. Dried frog gris-gris is useful if you want to practice a little black magic on a bad neighbor. Or maybe you just need some love potion No 9. For potions, take your pick from Zombie's House of Voodoo (☎ 504-486-6366, 723 St Peter St), where you'll also find a large selection of books on the occult; Marie Laveau's House of Voodoo (☎ 504-581-3751), 739 Bourbon St; or the Witch's Closet (☎ 504-593-9222), 521 St Philip St. Starling Books (☎ 504-595-6777), 1022 Royal St, is less a curio shop than a serious alternative New Age store where literature, herbs, and voodoo paraphernalia are sold. (These sites can all be found on Map 2.)

French Market

The French Market houses a vibrant Flea Market filled with bargains on everything from music CDs to crafts, along with a

Farmer's Market emphasizing local food-stuffs and cooking supplies.

Merchants in the Farmer's Market offer fresh fruits and vegetables, including mangos, papaya, green beans, bananas, plantains, peaches, strawberries, watermelon, apples, pecans and cold drinks. In addition, there are lots of kitchen supplies, spices (including a large selection of hot sauces), garlic and chili strings, and cookbooks for the tourist trade.

The flea market attracts a motley assortment of T-shirt and sunglasses vendors, but you will also find authentic African art, well-priced handcrafted sterling silver jewelry, inexpensive Mardi Gras masks, music CDs of dubious origin and enough preserved alligator heads to populate a swamp.

Malls
The Jackson Brewery (☎ 504-566-7245), 600 Decatur St, has been redeveloped into a small shopping mall. The Riverwalk Mall (☎ 504-522-1555) is on the riverfront upriver from the aquarium and is occupied by many chain stores. Adjoining the Superdome at LaSalle St and Poydras Ave, the air-conditioned New Orleans Centre (☎ 504-568-0000) is yet another downtown shopping emporium with Lord & Taylor and Macy's department stores.

GETTING THERE & AWAY
Air
New Orleans International Airport (☎ 504-464-0831) is not a large airport. A single terminal is connected to four concourses. Finding your way around is quite easy.

The main information booth, located downstairs at the A and B concourse (near the baggage claim), is open 8 am to 8 pm daily. Ask for a free copy of the *New Orleans Street Map*. The airport post office is near Concourse C.

A Whitney National Bank branch (☎ 504-838-6432) and ATM are in the terminal near Concourse C. Whitney charges a flat $5 foreign exchange service fee. It's open 8:30 am to 3 pm weekdays (till 5:30 on Friday). Also take a look at the exchange rates at Travelex (☎ 504-465-9647). Travelex

charges a sliding service fee and stays open later (till 6:30 pm).

White courtesy phones and a free phone connection to various airport services are scattered through the terminal. Pay phones that accept credit cards are widely available. See the Getting Around section for options on getting from the airport to your lodging.

Bus
Greyhound (☎ 800-231-2222, 800-531-5332 for Spanish-language service) is the only regular long-distance bus company serving the city. All trains and Greyhound buses share the New Orleans Union Passenger Terminal (Union Station), 1001 Loyola Ave, seven blocks upriver from Canal St. It's online at www.greyhound.com.

From New Orleans, there are two morning, three afternoon and four evening Greyhound buses to Baton Rouge. Travel time is under two hours, and the roundtrip fare (quoted recently on Greyhound's Web site) is $18.50. Other frequent departures and sample roundtrip fares include the following:

Atlanta	$74
Chicago	$125
Houston	$72
Jackson	$50
Lafayette	$31
Memphis	$71
Mobile	$44
Nashville	$48

Bicycles must be boxed (boxes are not available from Greyhound) and cost an additional $10 each way.

Train
Three Amtrak trains (☎ 800-872-7245, www.amtrak.com) serve New Orleans at the Union Passenger Terminal (Map 3; ☎ 504-528-1610), 1001 Loyola Ave.

The *City of New Orleans* runs to Jackson, Memphis (via towns in the Mississippi Delta) and Chicago. The *Crescent Route* serves Birmingham, Atlanta, Washington,

DC, and New York City. New Orleans is also on the *Sunset Limited* route between Los Angeles and Miami.

Car

Interstate 10 is the nation's major east-west route along the southern boundary, linking Jacksonville with Los Angeles via Mobile, New Orleans and Houston. Baton Rouge and Lafayette are also on I-10 west of New Orleans.

The north-south routes I-55 (to Chicago via Jackson and Memphis) and I-59 (to Chattanooga) meet I-10 to the west and east of New Orleans on either side of Lake Pontchartrain.

Call Auto Driveaway Co (☎ 504-737-0266), 7809 Airline Hwy in Kenner, if you're interested in a drive-away.

Bicycle

The interstate freeways and highway bridges near New Orleans are closed to bicyclists. Instead, use Hwy 90 or Hwy 61. All of New Orleans' free state-operated ferries crossing the Mississippi River offer bicycle transport. Outside of the city, the crossings cost $1.

GETTING AROUND
To/From the Airport

New Orleans International Airport is in Kenner, 11 miles west of the city center.

Most visitors take the Airport Shuttle (☎ 504-522-3500) to and from the airport. It offers frequent service between the airport and downtown hotels for $20 per passenger (fare includes passage back to the airport at the end of your visit). At the airport, purchase tickets from agents in the baggage area below the arrival gates. To get from your hotel to the airport, call a day ahead to arrange for a departure pickup.

The Louisiana Transit Company (☎ 504-737-9611) offers the cheapest ride to downtown aboard its Jefferson Transit Airport Express, route E2, for $1.50. The airport bus stop is opposite door No 5 on the upper level of the main terminal; a downtown stop is on Tulane Ave at Elks Place opposite the public library. After 6:30 pm, this bus doesn't go all the way downtown – ask your driver about transfers.

The quickest way to drive between the airport and downtown is to take I-10.

Taxi service to downtown costs $24 for one or two people, $30 for three people, $40 for four, $50 for five. Taxi stands are on the lower level, immediately outside the baggage claim area.

To/From the Train & Bus Station

As incredible as it may seem, local buses do not directly serve Union Passenger Terminal. In front of the station, arriving passengers must search for the sheltered stop across Loyola at Howard Aves. The No 17 S Claiborne Ave bus goes to the edge of the French Quarter at Canal and Rampart Sts ($1.25 fare plus 25¢ for a transfer). During the weeks preceding Mardi Gras, a sign directs passengers to board one block down Loyola Ave at Julia St.

Bus

The Regional Transit Authority (RTA) offers decent bus and streetcar service (see Streetcar, below). Call the RTA Rideline (☎ 504-248-3900) for bus route information. Fares cost $1.25 and transfers are 25¢ extra, except on express buses, which charge a $1.50 fare. All buses require exact change.

From the French Quarter, most destinations are served by buses that stop at the intersection of Basin and Canal Sts.

Streetcar

New Orleans' historic St Charles Ave Streetcar runs the entire length of St Charles Ave, from the French Quarter to the Riverbend, passing the Garden District en route. The fare is $1.25 each way (exact change required), and a transfer to RTA buses costs 25¢. Service is 24 hours a day. Unfortunately, the streetcars are not wheelchair accessible.

The Riverfront Streetcar Line operates vintage red cars on the old dockside rail corridor wedged between the levee and flood wall. The 2-mile route runs from the Old US Mint, in the lower end of the French

Quarter near the Faubourg Marigny, to the upriver convention center, crossing Canal St on the way. The fare costs $1.25. It operates from 6 am to midnight.

Car
Downtown on-street parking is typically for short-term use. Parking meters offer 12 minutes for a quarter, with a two-hour limit, from 8 am to 6 pm weekdays. Exceptions are numerous, so be sure to read all posted restrictions to avoid citations or towing.

Parking lots are distributed throughout the French Quarter and CBD. Most offer an all-day $12 rate, or $3 or $4 for the first hour. The least expensive lots are on Rampart St and they're outdoors and unguarded.

Taxi
Except when parades are blocking streets and when peak events are taking place, hailing a cab is easy in downtown New Orleans. It can be more difficult Uptown and elsewhere.

Telephoned requests for a taxi are typically quickly met, yet none of the taxi companies can be recommended as being completely reliable. White Fleet Cabs (☎ 504-948-6605) and United Cabs (☎ 504-522-9771) will pick up passengers anywhere within New Orleans. Fares in New Orleans cost $2.10 for the flag drop plus about $1 per mile.

Bicycle
New Orleans is flat and relatively compact, but potholes make fat tires a near necessity. Bicycles can be rented for around $15 to $20 a day at the following shops:

French Quarter Bicycles (☎ 504-529-3136),
    522 Dumaine St
Joe's Bike Shop (☎ 504-821-2350),
    2501 Tulane Ave, Mid-City
Bicycle Michael's (☎ 504-945-9505),
    622 Frenchmen St, Faubourg Marigny

AROUND NEW ORLEANS
Heading out of New Orleans, it doesn't take long before you find yourself surrounded by swamplands. There are numerous spots within an hour's drive of the city that are worthy of a day trip.

South To The Swamp
Below New Orleans, the Mississippi River flows 90 miles to the bird's foot-shaped delta, where river pilots board ships entering from the gulf. Rather than drive for hours to Venice, the farthest downstream point accessible by automobile, you can satisfy the same desire to travel to the end of the road at Barataria Preserve, Lafitte or Westwego, each less than an hour's drive from New Orleans. For those in search of a wetlands adventure, the Barataria Preserve beckons. In the little fishing village of Lafitte, about 10 or so miles south of Barataria down Hwy 45, you will find a wonderful country inn and two great seafood shacks in a setting more reminiscent of the Mosquito Coast than suburban New Orleans. A bit further west of the Hwy 45 turnoff, but more easily accessible, is the little town of Westwego, home to one of the state's premier swamp tours.

Barataria Preserve The Barataria Preserve, a unit of southern Louisiana's Jean Lafitte National Historical Park and Preserve, is set in an area originally settled by Isleños (Canary Islanders) in 1779. It offers hiking and canoe trips into the swamp and a good introduction to the wetlands environment. It is not a pristine wilderness, as canals and other structures offer evidence of human activities, yet wild animals and plants are abundant. Even a brief walk on the boardwalks that wend their way through the swamp will yield sightings of gators and egrets aplenty.

The best place to start is the NPS Visitors Center (☎ 504-589-2330 ext 10), 6588 Barataria Blvd, 1 mile west of Hwy 45, where you can pick up a map of the 8 miles of hiking trails and 9 miles of dedicated canoe routes, which are all closed to motorized boats. A 25-minute introductory nature film, *Jambalaya: A Delta Almanac*, is also shown at the center, which is open daily from 9 am to 5 pm (closed Christmas day).

AROUND NEW ORLEANS

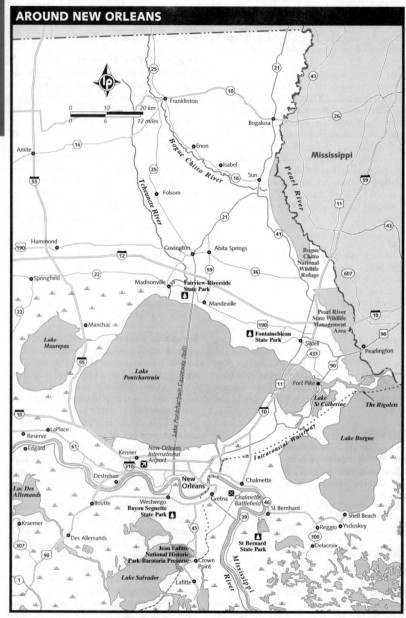

Trails in the preserve are open all the time, but parking lots close around dusk (signs are posted with the exact time – take note, when the gates are shut, your car is stuck). Call the visitor center to ask about ranger-led walks around **Bayou Coquille**. Other ranger-led activities require reservations, including a guided canoe trek and night walks.

Nearby *Jean Lafitte Inn* (☎ 504-689-3271, 800-339-8633), at the corner of Hwy 45 and Barataria Blvd, has nine modern air-con cabins for $60 to $75. Visit its Web site at www.jeanlafitteinn.com for more information. At the adjacent bar (formerly known as Earl's – the old sign may still be up), you can rent a canoe for exploring the park's waterways on your own; $25 gets you a canoe to seat three people, plus drop-off and pick-up service in the preserve. The bar is also a good spot for an ice cold one.

You can also rent canoes ($12.50 per person for the day) on the Bayou des Familles just outside the park at *Bayou Barn* (☎ 504-689-2663, 7145 Barataria Blvd), a pleasant compound of tin-topped weather-beaten buildings. Cajun or zydeco bands play to lively local crowds at the fais-do-do ($5) held here every Sunday from noon to 6 pm; add the Cajun buffet and the price is $10. Bayou Barn is closed on Monday.

Upscale dining at *Restaurant des Familles* (☎ 504-689-7834, 7163 Barataria Blvd), behind Bayou Barn, is a reward for a day of hiking or paddling. The cathedral-ceilinged dining room, which overlooks the bayou, features Cajun-tinged seafood lunches and dinners for $7 to $20. The soft-shell crabs (in season) smothered in a sauce of butter, artichokes and mushrooms are especially good. The restaurant also boasts a bar and lounge. It's closed on Monday.

Lafitte After you cross the high-rise bridge and double back onto Hwy 45 heading south, you will first come to the little town of Jean Lafitte. Quaint and remote though it may be, it has nothing on the little fishing village of Lafitte, some 8 more miles down the road. Soon the road narrows and you can almost feel the swamplands closing in around you. Due to frequent flooding, even the mobile homes down this way are set on stilts, and the Spanish moss hangs heavy – like green streamers tossed pell-mell onto the boughs of the live oak trees. This is a land remote, a land apart – once the province of the pirate Jean Lafitte and now home to a hardy camp of commercial fishers. Around these parts, 90% of the locals still make their living from the waters, and life owes its design to the patterns of the seasons and the sea. Though there are no typical tourist attractions to visit, the abundant waterside funk is worthy of a few hours of wandering.

Only 45 minutes from the French Quarter, the unconventional accommodations in Lafitte can serve as a base for exploring New Orleans to the north and the Cajun Wetlands to the west. At *Cochiara's Marina* (☎ 504-689-3701), on the left coming into town by the Goose Bayou Bridge, you can buy a fan belt for your car, Miracle-Gro for your garden and a cold beer from the bar. 'Folks around here like to tell their wife they're going to the hardware store,' says the proprietor, his face creased by a sly smile. 'Where else can you go shopping and catch a buzz?' Fishing charters and scruffy motel rooms ($55 and up) bordering on the bayou are also available. Though the rooms lack charm, they are in a nice spot right on the waterfront.

Farther south along the ever-narrowing roadway, you pass the turnoff for Lafitte's de-facto tourism office, the *Victoria Inn* (☎ 504-689-4757, 800-689-4797), on Hwy 45. The inn offers 14 rooms in two West Indies-style plantation homes surrounded by gardens. And just over the levee looms a lake, known locally as 'The Pen,' complete with a private dock available to inn guests. Some of the rooms can be a bit cramped for the price ($89 to $139), but the innkeepers are welcoming and extremely knowledgeable about the area, and the surroundings are sure to please guests. The innkeepers will also help you secure reservations for swamp tours and the like. Visit their Web site at www.victoriainn.com before your trip.

A mile or so farther south is **Boutte's Restaurant** (☎ 504-689-3889), a comfortable local joint with a great rooftop deck overlooking the Intracoastal Waterway. A half-shrimp, half-oyster po-boy costs just $5 and is sure to satisfy. Turtle soup at $3 a cup is damn near perfect. Steaks and chicken are also available, but why would you want to order them when the fishing boats dock just a block or two away? Boutte's (pronounced boo-TEE's) is open from 11 am to 10 pm every day but Monday.

Continuing south down Hwy 45, just before the road ends, keep a keen eye out for the barely legible sign for **Voleo's Seafood** (☎ 504-689-2482), in a humble structure fronted by a German-inspired beer garden. Local favorites include seafood-stuffed eggplant and trout topped with a crawfish and cream sauce for about $12 or so. If you fish, Voleo's will prepare your catch for you. It's open daily for lunch and dinner.

Westwego At Hwy 90 and Louisiana Ave is a sight you're not likely to see outside Louisiana, a huge **open-air fish market** – 20 little shacks clustered in a horseshoe fashion around a gravel parking lot – selling fresh-off-the-boat shrimp, crawfish, crabs and such at rock-bottom prices; at last pass, large shrimp were selling for around $2.50 a pound ($4 for jumbos). It's the perfect spot to pick up a sack or two of live crawfish for boiling later or to just take a gander at the bounty of the sea. The fish market is open daily from around dawn until dusk.

Make the turn south onto Louisiana St, and a block later the pavement gives way to dirt, and soon you are pulling up in front of the charmingly ramshackle home of Chacahoula Swamp Tours (☎ 504-436-2640), 422 Louisiana St. This family-owned business, run by Jerry Dupre, his wife and two daughters, offers a far more intimate **swamp experience** than larger operators. Converted shrimp boats seat about 20, rather than 50, and the narration is not amplified. Instead, you float along amid the stillness of the swamps and bayous as Captain Jerry points out the flora and

fauna, and coaxes an alligator to the side of the boat for the viewing pleasure of his passengers. Most tours last two hours and cost $22 per person. For an extra $16, the Dupre family will pick up passengers from New Orleans hotels – a bargain deal, especially on days when the Dupres have a big pot of gumbo waiting for guests at the end of the tour.

Still hungry? The Westwego area is home to two outstanding restaurants, each perched at the opposite end of the scale of affordability. **Mo's Pizza** (☎ 504-341-9650, 1112 Ave H) is just a mile or so east of Louisiana St off Hwy 90. Here you will find one of the metropolitan area's best muffulettas ($4) as well as wonderful pizzas, sausage rolls, po-boys and spaghetti with meatballs, all served at ridiculously low prices in a scruffy setting (where the jukebox seems to rattle and hum incessantly to a heavy bass beat). Draft beer is $4 a pitcher. Mo's is open every day but Sunday from 10 am to 10 pm.

Mosca's (☎ 504-436-9942, 4137 Hwy 90) is another 3 miles west in Waggman. Once a hangout for mafiosos (the original chef is said to have worked for Al Capone), it's now a favorite of slumming suburbanites and New Orleans swells, who make the trip to this dilapidated roadhouse for Italian oysters ($25), drowning in oil and garlic, and a crab salad ($11) fat with lump meat that everyone seems to love. Portions are huge – a single entree easily feeds two – and the wine list is reasonable if uninspired. Mosca's is open Tuesday through Saturday from 5 to 10 pm. No credit cards are accepted.

Bayou Segnette State Park This state park (☎ 504-736-7140) was established at the confluence of several canals that have partially drained the former swamp, creating a bottomland hardwood environment with good boat access to remaining swamps and bayous all the way to the Gulf Coast. The popular boat launch is open 24 hours a day.

Visitors can *camp* here. The park offers 100 reservable campsites with water and electricity for $12. Cabins, which can accommodate eight people, are available for $65, including linens and cookware.

Getting There & Away

From New Orleans, motorists heading to the Barataria Preserve should take Business Hwy 90 across the Greater New Orleans Bridge to the Westbank Expressway (Hwy 90) and turn south on Barataria Blvd (Hwy 45) to Hwy 3134, which leads to the national park entrance. The trip takes about 30 minutes.

To reach Lafitte, continue south on Hwy 45 past the turnoff for the park. You will take a switchback turn on a high-rise bridge and then pass through the town of Jean Lafitte before reaching land's end at Lafitte. Total travel time is 45 minutes or so.

Just 30 minutes from New Orleans, Westwego is just off the Westbank Expressway, west of Marrero.

To get to Bayou Segnette State Park, cross the Greater New Orleans Bridge and follow Business Hwy 90 upriver about 10 miles to the bayou entrance at Drake Ave, on your left.

North Shore

There was a time, not long past, when the northern shore of Lake Pontchartrain was a resort destination for New Orleans residents, who came – first by boat, then train and finally, in 1956 with the completion of the 24-mile causeway, by car – to enjoy the cool lake breezes and calm restful atmosphere. Today these North Shore communities are not quite resort destinations so much as they are bedroom communities for New Orleans.

Of the towns on the North Shore, the jewels are undoubtedly Covington and Abita Springs, with Hammond, Madisonville and Slidell having little to offer beyond their comparatively economical overnight accommodations. Mandeville is the site of a lovely state park and campgrounds, as well as a trio of good restaurants. The St Tammany Parish Tourist & Convention Commission (☎ 504-892-0520, 800-634-9443 ext 116), 68099 Hwy 59, Mandeville, LA 70471, is located off I-12 at exit 65. It's open daily 8:30 am to 4:30 pm.

Fontainebleau State Park What a gem! The 2700-acre park sprawls along the north shore of Lake Pontchartrain in **Mandeville**. It has nature trails, the ruins of a plantation brickyard and sugar mill, sandy beach, swimming pool (open in summer), campground (see the Places to Stay section, later) and lots of picnic areas. It's bordered by Lake Pontchartrain, Bayou Cane and Bayou Castine, making it an excellent spot for bird and wildlife watching. The Tammany Trace passes through here. Day use costs $5 per vehicle.

Tammany Trace An old railroad track was converted into this 32-mile trail. So far 15 miles have been paved – from Mandeville to Abita Springs, including a section through Fontainebleau State Park – for **outdoor activities**, including biking, hiking and in-line skating. An unpaved equestrian trail parallels the trace.

Abita Springs North of Mandeville, along Hwy 59, is the bucolic little burg of Abita Springs, once popular in the late 1800s as a spot to take in what were thought to be curative waters. Today, the springwater still flows from a **fountain** in the center of the village, but the real attraction is the **Abita Brewery** (☎ 504-893-3143), 21084 Hwy 36, just a mile or so west of town. Abita was the first microbrewery in the southeast, and its popular Turbo Dog, Purple Haze and Amber beers are top sellers throughout the state. Housed in a jumble of prefabricated metal and block buildings, with an overgrown auto-repair shop at its core, the brewery is not picturesque, but the personalized tours are quite charming and idiosyncratic – proof positive that beer making is not just the province of multinational conglomerates. And, as an added bonus, tours begin and end in the employees' break room, where a variety of beers – and a non-alcoholic root beer – are always on tap, and you are urged to help yourself. Tours of the brewery are free and offered at 1 and 3 pm on Saturday, and 3 pm on Sunday. Other times may be arranged by appointment. On your way home, you may want to stop off at the Abita Brew Pub (see the Places to Eat section, later) for a more formal tasting of their brews.

Covington Founded in 1816, Covington was a port city of some import on the Bogue Falaya River and emerged as the seat of government for St Tammany Parish in 1819. In the ensuing years, the city served as a center of commerce for North Shore communities until 1956, when the causeway was completed across Lake Pontchartrain. Covington then became a bedroom community for nearby New Orleans.

Long the haunt of artists and writers, Covington was home to the revered 20th-century author Walker Percy, whose novels examining what he termed the 'modern malaise' – *The Moviegoer, Lancelot, Love in the Ruins* – won wide acclaim. Today, the quaint little town is enjoying a renaissance, as artists and writers are joined by entrepreneurs in remaking the brick storefronts in the downtown area into a shop and gallery district reminiscent of New Orleans' Magazine St corridor. Along Columbia St and, to a lesser degree, Lee and Boston Sts, are a delightful selection of antique shops, modern-art galleries and furnishing stores worthy of an afternoon of ambling about.

Places to Stay For motels, the Hwy 190 corridor leading north from I-10 offers the most choices at the widest range of prices. No matter if you stay in Covington or Abita Springs, all North Shore attractions are just a 10- or 15-minute drive from one another. And New Orleans is a 35-minute drive away.

Camping The *Fairview-Riverside State Park* (☎ 504-845-3318) has a North Shore campground on the bank of the Tchefuncte River. It offers sites for $12 on a first-come, first-served basis. During the 19th century, the site was a lumber camp. Now the river and woodlands are recovering only to be assaulted by encroaching suburban development near the margins of the park. The park is 3 miles west of the Lake Pontchartrain Causeway on Hwy 22.

A better choice can be found at *Fontainebleau State Park* (☎ 504-624-4443, 888-677-3668). The campground has well-spaced, shaded sites with picnic tables and grills. Some sites have clean bathhouses and restrooms and a public phone. Standard sites cost $10, while those with extras are $12. For groups, there's a separate camping area and a lodge that sleeps nine to 13 people ($90).

Abita Springs There are a couple of B&Bs downtown, the most appealing of which is *Trail's End Bed & Breakfast* (☎ 504-867-9899, 71648 Maple St), a charming Victorian cottage close to the Tammany Trace and well within walking distance of two popular restaurants and the town springs. Rates are $75/85 a single/double, $20 more on weekends. Breakfast at the Abita Springs Café (see Places to Eat) is included.

Covington The *Mt Vernon Motel* (☎ 504-892-1041, 1110 N Hwy 190) is a spiffy little 30-room property, which was recently renovated. Though the desk clerk can be gruff, the rates are right: $40 for one bed (one or two people), $50 for two beds. Better yet, just a mile or so north along Hwy 21 on the edge of Covington, is the *Green Springs Motel* (☎ 504-892-4686, 72533 Hwy 21), a simple, single-story brick motel tucked into a neighborhood of beautiful homes. Rates are $35/45, and there is a nice pool (open summers only).

Closer to the interstate are a number of chain motels, the choicest of which is *Best Western Northpark Inn* (☎ 504-892-2681, 625 N Hwy 190), just north of I-12. Among the amenities are a better-than-average continental breakfast, a swimming pool and a fine adjoining restaurant, Dakota (see Places to Eat). Rates are $60 to $80.

Places to Eat Many of the restaurants that line Hwy 190 claim a Mandeville address but are in fact as close to Covington.

Mandeville The local favorite for breakfast, *Mande's Restaurant* (☎ 504-626-9047, 340 N Causeway) serves bounteous platters of grits and eggs ($4) along with plate lunches ($6), which are rib-sticking if not inspired. It is open daily for breakfast and lunch. Just west of town and open for lunch and dinner every day but Sunday is *Rag's Po-Boys* (☎ *504-845-3327, 4960 Hwy 22)*, purveyor of the best po-boys in town. Get your roast beef sandwich ($4) 'dressed' (with mayo, lettuce, tomatoes and a dab of mustard) and eat it quickly before the gravy soaks through the loaf.

Trey Yuen (☎ 504-626-4476, 600 Causeway Blvd), on the Service Rd, is a revelation: a well-appointed, even fashionable, Chinese restaurant serving inventive cuisine. Among the perennial favorites are pot stickers, shrimp in a cloud and a velvety-rich lobster in black-bean sauce. Lunch will cost $10 or more, dinner $20 and up. Trey Yuen is open for dinner daily and lunch Wednesday through Friday and Sunday.

Abita Springs At the *Abita Brew Pub* (☎ *504-892-5837, 72011 Holly St)* you can gaze at the vats full of beer while savoring seafood, salads, sandwiches and steaks. Try the blackened shrimp and avocado salad ($8) or the seafood muffuletta ($8). The brew sampler ($4.50) features five 4oz glasses of different beers. It's open daily for lunch and dinner.

Better yet is the *Abita Springs Café* (☎ *504-867-9950, 22132 Level St)*, open from 8 am to 2 pm every day but Monday. Try the seafood omelete ($6), a po-boy ($5) or a daily soup such as crawfish and corn ($3 a cup).

For haute cuisine in a refined setting, *Artesia (☎ 504-892-1662, 21516 Hwy 36)* is the choice. Recently voted one of the best new restaurants in greater New Orleans, this subdued restaurant, set in a restored Victorian home, serves dinner Wednesday through Saturday. Dishes like medallion of monkfish with a black-truffle crust ($24) and quail over a bed of smoked porcini mushrooms and whipped potatoes ($18) draw a crowd from New Orleans as well as the surrounding suburbs. Lunch, served Wednesday through Friday, can be had for $10 to $15.

Covington Open daily from 8 am to 5:30 pm, *Coffee Rani (☎ 504-893-6158, 226 Lee Lane)*, at Boston, is the spot for pastries and sandwiches. The cafe exhibits work by local artists, and the staff are a font of information on what's doing in town.

Judice's (☎ 504-892-0708, 421 E Gibson St) is a bright sunny restaurant, just off Columbia St. Lunch offerings include a shrimp salad with spicy pecans ($8), but the best meal here is breakfast. A heaping bowl of stone-ground grits swimming in a rich sauce of roast beef debris and gravy costs but $1.50, and a full breakfast is just $4. They're open every day but Monday for breakfast and lunch, and dinner is served on Friday and Saturday.

Adjoining the Best Western Northpark Inn, *Dakota (☎ 504-892-3712, 628 N Hwy 190)* may well be the best restaurant on the North Shore. At dinner, try the sweet-potato nachos with ground lamb in a tomato-currant chutney topped with Roquefort cheese ($7) for an appetizer, and the vanilla- and maple-cured duck atop risotto with grilled asparagus ($18) for an entree. Dakota has an excellent wine list and an attentive but not overbearing staff. It's open for lunch weekdays, dinner Monday through Saturday, and brunch on Sunday.

Entertainment Most locals head to New Orleans for a night on the town, but, as in most of southern Louisiana, you can count on restaurants having an adjacent bar that is more than an afterthought. For live entertainment, try the *Abita Brew Pub*, in Abita Springs, or Covington's *Columbia St Tap Room (☎ 504-898-0899, 434 N Columbia St)*, a boisterous barroom, which hosts rock and blues acts most Thursday through Saturday nights. It stays open until 2 am on the weekends.

Getting There & Away A car or motorcycle is almost essential for exploring the North Shore. The most direct access from New Orleans is via the Lake Pontchartrain Causeway. However, if the thought of a 24-mile-long trip across Lake Pontchartrain on a four-lane ribbon of concrete is not enticing, take I-10 west to I-55 north toward Hammond, or I-10 east toward Slidell and then I-12 west; the Slidell detour should add another 25 or so minutes of driving time, the Hammond route, maybe an extra 35.

Slidell & Around

There's little of interest for tourists in Slidell, an industrial center and New Orleans bedroom community on the eastern shore of Lake Pontchartrain. It's value to tourists is as gateway to several pristine nature preserves with terrific bird and wildlife watching and excellent boat tours. The Pearl River is a winding, slow-moving river that flows along the border of Louisiana and Mississippi. It floods into the Pearl River basin, a bottomland hardwood forest that drains into almost 9000 sq miles of both states.

Two public areas in this basin include the Pearl River State Wildlife Management Area (55 sq miles) and Bogue Chitto National Wildlife Refuge (63 sq miles). These areas offer opportunities for canoeing, hiking, fishing and camping. For boaters and canoeists, winter and spring floods provide the best conditions. For hikers and campers, summer and autumn offer the most dry land. The weather page of the New Orleans *Times-Picayune* lists water levels daily.

Tours to this area are easy to book from New Orleans, but if you want to spend more time and visit areas north (Bogue Chitto Refuge and Bogalusa) and west (Covington, Mandeville and Madisonville), you should rent a car.

Orientation & Information Slidell is about 22 miles northeast of New Orleans. The city centers around Gause Blvd, exit 266 on I-10, which is where you'll find most hotels, restaurants and shopping centers. The city is bounded by Lake Pontchartrain to the south and the Pearl River to the east. I-12 cuts across east-west, I-10 north-south before it veers east to Mississippi's Gulf Coast.

To thoroughly explore the Pearl River area, consider purchasing the USGS maps

for Bogalusa (Louisiana) and Gulfport (Mississippi) or a topographical map. For a map and information about Bogue Chitto National Wildlife Refuge, contact the US Fish and Wildlife Service (☎ 504-646-7555), 1010 Gause Blvd, Building 936, Slidell, LA 70458. For information on Pearl River Wildlife Management Area, see below. For information on St Tammany Parish, see the North Shore section, earlier in this chapter.

Pearl River State Wildlife Management Area Most of the 55-sq-mile protected area is cypress and tupelo swamp and hardwood forest. It adjoins the Honey Island Swamp and the Nature Conservancy's White Kitchen Nature Preserve and is especially popular with boaters, canoeists and hunters.

The land area has a short nature trail, campground, boat ramp and abundant wildlife. The water area has gorgeous trees dripping with Spanish moss, lubbers, turtles, snakes and other reptiles, wood ducks and abundant water fowl, song birds, perch, bass, bream, catfish and crawfish. There are inlets and coves with water hyacinths, cutgrass and yellow and white water lilies with unusual and colorful floating fishing villages.

If you really enjoy the outdoors, consider bringing your own canoe or renting one in New Orleans and setting up camp here. The *campground* consists of a large fenced area with lots of grass and oak trees. The sites are unmarked and facilities are limited to fresh water. A wildlife officer lives next door.

The area (☎ 504-646-6440, 225-765-2800) is on Holly Ridge Drive, two miles east of Slidell. Get off I-10 at exit 266 (Hwy 190 or Gause Blvd). Take Hwy 190 east two miles to Military Rd (Hwy 1090) and turn left. Drive north one mile and go over I-10, then take the first right onto Crawford Landing Rd (the I-10 service road) and continue 1½ miles to the end of the road. Admission is free.

For additional information, contact the Louisiana Department of Wildlife and Fisheries (☎ 225-765-2360).

Honey Island Swamp Covering nearly 70,000 acres of wild and protected swamplands, Honey Island abounds with wildlife. Taking a **Honey Island Swamp tour** is a highlight of the numerous day trips you can take from New Orleans.

Most companies operate 12- to 20-passenger motorized, flat-bottom boats and cover about 10 miles. Almost all of the operators offer two prices, one if they pick you up from your hotel in New Orleans ($35 to $40), the other if you drive yourself to the dock ($20). Typically, there is a tour in the morning and another in the afternoon. Some also run evening and overnight trips.

'Up close and personal' aptly describes Mr Denny's Canoe Swamp Tours, which last two hours and are run by former school teacher Denny Holmburg (☎ 504-643-4839, http://home.communique.net/~mrdenny). Up to seven canoeists paddle through the cypress and tupelo of Honey Island Swamp as Mr Denny points out flora and fauna. The highlight is the Nature Conservancy's Eagle Slough, which is off-limits to power boats. In spring it serves as a rookery for anhinga, egrets, herons and other water fowl, as well as nutria and raccoons. By summer, the young birds are attempting flight and the canopy is filled with chatter. Tours cost $20/12 for adults and children under 12. He also offers evening tours and two-day camping tours. Credit cards are not accepted.

Except for feeding gators marshmallows (they're not good for humans, so how could they be good for alligators?), Dr Wagner's Honey Island Swamp Tours provide visitors an acceptably entertaining and educational motorized visit to the Honey Island Swamp.

Drinks on the Tickfaw & Catfish at the Roadhouse

West of I-55 and south of I-12, just 10 miles or so beyond Ponchatoulaon, on Hwy 22 is the little town of Springfield, epicenter of an odd waterborne phenomenon. Arrayed along the Tickfaw River, which runs parallel to I-55 south from Mississippi and into Louisiana before pouring forth into Lake Maurepas and finally Lake Ponchatrain, are a collection of bars, many of which are accessible only by boat. Rather than being little dives, these bars are behemoths, sprawling out over the water, offering ample deck space for sunning and ample bar space for quaffing cocktails.

Among the ones that are accessible by car are *Tin Lizzies* (☎ 504-695-6787, 29592 Hwy 22), open Friday to Sunday only and closed during the late fall and winter. From a perch on the deck, you can watch cigarette boats ply the waters and hope to hitch a ride to one of the bars, like the Prop Stop, which is only accessible by water.

During the spring and summer, boat parades and poker runs are infrequently held – the latter is a floating game of five card stud, where the players are dealt one card at each bar they stop in, and the winning hand is announced around dusk. For those in search of an adventure, these hinterland hideaways promise drinking and debauchery, far from the maddening tourist milieu.

Many of the bars on the river offer decent to good food, but for a great meal, head to *Middendorf's* (☎ 504-386-6666), at exit 15 off I-55, a gussied-up roadhouse hard by Lake Mauepas. In business since 1934, Middendorf's is famous for its thin-cut catfish fillets ($7 for an ample small order served with green onion-flecked hushpuppies and forgettable fries), cooked to a crisp – fried so crisp in fact that they resemble more of a fish-flavored potato chip than a traditional fillet. That said, they are delicious, as is the oyster stew ($4.50) and the Italian salad ($5), an oily morass of lettuce, olives and parmesan cheese. But the real treat to behold is the timeless wood-paneled interior, where waitresses with beehive hairdos trundle back and forth bearing platters piled high with deftly fried seafood and icy beers. Middendorf's is open 10:30 am to 9 pm or so every day but Monday.

– John T Edge

Dr Wagner, a wetlands ecologist and environmental consultant on southern Louisiana swamps, leads many of the two-hour, 12-mile tours himself. To arrange a tour call ☎ 504-641-1769 (☎ 504-242-5877 from New Orleans), or write to 106 Holly Ridge Drive, Slidell, LA 70461. The cost is $20/10 for adults/children, or $40/20 for New Orleans pick up. Credit cards are not accepted.

White Kitchen Eagle Preserve Bird watchers have come here for decades to watch bald eagles, which have nested in the area in winter for more than 50 years. To give birders better access, the Nature Conservancy teamed up with Chevron Corporation to build a 300-foot boardwalk over the swamp at a rest stop with picnic tables. The scenery of live oaks heavy with moss, cypress and cypress knees, pickerel, marshmallow and waterbirds is as beautiful as the soaring eagles above. Bring binoculars and a lunch.

The White Kitchen Preserve is administered by the Nature Conservancy (☎ 225-338-1040) in Baton Rouge. It's at the intersection of Hwy 190 and Hwy 90; from I-10, take exit 266, then take Hwy 190 east to Military Rd (Hwy 1090) and turn right. At the dead end (at the cemetery), turn left. Go five miles to Hwy 90. The preserve is on the left.

Bogue Chitto River The Bogue Chitto River (BO-gay SHEE-to) joins the Pearl River about 25 miles north of Slidell. Like the Pearl, it offers lots of opportunities to canoe, hike, fish and camp.

Bogue Chitto Canoeing and Tubing Center (☎ 504-735-1173), on Hwy 16 in Isabel, is a fun mom-and-pop operation that rents two-person canoes ($30 a day) and inner tubes ($8), including shuttle service. They shuttle you up river and you float or paddle down. It takes three to four hours, unless you stop at one of the sandbar beaches to picnic and look for wildlife.

The small *campground* accommodates tents ($15 with water and electricity).

Restrooms and showers are available for day canoeists and tubers as well as campers,

and there's a small store for tackle, bait, ice and beverages.

To get there take Hwy 41 north to Sun, then Hwy 16 west for seven miles to Isabel. Turn left at the Isabel store and go two blocks. For advance reservations, write to 10237 River Rd, Bogalusa, LA 70427.

Places to Stay To camp in the Pearl River Wildlife Management Area and on the Bogue Chitto River, see above. There's a *KOA* (☎ 504-643-3850, 56009 Hwy 433) east of I-10 (take exit 263) with tent sites ($20) and fake log cabins.

Econolodge (☎ 504-641-2153, 58512 Tyler Drive), at I-10 and Hwy 190, has 57 rooms with free cable movies. Rooms ($50 to $120) are basic, but clean. It's close to restaurants and the road leading to the swamp tours.

Days Inn Slidell (☎ 504-641-3450, 1645 Gause Blvd) is on the main road through town, with easy access to I-10, I-12 and I-59. It has a restaurant, pool and free in-room movies. Rates start at $55.

For groups, *The Garden Guest House B&B* (☎ 504-641-0335, 34514 Bayou Liberty Rd/Hwy 433), in a picturesque setting in Slidell, is worth calling or checking out its Web site at www.gardenbb.com. For a rate of $250 and up, you get your own antique-filled three-bedroom, 2½-bath house with laundry, kitchen, a large glass-enclosed sun porch and a deck. Parts of the house can also be rented separately ($95 to $135 for a one-bedroom suite, $150 to $225 for two-bedrooms). The owners, Bonnie and Paul Taliancich, live nearby and love to garden and collect antiques. They cater to guests' dietary needs and special interests.

Places to Eat *Mike Schaeffer's* (☎ 504-646-1728, 158 S Military Rd) specializes in catfish, but also has shrimp, crawfish and Louisiana specialties. Lunch runs $6 to $9, dinner $6 to $12. It's open for lunch daily; dinner is served Tuesday to Saturday.

Indian Village Catfish Restaurant (☎ 504-649-5778, 115 Indian Village Rd), off Hwy 190, is a ramshackle little place on the Pearl River that serves some of the best catfish in the area. Because it caters to weekend anglers and hunters, it's open only Thursday to Sunday 11 am to 8 pm.

Getting There & Away If driving, which makes most sense, take either I-10 or the scenic Hwy 90 to Hwy 11 or to Hwy 190. If you take Hwys 90/190, you cross Rigolets (pronounced like the gum, Wrigley's) Harbor, a narrow channel that feeds water into Lake Pontchartrain from Lake Borgne and the Mississippi Sound near the Louisiana and Mississippi border. It also passes Fort Pike and puts you closest to the wildlife areas and the river, where the swamp tours depart.

Greyhound (☎ 504-643-6545), 3735 Pontchartrain Drive, Slidell, has twice daily service from New Orleans ($8). Amtrak trains stop at the small Slidell station, 1827 Front St. There is no local bus service, so to get from the station to your destination call Parish Cab (☎ 504-641-9479).

Plantation Country

Much of the early settlement of Louisiana followed the Mississippi River upriver from New Orleans. Missionaries drew parish boundaries (many of which remain today) so that each straddled the river. Plantations large and small required river frontage for transportation of goods and people, so most parcels of land were long and narrow, extending away from the riverbank.

Throughout the 1700s, many European planters, Creoles (the born-in-the-colony offspring of free foreign immigrants) and their slaves raised indigo, cotton, rice, tobacco and sugar cane. In the late 1700s, a man named Etienne Boré developed a method of crystallizing sugar on a commercial scale, and soon the flourishing sugar in-

Highlights

- Laura Plantation, a Creole house in Vacherie, where the story of plantation life includes Native Americans, African-Americans and European Americans

- The Rural Life Museum in Baton Rouge, focusing on the state's rural laboring classes of the 19th century

- Ferry rides across the Mississippi

- The historic district of Donaldsonville

dustry formed the state's first sound economic base. When the area was acquired as a US territory in 1803, it provided the country's first domestic sugar crop. By the eve of the Civil War, it was producing nearly 95% of the country's sugar.

Most of the largest sugar plantations lay between New Orleans and Baton Rouge; the area north of Baton Rouge, where the terrain is higher and drier, came to be dominated by cotton plantations. Both required much labor, and the demand for slaves increased dramatically.

In 1808, the US Congress forbid the importation of slaves from abroad; thereafter, the majority of the territory's new slaves were 'sold down the river' – from other slave states to southern slave states (others were smuggled in by pirates such as Jean Lafitte). Slaves greatly feared being sold to the sugar plantations – the harsh conditions of which were well known. In 1811, one of the largest slave uprisings in US history occurred involving around 500 slaves. It was successfully suppressed, and its leaders beheaded. By 1840, the state claimed 168,452 slaves – a substantial increase from 1810 when there were 34,660 slaves. Approximately half the state's population (more than 331,000) was made up of slaves, the vast majority living in the plantation parishes.

The cotton and sugar cane plantations created phenomenal wealth for their owners. By the time the Civil War began, at least half of the country's millionaires lived between Natchez and New Orleans. During the Civil War, the Mississippi River provided the Confederacy with a crucial route for supplies from Texas, the eastern seaboard and foreign allies. In response, the Union formulated the Anaconda Plan, which sought control of the river to 'strangle' the flow of supplies. While undertaking this plan, Union forces pillaged and destroyed nearly all the river plantations. By the war's end, only 180 of the 1200 sugar

PLANTATION COUNTRY

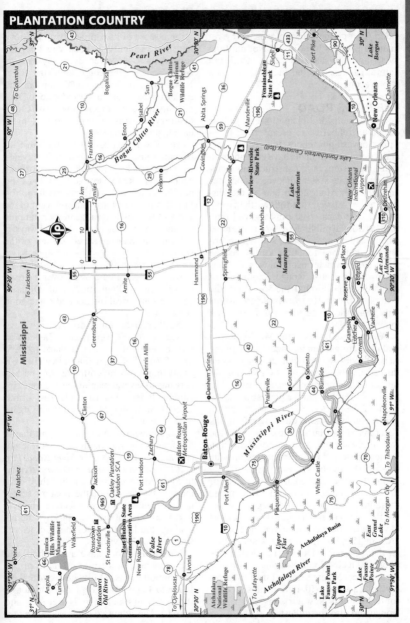

plantations remained. Without free labor and without the collateral that slaves provided for obtaining bank loans, many remaining planters went broke. Not until the 1900s and the discovery of vast oil and natural gas reserves did the state regain a strong economy.

THE RIVER ROAD

For settlements and plantations, as well as cities and refineries, to escape the Mississippi's devastating floods, the parish, state and federal governments have expended astonishing resources to construct and maintain an intricate system of levees, floodgates and spillways. Along either bank of the Mississippi lies a levee that follows the river's bends. Atop each levee runs a gravel road with occasional public access from a parallel paved road along the outer side. These two paved roads are together known as the River Road, which runs from New Orleans northwest to Baton Rouge. Thousands of freighters from around the world ply the waters to Baton Rouge, visible to visitors only from the levee tops, car ferries and immense bridges.

Along these banks of the Mississippi, no real plantations remain. Today, much of the rich alluvial soil in which sugar cane thrived has been covered by immense oil refineries and petrochemical plants, a shift uncannily captured in the plantation-house motif of the modern Chevron office building (on the west bank, downriver from the Veterans Memorial Bridge). Dwarfing the remaining 40 or so restored plantation homes, these industrial fortresses provide most of the region's jobs and wealth. The toxins they spew have earned the corridor the name Cancer Alley. Tucked in among these industrial plants and elegant homes are the edges of small country towns, most of which run between the river and Hwy 61 (Airline Hwy) on the east bank and Hwy 1 on the west bank. Despite the dominance of oil and its byproducts, farmers still raise sugar cane, soybeans and a bit of tobacco. Farther east lies I-10, by far the speediest route between New Orleans and Baton Rouge and also the dullest.

Planning

It's best to drive through the region to really glean a sense of its complexity and history, and there's plenty to keep you busy for several days. However, even day-trippers can experience the contrasts of the River Road. In a day, drivers could loop out and back from New Orleans; wander up to Donaldsonville and drop down to Cajun Country; or traverse the entire length, ending up in Baton Rouge.

The River Road is by far the most intriguing route, but it's also heavily traveled by large trucks and industrial workers, which can make for slow going at times and at others can pressure sightseers to go too fast. If you're in a hurry but still want to see some of the River Road, consider jumping off and onto the faster parallel highways. If you can only manage to see one side of the river, head for the east bank, which has a greater variety of terrain and buildings; however, do consider crossing over the river to see Laura Plantation, and Donaldsonville's historical district and some good restaurants.

Neither Greyhound nor Amtrak have service to the River Road. The closest Greyhound station is in LaPlace (☎ 225-651-2570), 1514 W Airline Hwy/Hwy 61. Many tour companies offer daylong bus excursions to several plantations for tours, including lunch at a roadside restaurant. These cost around $65 to $75 (see Organized Tours, below).

Visitors who plan to spend more than a few hours exploring the River Road should consider finding *Along the River Road: Past and Present on Louisiana's Historic Byway*, by Mary Ann Sternberg. The first third summarizes the history of the region's settlements, economy and architecture; the rest traces each side of the river mile by mile, revealing hidden histories behind what's visible to today's visitors.

Most plantations have a gift shop, and some include a restaurant and pricey accommodations. Daily hours are 9 or 10 am to 4 or 5 pm (except major holidays; shorter hours between November and March). The admission fee, which ranges

LOUISIANA

RIVER ROAD

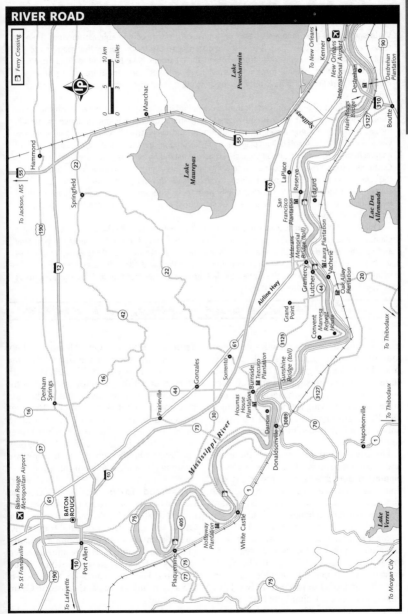

Ferry Crossing

10 km
6 miles
0 3 5
0

Lake Pontchartrain

Manchac

To New Orleans
Kenner
New Orleans International Airport
Destrehan
Destrehan Plantation
Boutte

Hammond

To Jackson, MS

Lake Maurepas

Springfield

Hale-Boggs Bridge

LaPlace
Reserve
Edgard

San Francisco Plantation

Lac Des Allemands

Laura Plantation
Vacherie
Oak Alley Plantation

Veterans Memorial Bridge (toll)
Gramercy
Lutcher

Airline Hwy

Grand Point

Convent
Manresa Retreat House

To Thibodaux

Denham Springs

Gonzales
Sorrento

Prairieville

Texcaxo Plantation
Burnside
Sunshine Bridge (toll)

Houmas House Plantation
Darrow

Napoleonville

To Thibodaux

Baton Rouge Metropolitan Airport

Mississippi River

Donaldsonville

Lake Verret

BATON ROUGE

White Castle

Nottoway Plantation

Port Allen

Plaquemine

To St Francisville

To Lafayette

To Morgan City

The Lowdown on Escapism

Visitors who plan their itineraries based on tourist office hype could easily assume that the only reason to travel the River Road is to visit the dozen or so plantation homes that are open to the public. Most of these impressive structures and their gardens have been authentically restored. Though some have original furnishings, most have antiques appropriate for each plantation's grandest period. Some also have out buildings, including overseers' homes, barns and stables and slave cabins.

Travelers fond of antiques, historical interiors or tidbits of family intrigue will relish the tours. Those who have seen these luxurious homes, moss-hung oaks and highly designed gardens in movies or on TV will enjoy seeing them in person, and even jaded travelers can gain a narrow window on the lives of antebellum plantation masters and mistresses. If nothing else, the variety of architectural styles, drawing upon Spanish, French, West Indian and Anglo antecedents, is striking. Costumed guides typically lead the 45- to 60-minute tours during which historical continuity or interpretation rarely come into play. Instead, these tours are driven by the rooms and the items they contain, with the guides interspersing family histories as appropriate. Many plantations contract with specific tour-bus companies, some with steamboat cruises, and tours can be crowded if you arrive with the hoards.

Only Laura Plantation succeeds in providing visitors with a sense of the business of running a plantation and the paternalistic organization that was the foundation of the plantation economy and society. With this exception, and to a lesser degree Nottoway (see West Bank, later in this section), the plantation-house tours ignore the story of the hundreds of thousands of slaves, who made the bricks, constructed the homes, tended the fires and worked the fields. Likewise, no tours address the role of working and poor whites.

from $2 to $10, usually includes a guided tour of the main house as well as self-guided tours of the grounds. If you've had enough of tours but simply want a cursory glance at the mansions' exteriors, you can drive into the parking lots without paying a fee. Photography is permitted outdoors only. Lavish Christmastime decorations are common.

Directly along the River Road, there are few accommodations other than B&Bs at plantation houses and even fewer gas stations. The closest campgrounds are a several miles east of Baton Rouge and west of New Orleans. You have a handful of food and gas options in the small towns just off the River Road and more accommodation choices along the parallel highways, but even there the options are limited. Alternatively, travelers can easily drop south from Vacherie (on Hwy 20) or Donaldsonville (on Hwy 1) to Thibodaux (see the Cajun Country chapter).

Special Events On Memorial Day weekend, the town of Gonzales hosts the Jambalaya Festival (☎ 225-622-1998). In December, all the plantations gussy up for the holidays. On the second full weekend in December, the Festival of the Bonfires draws folks from around the world to Lutcher to see bonfires on the river levees (see the boxed text; ☎ 225-869-4303, 800-367-7852). On Christmas Eve, bonfires are lit along a 12-mile stretch of the levee.

Organized Tours Lucille and Chester Le'Obia of Le'Ob's Tours (☎ 225-288-3478, fax 225-288-8517), 4635 Touro St, New Orleans, 70122, offer a realistic tour of historic Plantation Country, stopping at Laura Plantation, Houmas House and Tezcuco and its African-American River Road Museum. The five- to-six-hour tour costs $75 and includes lunch at the historic Cabin Restaurant.

LOUISIANA

Otherwise, hotels and the visitor centers in Baton Rouge and New Orleans provide brochures for companies offering full- and half-day Plantation Country tours. Full-day tours ($60 to $75) include two or three plantations and lunch. Half-day tours (around $40) usually include one long plantation stop and perhaps lunch. Many tours provide multilingual narration. In the narratives given between stops, some tour operators paint a less-than-realistic picture of plantation life. Before signing up for a tour, decide which plantations you want to see, find the companies that go there (the brochures make this clear) and inquire about the narrative riders will hear.

Orientation

The two-lane River Road runs along both river banks through St John, St James, Ascension and Iberville parishes. Both halves change road numbers frequently, but it's not hard to stay on course – just keep hugging the levee. Each bank has a series of parish and state highways that run farther east and west of River Road. On the east side these faster routes are Hwy 61 and I-10 (though smaller parish roads intercede occasionally), ending in Baton Rouge. On the west bank, faster routes include Hwy 90 (between New Orleans and Hwy 310), Parish Rds 3127 and 3089 and Hwy 1, ending in Port Allen across the river from Baton Rouge.

The *Great River Road Plantation Parade* brochure, available for free at some tourist offices, has a pretty good map showing the River Road, plantations and other historic sights. Even better is the *Historic Plantation Country* descriptive map available from the Baton Rouge Convention & Visitors Bureau (☎ 225-383-1825, 800-527-6843).

River Crossings Traffic crosses the river on bridges and ferries. The bridges are open daily and some charge a small toll. The ferries run Monday to Friday and charge a $1 toll heading west only. The Hale-Boggs Bridge (1983) carries Hwy 310 across the river and is about a half-hour's drive from New Orleans; it's very close to Destrehan Plantation.

Heading upriver, the next chance to cross the river is the ferry between Reserve and Edgard. It runs from 5:15 am to 8:30 pm and is not far from San Francisco Plantation. The next crossing is the Veterans Memorial Bridge (1995), which links Gramercy and the west bank. Upriver from that is a ferry between Lutcher and Vacherie near Laura and Oak Alley Plantations. The next crossing is the Sunshine Bridge just south of Burnside and Donaldsonville (50¢ toll) near Tezcuco Plantation. A ferry crosses just downriver from White Castle, and another runs at Plaquemine.

Information

The following tourist offices provide information on accommodations, attractions, restaurants and local history.

In LaPlace, St John Parish Economic Development Department (☎ 225-652-9569), 1801 W Airline Hwy/Hwy 61 (east bank), is open 8 am to 4:30 pm weekdays.

In Lutcher, the St James Parish Tourist Center (☎ 225-869-9752, 800-367-7852, www.stjamesla.com/index.htm), in the St James Historical Society Museum, 1988 Hwy 44/River Road (east bank), is open 8 am to 4 pm weekdays.

Ascension Parish Tourist Commission (☎ 225-675-6550, 800-967-2780), 6470-A Hwy 22, Sorrento, 70778, just off Hwy 61 (east bank), is open 9 am to 5 pm daily. It's in Cajun Village, a cluster of restored buildings now housing a handful of tourist-oriented businesses. It covers the towns of Burnside, Darrow and Donaldsonville.

Iberville Parish Tourist Commission (☎ 225-687-5190, 800-967-2478), Main St at Hwy 1 (west bank), PO Box 389, Plaquemine, 70765, is open 8 am to 4:30 pm daily; it covers White Castle.

East Bank

Destrehan Plantation The oldest intact plantation house (1787) located in the lower

Mississippi River Valley, it was originally designed and constructed in a colonial West Indies style by Charles Pacquet, a free man of color. It was remodeled to Greek Revival from 1830 to 1840. At its peak, the plantation had 6000 acres of sugar cane. During and after the Civil War, it was occupied by Union troops and housed a freedmen's center, where nearly 800 former slaves learned new skills and trades. Amoco, the oil corporation, donated the house and grounds to a historical society in 1971. Scenes from the movie *Interview with a Vampire* were shot here.

The 50-minute tour begins with a short video; the guided tour covers the building's construction, the antique furnishings and family anecdotes. The plantation (☎ 504-764-9315, 504-524-5522 from New Orleans), 13034 Hwy 48/River Road, is in Destrehan about 15 minutes southwest of the New Orleans airport. Take I-10 and then Hwy 310; exit just before the bridge and head downriver. It's open daily 9:30 am to 4 pm (last tour at 4). Admission is $8 for adults, $2 for kids.

San Francisco Plantation Frenchman Edmond Bozonier Marmillion built this stunning old-Creole-style house in 1856. With $100,000 and 100 slaves, Marmillion's son, Valsin, built a grand sugar plantation. Over the years, setbacks resulting from changes in the course of the river brought the levee up nearly to the mansion's front porch. From 1974 to 1977, $2 million was spent to return the house – from the curtains and ceiling murals to the carpets and wall paint – to its original state, jokingly referred to as 'steamboat Gothic.' The restoration was subsidized by Marathon Oil, as are its current operations. Oil storage tanks abut the property in clear view of the house.

San Francisco Plantation (☎ 225-535-2341, 888-322-1756), on Hwy 44/River Road, is in Reserve, 20 miles upriver from I-310. It's open daily 10 am to 4:30 pm March to October, till 4 pm November to February. Admission is $8 for adults, $3 for children.

St James Historical Society Museum
This extraordinary gem of a museum (☎ 225-869-9752, 800-367-7852), 1988 Hwy 44/River Road in Lutcher, tells the story of the River Road, from the plantations to the lumber mills to the tobacco companies to the levee bonfire tradition (see the boxed text). The main building houses artifacts and documents. Outside is an example of the wooden pyramid of logs that is set afire during December. Admission is free (donations accepted), and opening hours are weekdays 8 am to 4 pm. This is also the site of the St James Parish Tourist Center.

Convent Built in 1842 and formerly a college, the **Manresa Retreat House** has been a Jesuit-run retreat since 1931. Over 5000 people seek peaceful reflection here each year. Though it's not open to the public for tours, the impressive building and grounds are clearly visible from River Road. Just upriver from Manresa is **St Michael's Church**, a Gothic Revival building constructed in 1833. Its interior is worth a peek. If you've wandered as far as Convent, consider stopping to eat at Hymel's (see Places to Eat, later in this section).

Festival of the Bonfires

Just after Thanksgiving, residents in St James Parish (about 25 miles upriver from New Orleans) heed the century-old tradition of building 20-foot-tall tepee-shaped wooden structures 100 feet apart along the levee. On the second full weekend in December, residents stage a festival in Lutcher with bonfires, gumbo competitions, music, dancing and fun for kids. Each night thereafter, a few bonfires are lit. On Christmas Eve, the fire marshal checks the wind's direction. If all is well, he gives the OK signal, and a 12-mile stretch of the levee lights up with bonfires from Gramercy to Convent. As many as 50,000 spectators come to watch the fiery spectacle.

Tezcuco Plantation Built in 1855, this Greek Revival raised cottage is the centerpiece of a complex that includes gardens, a gift shop, museum, restaurant, antique shop and guest cottages in historic buildings and slave quarters, three of which are original to the property.

A must-see on the grounds is the small but important **River Road African-American Museum** (☎ 225-644-7955), started by Kathe Hambrick, a local African-American woman. Through grants and donations, she's assembled a collection of photos, recipes, documents, musical instruments, clothing, masks, tools and other items to tell the story of rural Louisiana and slavery. Exhibits change regularly (the museum's collection far exceeds the museum's display space). It's open Wednesday to Saturday 9 am to 5 pm, Sunday 1 to 5 pm, otherwise by appointment. Admission is a $3 donation. (Hambrick plans to open another museum in Donaldsonville.)

The plantation's B&B cottages are in comfortable cottages with rockers on the porches. Most have kitchens, but none has a telephone. Rates range from $65 for a one-room duplex cottage to $160 for the two-bedroom, two-bathroom suite in the main house. Full breakfasts are delivered to each room. At night you can wander down to the levee and watch the boats go by. Consider Donaldsonville's numerous restaurants for good meals.

The plantation (☎ 225-562-3929), 3138 Hwy 44/River Road, is in Burnside a mile upriver from the Sunshine Bridge. It's open daily 9 am to 5 pm. The restaurant is open 11 am to 3 pm. Admission is $8 for adults, $3.25 for children.

Houmas House Plantation In the late 1700s, the owners built a humble four-room dogtrot house; in 1840, new owners built the massive Greek Revival mansion that stands today (the original house was eventually joined to the main one). This plantation was spared the wrath of Union troops because its owner, an Irishman, claimed protection as a British citizen. At its height of production in the late 1880s, Houmas Plantation (named for Houma Indians who had a village here) was the largest sugar plantation in the state; its 20,000 acres produced 20 million pounds of sugar annually. In 1940, the Crozat family purchased the house and grounds, and restored them; Crozat family members still live here today. Of all the plantations, it has the most formal gardens and grounds.

The plantation house (☎ 225-473-7841, 504-522-2262 from New Orleans), 40136 Hwy 942/River Road, is on the town borders of Burnside and Darrow. It's open 10 am to 5 pm daily February to October, till 4 pm daily November to January. Admission for the 45-minute guided tour is $8 for adults, $6 for children.

West Bank

Laura Plantation Travelers who can only visit one plantation should choose this one. Laura Plantation was in the hands of two Creole families, one French, one German, for 180 years. It was here in the 1870s that Alcée Fortier interviewed the descendants of Senegalese slaves and recorded the tales that would come to be known as the Tar Baby stories and Br'er Rabbit legend (he published them a decade before Joel Chandler Harris published his version).

Today, the cottage's exterior is multicolored, underscoring its heritage as a Creole plantation (white façades were a feature of Anglo homes). The raised Creole cottage (1805) is now undergoing careful renovation. The house's peeled-back wallpaper and exposed bricks echo the efforts to interpret the plantation's history, which local historians Sand and Norman Marmillion have been researching from numerous sources. One primary source is the soon-to-be published memoirs of the first owners' great granddaughter, Laura Locoul, who the plantation is named after. Another source is 5000 pages of documents, among them slave and tax records, that were discovered in the Archives Nationales de Paris.

The one-hour tour, given by knowledgeable guides, integrates historical details from these and other sources. It's the only tour that addresses the role of Native

Americans (who lived here until 1915) in plantation life, and it doesn't gloss over the role of slaves (at its peak, Laura had 200). In fact, this is the only plantation that has original slave cabins. The tour also covers the role of the female family members, who largely ran the plantation while the men were away in New Orleans and Europe, or involved in fighting wars (as was common among wealthy planters).

Laura (☎ 225-265-7690, 504-488-8709 from New Orleans), 2247 Hwy 18/River Road, is in Vacherie. It's open daily 9 am to 5 pm for tours (last one at 4), which cost $8. Daily at 10:30 am there is a 15-minute tour of the slave quarters, which is included in the tour price. Tours in French are offered on Monday, Wednesday and Friday.

Oak Alley Plantation A quarter-mile canopy of majestic live oaks runs from the River Road to this elaborate 1839 Greek Revival house. The 28 trees, 14 on each side of the driveway, predate the house by a hundred years. More symmetry awaits at the house, which has 28 columns, each eight feet in circumference. The nearby sugar cane fields and woodlands are a pleasant contrast to the chemical plants that crowd other plantations, yet Oak Alley is the most commercial in feel. The grounds include a restaurant serving breakfast and lunch, B&B, gift shop, seasonal dinner theater and RV overnight parking. The complex is a favorite stop on the bus-tour circuit.

Overnight guests stay in cottages (nonsmoking) behind the mansion; these feature full kitchen, bathroom, living and dining room and porches overlooking attractive gardens. Rates run $95 to $125, which does include a full breakfast but not a house tour.

Oak Alley (☎ 225-265-2151, 800-442-5539, oakalleyplantation@att.net), 3645 Hwy 18/River Road, is in Vacherie, just upriver from Laura Plantation. Tours run from 9 am to 5 pm daily November through February, until 5:30 pm from March to October. Admission is $8 adults, $5 children (no credit cards accepted).

Donaldsonville At the confluence of Bayou La Fourche and the Mississippi, Donaldsonville is the most interesting town between New Orleans and Baton Rouge. Razed in the Civil War, it was the site of the only Union victory led by freed slaves. Its historic district has over 600 buildings dating from the war's end to 1930. A few of these have been restored, but many of them have been only sporadically maintained. Home to many longtime African-American residents, this is a real if poor neighborhood, utterly devoid of the mindnumbing perfection of many of the more quaint historic districts. Surprisingly, the cemetery on St Patrick St has a Jewish section with graves dating from the mid-1800s. With a welcome cluster of good restaurants, the town makes an excellent stop for River Road explorers.

Other than the historic district, the main attraction is **Rossie's Custom Framing** (☎ 225-473-8536), 510 Railroad Ave, in the former Ben Franklin store, which houses the studio of self-taught painter Alvin Batiste (see the boxed text 'Visions, Stories, Street Life'). Born and raised in Donaldsonville, Batiste draws inspiration from life in his hometown, depicting the courage, sorrows and wit of its residents. Hundreds of his pieces, large and small, line the walls, and the prices are very reasonable. Most days between 10 am and 3 pm, Batiste sets up his easel in the shop's window, so he can watch the street life passing by. Owned by the personable Sandra Imbraguglio and her son David, the shop is open from 8 am to 5 pm weekdays, till 4 pm Saturday, and from 10 am to 3 pm Sunday.

A few blocks down Railroad Ave at the corner of Mississippi St is the **Historic Donaldsonville Museum** (☎ 225-746-0004). It's a charming paean to small-town life set in a majestic white masonry building (1873) that was once home to the Lemann Department Store. Plans are in the works to turn it into a hotel with a second restaurant headed by chef John Folse (see Places to Eat, later in this section, for a description of the first). It's open 10 am to 4 pm Tuesday, Thursday and Saturday.

Nottoway Plantation Built in 1859 by a wealthy Anglo planter from Virginia, this 53,000-sq-ft home comprises 64 rooms. Greek Revival and Italianate in form, it is surprisingly understated and British in decor. With the labor of 200 field slaves and 20 house slaves, the 7000-acre sugar plantation prospered.

The largest extant plantation house in the South, is today owned by Australian Paul Ramsey. Guides wear no costumes and deliver no drama, yet the tours are rich in personal history thanks to business records; *The White Castle of Louisiana*, the diary written by the original owner's daughter, Cornelia Randolph; and recently recovered family letters. The house has original furnishings and period pieces, 200 windows and 165 doors – an opening for each day of the year. It is also still home to a 90-something former resident.

The pricey restaurant serves Cajun specialties daily 11 am to 3 pm and 6 to 9 pm; lunch prices hover around $12 and dinner prices around $20. (If you're looking for a special meal, consider Lafitte's Landing in Donaldsonville.)

Nottoway has 13 luxurious and comfortable guest rooms, all filled with antiques. Six rooms are in the mansion, the rest in out buildings. Rates range from $95 to $190 for a single, and from $135 to $200 for a double; suites are $225 to $250. Stays include a tour, plantation breakfast and use of a pool and the gardens.

Nottoway (☎ 225-545-2730, fax 225-545-8632), Hwy 1/River Road, is 2 miles north of White Castle. Guided tours run continuously between 9 am and 5 pm daily, except Christmas. Admission is $10 adults, $3 children. Tours in Parisian and Cajun French are also available. Visit its Web site at www.nottoway.com.

Places to Stay

East Bank Tezcuco Plantation features moderate-to-expensive B&B cottages (see earlier).

At I-10 exit 177 in Gonzales, there are plenty of chain hotels. ***Budget Inn*** (☎ 225-644-2000) has singles/doubles for $36/46. The new ***Quality Inn*** (☎ 225-647-5700, 800-228-5151) has rooms for $59. ***Holiday Inn*** (☎ 225-647-8000, fax 225-647-7741, 1500 Hwy 30) has a lounge offering entertainment and a seafood restaurant. Room rates are $68/73.

West Bank Oak Alley and Nottoway allow visitors to stay overnight (see entries, earlier, for details). Travelers might also consider staying in Thibodaux (see the Cajun Country chapter), which is accessible from Vacherie and Donaldsonville.

Bay Tree Plantation B&B (☎ 225-265-2109, 800-895-2109, baytree@eatel.net, 3785 Hwy 18/River Road), in Vacherie, is within viewing distance of Oak Alley. The property has six bedrooms and suites split between two buildings – an antique-filled Creole cottage (1850) and a house – both surrounded by informal gardens. Another recently renovated cottage has a kitchen, living room and spa. A full Southern breakfast is included in the rate of $75 to $190. Children are welcome.

Visions, Stories, Street Life

The walls of Rossie's Custom Framing pulse with vibrant dancers, gospel choruses, swaying canefields and jazz musicians plying their trade. Inside an otherwise humble storefront, lifelong Donaldsonville resident Alvin Batiste paints not only on canvases, but also on windows, jars, saws, egg cartons – whatever is handy – working his unique voodoo with acrylic paints to bring alive the street life outside the window, the stories his mother told him and the visions that come to him in dreams. Completely self-taught, Batiste began painting in his early thirties, and his growth as an artist is quickly evident upon comparing a recent work with one only a year or two old. Studying shadow, strokes and color, he conjures his subjects in their bedrooms, at the corner store and in the field, but they quickly demand the right to tell their own tales.

In Donaldsonville, the very simple *Magnolia Motel* (☎ 225-473-3146), on Hwy 1, has singles/doubles for $38/45. There's also a *Best Western* just outside town. Upriver the next motel cluster is in Port Allen.

Places to Eat

East Bank In LaPlace you'll find the *Airline Motors Restaurant* (☎ 225-652-9181, 221 E Airline Hwy/Hwy 61), a rough-edged art-deco palace, embellished with enough glass blocks, chrome and neon to send you reeling. Grab a seat at the counter and take it all in while enjoying a bowl of surprisingly good chicken andouille gumbo ($5) or one of the fish platters. It's closed only between 10 pm Sunday and 6 am Monday.

Don's Market (☎ 225-536-2275, 318 Central Ave), about a mile from River Road in Reserve, is the place to pack a picnic lunch. Try their homemade hogshead cheese and andouille sausage (turkey or chicken variations available). It's open Monday to Saturday 7 am to 7 pm, Sunday 8 am to noon.

The Stockpile (☎ 225-869-9917), on Hwy 3125 in Grand Point, serves fried or broiled seafood and steaks ($8 to $16) and sandwiches ($2 to $8) in a rustic-looking cypress-wood setting. The adjacent bar has pool tables and gaming machines. Lunch and dinner are served daily. From River Road take Hwy 642, just upriver from Lutcher, about 2 miles.

A local favorite for 40-plus years and also on the tour-bus circuit is *Hymel's Seafood* (☎ 225-562-7031, 8740 Hwy 44/River Road), 4 miles downriver from the Sunshine Bridge. This former filling station now serves a fine platter of soft-shell crab ($8) as well as turtle sauce piquant ($7) and weekday lunch specials for around $5. In the bar, heads of various beasts oversee the beer drinking. It's open daily for lunch, and Thursday to Sunday for dinner (no food service between 2:30 and 5 pm).

The *Cabin Restaurant* (☎ 225-473-3007), at the corner of Hwys 44 and 22, is set in a collection of out buildings rescued from several demolished plantations. Besides po-

boys you can get dishes such as red beans and rice with sausage for about $5 or an omelet filled with crawfish étouffée ($7). Broiled or fried seafood plates cost around $9. Though the restaurant courts the tourist crowds, the food is actually pretty good. Lunch is served daily, dinner every day except Monday. From River Road in Burnside take Hwy 44 2 miles north.

West Bank In Vacherie, just downriver from Laura Plantation, *B&C Seafood Market & Cajun Deli* (☎ 225-265-8356, 2155 Hwy 18/River Road) specializes in boiled fresh seafood and also serves gumbo, po-boys, burgers, alligator and turtle ($5 to $8). The deli is open weekdays as well as Saturday.

For those on a River Road ramble, Donaldsonville is by far the best place to stop for a meal. Near the base of the Sunshine Bridge, it's an easy drive from most attractions. *First & Last Chance Café* (☎ 225-473-8236, 812 Railroad Ave) is a trackside joint serving great burgers ($3) and toothsome steaks smothered in garlic sauce ($15). It's open 9 am to midnight every day except Sunday. It's one block west of Hwy 3089.

Also in Donaldsonville, set in an old grocery store, the *Railroad Café* (☎ 225-474-8513, 212 Railroad Ave) is *the* spot for an oyster po-boy and a side of onion rings. Po-boys and plate lunches run $5 to $7. It's open Monday to Wednesday 10 am to 2 pm, Thursday to Saturday 10 am to 7:30 pm.

Ruggiero's (☎ 225-473-8476, 206 Railroad Ave) is a creaky old bar and restaurant serving a wide range of Italian dishes, among them garlicky shrimp and pasta dishes ($12) and traditional spaghetti and meatballs. It's open for lunch Tuesday to Friday 11 am to 1 pm and for dinner Tuesday to Saturday 5 to 9:15 pm.

At bayou-side *Café La Fourche* (☎ 225-473-7451), on Bayou Rd just east of Hwy 1 in Donaldsonville, creative seafood dishes ($9 to $15) dominate the menu, but the po-boys, stews and salads ($6 to $8) are equally appealing. It's open weekdays for lunch and dinner (closed between 2 and 5 pm), Saturday for dinner, and Sunday for brunch. Next door is *J's Diner*, serving cheap breakfasts all day, po-boys and plate lunches.

Lafitte's Landing at Bittersweet Plantation (☎ 225-473-1232), on Railroad Ave in Donaldsonville's historic district, serves the best haute cuisine between New Orleans and Baton Rouge (and is comparable to New Orleans' best). Chef John Folse has won a large following for his inventive Cajun-influenced cuisine, and his fans don't mind paying $20 for seafood, veal or lamb entrees. It's open Tuesday to Saturday for dinner, Sunday for brunch.

Upriver in Plaquemine, the family-oriented *City Café* (☎ 225-687-7831), on Main St across from the Plaquemine lock, has been serving up tasty seafood and steak meals for over 90 years. Full meals run $9 to $20, burgers and po-boys $5 to $7. It's open Monday to Saturday for lunch and dinner. On Thursday night, *Humphrey's Restaurant*, around the corner on Eden St, is a favorite spot for bikers.

BATON ROUGE
• pop 250,000 • metro area 600,000

The Native Americans who lived here prior to European contact called the area *Istrouma*, which meant 'red stick,' referring to the practice of painting cypress poles with blood to mark off the boundaries of hunting territories. *Baton rouge* is French for red stick.

This Mississippi River city is the home of two of the state's largest universities – Louisiana State University (LSU) and Southern University – as well as the nation's tallest capitol, the fifth-largest port and the second-largest petrochemical industry. The latter is what defines Baton Rouge physically and economically. Without question, though, politics has shaped the city's culture since Baton Rouge became the state capital in 1849. For those interested in Louisiana's peculiar and picaresque political history, Baton Rouge is worth exploring. The city also has a handful of attractions for kids.

Orientation
I-10 crosses the river to Port Allen (this bridge can get quite backed up during the morning and evening rush hours). The new and old state capitols, casinos, a riverfront plaza and an entertainment complex are downtown off I-110 and just north of I-10. North Blvd is the east-west divider for north/south directionals – N 22nd St north of North, S 22nd St south of North. LSU is in the southwest quadrant of the city. Nicholson Drive/Hwy 30 and Highland Rd both head south from downtown and run through campus; the neighboring streets are home to parks, inexpensive restaurants, nightclubs, movie theaters and shops.

There are decent maps of the city and campuses in the front of the city's yellow pages, and the tourist offices have some as well.

Information
Tourist Offices The Baton Rouge Area Convention & Visitors Bureau (☎ 225-383-1825, 800-527-6843), 730 North Blvd, in downtown, is open 8 am to 5 pm weekdays. Its Web site is www.batonrougetour.com. There's a smaller branch, along with a state tourism office, in the capitol lobby (open till 4:30 pm). All have city maps.

The West Baton Rouge Visitor Information Center (☎ 225-344-2920) is on Frontage Rd next to Motel 6 in Port Allen (just off I-10 exit 151). The Baton Rouge office of AAA (☎ 225-293-1200, 800-926-4222) is at 5454 Bluebonnet Rd.

Post The two-story main branch (☎ 800-275-8777), 750 Florida Blvd at 7th St in downtown, is open weekdays 8:30 am to 5 pm, Saturday 9 am to noon.

Internet Access All of the city's public libraries have computers with Internet access. Anyone can use these free of charge. If you need to check your email round the clock, Kinko's has two locations offering Internet access for 20¢/minute or $12/hour. The downtown store (☎ 225-378-3000) is at 525 Florida between 5th and 6th Sts; it's open 24 hours. The store near LSU, at 159 W State St, is open 7 am to 3 am weekdays, till 11 pm weekends.

BATON ROUGE

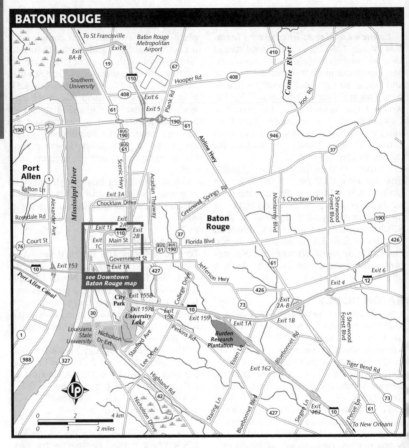

Media The main daily newspaper is *The Advocate*. The *Gambit* is a free weekly with extensive entertainment listings. *Rhythm City* is a free biweekly focusing specifically on music and clubs.

The local public radio station is at 89.3 FM. Gumbo Radio (104.5 FM) plays old R&B and zydeco.

Bookstores The Southern chain Books-A-Million (☎ 225-343-9584), 3525 Perkins Rd between I-10 and Acadian Thruway, has a strong regional section. It also has a large magazine section and it carries some titles in French. It's open daily from 9 am to 11 pm.

The discreet Hibiscus Bookstore (☎ 225-387-4264), 635 Main St between 6th and 7th Sts in downtown, is the city's gay bookstore. It's a good source of information about the local scene.

Libraries The Baton Rouge Main Library (☎ 225-231-3750), 7711 Goodwood Blvd, between Jefferson Hwy and Airline Hwy/ Hwy 61, is open Monday to Thursday 8 am to 10 pm, Friday and Saturday 8 am to 6 pm, Sunday 2 to 10 pm.

Medical & Emergency Services For emergency medical care, go to Our Lady of the Lake Medical Center (☎ 225-765-6565), 5000 Henessy Blvd at Essen Lane near the Burden Research Plantation, or Baton Rouge General Medical Center (☎ 225-387-7000), 3600 Florida Blvd at Acadian Thruway. For nonemergencies, call ahead; they may send you to local clinics.

Louisiana State Capitol

Among Huey Long's more brazen acts was the building of an art deco capitol (☎ 225-342-7317) in 1931 during the height of the Great Depression at a cost of more than $5 million and against the will of the state legislature. It would prove to be his most visible legacy – and the scene of his denouement. Today, the 34-story skyscraper, a towering palace of marble, is a beauty to behold. It's just north of downtown next to Capitol Lake.

In the lobby, what isn't covered with bronze friezes (ornamented bands) or sculpted metal panels is painted with murals or plastered with gold leaf. Behind the bank of elevators, a small display of mementos sits next to the bullet-pocked marble wall where Long was gunned down in 1935. On the 27th floor there is an **observation tower** offering sweeping views of the city, the industrial works to the north, and barges chugging by on the river.

The capitol building is open daily 8 am to 4:30 pm, the tower till 4 pm. When the state senate is in session, visitors can observe the action from balconies (photography is not permitted).

Outside, facing the capitol, is a massive bronze sculpture of Long, his left hand resting on a marble replica of the capitol as if it were a scepter. His body is buried beneath.

Old State Capitol

A few blocks away from the 'new' state capitol is the old one (☎ 225-342-0500, 800-488-2968), 100 North Blvd. The 150-year-old imposing Gothic-style structure sits on a bluff overlooking the Mississippi River and now serves as the Center for Political &

Governmental History. Don't let that discourage you: Louisiana's often-scandalous political history provides an entertaining insight into its culture. There are interactive exhibits, including an extensive video archive that visitors can sample and a small collection of historical maps. Even if political history doesn't interest you, the stunningly restored main rotunda, cast-iron staircase and stained-glass windows are worth a gander. It's open Tuesday to Saturday 10 am to 4 pm, Sunday noon to 4 pm. It costs $4 for adults, $2 for students.

Rural Life Museum & Windrush Gardens

This peaceful living history museum (☎ 225-765-2437), 4600 Essen Lane just off I-10 southeast of downtown, is on the site of the former Windrush Plantation, now the Burden Research Plantation operated by LSU. Instead of the opulent image of plantation life presented at many plantation homes, the focus here is on the everyday life of the laboring classes in the 19th century.

A working sugar plantation includes authentically restored and furnished rural buildings, including slave cottages, a sugar

For Faithful Service

Most visitors to the Rural Life Museum hardly note the sculpture that stands at the entrance to the museum grounds. It depicts a kindly African-American gentleman, his head bowed and hat tipped. Known to locals as 'Uncle Jack,' the sculpture was originally erected in 1927 in Natchitoches as a tribute to 'the arduous and faithful service of the good darkies of Louisiana.' During the Civil Rights movement, the sculpture was torn from its base and tossed in a patch of weeds. By 1974, the Rural Life Museum in Baton Rouge had acquired the sculpture, and today it greets visitors without explanation, an ironic reminder of one moment of a not-too-distant paternalistic past.

LOUISIANA

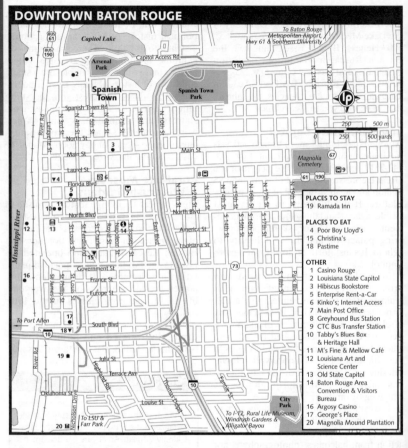

DOWNTOWN BATON ROUGE

To Baton Rouge Metropolitan Airport, Hwy 61 & Southern University

Capitol Lake

Arsenal Park

Capitol Access Rd

Spanish Town

Spanish Town Park

Spanish Town Rd

North St

Main St

Laurel St

Florida Blvd

Convention St

North Blvd

North Blvd

America St

Louisiana St

Government St

France St

Europe St

South Blvd

Julia St

Terrace Ave

Oklahoma St

Louise St

Magnolia Cemetery

Mississippi River

To Port Allen

To LSU & Farr Park

To I-12, Rural Life Museum, Windrush Gardens & Alligator Bayou

City Park

0   250   500 m
0   250   500 yards

PLACES TO STAY
19 Ramada Inn

PLACES TO EAT
4 Poor Boy Lloyd's
15 Christina's
18 Pastime

OTHER
1 Casino Rouge
2 Louisiana State Capitol
3 Hibiscus Bookstore
5 Enterprise Rent-a-Car
6 Kinko's; Internet Access
7 Main Post Office
8 Greyhound Bus Station
9 CTC Bus Transfer Station
10 Tabby's Blues Box
    & Heritage Hall
11 M's Fine & Mellow Café
12 Louisiana Art and
    Science Center
13 Old State Capitol
14 Baton Rouge Area
    Convention & Visitors
    Bureau
16 Argosy Casino
17 George's Place
20 Magnolia Mound Plantation

house with a 'Jamaica train' of open kettles, and a functioning blacksmith shop. A huge barn houses exhibits of African and slavery artifacts, carpenter's and weaver's tools, Civil War items, a hearse and carriage and more. Don't miss the Lucy Vargas figures of wax and cloth depicting rural African-Americans, and museum founder Steele Burden's comical clay figurines drawn from daily Louisiana life. The 25-acre gardens overflow with crape myrtles, azaleas and camellias. The museum is open daily 8:30 am to 5 pm, and admission is $5 for adults, $3 for children.

Louisiana State University

LSU is the state's best endowed public university. Despite having around 30,000 students, the campus is surprisingly calm (except during fall football games). The campus' main buildings are grouped on a 650-acre plateau in southwestern Baton Rouge. On the western edge is the Mississippi; on the eastern edge is the small University Lake (where it's possible to swim at city-run Stanford Park).

For visitors the most important area on campus is the LSU Museum Complex, which features the LSU Museum of Art

(☎ 225-388-4003) as well as the Museum of Natural Science (☎ 225-388-2855). For visitor information, call ☎ 225-388-5030; for a special events calendar, call ☎ 225-388-8654. Collegiate sports fans can purchase tickets for Tiger games and events by calling the LSU athletic department at ☎ 225-388-2184, or if you're out of town, call Ticketmaster at ☎ 225-761-8400.

Southern University

This institution was the founding campus for the largest predominantly black university system in the country. With around 9000 students, the campus spreads across the north end of Baton Rouge on the Mississippi a few miles west of the airport. Campus attractions include a small Gallery of Fine Arts (☎ 225-771-2070) with changing exhibitions and a Black Heritage Exhibit on the 3rd floor of the library (☎ 225-771-2843), which has an extensive collection of books and artifacts pertaining to African-American life. The music department (☎ 225-771-3440) is strong in jazz; call for information on upcoming concerts.

Other Things to See & Do

Just east of the state capitol, bounded by N 5th St, North St, N 9th St and State Capitol Drive is the **Spanish Town Historical District**, established in 1805 to accommodate Spanish families wishing to remain under the Spanish crown upon the region's cession to the US. The city tourist desk at the state capitol can provide you with a walking-tour brochure.

The **Louisiana Arts and Science Center** (☎ 225-344-5272), 100 S River Road across from the Old State Capitol, hosts art and science exhibits, many aimed at kids. It's open weekdays 10 am to 3 pm, Saturday till 4 pm, Sunday 1 to 4 pm, closed Monday. The entrance fee is $4 for adults, $2 for kids. The adjacent riverfront plaza is great for watching passing ships or downing a take-out meal.

Right on the river and hard to miss are two 24-hour casino boat complexes: the recently renovated **Argosy Casino** (☎ 225-378-6000), on France St near the I-10 bridge,

and **Casino Rouge** (☎ 225-709-7777), across from the state capitol. If you want a glimpse of the gambling scene, take a few minutes to wander through; they also offer all-you-can-eat buffets.

French Creole-style **Magnolia Mound Plantation** (☎ 225-343-4955), 2161 Nicholson Drive/Hwy 30 several blocks south of I-10, is the oldest plantation house (circa 1791) in the area. Also on the 16-acre grounds are an overseer's house, open-hearth kitchen (demonstrations Tuesday and Thursday), carriage house, food gardens and gift shop. There's also a slave cabin that is the focus of the 'Beyond the Big House' tour (by reservation only). It's open Tuesday to Saturday 10 am to 4 pm, Sunday 1 to 4 pm. Admission is $5 for adults, $1 for children.

The city-owned 101-acre **Bluebonnet Swamp Nature Center and Conservation Area** (☎ 225-757-8905), 10503 N Oak Hills Parkway, one block off Bluebonnet Blvd, has a 1-mile boardwalk with two observation decks. It winds through an upland hardwood forest before descending to a cypress swamp. The nature center features wildlife folk art and ecology displays. It's open Tuesday to Saturday 9 am to 5 pm, Sunday noon to 5 pm, closed Monday. Admission is $3 for adults, $2 for kids.

Gilley's Gallery (☎ 225-922-9225), 8750 Florida Blvd near Airline Hwy/Hwy 61, displays the works of many self-taught artists, including Clementine Hunter. To see pieces by her and other artists as well, check out www.eatel.net/~outsider.

Every weekend from 9 am to 5 pm, bargain hunters and people watchers descend on the 400 booths at the **Greater Baton Rouge Flea Market** (☎ 225-673-2682) at the corner of Hwys 73 and 61, just south of the city in Prairieville.

Outdoor Activities

Information & Gear The Backpacker (☎ 225-925-2667), 7656 Jefferson Hwy/Hwy 73 at Old Hammond Hwy, opposite Bocage Village Mall, is one of the best sources of outdoor information in the South. Downstairs near the entrance is a rack of free maps and lists showing trails in Louisiana and southern and western Mississippi. There's a book section that carries the *Trail Guide to the Delta Country* by the New Orleans chapter of the Sierra Club (☎ 225-885-8518); it covers hiking, cycling and paddling. The Baton Rouge chapter of the Sierra Club also sponsors outings; call ☎ 225-766-7784 for events listings.

The Backpacker staff can steer you to their favorite trails and help you with rentals of backpacks, sleeping bags and two- and four-person tents. If you want to get out on the water, ask the staff for the contact number of the Bayou Haystackers Paddling Club, which sponsors outings. The store sells equipment as well as maps and kayaks (no rentals). It's open Monday to Friday 10 am to 7 pm, Saturday 9 am to 6 pm.

Canoeing If you want to see swamp creatures up close, rent a canoe from Alligator Bayou Tours (see below; $10 for first hour, $5 each additional hour, for canoe, paddle, life jacket and map). Paddlers put-in at Alligator Bayou, part of the pristine 13,000-acre Spanish Lake Basin, a cypress swamp with many smaller bayous, islands and lakes. Paddling is a year-round activity. Located on the southern outskirts of Baton Rouge, the rental shop is open all year Monday to Friday 8 am to 6 pm, Saturday and Sunday 7 am to 6 pm.

Swamp Tours Alligator Bayou Tours (☎ 225-642-8297, 888-379-2677, gatrtour@ bellsouth.com), 35019 Alligator Bayou Rd in Prairieville, 15 minutes from downtown, offers 1½-hour sightseeing tours of Alligator Bayou on a canopied pontoon boat that holds up to 50 passengers. On the way to the dock, don't be thrown off by the suburban neighborhoods you have to drive through; you'll soon be seeing real swamp, where wildlife is abundant. Tours depart promptly at 6:30 pm Wednesday to Friday, at 10:30 am, 4 and 6:30 pm Saturday, and at 4 and 6:30 pm Sunday (call for other departures). Plan to arrive a half-hour early. Tours cost $15 for adults, $10 for children.

Occasionally on weekends there's live Cajun music under an outdoor pavilion. The operators plan to start giving nature-walk tours on a raised wooden walkway in a nearby preserve.

Swimming If the kids are boiling over with post-plantation yayas, **Blue Bayou Water Park** (☎ 225-753-3333), on Perkins Rd 7 miles south of town (I-10 exit 166), might just cool them (and you) off. It's open 10 am to 6 pm Memorial Day through Labor Day. Admission is $18 for those over 4 feet tall, $15 for those under.

Special Events
In mid-April, Port Allen, just across the river, hosts an annual blues festival (☎ 225-357-8518). City-run Farr Park (☎ 225-769-7805, 225-766-8828), 6400 River Rd south of LSU, is the site of many equestrian events throughout the year.

Places to Stay
Many of the moderate to expensive chain hotels are located just off I-10 around College Drive (exit 158) and Acadian Thruway (exit 157B). Less expensive chains are clustered along the north side of I-12 near Airline Hwy/Hwy 61 within a mile of I-10. Some hotels increase rates 20% to 30% on football-game weekends in fall. In Port Allen just across the river and only five minutes from downtown, there's a cluster of chain hotels at Lobdell Hwy (exit 151).

Camping City-owned *Greenwood Park Campground* (☎ 225-775-3877, 13350 Hwy 19), at Thomas Rd, is north of downtown near the Baton Rouge Zoo and features RV ($7) and tent ($2) sites with water, electricity, bathhouses, restrooms and picnic tables. The wooded park, which also has tennis courts and a 30-acre fishing lake, is near golf courses and Cohn Arboretum.

Baton Rouge KOA (☎ 225-664-7281, 800-562-5673, 7628 Vincent Rd) is 7 miles east of downtown off I-12 in Denham Springs. It's a peaceful setting with lots of trees, a pool, playground, game room, store and picnic tables at each well-shaded site.

Rates are $19 for tents, $26.50 for RVs with hookups. There's also a pair of small single-room log cabins that sleep up to four ($35; no linens provided).

If you can't get into one of the closer campgrounds or are headed north to St Francisville and prefer to take back roads, consider *Tranquility Lakes Campground & 3-D Archery Range* (☎ 225-777-4393), on Hwy 16, 18 miles north of I-12 in Dennis Mills. It's a low-key family-run campground on a 35-acre lake. There's a pool, coin laundry and three bathhouses. Tent sites are $14 to $16, RV sites are $17 for full hookups. Cabins (sleeping four or more) have air-conditioning, refrigerators, bathrooms and barbecue pits for $45; add $10 for units with a stove.

Motels & Hotels Cross the river and save at *Motel 6* (☎ 225-343-5945), on Frontage Rd at I-10 exit 151 in Port Allen. It has 121 rooms and a nice pool. Rates are $36/42 singles/doubles. It's only five minutes from downtown Baton Rouge. Also at this exit is *Super 8* (☎ 225-381-9134) with rooms for $41, *Holiday Inn Express* (☎ 225-343-4821), *Best Western* (☎ 225-344-3638) and *Ramada Inn* (☎ 225-383-7188).

If you'll be spending much time near the LSU campus, consider staying right on campus at *Pleasant Hall* (☎ 225-387-0297, fax 225-387-3317). Basic rooms go for $45, suites for $65.

Near downtown and the Argosy casino, just south of the I-10 bridge, is the recently renovated *Ramada Inn* (☎ 225-387-1111, 1480 Nicholson Drive), which has rooms for $65.

Shoney's Inn (☎ 225-925-8399, 9919 Gwen-adele Drive) is conveniently located at I-12 exit 2B at Airline Hwy (Hwy 61/190). It features attractive but smallish rooms and suites. Rates are $49/57. Also at this exit is another *Motel 6* (☎ 225-924-2130); singles/doubles are $40/46.

Comfort Inn University Center (☎ 225-927-5790, 2445 S Acadian Thruway), off I-10 exit 157B, has an ideal location for trips to LSU, a variety of restaurants along College Drive and Perkins Rd, and easy access to I-10, I-12 and I-110. There's a pool and 24-hour coffee shop next door. The spacious rooms go for $70/76.

Hawthorn Suites (☎ 225-923-3377, 800-945-7667, 3045 Valley Creek Drive), between I-10 and Perkins Rd, just east of College Drive, has 110 rooms with in-room refrigerators. Rates for rooms are $55/60 weekdays/weekends. The nearby *Embassy Suites* (☎ 225-924-6566, 4914 Constitution Ave) is one of the nicest hotels in the city. Its two-room suites feature a galley kitchen. There's an indoor pool with a sauna and whirlpool, airport shuttle service, and a complimentary full breakfast. Rooms are $129, with weekend discounts.

Places to Eat
Baton Rouge has a surprisingly high number of excellent restaurants, making it easy to avoid the chains.

Downtown Convenient *Poor Boy Lloyd's* (☎ 225-387-2271, 205 Florida St), at Lafayette, is famous for its chicken and dumplings ($5), not to mention the po-boys (try the oyster one). It's open weekdays 7 am to 2 pm.

There is a *cafeteria* (☎ 225-342-0371) in the basement of the state capitol offering the best breakfasts and lunches that government money can subsidize (open weekdays). Or try the burgers at *Pastime* (☎ 225-343-5490, 252 South Blvd), in the shadow of the I-10 bridge.

Christina's (☎ 225-336-9512), at St Charles and Somerulos, tucked half a block off Government St, is a favorite among downtown workers. Breakfast ($5) and lunch (salads, po-boys and plates $5 to $7) are served Monday to Saturday, closed Sunday.

East of Downtown There's a handful of places along Government St as it heads east out of downtown. A neighborhood joint, *Phil's Oyster Bar* (☎ 225-924-3045, 5162 Government St) has a bar on one side of the room, booths on the other. The oyster shuckers keep up a steady banter as they slide dozen after dozen across the bar to waiting customers. Lunch or dinner runs $8 to $10. Thursday night Phil's hosts a jazz and blues jam session.

Arzi's Café (☎ 225-927-2111, *5219 Government St*) may well be one of the few Louisiana places outside New Orleans where you can eat a delicious vegetarian meal. Try the falafel, baba ganoush, spanakopita and dolmas; the best deal is an appetizer assortment to share for $18. There are lamb, beef and chicken dishes, also. Prices for lunch or dinner start at about $10 and continue up. There's another location just north of LSU on W Chimes St.

Fleur-De-Lis Cocktail Lounge (☎ 225-924-2904, *5655 Government St*) is a funky Baton Rouge favorite that's been in business since the 1940s. The Pepto Bismol-pink exterior and art deco-tinged interior are a kick, and its 'Roman' pizzas are famous. It's open Tuesday to Saturday 10 am to 10 pm.

Near LSU Just north of campus near the famous Varsity Theater on Highland Rd is a cluster of good and cheap restaurants. Recently relocated ***Silver Moon*** (☎ 755-2553), on W Chimes St, serves monstrous portions of some of the best Creole soul food in the state at very low prices (around $5). Fridays only, jambalaya is offered and it's so good that it always runs out early. It's open Monday to Saturday for lunch. There's an ***Arzi's*** down the block (see above).

Serving the university community since 1941, ***Louie's Café*** (☎ 225-346-8221, *209 W State St*) is the best 24-hour eatery in town according to some locals. It's famous for its hash browns, and the veggie omelet is tasty. The decor is vintage 1950s-style diner counter. Meals run $5 to $10.

In the same block as the Varsity Theater, ***Raising Cane's*** serves up cheap and tasty fried chicken 'fingers'; with fries, slaw, toast and sauce, lunch or dinner will cost you $4.50. (This is a local chain, and other locations are also good bets.)

The area just east of LSU holds another smattering of restaurants. Grab a cup of brew and a beignet or muffin at ***Coffee Call*** (☎ 225-925-9493, *3010 College Drive*), off

I-10 exit 158. It's open daily for breakfast and lunch (Saturday it's open all night). The weekday lunch consists of po-boys and a soup and salad bar.

The most expensive item on the deli menu at ***Zeeland Street Market*** (☎ 225-387-4546, *2031 Perkins Rd*), between Acadian Thruway and I-10, is the club-style po-boy at $7. That's just one of the reasons for its popularity. Others are mouth-watering omelets served from 7:30 to 10:30 am, fresh salads like the Zeeland Zen with tender baby greens, walnuts, sprouts and blue cheese, and a sophisticated (but not necessarily expensive) selection of wines. It's open weekdays 7:30 am to 7:30 pm.

Our Daily Bread (☎ 225-924-1215, *9414 Florida Blvd*), between Monterrey and Cora Drives, two blocks east of Cortana Mall, serves vegetarian lunches Monday to Saturday 11 am to 3 pm. It offers a menu of healthful sandwiches, including veggie po-boys ($4 to $7), salads and a generously sized lunch special ($4). They bake their whole-grain breads daily.

Though set in a shopping strip, ***Juban's Restaurant*** (☎ 225-346-8422, *3739 Perkins Rd*), at S Arcadian Thruway, is surprisingly upscale; in fact, it's arguably the best restaurant in town, serving sophisticated nouveau Creole dishes. At lunch, the $10 daily special is the best deal. The dinner menu has grilled items as well as seafood, lamb, veal and fowl ranging from $12 to $28. Start the meal with a bowl of subtle gumbo ($4.50). It's open weekdays for lunch and dinner, and Saturday for dinner only.

Other Parts of Town Close to the Rural Life Museum, ***Louisiana Pizza Kitchen*** (☎ 225-763-9100), just off Essen Lane south of I-10, serves thin-crust, wood-fired individual-size pizzas for around $8, including one with smoked salmon and caviar and another with goat cheese and chicken. A tasty mozzarella salad and pastas cost about $9. It's open daily for lunch and dinner.

DeAngelo's (☎ 225-761-4465, *7955 Bluebonnet Rd*) serves rich pizzas ($8) that have homemade tomato sauce, imported cheeses, hand-tossed crusts and fresh toppings. Then there are freshly baked focaccia and bruschetta, fabulous calzones and salads. It's open Monday 10 am to 3 pm, Tuesday to Saturday 11 am to 10 pm, Sunday 11 am to 9 pm. There are three additional locations: ☎ 225-927-2762, 9634 Airline Hwy in the Hammond Shopping Center; ☎ 225-757-3877, 250 W Lee Drive; and ☎ 225-624-8500, 2820 E Causeway Approach.

India's Restaurant (☎ 225-769-0600, 5230 Essen Lane) across from Denny's Car Wash serves large portions of excellent standard Indian dishes and a few unusual crab, scallop, and lobster ones, all for $7 to $15. Its unremarkable exterior fits its surroundings, so its elegant dining room is a pleasant surprise. There's a lunch buffet, and dinner is served daily.

If you're craving fresh Mexican food, head for *El Rio (☎ 225-926-1348, 8334 Airline Hwy)*. Locals say the margaritas here are the best in town.

Entertainment

Near the old capitol, *M's Fine & Mellow Café (☎ 225-387-3663, 143 N 3rd St)* hosts folk, jazz and the occasional poetry slam from Wednesday to Saturday. It also serves soup, salad, sandwiches and pizza. Not far from there is the new location of *Tabby's Blues Box and Heritage Hall (☎ 225-387-9715, 244 Lafayette)* across from the Capitol House Hotel.

While the neighborhood is questionable, there's no doubt about the quality of blues at *Phil Brady's (☎ 225-927-3786, 4848 Government St)*. The clientele averages mid-30s and 40s.

In north Baton Rouge, *Flava's Entertainment (☎ 225-357-1500, 6046 Airline Hwy)* features a different style of music each night of the week, including hip hop, reggae, jazz and soul. The bar specializes in exotic mixed drinks and ice-cold beer, and there's a dance floor and pool tables.

Dating from the '40s, the *Gator Bar* at the departure point for Alligator Bayou Tours (see Swamp Tours, earlier in this section) has live music on weekend nights (Sunday is the busiest night).

Gay & Lesbian Clubs At Polk St between downtown and LSU (look for the rainbow awning) is *Evolution (☎ 225-344-9291, 2183 Highland Rd)*, a multiroom dance club with two bars catering to gays and lesbians, and the straights who love to dance with them. The recently expanded *Hide-A-Way (☎ 225-923-3632, 7367 Exchange Place)*, near the intersection of Airline Hwy and Florida Blvd, is a women's dance club. Over at *George's Place (☎ 225-387-9798, 860 St Louis St)*, the clientele that shows up for the drag show, live music or karaoke is gay and heterosexual friendly. It's across from the Pastime restaurant in a small brown building without a sign just north of the I-10 bridge.

Around LSU The new *Reilly Theatre* (on the southwest side of campus) is home to Swine Palace Productions, which stages several plays each season. For information and tickets, call ☎ 225-388-3527.

The cult film *Sex, Lies and Videotape* was filmed at *The Bayou (☎ 225-346-1765, 124 W Chimes)*, and REM played here in its early days. It hasn't lost its appeal and the quality of rock and jazz remains high. There are also half a dozen pool tables. The *Varsity Theatre (☎ 225-383-7018, 225-383-5267, 3353 Highland Rd)*, is *the* place for live music – there's a variety of acts, large and small, such as Wilco, String Cheese Incident, and Cowboy Mouth (call after 2 pm for information).

Next to the Varsity, the *Chimes (☎ 225-383-1754, 3357 Highland Rd)* serves 120 varieties of bottled beer and 30 on tap to the college crowd and their elders. The college crowd also lingers at the *Caterie (☎ 225-383-4178, 3617 Perkins Rd)*, at Acadian Thruway in a shopping mall, where the nightly draw is live local talent. (It also serves seafood, po-boys and sandwiches until midnight.)

Getting There & Away

Air Recently expanded Baton Rouge Metropolitan Airport (☎ 225-355-0333), 9430 Jackie Cochran Drive north of the city off I-110, is served by major US airlines. Most direct flights arrive from airline hub cities – Dallas for American Airlines, Atlanta for Delta, Houston for Continental, Memphis for Northwest. All roundtrip fares into Baton Rouge are over $100. American has begun a direct flight from Chicago.

Bus Greyhound (☎ 225-383-3811, 800-231-2222), 1253 Florida Blvd at N 12th St, has daily one-way buses to Biloxi (four to five hours, around $34), Lafayette (one hour, $12), New Orleans (1½ to two hours, $12), Shreveport (five to six hours, $32) and other cities. The station is on a well-lit major street about a mile east of downtown. It's easy to catch a cab from here.

Amtrak Thruway Bus Service (☎ 800-872-7245) offers four trips daily from New Orleans to Baton Rouge ($14), but it does not carry passengers from Baton Rouge to New Orleans. It stops at the Greyhound station.

Car Before I-10 connected New Orleans and Baton Rouge, Hwy 61/Airline Hwy was the main strip. Via either route the trip is about 80 miles. I-12 runs east/west from Slidell, joining I-10 just east of downtown Baton Rouge. I-10 crosses the river to Port Allen and heads 55 miles to Lafayette. I-110 parallels the river just east of downtown, joining Hwy 61 north of Southern University and heading up to St Francisville and the state border.

Getting Around

To/From the Airport Yellow Cab (☎ 225-926-6400, 800-259-2227) and Tiger Taxi (☎ 225-921-9199) serve the airport. A ride from the airport to downtown costs from $15 to $20.

Bus The Capitol Transportation City Bus (☎ 225-389-8920 for general information, ☎ 225-336-0821 for rider information) costs $1.25, 25¢ for a transfer. Look for blue signs with the letters 'CTC.' Drivers also stop when flagged. City buses require exact change and run Monday to Saturday from 6 am to 6 pm.

The system revolves around a transfer station at 2222 Florida St, where riders can get a system map. From this station, you can pick up the North Blvd Shuttle to the new and old state capitols and other downtown and waterfront attractions. Buses to LSU (University line) and Southern (Scotlandville line) also run through the transfer station. A special 30-minute shuttle runs between LSU and Southern University. It departs LSU on the half-hour, Southern on the hour.

Car The national rental chains have counters at the airport. Enterprise has several offices around town. The downtown branch (☎ 225-346-5487), 641 Convention St, is convenient for bus and train travelers; it offers a car drop-off and pick-up service.

Taxi You must call for cab service. Yellow Cab (☎ 225-926-3260) serves Baton Rouge; the meter starts at $1.95 and runs $1.40 per mile.

BATON ROUGE TO CAJUN COUNTRY

West of Baton Rouge flows the Atchafalaya River, a main distributary of the Mississippi. Surrounding it is the vast Atchafalaya Basin, the country's largest freshwater swamp, forming the eastern edge of the region known as Cajun Country. Over this watery landscape runs elevated I-10. Completed in 1973, it connected Baton Rouge and New Orleans with a region that until then had remained physically and culturally isolated.

Travelers heading west on I-10 will arrive in Lafayette in about an hour. If you'd like a closer look at the swamp, consider a levee walk or swamp tour in Henderson (see the Cajun Country chapter).

Those heading to Lafayette on I-10 (and who don't mind a 12-mile detour north) or to Opelousas via Hwy 190 should make a point of stopping at *Joe's Dreyfus Store Restaurant* (☎ 225-637-2625), on Hwy 77 South in Livonia. The store, opened just after the Civil War, now houses a casual restaurant famous statewide for its fried and broiled dishes. Try the turkey and andouille gumbo ($4.50), fried chicken ($6), crawfish étouffée ($13), stuffed quail ($7.50) or steaks ($15). It's open daily for lunch and dinner (closed on Sunday evening and on Monday).

If you feel too full after dinner to continue the drive, consider staying at the **Dreyfus House** (☎ *225-637-2094, 888-757-3120, 2741 Maringouin Rd West*) in Livonia. In an 1850 Victorian, its four B&B suites, each with bathroom, cost $65 to $85. About 12 miles west of Livonia along Hwy 190 in Krotz Springs is the **Country Store B&B Inn** (☎ *337-566-3501, 888-900-6090, 204 Main St*). Above a country store are four rooms that go for $45 to $75.

BATON ROUGE TO MISSISSIPPI

Just north of Baton Rouge the elevation begins to climb, and herds of cattle and horses graze in fields. The architecture and culture starts to change as well, having more in common with Anglo Mississippi culture to the north than the Creole and Cajun culture to the south. A network of ravines made this a Confederate stronghold in the battle for control of the river, and the riparian habitat attracts an astonishing variety of bird life that kept artist John James Audubon coming back.

Port Hudson SCA

In the longest siege in US military history, the Confederate and Union armies struggled for 48 days in the summer of 1863 for control of the Mississippi. Among the Union troops were the Louisiana Native Guards, the first African-American soldiers to enter battle, paving the way for the acceptance of black soldiers in the war effort. After 6800 Confederate and 30,000 Union casualties, Port Hudson finally fell to the Union.

Today, this state commemorative area has a museum, outdoor exhibits, picnic areas and 6 miles of wooded trails that connect battery positions and earthworks used during the battle. These trails keep bird watchers busy. The park (☎ 225-654-3775), 756 W Plains-Port Hudson Rd (off Hwy 61), is 13 miles southeast of St Francisville and just north of Port Hudson. It's

open daily 9 am to 5 pm. Admission is $2 for adults and free for seniors and children.

St Francisville
• pop 1700

In the mid-1700s, Spanish Capuchin monks found the highland bluffs here more suitable as a burial ground than the lowlands across the river in Pointe Coupee Parish. Soon the area took on the name of the monks' patron saint, St Francis. By the late 1700s, northern British loyalists began arriving to escape the Revolutionary War. Cotton plantations sprang up around the town. Its most well-known resident was John James Audubon, who lived a few months at Oakley Plantation; he returned to the town many times to draw its birds. Restoration of the town has taken place since the early 1970s thanks to the efforts of the local historical society, which raises funds through its annual Audubon Pilgrimage (see Special Events, later in this section).

Today this tranquil town retains nearly 150 of its 18th- and 19th-century houses and buildings, some of which are open to the public for tours. For travelers interested in architecture, antiques, birding and B&Bs, St Francisville makes a pleasant day trip from Baton Rouge or a first stop heading south from Natchez. The ferry provides easy access to Cajun Country to the west.

Orientation & Information St Francisville is about 25 miles north of Baton Rouge on Hwy 61. The highway passes the intersection of Hwy 965 (which heads to Oakley Plantation/Audubon SCA) just before entering the southeast side of town; it continues through the town and toward the state border. Hwy 10 cuts diagonally across the center of town, running northeast to Rosedown Plantation and southwest to St Francisville's historic district and the ferry. B&Bs and restaurants are scattered around town. There's no commercial transportation into St Francisville.

The West Feliciana Parish Tourist Commission (☎ 225-635-6330), 11757 Ferdinand St, St Francisville, 70775, is open Monday to

Saturday 9 am to 5 pm, Sunday 9:30 am to 5 pm. The Web site is www.n-sf.net. It's also home to the West Feliciana Historical Society and has a small museum and restrooms. The West Feliciana Parish Hospital (☎ 225-635-3811) is on Commerce St just west of Hwy 61. The Audubon Regional Library (☎ 225-635-3364), on Ferdinand St, has Internet access.

Historic District Most historic buildings are along Ferdinand St/Hwy 10 and Royal St, as well as Johnson, Prosperity and Fidelity Sts, all of which run perpendicular to Ferdinand as it heads to the river and the ferry dock. The historical society has a detailed walking-tour brochure; numbers on the brochure correspond to numbered plaques at the buildings.

Oakley Plantation/Audubon SCA In 1821, John James Audubon came to Oakley to teach painting to the daughter of owner James Pirrie. Though his assignment lasted only four months, he and his assistant worked on 32 paintings of birds found in the plantation's surrounding 100-acre forest (he returned many times to the town to continue his work). Guided tours of the West-Indies-influenced house (1806) start every half-hour (last tour at 4 pm). Self-guided tours of the 100-acre grounds include a lovely herb and vegetable garden, two slave cabins, a working kitchen and a barn. You can picnic on the grounds or hike the short, wooded Cardinal Trail (good for bird watching). Oakley Plantation (☎ 225-635-3739, 888-677-2838), on Hwy 965, charges a mere pittance for its plantation tour – $2 for adults and free for seniors and children. It's open daily 9 am to 5 pm.

Other Things to See & Do An *allée* of oak trees forms a canopy over the driveway to the 1832 **Rosedown Plantation** mansion (☎ 225-635-3332), 12501 Hwy 10. Many of the mansion's current furnishings were purchased in the mid-19th century by the original owners, cotton planters Martha and Daniel Turnbull. For $10, visitors can view these furnishings in immaculately restored rooms only through windows and Plexiglass

JERRY ALEXANDER

Strut your stuff over to Oakley Plantation to picnic with the peacocks.

doorways while listening to recorded monologues. Rosedown is a major stop on the tour-bus circuit.

The Nature Conservancy's 109-acre **Mary Ann Brown Nature Preserve** (☎ 225-338-1040), on Hwy 965 a few miles west of Oakley Plantation, has 2 miles of trails, a pond with a viewing deck, and picnic grounds. Hwy 965 itself makes a very scenic drive.

Though **Hemingbough** (☎ 225-635-6617) is privately owned, its 238 rolling acres, 45-acre lake, and gardens with 2000 azaleas are open to the public free of charge. Its owner, Arlin Dease, created the complex to foster peaceful contemplation, appreciation of nature, and an exchange of ideas. A 20,000-sq-feet museum opening in summer 2001 will house Audubon's Birds of America (all 437 paintings). The grounds also have an outdoor stage hosting the Baton Rouge Symphony (☎ 225-927-2776) in May and June and B&B accommodations (see Places to Stay, later in this section). Hemingbough is on Hwy 965 west of Hwy 61 just south of town.

In 1963, the Gothic Revival **Afton Villa** mansion burned down, but visitors can wander its gardens (☎ 225-635-6330), some within the ruins, daily during fall and spring. It's on Hwy 61, 4 miles north of town. Admission is $5.

Outdoor Activities Although hundreds of species of bird are visible throughout the year, the best times to **bird watch** are spring and fall. Expect to see waterfowl as well as songbirds. The bird checklist produced by the Dept of Culture, Recreation and Tourism (☎ 225-342-8111) covers species at Oakley Plantation, Port Hudson and Tunica Hills. It's available at the tourist office. Naturalist and wildlife artist Murrell Butler (☎ 225-635-6214) leads birding tours through a 350-acre upland forest.

The quiet, shady roads and rolling hills around St Francisville are ideal for **cycling**. In fact, the state cycling championships have been held here. One route favored by the Baton Rouge Bicycle Club is the Audubon Ramble starting at the Audubon

State Commemorative Area. Another route starts in Jackson and goes through the East Felicianas. Maps of these routes are available at the Backpacker in Baton Rouge and sometimes at the St Francisville tourist office. They're also in the Sierra Club's *Trail Guide to the Delta Country*. No bike rentals are available in town.

Cross Creek Stables (☎ 225-655-4233) offers **horseback trail rides**. Call after 5 pm.

Special Events Guides outfitted in antebellum-period costumes lead tours of historic plantations, houses, churches and gardens during the annual Audubon Pilgrimage (☎ 225-635-6330) the third weekend in March. The cost is $20 and proceeds benefit the historical society. Every weekend in October, Angola Prison hosts a famous rodeo (see the Angola Prison section, later in this chapter).

Places to Stay There's water, electricity and full hookups at *Green Acres Campground* (☎ 225-635-4903, 11907 Hwy 965). It has a few tent sites next to the pond ($13) and 47 RV sites ($15). Guests can swim in the large pool, hike a nature trail and prepare meals either on a grill or in a pavilion with a kitchen. There are clean restrooms and showers, laundry facilities and a store.

Those in search of Americana will find it at the ramshackle *3V Tourist Court* (☎ 225-635-3120, 877-313-5540), centrally located at the intersection of Ferdinand and Commerce Sts. Built in the 1920s, it was the first motor court in the South. Small cabins with kitchenettes cost $50 to $65, $75 for four or more guests. The cabins vary considerably; look before you pay.

Set back off Hwy 61 at Hwy 10, the recently renovated *Best Western St Francis Hotel on the Lake* (☎ 225-635-3821, 800-826-9931 in state, ☎ 800-528-1234 out of state) has 5 acres of lawns and a small lake that give it a bit of charm. It has 96 rooms and a pool. Rates are $65 to $75 for a double.

Historic accommodations abound in St Francisville, including guest rooms in several of the houses open for tours. Rates run from $65 to $195. For advance written reservations, all addresses are St Francisville, LA 70775.

Next to a small park, the *St Francisville Inn* (☎ *225-635-6502, 800-488-6502*), PO Drawer 1369, at the intersection of Commerce and Ferdinand Sts, is in walking distance of the historic district, shops and restaurants. The 10 comfortable rooms in this 1880s Victorian range from $55 to $75 and include a buffet breakfast. There's a brick courtyard and a pool.

Guests at *Hemingbough* (☎ *225-635-6617, fax 225-635-3800*), PO Box 1640, along Hwy 965 just off Hwy 61 south of town, can relax in one of eight antique-filled rooms (two of them in suites) with private bathrooms. Its peaceful grounds are most relaxing (see Other Things to See & Do, earlier). One or two guests pay $90 for a room, $110 for a suite, including continental breakfast.

The *Butler Greenwood* (☎ *225-635-6312, ButlerGree@aol.com, 8345 Hwy 61*) has seven peaceful guest cottages scattered around oak-shaded grounds and a small lake. Stays include continental breakfast, use of the pool and a tour of the owner's antebellum home, which has been in the same family since 1810. Rates are $100 to $110 for one or two guests in one bedroom, $160 for four guests in two bedrooms. All cottages have kitchens.

A 4-mile drive north of St Francisville takes you to *Green Springs Inn* (☎ *225-635-4232, 800-457-4978, 7463 Tunica Trace/Hwy 66*), a country house on 150 lovely acres. The spacious rooms have large beds, and come with a full Southern breakfast. Upstairs rooms in the main house for one or two guests run $95 to $105. Six semiprivate cottages, all with kitchenettes and decks overlooking the woods, go for $175.

Places to Eat Restaurants, though numerous, are not the draw of this town. For breakfast, check out the buffet at the *St Francisville Inn*, served 7 to 9 am. Popular *Magnolia Cafe* (☎ *225-635-6528, 5687 E Commerce St*) has tasty salads, pizzas, po-boys and Mexican selections for $4 to $10.

It's open Wednesday to Saturday for lunch and dinner, Sunday 11 am to 4 pm. Down the street, *Sammy's Grill* (☎ *225-635-9755*) has po-boys ($6), specialty sandwiches ($4 to $8) and seafood plates ($8 at lunch, $12 at dinner). It also serves a simple Sunday brunch.

The *Road Side Bar-B-Q* (☎ *225-635-9696*), on Hwy 61 just south of town, serves inexpensive barbecue, catfish and steaks. It's open Monday to Wednesday for lunch, Thursday to Sunday for lunch and dinner (closing Sunday at 5 pm).

Elegant newcomer *Keane's Carriagehouse*, at the Myrtles Plantation (☎ *225-635-6276, 7747 Hwy 61*), serves such upscale dishes as braised duck breast, osso bucco and filet mignon. Prices range from $18 to $21. There's an extensive wine list. It's open for dinner Wednesday to Saturday, for brunch Sunday.

Tunica Hills Wildlife Management Area

This 3366-acre area has rugged ravines, bluffs and mixed hardwood forests ideal for hiking, birding and wildlife watching. The woods are thick, and the climbs challenging due to rough footing and hills. There are waterfalls in the Clark Creek Natural Area. February and March, when it's cool and the spring flowers are blooming, are the best months to go. As in many wilderness areas, beware of snakes. Hunting is permitted, so call ahead to speak to an official and get a map of these areas.

Tunica Hills (☎ *225-765-2360*) is located off Hwy 66 near Tunica. From St Francisville, take Hwy 61 north about 3½ miles; turn west onto Hwy 66 for 17 miles. You'll see an Exxon Country Grocery (with a friendly proprietor). Turn left and go one hundred yards past the grocery onto a blacktop road, which turns to gravel. Small signs are posted on an iron gate indicating the entrance. You can pick up a free map at the West Feliciana Parish Tourist Commission in St Francisville (see Orientation & Information in the St Francisville section, earlier in this chapter) or at the Backpacker in Baton Rouge.

Angola Prison

Since its establishment in the late 1800s, the Louisiana State Penitentiary's reputation has been marred by poor conditions and brutality, and from the early 1970s to 1999, the prison was under federal oversight. Bordered on three sides by the Mississippi and on the fourth by Tunica Hills, this remote maximum-security facility, commonly known as Angola, today houses 5100 prisoners, many of whom farm the adjoining 18,000 fertile acres. At this facility, Sister Helen Prejean worked with death-row inmates, and her memoir, *Dead Man Walking*, was later made into the film by the same name, scenes from which were shot here. Inmate journalists produce *The Angolite*, an award-winning newsmagazine. Famous former prisoners include bluesman Leadbelly and pop singer Freddy Fender.

Just outside the main gate is the recently expanded **Louisiana State Penitentiary Museum** (☎ 225-655-2592). The collection's point of view is that of correctional staff, not inmates. Historical photos and articles convey some of the horror of prison conditions in the distant past, but the more recent conditions that led to federal oversight are not discussed. Along one wall is the history of the death penalty in Louisiana; an adjacent room houses a former electric chair and photos of executed prisoners. A display case of confiscated prisoner-made weapons reveals real ingenuity. A row of prisoners' artwork appears near photos of correctional staff killed on duty. Nearby, a video shows harrowing events from the annual prisoner rodeo, among them one in which contestants try to grab a token off a bull's forehead. The museum is open Monday to Friday 8 am to 4:30 pm, Saturday 9 am to 5 pm, and Sunday 1 to 5 pm. Donations are much appreciated.

In early May, the prison hosts an arts and crafts festival (☎ 225-655-2001). Every Sunday in October, the prison puts on an all-prisoner rodeo (☎ 225-655-4411), a tradition for more than 35 years. Five thousand spectators watch nonprofessional cowboys in prison stripes compete for prizes and the coveted champion's belt buckle. Proceeds go to the Inmate Welfare Fund, which subsidizes prisoner expenses not covered by the state.

Cajun Country

Officially called 'Acadiana,' Cajun Country encompasses a 22-parish region of southern Louisiana, forming a triangle from the Mississippi River delta and wetlands south of New Orleans to a peak in the uplands above Ville Platte to the Texas border west of Lake Charles. Home to the largest French-speaking minority in the US, the region is named for the French settlers from L'Acadie (now Nova Scotia) who were exiled by the British in 1755 and almost 10 years later began seeking refuge in the bayou country.

Cajun Country consists of three distinct subregions revolving around Lafayette, the self-proclaimed Capital of French Louisiana

Highlights

- Bayous, cheniers, marshlands and swamps
- Cajun and Creole delicacies, including fresh crawfish and catfish; boudin, andouille and head cheese; jambalaya and red beans and rice; and deep-fried just-about-anything
- Cajun and zydeco and their infectious beat, which will tickle your feet at festivals, clubs, restaurants and community halls
- People watching and 'passing a good time' at festivals large and small

(also known as the Hub City). South of Lafayette, swinging east in an arc below New Orleans, is a maze of bayous and swamps where the earliest Cajuns settled. Northwest of Lafayette is the Cajun prairie, an area of cattle ranches and rice and craw-fish farms settled by Acadians and Creoles; today, it's a center of Cajun and zydeco music. Southwest of Lafayette is the Cajun coast, a ruggedly remote region along the Gulf of Mexico. It's on both the Mississippi and Central Flyways, making it a prime area for birding.

Few specific sites in Cajun Country are destinations in themselves. Instead, the draws are seeing the lush landscapes and their wildlife (preferably from a boat) and experiencing the joie de vivre of its proud people, evident in their love of food, dancing and music. Any celebration usually involves all three, and communities embrace most any excuse for partying with the whole family. Hundreds of regional festivals focus on local crops and dishes or on historical, religious, or cultural events. Local celebrations provide visitors with a window into family and community life, and visitors are welcome – indeed, tourism is second only to mineral extraction and refining in the economies of many towns. Except in January and the hottest summer months, it's easy to find several events every weekend, and a few merit planning trips around (see Special Events, later in this chapter). If you plan on spending a good stretch of time in the area, pick up a copy of *Cajun Country*, by Macon Fry and Julie Posner, whose deep affection for and knowledge of the region and culture are evident on every page.

Outside of Lafayette, few towns have plentiful accommodations, and of these, budget pickings are slim. If a large festival is happening or if several smaller ones are taking place in neighboring towns, you may be out of luck without a reservation. Even on a weekend without a festival in town, if you plan on arriving in the evening and

CAJUN COUNTRY

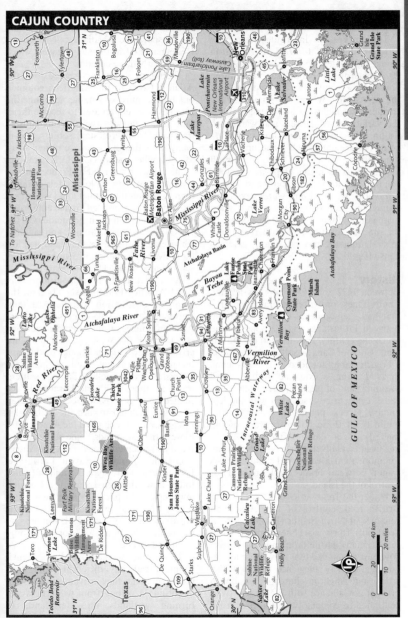

don't want to be stuck paying for a pricey room, call ahead.

The quickest driving routes from New Orleans to Lafayette are I-10 via Baton Rouge (129 miles, 2½ hours) and I-49/Hwy 90 through the wetlands (165 miles, three hours). However, you won't see much from the interstates. Whenever possible, take smaller state highways and parish roads – the variety of wildflowers and waterfowl, Cajun cabins and mobile homes, fishing boats and freighters will make up for the time and wrong turns you'll take. And by all means, grab as many maps as possible. Country and town roads south and west of Lafayette wind along waterways, and signage is often poor. Even with a good map, visitors (and locals) get lost often. In the prairies north of Lafayette, roads tend to straighten out into more easily comprehensible grids.

History

Between 1632 and 1654, colonists left the Centre-Ouest provinces of France, an area that had seen some of the worst fighting between Protestants and Catholics in the preceding century. They headed for the Atlantic Coast of Canada, settling in La Cadie, a French colony founded in 1604, its name derived from a Micmac Indian word meaning 'land of plenty.' (Eventually, 'L'Acadie' came to be associated with the legendary Greek paradise, Arcadia.) The majority of these colonists were of the highest caste of peasant farmers, and Acadians lived a relatively peaceful agrarian life for more than a century despite contests waged between France and England for control of the island.

Under the Treaty of Utrecht in 1713, the British took control of the island and renamed it Nova Scotia (Latin for 'New Scotland'). Thirty years later, with an eye on the Acadians' fertile farmlands, the British governor demanded that they swear an unqualified oath of allegiance to the British crown and Anglican church, ostensibly to prevent any alliance with the French (who continued to compete with the British for other North American territories). The Acadians refused, and in 1755, the governor ordered their forced deportation, beginning the diaspora the Acadians call 'le Grand Dérangement' (the Great Upheaval), which lasted nearly three decades.

Thousands of survivors headed down the Atlantic Coast to the American colonies, but by the most charitable accounts, the colonies were unprepared to receive them. Often the Catholic peasants endured hostile treatment from Protestant settlers, and in many cases, the refugees were turned away. Many families endured lengthy separations. Some refugees returned to France, only to discover that they no longer felt at home there. Yet their ill treatment and violent expulsion by the British led French authorities to charge Britain with genocide. Of the 10,000 Acadian men, women and children who were banished from the island, half lost their lives to violence, drowning, disease, starvation and neglect in prisons.

As a historically French settlement in North America, Louisiana soon became the idealized destination for the Acadians. Between 1765 and 1785, dispersed groups of Acadian refugees from American colonies, Nova Scotia, the West Indies and France arrived in New Orleans. Though by this time the territory was governed by Spain, the Spanish welcomed fellow Catholic settlers, especially those with agricultural skills. The refined Creoles of New Orleans, however, were less inclined toward the bedraggled refugees, and they shunted the Acadians off to western swamplands. Some of the earliest Acadian settlements were along the Mississippi and adjoining Bayou Lafourche, Bayou Teche and Bayou Vermilion (which today flows through Lafayette). Longfellow's epic 1847 poem *Evangeline* – much revered in Acadiana – relates the tragic Acadian history from L'Acadie to Louisiana through the story of long-separated lovers.

Though the Acadians faced a new environment radically different from their Canadian home, they arrived with a history of forging a colony from wilderness and turning wetlands into farmland. In Louisiana, they were helped by the local

Houma and Chitimacha Indians, who taught them to trap, hunt and catch fish with their bare hands (a technique still practiced today). Indian guides showed them through the watery mazes in canoes hewn from cypress. They also taught the refugees about the sacred crawfish – a crustacean native to the bayou that figures prominently in the Chitimacha creation myth as well as in their diet. Though the settlers benefited from these valuable lessons, they brought smallpox and other diseases that continued the decimation of the Indian tribes begun by earlier explorers and missionaries. (Historians estimate that the Louisiana region was home to around 15,000 Native Americans in the early 1700s; by the 1950s, the census bureau counted 490.)

Despite devastating floods and hurricanes, the Acadians endured. Within a generation these exiles had so firmly reestablished themselves that they became the dominant culture in southern Louisiana, absorbing other ethnic groups around them. Most of the French Creoles, Spanish, Anglo-Americans, Afro-Haitians and Germans eventually adopted Acadian traditions and language (though many English-speaking Anglo Protestants remained culturally isolated). Acadian surnames such as Soirez, Castille, Farris, Reed, McCauley, O'Connor and Israel illustrate the Acadian absorption of many groups. (Many last names, however, were gallicized.)

During the antebellum period, cotton ruled much of the South, but sugarcane came to dominate southern Louisiana. Though some Acadians became planters, many were forced off fertile land by Creoles, Anglo planters arriving from the north, and wealthy French immigrants, and driven farther into isolated swamps. During the Civil War, as Union troops invaded and confiscated many plantations, Acadians joined Confederate forces and fought in the Battle of Lafourche Crossing (near Houma). However, small-plot farming Acadians had little stake in the war, and many deserted. After the war, freed slaves joined communities of free people of color, Afro-Haitians and other Louisianans with African heritage. These French-speaking blacks came to define themselves and their culture as Creole.

On the prairies north of Lafayette, Acadians and Creoles maintained Brahmin cattle ranches and developed traditions more closely associated with neighboring Texas than wetland Acadiana. In fact, many of America's earliest cowboys were Cajuns and black Creoles. (Le Courir de Mardi Gras is a horseback run common on the prairies – see the boxed text in the Cajun Prairie section.) On the prairies, the solid clay foundation holds the water necessary for rice cultivation, and rice came to replace cotton after the Civil War.

Many Acadians were largely unschooled and unlettered, and so speaking French became associated with cultural inferiority in Louisiana. During WWI, the US saw an upsurge in nationalism, and regional cultures bore the brunt of acculturation efforts. In 1916, Louisiana's Board of Education implemented a ban forbidding students from speaking French in school and on school grounds; those caught doing so were disciplined. The next 40 years came to be known as the Heure de la Honte (Time of Shame).

In the 1940s, WWII had a tremendous impact on local soldiers, especially those who had never been outside the region. Blacks identifying themselves as Creole often found that the army did not classify them among black troops, who received more prejudicial treatment. Acadian soldiers in France discovered that the language and culture they'd been told to forget helped them survive and made them valuable as interpreters. After the war, returning GIs immersed themselves in their own culture, sparking a renewal of cultural pride.

In 1955, local politician Dudley Le Blanc used the bicentennial anniversary of Acadian expulsion from Nova Scotia to remind the community of its enduring roots and rally them in support of their heritage. Cajun musicians including Dewey Balfa were invited to perform at the 1964 Newport Folk Festival, exposing Cajun folk music and culture to a national audience. In 1968, Louisiana officially recognized the

Cajun cultural revival by creating the Council for the Development of French in Louisiana (Codofil) to encourage the use of the suppressed local language. Teachers from France, Belgium and Canada were brought in to reintroduce French to schoolchildren and to inspire pride in French heritage. Efforts were not restricted; Codofil also organized music festivals, including the successful 1974 Tribute to Cajun Music in Lafayette, which helped to popularize Cajun music locally. Likewise, zydeco was beginning to get some play outside the region. By the late '70s Clifton Chenier had spread the sound, enhancing traditional zydeco with new inflections.

Other developments exacerbated the strain on regional culture, namely the rise of the oil industry in the state and the influx of tourists. Though oil was first discovered in the region as early as 1901, the first commercial oil well was dug in 1947. Oil companies cut canals through the swamps and marshes and built refineries. The oil boom in the 1970s drew workers from around the country, and local workers again received a large dose of mainstream American culture. However, only a few Acadians were enriched by oil profits, and in the haste to extract oil, many companies degraded previously wild areas. Most local oil workers and many towns in Acadiana were devastated when prices plummeted in the 1980s; many workers left the region in search of jobs.

In 1973 after seven years of construction, the I-10 bridge (an engineering marvel) across the 18-mile-wide Atchafalaya Basin was completed. This arduous last link of the nation's interstate network made this region of southern Louisiana readily accessible to outsiders for the first time. Communities that had been relatively isolated for centuries began to see radical change. From the late 1980s to the present, a renaissance of national and international interest in things Cajun and Creole has brought an unprecedented number of visitors to Acadiana to celebrate the crawfish once decried as 'poor man's lobster,' to listen to the language once banned, and to hear the homespun accordion music local youth had once been embarrassed to admit their families played. While cultural adaptation has been a hallmark of community survival for centuries, many southern Louisianans are concerned that Cajun and Creole culture will be commercialized beyond recognition.

Acadian Folklife

The National Park Service (NPS) maintains three sites in Cajun Country that focus on Acadian heritage under the umbrella of Jean Lafitte National Historical Park and Preserve. The Acadian Cultural Center in Lafayette is the most comprehensive. The Cajun wetlands center is in Thibodaux, and the Cajun prairie center is in Eunice. All three have thoughtful, well-presented exhibits, artifacts and interpretive captions that provide an excellent introduction to regional history and cultural heritage. Available at their gift shops is *Cajun Country*, by Barry Jean Ancelet, Jay Edwards and Glen Pitre, which focuses on Cajun history, folkways, architecture, religion, music and more.

Until the late 19th century, the geographically isolated Acadians lived off the bounty of the land. The swamps provided plentiful fish, crawfish, bullfrogs and turtles. (Alligator meat was not generally consumed before the 1970s.) In the spring, families would harvest crawfish and live on commercial fishing; net-making was an important skilled craft. When water levels dropped in summer and fall, families trapped furbearing animals and sold their pelts. Spanish moss – used for mattress stuffing – was harvested as their only cash crop.

Bayous provided the primary routes for travel and commerce. While steamboats and then railroads opened up the region somewhat, many Acadian villages remained isolated well into the 20th century. Boatmaking was a highly prized craft. The *pirogue* – a shallow wooden skiff poled standing up – was an indispensable means of transportation in bayou country. Originally, pirogues were made from cypress trunks; after the cypress was clear-cut around the beginning of the 20th century, the boats were generally made of plywood or fiberglass. Small wooden pirogues remain in common use today.

Acadian vernacular architecture was also distinctive. A popular image of Cajun life is of swampers living on houseboats and in island cabins, but there were also town houses – some still standing today – that reflected European design. As easily seen at Acadian village attractions in Lafayette, the typical Acadian cottage was a 1½-story, four-room house with a front porch and steep-gabled roof. Because of the heat and fear of fire, detached kitchens were positioned behind the house. Roof supports evolved from early European design, and exposed beams reflect French influence. *Bousillage*, a mixture of Spanish moss, clay and even animal hair, served to insulate walls and chimneys. Unusual features on some houses included a *garconniére*, an attic reserved for young men, which had its own entrance from the front porch, and another separate entrance for guests or travelers. Access to the bayou was critically important, so waterside lots in town tended to be long and narrow.

Close-knit extended family life has been the foundation of Acadian society. An interesting facet of weddings is the Money Dance, during which participants pin money to the bride's veil. Another traditional communal gathering was *la boucherie*, a hog slaughter held frequently in the years before refrigeration became common. *Les coups de mains* ('helping hands') was the Acadian equivalent of barn-raising.

Devout Catholics, the Acadians focused their community spiritual life in churches, though geographic isolation led to *la messe blanche* ('the white Mass'; prayer services conducted by laity, often women), and home altars once supplemented churches as a place to worship. On All Saints' Day, the aboveground crypts of ancestors were washed and decorated, and a priest delivered Mass by candlelight in the cemetery. Shrines to the saints, particularly to St Mary, considered the patron saint of Acadians, were built throughout the region. Even today, statues of Mary commonly populate yards and gardens.

TOM DOWNS

Acadian rhythms are as spicy as Cajun cookin'.

While most surrounding ethnic groups came to adopt Acadian traditions – even isolated local Indians continue to speak an archaic form of French – their various influences can perhaps best be recognized in the Cajun music distinct to southern Louisiana. From the Indians, the Acadians borrowed wailing styles and dance rhythms; from blacks they learned the blues; and from Anglo-Americans they picked up new fiddle tunes tailored for Virginia reel dances and hoedowns. The Spanish contributed the guitar, Afro-Haitians brought in a syncopated West Indian beat, and Jewish-German immigrants imported accordions. Zydeco developed concurrently as a more blues-influenced style performed by black Creoles. With the introduction of rock & roll, 'swamp pop' was born, with Cajun rhythms and French lyrics transforming American popular music. Local radio programs today broadcast a great variety of authentic southern Louisiana music; some programs are in French.

A Cajun dance is called a *fais-do-do*, a name taken from the phrase that mothers would murmur to encourage their babies to fall asleep at dance halls. A high-stepping waltz and two-step jitterbug were common dances at a fais-do-do. (The uninitiated will find that locals are happy to demonstrate traditional steps to newcomers.)

Beyond the famous crawfish of Acadiana, visitors today feast on such traditional foods as cracklins (fried pork rinds) and *boudin* – a sausage that can be 'blanc' or the

Boudin: Rouge et Blanc

'What's a seven-course Cajun meal?' asks the old joke. 'A six-pack of beer and a link of boudin.'

Boudin (BOO-danh) is Cajun convenience food, pure and simple. Spend any time driving the backroads of the state and you will begin to notice the little signs that dot the landscape: 'Hot Boudin & Cold Beer.'

Of the two types available – rouge and blanc – boudin blanc is by far the more popular. Ground pork and liver is cooked, seasoned with (among other things) cayenne pepper, combined with rice, and then stuffed into sausage casings. As for the rouge version, it acquires its distinctive coloring and its name through the addition of pig's blood. It's not for the squeamish.

After being steamed or boiled, the sausage is eaten by hand. A nibble is taken from the top of the link and then the sausage is pushed up from the bottom, in the same manner that you would extract toothpaste from a tube. It takes a little getting used to, but by your fourth link, you'll be an old hand at it.

And, yes, boudin goes fine with a cold beer.

more daring 'rouge.' Andouille sausage, jambalaya, gumbo, alligator and turtle are also found at restaurants throughout the region.

Ecology & Environment

The Atchafalaya (atch-ah-fah-LIE-ah) Basin, which dominates the eastern edge of Acadiana, is the largest freshwater swamp in the US. Through its center flows the Atchafalaya River, a regulated distributary of the Mississippi, which courses from near the southwest corner of Mississippi state along a straight shot south to the Gulf of Mexico. As it is the most direct and steepest route, the Mississippi River would have long ago taken this course if it weren't for extraordinary efforts undertaken by Army

Corps of Engineers to confine the Mississippi to the channel around New Orleans. The corps has also contained the Atchafalaya flood plain into a basin 20 miles wide and 80 miles long by constructing earthen levees along its length down to Morgan City, where the river pours into the Gulf. One of the most complex managed water systems in the world, the basin drains floodwaters from as many as 38 states.

The watery 134-sq-mile wilderness within the basin is dense with the stumps of bald cypress (the official state tree) that remain from the clear-cut lumbering in the first half of the 20th century. Fields of white water lilies and other aquatic plants fill the landscape. The common black willow is not native; nor is the water hyacinth, which was imported from Japan. Though it blooms with a beautiful lavender flower, the hyacinth is actually a nuisance that easily chokes bayous and channels.

Throughout the swamp, you can see alligators, frogs, turtles, snakes and nutria, a plump fur-bearing South American rodent. (A small number of caged nutria on Avery Island escaped into the wild during a hurricane in 1940 and rapidly reproduced, displacing the muskrat and boosting the local fur industry.) Deer, raccoons, rabbits, squirrels and snakes inhabit the larger swamp islands. Herons (with yellow legs), egrets (with black legs) and ibises are common. Owls, anhingas and brown pelicans (the official state bird) are a few of the hundreds of bird species seen in the swamp. Besides serving as breeding grounds for crawfish, swamp waters are rumored to harbor elusive giant catfish – a world record 128-pounder was caught in the basin in 1986.

Oil deposits under the basin drew interest as far back as 1901. Today the basin is dotted with oil rigs, and the petroleum industry is a mainstay of the local economy. Drilling and canal dredging has greatly hastened natural erosion. In the Chenier plain alone, more than 2000 miles of canals have been cut.

Mismanagement of coastal lands in combination with natural forces has led to a catastrophic land-loss problem, and the

The fur industry digs the goofy-looking nutria.

intrusion of saltwater is killing off many freshwater species. The state is now losing an acre of land every 24 minutes; the Coalition to Restore Coastal Louisiana estimates that 25 sq miles of coastal land are reclaimed by the Gulf each year. At this rate, they project that Houma and New Orleans will be on the coast within 50 years. In 1989, a state initiative committed petroleum taxes to try to reverse this trend, and federal monies are being funneled to the state as well. The Louisiana Coastal Restoration Web site provides extensive background on the issue and disseminates news. There are also land loss as well as satellite maps (www.lacoast.gov).

Language

The 700,000 Acadians in southern Louisiana constitute the largest French-speaking minority in the US (about 45% speak French as a second language). Acadians who learned French from their parents speak a dialect that is as different from Parisian French as hard-core Southern-accented English is from upper-class British English. French-speaking travelers will find that bilingual folks in the tourist industry and schoolchildren speak a more easily understood dialect than local swampers and older residents.

For four decades in the middle of the 20th century, speaking French was prohibited on school grounds in Louisiana, and even when this policy was overturned, the stigma formerly associated with speaking French lingered. In recent decades, French language instruction in schools has become increasingly common; in fact, the Lafayette school district has several immersion schools where students spend half the day in classes conducted in French. Teachers – often from France and French-speaking Canada – are teaching the standard form.

Many printed materials are in both French and English, as are many street signs. Much Cajun music has French lyrics, as does more traditional zydeco. Many radio stations offer news programs in French. The University of Louisiana at Lafayette is a center for Francophonic studies. Each April Lafayette's Festival International de Louisiane celebrates French-speaking cultures around the globe and draws visitors from those countries as well.

Special Events

Visitors should try to plan a trip that takes in as many Acadian festivals as possible. Here is a listing of only the major festivals (contact details are provided under specific towns), but there are dozens of smaller, more homespun events as well, some of which are listed under the town entries. For a list of many annual events and dates, contact the Lafayette Convention and Visitors Commission. The parish tourist offices can help as well. For a more descriptive listing, purchase a calendar of regional events from Huli Publishing (JuliePosner@aol.com), PO Box 851, Metairie, 70004.

February/March

Throughout the region, krewe balls, pageants and dances are held the month prior to Mardi Gras, when parades and the unique Acadian Courir de Mardi Gras take place (see the boxed text in the Prairie section). Some towns have a Queen Evangeline and King Gabriel reigning over Mardi Gras festivities; this royal couple symbolizes the long-separated Acadian lovers of Longfellow's epic poem. Major festivals are held in Church Point, Eunice, Iota, Lafayette and Mamou.

Eunice hosts the World Championship Crawfish Étouffée Cook-Off late in the month.

LOUISIANA

April

At the end of the month, Lafayette's six-day Festival International de Louisiane celebrates French-speaking cultures around the world with films, visual arts, theatrical performances, and, of course, plenty of French-influenced food and music (five stages' worth on the weekend).

May

The first full weekend of the month, Opelousas hosts the Cajun Music Festival, and Breaux Bridge simultaneously celebrates the Crawfish Festival with Cajun and zydeco music and the Creole Crawfish Festival with zydeco music.

August

The Cajun French Music Association Festival is held in Lafayette on the third weekend.

The Louisiana Shrimp & Petroleum Festival in Morgan City takes place toward the end of the month.

September

On Labor Day weekend, the Southwest Louisiana Zydeco Music Festival brings together a dozen zydeco bands for a 15-hour-long concert in Plaisance near Opelousas. On Labor Day, zydeco star Boozoo Chavis hosts a zydeco party and BBQ at his home just outside Lake Charles.

Midmonth Lafayette's Festivals Acadiens draws crowds of 100,000 to this music festival featuring Cajun and zydeco bands, a bayou food festival, and a native crafts festival with 300 artisans, storytellers and boat-builders.

October

There's a large Germanfest in small Roberts Cove early in the month.

Eunice hosts the Cajun Prairie Folklife Festival in mid-October.

November

Early in the month, Abbeville's Celebration of the Giant Omelet sees attendees consume 5000 eggs cooked all at once.

December

Throughout the month, Lafayette and surrounding parishes light up special decorations for Christmas, notably at Lafayette's Acadian Village and in St Martinville. Just about every town has seasonal celebrations.

One important footnote: it is worth planning a trip around the Saturday morning music, dancing and drinking festivities at Fred's Lounge in Mamou; the morning Cajun jam sessions at the Savoy Music Center in Eunice; and the evening Rendezvous des Cajuns live radio show at the Liberty Center Theatre in Eunice.

Getting Around

Most travelers drive through Cajun Country. Unless you're bringing along a boat or prepared to rent one long-term, you'll need a car.

Bus Greyhound (☎ 800-231-2222) has main offices in Lafayette and Lake Charles, and there are Greyhound counters in various towns including Eunice, Houma, Opelousas, Thibodaux, Ville Platte, New Iberia and Schreiver (these last two are also Amtrak stops). Other minor Cajun Country stops include Crowley, Morgan City and Lawtell.

Train Amtrak's *Sunset Limited* transcontinental route from Los Angeles, California, to Jacksonville, Florida, stops several times in Acadiana before reaching (or leaving) New Orleans. The train roughly follows Hwy 90, stopping in Lake Charles; in downtown Lafayette; in New Iberia at a relatively inviting station in a developed area, just a short drive from the central commercial district (too long a walk with luggage); and in Schreiver (where Greyhound also stops) at an isolated outpost 4 miles south of Thibodaux. These stations all offer little more than a pay phone and waiting room, but taxi service is available from all of them. Trains run every other day. Call for current schedules (☎ 800-872-7245).

Car Though intertown distances aren't great in most areas, getting from one side of Cajun Country to the other will take half a day on the interstates, and all day or longer on smaller highways and parish roads. Off the interstates, it's hard to predict the condition of roads. Many are in rough shape, but a surprising number have been recently paved. Most are narrow and winding and have little or no shoulder.

It's extremely easy to lose your sense of direction in the wetlands areas; roads wind around and around following and crossing waterways. Pick up as many maps as possible before you start out. The parish tourist offices have maps that can be quite helpful.

Signage is often poor. It's common for intersections and exits to be unannounced until you're at them – be very watchful of surrounding and oncoming traffic before slamming on the brakes or crossing lanes. In many towns, signs indicate only cross streets, leaving newcomers wondering what road they're on. Though businesses give their addresses in English, many street signs have the French name in large lettering and the English name in tiny type. In addition, most highways have local names as well as numbers (when asking for an address, get both).

Drivers in Cajun Country seem hell-bent on getting where they're going as quickly as possible. Drivers who stick to the speed limits will find themselves being passed whether passing is permitted or not. Tailgating also seems to be a peculiar obsession among the region's drivers, even when they don't want to pass; they seem driven to minimize the space between cars and usually intend no rudeness in doing so.

During the warmer months of crawfish season (roughly April through June), the little fellas often crawl across highways in search of more hospitable conditions, and it's impossible to avoid running them over. When their peers don't heed the telltale mess, the carnage-covered roads can get dangerously slippery.

Bicycle Cyclists will have to bring their own bikes or buy one upon arrival. Most of the roads in Cajun Country are scenic and flat, and have little if any shoulder. Many of the smaller highways carry little traffic. Cyclists' primary concerns will be weather and navigating. In addition, storms and heat in summer are fairly daunting.

Cajun Cyclists, a cycling club based in Lafayette, has numerous weekly rides, most beginning in Lafayette. On most Saturdays, the club has a ride that departs from Pack &

Paddle at 8 am, weather permitting. The club's Web site is a good source for information about cycling throughout the region (www.cajuncyclists.org).

French Louisiana Bike Tours (☎ 504-488-9844, 800-346-7989, info@flbt.com) offers spring and fall tours of Cajun Country that focus on the region's culture and cuisine. Trip leaders are knowledgeable locals. The five-day food and music tour takes in Breaux Bridge, Washington, Mamou, Eunice, Chretien Point and Grant Couteau ($995 including hotels and most meals). The seven-day Cajun Experience goes to the same towns as well as Lafayette, St Martinville and Lake Fausse Point State Park ($1295). Bike rental is another $109. Cyclists on both trips average 30 to 50 miles a day. Their Web site is www.flbt.com.

Bayous, Swamps & Marshes

The heart of the Cajun wetlands lies between Grand Isle south of New Orleans, the Atchafalaya Basin west of the Mississippi, and the Gulf coast south of Abbeville. Covered with dense, lush growth, this lowland is a watery maze of swamps, bayous and lakes. Spanish explorers and missionaries traversed the Old Spanish Trail through these wetlands on their way from St Augustine to Los Angeles. Today, I-49/Hwy 90 roughly follows that route.

Many of the earliest Acadian settlements lined Bayou Lafourche (pronounced la-FOOSH) and Bayou Teche (pronounced tesh), and this region retains many historic sights. Bayou Lafourche leaves the Mississippi at Donaldsonville and empties into the ocean near Grand Isle; Hwy 1 traces its course, passing through tiny settlements and Thibodaux. The Atchafalaya River flows between the Mississippi and I-49; its swampy basin, dotted with oil and gas fields, can be explored only by boat. East-west I-49/Hwy 90 runs just south of Bayou Teche, providing the fastest route between sites. Between I-49 and the bayou lies

The Patron Reptile of Acadiana

The American alligator *(Alligator mississipiensis)* inhabits coastal marshes and swamps from the Carolinas to Texas, but one of the largest concentrations is in Louisiana. Louisianans have hunted alligators for their skins since the mid-1800s, and by the 1930s, hunters and biologists were noting a serious decline in the alligator population. By the 1960s, there were only about 40,000 wild gators left in the state. An enforced and limited hunting season, research and conservation efforts (much of it conducted at Rockefeller Wildlife Refuge), and the development of commercial alligator farms have contributed to a resurgence in the animal's population. Classified as an endangered species in 1967, the American alligator was removed from the list by 1975. Louisiana wetlands are today home to an estimated 670,000 gators.

Gator sightings – whether from a boat or swamp cabin or on a menu – have tugged plenty of greenbacks from tourist wallets. Tourism dollars in southern Louisiana quadrupled from $10.9 million in 1987 to $54.3 million in 1994 'thanks largely to so-called gator dollars,' according to a 1995 *Wall Street Journal* report. Despite all the hype, spotting one of these truly odd prehistoric reptiles grinning in the mud is sure to be a highlight of any trip. To estimate an alligator's length, eyeball the inches from the tip of the snout to the line across the base of its eyes. 10 inches? That's a 10-footer.

The alligator gets its name from Spanish sailors, who called it *el lagarto* – 'the lizard.' It belongs to the order Crocodylia and can be distinguished from its crocodile cousin by snout shape and overbite. Gators have rounded snouts; crocodiles have pointed ones. Unlike gators, crocodiles expose a lower tooth outside the upper lip. Alligators take 10 years to reach sexual maturity, at which point they are about 6 feet long; once they reach this size, their only predators are larger gators and humans. The average length of gators is 6 to 8 feet, though some have been known to

Hwy 182, a far more scenic and less crowded route.

Tempting though it is to speed along I-49/Hwy 90 toward better-known tourist destinations, travelers should not miss the chance to explore the bayous south of Houma, drive along narrow ridges only inches above water, and observe the houses held aloft by telephone-pole stilts.

HOUMA
• pop 33,000

Houma (pronounced HOE-ma) is named for the Houma Indians, who lived in the area before being pushed far into southern marshes. In the early 1900s, oil workers happened upon small bands of Houmas who still spoke French. Aptly nicknamed the 'Venice of America,' this urban hub, 57 miles from New Orleans, is perched along three bayous and the Intracoastal Waterway, its streets forming a maze sure to baffle any visitor. Hwy 90 formerly ran through the commercial center along Bayou Terre-

bonne, but I-49/Hwy 90 now bypasses it north of town, and some highway numbers have changed. Pick up a current map at the tourist office (☎ 504-868-2732, 800-688-2732) at the westernmost Houma exit off I-49/Hwy 90. You can also find information at www.houmatourism.com.

Hwy 24 runs along each side of Bayou Terrebonne, on the north side as Park Ave and on the south as Main St. It goes right through the small downtown, which has a handful of decent restaurants.

The new **Bayou Terrebonne Waterlife Museum** (☎ 504-580-7200), 7910 Park Ave, offers an introduction to the parish and its history, ecology and economy. It houses a Robert Dafford mural of the wetlands that's quite detailed and beautiful. The museum is open Monday to Saturday 10 am to 4 pm and is closed on Sunday. Admission is $3.

Those wishing to experience the swamp could try **A Cajun Man's Swamp Tour** (☎ 504-868-4625), which explores Bayou

The Patron Reptile of Acadiana

reach 20 feet. Alligators in captivity live around 40 years; in the wild they can live much longer – some beyond 100 years.

Alligators are most at home in the water, where they swim with snakelike movements. On land, they travel forward in a straight direction, sometimes surprisingly quickly. They eat anything in close range that moves, but they have a particular fondness for nutria and muskrat. In the winter, their metabolism slows, and they retreat to their underwater dens, occasionally surfacing for air. The warming temperatures of spring draw the gators from their dens, and males begin to bellow. A bull alligator's bellow – which has been compared to a lion's roar – sounds a territorial warning throughout the year, but in late April and May the cry has special meaning. Females follow this sound to the love shack, lured also by the musky odor of the bull's emissions. 'Bulls' fend off competing males in a show of strength: the two prehistoric giants lock jaws and thrash about until the exhausted party gives up and slinks off. The victor then begins an equally tumultuous ordeal with the female. Nest building occurs in late May and early June.

All crocodilians are egg-laying. Females lay 20 to 80 eggs on a bank, covering them with decaying vegetation that provides insulation. The nest temperature between the 14th and 35th days determines the sex of the hatchlings: 86°F and below produces females, 93°F and above produces males; temperatures in between produce both. After an incubation period of 60 to 90 days, 'clucking' cries alert the mother to uncover her 9-inch hatchlings. The babies frolic around their mother for months in an unusually familial relationship for reptiles (though alligators have been known to eat their young in hard times). Baby gators stay close to their mother's den until they reach about 3 feet.

Black. 'Black' Guidry serenades his passengers, with his trusty dog Gator Bait (a blue-eyed Catahahoula) at his side. He charges $15 for adults and $10 for kids for an hour-and-a-half tour. Call for reservations. Tours start 10 miles west of Houma on Hwy 182 (formerly Hwy 90).

Fishing, both fresh- and saltwater, is the primary regional activity. Houma and surrounding towns are home to dozens of charter boats. The tourist office has a brochure listing them all and their specialties. In summer, visitors can attend numerous fishing rodeos.

Throughout the year, Houma hosts a variety of noteworthy special events. Its Mardi Gras is one of the largest in the state. In March, there's the Calling of the Tribes Powwow. April sees the Blessing of the Shrimp Fleet. Over the Fourth of July weekend, there's a Gospel & Soul Festival. In September, the town hosts the Grand Bois Inter-Tribal. Contact the tourist office for details.

Places to Stay

The oldest motel in town and still a decent budget choice is the *Sugar Bowl* (☎ 504-872-4521), on Hwy 182 E at Park Ave just across the bayou from the central commercial district. Rooms are $38, and there's a 24-hour restaurant next door. Across town on Bayou Black Drive/Hwy 182 W, the good-value *Red Carpet Inn* (☎ 504-876-4160, 800-251-1962, No 2115), near St Charles St offers basic singles/doubles for $35/38, including a hot breakfast. It has a pool. A step up is the *Plantation Inn* (☎ 504-868-6500, 800-373-0072, 1381 W Tunnel Blvd), where comfortable rooms cost $45/55. The outdoor covered pool adjoins a grassy lounge area, and there's a restaurant. Tunnel Rd runs parallel to and south of Hwy 24.

Places to Eat

Downtown has a smattering of small, convenient restaurants. *Aromas Coffeehouse* (☎ 504-580-4044, 7832 Main St) is a good place to grab a simple breakfast or late-night cuppa (it's open daily). *Bayou Vue Café (☎ 504-872-6292, 7913 Main St)*, with a patio overlooking the bayou, has a daily menu of Cajun and Creole breakfasts and lunches (around $5) and dinners ($10 to $15; Thursday through Saturday). There's live Cajun music on weekends. Down the block, *Castalano's Deli (☎ 504-853-1090, 7881 Main St)* offers reasonably priced Italian lunch specials and simple Italian dinners (with a few vegetarian options). It's closed on Sunday.

Tiny *A-Bear's Cafe (☎ 504-872-6306, 809 Bayou Black Drive)* has filling plate lunches (around $10 including dessert) and live Cajun music on Friday night (this is the only night dinner is served, and then it's all-you-can-eat catfish). About 7 miles farther west on Bayou Black Dr/Hwy 182 W is the *Bayou Delight (☎ 504-876-4879)*. Try the onion rings ($2) and fried catfish dinner ($9). It's open daily for lunch and dinner. There's Cajun or country music on Friday and Saturday night.

Dula & Edwin's Seafood Restaurant (☎ 504-876-0271, 2821 Bayou Blue Rd/Hwy 316 N), north of town, is known for its boiled crabs and crawfish. It's open Tuesday through Friday for lunch and dinner and Saturday for dinner only, and closed Monday. There's a Cajun band on Tuesday.

The *Jolly Inn (☎ 504-872-6114, 1507 Barrow St)* has Cajun or zydeco bands on Thursday and Friday nights and 4 to 8 pm Sunday.

AROUND HOUMA

A short distance south of Houma, the land-to-water ratio shifts drastically, the concentration of birds intensifies and the number of sightseers drops. Many extended Cajun families have called this maze of canals and bayous home for many generations, and their culture and livelihoods depend on the tides and weather, schools of fish and oil deposits. The main highways follow the bayous; on one side of the road, fishing boats of every description come and go, while along the other, homes are raised 15 feet high on telephone poles to survive hurricanes. Farther south, stands of dead cypress mingle with marsh grasses and cattails, and the roads, with water lapping both sides, are built atop ridges of gravel and seashells. Though Grand Isle to the east draws more tourists and offers more tourist services, it's a shabby echo of the magic that permeates these wetlands.

Head south of Houma on one of four small highways: Hwy 315 through the small fishing village of Theriot, Hwy 57 through Dulac, Hwy 56 through Chauvin and ending at Cocodrie, or Hwy 665. Drivers can travel down any of the first three and come back via another. Hwy 315 along Bayou du Large is busy with fishing fleets, particularly in the late afternoon when boats dock to off-load the day's catch. A road along the Flagout Canal connects Hwy 315 with Hwy 57.

Hwy 57 follows Bayou Grand Caillou, eventually passing a small Houma Indian settlement on the way to Cocodrie (26 miles south of Houma). Along the road just before its end is **Lumcon** (the Louisiana Universities Marine Consortium), a research center open to the public daily (free). There's a viewing platform and an aquarium (☎ 504-851-2800). The *CoCo

HOUMA & AROUND

To Donaldsonville · To Vacherie · To New Orleans · Thibodaux · Schriever · Gibson · Donner · Raceland · Bayou Black Drive · To Morgan City · Houma · To Grand Isle · Intracoastal Waterway · Theriot · Dulac · Chauvin · Falgout Canal Rd · LUMCON (Research Station) · Cocodrie · Terrebonne Bay

0   14 km
0 4 8 miles

Marina & Motel (☎ 504-594-6626, 800-648-2626) is a popular spot for those heading out early on fishing charters. Motel rooms sleeping four cost $50, a studio sleeping four $125 and a condo sleeping five $150. There's a restaurant. From May to December, the Indian Ridge Shrimp Co provides tours of its shrimp-processing plant (by appointment only; ☎ 504-594-3361).

Hwy 56 is busy with cars and pickups hauling boats. Chauvin has several small restaurants. Scenic Hwy 665 is the most remote route, ending at another small Houma community.

GRAND ISLE

If heading to the end of the road appeals to you, then Grand Isle provides a goal but no gold. (A much better bet for a ramble is a trip to Cocodrie; see Around Houma.) Vacationers head along busy Bayou Lafourche to Grand Isle to swim year-round and fish for the 280 coastal species (a dozen fishing rodeos take place between May and September). The beach at Grand Isle is a narrow strip of dark, hard-packed sand, and oil rigs are in plain view.

At the Raceland exit off I-49/Hwy 90, the Lafourche Parish Tourist Information Center (☎ 504-537-5800) provides maps and brochures for the whole region.

On the bayou's north side, Hwy 308 passes many residences; on its south side, Hwy 1 runs through a string of small commercial districts lined with chain restaurants, gas stations, and a few unappealing motels courting derrick workers and travelers who got a late start. After crossing the high bridge over the Intracoastal Waterway, the busy shipping channel is within view, brimming with ocean freighters, oil tankers, tugboats and fishing vessels of every size. The bayou diffuses into expansive marshlands as it approaches the coast. After an hour-and-a-half drive, travelers reach the ramshackle strip of Grand Isle. (On the way, tune to KLEB 1600 AM for Cajun music from 6 am to 10 am.)

The highlight is **Grand Isle State Park** (☎ 504-787-2559, 888-787-2559), on the far eastern tip of the island. The only state-owned and operated beach on the Louisiana Gulf Coast, and a popular destination for bird watchers, the park provides modern bathhouses and an observation tower. A 400-foot fishing pier offers anglers easy access to the saltwater. Admission to the park is $2 per car.

The park's *campground* charges $10 a night and is simple: those willing to risk getting stuck in the sand can pull up to the water's edge; those seeking a bit of protection from the wind can set up behind a strip of dunes. Motels and cabins along the Grand Isle strip are built on stilts; the majority are surprisingly shabby, and rates start at $60 a night and more during busy weekends.

THIBODAUX & AROUND
• **pop 15,000**

Thibodaux (TI-ba-doh), at the confluence of Bayou Lafourche and Bayou Terrebonne, was the most important town between New Orleans and Bayou Teche when commerce was restricted to travel by boat. Early settlement followed the 'Main St' of the bayou, leading to thousands of narrow lots, each with a few hundred feet of bayou access and a depth of a mile or more. Early French and German farmers produced crops for the New Orleans market. Isleños arrived about 1780 on the upper Bayou Lafourche. By 1800, Acadians and Americans extended down the bayou to Thibodaux. The town has been the Lafourche Parish seat since 1820.

I-49 runs about 10 miles south of town. Hwy 24 intersects it and becomes Hwy 20 heading north toward town. Eventually it passes through downtown and crosses Bayou Lafourche (in town Hwy 20 is Canal Blvd). Along the south side of the bayou runs Hwy 1 (west of Hwy 20, it's St Mary St; east it's 1st St); along the north side runs Hwy 308/Bayou Rd.

The Thibodaux Chamber of Commerce (☎ 504-446-1187), 1058 E Canal St near the freight train tracks, distributes maps, including one of the historical district, and information on local events, among them the annual Firemen's Fair in early May, featuring country, Cajun and blues bands. This fund-raiser for the volunteer fire department has its origins in the first annual Firemen's Parade in 1866. For its first 50 years, this annual parade gave the many local Dixie bands a chance to show off.

Downtown Thibodaux

The bayouside compact downtown has seen some renovation in recent years. It has small eateries, a handful of lively bars, and a few antique stores. Surrounding downtown is the historical district, with over 50 well-maintained homes, among them the striking three-story pink **Dansereau House** (☎ 504-447-1002), 506 St Philip St, today a pricey restaurant and inn. The huge brick **St Joseph Co-Cathedral** (built in 1923), 721 Canal Blvd, is worth a look.

Wetlands Acadian Cultural Center

Part of Jean Lafitte National Historical Park, this center (☎ 504-448-1375), at 314 St Mary St, a few blocks west of downtown, operates an impressive museum, gallery, and gift shop with books and CDs. Enlightening displays focus on how the Acadians adapted to the wetlands environment. Videos are shown in a small auditorium, and the gallery hosts changing exhibits of works by Louisiana artists. There are regular demonstrations of boat-building or net-making; storytellers relate Acadian folktales. The center also showcases Cajun musicians: jam sessions are scheduled on Monday night from 5:30 to 7 pm, and there are Sunday concerts in October and March. The center opens daily at 9 am. Closing times vary: 6 pm on Tuesday through Thursday, 5 pm Friday through Sunday, and 8 pm Monday.

A local library upstairs maintains an exhaustive collection of reference works on southern Louisiana, from volumes on Acadian crafts and local botany to cancer statistics in the industrial corridor along the Mississippi River.

Laurel Valley Village

This nonprofit history village (☎ 504-446-7456), about 2 miles east of town on Hwy 308 (down Bayou Lafourche), oversees the largest remaining sugar-plantation complex, including the best-preserved slave cabins in the state. Exhibits in the general store next to the highway describe the now-abandoned settlement. About a half-mile down Laurel Valley Rd, which passes through sugarcane fields, visitors can view over 60 buildings, some in ruins, but only from a distance. For a tour, call ☎ 504-447-2902 or 504-447-5216. Hours at the general store are Tuesday through Friday 10 am to 3 pm and weekends noon to 3 pm; it is closed on Monday. The store also closes if no volunteers are available (call first to confirm). Donations fund repairs and upkeep.

Center for Traditional Louisiana Boat Building

South of downtown is the 166-acre campus of Nicholls State University, home of the Center for Traditional Louisiana Boat Building (tours by appointment; ☎ 504-448-4626). The center has photographs, slides and audio tapes that trace the history of boat building in southern Louisiana. The region's boat builders are known for their ingenuity in designing vessels that could ply the shallow waters of the swamps, bayous and marshes for transportation, hunting, fishing and moss picking. The center has various *bateaux*, including pirogues and a sailing lugger. A few boats are on display in the library, but most are stored in a barn on campus.

Places to Stay

Budget accommodations can be found at the recently renovated ***Economy Inn*** (☎ *504-446-3667, 1113 St Mary St*), six blocks west of the Acadian Cultural Center. Comfortable singles/doubles cost $35/45 including tax, and most have a minifridge and microwave. The modern ***Howard Johnson's*** (☎ *504-447-9071, 800-952-2968, 201 N Canal Blvd*), north of the bayou from downtown, has a pool and a lounge. Rooms are $67/75. The ***Holiday Inn*** (☎ *504-446-0561, 400 E 1st St*) has a pool and a restaurant. Rooms cost $65/73. On a side street next to the Holiday

Inn, the 100-year-old Queen Anne-style *Robichaux House* (☎ 504-447-4738, 322 E 2nd St, 70301) offers B&B rooms for $90 including full breakfast.

Places to Eat & Drink

The dining options in Thibodaux are unimpressive, at least compared to the rest of the region. Not far from downtown, locals crowd into *Politz's* (☎ 504-448-0944, 100 Landry St), at St Mary St, for a heaping plate of corn-flour crusted seafood, or a broiled catfish lunch or dinner for about $12; it is closed Monday. Down the street, the *Rinky Dink Café* serves simple po-boys, burgers, daily lunch plate specials and fountain treats. There's a bayouside eating area. For a big platter of boiled seafood, head to *Seafood Outlet* (☎ 504-448-1010, 100 St Patrick Hwy), just across the bayou from downtown.

For a place devoted to cranking out steaks, *Western Sizzlin* (☎ 504-447-1983), on N Canal St, has a good salad bar ($5). The nearby *Casa del Sol* (☎ 504-446-2576) is the spot favored by locals for Mexican meals; it also serves a good margarita. If you've been tempted to join in the daiquiri craze, stop for one at *Norm's*, on N Canal St a block above the bayou.

South of Thibodaux on Hwy 20 S in Schriever, the *Bourgeois Meat Market* (☎ 504-447-7128) is one of the few remaining markets with its own slaughterhouse. Since 1891, it's been selling 'miracles in meat' – boudin blanc, zesty boudin rouge (blood sausage), andouille sausage and its specialty beef jerky. Grab some links, French bread and mustard and find a shady spot to enjoy it all.

Getting There & Away

The Greyhound bus stop is at 213 West Park. Buses run from New Orleans to Thibodaux (two hours, $14.50) with a stop in Schriever (same price) and continue on to Lafayette (2½ hours, $19.50).

Amtrak deposits *Sunset Limited* passengers 4 miles south of Thibodaux at a forlorn station outpost in Schriever at the junction of Hwys 20 and 24. From New Orleans, the train ride costs $12 and takes 1½ hours; from Lafayette, it's $16 and takes two hours.

THIBODAUX TO NEW IBERIA

West of Houma along Hwy 20 and just off I-49/Hwy 90, **Gibson**, along Bayou Black, and Donner are two tiny towns not discernible at 60 mph. However, some of the best swamp adventures in Acadiana start out in Gibson.

Atchafalaya Basin Backwater Adventure Tours (☎ 504-575-2371, rgs52@earthlink.net), 6302 N Bayou Black Drive, is in Gibson a few blocks down the bayou from the Caroll St bridge. Guide Jon Faslun, the first in the state to offer swamp tours, has been running motorized boat tours deep in the Great Chacahoula Swamp for nearly 25 years. In 2½ hours, Faslun's tours wind through 10,000 years of natural history: the swamp's early inhabitants, its evolution, flora and fauna, swamp survival and swamp medicine. This is no jokey-Cajun show – Faslun's a serious swamper with a strong respect for nature and a firm policy against feeding alligators.

For basic tours he charges $50 per person with a two-person minimum; the maximum boat capacity is eight. During the high season from Mardi Gras through May, and again December to February, he runs one boat daily at 11 am. All tours are weather permitting, and reservations are essential. He also rents pirogues for $20 per person per day with a map that will direct you to an abandoned cypress mill. As with any trip into the deeper swamp, you'll be more comfortable in socks and boat-worthy shoes and in clothes that cover your limbs.

Though the swamp has plenty of active wildlife by day, it positively teems with creatures by night. Faslun can motor hardy adventurers to a small island about 20 yards in diameter, dropping them off for an overnight stay. He charges passengers who bring their own equipment $20 each for the ride. If he provides equipment, he charges $50 each. If passengers want Faslun to spend the night, it's $100 each. If he provides food, it's a bit more. He can outfit up

to four people. His Web site is at www
.atchafalayabasinbackwateradventure.com.

A few miles down the road at *Wildlife
Gardens* (☎ 504-575-3676, 5306 N Bayou
Black Drive), owner Betty Provost leads
visitors on tours over the shady paths she
and her husband cut through their 30-acre
private swamp preserve. The couple keeps
ostriches, nutria and alligators on display in
cages, and peacocks roam the grounds. But
even more intriguing are the one-of-a-kind
B&B accommodations. Their four little
'trappers cabins' are adjacent to a small
swamp, and each has its own front porch
overlooking the water and gators. At night
the chorus of swamp creatures provides
plenty of entertainment. The rustic cabins
are spare but comfortable, with big high
beds, air conditioning, ceiling fans and stall
showers. Cabins rent for $80 for two includ-
ing breakfast, a tour, and use of the nature
trails. Though staying here is hardly rough-
ing it, it is a unique experience and one kids
especially will love.

Chester's Cypress Inn (☎ 504-446-6821),
visible on Hwy 20 in Donner a couple
miles east of Gibson, is an old dining hall
serving Dixie beer and frog legs. It's
famous for chicken (which tastes like frog
legs); it comes regular, spicy or no-batter
for $6 a plate. Chester's is open for dinner
from 5 to 9 pm Thursday through Saturday
and all day Sunday. Chester's is convenient
for travelers returning from a swamp tour.
But don't let a few miles deter you – locals
from as far as 20 miles away frequent
Chester's.

East along I-49/Hwy 90 lies **Morgan City**,
at the confluence of the Atchafalaya River
and the Intracoastal Waterway. Though it
began as a fish-processing hub, fish oil has
given way to crude oil, but both are celebrated at the annual Shrimp & Petroleum
Festival over Labor Day weekend (☎ 800-
256-2931). The rest of the year, the unique
International Petroleum Museum & Exposition (☎ 504-384-3744), 111 First St on the
city's riverfront, offers visitors the chance to
experience life aboard Mr Charlie, a retired
offshore drilling rig that once housed more
than 50 workers. It's open weekdays.

Lake End Park (☎ 504-380-4623, 2300
Hwy 70), north of town on Lake Palourde,
has 118 sites and a small beach. Tent sites
are $13.50, and RV sites are $16.75. There
are several chain motels in town. Morgan
City is also the southern end of Henderson
Levee Rd (see the Henderson section, later
in this chapter, for coverage of Henderson
Levee Rd).

A few miles north of Franklin, a short
detour off I-40/Hwy 90 or Hwy 182 leads to
Charenton and the 1260-acre **Chitimacha
Indian Reservation**. The Chitimacha, famed
basket weavers, are the only Native Americans in Louisiana to retain federally recognized sovereignty over a portion of their
ancestral lands. With the arrival of the Acadians and subsequent intermarriage, many
Chitimacha began speaking French and
adopting Catholicism. The estimated population of 20,000 around colonial times was
decimated by European diseases. Today
about 375 tribal members live on the reservation; total tribal membership is now
around 1000. The Chitimacha language,
dormant for most of the 20th century, is now
being taught in the tribe's elementary
schools and to adults as well.

The **Chitimacha Museum** (☎ 337-923-
4830), at 3283 Chitimacha Trail, has been recently remodeled and contains tribal
objects and displays focusing on traditional
and contemporary life, education, assimila-
tion, veterans and government; admission is
free. The tribe's largest commercial development is the 115,000-sq-foot *Cypress
Bayou Casino*, which includes two restaurants and a cocktail lounge, and is open and
busy 24 hours a day. A portion of the revenues from the casino are used to purchase
adjacent lands to expand the reservation.

Along Hwy 182 near Jeanerette is the
Yellow Bowl Restaurant (☎ 337-276-5512),
in a tidy yellow building with a corrugated
tin roof. The seafood lunches (around $7)
and dinners ($10 to $14) are worth a stop.
On weekends there's a seafood buffet. It's
closed Monday and Tuesday.

Amid coastal marshlands 24 miles south
of Jeanerette, **Cypremort Point State Park**
(☎ 337-867-4510) is the only place near the

Gulf of Mexico that can be easily reached by car between here and Cameron near the Texas border. Visitors to the 185-acre day-use park can swim at the half-mile stretch of landfill beach, launch private sailboats or windsurfing boards, or cast a line off a 100-foot fishing pier. Bring sunscreen – shade is sparse. Admission is $2 per car. From I-49/Hwy 90 near Jeanerette, follow signs south on Hwy 83, then left on Hwy 319. From New Iberia, head south on Hwy 83 and turn right on Hwy 319.

NEW IBERIA & AROUND

Named for the Iberian Peninsula, New Iberia was settled by the Spanish in 1779. The town prospered on the sugarcane of surrounding plantations. Of the state's 18 sugar-producing parishes, Iberia Parish now grows the most sugarcane. The town's best-known current resident may well be mystery writer James Lee Burke, whose novels often take place in and around New Iberia and feature Detective Dave Robicheaux.

The convenient Iberia Parish Visitors Bureau (☎ 337-365-1540; www.iberiaparish .com) is on Hwy 14/Center St just east of I-49/Hwy 90. It's open daily 9 am to 5 pm. The Greater Iberia Chamber of Commerce (☎ 337-364-1836), 111 W Main St in down-town, can provide information on special events, and it has parish maps and brochures.

Hwy 14/Center St and Hwy 182 meet in the compact downtown along Bayou Teche. Hwy 182 splits and becomes Main St north-bound and St Peter St southbound.

A walking tour of downtown could start at **Shadows on the Teche** (☎ 337-365-5213), at 317 E Main St, a Greek Revival–Louisiana Colonial plantation house open daily for tours from 9 am to 4:30 pm. Admission is $6 for adults and $3 for kids. The tours are enriched by stories gleaned from 40 trunks' worth of family documents. Anyone can wander the grounds for free. Continue along Main St to surf the Web at the public library, or browse through the titles at the fine little Books Along the Teche. More sights

include the art deco Evangeline Theatre and the central plaza across from the chamber of commerce. (In spring 2000, a train carrying toxic chemicals derailed in downtown, forcing an extensive evacua-tion of the surrounding areas and closing the downtown for several days.)

Three miles north of downtown along Hwy 182 is **Spanish Lake** (☎ 337-364-0103), a prime spot for bass fishing and wildlife watching. From five piers and a paved road, visitors can spot 53 species of nesting birds, nutria, beavers and alligators. There are also picnic tables. Entrance is $2.

Every spring, the town sponsors a Courir de Mardi Gras. The 1920s jazz trumpeter Bunk Johnson, one of Louis Armstrong's mentors, lived here, and in April, the town hosts the Bunk Johnson Jazz, Arts & Her-itage Festival. Also in April there's a Laotian New Year's Festival.

The first week of May, the town is the starting and ending point for the Cycle Main St bike tour. Every year in early May, hundreds of cyclists from around the country gather in New Iberia and head out for a weeklong ride, averaging between 45 and 50 miles a day and overnighting in six towns. The towns, which vary each year, are all designated Main Street America towns, hence the event's name: Cycle Main Street. For more information, contact the ride di-rector at ☎ 337-369-2330.

The Louisiana Sugarcane Festival is held the last weekend in September, and the World Championship Gumbo Cook-Off takes place in mid-October. On Saturday and Sunday from 7:30 to 10:30 am, tune to KANE 1240 AM for Cajun music.

A cheap place to stay is the *Teche Motel* (*☎ 337-369-3756, 1830 Main St*), six blocks south of Jefferson Terrace. The simple rooms in duplex units cost $35. The town has numerous B&Bs, and among them is the comfortable 100 year-old *Estorage-Norton House* (*☎ 337-365-7603, estnortbb@ bbhost.com, 446 E Main St*). The four rooms, each with private bath, range from $65 to $90 and include a full breakfast. There's a *Holiday Inn* and a *Best Western* on Hwy 14 just off I-49/Hwy 90.

A favorite weekday breakfast and lunch spot is the ***Lagniappe Too Café*** (☎ *337-365-9419, 204 E Main St)*. It also serves dinner on Friday and Saturday. For boiled seafood, locals head out a few miles north of town along I-49/Hwy 90 to the simple ***Guiding Star*** (☎ *337-365-9113)*. If you need crawfish-cracking lessons, this is the place to come. On the east side of the interstate near a truck stop, it's open daily.

The Amtrak station (☎ 337-364-9625), 402 W Washington St at Railroad Ave, is in a 1910 depot a few blocks north of downtown. The Greyhound station (☎ 337-364-8571) is on E Main St and Darcey, about a mile south of the central commercial district (and near the Teche Motel).

Teche City Taxi can be reached by calling ☎ 337-367-1752.

Avery Island

A detour southwest of New Iberia along Hwy 329 leads through cane fields and along a small bayou to Avery Island, the home of McIlhenny Tabasco factory and a wildlife sanctuary. The island is actually a salt dome that extends 8 miles below the surface. Hundreds of salt domes exist throughout coastal Louisiana, but only a few rise above the surface (another is Jefferson Island). And yes, the salt that's mined here goes into the sauce, as do locally grown peppers, which are mashed and combined with the locally mined salt. The mixture ferments in oak barrels and eventually vinegar is added and the mixture is strained and bottled.

McIlhenny Tabasco factory tours (☎ 337-365-8173) are a touchstone for many gourmet travelers who appear by the busload, but visitors no longer enter the factory itself, and the exhibits and presentations in the tour room leave visitors wanting more. Tours run 9 am to 4 pm daily. The gift shop offers a fun collection of Tabasco souvenirs.

In the adjacent **Jungle Gardens** (☎ 337-365-8173) visitors can drive and walk through 250 acres of exotic subtropical jungle flora. Though the mosquitoes can be fierce, even drivers who stay safely en-

sconced in a car can see an amazing array of waterbirds (especially snowy egrets, which nest here), turtles and even alligators. Watch for turtles and peacocks in the road. Admission is $5.75 for adults and $4 for children; the garden is open 8 am to 4:30 pm daily.

LOREAUVILLE

From New Iberia, Bayou Teche snakes around in a big loop before reaching St Martinville. On the east end of the loop is Loreauville, a small town set among cane fields near the edge of the Atchafalaya Basin. Hwy 86, which heads east out of New Iberia, traces the loop and becomes Main St in central Loreauville. North of town, it crosses Hwy 347 and Hwy 31, both of which head to St Martinville.

The **unmarked grave** of the legendary zydeco accordionist Clifton Chenier (see the boxed text in the Opelousas section) is just outside Loreauville. From Hwy 86/Main St, take Hwy 3242 east toward Dauterive Lake; after around 1½ miles, turn left on Harold Landry Rd, and go 1½ miles to the cemetery (on the right). His grave, often decorated with flowers, is parallel to the Veret and Broussard graves.

Nearby, ***Clifton's Club*** (☎ *337-229-6576)*, formerly operated by Chenier's widow, Margaret, is still in the family. Bands still manage to pack the 700-seat remote dance hall. Schedules are unpredictable; call first to see if a band's playing. To find it, follow directions to the cemetery; then continue up Landry Rd a half-mile farther north, and turn right onto Crochet Lane. The club is a mile up on the right beyond Braquet Rd.

For those who want to join a **swamp tour**, guides with Airboats Inc (☎ 337-229-4457) run surface-skimming skiffs with huge motors in the back, allowing the boats to access extremely shallow channels deep in the basin. The motor's roar is so loud that the guide provides ear protection for the ride, and instead of a running narration, he buzzes through the marsh and then cuts off the engine to discuss the surroundings. One-hour tours cost $15 per person when it's fully reserved (when calling, ask if you can join another tour to keep down costs); the minimum cost per tour is $60. Tours in French are possible (ask when making reservations). They operate Tuesday through Sunday 8 am to 5 pm February through October; boats leave from Marshfield Landing. If you're staying at Lake Fausse State Park, they'll pick you up there.

The *Patio Restaurant* (☎ 337-229-8281), on Main St/Hwy 86 in downtown Loreauville, is a good place to end up after a day in the swamp. The small restaurant serves ambitious seafood dishes such as stuffed-catfish Cajun delight ($14); a salad bar is also available. They are open for lunch from 11 am to 2 pm every day but Monday, and serve dinner Tuesday through Saturday from 5 (5:30 in summer) to 9 pm. *Danna's Bakery* right across the street makes yummy cookies.

ERATH & ABBEVILLE

The small town of **Erath** lies southwest of New Iberia along Hwy 14, which now bypasses its tiny downtown. The town is also a straight shot south of Lafayette on Hwy 339 about 18 miles. And folks are happy to drive the distance to get to *Big John's Seafood Patio* (☎ 337-937-8355). In these parts, a 'patio' is about as barebones as it gets. But no matter, from January to June, they boil crawfish in spice-laced water (rather than slopping on the spices afterward) and serve them up on a heaping tin tray with condiments. From Lafayette, follow Verot School Rd/Hwy 339 south (with a slight eastward jog) to Broadview and turn right. From Hwy 14, head north on Hwy 339 to Broadview and turn left.

Perate's Seafood Patio (☎ 337-937-5037), Hwy 14, in downtown Erath, has boiled crawfish and shrimp, but also serves crawfish bisque and po-boys. It sets up a seafood buffet on Friday and Saturday nights, and has Cajun music on Friday night. It's open for dinner Tuesday to Saturday, closed Monday.

Smiley's (☎ 337-937-4591) is a traditional Cajun dance hall featuring live music and dancing most Friday and Saturday nights, and in the late afternoons and early evening on Sunday. It's on Hwy 14 east of downtown Erath toward Delcambre.

Seven miles west of Erath on Hwy 14 and 24 miles south of Lafayette on Hwy 167 lies **Abbeville**, the jumping-off point for long drives into western Acadiana. Hwys 167 and 14 (not the bypass) lead to the town's two historic squares in its compact downtown along Bayou Vermilion. This center holds the town's main attractions – its legendary oyster bars. To find them, look for the spire of St Mary Magdalen Church (1910). Nearby is Steen's Syrup Mill – in the fall, warm-sugar aromas waft from the mill. St Magdalen Square hosts many of the town's festivals, along with performances by the Abbey Players theater troupe. There's Cajun music on the radio on KROF 960 AM daily from 6 am to noon. As the seat of cattle-producing Vermilion Parish, Abbeville is well recognized for its Louisiana Cattle Festival (☎ 337-893-6328) the first weekend in October. The Giant Omelet Festival (☎ 337-893-6517), the first weekend in November, entails the cooking and consuming of a 5000-egg omelet. The tradition harkens back to Napolean's delight with an omelet prepared by an innkeeper in Bessière, France, which inspired him to order that all the eggs in town be gathered for a huge omelet. Today the giant omelet is a symbol of friendship and pride in things French.

At 1903 Veterans Memorial Drive/Hwy 14 Bypass, the *Sunbelt Lodge* (☎ 337-898-1453, fax 337-898-1463) offers decent singles/doubles for $42/45. It's right behind the visitor center (☎ 337-898-4264).

Dupuy's (☎ 337-893-2336, 108 S Main St), established in 1869, and *Black's* (☎ 337-893-4266, 319 Pere Megret St), operating for over 30 years, offer huge, incredibly fresh oysters for around $4 a dozen, as well as other tasty seafood dishes. A short block apart and one block from the bayou bridge, they are open for lunch and dinner. Dupuy's is closed Tuesday; Black's is closed Sunday and Monday. Just across the bridge, the new *Riverfront Restaurant* (☎ 337-893-3070, 503 W Port St) serves – what else? – oysters, in addition to other seafood, steaks and pasta. From 5 to 7 pm Tuesday through Saturday, oysters cost

25¢. It's closed Monday. Down the block, the folks who formerly ran Black's now serve up oysters at **Shucks** (☎ 337-898-3311, 701 W Port St), where Hwy 167 dead-ends. They also have oyster loaf sandwiches for under $5, and a drive-through for those in need of a quick slurp. It's open every day but Sunday.

ST MARTINVILLE & AROUND

A group of Acadians who had sought refuge in St Domingue (now Haiti) was the first to settle in Louisiana. From Plaquemine on the Mississippi, they traveled 111 miles down Bayou Teche to St Martinville, arriving in 1765. They found a town busy with wealthy Creoles from New Orleans (who were later joined by aristocrats fleeing the French Revolution). Few Acadians stayed in town, but today, St Martinville has become the spiritual center of Acadiana. Visitors can see the Evangeline Oak made famous by Longfellow's 1847 epic poem *Evangeline*, which recounts the story of betrothed lovers Evangeline and Gabriel, separated during le Grand Dérangement. (The story is loosely based on real people.)

The quiet town carries much of the charm befitting such a legend. At the intersection of Hwy 31 (running between New Iberia and Breaux Bridge) and Hwy 96 (running west to Hwy 182 and I-49), a quaint downtown of old wooden storefronts with wide 2nd-story galleries faces the manicured square surrounding the historic **St Martin de Tours Church**, on Main St/Hwy 31. Though the church was built circa 1844, the congregation dates back to 1765. The church is open daily; for a tour, call ☎ 337-394-7334. A statue of Evangeline stands beside the church. Behind the church on the bayou is the **Acadian Memorial**, housing a mural depicting the early settlers, history exhibits and an eternal flame (admission $3).

On Evangeline Blvd facing the church, the **Acadian Arts & Crafts Gallery** has an eclectic collection of reasonably priced art and gifts (open daily). Down the block and right next to the famed oak, the three-story brick **Old Castillo Hotel** (☎ 337-394-4010, 800-621-

3017, 220 Evangeline Blvd) is the oldest building in town. Once a trading post, then an inn, then an all girls' high school, it again operates as an inn, offering five comfortable rooms for $50 to $80, including breakfast. There are half a dozen other B&Bs around town and a few restaurants (though you'll be better off eating in Breaux Bridge). **Danna's**

Longfellow's Evangeline

Excerpts follow from Part the Second, II, from Henry Wadsworth Longfellow's 1847 epic *Evangeline*, about Acadian sweethearts separated during le Grand Dérangement:

Thus ere another noon they emerged from the shades; and before them
Lay, in the golden sun, the lakes of the Atchafalaya.
Water-lilies in myriads rocked on the slight undulations
Made by the passing oars, and, resplendent in beauty, the lotus
Lifted her golden crown above the heads of the boatmen.
Faint was the air with the odorous breath of magnolia blossoms,
And with the heat of noon; and numberless sylvan islands,
Fragrant and thickly embowered with blossoming hedges of roses,
Near to whose shores they glided along, invited to slumber.

On the banks of the Teche are the towns of St Maur and St Martin.
There the long-wandering bride shall be given again to her bridegroom,
There the long-absent pastor regain his flock and his sheepfold.
Beautiful is the land, with its prairies and forests of fruit-trees;
Under the feet a garden of flowers, and the bluest of heavens
Bending above, and resting its dome on the walls of the forest.
They who dwell there have named it the Eden of Louisiana.

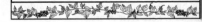

Bakery, on E Bridge St facing the church, makes great fig bars and pastries.

If you see one thing in town, make sure it's the **Longfellow-Evangeline State Historical Site** (☎ 337-394-3754), on Hwy 31 a mile or so north of downtown. Formerly a sugar plantation, today the lush grounds hold huge moss-draped trees and a narrow bayou, a beautiful setting for the restored three-story raised Creole cottage (1815), which is open for tours. The visitor center has exhibits on Acadian immigration, and there's a restored Acadian farmstead. Occasional living-history programs shed light on 19th-century life here. The park is open daily 9 am to 5 pm; admission is $2.

Lake Fausse Pointe State Park

This impressive 6217-acre wildlife sanctuary and state park (☎ 337-229-4764), along the levee road 18 miles southeast of St Martinville, is scenically poised on a lake adjacent to the Atchafalaya Basin. Three short nature trails wind through swamp woodlands. There's a boat launch and boat rentals: a motor boat rents for $20 per hour or $40 per day; canoes for $5 per hour or $25 per day; kayaks for $7 per hour. On a summer weekend, the park can get busy with families from northern Louisiana who love their speedboats.

Eighteen modern, spacious cabins that sleep up to eight are built on stilts, some at the water's edge. They rent for $65 a night (and are often reserved far in advance). Cookware, dishware, flatware and bed linens are provided; bring your own towels. The well-tended campsites ($10, $12 with hookups) are spacious, shady and private. Bring all the food you need – the closest markets are very small. The park store has little more than cold drinks, bait and snacks.

From St Martinville, the drive will take about a half hour. The roads are small and signs are few. Take Hwy 96 to Hwy 679. Stay on Hwy 679 for seven miles to Hwy 3083. Cross the canal and turn right on Henderson Levee Rd. The park is about 5 miles farther. Alternatively, the park is also a straight shot down the levee road from Henderson off I-10, but much of the road is gravel.

BREAUX BRIDGE

Nine miles east of Lafayette, the sign on the namesake drawbridge in downtown Breaux Bridge welcomes you to La Capitale Mondiale des Écrevisses (the Crawfish Capital of the World), a title bestowed on the town by the state legislature in 1959. Since then, the town of 7000 has hosted an annual Crawfish Festival (☎ 337-332-6655) on the first complete weekend in May, featuring a crawfish étouffée cook-off, crawfish-eating contests (the record is 55¾ pounds in 45 minutes), parade replete with crawfish royalty, and even crawfish races. Cajun and zydeco bands play all day and well into the night. Daily admission costs $5 (a three-day pass is $10). Simultaneously, there's a small Afro-American Crawfish Festival with zydeco and R&B at the National Guard Armory Grounds.

Breaux Bridge is just south of I-10 exit 109, but travelers heading there from Lafayette should take the calmer Hwy 94, turning right on Hwy 31 to reach downtown. Hwy 31 continues south to St Martinville. Downtown Breaux Bridge is an old-fashioned row of shops along Bayou Teche, a block from the drawbridge. A tiny park at the water's edge commemorates the establishment of the town in the late 18th century. Next to the bridge, the Bayou Teche Visitors Center (☎ 337-332-8500, 888-565-5939) can provide maps, B&B brochures and festival dates.

Lake Martin

South of Breaux Bridge, Lake Martin offers the unusual opportunity to see swamp wildlife from a hiking trail – or even from a car. The beautiful lake is the state's largest nesting area for wading birds. White ibis, herons, egrets, owls, eagles, and ospreys populate the cypress and tupelo, and nutria and alligators wander through the duckweed below. A few virgin cypress are more than 1000 years old. It's a wonderfully still and peaceful place surprisingly close to all the activity.

The Nature Conservancy's **Cypress Island Preserve** at the lake's south and west sides has the largest white ibis rookery in

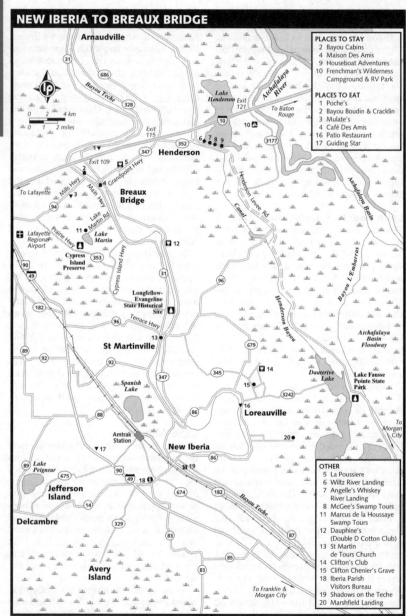

NEW IBERIA TO BREAUX BRIDGE

PLACES TO STAY
2 Bayou Cabins
4 Maison Des Amis
9 Houseboat Adventures
10 Frenchman's Wilderness
   Campground & RV Park

PLACES TO EAT
1 Poche's
2 Bayou Boudin & Cracklin
3 Mulate's
4 Café Des Amis
16 Patio Restaurant
17 Guiding Star

OTHER
5 La Poussiere
6 Wiltz River Landing
7 Angelle's Whiskey
  River Landing
8 McGee's Swamp Tours
11 Marcus de la Houssaye
   Swamp Tours
12 Dauphine's
   (Double D Cotton Club)
13 St Martin
   de Tours Church
14 Clifton's Club
15 Clifton Chenier's Grave
18 Iberia Parish
   Visitors Bureau
19 Shadows on the Teche
20 Marshfield Landing

Arnaudville

Lake Henderson

Atchafalaya River

To Baton Rouge

Henderson

Bayou Teche

Breaux Bridge

To Lafayette

Lafayette Regional Airport

Lake Martin

Cypress Island Preserve

Henderson Levee Rd

Henderson Bayou

Bayou L'Embarras

Atchafalaya Basin

Longfellow-Evangeline State Historical Site

St Martinville

Spanish Lake

Atchafalaya Basin Floodway

Dauterive Lake

Lake Fausse Pointe State Park

Loreauville

To Morgan City

Amtrak Station

New Iberia

Lake Peigneur

Jefferson Island

Delcambre

Avery Island

To Franklin & Morgan City

0   2   4 km
0   1   2 miles

Grandpoint Hwy
Mills Hwy
Main Hwy
Lake Martin Rd
Prairie Hwy
Cypress Island Hwy
Terrace Hwy

the world. A 3½-mile trail runs along the north edge of the lake; a public gravel road hugs the southern half. Those disinclined to leave the air conditioning of their car can bird and gator watch in comfort. Because it's a preserve, there are no services, stores or restrooms.

Marcus de la Houssaye (☎ 337-845-5332, 337-298-2630) leads guided **swamp tours** here aboard a 20-foot aluminum skiff and also rents canoes and johnboats – all by calling in advance. He offers four daily 1½-hour tours on weekdays ($25 for adults and $5 for children). Pack & Paddle in Lafayette also arranges kayak trips on Lake Martin (see Activities in the Lafayette section for more information).

From Breaux Bridge, take Hwy 31 south and turn right on Lake Martin Rd. At the lake, tours depart from a landing on the right. From Lafayette the lake is about 15 minutes; go east on Hwy 94 and turn right on Hwy 353. In about 5 miles, there's a sign and entrance on the left; the trail begins on the left, and a gravel road veers right. To reach the boat landing, drive 2 miles down the road.

Places to Stay
Though it's set back from a busy highway, the eight cozy units at **Bayou Cabins** (☎ 337-332-6158, 100 Mills Hwy/Hwy 94) feel wonderfully removed. (The postal address of Bayou Cabins is PO Box 3, 70517.) Rocky and Lisa Sonnier have lovingly restored the Acadian cabins, all of which have porches, some overlooking the bayou. For breakfast, guests can choose between a lagniappe of excellent boudin, cracklins and hogshead cheese, or beignets, eggs and ham. Rates range from $50 to $90. It's walking distance to Mulate's (see Places to Eat).

At **Maison Des Amis** (☎ 337-332-5273, 140 E Bridge St, 70517), right in downtown on Bayou Teche, the Breaux family will put you up in their charming Creole cottage, which dates back to 1870. Here, you'll pay from $75 to $95 for a room. The price includes breakfast the next morning at Cafe Des Amis.

Places to Eat & Drink
In a corner storefront built in the 1920s, the **Cafe Des Amis** (☎ 337-332-5273, 140 E Bridge St), in downtown, is a homey place for breakfast, serving beignets, crawfish omelets, *pain perdu* (French toast) and boudin and eggs. It is also an intimate dinner spot where you can sit under the pressed tin ceiling and hear French spoken all around. The place is packed on Saturday starting at 8:30 am for zydeco breakfast, featuring live bands.

Bayou Boudin & Cracklin (☎ 337-332-6158, 100 Mills Hwy/Hwy 94) is the place to go for hearty Cajun cooking. Get the regular or crawfish boudin, prize-winning pork cracklins, surprisingly light hogshead cheese and other tasty lunches and dinners, and eat it all on the screened-in porch.

Just a block away is **Mulate's** (☎ 337-332-4648, 325 Mills Hwy/Hwy 94), where every night great Cajun bands draw crowds onto the well-worn dance floor. Mulate's (MOO-lotz) offers a full selection of Cajun dishes for lunch ($8 to $12) and dinner ($12 to $15); the house specialty is catfish. It's open daily, and there's no cover charge.

A historical marker outside **Poche's** (☎ 337-332-2108, 3015-A Main Hwy/Hwy 31), north of I-10, confirms its credentials as a legendary local charcuterie. Poche's (po-SHAYZ) specializes in boudin and cracklins and serves daily Cajun lunch specials and barbecue on weekends. It's open daily from 5:30 am to 9 pm; lunch is served from 10:30 am to 2 pm. The large and simple dining area is overseen by a herd of pensive deer heads. From I-10, head north 3 miles on Hwy 31; it's on the right.

A traditional Cajun dance hall, **La Poussiere** (☎ 337-332-1721, 1301 Grandpoint Hwy/Hwy 347) gained considerable notoriety when it was sued by two African-American lawyers for being barred from admittance. The fais-do-do, now open to everyone, is Saturday night from 8 pm to midnight (admission $3). On Sunday, there's music from 4 to 8 pm (admission $4). From downtown, cross the bridge; take the first right and then the first left on Grandpoint Hwy. The hall is a half mile down on the left.

The Sacred Mudbug

In Australia, they call them 'yabbies,' in Germany, 'flusskrebse.' In the rest of the US, it's 'crayfish.' But in southern Louisiana, it's crawfish or *écrevisse*. This is also where the phrase 'Bugs on Hogs' refers not to a swine disease, but rather to Harley-driving bikers who flock to the annual Breaux Bridge Crawfish Festival.

The ongoing love affair with this cute crustacean is hard to miss. Emblazoned on T-shirts and coffee mugs, gracing menus in the form of étouffée, bisque and balls, the ubiquitous crawfish reigns supreme. Though crawfish was formerly known as the 'poor man's lobster,' south Louisianans can now justifiably refer to Maine's larger cousin as the 'rich man's crawfish.' No trip to Cajun Country is complete without sampling the tail meat. If you arrive in springtime, head straight for a 'boiling point,' stare down 50 sets of beady black eyes and start cracking those red shells. If you need help with technique, humbly seek out an expert.

According to the mythology of the Chitimacha, a local Native American tribe, the universe was founded by the crawfish, a freshwater crustacean native to the swamps of southern Louisiana. The Chitimacha and other tribes relied on crawfish as a primary food source, and when the Acadians arrived in southern Louisiana in the mid-1700s, the Indians taught them to catch and eat these crustaceans. In the 1930s, crawfish were served free in local pubs to push beer sales. After WWII, an industry of harvesting wild crawfish developed in the Atchafalaya Basin near Henderson.

Annual crawfish yields vary greatly depending on water levels, and wild catches could not always meet demand. In the 1960s, researchers began studying crawfish aquaculture and discovered that crawfish could be raised in shallow artificial ponds and made an ideal rotation crop in rice fields. Today ponds ranging in size from 1 to 100 acres are flooded in fall and drained in summer. Crawfish can be harvested as early as November, but the crawfish season peaks in April and May. According to LSU's Agricultural Center, the combined annual yield of wild and cultivated crawfish ranges from 75 million to 105 million pounds, generating $125 million annually. Nearly 7000 people, almost all in Acadiana, depend directly or indirectly on the crawfish industry.

Eighty-five percent of the crawfish harvest is consumed locally, and in this case, these numbers tell the 'tail.' The crawfish tail meat, often frozen, is available year-round and is used by home cooks and haute chefs alike. But the humble crawfish has spawned a tradition in Cajun Country: the crawfish boil, a communal gathering of family and neighbors that often includes music and dancing. Cleaned live crawfish are boiled in a vat of water laced with spices (though some cooks prefer boiling them in plain water and covering them in spices afterward); for variety, the cooks might also toss in whole potatoes and ears of corn. The now-bright-red crawfish are typically served on large tin trays, and empty trays are on hand for discarded shells. Accomplished mudbug eaters tear off the head, suck out the 'butter,' tear off the back fin, pull out the vein and squeeze out the morsel of tail meat. Whatever you do, don't leave Cajun Country without 'sucking head' – and if you can't quite manage that, at least invest in a lifelike refrigerator magnet.

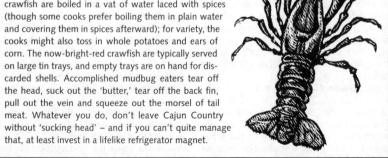

For zydeco, head to ***Dauphine's*** *(☎ 337-394-9616)*, also known as the Double D Cotton Club, just outside the country town of Parks south of Breaux Bridge, halfway to St Martinville. There's usually music on weekend nights. Inside, the theme is wood – wood ceiling, walls and floor. Polish your shoes and then polish the floor. Take Hwy 31 5 miles south of Breaux Bridge to Parks, turn left onto Hwy 350, turn right onto Hwy 347, drive 600 yards and turn left onto St Louis.

HENDERSON

Henderson is the most convenient access point to the Atchafalaya Basin, a tremendous recreational resource for boating, fishing and hunting. Swamp tours, canoe and motorboat rentals, houseboats and restaurants are in town and on landings that line the levee road. To reach the levee, take I-10 exit 115, head south, and make a fairly immediate left turn onto Hwy 352. Follow this route 3 miles through the small community. Across the bridge over the canal, you will see the levee. Turn right and watch signs for landings open to the public. Drivers can also take I-10 exit 121 and head south on Hwy 105, which becomes Hwy 3177; with swamp on both sides, it eventually joins the levee road 4 miles south of Henderson.

Henderson Levee Rd itself makes an interesting ramble; it snakes along next to the levee 50 miles south, passing Lake Fausse Pointe State Park on the way to Morgan City. It is mostly a decent gravel road (best navigated when dry if you are driving a passenger car), but it is intermittently paved. The basin is out of sight unless you drive up and over into a public landing, but houses, shacks and trailers line the remote route. Boat rentals are available from **Wiltz River Landing** (☎ 337-228-2430), off the levee road just south of the Hwy 352 bridge. Motorboats rent for $38 per day, canoes for $15 per day, paddles and lifejackets are extra.

The family-run McGee's Swamp Tours (☎ 337-228-2384), 1337 Henderson Levee Rd, takes party boats holding up to 50 passengers into the basin for 1½-hour guided tours given by local Cajun old-timers. The four daily tours (none in January) are convenient and cheap ($12 for adults and $6 for children), but this portion of the swamp – practically under the I-10 bridge – is hardly remote. They also feed the gators. Reservations are recommended. Buy tickets from the cashier inside. The restaurant serves seafood specialties (alligator, frog legs) along with inexpensive sandwiches (a decent catfish po-boy for $5). Boat passengers might want to pick up a cold drink for the ride.

Very similar tours – on similar boats and for the same price – are offered at nearby Angelle's Whiskey River Landing (☎ 337-228-8567). Tours here are also given in French. Every Sunday from 4 to 8 pm, there's a flurry of Cajun music and dancing at the landing, providing visitors an excellent chance to learn the steps.

For campers, the 108-site ***Frenchman's Wilderness Campground & RV Park*** *(☎ 337-228-2616)* is just south of I-10 exit 121 (at Butte La Rose). It charges $13 for tents, $15 for hookups and $1 to use the pool (noncampers pay $4).

Houseboat Rentals

One of the most distinctive overnight experiences you can find anywhere is a night aboard a houseboat in the Atchafalaya Basin. Doug Sebatier and his wife, Diane, run Houseboat Adventures, and will 'push you out' from their landing in Henderson into a protected cove for a stay aboard a comfortable modern houseboat. The boats are equipped with generators to power the TV, VCR, lights and air-conditioning, or you can skip the noise and go natural. Boats have two-burner ranges and some have mini-refrigerators.

You will need to bring your own food and drinking water, and an ice chest for cold drinks. A flashlight will also come in handy, as will insect repellent and fishing gear. They provide linens and towels, dishware, candles, matches and quick generator-operating lessons. They'll even throw in a pirogue or motorized skiff so that you can

Swamp Tours

You haven't been to Cajun Country until you've been out in the swamp. There are dozens of kinds of swamp tours, each with its particular advantages and disadvantages, but anything that gets you out onto the water is a good move. Many larger tours leave from the town of Henderson, accessing the Atchafalaya Basin. Others farther south leave from Loreauville, a smaller landing that accesses the deeper basin. Trips out into the smaller bayous and swamps are scattered in the region around Houma, from Gibson to Des Allemands.

Tours run on many types of boats. The most common are party boats – open-sided pontoon boats that seat 40 or more. These tours are inexpensive and easy to find, and usually run at regularly scheduled times year-round. The disadvantage is that such big boats can't hope to nuzzle their way into the narrow, shallow channels where most of the swamp wildlife seeks refuge. Operators who use smaller craft can get deeper into the swamp, but their tours may run only seasonally or on a less predictable schedule, and reservations are required. Prices on the smaller boats may vary according to how many seats are filled – if the boat is full, it may be comparable to the cost of a party boat, but if you end up getting a personal tour, it will cost considerably more.

One of the highlights of a swamp tour is having an engaging local guide who is familiar with the area and who can point out wildlife and relate stories. Some operators provide more folksy banter (and even songs) than lessons on ecology, wildlife and history. Another highlight of a swamp tour is alligator sightings, and a tour without such appearances tends to disappoint. This has engendered a wide philosophical divide between operators who feed the alligators and those who don't. Most do, throwing chicken parts or marshmallows to lure alligators into camera range. At least one guide even catches a small alligator for a close look before releasing it. These are not the most ecologically sensitive practices, and operators who do not feed the gators make it their calling card. Another high-impact tour is aboard an airboat that buzzes through fields of lily pads at 40 mph making such a racket that passengers wear ear-protective headphones. Airboat tours are popular for speed thrills and to access shallow channels, but most animals are seen only as they flee from the noise.

On any tour, a camera, binoculars, insect repellent, sunscreen, sunglasses, hat and cool drink come in handy. On deeper swamp tours, you might be more comfortable in clothing that covers your limbs and sporting socks and boat-worthy shoes. It's better to organize a tour either in the early morning or early evening. This allows you to avoid the heat of the day and also to see wildlife when it's most active.

You can also rent canoes and kayaks at several locations and get out into the swamp independently, but a guided paddling expedition lets you see the swamp up close while learning all about it. Pack & Paddle (☎ 337-232-5854, 800-458-4560) in Lafayette, the premier outfitter in the region, organizes paddling expeditions into the basin, bayous and area lakes, including night rides. Group tour prices start around $25 per person, including a naturalist guide and canoe; prices increase if trips require shuttles or meals.

row around or motor back and forth to shore and nearby restaurants.

The peak rate from March through October is $145 a night for a small boat that will sleep four to six people or $175 for a large boat that will sleep up to eight (two-night minimum on weekends), plus a $25 towing fee. Discounts are available off-season and for three or more nights. To arrange a stay with **Houseboat Adventures**, call the Sebatiers (☎ 337-228-7484, 800-491-4662, 1399 Henderson Levee Rd, Breaux Bridge, 70517); they require advance reservations and your estimated arrival time. An airport shuttle is available from Lafayette.

Lafayette

Lafayette (lahf-ee-ET; population 112,000) has an older downtown that has been the focus of recent redevelopment. Chain stores line Evangeline Thruway/I-49, the central four-lane route through town, as well as all the other main routes. Though few districts are visually remarkable, the rapidly expanding Hub City is abuzz throughout the year, and its residents partake of its rich musical scene every chance they get. The 17,000 Ragin' Cajuns at the University of Louisiana at Lafayette (UL) boost the energy level considerably, but a college town this ain't. For visitors the city's charm lies in its warm welcoming attitudes, festivals large and small, a wealth of restaurants and accommodations and proximity to the rest of Acadiana.

Three attractions shed light on Acadian heritage and make good stops for travelers venturing out into the rural areas – the NPS-run Acadian Cultural Center, Vermilionville next door, and Acadian Village across town. If you have kids in tow, take them to the downtown Children's Museum and the Natural History Museum. Many festivals cater to children. In fact, one of the pleasures of attending the city's events is watching whole families enjoy the myriad festivities.

Though Lafayette has plenty of distractions, no trip to Cajun Country should begin and end here. After a day or two, venture out to the small rural communities to experience a more traditional Cajun life.

History

In 1821, Jean Mouton, a local Acadian, donated a portion of his lands near the Bayou Vermilion for the construction of a church. Vermilionville grew around the church, and in 1823, the Louisiana legislature created Lafayette Parish, named after the Marquis de Lafayette, and the town became the new parish seat. In 1844, the town was renamed Lafayette. The rich soil in Lafayette Parish fostered many small farms and provided excellent cattle and horse grazing, and the town was the center of agricultural and cattle trade. In the 1970s, Lafayette boomed with the oil industry, becoming home to industry offices managing offshore operations. During the oil bust of the '80s, the city weathered hard times. Better oil fortunes in the '90s, as well as the growth of tourism, have fostered redevelopment and expansion.

Orientation

I-10 traverses the north side of town; around exits 101 and 103A are clusters of chain hotels and restaurants. Evangeline Thruway (Hwy 167/Hwy 90/I-49) runs north/south through the center of town along two parallel one-way streets. Jefferson Blvd traces a half circle through the small, compact downtown. University Ave/Hwy 182 crosses I-10 and heads south to the eastern edge of the university and the western edge of downtown. Ambassador Caffery Parkway is a busy route through the west side of town along which lies many shopping strips and malls. None of the main roads and few smaller ones in town are linear. Get a map as soon as possible.

Information

Tourist Offices A mile south of I-10 in between the north- and southbound lanes of the Evangeline Thruway is the main visitor center. It distributes maps, guides and brochures daily until 5 pm, and the staff is very helpful.

For advance information, contact the Lafayette Convention & Visitors Commission (☎ 337-232-3808, 800-346-1958, info@ lafayettetravel.com), Box 52066, Lafayette, LA 70505. From Canada, call ☎ 800-534-4340. The Web site is www.lafayettetravel.com; it has a good list of Cajun Country links.

Money All of the Whitney National Bank branches exchange foreign currency. There's one at 911 Lee Ave (☎ 337-264-6158).

Post & Communications The main post office downtown (☎ 337-232-4910), 101 Jefferson Blvd at E Cypress St, is just east of

LOUISIANA

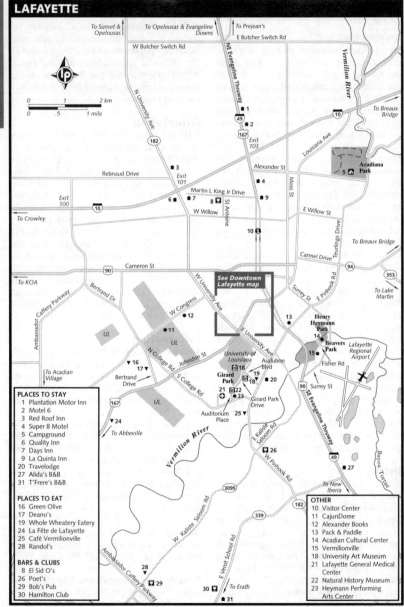

LAFAYETTE

To Sunset & Opelousas

To Opelousas & Evangeline Downs

To Prejean's

E Butcher Switch Rd

W Butcher Switch Rd

W Butcher Switch Rd

NE Evangeline Thruway

Vermilion River

To Breaux Bridge

N University Ave

182

49

167

Exit 103

1

2

Louisiana Ave

Alexander St

Acadiana Park

Rebnaud Drive

Exit 101

3

Moss St

4

5

Exit 100

Martin L King Jr Drive

St Antoine

6

7

8

9

E Willow St

To Crowley

W Willow

10

E Willow St

Teurlings Drive

To Breaux Bridge

Carmel Drive

94

353

Cameron St

To Lake Martin

90

See Downtown Lafayette map

Surrey St

E Pinhook Rd

To KOA

Bertrand Dr

Ambassador Caffery Parkway

W University Ave

W Congress

12

13

Henry Heymann Park

14

Beavers Park

Lafayette Regional Airport

UL

11

UL

N College Rd

Johnston St

University of Louisiana

Audubon Blvd

15

Fisher Rd

To Acadian Village

16

17

Bertrand Drive

S College Rd

Girard Park

18

19

20

Surrey St

90

SE Evangeline Thruway

49

To Abbeville

167

UL

21

22

23

Girard Park Drive

25

Auditorium Place

24

E Kaliste Saloom Rd

26

W Pinhook Rd

27

Bayou Tortue

Vermilion River

3095

339

To New Iberia

182

28

29

30

31

W Kaliste Saloom Rd

Ambassador Caffery Parkway

E Verot School Rd

To Erath

PLACES TO STAY
1 Plantation Motor Inn
2 Motel 6
3 Red Roof Inn
4 Super 8 Motel
5 Campground
6 Quality Inn
7 Days Inn
9 La Quinta Inn
20 Travelodge
27 Alida's B&B
31 T'Frere's B&B

PLACES TO EAT
16 Green Olive
17 Deano's
19 Whole Wheatery Eatery
24 La Fête de Lafayette
25 Café Vermilionville
28 Randol's

BARS & CLUBS
8 El Sid O's
26 Poet's
29 Bob's Pub
30 Hamilton Club

OTHER
10 Visitor Center
11 CajunDome
12 Alexander Books
13 Pack & Paddle
14 Acadian Cultural Center
15 Vermilionville
18 University Art Museum
21 Lafayette General Medical Center
22 Natural History Museum
23 Heymann Performing Arts Center

the central commercial district near the train tracks. Mailboxes Etc (☎ 337-233-2139, fax 337-233-3256), near Kmart at the intersection of E Kaliste Saloom and W Pinhook Rd, provides mailing, packaging and fax services. Kinko's Copies (☎ 337-989-2679, fax 337-989-2779), at 3808 Ambassador Caffery Parkway, provides photocopy, fax and Internet services 24 hours a day.

Media *The Times of Acadiana* – simply called the *Times* – is a free weekly tabloid that covers the news and events for the region much better than local newspapers. Look for it at the visitor center and select outlets or online at www.timesofacadiana .com and www.acadiananow.com.

Radio Acadie out of UL (KRVS 88.7 FM; ☎ 337-482-6108) broadcasts great programs devoted to authentic southern Louisiana music. They play Cajun music weekdays 5 to 7 am, Saturday 6 am to noon, and Sunday 4 to 5 pm, and they broadcast the Liberty Center Theater *Rendez-vous des Cajuns* on Saturday evening. During the Festival Internationale, the station broadcasts live from the various stages. It also broadcasts on the Web (http://krvs.louisiana .edu). R&B, hip-hop and rap are featured on 95.5 FM.

Bookstores & Libraries Alexander Books (☎ 337-234-2096), 2001 W Congress St near the university, sells new, used and rare editions as well as periodicals.

The main public library (☎ 337-261-5775), 301 W Congress St in downtown, has public Internet access.

Medical & Emergency Services Lafayette General Medical Center (☎ 337-289-7991) is at 1214 Coolidge Blvd near S College Rd. It runs two Quick Care centers for minor emergencies; one is in the emergency room of the hospital (weekdays noon to 10 pm, weekends 9 am to 9 pm) and another at Southpark Shopping Center near Broussard (☎ 337-232-2273; open weekdays 8 am to 8 pm, weekends 8 am to 4 pm). The Lafayette police department, 731 Jefferson Blvd, can be reached at ☎ 337-261-8630.

Acadian Cultural Center

The Lafayette branch of the Jean Lafitte National Historical Park and Preserve has very good exhibits and artifacts that interpret the distinct Acadian history and heritage in the wetlands and on the prairies. The signage is an interesting mix of English and Cajun French. There's a 40-minute film (with French subtitles) that dramatizes the plight of the 18th-century Acadians at the hands of the British. Rangers speak French and have brochures in French. The shop has a fine collection of books on history and cultural arts as well as CDs.

The center (☎ 337-232-0789), 501 Fisher Rd, is open daily 8 am to 5 pm; admission is free. To reach it from the Evangeline Thruway, follow signs east on E Pinhook Rd, turn right on Surrey St just north of the airport, and then right again on Fisher Rd. It's next to Vermilionville.

Vermilionville

This refined Acadian living history and folklife museum (☎ 337-233-4077), 1600 Surrey St near the airport, spreads out across 23 acres. Nicely landscaped walkways along a bayou and lake lead past craft shops as well as restored cabins and houses typical of Acadian villages from the mid-1700s to late 1800s. Docents in period costumes guide groups through the homes and explain the furnishings, architecture and folkways. Tours depart at 10:15 am and 12:30 and 3 pm; at other times, visitors can follow a walking tour described in a brochure. Craftspeople demonstrate whittling, blacksmithing, weaving and other traditional crafts. Cajun bands perform shows daily in the barn (1:30 and 3:30 pm weekdays, 2 to 5 pm weekends), and there are daily cooking demonstrations with sample tastings (11:30 am and 1:30 pm). A cafe on the premises serves lunch, and a gallery sells items crafted by local artisans. A gift shop has a good assortment of regional books. The museum is open daily from 10 am to 5 pm. Admission is $8 for adults and $5 for students. While here, visit the nearby Acadian Cultural Center.

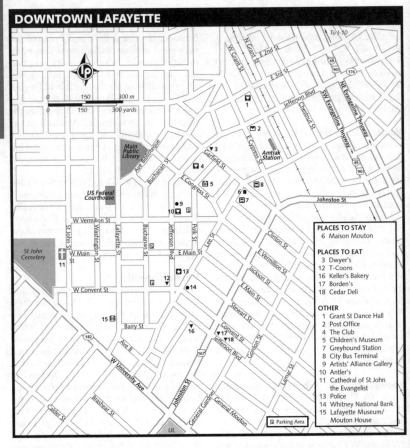

DOWNTOWN LAFAYETTE

To I-10

0　150　300 m
0　150　300 yards

Main Public Library

US Federal Courthouse

St John Cemetery

PLACES TO STAY
6　Maison Mouton

PLACES TO EAT
3　Dwyer's
12　T-Coons
16　Keller's Bakery
17　Borden's
18　Cedar Deli

OTHER
1　Grant St Dance Hall
2　Post Office
4　The Club
5　Children's Museum
7　Greyhound Station
8　City Bus Terminal
9　Artists' Alliance Gallery
10　Antler's
11　Cathedral of St John the Evangelist
13　Police
14　Whitney National Bank
15　Lafayette Museum/ Mouton House

P　Parking Area

Acadian Village

This living-history village (☎ 337-981-2364), 200 Greenleaf Drive on the city's western periphery, is older, more folksy, smaller and more tranquil than Vermilionville. Visitors follow a rippling brick path around a tiny bayou and over bridges to authentically restored houses, craft shops, a church and outbuildings, where signs describe aspects of 19th-century Acadian life. Ducks and geese roam about. Occasional Cajun music performances are held, and special events are hosted here.

The **Mississippi Valley Museum** is a sight in itself – huge paintings by Robert Dafford (whose murals appear on downtown buildings) depict pivotal events in local Native American history, and there are examples of cypress canoes and other Indian artifacts. An Indian historian is usually on hand to provide further explanation.

The village and museum are open daily 10 am to 5 pm. Inclusive admission is $6.50 adults/$2 children (proceeds benefit the local chapter of the Association of Retarded Citizens). From Ambassador Caffery

Parkway, turn west onto Ridge Rd, and then south (left) onto W Broussard Rd (watch for signs).

Children's Museum

In the old brick Heymann's Grocery in the heart of downtown, this museum (☎ 337-232-8500), 201 E Congress St, entertains and educates children ages one to 12 by encouraging learning by doing. There's a hands-on operating room and full-size ambulance, a mini TV studio, a recyclables-into-art station, a bubble area and even an Acadian-style cottage. The museum is open Tuesday to Saturday from 10 am to 5 pm and is closed Sunday and Monday. Admission is $5. Free parking is available at the Polk and Taylor Sts entrances.

Natural History Museum

This glass-walled museum (☎ 337-291-5544), 637 Girard Park Drive, features changing exhibits on southern Louisiana's exotic natural environment and other science and nature displays. The planetarium here has a schedule of shows and telescope observation times. The museum is open weekdays 9 am to 5 pm, Tuesday till 9 pm, weekends 1 to 5 pm; admission is free. It's tucked behind the Heymann Performing Arts Center. This is also the site of Bach Lunch (see Entertainment, later in this section).

University of Louisiana

With 17,000 students and the most diverse student body in the state, UL (formerly the University of Southwestern Louisiana) is the intellectual center of Acadian culture. It's home to the Center for Louisiana Studies, a library with extensive historical archives, the National Wetlands Research Center, and a doctorate program in global Francophonic studies, one of only three such programs in the world. The university also hosts an extensive Elderhostel program covering Cajun culture, music and dance (☎ 337-482-6371).

The highlight of a UL tour for many visitors is **Cypress Lake**, an incongruously civilized swamp in the center of campus behind the student union. The **University Art**

Museum (☎ 337-482-5326) maintains a permanent collection of primarily 18th-, 19th- and 20th-century paintings and photographs by state and American artists, along with some Southern folk art and Japanese prints. It houses them in two locations a block apart: modern Fletcher Hall on E Lewis St and Girard Park Circle and a Greek Revival plantation-style house at 101 Girard Park Drive at St Mary Blvd. They're open weekdays 9 am to 4 pm (Fletcher Hall is also open Saturday 10 am to 4 pm). Admission is free.

Acadiana Park

This 42-acre mature bottomland forest park (☎ 337-291-8448) is preserved by the city in cooperation with the Natural History Museum. A subdivided 3-mile **loop trail** winds under a canopy of hardwoods and over a stream. The park is an oasis in the midst of urbanization for birds, fish and mammals such as squirrels, opossum, raccoons, swamp rabbits, armadillos and even gray foxes. Spring is the best time for spotting the park's 157 bird species. The park is driest in October and November, when most of the flowering plants display a second bloom. From the first summer rain until fall, mosquitoes reign.

The three-story wheelchair-accessible **nature station** offers exhibits on the local habitat along with guided bird walks (which are held 8 am on the first Saturday of the month) and night hikes (last Saturday of the month), both by reservation only. The station is open weekdays 9 am to 5 pm, weekends 11 am to 3 pm. Just south of I-10 exit 103, go to the frontage road along the east side of Evangeline Thruway. Head north (beyond the Super 8) to Alexander St; turn right (east) and follow the signs for a few miles. (Camping is also available here; see Places to Stay.)

Other Attractions

The **Cathedral of St John the Evangelist** (☎ 337-232-1322), on St John St in downtown (look for the 10-story tower), offers daily services and guided tours by request in the dramatic 700-seat Romanesque brick sanctuary built in 1916. A 450-year-old live oak stands alongside. The cemetery just behind the church is worth a look.

The new US federal courthouse on Lafayette St just north of W Vermilion is large and impressive, but its most remarkable feature may well be the pair of 7-foot marble heads flanking each side of the front. The mirror images of blindfolded justice are missing cranial domes, but an optical illusion forces viewers to hopefully imagine brains intact.

The **Lafayette Museum/Mouton House** (☎ 337-234-2208), 1122 Lafayette St, opens the 19th-century home of the city's founder and first Democratic governor to the public. It's open Tuesday through Saturday 9 am to 5 pm, Sunday 3 to 5 pm. Admission is $3 for adults and $1 for students and children. They decorate lavishly at Christmastime.

The **Artists' Alliance Gallery** (☎ 337-233-7518), 551 Jefferson Blvd in downtown, showcases local artists' work. Songwriters perform on Tuesday nights. During the Festival Internationale, works are displayed in the juried Southern Open competition.

Activities

For outdoor adventures, the primary resource is Pack & Paddle (☎ 337-232-5854, 800-458-4560), 601 E Pinhook at Evangeline Thruway. This outfitter schedules kayaking, canoeing and hiking trips throughout the region (advance reservations required). They distribute bike maps and guides, and publish a free tabloid, *Outside Scoop*, listing their full slate of events; it's available in their store and around town. Particularly scenic paddling trips include their sunset tour on Bayou Teche between Loreauville and New Iberia and their Lake Martin tour during the spring and fall bird migrations (around $25 for canoe or kayak, guide and transportation). Recreational maps and information about trips are available online at www.packnpaddle.com.

Special Events

On the second Saturday of each month, galleries, coffeehouses, and restaurants on Jefferson Blvd stay open from 5:30 to 8:30 pm for Artwalk. Many host special events such as artist appearances, readings, and food and drink tastings.

In January, the Boudin Festival takes place just south in Broussard. In late February or early March, Lafayette has Mardi Gras parades, a Courir de Mardi Gras at Vermilionville, a free public ball and a five-day festival preceding Fat Tuesday (☎ 337-235-2471, 800-346-1958). There's also a Krewe des Chiens parade and ball that raises funds for homeless and ill-treated animals (☎ 337-984-7611). In April, Acadian Village hosts the Beef, Rice, and Gravy Cookoff (☎ 337-981-2364); in addition to high-calorie tastings, there are Cajun and zydeco bands.

For six days at the end of April, the free Festival Internationale de Louisiane (☎ 337-232-8086) draws over 150,000 people for music from the French-speaking world (www.festivalinternational.com in English and French). On Sunday night after the last performance, there's a jam session at the Grant St Dance Hall. Also that weekend, Art House Jive is a juried show of work by artists under 21 (attendees must also be under 21; ☎ 337-233-7518).

On the third weekend of August at Blackham Coliseum, the Cajun French Music Association Festival (☎ 337-232-3737) involves Cajun music and an awards ceremony (www.cajunfrenchmusic.org). In mid-September, the Festivals Acadiens (☎ 337-232-3737, 800-346-1958) celebrates Acadian music, food, crafts and wetlands folklife. In December, Cajun and Creole Christmas activities are ubiquitous; Acadian Village becomes a wonderland of lights.

Places to Stay

Lafayette has the widest choices of accommodations in the region, offering nearly 4000 hotel and 60 B&B rooms. Despite the wealth of options, visitors should be aware that the city and surrounding towns can completely fill up for large festivals or on weekends in which several adjoining towns host special events; rates can also skyrocket up to 50%. At these times, make reservations – otherwise, you may end up unexpectedly driving to Baton Rouge for a room.

All the usual chains are present. The budget and moderate motels are relatively new, well maintained and easily accessible. Most offer pools and at least continental breakfast. Budget rates are fairly consistent from around $35 to $45 for doubles. B&B choices are plentiful; if you're looking for a more peaceful setting, consider staying in nearby St Martinville, Breaux Bridge, or Sunset.

Camping The convenient city-run *Acadiana Park* (☎ 337-291-8448 for reservations, 1201 E Alexander St) offers 75 woodsy, basic sites (some for tents only) for $9 a night in a bottomland forest (see Acadiana Park, earlier). It has flush toilets and showers.

On higher ground but more exposed, the *KOA Kampground* (☎ 337-235-2739, 800-224-7724), on I-10 exit 97 in Scott, 5 miles west of town, offers 200 sites and air-conditioned cabins right off the interstate. There are two pools, mini-golf and a playground. Campsites cost $19 a night. One-room cabins sleeping four to six are $38; two-room cabins sleeping six to eight cost $48 (there's a two-night minimum on summer weekends).

Motels The *Super 8 Motel* (☎/fax 337-232-8826, 2224 NE Evangeline Thruway), just south of I-10 exit 103B, is in a developed strip. Singles/doubles go for $33/43 including tax. Guests get a large continental breakfast and have pool access. The decent *Motel 6* (☎ 337-233-2055, fax 269-9267, 2724 NE Evangeline Thruway), just north of I-10 exit 103B, is on the outskirts of town. Rates are $36/40. Just a bit farther north is the slightly worn *Plantation Motor Inn* (☎/fax 337-232-7285, 800-723-8228, 2810 NE Evangeline Thruway), offering singles/doubles for $30/36. Just north of I-10 exit 101, the *Red Roof Inn* (☎ 337-233-3339, 800-843-7663, 1718 N University Ave) is also on the outskirts; rooms here go for $40/50.

Just south of I-10 exit 101, the good-value *Quality Inn* (☎ 337-232-6131, fax 337-232-2682, 800-228-5151, 1605 N University Ave) has rates that start at $45. There are in-room safes, and it's next door to a Cracker Barrel Restaurant. Across the street is a recently renovated *Days Inn* (☎ 337-237-8880, fax 337-235-1386, 1620 N University Ave), which charges $59/62 and allows pets. Both motels have a pool.

If you want to be centrally located but off the noisy strips, try *Travelodge* (☎ 337-234-7402, fax 337-234-7404, 800-578-7878, 1101 W Pinhook Rd), at Audubon just south of the university. Decent rooms go for $48/52.

One of the nicer hotels in town is *La Quinta Inn* (☎ 337-233-5610, fax 337-235-2104, 800-531-5900, 2100 NE Evangeline Thruway). Though it's on a noisy strip, the comfortable rooms ($69) are well insulated and have a recliner. There's a filling continental breakfast and nice pool. It also offers free shuttle service to the airport.

B&Bs You can't get closer to downtown than at the friendly *Maison Mouton* (☎ 337-234-4661, fax 337-235-6755, 402 Garfield St); for those attending the Festival Internationale, it's right behind the main stage (as well as between the Greyhound and city bus station). The 100-year-old inn has been recently renovated, and creatively decorated rooms cost $59 for a shared bath, $89 with private bath.

Near the airport, *Alida's* (☎ 337-264-1191, 800-922-5867, info@alidas.com, 2631 SE Evangeline Thruway) offers four comfortable rooms for $90 to $125, each with private bath, in a pink 1902 Queen Anne house. Gourmet breakfasts are a highlight, and the gracious hosts are knowledgeable about the area. It's at Verot School Rd about 10 minutes from downtown.

T'Frere's (☎/fax 337-984-9347, 800-984-9347, tfreres@mindspring.com, 1905 E Verot School Rd), on a main street farther away from traffic (and walking distance to the zydeco Hamilton Club), offers four rooms in a tidy 1880 two-story house and two garden rooms in a side building. Rates of $80/95 for singles/doubles include a Cajun breakfast. All rooms have private baths.

Places to Eat

Locals seeking a quick, cheap bite all head to a favorite market, convenience store and even gas station, nearly all of which seem to keep a crock pot of hot boudin by the cash register and often serve lunch plates. The visitor information office has a handy English-French brochure called 'The Boudin Trail' that steers folks to the links.

For early starts or late nights, *Dwyer's* (☎ 337-235-9364, 323 Jefferson Blvd), in downtown, serves very affordable and plentiful breakfasts, daily plate lunches (order at the back counter) and a large menu of seafood and sandwiches at tables inside or on the patio. Down the street *T-Coons* (☎ 337-232-3803, 740 Jefferson Blvd) is known for its zydeco breakfasts and lunches of rice and beans with homemade sausage, fried catfish, pork-and-turkey jambalaya, and plate lunches; it is open weekdays.

Not far away is the Syrian-owned *Cedar Deli* (☎ 337-233-5460, 1115 Jefferson Blvd), serving falafel, veggie and meat muffulettas, gyros, chicken tandoori and Middle Eastern appetizers for breakfast and lunch (closed Sunday). The nearby '60s-era *Borden's* (1103 Jefferson Blvd), at Johnston St, dishes up fountain treats and milkshakes. Enjoy it all in red vinyl booths under Elsie the Cow's wide-eyed gaze. If you'd prefer an éclair or mini pecan pie, head for *Keller's Bakery* (1012 Jefferson Blvd); it's open daily.

Several restaurants offer one-stop live nightly Cajun entertainment and dancing along with full menus of regional cuisine. All of these are firmly on the beaten path and often draw a family-oriented crowd. *Prejean's* (☎ 337-896-3247, 3480 Hwy 167 N) is lined with chefs' cooking trophies, as well as stuffed critters including an 8-foot gator. Entrees start around $15. You could also choose a meal's worth of appetizers such as alligator, boudin balls and popcorn crawfish (from $7). The bands start at 7 pm. Prejean's (PRAY-jhonz) is visible off I-49 near Evangeline Downs; from exit 2 go north on Hwy 167 almost a mile. On the south side of town near Ambassador Caffery Parkway, *Randol's* (☎ 337-981-7080, 2320 W Kaliste Saloom Rd) offers Cajun dishes that run $12 to $17. It has a large and lively dance floor. Though whole families meet up here, it tends to draw an older crowd. (Another option is nearby Mulate's, which is covered in Places to Eat & Drink in the Breaux Bridge section, earlier in this chapter.)

Deano's (☎ 337-233-5446, 305 Bertrand Drive), three blocks north of Johnston near the west side of campus, is famous for its Cajun pizzas. It also serves po-boys, pastas and salads. It's open Monday to Saturday for lunch and dinner (Sunday for dinner only).

The simple *Green Olive* (☎ 337-234-0004, 2441 W Congress St), out past the Cajun-Dome, offers Lebanese specialties, including many meatless dishes. Their $6 vegetarian combination plate includes a stuffed grape leaf, falafel, tabbouleh, lentils-and-rice mujadara and hummus with pita bread. It's open for lunch on weekdays. A wholly vegetarian place near campus is the *Whole Wheatery Eatery* (☎ 337-269-0144, 927 Harding St), at Travis St. It's open weekdays for breakfast and lunch, Saturday for lunch, and adjoins a health-food store.

La Fête de Lafayette (☎ 337-981-9979, 4401 Johnston St), west of College Rd, offers an all-you-can-eat Cajun seafood buffet with a daunting variety of boiled, fried, stuffed or smothered choices. The $8 lunch buffet is available 11 am till 2 pm, the $17 dinner buffet 5 to 9 pm (Friday and Saturday till 10 pm; closed Sunday and Monday). There's also a regular menu.

A step up is the grilled seafood at *Charley G's* (☎ 337-981-0108, 3809 Ambassador Caffery Parkway). It's open weekdays for lunch and Monday to Saturday for dinner. Sunday, when there's a live jazz trio, it's brunch only. Lunch entrees cost around $15, dinner entrees a bit more.

In a category by itself is the elegant *Café Vermilionville* (☎ 337-237-0100, 1304 W Pinhook Rd), near S College Rd in the historic 1818 Vermilionville Inn. Under the eye of chef-owner Ken Veron, the kitchen turns out award-winning seafood dishes laced with fresh herbs. It's open weekdays for lunch and dinner, Saturday for dinner only.

Expect to pay at least $20 for lunch and $30 for dinner (without wine). No tie required.

Entertainment

To find out who's playing throughout Acadiana, look around town for the free weekly *Times*. Upcoming performance schedules are also broadcast on Radio Acadie KRVS 88.7 FM.

In temperate months (April through June and September through October), the weekend gets started at the free *Downtown Alive* block party from around 6 to 8 pm on Friday only (check the area bounded by Polk, Garfield, Taylor and Congress Sts, but you'll hear the band wherever it is). Favorite local bands – playing everything from rockabilly and country to R&B and blues, with plenty of Cajun and zydeco music – pack the streets with revelers, stands sell beer and snacks, and the party continues at downtown bars. March through May and mid-September through mid-October, the grounds of the Natural History Museum are the site of free Friday concerts from noon to 1 pm; though the series is called *Bach Lunch*, the musical offerings are diverse.

El Sid O's (☎ 337-237-1959, 1523 Martin Luther King Drive), at St Antoine St, is a big and welcoming cinder-block joint famous as a venue for zydeco and blues on Thursday, Friday and Saturday nights starting around 9:30 pm. The kitchen out back cooks up chicken, fish or pork-chop plates. From Willow St, turn north on St Antoine St; you'll see it in a half mile. The *Hamilton Club* (☎ 337-991-0783, 1808 Verot School Rd) is a zydeco spot south of the airport.

In downtown, the cavernous *Grant St Dance Hall* (☎ 337-237-2255, 113 W Grant St) near the train depot books a variety of bigger acts (some nationally known) including blues, reggae, classic rock and a good dose of zydeco. *Antler's* (☎ 337-233-7518, 555 Jefferson) has a variety of live acts Wednesday through Saturday. The *Club* (425 Jefferson Blvd) caters to a gay clientele and has a dance floor (look for the rainbow flag); it's open nights Wednesday through Sunday.

Bob's Pub (☎ 337-984-9540, 104 Republic St) is a comfortable place to hear live blues Wednesday through Saturday. It's in the strip mall across from Randol's on W Kaliste Saloom Rd.

The popular *Poet's* (☎ 337-235-2355, 119 James Comeaux Rd), tucked in the shopping center behind Pinhook and Kaliste Saloom Rds near Kmart, draws clean-cut college-plus audiences for loud dance music, including rock & blues, swamp pop, and zydeco.

Spectator Sports

The **CajunDome**, on W Congress St a couple miles west of downtown Lafayette, is the home of the University of Louisiana's Ragin' Cajuns ('Geaux Cajuns!' is their rally cry). The CajunDome also holds major concerts, theatrical performances, and fairs and festivals. The Lady Cajuns, a fast-pitch softball team, are often regional and national champions; they play in the spring at Lady Cajun Field. For sporting events tickets, call ☎ 337-482-2586.

The horse-racing track a mile north of I-10 on I-49 is **Evangeline Downs** (☎ 337-896-7223). It's also commonly cited as a landmark when giving directions. When the owners wanted to add slots and video poker, the antigambling sentiment in the parish prevented them, so they have decided to build a new and improved track north along I-49 just inside St Landry Parish.

Getting There & Away

Lafayette is most practically approached by car, but it has more varied alternatives to personal automobiles than many cities this size.

Air Lafayette Regional Airport (☎ 337-266-4400) is served by four major carriers and their subsidiaries: American Airlines/American Eagle (eight daily flights from Dallas), Delta/Atlantic Southeast (three daily from Dallas and Atlanta), Continental Express (six daily from Houston) and Northwest Airlines/KLM/Northwest Airlink (three daily from Memphis). US Airways and

United also have connections. There's an information desk (☎ 337-266-4414) on the 1st floor of the terminal. The airport is next to Evangeline Thruway (Hwy 90/I-49) south of town. Avis, Hertz and National have car-rental offices here. Airport Shuttle (☎ 337-993-8511) offers rides to town 24 hours a day for about $12. Call at least 15 minutes in advance.

Bus Greyhound runs bus service out of its station (☎ 337-235-1541) at Clinton and Lee Sts near downtown and a block from the main city-bus transfer station at Lee and Garfield Sts. The area's not bad and a huge police station is nearby. The station is within walking distance of downtown businesses, but travelers will likely need a cab to reach their destinations. There are 11 buses a day to and from New Orleans ($17.50 one way), 11 buses daily to and from Baton Rouge ($12.50), and six buses daily to and from Lake Charles ($11.50).

Train The Lafayette station is decrepit, but it's conveniently located near a huge police station and a block from transit terminals for Greyhound and city buses.

Car Lafayette is 52 miles east of Baton Rouge, 130 miles east of New Orleans, 89 miles south of Alexandria, and 71 miles west of Lake Charles.

I-10 runs east/west connecting Lafayette with Baton Rouge and Lake Charles. Parallel to it and just to the south is Hwy 90, which runs west to Rayne and Crowley.

I-49/Hwy 90 runs north/south connecting the city with Opelousas and with New Iberia, Morgan City, and Houma; in town it's called Evangeline Thruway. Parallel scenic Hwy 182 runs north through Sunset, Opelousas, and Washington; south of town it heads to New Iberia.

Hwy 94 northeast of town runs to Breaux Bridge. Hwy 167 runs southwest to Abbeville.

Bicycle The outfitter Pack & Paddle (☎ 337-232-5854), 601 E Pinhook Rd at the Evangeline Thruway near the airport, distributes maps and guides to more than 60 miles of marked bike routes in the region. However, no store in town rents bikes.

Getting Around

A car is indispensable for seeing the widely dispersed sights.

Car rentals are available from Thrifty Car Rental (☎ 337-237-1282), 401 E Pinhook Rd; Enterprise (☎ 337-237-2864), 1800 W Pinhook Rd; and Budget (☎ 337-233-8888), 1711 Jefferson Blvd in downtown. The latter offers local pickup and drop-off.

Driving in Lafayette is not a relaxing experience. The city is growing quickly, and road improvements aren't quite keeping pace with traffic. Many of the main thoroughfares have surprisingly high speed limits and intermittent access to frontage roads, where the businesses are. Jumping on and off these frontage roads can be harrowing, and if you miss your destination, it can take a while to backtrack.

City of Lafayette Transit (Colt; ☎ 337-291-8570) runs buses from a convenient central terminal (☎ 337-237-7945) between the Greyhound station and the Amtrak station. Buses operate from 6:30 am to 6:30 pm Monday to Saturday (no service on most major holidays). The fare is 45¢ for adults and 30¢ for children five to 12 (exact fare required); transfers are free. Routes are not designed with tourists in mind, yet a few routes serve major sights. Bus No 15 goes downtown and out to the CajunDome; bus No 25 goes to UL. A bus route map is available at 1515 E University Ave at the Pinhook Rd intersection.

Try Affordable Cabs of Acadiana (☎ 337-234-2111) or call Yellow Checker Cab (☎ 337-237-5701).

The Prairie

As the elevation slowly climbs to the north, the land dries out a bit, crypts in cemeteries rise only a few inches above ground, and highway routes and street grids become far more predictable than in the southern wetlands. The simple geometry of grain silos and elevators echoes that of Midwestern prairies, and in fact, both regions were once covered with tall prairie grasses and shared many species of wildflowers. Transplanted Midwestern farmers were some of the earliest rice growers in the region.

The region is a center for Cajun and zydeco music, and its spoon-struck washboard rhythms and insistent accordion chords permeate the local life of rice cultivation, fishing camps, crawfish boils, family-oriented traditions and *le courir*. Unlike many areas, there's actually local music on the radio (try KBON 101.1 FM). The Central Acadiana Gateway provides history and current information about the region (www.lsue.edu/acadgate).

LAFAYETTE TO OPELOUSAS
Sunset

North of Lafayette and just outside Sunset, the **Chretien Point Plantation** (☎ 337-662-5876, 800-880-7050) opens the 1831 Greek Revival house and grounds of a former 10,000-acre cotton plantation to the public for guided tours and B&B accommodations. The plantation is rife with legend. A young Hypolite Chretien (later the plantation owner) saved the life of another soldier in the War of 1812; that soldier happened to be Jean Lafitte. Years later, Lafitte contacted Chretien, by then a wealthy planter, and convinced him to act as a middleman for Lafitte's stolen booty. After Chretien's death, pirates descended on the plantation, then run by his wife, who shot and killed a would-be thief; traces of bloodstains remain on the stairs under the carpet. In less glorious days following the Civil War, the house was used for storing hay and keeping livestock.

Now completely restored, the house – a rare pairing of a Greek Revival exterior with a French floor plan – is open daily for tours ($6.50) and B&B lodging. Rates range from $110 for downstairs rooms to $225 for the upstairs room with its own jacuzzi. Children are welcome. From I-49 exit 11, head south on Hwy 93 to Hwy 182; turn right and head through Sunset; turn left on Hwy 93,

right on Hwy 356, and right again on Chretien Point Rd.

If railroads appeal to you more than plantations, head to *La Caboose B&B* (☎ 337-662-5401, 145 S Budd St, 70584), one block off Hwy 182. Just a few minutes from I-49, the Brinkhauses put up guests in their comfortable caboose, depot, train car and ticket office. The accommodations face three acres of lovely gardens. Rates are $75 to $95.

Grand Coteau

Between Opelousas and Lafayette, the tiny community of Grand Coteau is set on an ancient Mississippi River levee *(coteau* means 'ridge'). It's home to the landmark **Academy of the Sacred Heart** (☎ 337-662-5275), off Church St. Founded in 1821 by a local couple to provide Catholic education for the parish, Sacred Heart was the scene of a bona fide miracle in 1866. Today, a shrine marks the place where a dying young girl saw the saintly vision of the Blessed John Berchmans, who as a result of his appearances was later canonized a saint. Also on the grounds are a school, chapel and Jesuit retreat house, built in the Spanish Mission style around 1850. Guided weekday tours ($5) are available; it's best to call first to confirm times. The neighborhood around the academy has an interesting variety of historic homes.

On Hwy 93 right across from Sacred Heart in a former country store is *Catahoula's* (☎ 337-662-2275), which puts a sophisticated twist on traditional Cajun fare for moderate prices. It's open for dinner Tuesday through Saturday and for brunch on Sunday.

Grand Couteau is just east of I-49 on Hwy 93.

Church Point

West of Sunset (on Hwy 178) and 16 miles north of I-10 (on Hwy 5) lies the small community of Church Point, known for celebrating its French-Acadian traditions, particularly Cajun music. Church Point (population 4500) claims to be home to more Cajun musicians (including the

'Father of Cajun Music' Iry Lejeaunethan) than anywhere else in Acadiana. On Wednesday nights from late spring to early fall, there's free Cajun music at Le Parc du Vieux Depot (the old train depot). Handmade Cajun musical instruments are sold at Le Vieux Moulin (the Old Mill; ☎ 337-684-1200), 402 W Canal St.

The town's Courir de Mardi Gras is held the Sunday before Mardi Gras. Riders assemble at the town's Saddle Tramp Riding Club (☎ 337-684-2739), 1036 E Ebey St, early in the morning, and the party starts here and then moves over to Main St for the afternoon parade as the riders return for more fais-do-do. The party shuts down by 6 pm to commemorate the beginning of Lent.

The town's Buggy Festival (☎ 337-684-2739) on the first weekend in June harkens back to the 1920s, when worshipers from all over rode horse-drawn buggies to attend Sunday services at local churches.

OPELOUSAS
• pop 19,000

The third oldest city in Louisiana, Opelousas is the seat of St Landry Parish and the largest city in the prairie region. Its position at the intersection of I-49, Hwy 182

King of Zydeco

Clifton Chenier (1923–87), a native of St Landry Parish, is widely credited with popularizing zydeco music. Nicknamed the King of Zydeco, Chenier (pronounced sha-NEAR) toured the US and Europe with his Red Hot Louisiana Band and often performed wearing a crown. Such headgear might have appeared ridiculous on a musician of lesser stature and skill, but on Chenier, it was fitting, and he wore it with dignity and pride.

Zydeco, the traditional music of black Creole southern Louisianans, developed concurrently with Cajun music, and it similarly featured accordions and washboards with lyrics sung in a local French dialect. It was then called 'la la' music and inspired the la la dance (the two-step). Chenier's landmark lament, 'Zydeco Sont Pas Sale,' is from a dance tune in both the Creole and Cajun traditions called 'Les Haricots Sont Pas Sales' – Louisiana French for 'the snap beans aren't salted,' a reference to times so hard you can't even afford the salt pork to flavor the beans. The corruption of *les haricots* into *zydeco* is how many believe the genre got its name. (Dissenters suggest the term may actually be rooted in West African languages.) The term 'zydeco' also refers to the party or venue at which zydeco music is played.

Chenier melded traditional zydeco sounds with a hard-driving blues beat and electric guitars. The recipient of a Grammy and a National Endowment for the Arts Heritage Award, Chenier inspired many Creole musicians, and his legacy continues today. While such performers as Beausoleil, Queen Ida and Buckwheat Zydeco continue to bring the music of Clifton Chenier to national audiences, keepers of the zydeco flame in south Louisiana include Boozoo Chavis, Geno Delafose, Keith Frank, Walter Mouton, Chris Ardoin, Ann Goodly, CJ Chenier (Clifton's son), and Nathan and the Zydeco Cha Chas. 'Nouveau zydeco,' which blends traditional zydeco with the heavy bass of hip hop and edginess of rap, is played by the likes of Rosie Ledet and Lil' Pookie. All of these artists draw devoted crowds of dancers to clubs and festivals throughout the region, and many performers extend their range by traveling to Texas and California to play for homesick former Louisianans. Despite their skill and talent, none has attained the throne built by Clifton Chenier.

and Hwy 190 makes it a natural thoroughfare for folks seeking more far-flung attractions, clubs, accordion factories and boudin markets. The town is known as the birthplace of zydeco, as well as of Clifton Chenier. Chef Paul Prudhomme was born here, too, as was Olympic gold medalist Rodney Milburn, who set a world record in the 120m hurdles at the 1972 Munich Games and was inducted into the National Track and Field Hall of Fame.

In town, Hwy 190 becomes Landry St running west and Vine St running east; Hwy 182 is Main St. The historic city center revolves around the county courthouse square bounded by Market, Court, Landry and Bellevue Sts, which is surrounded by 19th-century shops and offices. Every Friday from late March to early June, weekends kick off at 5:30 pm with street concerts in downtown at Bellevue and Main Sts.

Three blocks away near City Hall, the **Opelousas Museum & Interpretive Center** (☎ 337-948-2589), 329 N Main St/Hwy 182, focuses on the city's Native American, Acadian and Creole history. Visitors can watch zydeco concert videos from the center's large archives. There's also stunning photos of 1940s Louisiana from the Standard Oil Project. For maps and information about special events, head to the Opelousas Tourist Information Center (☎ 337-948-6263, 800-424-5442), 941 E Vine St/Hwy 190. Clustering around it is a half a dozen restored buildings. The town's Web site is www.lsue.edu/acadgate/opelous.htm. You'll find the St Landry Parish Web site at www.cajuntravel.com. Greyhound stops in town at 238 W Landry St.

In April, humorists descend on the town for an International Cajun Joke Telling Contest (☎ 337-948-4731). In early May, the town hosts the Cajun French Music Association's Music Festival (formerly held in Eunice). The Saturday before Father's Day in June, the town celebrates Juneteenth with an African-American folklife festival (☎ 337-826-3934). During Labor Day weekend, the Southwest Louisiana Zydeco Music Festival (☎ 337-942-2392, www.zydeco.org) in nearby Plaisance spotlights a 15-hour concert and various activities; a kick-off concert at one of the local zydeco clubs usually occurs the night before. On the last full weekend in October, the town goes crazy over yams at the Yambilee, a 50-year tradition. Every Wednesday, Thursday, and Saturday evening, KSLO 1230 AM plays Cajun music.

Places to Stay

Simple and clean rooms at the *Town House Motel* (☎ 337-948-4488, 343 W Landry St) cost $30/40 for a single/double. Rooms at the *Best Western* (☎ 337-942-5540, 888-942-5540), on Frontage Rd along I-49, go for $61/66. For a leap into blissful luxury, head to the women-owned *Estorage House B&B* (☎ 337-942-8151, 417 N Market St). Large rooms in the opulent 1827 home are furnished with antiques and cost $125, including full breakfast.

Places to Eat

Right on the main square, the landmark *Palace Café* (☎ 337-942-2142) has been drawing a great mix of people since 1954 with its inexpensive Southern breakfasts, plate-lunch specials and fried chicken dinners; it closes at 3 pm Sunday.

South of downtown, *Kelly's Country Meat Block & Diner* (☎ 337-942-7466, 1531 S Vine St) serves tasty seafood or pork plate lunches and fried chicken for around $6. On Thursday and Sunday, there's barbecue. It's open Monday to Saturday for lunch and dinner but closes at 2 pm on Sunday.

Entertainment

Around Opelousas are two famous zydeco venues. North of town on Hwy 182 a few miles from the square, *Slim's Y-Ki-Ki* (☎ 337-942-9980) is across from the Piggly Wiggly. In Lawtell 8 miles west of Opelousas, *Richard's* (REE-shardz; ☎ 337-543-8233) is on a rural stretch of Hwy 190. On weekend nights, you should have little trouble finding either place; if a band is playing, the buildings are surrounded by cars, as folks come from all over to hear the likes of Chris Ardoin, Keith Frank, Boozoo Chavis and T-Mamou.

WASHINGTON

Six miles north of Opelousas on either Hwy 182 or I-49 (exit 25), this sleepy town on a bluff, settled in 1720, holds a large restored historic district with several B&Bs and antique shops. At the head of navigation on Bayou Courtableau, Washington boomed with activity in the late 1800s, shipping out cotton, lumber, sugar and cattle, and becoming the largest inland steamboat port between New Orleans and St Louis. Wealthy merchants, brokers and steamboat captains built the antebellum houses that remain in the historic district today. In fact, 80% of the buildings in town are now on the National Register of Historic Places.

Begin a tour at the **Washington Museum & Tourist Center** (☎ 337-826-3627) at the town's only traffic light, on the corner of Main and Dejean Sts. The museum explains the town's history and distributes a self-guided walking-tour map. It's open daily and is closed for lunch from noon to 1 pm. The town hosts its Festival du Courtableau the third weekend in March and a Heritage Festival in May.

The **Hinckley House** (☎ 337-826-0397), 405 E Dejean St, has been in the same family since the 18th century. The cypress house is constructed with wooden pegs, and its original plaster walls are bound with cattle and deer hair. It and several other homes in the historic district open their doors for personal tours by advance reservation only (most can be arranged at the museum).

Four blocks east of the museum on Dejean St is **Magnolia Ridge**, a plantation house built in 1830 and its grounds. Though the home is a private residence, its owners have opened 6 acres of landscaped grounds and 3 miles of paved trails to the public from dawn to dusk. Visitors are free to enjoy thousands of daylilies and a small swamp, and to bird watch in a meadow. Parking is on Prescott St.

Plenty of antique stores line Main St/ Hwy 182. Six blocks east of Main St, on Vine St, the **Antique School Mall** in the former Washington High School houses over 100 antique dealers. It's open weekends.

Several B&Bs offer pampered overnight lodging in historic homes filled with antiques. One block off Main St, *Camellia Cove* (☎ 337-826-7362, 211 W Hill St), at St John St, provides three huge guest rooms – two that share a bath and one with a private bath ($75 to $85) – in an 1823 house on 2 acres. At the corner of Sittig, *De la Morandiere* (☎ 337-826-3510, 509 St John St), built around 1830, offers two rooms, both with private baths ($75 to $95 per night).

Stop for a drink or bowl of gumbo ($8 for a meal-size bowl) at *Jack Womack's Steamboat Warehouse* (☎ 337-826-7227) on Main St, a bayouside restaurant in an 1830 steamboat warehouse. It's open Tuesday through Saturday for dinner; on Sunday, it's open for lunch only, and is closed on Monday. Adjacent to the restaurant, Frankie Elder rents two modern *multiroom cottages* sleeping up to four for $88 (☎ 337-826-7227).

VILLE PLATTE & AROUND
• pop 10,000

About 20 miles northwest of Opelousas on Hwy 167 is Ville Platte, named for this last stretch of level prairie bordering the rolling hill region to the north. The seat of Evangeline Parish, it's also the 'Smoked Meats Capital of the World,' and on the last weekend in June, crowds arrive for Le Festival de Viande Boucanée, celebrating this specialty. The town's Cotton Festival during the second weekend in October features a knightly *tournoi*; though this jousting tournament once featured dueling horsemen, riders now use lances to collect seven iron rings. The town also hosts a gumbo festival the first Saturday in November. The Chamber of Commerce (☎ 337-363-1878), 306 W Main St, can give you exact upcoming dates and city maps. Greyhound stops at Mikey's Donuts on W Main St, half a mile from downtown. (Main St is also Hwy 167.)

Open since 1956, the landmark **Floyd's Record Shop** (☎ 337-363-2138), 434 E Main St, maintains the largest collection of Southern Louisiana music around (closed Sunday). In addition to zydeco, Cajun, and swamp pop recordings, the store sells oldies on 45rpm records. Manager Cecil Fontenot knows the music and its musicians; he also builds accordions 'just for fun.' Owner Floyd Soileau, one of the main promoters of the region's music, runs a studio down the street where he produces recordings of local musicians on various labels. Tune in to Ville Platte's KVPI at 1050 AM/92.5 FM for local Cajun music broadcasts.

The **Platte Motel** (☎ *337-363-2148, 1636 W Main St*) has simple rooms ranging from $30 to $40 for singles or doubles. It's about a mile west of downtown. East of the Greyhound stop, on Hwy 167, **Best Western** (☎ *337-360-9961*) has single/double rooms for $61/68.

A block from Floyd's is a favorite barbecue joint, the **Pig Stand** (☎ *337-363-2883, 318 E Main St*). It goes beyond its popular pork barbecue to offer exotic sausages and stews with its trademark onion-and-garlic sauce. Hefty plate lunches cost $5. It's open for breakfast, lunch and dinner, and is often open late.

On Lasalle at the train tracks, the **Whistle Stop** serves some of the best boudin in town. The ascendant **Kernie's Restaurant** (☎ *337-2756*), on Tate Cove Rd, serves blackened redfish and such novelties as crawfish-stuffed filet mignon. To get there, head north of town on Hwy 29, and turn left on Tate Cove Rd; it's about 3 miles farther on the left. On the west side of town, the popular **Jungle Dinner Club** (☎ *337-363-9103, 1636 W Main St*) serves tasty po-boys for lunch and a large menu of fried and broiled seafood and steaks for dinner; it is closed on Sunday.

Chicot State Park & Louisiana State Arboretum

Here in south-central Louisiana, the 6400-acre state park and adjacent 300-acre arboretum encompass a sloping forested terrain that contrasts sharply with the flat prairie to the south. Chicot State Park (☎ 337-363-2403, 888-226-7652) is 6 miles north of Ville Platte along Hwy 3042. Surrounding 2000-acre Lake Chicot, there are boat launches, fishing piers, a pool (open summer only) and 22 miles of trail through the bottomland hardwood forest. The trail is

suitable for hiking, backpacking and mountain biking.

Twenty-seven fully equipped and air-conditioned lakefront cabins sleep four ($45) or six ($60); lodge rooms sleep groups of nine or 12 ($90). Some beds are in twin bunks. Bring your own towels. The park has over 200 campsites in two areas: those at the south landing are wooded, convenient, and a bit noisy when the park is full; those at the north landing are quieter. Sites cost $12 a night with hookups, $10 without. Admission is $2 per car.

The Louisiana State Arboretum (☎ 337-363-6289) preserves a mature forest dominated by beech and magnolia. Several miles of nature trails wind through the woodlands; signs identify native Louisiana plants. The arboretum is 8 miles north of Ville Platte off Hwy 3042, north of the main entrance to the state park.

Crooked Creek Recreation Area

Northwest of Ville Platte on Crooked Creek Reservoir, this parish park (☎ 337-599-2661) has a campground and offers opportunities to swim at a small beach, fish, boat, and water-ski. Sites are $12 for RVs, $10 for tents in a tent-only area near the lake (though unfortunately far from the bathhouse). Day-use admission is $2 per person. To reach the park from Ville Platte, head north on Hwy 167 for 10 miles to Bayou Chicot, and turn left on Hwy 106, which turns into Hwy 3197 after crossing Hwy 13. The park is about 6 miles down Hwy 3197 (follow the signs).

MAMOU

Tiny Mamou is about 15 miles west of Ville Platte (west along Hwy 10 and south on Hwy 13) and 10 miles north of Eunice (on Hwy 13). Six days of the week, it's a sleepy town where finding a bite to eat can be a challenge. But Saturday morning a few townsfolk head into downtown to meet the crowds arriving from Texas, Mississippi, Tennessee and the rest of the world. Everyone heads straight to **Fred's Lounge**, which is open six rollicking hours a week (see the boxed text 'No Standing on the Jukebox').

No Standing on the Jukebox

Tante Sue, her face framed by a halo of gray curls, is swigging Hot Damn cinnamon schnapps from a hip flask, squeezing her chest in time to the music as if playing an anthropomorphic accordion. Elegantly dressed elderly gents lead ladies young and old to the tiny dance floor, as a gaggle of middle-aged couples waltz with unstudied ease around the band. College kids from Baton Rouge gawk in the corner tightly clasping cans of Bud, and a few Australians are doing the same. It's 9:30 am on a Saturday morning, and **Fred's Lounge** (☎ 337-468-5411, 337-360-8390) is at full tilt.

Since 1950, this Saturday tradition has lured folks out of bed to the nondescript bar on 6th St, the main drag through Mamou. And for those lucky enough to squeeze through the front door, it may well be the best free entertainment to be had in Louisiana. The doors open at 8 am each Saturday, and from 9 am to 1 pm, a top-notch Cajun band broadcasts live from the bar over KVPI 92.5 FM, playing loping accordion-and drum-fueled waltzes interspersed with commentary in English and French. When Fred's quiets down around 2 pm, the party continues at one of the five other bars in Mamou's block-long commercial center. If beer for breakfast has left you with the hungries, head for eats in Eunice or Ville Platte.

Mamou was one of the first towns to revive Courir de Mardi Gras, and nowadays Mamou's celebration is the best known and most raucous of all. On the Monday night before Mardi Gras, there's a street party. On Tuesday, the riders take off, and the waiting crowd parties; when the riders return, the party just gets bigger. The town also hosts a Cajun Music Festival in May.

The aging **Hotel Cazan** (☎ 337-468-7187) on 6th St downtown across from Fred's has sparsely furnished rooms that have seen better days, but they fill up on Friday nights and during festivals. It was recently closed for renovations; call for prices and availability. The downstairs restaurant and bar were also closed.

After dancing all morning, go to **Ortego's Meat Market** (☎ 337-468-3746), around the corner from Fred's on South St, where they make a good, lightly-spiced boudin sausage. Locals vouch for their tasso (spicy, smoked pork or beef) as well. And if you really want to make friends at Fred's, stop off here beforehand to purchase a few pounds of boudin for the crowd. The 24-hour **Shell** gas station at the north edge of town dishes out simple breakfasts and Creole plates of fried chicken and rice and beans for around $2; a few benches are available inside.

Another unusual bar is the peculiarly swank **Holiday Lounge**, in a field west of Hwy 13 at the southern Mamou turnoff. Formerly a gaming house, it sports extensive Naugahyde and fake tropical flora. At night, the blinking neon is visible from the highway.

EUNICE
• pop 12,000

Founded in 1895, this friendly farm town has top-notch music venues, cultural museums and festivals that together have earned it a reputation as the family-oriented center for prairie Cajun heritage. Visitors can walk between most of the town's main attractions, which are sprinkled around the compact downtown bordered by S First St/Hwy 13, Laurel St/Hwy 190, Fourth St and Park Ave. The town is 20 miles west of Opelousas on Hwy 190 and about 20 miles north of I-10 exit 80 at Crowley. Greyhound stops in town (Baton Rouge $14.50 one way, New Orleans $26).

Eunice hosts the World Championship Crawfish Étouffée Cook-Off (the last Sunday in March unless it's Easter), a Courir de Mardi Gras and parade (from Sunday evening through Tuesday), and the Cajun Prairie Folklife Festival in mid-October. The chamber of commerce (☎ 337-457-2565, 800-222-2342) operates a visitor center, which is downtown on Hwy 13; it distributes maps and calendars of events. A block away, the mayor's office at city hall

(☎ 337-457-7389) can also provide useful information.

In May 2000, a train carrying dangerous chemicals derailed and caught fire near downtown; exploding train cars forced 2000 residents to be evacuated.

Prairie Acadian Cultural Center

In downtown at the corner of Third St and Park Ave adjacent to the Liberty Theatre, the center (☎ 337-457-8490) is a part of Jean Lafitte National Historical Park and Preserve. Displays introduce visitors to the Acadian prairie heritage, noting that more Caribbean immigrants settled here than in other parts of Acadiana, infusing the prairie with its still pronounced Creole heritage. Other exhibits relate the history of the region's cattle ranches, rice industry, and a Courir de Mardi Gras. The center helps operate the Liberty Theatre next door (call ☎ 337-457-7389 for programming information); there are craft demonstrations from 3 to 6 pm on Saturday. It hosts an Acadian jam session from 2 to 4:30 pm Sunday. The gift shop has a good selection of books. The center is open daily 8 am to 5 pm (Saturday till 6 pm); admission is free.

Liberty Center Theatre

This restored 1924 theater (☎ 337-457-7389), at the corner of S Second St and Park Ave, is best known for its *Rendez-vous des Cajuns*, a Saturday-night performance broadcast on local radio stations. The *Rendez-vous* features traditional Cajun and zydeco music and dance in sort of a Grand Ole Opry format. Bergen Angeley serves as the bilingual emcee, with his French and English quickening into a snappy Cajun Franglais. Many old-time couples and families circle the dance floor below the stage. Tickets go on sale at 4 pm, and the show runs from 6 to 8 pm. Admission is $3, children under 12 are free.

Other Downtown Attractions

The small but interesting **Cajun Music Hall of Fame** (☎ 337-457-6534), 240 First St at the end of Park Ave, showcases the photos of inductees as well as the year's nominees. It also displays instruments and memorabilia. The curators are knowledgeable about Cajun music and culture. The museum is open Tuesday through Saturday 9 am to 5 pm (8:30 am to 4:30 pm in winter; closed Sunday and Monday year-round).

A few doors down the block in the historic train depot that put Eunice on the map, the **Eunice Museum** (☎ 337-457-6540), 220 S First St at Park Ave, is overflowing with memorabilia donated by locals. Courir de Mardi Gras costumes are interesting, and the depot is itself evocative. It's open Tuesday to Saturday 8 am to 5 pm (closed between noon and 1 pm for lunch and all day Sunday and Monday). Admission is free.

Music Machine (☎ 337-457-4846), 235 W Walnut Ave, is a record shop that carries exclusively southern Louisiana music. The staff is extremely knowledgeable, and they mail-order hundreds of titles of Cajun, zydeco, swamp pop, compilation and festival recordings. It's open daily.

Just outside downtown, the **Cajun Prairie Restoration Project** (☎ 337-457-2016), at Martin Luther King Drive and Magnolia St, preserves a small piece of the once unbroken prairie.

Savoy Music Center

This music store (☎ 337-457-9563), on Hwy 190 about 3 miles east of downtown, houses the accordion factory of famed musician Marc Savoy (sahv-WAH). A key advocate for and promoter of Cajun music, Savoy has been featured in two films by Les Blank, *Laissez les Bons Temps Rouler* and *Marc and Ann*. Most Saturday mornings, Savoy hosts a Cajun music jam session here from around 10 am to noon; his wife, Ann, a guitarist, often joins him (her book *Cajun Music: A Reflection of a People* is a must for serious aficionados). The rest of the week, it's fascinating to see the artistry and variety of accordions in the shop, and there are CDs and cassettes for sale. It's open Tuesday through Saturday. Look for the huge Savoy Music Co sign 3 miles east of downtown (it's invisible to eastbound travelers); the store is west of the Cajun Campground.

Places to Stay

The well-maintained **Cajun Campground** (☎ 337-457-5753), on Hwy 190, 5 miles east of downtown, offers hookup sites for RVs

Le Courir de Mardi Gras

A Mardi Gras spectacle unique to Cajun Country is 'le courir' – a horseback run through the countryside held in Cajun prairie towns north and west of Lafayette. The ritual has its roots in the medieval tradition of ceremonial begging and resembles Christmas 'mumming' in Europe and the West Indies. On or around Mardi Gras, bands of masked and costumed men ride from house to house 'begging' for ingredients to add to a community gumbo in exchange for singing, dancing or clowning antics. A traditional Mardi Gras song is sung in French, recalling medieval French folk music.

Typical courir costumes and characters are quite different from the refined or outrageous dress of revelers in New Orleans or even Lafayette. The *paillasse* (straw man) who acts as the clown or fool wears a costume of burlap and straw decorated with other readily available materials such as buttons, fabric and metallic objects. Painted and decorated screens serve as masks. Other colorful characters wear tall cone-shaped hats called *capuchon* (French for 'hood') that symbolize a mockery of the upper class. A *capitaine* oversees the mêlée. The same ritual carried out in Creole communities tends to be more traditional and less brawling than in Cajun communities. The tradition is a rite of passage for many young men in small communities – such as Church Point, Eunice, Mamou, Ville Platte and Elton – known for their courir celebrations.

While the riders are out in the countryside, folks gather in town to await their return. After they gallop back in triumph, a communal supper is held with much more drinking and dancing. Visitors may join in the festivities – staking out a corner to watch the riders pass or joining the party.

($16) and an area for tents ($10). Seven cabins with kitchenettes go for $45 and $55. There's a pool, small store, playground and small lake, all surrounded by woods. (Noncampers pay $2 to swim.)

The recently renovated **L'Acadie Inn** (☎ 337-457-5211, dLpitre@cyber-designs .net), just off Hwy 190 about 4 miles east of town, has nice singles/doubles for $40/45. At the two-story brick **Howard's Inn** (☎ 337-457-2066, 3789 Hwy 190), a bit closer to town, clean rooms go for $36/46. The **Best Western** (☎ 337-457-2800, 800-962-8423, 1531 W Laurel Ave), west of downtown offers comfortable rooms for $64/70, including a pool and continental breakfast.

Pleasant B&B rooms and suites are available at the **Seale Guesthouse** (☎/fax 337-457-3753, 123 Seale Lane, 70535) on a lushly wooded 60-acre site 2 miles south of town on Hwy 13. Rates are $75 to $150 including breakfast.

Places to Eat

For a cheap and tasty breakfast or lunch, head to **Ruby's Cafe** (221 W Walnut Ave), where Ruby has been serving meals since 1958. It's open weekdays. The **Pelican Restaurant** (☎ 337-457-2323, 1501 W Laurel Ave), adjacent to the Best Western, makes plentiful breakfasts and lunches daily and dinners Thursday through Saturday. Try the grilled shrimp salad.

The smoke wafting up from **Allison's Hickory Pit** (☎ 337-457-9218, 501 W Laurel) indicates the barbecue is ready. **Johnson's Grocery** (☎ 337-457-9314, 700 E Maple Ave) is considered the high altar of boudin; it also sells tasso.

Mama's (☎ 337-457-9978, 1640 W Laurel/ Hwy 190) is adjacent to a poultry butcher, so the fried chicken is fresh, and the rest of the menu is surprisingly good. Mama's crawfish étouffée is famous.

About 20 minutes outside of town, **DI's Cajun Restaurant** (☎ 337-432-5141) is surrounded by crawfish and rice fields, but locals pack the parking lot for lunch and dinner. The menu focuses on boiled, grilled, and fried seafood and steaks ($7 to $13). The sizable dining room has a stage and dance floor, and on Tuesday, Friday and Saturday nights, the place is jumping with families whirling and twirling. Wednesday night there's a Cajun jam session. From Eunice, take Hwy 190 west to Basile; turn left (south) on Hwy 97 and go about 5 miles. DI's will be on your left (if you reach Hwy 98, you've gone too far).

WHISKEY CHITTO RIVER

From its headwaters in the Kisatchie National Forest, the Whiskey Chitto Creek flows 65 meandering miles south, passing mixed pine and hardwood forests amid low hills. On its banks are a dozen Native American archaeological sites dating between 400 and 1500 AD. The creek offers some of the best canoeing in the state. The small town of **Mittie** lies along one of the prettiest stretches, and it's home to several canoe outfitters. (Mittie is located about 50 miles northwest of Eunice and 70 miles north of Jennings).

Arrowhead Canoe Rentals (☎ 337-639-2086, 800-637-2086) offers both day and overnight trips. Ten- or 14-mile day trips cost $22 per canoe, a bit more on weekends; up to 24-mile overnight trips cost $40 to $45. Weekends are often very busy; call as far ahead as possible. For information about other outfitters and nearby accommodations, contact the Allen Parish Tourist Commission (☎ 337-639-4868, 888-639-4868).

RICE BELT

Off I-10 between Lafayette and Lake Charles is the Rice Belt of the Cajun prairie. In the late 1800s, a group of British companies with local landholdings sent an operative to study how they could make money in the region. He sent back word that the area between Lake Charles and Lafayette was ideal for rice growing. The company lured many Midwestern farmers to the area, and within 20 years, the region was producing half the rice grown in the US. Nineteenth- and early-20th-century railroad towns here hold rice landmarks and other small-town pleasures.

After the Civil War, frog legs became a delicacy and **Rayne** was a main distribution point for them. Though the demand for the 'chickenlike' meat has diminished, the town is still known as the Frog Capital of the World, a title supported by whimsical frog murals on downtown walls and storefronts that set the scene for the town's Frog Festival (☎ 337-334-2332) over Labor Day weekend. The festival, which draws 75,000 revelers, features a frog-legs eating contest, a frog race, more than two dozen Cajun and zydeco bands, an accordion contest, parade and traditional fais-do-do. Be sure to get a bite of the frog legs étouffée.

Three miles north of Rayne on Hwy 98 is the small German Catholic community of **Roberts Cove** (founded 1880), which centers around St Leo's Church. The first full weekend in October it puts on a German-fest (☎ 337-334-8354) with German and Cajun music, food and crafts.

Crowley, Rice Capital of Louisiana, celebrates its primary industry at the Rice Festival on the third weekend in October (☎ 337-783-3067). The downtown Rice Theater hosts a gospel concert the first Saturday of each month, a country music concert on the third Saturday, and a Cajun music concert on the last Saturday (☎ 337-783-0824). Monuments to rice can be found at the Rice Museum (☎ 337-783-6842), on Airport Rd/Hwy 90 west of town. Once the rice experiment station of the Louisiana State University, the museum tells the story of the grain with vintage machinery and a demonstration rice mill (hours are irregular; call first). The Crystal Rice Plantation (☎ 337-783-6417), on Airport Rd south of town (via Hwy 13), gives an aquaculture

Creole Rose, the Crowley treat

JERRY ALEXANDER

tour, which describes the crop rotations of rice and crawfish common to the region. There's also an 1848 Acadian cottage and a vintage automobile collection. It's open weekdays (Saturday by appointment).

On Hwy 13 south of I-10, *Boudin King*, a local fast-food chain, serves up the links as well as fried chicken, gumbo, po-boys and fried seafood (closed Sunday). Motels are clustered around I-10 exit 80. Among them is the good-value *Crowley Inn* (☎ 337-788-0970, 800-256-4565), north and east of the interstate exit, offering decent singles/doubles for $45/50. There's an adjacent restaurant.

Fourteen miles northwest of Crowley, **Iota** celebrates Mardi Gras with a courir and folklife festival retaining traditions no longer found elsewhere. In downtown at a free Mardi Gras street festival, a hundred riders return wearing the traditional hand-made screen masks, capuchon hats, and costumes. Cajun and zydeco bands, prairie Cajun food specialties and a lively dance are all part of the event.

In 1901, oil was discovered in **Jennings**, and it was here that the first well was drilled. Today, the city's 31-acre Oil and Gas Park, right off I-10 exit 64, is a handy pit stop for I-10 through-travelers. It has the Jefferson Davis Parish Tourist Office (☎ 337-821-5521), a small lake, playground, picnic tables and an oil-well replica. In Jennings, listen to KJEF 92.9 AM for 24-hour Cajun music.

Several chain motels surround I-10 exit 64, including the *Holiday Inn* (☎ 337-824-5280). The budget *Sundown Inn* (☎ 337-824-7041), on Hwy 26 a half mile north of I-10, charges $30/35 for singles/doubles. Next door, *Donn E's* (☎ 337-824-3402) serves reasonably priced Cajun buffets daily.

LAKE CHARLES

With around 75,000 residents, Lake Charles is the largest city in the state's southwestern corner. It's on the edge of the prairie; just south of town, solid ground quickly gives way to marshes that are known for some of the best bird watching in the state. The city is primarily a deepwater industrial port and tourist hub. For travelers entering the state from Texas or planning to spend a few days bird watching, Lake Charles makes a decent place to spend the night or a few dollars gambling. Lake Charles is 71 miles west of Lafayette and 140 miles west of Baton Rouge.

During the first two weeks of May, the city celebrates Contraband Days (☎ 337-436-5508, 800-456-7952), which includes power-boat races; a variety of Cajun, zydeco, and gospel concerts; and children's activities. On Labor Day, zydeco star Boozoo Chavis hosts a large barbecue and concert (☎ 337-478-5855) next to his home just outside the city.

The commercial center hugs the eastern shore of the Calcasieu River just before it empties into the north side of the lake. I-10 passes through town along the downtown's northern edge and crosses the river to Westlake, with its gray expanse of petrochemical plants and flaming smokestacks. On the lakeshore south of I-10 near the Lake Charles end of the bridge is the large Southwest Louisiana Visitor Center (☎ 337-436-9588). Just west of it is **North Beach**; though I-10 is within view, the white-sand beach does offer a chance to cool off, and there's a bathhouse and barbecue stand.

Casinos dot the landscape. Just east of the tourist office is the Players Island Casino (☎ 800-977-7529). Across the bridge in Westlake is the Isle of Capri Casino (☎ 800-843-4753), off I-10 exit 27. Both casinos are open 24 hours a day and have all-you-can-eat buffets (around $5 breakfast, $7 lunch and $11 dinner). The gambling rooms are on actual boats; there are two at each casino that alternate trips around the lake to satisfy state gaming laws. Unlike most casinos, these have windows so passengers can enjoy the view (which is actually pretty at night).

There's good camping just north of town at *Sam Houston Jones State Park*. Thirty miles west of Lake Charles on the Sabine River, which forms the state border, is the wooded *Niblett's Bluff Park* (☎ 337-589-7117), offering 48 camping sites (without hookups $5, with $10). Five simple cabins sleeping up to four cost $21. Facilities include showers, a beach, playground and fishing pond. Take I-10 exit 4, head north on Hwy 109 about 4 miles to Niblett's Bluff Rd, and turn left.

Accommodations at both casinos are around $80 weekdays and $115 weekends; however, there are plenty of better-value chain hotels along or not far from I-10, and also in the town of Sulphur to the west. Right across I-10 from Players Island on N Lakeshore Drive is the tidy **Lakeview Motel** (☎ 337-436-3336), with singles/doubles for $43/58. Just west of it is the nicer **Travel Inn** (☎ 337-433-9461, 888-436-2580), which has a pool, restaurant and shuttle to the casinos. Rooms are $53/59. Away from the noise of the interstate and on the edge of the historic district, the new **Howard Johnson Express Inn** (☎ 337-436-4311, 800-446-4656, 825 Broad St) has kitchenettes in some rooms and restaurants nearby. Rooms go for $59. It's only a few blocks from **Dagostino's Bistro & Cigar Bar** (☎ 337-436-3246, 1025 Broad St), which offers moderately priced New York–Italian fare in a renovated house. The recently remodeled **Motel 6** (☎ 337-433-1773, 335 Hwy 17), just off I-10 exit 32, offers comfortable rooms for $36/42; it has a pool.

Greyhound (☎ 337-439-4576) runs a main office in town at 3034 Legion St. Daily buses run to Lafayette ($11.50 one way), Baton Rouge ($15.50) and New Orleans ($21.50). Amtrak's *Sunset Limited* train stops in town every other day on the way to and from Lafayette ($16 one way) and New Orleans ($51).

SAM HOUSTON JONES STATE PARK

This inviting state park (☎ 337-855-2665, 877-226-7652), 12 miles north of Lake Charles, is well worth the detour for folks looking to camp or needing a refuge from interstate travel. At the confluence of the Calcasieu and Houston Rivers and Indian Bayou, the 1087-acre park has a small cypress lagoon. Two short hiking trails wander through the pine and hardwood forest. Wildlife includes waterbirds, nutria, deer, bobcats and alligators. Fishing and boating ($10-per-day rentals) are primary activities.

The 73 campsites ($12 a night, hookups available) are in two clusters by the lagoon. Twelve waterside vacation cabins that sleep up to six are also available for $60 a night, but note that state park cabins are often booked far in advance (linens and dishware provided; bring towels and dish soap). Outside the entrance to the park is a small, friendly market and gas station beside a small marina.

From I-10 exit 33 in Lake Charles, head north on Hwy 171 for 7 miles; turn left on Hwy 378 and go about 5 miles. From I-10 exit 27 in Westlake, head north on Hwy 378 for about 5 miles.

Coast & Chenier

The state's western region near the Texas border and along the coast is the most remote in Cajun Country. Several wildlife refuges provide prairie and marsh sanctuaries for birds migrating along the Mississippi and Central Flyways. From Vermilion Bay south of Abbeville in the east to Sabine Lake at the state border, a 20-mile band of chenier (shi-NEAR) plain is home to about 6000 residents. Cheniers – oak-covered ridges of sand and shells – parallel the coast and have long harbored remote, largely Cajun cultural pockets and provided cattle grazing.

The appeal of southwest Louisiana lies in walks and scenic drives through the quiet marshlands, and drives along the oak-shaded cheniers. Though the region is officially Acadiana, culturally it borrows many traditions from neighboring Texas. Visitors intrigued by the region should track down geography professor Gay M Gomez' *A Wetland Biography: Seasons on Louisiana's Chenier Plain*, a thoughtful study of the land, its wildlife and the influence of humans on them.

CREOLE NATURE TRAIL

This 180-mile scenic byway takes the better part of a day to drive. Those who intend to stop along the way should plan on a whole day. West of Lake Charles, Hwy 27 drops south from Sulphur, passing first through prairie and then through fresh- and saltwater marsh and along the eastern edge of the Sabine National Wildlife Refuge on the way to Holly Beach, a jumbled cluster of ramshackle cabins and trailers. There Hwy 27 joins Hwy 82, the east-west coastal route. Together they head east to the free car ferry over the Calcasieu River. On the east bank is Cameron, which services the oilfield industry and has several restaurants, motels, a gas station, and an ATM. At Cameron, visitors start seeing the oaks that line the cheniers and which continue along for 50 miles. Fifteen miles east of Cameron is the tiny community of Creole; there Hwy 27 runs north, passing through the Cameron Prairie National Wildlife Refuge, and eventually hitting Hwy 14 W, which runs back to Lake Charles.

The route is remote and peaceful. Visitors can stop at roadside parking strips and at a few parking areas, where they can view the spectacular migrations of birds flying along the Central and Mississippi Flyways as well as alligators, nutria, turtles and other marsh wildlife. Another marsh denizen, the mosquito, greets all comers. The area is very popular with fishermen; those not in boats cluster along bridges and channels. Though it's possible to swim at **Holly Beach**, the beach itself is usually strewn with debris, especially in the summer, when thousands flock to the so-called 'Cajun Riviera.' However, self-contained camping is permitted on Gulf beaches. Here as everywhere along the state coast, oil wells and gas pumps dot the horizon, and pipelines (many below water) crisscross the region. The Calcasieu River is busy with oceangoing freighters heading to and from Lake Charles. Provisions are minimal, and it would be good to head out with enough gas, cash, insect repellent and cold drinks for the trip.

Sabine National Wildlife Refuge

The 196-sq-mile Sabine Refuge is the largest coastal refuge on the Gulf. On both the Mississippi and Central Flyways, it preserves wetlands for wintering and migrating waterfowl. Over 250 bird species have been observed at the refuge, 50 of which nest here. Abundant snow geese are present from November through February. March sees the most wildflowers, and in April, the spring bird migration peaks. In June, alligators build their nests, and their eggs hatch in August. In September, the blue-winged teal population peaks, and in October, the peregrine falcons return. The waterfowl population peaks in December.

The refuge is a major nursery for marine species and provides wetland habitat for alligators, turtles, furbearers, and numerous wading, water, and marsh birds. The marsh landscape is streaked with salt-meadow cordgrass; narrow estuary streams cut through tufts of the green reeds, which give way to bullwhip, cattails, and water lilies in the fresher areas. Elm, willow, and palmetto grow on patches of higher ground.

At refuge headquarters on Hwy 27, a small **visitor center** (☎ 337-762-3816) provides maps and distributes information on boating through 150 miles of waterways, as well as recreational fishing, crabbing, shrimping, crawfishing and duck hunting. There's also an amazingly lifelike button-activated animatronic Cajun, who provides a brief, folksy introduction to the area. The center is open weekdays 7 am to 4 pm, weekends noon to 4 pm.

The 1½-mile **Marsh Trail** is 4 miles south of the center. The all-access trail enters the tranquil marsh and allows opportunities to see alligators (most visible on windless, bright, warm days) and other wildlife.

Cameron Prairie National Wildlife Refuge

North of Creole on Hwy 27, this 9600-acre refuge of prairie and freshwater marsh is a prime bird watching area. About 12 miles north of Creole and on the east side of the road is the 3½ mile **Pintail Wildlife Drive**, which circles a peaceful marsh area teeming with birds, alligators, turtles, and snakes. Visitors can either walk or drive the gravel loop. If you drive it, do so slowly and plan to spend about half an hour. A few miles north along Hwy 27 is the **Interpretive Center** (☎ 337-598-2216), which has a female animatronic Cajun describing human and wildlife in the refuge. The ponds adjacent to the center are home to small gators and turtles. The center is open weekdays 7 am to 4 pm and weekends noon to 4 pm.

HWY 82 SCENIC DRIVE

In Creole, Hwy 27 turns north and Hwy 82 drops south 3 miles before heading east along chenier ridges through the village of **Grand Chenier**, the northern edge of the Rockefeller National Wildlife Refuge, and the village of Pecan Island before heading north to Abbeville, a drive of about 120 miles. These two villages are the only chenier communities accessible by car, and though the roads connected them to more developed areas in the 1950s, they are still fairly isolated and independent. A scenic arcade of oaks follows much of the route, and cattle graze small meadows.

Rockefeller National Wildlife Refuge

The 131-sq-mile Rockefeller Refuge provides an opportunity to see the same wildlife species and landscapes as at the Sabine Refuge (see earlier), but in a more remote location bordering the Gulf of Mexico. Aerial inventories conducted by refuge biologists list the midwinter duck population at about 400,000.

The headquarters (☎ 337-538-2276) is at the northwestern corner of the refuge outside Grand Chenier, and it is open to visitors from March 1 to December 1. The primary access into the marsh is Price Lake Rd, just west of the headquarters, where there's a three-story observation tower.

Central Louisiana

There is no Maginot Line equivalent that divides northern from southern Louisiana. Instead, there is central Louisiana (Cenla), a region with various pockets of cultures from all directions – from Natchitoches with its strong and proud French heritage; and Marksville, home of the Tunica Indian tribe; and Alexandria, a city described in AJ Liebling's brilliant book *The Earl of Louisiana* as 'the political navel of Louisiana (where) Southern bilingual, French Catholic Louisiana, the land of the bougalees, shades into Northern monolingual, Anglo-Saxon Protestant Louisiana, the land of the rednecks.'

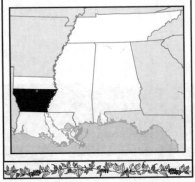

Liebling's characterization of Alexandria might well be applied to the whole region east and south of Natchitoches. Though tagged as Cenla, the culturally diverse parishes of the region have little in common beyond geographical proximity.

Much of central Louisiana is a lonely place, densely forested and sparsely populated. Around 1900, lumber companies began flocking to the region, intent upon harvesting the monstrous virgin pines. Today there may be more reforestation than deforestation going on, but pulpwood trucks still clog the highway. What is left of the virgin forests is a direct result of the efforts of one woman: Caroline Dormon, who was the first female forester in the nation. By sheer will alone, she convinced the state of Louisiana and the US Forest Service to establish the Kisatchie National Forest in 1930, comprised of 937 sq miles stretching over seven parishes.

History

On the western fringe of the region, Natchitoches is still under the sway of the French explorers who first came to the area in 1714. Under the direction of Louis Juchereau de St Denis, they established the first European settlement in what is now Louisiana, Fort St Jean-Baptiste. Three years later, the Spanish, intent upon stemming westward migration of the French, built a fort just 15 miles away and named it Los Adaes. The frontier standstill ended in 1762 when France ceded Louisiana to Spain. Save a few minor conflicts, the French and Spanish never really did battle. What they did do was trade with Caddo Confederation Indian tribes like the Adaes and the Natchitoches.

Despite 40 years of de facto Spanish rule, by the time of the Louisiana Purchase in 1803, Natchitoches fancied itself to be a decidedly French town – so much so that most of the local gentry looked upon the coming of the Americans as tantamount to an invasion of vulgarians.

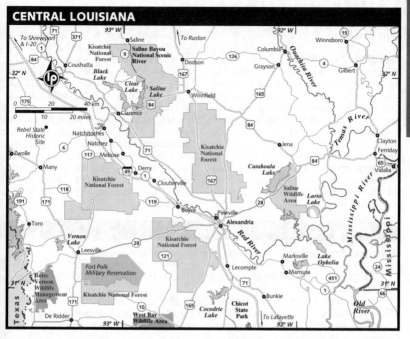

CENTRAL LOUISIANA

Today, Natchitoches still clings tenaciously to its French ancestry. Equally proud, and just as disdainful of the Anglo-Saxon Protestants in their midst, are the Franco-African people who live along the Cane River just south of Natchitoches and are known as Creoles of Color.

Surrounded as it is by the Kisatchie National Forest, Natchitoches feels a bit removed from other population centers in the state. But, just 35 miles northeast is what may well be (with apologies to Mr Liebling) the epicenter of Louisiana politics – Winnfield, seat of government for Winn Parish and birthplace of the state's strongest and strangest political legacy. Once known as the Free State of Winn because of its resistance to secession during the Civil War, Winn Parish remains a hotbed of rancorous populist politics where voters look for character, charisma and charm, and are more impressed by a good stump speech than promises of a tax cut.

South of Winnfield, the landscape changes from rolling hills to flatter, oftentimes swampy land. Though the French settled along the Red River here in 1723, the present-day French influence is not as strong as it is upriver.

By the 19th century, Rapides Parish was the economic hub of the region. But during the Civil War most of the towns along the southern stretch of the Red River were burned. It was not until WWII, when troops came to train at Camp Beauregard in Rapides Parish, that Cenla came to life again.

Flora & Fauna

This is timber farming territory. Accordingly, there are huge tracts of dense pine forests scattered about the region. The whole of the area is alive with squirrels, deer, armadillos, opossum, raccoons and wild turkeys, while the waterways teem with gaspergou, gar, crappie, catfish and crawfish. On and around the bayous, lily pads and iris bogs flourish beneath moss-draped cypress trees. Azaleas take over the landscape in early spring.

Outdoor Activities

Thanks to the 937-sq-mile Kisatchie National Forest, located to the northeast and southwest of tiny Natchitoches, central Louisiana abounds with hiking and other recreational opportunities. Once you're 50 feet into these piney hills, all traces of the modern world quickly recede, for though this is beautiful country it's not highly trafficked by either tourists or locals. Take advantage of the lakes and rivers scattered all about and try canoeing around the Kisatchie Bayou.

Getting There & Away

Alexandria boasts a regional airport with regular connections to hub cities such as New Orleans, Houston and Dallas. Train service is unavailable to and from any of the major population centers, but Greyhound buses provide service throughout the region. As a rule, a car is the preferred mode of transportation. For those traveling through the western part of the region, I-49 and Hwy 71 connect Natchitoches and Alexandria, but elsewhere you will travel circuitous (but often scenic) routes. Continuing southward, I-49 is the primary route, with the Cajun capital of Lafayette just 90 miles down the road (see the Cajun Country chapter).

Louisiana Politics – The Long Way

For years, when it came to Louisiana politics, the Long way was the only way.

Huey Long, a flamboyant and charismatic populist politician, served as governor from 1928 to 1932 before entering the US Senate in 1932. At the height of his power, he had a virtual stranglehold on the state.

With a promise to 'make every man a king,' the 'Kingfish' won the undying faith of the working men and women of Louisiana, on whose behalf he embarked upon a massive series of public works programs – building hospitals, schools and highways throughout the rural parishes. But along with such good works came a good measure of graft.

Through intimidation and bribery, Huey Long squashed any challenges to his authority, until, in September of 1935, he was assassinated by a Baton Rouge physician. At the time of his death, Huey Long was poised to challenge Franklin D Roosevelt for the White House. Earl Long, while not as ambitious or as controlling as his brother Huey, was nevertheless a singular political personality. His three terms as governor during the 1940s and 1950s provided both comic relief and strong leadership. Infamous for his liaisons with strippers and affinity for strong drink, 'Uncle Earl' was at one time during his administration committed to a hospital for the insane. Elected to Congress in 1960, Earl died 10 days later.

For a more in-depth portrait of these men, pick up a copy of T Harry Williams' voluminous biography *Huey Long*, AJ Liebling's brilliant and witty portrait *The Earl of Louisiana* or Robert Penn Warren's fictionalized story *All the King's Men*.

Or, if you're in search of the roots of these two political titans, you might want to visit the town of **Winnfield**, just 35 miles northeast of Natchitoches. Aside from the bronze statue of Huey at the courthouse and the imposing sculpture of Earl at the Earl K Long Memorial Park on Elm St, the prime attraction is the **Louisiana Political Museum and Hall of Fame** (☎ 318-628-5928), 499 E Main St. It is open weekdays 9 am to 4:30 pm and Saturday 10 am to noon.

Located in an old railroad depot, this cozy little museum is filled with political ephemera. Though life-size statues of the Longs dominate the room, the more interesting artifacts are more mundane, from an old voting machine to campaign buttons that read 'Vote for Uncle Earl. I ain't crazy.' Even the bathrooms are plastered with political bumper stickers.

NATCHITOCHES
• pop 17,000

Despite its storied history and charming French architecture, Natchitoches (pronounced NA-kid-esh or NAK-a-tush) remained a sleepy little backwater town with hardly a tourist on the street until, in 1988, Hollywood filmmakers arrived to make the blockbuster movie *Steel Magnolias*. Based upon the play by native son Robert Harling, the film's cast – Shirley MacLaine, Darryl Hannah, Dolly Parton, Julia Roberts, Sally Field and Olympia Dukakis – brought along a lot more star power to the town's nighttime sky.

In their wake, Hollywood left Natchitoches transformed. Before *Steel Magnolias* it was hard to find a decent hotel in town. Now there are at least 27 B&Bs ranging from opulent homes to converted duplexes.

The oldest settlement in the Louisiana Purchase Territory, Natchitoches was founded in 1714 by Juchereau St Denis and established as an outpost for trade with the Spanish in Mexico, near a village of Natchitoches Indians. Several overland highways met at the town, including the El Camino Real from Mexico. This was a thriving transportation center and cotton crossroads, but Natchitoches river commerce literally dried up when, in the 1830s, the Red River began changing course. Now the former part of the Red River that bordered Natchitoches is a tranquil oxbow lake called Cane River Lake, and the economy depends upon tourists and college students from Northwestern State University for sustenance.

Today, Natchitoches is an enchanting blend of genteel French town and thriving tourist destination. The riverfront bustles with tourists shopping for souvenirs and gawking at the elaborate wrought ironwork on Front St townhouses. But don't think that the city's rich history has been tossed aside in a grab for the almighty dollar. Natchitoches residents are dead serious about their history. Stop a local on the street to talk, and chances are that 10 minutes later you will walk away with a head full of names and dates. And, halfway through that same conversation, you can be sure that he

or she will mention, in an offhand manner, that Natchitoches just happens to be older than New Orleans.

Orientation & Information

At the heart of Natchitoches is a 33-block National Historic District situated along the west bank of Cane River Lake. It's one of only two such districts in all of Louisiana, the other being the Vieux Carré in New Orleans. Most west-bank commercial activity is on Front, Washington and 2nd Sts, while Williams Ave (Business Hwy 1) is the core east-bank thoroughfare. Hwys 1 and 6 form a de facto perimeter around the city.

The convention and visitors bureau (☎ 318-352-8072, 800-259-1714) is at 781 Front St, in the heart of the historic district. It is open 9 am to 5 pm Monday to Saturday and 10 am to 3 pm on Sunday. Visit its Web site at www.natchitoches.net.

ATMs are found on Church St and 2nd St downtown, or on Keyser Ave on the eastern edge of town. The main post office (☎ 318-352-2161) is at 240 Rue St Denis.

As for newspapers, the meager *Natchitoches Times* is published daily and the Shreveport paper is widely distributed in town. The main library (☎ 318-357-3280) is at 431 Jefferson St and is open 9 am to 6 pm on weekdays and until 5 pm on Saturday.

The Book Merchant (☎ 318-357-8900), 512 Front St, is a cozy bookstore with a strong selection of regional history and Southern fiction. As a bonus, the helpful staff seems to always be well informed about live entertainment offerings in town. If you're longing for a real newspaper, the store sells the Sunday *New York Times*. The store is open 10 am to 6 pm daily and until 3 pm on Sunday.

For laundry, try Agape Washateria (☎ 318-357-0271), 137 Caspari St near the university. It's open 8 am to 8 pm daily.

Natchitoches Parish Hospital (☎ 318-352-1200), 501 Keyser Ave on the east bank, offers emergency services.

Things to See & Do

No matter what the folks who run the little motorized trolley tell you, Natchitoches is

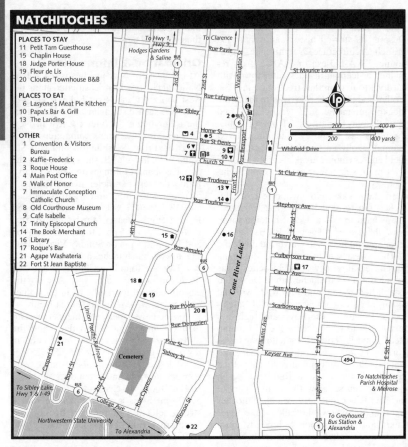

NATCHITOCHES

PLACES TO STAY
11 Petit Tarn Guesthouse
15 Chaplin House
18 Judge Porter House
19 Fleur de Lis
20 Cloutier Townhouse B&B

PLACES TO EAT
6 Lasyone's Meat Pie Kitchen
10 Papa's Bar & Grill
13 The Landing

OTHER
1 Convention & Visitors Bureau
2 Kaffie-Frederick
3 Roque House
4 Main Post Office
5 Walk of Honor
7 Immaculate Conception Catholic Church
8 Old Courthouse Museum
9 Café Isabelle
12 Trinity Episcopal Church
14 The Book Merchant
16 Library
17 Roque's Bar
21 Agape Washateria
22 Fort St Jean Baptiste

best enjoyed on foot. A **walking tour** begins with a stroll down Front St between Rue Touline and Rue Lafayette; it's the ideal way to get your bearings and appreciate the Creole townhouses with their lacy cast-iron balconies overlooking the lake.

From Front St, turn away from the river and just wander the back streets. Along the way, you'll encounter a plethora of older homes ranging in style from Georgian to Victorian and everything in between. On Rue St Denis between Front St and 2nd St, be sure to check out the **Walk of Honor**, where inscribed fleurs-de-lis are cemented into the sidewalk in tribute to anyone who has made a significant contribution to the town. Famous visitors and locals who have received the honor include everyone from Dolly Parton and John Wayne to the Dixie Debs, 1994 World Series Girls Fastpitch Softball Champions.

At the corner of 2nd and Church Sts, the **Old Courthouse Museum** (☎ 800-568-6958), a beautiful 1896 Romanesque building, hosts frequently changing exhibits but is, quite frankly, not worth the $3 admission. Across the street you will find Immaculate Conception Catholic Church, built in 1856,

LOUISIANA

while one block south at the corner of Rue Trudeau and 2nd St is the graceful Trinity Episcopal Church. If you continue in a south to southwesterly direction, you will become happily lost along the town's narrow back streets.

Below the tourist offices on Rue Beauport next to the lakefront is **Roque House**, an 18th-century plantation outbuilding moved to this site to serve as a museum displaying the works of folk artist Clementine Hunter (see Melrose Plantation in the Cane River Country section, later in this chapter). It also houses special exhibitions focusing on local architecture and the arts. Unfortunately, the proprietor's hours of operation defy logic. People can visit the Roque House's exterior anytime; call the convention and visitors bureau before making a special trip.

Just south of downtown is **Northwestern State University**, a liberal arts college founded in 1884. Now home to 10,000 students, Northwestern is the site of a new $20 million National Center for Preservation Technology (☎ 318-357-6464), dedicated to the preservation of architecturally important sites throughout the nation. Located in South Hall, it's open to visitors weekdays 8 am to 5 pm. Those interested in Native American archaeology are encouraged to visit **Williamson Museum** (☎ 318-357-4364), 210 Keyser Hall, a research repository of over 500,000 artifacts; it's open weekdays 9 am to 4 pm. Visitors who wish to explore more of the region's culture should stop by the university's **Folklife Center**. It houses 800 artist and subject files, 1500 audio recordings, 100 video tapes, a small but growing print library of books and periodicals and 5000 photographs. The campus hosts special lectures and concerts during the academic year; call university information (☎ 318-357-6361) for details.

Off Jefferson St, near the university at 130 Moreau St on Cane River Lake, is **Fort St Jean Baptiste** (☎ 318-357-3101, 888-677-7853). Step inside the full-scale replica of a French Colonial fort, and all reminders of 20th-century life vanish before your eyes. Reconstructed in 1979 from drawings made by the architect Ignace François Broutin in 1733, the five-acre compound features eight wood-and-mud buildings, all surrounded by a pointy wood fence. If you're lucky, one of their frontier reenactments will be taking place when you visit. One look at the actors' buckskin clothing and coonskin caps, and you'll want to join in (or burst out laughing). The fort is open 9 am to 5 pm daily.

Special Events

Call the visitors bureau (☎ 318-352-8072, 800-259-1714) for more information on special events.

Each October, Natchitoches holds a somewhat subdued celebration as locals dress in colonial-period attire and open their homes for tours during the Natchitoches pilgrimage.

On the first weekend in December, Cane River Lake is ablaze with lights as Natchitoches celebrates its renowned Festival of Lights with boat parades and Christmas decoration competitions capped with fireworks. The festival attracts hundreds of people from all around the area.

Places to Stay

Camping *Hodges Gardens* (☎ 318-586-3523), 35 miles southwest on Hwy 171 (via Hwy 6 south from Natchitoches) between the towns of Many and Leesville, may be your best bet for camping (see the Around Natchitoches section, later in this chapter). Campsites cost $10. Or drive north and east to the *Kisatchie National Forest*, where numerous campsites await (see the Kisatchie National Forest section, later in this chapter).

Motels For budget rooms, the *Lakeview Inn Motel and Apartments* (☎ 318-352-9561, 800-535-5672, 1316 Washington St), on the northern edge of town near the Hwy 1 Bypass, has some of the cheapest rates in town. Though simple, the rooms are clean and the desk clerks are accommodating – some of the rooms even overlook Cane River. Rooms are $40 a night. Be aware that the inn's office is only open weekdays 8 am to 5 pm and Saturday 8 am till noon.

Cheaper still, *Louisiane Motel* (☎ 318-352-6401, 340 Hwy 1 S) is south of town on the east bank and is advertised as 'The Working Man's Motel.' Rooms are priced at $32 for a single or double. The motel is located across from the Greyhound bus stop.

The chain motels located west of town, near the intersection of Hwy 6 and I-49, are overpriced at $45 and up. You are better off splurging and staying in one of the B&Bs in Natchitoches, where, with a little luck, you might be able to negotiate a lower rate.

B&Bs When there is an excess of something, Southerners are fond of saying, 'You can't swing a dead cat without hitting a (lawyer, junked car, pine tree – pick a noun).' In Natchitoches, that swung dead cat is likely to hit a B&B, and lucky for you. With over 27 in town, the rates are reasonable and the rooms are nice. One caveat: All rates go up approximately 25% in the month of December because of the Festival of Lights.

Established in 1983, *Fleur de Lis* (☎ 318-352-6621, 800-489-6621, 336 2nd St), at Rue Poete, is Natchitoches' first B&B. This brightly painted Queen Anne home has five rooms that go for $65 to $80 a night. It also offers a guest house called Abigail's Cottage, which can accommodate up to eight people. The owners give guests free run of the house, encouraging them to help themselves to wine or soft drinks from the refrigerator whenever the mood strikes. In the morning, everyone sits down to a big communal breakfast before parting ways. It's Web site is www.virtualcities.com.

The *Chaplin House* (☎ 318-352-2324, 434 2nd St), near Rue Amulet, is an 1892 home with a wonderful front porch (called a gallery around these parts) that just begs for a book and a pitcher of iced tea. Upstairs, there is one long room built into the eaves that the owners rent for $55 to $100 a night depending upon the number of guests. As the only guest(s), you enjoy a sense of privacy that you don't find with many B&Bs. The upstairs kitchen has a microwave and refrigerator.

Beautifully restored, the imposing 1912 *Judge Porter House* (☎ 318-352-9206, 800-441-8343, 321 2nd St) has a clean, airy feel to it. One- and two-bedroom suites, complete with coffeemakers and bathrobes, are available for $95 to $160. The upstairs two-bedroom suite has a huge bathroom as well as floor-to-ceiling windows that allow access to the wraparound gallery. It's Web site is www.judgeporterhouse.com.

For a spooky night's lodging, try the *Breazeale House* (☎ 318-352-5630, 800-352-5631, 926 Washington St), which was featured during the opening scenes of *Steel Magnolias*. Built in the late 1800s for Congressman Phanor Breazeale, the house is said to have 'unknown occupants.' According to the innkeepers, Willa and Jack, 'guests have experienced some unexplainable activities.' You can be one of them for $60 to $85 a night. The Breazeale has eight rooms, 11 fireplaces and a swimming pool.

If you prefer to be alone, the *Petit Tarn Guesthouse* (☎ 318-352-5242, 877-699-8471, 612 Williams Ave), across the Cane River from the historic district, is the perfect spot. Run by Conna Cloutier, who also runs the *Cloutier Townhouse Bed & Breakfast* (same ☎, 416 Jefferson St), the Petit Tarn offers three ideal options: the Treehouse, hidden among the trees on the upper floor; the Library Suite, featuring a cozy collection of Louisiana history, art and literature; or the River Room, with a private riverside patio. All three have private entrances and balconies, whirlpool baths and kitchenettes. Prices range from $95 to $110 per night, double occupancy. The B&B's Web site is at www.cloutierbandb.com.

Places to Eat

It seems like every restaurant in town serves 'authentic' Natchitoches meat pies – crusty, crescent-shaped little turnovers, stuffed with spicy ground beef, pork and onions and then fried. Once sold from street corner carts, these savory pies were on the verge of extinction when, in 1967, James Lasyone opened *Lasyone's Meat Pie Kitchen* (☎ 318-352-3353, 622 2nd St). Today, his pies are still the best. Order a meat pie platter and you get a pie, dirty rice, a choice of vegetable (try the cabbage) and salad bar, all for $7. Or, if you crave vegetables, get the four-vegetable plate lunch with cornbread for $4. Fridays feature all-you-can-eat catfish for $9. Lasyone's is open 7 am to 7 pm Monday through Saturday. Credit cards are not accepted.

Locals swear by *Almost Home* (☎ 318-352-2431), on Hwy 1 near Sibley Lake, which offers a breakfast and lunch buffet of rib-sticking home cooking; it is open Sunday to Friday 6 am to 2:30 pm and Friday nights from 5 pm until 8 pm for an all-you-can-eat catfish buffet (under $10).

If you're willing to drive a few miles, *Grayson's Bar-b-q* (☎ 318-357-0166, 5849 Hwy 71) just north of Hwy 84 in Clarence, is worth the trip. First-time visitors should order the mixed plate ($7), piled high with pork ribs, ham, beef, potato salad, beans and bread. If you just want a snack, order a ham sandwich on what the locals call a 'frog bun' – a fresh baked French roll. If you ask nicely, the owner might let you sneak a peek at the pits out back where that delectable hunk of ham you just ate spent the last 48 hours. On your way out the door, pick up a half-dozen chocolate or ginger cookies to go. It is open Tuesday to Sunday from 8 am to 9 pm.

At *Papa's Bar & Grill* (☎ 318-356-5850, 604 Front St) order grilled pork chops stuffed with sausage for $9, or any of the nightly seafood specials. And if the waitress mentions something about having a few servings of catfish court bouillon left, for heaven's sake, order it; their version of this tomato-smothered dish is one of the best you'll find north of New Orleans. This comfy locals' spot is open Monday to Saturday from 11 am to 10 pm.

For pizza, *Beaudions's Pizza Pub* (☎ 318-356-9200, 302 Hwy 1 S), at Magnolia St, near the city limits, packs 'em in weekdays 11 am to 2 am and weekend nights from 4 pm to 2 am. The cinderblock building doesn't look like much, but the pizza is the best in these parts.

Some Louisianans will tell you that alligator makes good eating for their dogs but they wouldn't touch it. With that in mind, you should steer clear of restaurants that serve wild alligator in any form. One exception to that rule is *The Landing* (☎ 318-352-1579, 530 Front St). Owner/chef Kent Gresham swears that the trick is to use farmed alligator – his experiences with buckshot-riddled wild alligator confirmed the notion that alligator is bad eating otherwise. Kent serves a delicious blackened alligator, and also serves some of the town's best seafood, including a great crawfish étouffée. But no matter what, start your meal with a plate of fried green tomatoes. Main dishes start at about $9. This elegant restaurant is open Tuesday to Friday 11 am to 2 pm and 5 to 10 pm, Saturday 11 am to 10 pm and Sunday 11 am to 9 pm. On Sunday it features a champagne brunch buffet until 2 pm.

Also worth considering is *Monjuni's Italian Café & Grocery* (☎ 318-352-0401, 5909 Hwy 1 Bypass), near Dean St just east of Sibley Lake. Though this location is not as good as the original in Shreveport, the po-boys, pastas and salads are still tasty and cost between $4 and $7. Dinner dishes cost about $7 to $12. It is open for lunch Monday to Saturday from 11 am to 2 pm and for dinner weekdays 4:30 pm to 9 pm and closes on weekends at 10 pm.

Entertainment

Café Isabelle (☎ 318-357-1555, 624 Front St), a trendy little bohemian coffeehouse, is popular for its poetry readings and live acoustic music. It's open weekdays 10 am until 6 pm and weekends around 11 am or noon until 8 pm if there's no evening entertainment. Your best bet is to call first and find out what's going on.

A good place for a drink is the *Cove Bar and Grill* (☎ 318-357-1223), in the Mariner's Restaurant located on Sibley Lake, off the Hwy 1 Bypass heading north. The Cove offers live music on Friday and Saturday evenings and locals stop by to dance.

If you're really lucky, you'll be in town on the last Friday of the month when *Roque's Bar* (☎ 318-352-6586, 235 Carver Ave) comes alive to the sounds of a blues jam. On most other days, a lively group of older gentlemen – most of them proud Creoles of color – hold forth at this bar they call home. The beer is cheap ($1 for a 16-ounce Schlitz), and first-time visitors shouldn't be surprised when one of their bar-mates picks up the tab.

Shopping

Kaffie-Frederick (☎ 318-352-2525), 758 Front St, open since 1863, is a treasure trove of upscale hardware and home furnishings. They stock the largest selection of little red wagons you have ever seen. It is open weekdays 7 am to 5 pm and Saturday from 7 am to 4 pm.

For life's essentials there is a WalMart (☎ 318-352-5607) at 925 Keyser Ave near Williams Ave, on the east side of Cane River Lake. Grocery stores are also located along this stretch.

Getting There & Away

There is neither air nor train service to Natchitoches.

Buses arrive and depart from the Greyhound station (☎ 318-352-8341, 800-231-2222) at 331 Cane River Shopping Center just off Business Hwy 1 S. The station is open weekdays 8 am to 11 am and again from noon to 4 pm. You have to arrange to meet buses on Saturday; the station is closed on Sunday and holidays. Three buses come through daily headed to and from Shreveport ($31 roundtrip; two hours) and three more travel to Alexandria ($25; one hour), with connecting service throughout the region.

Though you won't need a car around Natchitoches, you will need one to explore the Cane River country and Hodges Gardens south of town or Briarwood Nature Preserve north of town.

AROUND NATCHITOCHES
Hodges Gardens

In the 1940s, AJ Hodges reclaimed 4700 acres of land as a tree farm and experimental arboretum. Where turn-of-the-century workers left an abandoned rock quarry, Hodges fashioned formal gardens and a 225-acre lake.

Today Hodges Gardens (☎ 318-586-3523) are encircled by a 10-mile loop road that offers access to forested hiking trails as well as 60 acres of formal terraced gardens. The gardens are a maze of switchback, paved trails skirted by babbling brooks. Occasionally, a deer will sprint across the path ahead of you.

Fishing boats are available for rental at $50 to $75 for a whole day. The catch is catfish, bass and bream, and you must bring your own tackle.

Campsites rent for $10, but be aware that the admission fee, $6.50 for adults and $3 for children, is still charged. Drive 25 miles west of Natchitoches on Hwy 1 and then turn south for about 10 miles on Hwy 171 to reach Hodges Gardens.

Across the street is **Emerald Hills Golf Resort** (☎ 318-586-4661), a 100-room hotel with nice accommodations for $70/75 for singles/doubles. A round of golf is $26 Monday to Thursday and $39 Friday to Sunday.

Briarwood Nature Preserve

Briarwood (☎ 318-576-3379), also known as the Caroline Dormon Nature Preserve, is as remote and rustic as Hodges Gardens is accessible and well groomed. It's 120 acres of wild woods and wildflowers surrounding the old log cabin of environmentalist Caroline Dormon, who set up shop here to study horticulture. The preserve is open during the months of April, May, August and November, but only on Saturday from 9 am to 5 pm and Sunday noon to 5 pm. It's located about 37 miles north of Natchitoches via Hwy 84 east and Hwy 71 north, and 3 miles south of the town of Saline on Hwy 9. Admission is $5.

Rebel State Historic Site

The Rebel site harks back to Civil War days when, as legend has it, a lost 'rebel' soldier who stopped to take a drink from a spring was killed by Union cavalrymen. Today, a gravesite marks the spot of the Unknown Confederate Soldier, for whom locals hold memorial services once a year. On a less somber note, Rebel also brings people together to revel in the area's country and gospel music in a open-air amphitheater. The soldier's memorial has expanded to include local performers as well as nationally known music acts; other times of the year, folk artists are invited to play. There's an Annual Fiddling Championship the first weekend of April. When live music isn't on, visit the **Louisiana Country Music Museum** (☎ 318-472-6255), which tells the story of how different folk music traditions developed in the this part of Louisiana, including gospel and string band. Leave time for the listening room. Rebel State is about 25 miles west of Natchitoches on Hwy 1221. The museum is open daily 9 am to 5 pm. Admission costs $2 for adults; free for children 12 and under and seniors.

CANE RIVER COUNTRY

Once you've spent any time driving through Louisiana and Mississippi, columned plantation houses begin to draw about the same amount of attention as double-wide mobile homes. They're everywhere.

From bayou-front palaces to hill country showplaces, these homes all begin to look the same. And, should you choose to tour one of these mansions, chances are that some hoop-skirt-wearing guide will regale you with a tall tale of brave Southern belles defying 'Damnyankee' looters – all in the name of saving 'the old home place.' If you saw *Gone With the Wind*, you know the shtick.

The Cane River country, formally known as the Cane River National Heritage Area, just south of Natchitoches, is different – far different. Sure, there are some fairly typical plantations along the 35-mile stretch of Hwy 119 that leads to Cloutierville. But the monotony of all those white columns is broken by two outstanding attractions: Melrose Plantation, home of folk artist Clementine Hunter and Creole dowager Marie Thérèse Coincoin; and the Bayou Folk Museum, residence of Kate Chopin, who wrote an early feminist novel titled *The Awakening* in 1899.

South from Natchitoches, the highway hugs the bank of the Cane River Lake, and you'll pass locals dipping fishing poles into the lazy river or whiling the afternoon away on front gallery rockers.

Along the western bank of the lake you pass four plantations in quick succession: Oak Lawn (which has been restored by *Steel Magnolias* author Robert Harling), Cherokee, Beau Fort and Oakland, all suitably white and predictably unimpressive. Drive a bit farther on this two-lane meandering blacktop and you begin to notice that this is not just a land of wealth. Poor folks live here, too. Their jauntily painted shotgun houses and hard-listing trailers are proof-positive of their claim to this land. For more information on this fascinating part of Louisiana, call the Cane River National Heritage Area (☎ 318-356-5555).

Melrose Plantation

Just north of the Hwy 119 intersection with Hwy 493 is Melrose Plantation (☎ 318-379-0055), a fascinating complex of three main buildings and various outbuildings dating as far back as 1790. Though the 'big house' looms large from the road, the most compelling features are the African and Yucca Houses, which are found out back. The plantation is open daily 1 pm to 4 pm. There are only guided tours, which take about a half-hour. Admission is $6/4/3 for adults/students/children.

The **Yucca House**, built around 1796, was the original dwelling on the plantation, but it is perhaps best known as the guesthouse where, in the early to mid-1900s, hostess Cammie Henry offered lodging to artists and writers such as William Faulkner and John Steinbeck. This is where folklorist Lyle Saxon lived while writing about Louisiana (his *Children of Strangers* is about the Cane River area) and where the artist François Mignon stayed for 32 years after being invited for only six weeks.

The **African House**, of Congo-style construction, is just about the most African-looking building you are likely to see in the US. This two-story structure, capped by an enormous roof with a 12-foot overhang,

The Creoles of Cane River Country

Indiscriminate use of the term Creole can get you in a lot of trouble when in Louisiana. Ask any two natives who or what is Creole, and most likely the only thing they'll agree on is that, whether you are referring to people, architecture or food, Cajun and Creole are not synonymous.

From there, it gets kind of murky.

When the term came into frequent use in the 1700s, it was used to refer to people of European parentage who were born in the colonies. By the 1800s usage had expanded to embrace all things and peoples that were native to Louisiana. Then, people born of mixed European and African ancestry began claiming the mantle of Creole, much to the consternation of aristocratic natives of pure French ancestry, who felt it was theirs. And, to further confuse the matter, many people began to use the term 'Creole' to refer to the architecture and foods of New Orleans.

Today, the debate rages on. Only around Natchitoches and Cane River country are you likely to find a consensus among residents as to who is and who is not a Creole. There, the term is most often used to refer to *les gens de couleur libre*, translated from the French as 'free people of color.'

These Creoles of color, as they are also known, trace their origins to the union of a slave, Marie Thérèse Coincoin, and the scion of a noble French family, Claude Thomas Pierre Metoyer, whose 10 children have produced as many as 10,000 descendants. Long a wealthy people (during ante-bellum days, many owned plantations worked by slaves), these Creoles still consider themselves neither white nor black but a distinct race, a Creole race, *les gens de couleur libre*. Theirs is an insular community, as constrained by the dictates of society and parentage as any you might find. Centered along the Cane River near the Melrose Plantation at Isle Brevelle, this micro-culture is one of the most unique you will encounter during your travels in the Deep South. While there, be sure to drop by the St Augustine Church, established in 1803 by Marie Thérèse and Pierre Metoyer's eldest son Augustin, and wander around the church's cemetery – you're sure to see a lot of wrought iron crosses and tombs inscribed with the Metoyer name.

looks like a squat brick mushroom. Built in 1800, the ground floor once served as a jail for rebellious slaves, and the top floor is where folk artist Clementine Hunter, a longtime employee of the plantation, painted a vivid, colorful 50-foot mural depicting life as she knew it on the plantation. Though Hunter was a prolific artist (she died at the age of 101 in 1988), and many of her paintings are on display in museums across Louisiana, this is her masterwork. To see this work alone is worth the price of admission.

More so than the architecture or art, Melrose Plantation is unique as a place where women rather than men were the dominant forces. From Cammie Henry and Clementine Hunter back to Marie Thérèse Coincoin, the home bears the imprint of a long line of forceful, enterprising and artistic women. Foremost among them was

perhaps Coincoin. Born a slave in 1742, she became the mistress of a Frenchman named Metoyer, with whom she had 10 children.

By 1778 Metoyer had granted Coincoin her freedom and a parcel of land, including what is now Melrose Plantation. For years Coincoin worked the land with slaves of her own, eventually earning enough money to purchase the freedom of her children not already freed by Metoyer. At the time of her death in 1816, the family owned over 1200 acres of land and almost a hundred slaves. Though the plantation was later lost due to mounting debt, her heirs and those of Metoyer still live in the Cane River area today and proudly boast of their lineage as Creoles of color.

Magnolia Plantation

Eight miles of narrow roadway separate Melrose from the town of Cloutierville.

Along the way, you pass beautiful Magnolia Plantation (☎ 318-379-2221), 5487 Hwy 119, which, with 27 rooms, including a Catholic chapel, is one of the largest plantation homes in the area. The land grant for Magnolia was obtained in the late 1700s and the home was built in 1835. This plantation is one of only two National Bicentennial Farms (given to farms that have been in the same family for over 200 years) west of the Mississippi and contains the only cotton press still in its original location. Magnolia is open Monday to Saturday 1 to 4 pm. Admission is $5/4/2 for adults/students/children.

Bayou Folk Museum

Just off Hwy 1 on the eastern edge of Cloutierville, the Bayou Folk Museum (☎ 318-379-2233) is an authentic restoration of the plantation home once managed by author Kate Chopin (1851–1904). The museum doesn't feature many mementos of Chopin's life but is nevertheless an interesting place to visit. Fans of Chopin are probably most familiar with her 1899 novel *The Awakening*, which depicts a woman's sexual and emotional coming of age, but they may be less familiar with her colorful work *Bayou Folk*, for which the museum is named.

Wander from room to room, taking in the museum's enjoyable collection of ephemera and oddities, including a cross-emblazoned cookie cutter once used by the local Catholic church when making communion wafers. Those with more morbid tastes should ask to see the hand-hewn coffins stacked up in the attic.

With a little luck, you will get the guide who, when queried about a bright, almost surreal painting in one of the front rooms, answered, 'Oh, Father Albert must have done that after taking LSD.'

The two-story house, built around 1806, is nothing grand, but it's surrounded by a variety of outbuildings that bear a look, including a doctor's office dedicated to the area's first woman doctor. Jammed full of antique medical equipment, the building was moved to the site in 1938, while a

nearby blacksmith shop was added several years later.

On your way out, catch a glimpse of Chopin's well-worn copy of Thomas Hardy's *Jude the Obscure*, displayed in a showcase on the bottom floor. The museum is open Monday to Saturday from 10 am to 5 pm, Sunday from 1 pm to 5 pm. Admission is $5/3/2 for adults/students/children ages six to 12.

KISATCHIE NATIONAL FOREST

It's not hard to stay off the beaten path in Louisiana. Outdoor enthusiasts can explore a vast wilderness, which, thanks to its dispersal across the state, is never more than an hour's drive from any of the region's population centers. Though attempts made during the 1920s to save some of the area's virgin forest failed, what remains is as densely forested and remote an environment as you are likely to encounter in the state. While roaming under cover of immense longleaf pine trees, you may well

Clementine Hunter, Creole folk artist

encounter bears, opossums, deer and other animals, but you'll rarely see another group of hikers, for this is truly a wilderness and humanity's imprint is rarely seen.

Spanning 937 sq miles in northern and central Louisiana, Kisatchie National Forest, the only national forest in Louisiana, is comprised of two main districts: **Kisatchie**, which has ranger headquarters in Natchitoches (☎ 318-352-2568); and **Winn**, headquarters in Winnfield (☎ 318-628-4664). Four other districts, not covered here, are **Catahoula**, which has headquarters in Bentley (☎ 318-765-3554); **Evangeline**, in Alexandria; **Caney**, in Homer (☎ 318-927-2061); and **Calcasieu**, in Leesville (☎ 318-239-6576).

The national forest offers campgrounds, automobile tours, canoeing and hundreds of miles of hiking trails. Camping is permitted anywhere in the forest all year long, unless posted otherwise – with one notable exception. During hunting season, which is from October through April, visitors to the Catahoula and Kisatchie districts should only camp where designated. Fees are charged for use of a few facilities, but in all cases rates are reasonable. Camping permits, with the sole exception noted above, are not required.

The following is a sampling of the variety of recreational opportunities available in the two main districts. For more detailed information, or to obtain maps, contact the Kisatchie Supervisor's office (☎ 318-473-7160), 2500 Shreveport Hwy, Pineville, 71360.

Longleaf Scenic Byway

Located between the cities of Natchitoches and Alexandria, the Kisatchie Ranger District is home to the Longleaf Scenic Byway, a 17-mile route that runs from Hwy 119 (near the intersection with I-49), just west of the town of Derry, connecting with Hwy 117 in the west.

Along this narrow, blacktop road are nine campgrounds, ranging from rustic to improved. One of the most beautiful is the *Kisatchie Bayou campground*, where sandy, level campsites are arrayed along the waterfront. To get there, turn off Hwy 117 in the direction of Middle Branch Overlook onto Forest Service Rd 321, travel for 6 miles, then turn left onto Forest Service Rd 366. The camping fee is $2 per night.

Also worth noting here are the pock-marked trees just east of the turn off for Middle Branch Overlook. These pine trees, infected with red-heart decay from past logging operations, are the favorite haunt of the endangered red-cockaded woodpecker.

From the campground, head out on the **Caroline Dormon Hiking and Horse Trail**, a 12.8-mile trail that also passes through – and is well-marked – from the main road. It extends all the way to the Kisatchie Hills Wilderness campground. Dedicated to the mother of the Kisatchie, the Caroline Dormon hike gently meanders through beautiful fields of wildflowers and pine trees. For more of a challenge, consider hiking part of the 8700-acre **Kisatchie Hills Wilderness**, which juts to the north along the first several miles of the Longleaf Scenic Byway's start at Hwy 119. Locals call it the 'Little Grand Canyon' due to its steep slopes, rocky outcrops and other rugged topographic features. It's pretty different from the pine forests that dominate most of the hiking spots in this part of the state.

Five miles south on Hwy 117, at the corner of Hwy 118, is the **Kisatchie Country Store** (☎ 337-239-0119), where all the world seems to stop for bait, food and directions. The store is also headquarters for Kisatchie Cajun Expedition, which offers a variety of self-guided float trips on Kisatchie Bayou, suitable for beginner to expert canoeists. Trips are offered seasonally, usually from early January until the end of the rainy season. In addition to pointing people in the right direction, they rent canoes ($20 per day including shuttle), provide shuttle service to the Kisatchie Bayou ($7.50 to $10) and have facilities for hot showers ($2.50). It's open daily 6:30 am to 8 pm.

Dogwood Trail

Located between the cities of Natchitoches and Winnfield, Winn Ranger District is home to a spectacular, short hiking loop. Dogwood Trail, located on the side of Hwy 84 near Natchitoches approximately a mile west of Hwy 477, is a 1.3-mile hiking trail that is at its best during the spring when the dogwoods are in bloom.

Gum Springs Horse Trail

Farther into the Winn District of Kisatchie, on Hwy 84, Gum Springs has two developed trails for hikers or horseback riders. The Blue Loop Trail is a little over 5 miles and often used by covered wagons. The trail goes through open forest of cedar and pine. The Yellow Loop travels for 18 miles along ponds and primitive campsites. Gum Springs is a very beautiful place to see wildflowers and has great campgrounds along both trails.

Saline Bayou National Scenic River

Beginning near the town of Saline and running 21 miles south to Saline Lake is Saline Bayou National Scenic River, a tranquil yet wild waterway that is ideal for a day of canoeing on the cypress-strewn waters. Short of idyllic at times, canoeing here can be downright challenging, so here are a few things to keep in mind before heading out: carefully consider the water level before departing on a trip, because high water can mean high danger; when the water level is low, portaging is often required; swift currents happen; and, lastly, water moccasins, wasps nests and alligators lurk below. Still, the variety of wildlife and undisturbed ecosystems that make up the Bayou are worth discovery. Developed campsites are available off Forest Service Rd 513 at Cloud Crossing Recreation Area, which is also the starting point for the Saline Bayou Trail, a wooded, waterside trail. The ideal time to hike is December and January – other times of the year, bring *lots* of mosquito spray and be prepared for flooded trail sections. Call the Winn Ranger District (☎ 318-628-4664) for current water levels and other information.

ALEXANDRIA & AROUND
• pop 46,000

Local chamber-of-commerce types like to call Alexandria the Crossroads of Louisiana. After visiting this compact city on the banks of the Red River, you might be inclined to agree that crossroads is a fitting moniker. With a few notable exceptions, Alexandria is truly a place one passes through en route to somewhere else.

Established, along with its cross-river neighbor Pineville, as a trading center in the mid-18th century, Alexandria prospered as the seat of government for Rapides Parish until, on May 13, 1864, Union General Nathaniel Banks burned almost every structure in town. By the early 1900s, Alexandria was reborn as a center for the Louisiana timber industry, as thousands of men flooded the area searching for work in the sawmills and lumber camps.

In 1941, Rapides and surrounding parishes played host to the largest peacetime military maneuvers in the history of the nation as over 500,000 troops under the leadership of General George Patton and Colonel Dwight Eisenhower (among others) engaged in war games and planning for battle in Europe.

In 1992, the area's largest employer, England Air Force Base, closed. Though doomsayers were quick to predict Alexandria's demise, local business leaders and civic organizations banded together. Now the base has been turned into an industrial park and retirement village, while the downtown area, on the wane since the 1970s, is slowly coming alive as a cultural and recreational center.

Orientation & Information

MacArthur Drive is the great octopus of a highway that encircles Alexandria. Also known as Hwy 71, this limited-access, four-to six-lane road is at the core of city life, its tentacle-like frontage roads ensnaring the whole of Alexandria in its vast grasp. As

N MacArthur, MacArthur, and S MacArthur Drive, it is a much busier and more useful thoroughfare than I-49, which runs north and south through the eastern flank of downtown. But once you have mastered MacArthur, you've got Alexandria licked.

The visitor center for Alexandria and Pineville (☎ 318-443-7049) is in the Alexandria Mall at 3437 Masonic Drive.

ATMs can be found all along the MacArthur Drive frontage roads, especially near Alexandria Mall, just east of the traffic circle. Also try downtown along 3rd St and in the 3700 block of Jackson Ave.

The main post office (☎ 318-487-9402) is downtown at 515 Murray St.

Though Waldenbooks operates a local branch at Alexandria Mall, the best bookseller in these parts is Books-A-Million (☎ 318-448-5116), 3660 North Blvd. Complete with a coffee shop, this large and well-stocked chain store is open daily 9 am to 11 pm. The Rapides Parish Library (☎ 318-445-2411) is downtown at 411 Washington St, at the corner of 4th St. The Alexandria Historical and Genealogical Library (☎ 318-487-8556) is just a few doors down, at 503 Washington St.

Emergency services are provided by Huey P Long Medical Center (☎ 318-473-6280), 352 Hospital Blvd, Pineville; Rapides Regional Medical Center (☎ 318-473-3000), 211 4th St; and St Frances Cabrini Hospital (☎ 318-487-1122), 3330 Masonic Drive.

Kent House

Owing to its location in a middle-class neighborhood just off MacArthur Drive, it's difficult to suspend a sense of 21st-century disbelief when visiting Kent House (☎ 318-487-5998), 3601 Bayou Rapides Rd. Rumor has it that this home, completed in 1800, was spared destruction during the Civil War in deference to its owner, who, like marauding Union General Sherman, was a member of the Masonic order. It is also said to be the oldest still-standing structure in central Louisiana.

Though the big house is a wonderful example of French colonial architecture, the collection of outbuildings recently moved to the property are more interesting. Among the structures are a blacksmith shop, two slave cabins and a kitchen where open-hearth cooking demonstrations are held every Wednesday from October through April. The guides are happy to answer questions about the antique farm equipment on display, taking special delight in pointing out a hand-rocked butter churn that local school children often mistake for a television set. Also of interest is the massive brick sugar mill where employees boil up a mess of syrup each November. Open Monday through Saturday from 9 am to 5 pm and Sunday by appointment, Kent House charges $5 admission for adults, with reduced prices for students and children.

Hotel Bentley

As much a sight to see as a place to spend the night, the Hotel Bentley (☎ 318-448-9600), 200 Desoto St, has, since its opening in 1908, achieved near mythical status in Alexandria. Though now owned by the Radisson chain, desk clerks at the Hotel Bentley relish telling the (apocryphal?) story of lumber magnate Joseph Bentley, who, when refused a room at the Rapides Hotel because of his shabby dress, built the Bentley and pledged that no one, including people of color, would ever be refused service in his hotel.

Dubbed the Biltmore of the Bayous (or the Waldorf of the Red River), the Bentley is an imposing neoclassical building with massive columns that looks like it belongs on Park Ave in New York instead of on a narrow street in a fourth-tier Southern city.

Inside, a marble fishpond and fountain are at the center of the lobby beneath a domed ceiling with stained-glass inserts. All in all, it's a fine spot to cool off on a hot summer day or to warm yourself on a cold one. Though the Bentley still impresses, it is no longer at the center of social life in Alexandria. Long gone are the days when Louisiana Governor Earl Long kept a suite of rooms here or when leaders like General George Patton used the hotel as a headquarters while planning WWII military offensives. (History buffs hungry for more should be sure to read the two historical markers out front.)

Arna Bontemps African-American Museum & Cultural Arts Center

The center (☎ 318-473-4692), 1327 3rd St, is more a cultural clearinghouse than a museum. Though the facility is housed in Bontemps' boyhood home (circa 1890), visitors only get to see a few books and lesser personal effects of this author, poet and scholar. Bontemps made his mark during the Harlem Renaissance of the 1920s alongside luminaries such as Richard Wright and Zora Neale Hurston, but he is perhaps best known as an author of children's literature. It is open Tuesday through Friday 10 am to 4 pm and Saturday 10 am to 2 pm; admission is free.

Wild Azalea National Recreation Trail

The Wild Azalea Trail is Louisiana's longest and is easily reached from Alexandria. Within Kisatchie's Evangeline Ranger District (☎ 318-445-9396), the Wild Azalea winds through 31 miles of pine woods and boggy creeks, decorated along the way with pink azaleas and dogwood trees, the latter of which turn sheer white when in bloom in early spring. The trail has five entry points, but from Alexandria, the easiest thing to do is head south on Hwy 165 until it connects with Hwy 287 (about 15 miles), head east on Hwy 287 and start from the trailhead on the right. Evangeline Camp, complete with water and restrooms, offers respite along the way.

Other Attractions

Founded in 1906, **Louisiana College**, 1140 College Drive in Pineville, is a Baptist-supported liberal arts school set on an 81-acre tract covered by native pines, oaks and dogwoods. At the center of the campus is the attractive columned facade of Alexandria Hall. Though home to only 1000 students, the college offers a surprising array of performances and lectures. Call ☎ 318-487-7011 for more information on campus events.

The impressively housed **Alexandria Museum of Art** (☎ 318-443-3458), 900 Main St, is worth a quick look. The museum features an extensive collection of Louisiana folk art as well as works by regional artists and local collections. It also includes an interactive art gallery for kids. From one of the top galleries, you can also sneak a peek at the improving riverfront area – a good place to stroll. The museum is open Tuesday through Friday 10 am to 5 pm and weekends 11 am to 5 pm. Admission is \$4 for adults and \$2 for children.

The wooden boardwalks that encircle the 500 animals at the **Alexandria Zoological Park** (☎ 318-473-1143), 3016 Masonic Drive (in Bringhurst Park), provide a good afternoon's diversion. Though this compact little park doesn't measure up to those you see in larger cities, this one is recently renovated and, at \$2 for adults and \$1 for children, a comparative bargain. It also features a Louisiana Habitat Exhibit that by itself is worth the price of admission – lots of alligators and snakes. The zoo is open daily 9 am to 5 pm.

For a glimpse of one of the most arresting neon signs, drive by **Hokus Pokus Liquor** (advertised as 'the house of many spirits'), 2130 Lee St, and watch the straw-hatted ghostlike angel flap its neon wings. You won't be the first person to drive out of the way to view the sign. Just to catch a glimpse of this wonderful piece of neon Americana, Governor Earl Long used to make a detour down Lee St on his way to the Hotel Bentley. If the tales they tell about Uncle Earl are true, he probably picked up a bottle or two while he was in the neighborhood.

Special Events

The Louisiana Nursery Festival (☎ 318-748-6832) brings bargain-hunting plant lovers to nearby Forest Hill, the Nursery Capital of Louisiana, during the third weekend in March.

The annual Cenlabration (☎ 318-473-1127) takes place along the Red River in Alexandria each Labor Day weekend, when the locals celebrate their heritage of 'levee livin' by racing boats, reenacting historical battles, scarfing food and drinking.

The Louisiana Pecan Festival – including the contest to choose the Pecan Festival Queen – is held the first weekend in November in nearby Colfax. Call the local chamber of commerce (☎ 318-627-3711) for more information.

Places to Stay

As with most things in Alexandria, the budget motels are strung out along MacArthur Drive. On the budget side, there are three decent choices – all with swimming pools. The *Alexandria Inn* (☎ 318-473-2302, 1212 MacArthur Drive) features simple, spare rooms for $29/34 for a single/double. Just up the road is the newly renovated *Economy Inn* (☎ 318-448-3401, 3801 Halsey St), with rooms at $34/46. At *Motel 6* (☎ 318-445-2336, 546 MacArthur Drive) rooms go for $34 and up.

Downtown, at 701 4th St, is the comparatively upscale *Holiday Inn* (☎ 318-442-9000), where rooms rent for $60 to $70 a night. With a business center and complimentary shuttle service, this hotel is preferred by many businesspeople.

Despite all the hoopla, a night's stay at the *Radisson Hotel Bentley* (☎ 318-448-9600, 200 Desoto St) is really not that expensive. Though the lobby of this grand old hotel still shines, the rooms are pretty standard. Still, at $79/89, it may be worth the splurge.

Matt's Cabin (☎ 318-487-8340, susan@inglewoodplantation.com), definitely worth the splurge, is a refurbished sharecropper's cabin stationed at the Inglewood Plantation, south of town off Hwy 71/167. Still a working plantation, the view from every window at Matt's looks onto rows of green corn and magnolia trees. Complete with full kitchen, outdoor barbecue, fireplace and an old-fashioned gallery and rocking chairs, Matt's is not just a night's stay – it's a step back in time into a different world. As part of your stay, the owners extend use of the big house's pool and tennis courts and will gladly give tours of the plantation. Rates

are $125 per night (Friday and Saturday) and $90 (Sunday to Thursday).

Places to Eat

The best restaurant in Alexandria is actually 12 miles down the road, just north of Lecompte on Hwy 71 S. Open since 1928, *Lea's* (☎ 318-776-5178, 1810 Hwy 71 S) serves simple Southern fare to a loyal cadre of regulars who make the pilgrimage for some of the best pies ($14 for a whole pie and $2 to $3 for a slice; boysenberry was one of the eight varieties available) and baked ham ($8) you will find in the South. Lea's is open Tuesday to Thursday 7 am to 6 pm and Friday to Sunday 7 am to 7 pm.

Just across the Jackson Street bridge in Pineville is *Lee J's on the Levee* (☎ 318-487-4628, 208 Main St). Their lunchtime buffet ($5) offers you a choice of meat (fried chicken comes highly recommended), three vegetables and cornbread in a cheerful little building with lots of windows. It is open weekdays 11 am to 2 pm.

Open since 1956, *Jim's Westside Bar-b-que* (☎ 318-443-9607, 3336 Monroe St) looks like a barbecue shack should – clean, functional and smoky. Lawrence (Jim's brother) and staff serve high-quality smoked sirloin beef, ham and sausage accompanied by near perfect potato salad, baked beans or dirty rice. Cooking starts at 4:30 am every day on the same cooker they've used since the beginning. Sandwiches are less than $3; a whole chicken will set you back $6.95. It is open Tuesday to Friday 10:30 am to 6 pm and Monday and Saturday until 3 pm.

For a taste of nostalgia try the *Sentry Grill* (☎ 318-445-0952, 1002 3rd St). Located in an old downtown drugstore, this vintage diner serves good, greasy breakfasts and better plate lunches for $4 to $5. It is open weekdays 7:30 am to 3 pm, Saturday 7:30 am to 1 pm. Also downtown and economical is *Critic's Choice* (☎ 318-442-3333, 415 Murray St). The Philadelphia-born owners serve a variety of sandwiches (including hoagies) Philadelphia-style, which means that the meat is sliced thin and everything is blanketed in cheese, onions and peppers. The place is open Monday through

Wednesday 10:30 am to 3 pm, Thursday and Friday 10:30 am to 9 pm and Saturday 5 pm to 9 pm.

For the best seafood in town, head to **Tunk's Cypress Inn** (☎ *318-487-4014, 888-350-2158, 9507 Hwy 28 W*). This restaurant and oyster bar is on the shore of Kincaid Lake, about 9 miles out of town and worth the pretty drive it takes to get there. Don't be surprised to arrive to an overflowing parking lot. Anyone you ask will say there's nowhere as good as Tunk's for crawfish ($14), oysters ($4.50 for six half shells) and any other kind of sea creature. It serves a good steak ($20), too. There's plenty of room at Tunk's, spread across a formal dining room upstairs, a downstairs oyster bar and an outside deck. Country bands play on the deck every night except Monday. Tunk's is open for dinner Monday to Saturday 5 to 10 pm.

Bangkok Restaurant (☎ *318-449-1950, 3648 North Blvd*), a hybrid Chinese, Thai and Japanese restaurant, serves economical noodle dishes and soups ($5) as well as more elaborate fish entrees daily 11 am to 10 pm. For the best of what this kitchen has to offer, choose exclusively from the Thai dishes.

El Reparo Mexican Restaurant & Grill (☎ *318-487-0207, 550 MacArthur Drive*) is the area's best Mexican restaurant, expertly run by the Melendez family and very affordable (most entrees cost under $10). It is open Sunday to Thursday 11 am to 10 pm and Friday and Saturday 11 am to 10:30 pm.

During the hot summer months, some locals like to cool off by resting their heads on the cool black-and-yellow tile bar at **Giamanco's Suburban Gardens** (☎ *318-442-6974, 3322 Jackson St*). Even when the summertime temperature is nearing 100°F, the bar is indeed cool to the touch, but the real reason to visit this funky (almost tacky) restaurant is to taste Alexandria's best Italian food. Among the specialties are oysters on the half shell ($6), chicken liver spaghetti ($5) and pollo à la Michelle ($10; chicken rolled in Italian spices and then deep fried). In business since 1951, Subur-

ban Gardens is open Tuesday to Saturday 4 pm to 10 pm.

Entertainment

It's not easy to find an evening's diversion in Alexandria. Though performances are held here infrequently, **Café Au Lait** (☎ *318-448-1802, 2312 MacArthur Drive*) is worth a try for poetry readings and acoustic music. Most of the customers, however, seem to be more interested in drinking coffee and surfing the Web on the computers scattered about the room.

Mojos (☎ *318-448-4890, 3425 Jackson St*), in the Emerald Square shopping mall, is a stomping ground for sports fans. A big screen TV broadcasts game after game from 11 am until 3 am; there is food service until 10:30 pm.

If not for dinner, head to **Tunk's Cypress Inn** (see the Places to Eat section) for the live country bands that play nightly.

Spectator Sports

If you happen to be in town from May through September, plan a trip to Bringhurst Field (☎ *318-473-2237*), 1 Babe Ruth Drive, home of the Alexandria Aces, a AA baseball team in the Texas-Louisiana minor league. You really haven't seen a pro baseball game until you've experienced the intimacy of a small ballpark like this one.

If hockey is more your style, the Alexandria Warthogs (☎ *318-449-4647*) play two to three times a week at Rapides Parish Coliseum from October through March. Tickets cost $7 to $20.

Shopping

If you're in search of a souvenir (or if you're just out of clean clothes), pick up a T-shirt from Lea's restaurant (see the Places to Eat section) in Lecompte. Made of heavy cotton and emblazoned with a picture of one of their famous pies, they're a bargain at $12.50.

Alexandria Mall (☎ *318-448-0227*), 3437 Masonic Drive, should suffice for more mundane shopping needs; it's open Monday to Saturday from 10 am to 9 pm, Sunday 12:30 pm to 5:30 pm.

Getting There & Away

They may call it Alexandria international airport, but with the exception of military flights, all service is regional, not international. Located at 1303 Billy Mitchell Blvd off England Drive, the airport is served by Delta, American, Continental and Northwest airlines with connecting flights to the hub cities of Houston, Dallas, Memphis and Atlanta.

Greyhound (☎ 318-445-4524), 403 Bolton St, which is open 24 hours a day, provides bus service to the larger cities in the region, including Shreveport (six daily; two to three hours) and Natchitoches (three daily; one hour), but a car is the preferable mode of transport whether traveling around town or between cities in the region.

MARKSVILLE
• pop 6000

The farther south and west you travel in Louisiana, the closer you come to the mythical Acadiana, home of the Cajuns. Once you're south of Alexandria, the only sure way to tell whether you're in Cajun Country

---

Ferriday – What a Gene Pool!

Located just across the Mississippi River from Natchez, Mississippi, Ferriday is a town in conflict with itself. Here, bars and churches compete for the same clientele. And, in this small town, much of that clientele is related.

Firebrand rock & roller Jerry Lee Lewis, country music singer Mickey Gilley and adulterous televangelist Jimmy Swaggart all hail from Ferriday, and though they have taken different paths to stardom, each is a strange and oddly similar amalgam of secular and sacred – of Saturday night and Sunday morning. The town of Ferriday operates a museum devoted to their favorite sons on Hwy 65, 2 miles north of town, but to be frank, it is a bit sterile. Housed in a former bank building, the displays give you an idea of what these men have done, but no rationale as to why.

Questions are better answered by a trip to the **Lewis House** (☎ 318-757-4422, 318-757-2563 for reservations), 712 Louisiana Ave, and its next-door neighbor, **Lewis Terrell Drive Thru**, a liquor store. Owned by Jerry Lee's sister Frankie Jean, this cultural compound is the wackiest and most wonderful spot you'll encounter north of New Orleans.

You enter the museum through what was once the garage of a ranch-style brick home. Soon after paying the $6.50 admission, Frankie Jean launches into a rapid-fire recitation of her family history, talking unashamedly about her father's moonshine still, her brother's antics and her cousin Jimmy's infidelities.

Pictures of Jerry Lee, Jimmy Swaggart and Mickey Gilley – all first cousins – cover nearly every surface in the house. A piano sits in every room. Baby portraits and bibles are displayed alongside framed, handwritten sermons by Jerry Lee 'during his religious phase.'

The dining room table is covered with publicity photos and mementos. Look closely for the check from Elvis A Presley to Frankie Jean in the amount of $10,403.99. Ask her about it, and she will tell you, 'Oh, Elvis, he was all on drugs; he thought I was a Chevrolet salesman.'

Give yourself a good hour or so to take it all in. And, when you've had enough, jump back in your car and get in line at Frankie Jean's drive-through liquor store. Even if you are a teetotaler with a taste for nothing stronger than a Coca-Cola, this tin hut, brimming with alcohol and kitsch, is worth a look. Terrell's offers over 40 different shots as well as a variety of mixed drinks, beer and wine – all of which can be consumed in the privacy of your own car. According to Frankie Jean, the only folks in town who don't patronize her store are the Baptists.

The museum is open daily from 1 to 8 pm. Children under 12 are not allowed. The liquor store is open from 9 am to midnight.

is to look for the crock pots. If you walk into a convenience store and spy a crock pot full of boudin sausage next to the cash register, then you are in Cajun Country. No crock pot? No Cajun.

Marksville, seat of government for Avoyelles Parish, is on the cusp of crock pot territory. Founded in 1783 as a French outpost, the city boasts of a long and proud French heritage. Of equal, if not greater, influence has been the continuing Native American presence in the area.

Marksville affords travelers a great introduction to both ancient and modern Native American culture. Today, you may tour the ancient burial mounds of the Marksville culture, view the reclaimed 'Tunica treasure' or try your luck at a local casino owned by the Tunica-Biloxi Indians.

If these Native American sites don't interest you, jump back in your car and drive 90 miles south to Lafayette, where you'll find a crock pot on every counter. (See the Cajun Country chapter for coverage of Lafayette.)

Orientation & Information

Marksville is a fairly compact town. Hwy 1 (known as Tunica Drive within the city limits) runs from the northeast corner of town to the southeast corner, where the Tunica reservation and casino are located, while Preston St runs from its intersection with Tunica Drive on the southern end of town to the northern suburbs. Downtown Marksville lies in the wedge between the two roads.

The tourism office (☎ 318-253-0585) is at 208 S Main St. It can put you in touch with Steve's Bayou Tours (☎ 318-253-9585). Steve will take small groups for hour-long boat rides on nearby Spring Bayou for about $20 per person.

ATMs are found on Tunica Drive and on Main St. The post office (☎ 318-253-9502) is at 207 N Monroe St.

The Avoyelles Parish Library (☎ 318-253-7559) is at 104 N Washington St and is open weekdays 8 am to 5 pm, except Wednesday (9 am to 6 pm) and Saturday 9 am to 1 pm.

Avoyelles Hospital (☎ 318-253-8611), out on Hwy 1192 on the northern outskirts of town, offers emergency services.

Marksville State Commemorative Area

When it comes to funding, this site (☎ 318-253-8954), 700 Martin Luther King Drive, gets short shrift compared to Poverty Point, a Native American site in the northeast corner of the state (see the Poverty Point section in the Northern Louisiana chapter). The Marksville facility makes do with displays and signage that the curator confesses to have retrieved from the attic. That said, there is a certain charm to the yellowed and water-stained map she encourages visitors to run their hands up and down, feeling for the little bumps that represent Indian mounds and their distribution across the Mississippi River Valley.

Dubbed the Marksville culture (a variant of the better-known Hopewell culture centered in Ohio and Illinois) by the archaeologists who discovered the site in the 1920s, this complex society originated around 2,000 years ago in this area (or as the guides like to put it 'when Columbus set foot on New World soil, the Marksville ceremonial center was already 1000 years old'). Archaeologists believe that the extant mounds were used for burial ceremonies rather than defensive purposes.

Along an old river bed in what is now a lower-middle-class neighborhood are five mounds of varying height. They are bordered by a lower half-moon-shaped earthwork. Though the site encompasses 42 acres, given a couple of hours, you can hike around and see most of the mounds. And, if you're lucky, your introductory site overview will be given by the guide who lovingly pokes fun at herself and the condition of the visitor center.

On some Saturdays, the museum sponsors classes where you can learn how to make pottery in the same manner that the Marksville inhabitants once did. The site is open daily 9 am to 5 pm. Admission is $2 for visitors between the ages of 12 and 62; if outside that spectrum, you get in free.

Tunica-Biloxi Museum

Across town from the Marksville State Commemorative Area is another burial mound of more recent construction. Home to the Tunica-Biloxi Museum (☎ 318-253-8174, 800-488-6674), located on the Tunica-Biloxi Reservation on Hwy 1 just south of town, this mound was built in the late 1980s for the symbolic re-interment of some 200,000 artifacts that were looted from graves in the Tunica Cemetery at Trudeau. Most of the objects are from the 1700s when the Tunica traded with French settlers in the area. There is even a story that some of the coins and china that are part of the treasure were given to the Tunica by King Louis XV in appreciation of services provided to French explorers.

The Tunica tout the artifacts as the world's largest collection of Indian and European artifacts from the colonial period in the Mississippi Valley, but the story behind their recovery and the Tunica nation's concurrent ascendance is also interesting.

Until the summer of 1968, what is now known as the Tunica treasure lay buried on the grounds of the Trudeau Plantation near St Francisville. That summer, Leonard Carrier of Bunkie found the centuries-old cache and then spent the next two years digging for more. By 1974, Carrier had unearthed enough artifacts to sell to a consortium of museums including the Peabody and the Smithsonian.

Carrier's gains, though, were short-lived. By 1976, he was embroiled in a lawsuit brought by the Tunica who were seeking return of the artifacts, which they claimed he had robbed from their ancestral graves. Over the next nine years litigation crawled at a snail's pace, but in March of 1985 a federal court ruled that the artifacts did indeed belong to the Tunica, and that they must be returned.

Since that time the Tunica have been hard at work restoring the artifacts, many of which had deteriorated since being exhumed. Today, much of the collection has been restored and shares exhibition space with a diorama that depicts French-Indian relations during the early colonial period. The museum is open daily 8:30 am to 4 pm and charges $2 admission. Its Web site is www.tunica.org.

Special Events

Nearby Bunkie has a Corn Festival (☎ 318-346-2575) the second weekend in June each year, while the burg of Mansura sponsors the Couchon de Lait Festival, where locals roast pigs and make cracklins on the second weekend in May. Call the Mansura Chamber of Commerce (☎ 318-964-2887) for more information.

Places to Stay

Unlike many towns with casinos, you can still find relatively inexpensive accommodations in Marksville. That said, rates are generally 20% higher on the weekends and during other times when the casino is crowded.

The best deal in town is the *Terrace Inn* (☎ *318-253-5274, 915 Tunica Drive W*), an inviting little motel with a pool and free shuttles to the casino. The Terrace charges $40/50 for singles/doubles. If they're all booked up, try the similarly priced *Deluxe Inn* (☎ *318-253-7595, 221 S Preston St*), which also offers free shuttles to the casino.

Directly adjacent to the casino off Hwy 1 is the *Grand Hotel Avoyelles* (☎ *318-253-0777, 800-642-7777, 709 Grand Blvd*), a newer luxury hotel with a large outdoor pool and spa and over 200 rooms for $50 to $99 a night during the week; $100 and up on the weekends. Members of AAA get a $10 discount no matter when they stay.

Places to Eat

The best meal in Marksville requires a little advance planning, but it's more than worth the effort for a taste of John Ed LaBorde's gooey, cheesy crawfish bread. *Panaroma Foods* (☎ *318-253-6403, 815 Tunica Drive W*), on the outskirts of town, has built a national reputation through appearances at the New Orleans Jazz and Heritage Festival every spring, where tens of thousands flock to John Ed's little stand for a taste of his stuffed bread creations ($4). Though most of his business is geared toward local catering, if you call 20 minutes in advance, they will have a crusty, hot sandwich waiting when you arrive. Most mornings they also serve hot cinnamon pecan rolls. All food is packaged to go, and they are open weekdays 6:30 am to 5 pm and Saturday 7:30 am to 11 am.

Locals vouch for **Nanny's** (☎ *318-253-6058, 333 W Tunica Drive*), at Center St, which features a bounteous steam table piled high with vegetables and fried meats for around $5. Nanny's is open weekdays 5:30 am to 10 pm, Saturday 7 am to 11 pm, Sunday 8 am to 2 pm. Bypass the fast food joints and turn your car into **Big Boys Drive In** (☎ *318-253-5219*), on Hwy 1, for a true American drive-in experience. Big Boys represents a dying breed, where the waitresses bring trays overflowing with burgers, shakes and fries straight to your car. Try the crab burger ($2) for something different, and do yourself a real favor by having a fresh strawberry shake (99¢) or a cherry limeade (90¢), made with fresh limes.

Entertainment
If locals are to be believed, when it comes to entertainment, the **Grand Casino Avoyelles** (☎ *318-253-1946, 711 E Tunica Drive*) is the only game in town. Located just south of the Tunica-Biloxi Museum on Hwy 1, this gambling hall, when approached in the heat of a Louisiana summer, looks as though it is floating on a sea of steaming black asphalt. Inside, the usual assortment of T-shirt-clad tourists clutch plastic cups as they pop quarter after quarter into the slot machines or play blackjack, poker, craps, roulette and the like. At least the profits from this casino benefit the local Tunica-Biloxi Indian tribe. Travelers in search of musical entertainment will be pleasantly surprised to find that the casino regularly features well-known entertainers (the Supremes, Waylon Jennings, KC & The Sunshine Band...) in its 30,000-sq-ft entertainment complex, as well as the best from the local music scene. The casino also offers a supervised child care center for kids under 12 and a huge arcade for kids of all ages.

Getting There & Away
Travel via bus or air is best arranged through nearby Alexandria, which is just 30 miles up the road via Hwy 107 or Hwy 1. Or you might try flying in and out of Lafayette, 90 miles south. Despite the popularity of the new casino, it's hard getting to, from or around Marksville without a car.

Northern Louisiana

Stretching from the rich, alluvial soil of Mississippi Delta cotton country in the east to the comparatively arid, mineral-rich lands of the west, northern Louisiana resists encapsulation.

Make no mistake: northern Louisiana is as far removed, culturally and historically, from New Orleans and the Cajun Country of southern Louisiana as Paris, Texas, is from Paris, France. But you would never know it from the profusion of roadside billboards advertising Cajun-this and New Orleans-that. It is also a region in transition – in effect, gradual decline. Many of the downtowns are burnt and empty, boarded

Highlights

- Caney Ranger District, the most far-flung of the Kisatchie National Park's six districts and a destination for hikers, canoeists and anglers
- Lincoln Parish Park, a mecca for mountain bikers
- Shreveport, a former frontier town, as Western as it is Southern and in the midst of a renaissance
- Poverty Point, one of the most important (and most interesting) Native American archaeological sites in the country

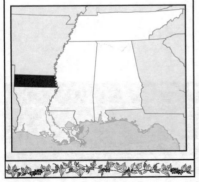

up, and abandoned by those who could abandon them. Commerce and community once centered downtown is more often than not taking place off the interstates as the middle class opt for malls over Main Street. Of course, the shift isn't only economic. It's sociologic, as well. Poor minorities tend to get left behind in these dilapidated areas of the city.

Community officials, chambers of commerce, businesspeople and residents are trying hard to revive once prosperous and architecturally rich old business districts with the Main Street Program. Created 20 years ago by the National Trust for Historic Preservation to help restore America's small towns, the program targets towns and cities with populations of less than 50,000. There are a lot of those in Louisiana. Communities receive grants, historic-district planning and tax incentives to help renovate commercial buildings. It's too soon to say whether Main Street will win over WalMart, but the fight is on.

History

Though drive-through daiquiri stands now dot the landscape, this remains a land apart, where Baptist churches, not neighborhood taverns, are the favored meeting spots, and locals tout a history that begins not with the first European settlement in the 1700s, but with early Native American inhabitants around 1500 BC in what is now known as Poverty Point.

At its height, the Poverty Point culture was the center of a network of more than 100 communities scattered throughout present-day Louisiana, Mississippi and Arkansas. The earthworks visible today hint at a culture that flourished long before Rome and Athens, before the Mayans, only to collapse inexplicably around 750 BC.

The eastern portion of the region had played host to French hunters and trappers for over 50 years when in the early 1790s, French pioneers built the trading post Fort

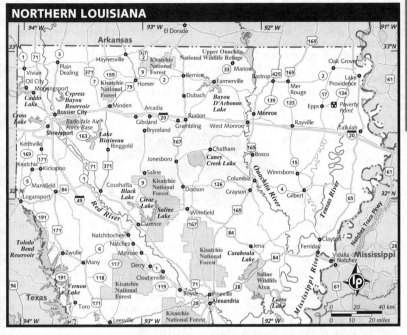

NORTHERN LOUISIANA

Miro, which would later become the city of Monroe.

Until the 1830s, a huge logjam, caused by logging and natural debris, on the Red River stifled westward expansion. Captain Henry Shreve used a snag boat (a steamboat with jaw-like bows) to pull up the tree trunks of the 165-mile floating barrier, in turn opening the area to trade with New Orleans. By 1863, Shreve's frontier-town, named Shreveport in his honor, was the capital of Louisiana, when the state belonged to the short-lived Confederate States of America.

During the early days of the Civil War, northern Louisiana remained on the fringes of the fiercest fighting, a positioning that led to one of the most bizarre acts of the war. In an attempt to bypass the strategic Confederate stronghold of Vicksburg, Mississippi, General Ulysses S Grant tried to dig a canal on the Louisiana side of the Mississippi River to connect Lake Providence to the lower Mississippi by way of a series of oxbow lakes. Stump-filled bayous, a shortage of labor, weather worries and an epidemic of influenza combined to thwart the project altogether. Despite Grant's failure, Union troops captured Vicksburg soon thereafter.

And what has become of Grant's Canal? It's now a lake, favored by local anglers who tell the story to anyone who will listen, relishing the opportunity to cast a line where a Yankee general once floundered.

As in antebellum times, the boom-and-bust cycles of a cotton-centered economy defined life in northern Louisiana in the early years of the 20th century. The discovery of natural gas in 1916 and oil in 1920 pushed the booms higher and the busts lower. Today, the area reels from the continual decline of farming as a way of life, the loss of the local oil economy and the 'Wal-Martization' of America; forces that segue into ongoing segregation between blacks and whites, rich and poor.

Flora & Fauna

The area has a diverse topography bursting with native plants and animals. Be on the lookout for deer, opossum and wild pigs while traveling in the region's forests. You are more likely to spot armadillos, another common species, dead on the roads then waddling through the forest. Herons, red-tailed hawks and woodpeckers make up just part of a thriving bird population. On and around the bayous and lakes, gnarly kneed cypress trees jut from the water and, in some spots, Spanish moss hangs heavy from the trees. Other landscapes are relatively flat with large stands of forests.

Why did the armadillo cross the road?

Outdoor Activities

Northern Louisiana is affectionately known as 'Sportsman's Paradise,' and whether you plan on toting a tent, fly rod or pair of binoculars, getting outside is a main reason to visit. Above Homer in the northwestern part of the state, the Caney District is the most far-flung of the six districts of the Kisatchie National Forest. It offers camping and hiking trails in a desolate and remote setting. For information on any district of Kisatchie, call the supervisor's office in Pineville (☎ 318-473-7160); see also the Central Louisiana chapter for coverage of other districts.

Fantastic fishing is found on the southeast outskirts of Homer, only 30 minutes from Ruston, on Lake Claiborne (☎ 318-927-2976), one of Louisiana's state parks, as well as on Lake Bistineau (☎ 318-745-3503), on Hwy 163 southeast of Shreveport, and Caney Creek Lake (☎ 318-249-2595), in Chatham along Hwy 4 southeast of Ruston, where nine of the state's 10 largest bass have been caught.

World-class mountain biking trails await you at Lincoln Parish Park (see the Ruston & Around section, later in this chapter, for more information). Farther east, the Ouachita River is recognized as one of the most beautiful waterways in the US.

Getting There & Away

Both Monroe and Shreveport boast regional airports with regular connections to hub cities such as New Orleans, Dallas and Houston, Texas.

Greyhound (☎ 800-229-9424) provides bus service throughout the region, as does Trailways, a local company. Most routes are along the primary north-south highway corridors, so reaching smaller towns by bus can be problematic.

Train service is unavailable to and from any of the major population centers around the area; the closest stop is in Lafayette, 180 miles south of Monroe.

On the whole, a car is the preferred mode of transportation. Fortunately, I-20 and I-49 (as well as the older Hwys 71, 80, 165 and 171) make a trip through the region a pleasant series of hourlong and half-hourlong tours from one city or attraction to the next.

MONROE

• pop 53,000 • West Monroe 13,000

Monroe proper traces its colonial origins to Don Juan Filhiol, a French soldier who wrangled a land grant from the Spanish King in 1785. Under Filhiol's direction, Fort Miro was built, and by 1805 it served as the seat of government for Ouachita Parish (WATCH-ih-tah or WASH-ih-tah). West Monroe, formerly Trenton, is a relatively new railroad town, founded in 1880. Both West Monroe and Monroe were part of the original colonial settlement and residents consider the two to be one town.

Due to its location on the Ouachita River, Fort Miro was a major trading center during the 1800s. It was not until 1819 and the arrival of the first steamboat, the *James Monroe*, that area residents impressed by the majesty of the vessel and caught in a sweeping tide of nationalism, renamed their city Monroe.

The early years of the 20th century were kind to Monroe and the surrounding area.

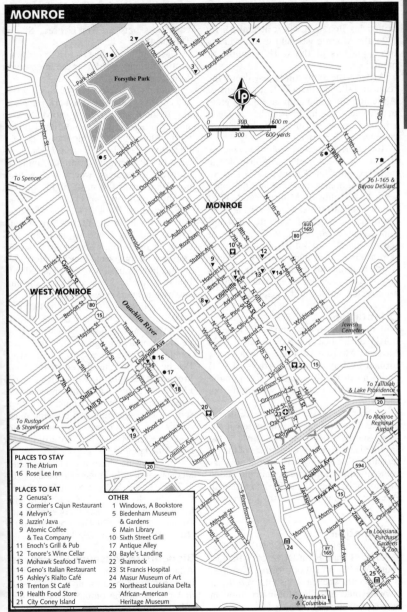

MONROE

Forsythe Park

MONROE

WEST MONROE

Ouachita River

To Spencer

To I-165 &
Bayou DeSiard

To Ruston
& Shreveport

To Tallulah
& Lake Providence

To Monroe
Regional
Airport

Jewish
Cemetery

To Louisiana
Purchase
Gardens
& Zoo

To Alexandria
& Columbia

PLACES TO STAY
7 The Atrium
16 Rose Lee Inn

PLACES TO EAT
2 Genusa's
3 Cormier's Cajun Restaurant
4 Melvyn's
8 Jazzin' Java
9 Atomic Coffee
   & Tea Company
11 Enoch's Grill & Pub
12 Tonore's Wine Cellar
13 Mohawk Seafood Tavern
14 Geno's Italian Restaurant
15 Ashley's Rialto Café
18 Trenton St Café
19 Health Food Store
21 City Coney Island

OTHER
1 Windows, A Bookstore
5 Biedenharn Museum
   & Gardens
6 Main Library
10 Sixth Street Grill
17 Antique Alley
20 Bayle's Landing
22 Shamrock
23 St Francis Hospital
24 Masur Museum of Art
25 Northeast Louisiana Delta
   African-American
   Heritage Museum

In 1916, according to local legend, Louis Lock flipped a half-dollar coin in the air and drilled his first well where it landed. By 1924, the Monroe gas field was producing three-quarters of the world's supply of natural gas.

Around the same time, just down the road in Tallulah, the US Department of Agriculture began a crop-dusting program that would result in the founding of Delta Air Lines, now one of the world's largest commercial air carriers.

Today, the economic boom is long gone. Where the beautiful mansions of the moneyed elite lined Monroe's Grand St, ramshackle homes now abut jails that once served as schools. Monroe and West Monroe appear, at first glance, to be nothing more than a tangle of concrete off-ramps and elevated highways. Well, maybe at second glance, too. But if you're willing to skip around town, there are a few things worth seeking out, including the world's largest Bible museum, an excellent regional art museum and the perfect chili dog.

Orientation

I-20, running east-west, and I-165, running north-south, bisect Monroe and West Monroe. Monroe is situated in a crook formed by Bayou DeSiard (deys-EERD) on the north and the Ouachita River on the west. West Monroe sprawls westward from the river.

In Monroe, the commercial center is around Louisville Ave, but increasingly, mega-shops, such as WalMart, have sprouted along the frontage roads of the interstates. West Monroe's riverfront area has some antique shops and restaurants along Trenton St between Louisville and Coleman Aves, extending westward to Cypress St (Hwy 80).

Information

The visitor center (☎ 318-387-5691, 800-843-1872), 1333 State Farm Drive, off I-165 just south of I-20, is for both towns. It is open 8 am to 5 pm weekdays. Visit its Web site at www.bayou.com/visitors for information on activities, events and lodging.

ATMs can be found on N 18th St and Louisville Ave in Monroe. In West Monroe, your best bets are on Cypress St and Thomas Rd.

The main post office (☎ 318-387-6161) is at 501 Sterlington Rd near the intersection with Desoto St.

Windows, A Bookstore (☎ 318-361-9004), 609 Park Ave near Forsythe Park, is a pleasant, if small, shop with a knowledgeable staff. It's open Monday to Saturday 10 am to 6 pm. While there, pick up a copy of John Dufresne's *Louisiana Power & Light*, a portrait of the fictional Fontana family of Monroe; this quirky, wacky, well-written novel is one of the most highly praised Southern works in years.

Serendipity Books (☎ 318-388-4202), 1012 N 4th St in the rear of the Atomic Coffee and Tea Company, is a cluttered closet of used books and records stacked among a jumble of old couches. Hours are erratic, but it's usually open Wednesday to Friday 10 am to 8 pm, with later opening and closing hours on weekends.

The main library (☎ 318-327-1490) is at 1800 Stubbs Ave at the corner of N 18th St.

The best musical offerings in Monroe can be found, oddly enough, on the radio. Each Sunday morning from 8 to 10 am Sister Pearlie Tolliver, 'the Queen of the Dial,' broadcasts a gospel program on KYEA 98.3 FM. Mike Luster, a fan of her show and the director of the Louisiana Folklife Festival, spins a wide spectrum of Louisiana music on his own show, *Creole Statement*, broadcast on KEDM 90.3 FM, Saturday night from 7 to 9 pm.

The following places provide emergency medical services: St Francis Hospital (☎ 318-327-4171), 309 Jackson St at St John St; Columbia Hospital (☎ 318-388-7875), 3421 Medical Park Drive just off Hwy 165 N; and Glenwood (☎ 318-329-4760), 503 McMillan Rd off Thomas Rd in West Monroe.

Biedenharn Museum & Gardens

Atlanta is not the only town that Coca-Cola built. After making a fortune in 1894 as the first bottler of the omnipresent caramel-colored sugar water, Joseph Biedenharn moved his family from Vicksburg to Monroe. While in Monroe, Biedenharn's business interests continued to thrive, but his achievements were eventually overshadowed by the artistic vision of his daughter, Emy-Lou Biedenharn. She created a singular cultural complex called Biedenharn Museum & Gardens (☎ 318-387-5281, 800-362-0983), 2006 Riverside Drive, which now includes ELsong Garden & Conservatory, the Biedenharn home and a Bible museum, all administered by the Emy-Lou Biedenharn Foundation.

In 1939, with much of Europe embroiled in war, Emy-Lou abandoned a successful international opera career to return home. While in Europe, she had become enamored of the formal gardens and biblical antiquities of the European elite, and upon her return to Monroe she set out to replicate such an environment. By 1947 her vision of a European garden began to take shape in the backyard of her family home.

Today, visitors stroll on the manicured lawn that once served as a ballet stage, and gawk at the wrought iron orchestra boxes amid a riot of colorful flowers. After touring the hothouse conservatory, the garden filled with plants mentioned in the Bible, and the Japanese pavilion, you are likely to forget you are in the backyard of a large rambling house in a nice but somewhat ordinary neighborhood in the middle of Louisiana.

Though the 45-minute escorted home tour can be a bit pedantic, the museum and gardens are worth an hour or two. Especially interesting is the current display of contemporary handmade Bibles done by renowned artists such as Jim Dine. The complex is open Monday to Saturday 10 am to 5 pm and Sunday 2 to 5 pm. Admission is free. More information, including a schedule of free summer concerts, can be found at www.bmuseum.org. Before you leave, pop a nickel in the Coke machine and fish out an icy-cold, 6½-oz bottle (subsidized courtesy of the Biedenharn family fortune).

Other Things to See & Do

Across town in the middle of a rundown residential area, the **Northeast Louisiana**

Delta African-American Heritage Museum (☎ 318-323-1167), 503 Plum St, is a study in austerity compared to the Biedenharn complex. Set in a converted shotgun house, the museum offers numerous outreach programs as well as art and dance classes and year-round art workshops. A small exhibit covers the African-American experience in Louisiana and includes African and slave artifacts, artwork and tools. Monthly exhibits feature the work of local artists. It also showcases major traveling art exhibits that pertain to its subject matter. It is open Tuesday to Saturday 9 am to 5 pm.

The **Masur Museum of Art** (☎ 318-329-2237), 1400 S Grand St at Morris Drive, is also worth a look. Exhibits take full advantage of the intimate spaces of the former mansion, wherein wandering from room to room you view a collection of contemporary Southern artwork. The house was originally built by a lumber tycoon. Sigmund Masur moved in during the early 1930s, and with his family owned the Palace Department Store and other real estate in town. The house is said to have been the first in Monroe with air conditioning and an elevator and he, his wife, Beatrice, and their three children lived there happily until both parents died. The children donated the house to the city in 1963 as a tribute to their parents, stipulating that it be used as a fine-arts museum. The museum is free and open Tuesday to Thursday 9 am to 5 pm and Friday, Saturday and Sunday 2 to 5 pm.

The **Louisiana Purchase Gardens and Zoo** (☎ 318-329-2400), on Bernstein Drive just two blocks west of Hwy 165, southeast of downtown, has a nice collection of the native flora and fauna as well as more exotic species, such as leopards and zebras. It is open daily 10 am to 5 pm and charges an admission fee of $3.25 for adults and $2 for children and seniors. The Bayou Safari boat ride ($1) provides a pleasant orientation to the park.

To answer the call of a wilder sort, head to **Black Bayou National Wildlife Refuge** (☎ 318-726-4400), off Hwy 165 north a tiny bit out of town. There you can fish, canoe and hike (but no camping is allowed). The

2000-acre wetlands are characteristically swampy and home to alligators.

On Riverside Drive at Forsythe Ave is **Forsythe Park** (☎ 318-329-2440), a well-manicured green space with tennis courts, a nine-hole golf course and public boat launch.

Special Events

Monroe is home to one of the state's best events: the annual Louisiana Folklife Festival, held the second week in September. Not only do you get a chance to hear some of the state's best musicians play everything from Cajun fiddle music to swamp pop to zydeco, but also you get a chance to learn more about the culture of the state – all made that much more palatable by bounteous supplies of cold beer. Call the festival office (☎ 318-329-2375) for more information or visit www.louisianafolklifefest.org.

The annual Black Heritage Parade (☎ 318-387-5691) features gospel music and marching bands. It's held the fourth Saturday in February.

Places to Stay

Shilo RV and Travel Resort (☎ 318-343-6098, 7300 Frontage Rd), off I-20 east of Monroe, offers tent sites with water for $19.95 and small cabins for $19 to $29. The compound features a small, stocked lake, a swimming pool, a hot tub and mini-golf.

Numerous chain motels are grouped around I-20 exits 114, 117 and 118.

The cheapest bed in town can be had on the outskirts of West Monroe at the **Canary Motel** (☎ 318-325-7383, 3002 Cypress St) for $22 a night. The rooms are scruffy, but the grounds are well tended and the parking lot is well lit.

The Atrium (☎ 318-325-0641, 800-428-7486, 2001 Louisville Ave) is a luxury hotel around these parts. Rooms are $73/78 for a single/double. Amenities include a Jacuzzi, pool, restaurant and complimentary in-town transportation. Reservations can be made online at the Holiday Inn Web site, www.basshotels.com/holiday-inn.

The **Rose Lee Inn** (☎ 318-322-1990, 318 Trenton St), in West Monroe, is a classic five-room B&B run by the same folks responsible for Chandler's Antiques downstairs. Rooms are clean, quiet, include private bathroom and are worth the $82 per night (hot breakfast included). They also rent rooms by the week.

Places to Eat

Health-conscious shoppers should check out the aptly named **Health Food Store** (☎ 318-325-2423, 801 Natchitoches St), at 4th St in West Monroe. Gourmands can find a nice bottle of wine and some cheese at **Tonore's Wine Cellar** (☎ 318-325-4100, 801 Louisville Ave).

The best meal in the area may well be one of the cheapest. The **Hollywood Snack Bar** (☎ 318-322-7984, 1810 Bernstein Park Drive), just a few blocks east of the zoo, serves hearty breakfasts and plate lunches ($5 to $6) featuring oxtails, chitlins, mustard greens, black-eyed peas and cornbread. It's open weekdays from around 8 am to 4 pm.

For a taste of the hip side of Monroe, pick up coffee and pastries at the **Atomic Coffee & Tea Company** (☎ 318-388-4202, 1012 N 4th St). It's open Wednesday to Friday 11 am to 8 pm and weekends noon to 8 pm.

For good food and a lively atmosphere – that sometimes includes performances by a local Elvis impersonator – try **Jazzin' Java** (☎ 318-324-9864, 819 N 3rd St). Thursday night features all-you-can-eat teriyaki and chicken stir-fry ($3.95). On other nights try the Louisiana-style tapas or homemade chips and salsa.

For lunch, do as the locals do and get a side order of gravy to dip your fries into at **Melvyn's** (☎ 601-325-2055, 200 18th St), at Forsythe Ave. Open Monday to Saturday 11 am to 10 pm, it also serves some of the best burgers in the state ($5 to $7).

If you're in search of really cheap eats, seek out **City Coney Island** (☎ 318-322-9159, 519 DeSiard St) for good and greasy chili dogs ($2 to $3).

In West Monroe, try the **Trenton St Café** (☎ 318-322-1444, 232 Trenton St) for po-boys on fresh-baked French bread, and daily plate lunches ($5). **Ashley's Rialto**

Barber takes a break between cuts, Mamou, LA.

Crawfish pond, Cajun Country, LA

Objects are bigger than they appear.

Pinch da tail, suck da head, Breaux Bridge, LA.

In the golden sun of the Atchafalaya Bayou, LA

Rosedown Plantation, 1832, St Francisville, LA

Destrehan Plantation bedroom, Destrehan, LA

Baton Rouge's Gothic-style Old State Capitol surely houses a ghostly scandal or two. LA

It's cotton-pickin' time.

Intracoastal highway, Morgan City, LA

Café (☎ 318-323-5004, 319 Trenton Ave) is a good place for standard breakfast fare ($4 to $5).

The *Hob Nob (☎ 318-396-9101)* is on the western outskirts of West Monroe at 5076 Cypress St near the intersection with Thomas Rd. A loyal cadre of regulars packs into this ramshackle roadhouse to eat oysters, gumbo and other local specialties. It is open Monday to Thursday 11 am to 10 pm (till midnight on Friday and Saturday). The beer is always cold, and on Wednesday night in season, the crawfish are super cheap.

Better yet, grab a seat at the bar or in one of the booths that line the back wall of the *Mohawk Seafood Tavern (☎ 318-322-9275, 704 Louisville Ave)*, near N 8th St. Settled amid a stuffed fowl and 1950s beer advertising, you can savor a bowl of gumbo, nut brown and pungent, with still-crunchy shrimp ($8). They also make their own shrimp delight sauce, which you can buy in town. The Mohawk is open Tuesday to Thursday 11 am to 9 pm, till 10 pm on Saturday.

Also popular and economical is *Cormier's Cajun Restaurant (☎ 318-322-0414, 1205 Forsythe Ave)*. Great boiled crawfish, boudin and red beans and rice ($6 to $9) are served on picnic tables in front of this shed of a building near Forsythe Park.

Genusa's (☎ 318-387-3083, 815 Park Ave) is Monroe's most popular Italian restaurant and features the town's best wine list. Especially good are the Portabella mushrooms, tomato and pesto salads and grilled fish dishes. Dinner ($10 to $20 per person) is the main meal served Monday to Saturday 5 to 10 pm. It is also open for lunch weekdays 11 am to 2 pm. *Geno's Italian Restaurant (☎ 318-325-5098, 705 N 8th St)*, just off Louisville Ave, is another local favorite for lunch and dinner.

Enoch's Grill & Pub (☎ 318-388-3662, 507 Louisville Ave) has live music on weekend nights and serves great pub grub Tuesday to Friday 11 am to 2 pm and again from 4:30 pm on. It's also open for dinner on Saturday.

Entertainment

Monroe is not exactly the live music capital of Louisiana, however, the *Sixth Street Grill (☎ 318-323-0010, 1026 N 6th St)* books college rock and folksy acts most weekends, while *Shamrock (☎ 318-325-8923, 500 DeSiard St)* hosts comedy most Thursday nights and has live music on the weekend.

Bayle's Landing (☎ 318-322-8278), 113 S Riverfront Rd, is a popular fish house in West Monroe. It's known more for the ambiance than the food. It's a great spot to sip a beer and take in a view of the Ouachita River.

Your best bet might be taking a drive out along Bayou DeSiard to the *Cypress Inn (☎ 318-345-0202, 7805 DeSiard St)* to have a drink or two and feed leftover hushpuppies (provided free of charge) to the turtles. The view of the moss-shrouded cypress trees is magnificent.

For a taste of what the locals like to do, head out to the *Twin City Drag Race (☎ 318-387-8563, 3695 Prairie Rd)*. The National Hot Rod Association (a big deal around here) sanctions this quarter-mile strip. Drag races take place on Saturdays from March to October. Gates open at noon, time trials start at 3 pm, races at 7 pm.

Shopping

Along a two-block stretch of Trenton Ave in West Monroe is an area known as Antique Alley, comprising a handful of restaurants, antique stores, art galleries and tchotchke shops of varying degrees of quality and appeal.

With more than 80 stores, Pecanland Mall, 4700 Millhaven Rd, should suffice for other shopping needs.

Getting There & Away

Monroe Regional Airport (☎ 318-329-2461), 4 miles east of town on Hwy 80, has a few more connecting flights than the norm owing to the city's still-strong ties to Delta Air Lines. Delta provides jet service six times a day to and from Dallas, Texas ($180), and Atlanta, Georgia ($300). Continental, Northwest, AmericaWest and US Airways provide commuter air service three times a day to Shreveport, Jackson, Mississippi and Houston, Texas; fares cost between $200 and $300. Flights to New Orleans and Memphis cost around $300.

Greyhound (☎ 318-322-5181) has bus service to and from Jackson four times a day ($24/47 one-way/roundtrip), and to New Orleans five times a day ($47/84). Its service to and from Chicago, Dallas and Atlanta is offered just once or twice a day. Trailways offers service to Baton Rouge twice a day.

Monroe's bus depot is at 830 Martin Luther King Jr Drive (Hwy 165) on the east side of town near the intersection with Roberta Drive. All tickets are sold at this location and the terminal is open 4 am to 10 pm daily. The only problem with bus service is that once you arrive in Monroe, you really need a car to get around.

AROUND MONROE

Traveling east from Monroe, the landscape becomes flatter and bleaker. You're in the Mississippi Delta now, a former swampland reclaimed with slave labor in the mid-1800s. The few surviving plantations – their main houses blinding white and columned – are relics from a long-forgotten past incongruously placed amidst acre upon acre of cotton fields now tended by monstrous machines. Driving through the flat, open fields, past row upon regimented row of crops, you can't help but think of the slaves who once worked these same fields. Where did those who attempted escape from their masters hide in a land so vast and open?

Lake Providence & Around

Fifty miles northeast of Monroe on Hwy 65 (via Hwy 165 N and Hwy 2 E), the town of Lake Providence is, quite frankly, a dump. Long a thriving settlement before Shreveport or Monroe, it is the oldest Louisiana town north of Natchitoches. Today, few vestiges of the town's cotton-enriched glory days remain, save the infamous Grant's Canal and the Louisiana Cotton Museum.

The historical marker for **Grant's Canal** (see the History section, earlier in this chapter) is directly across from the local visitor center in the **Byerley House** (☎ 318-559-5125), off Hwy 65 on the northern edge of town. The Byerley House is an intact and rare surviving example of the Queen Anne Revival style in Lake Providence. The façade of the house remains entirely unaltered. Many of the grand structures in Lake Providence were destroyed by two major incursions of the Mississippi River levee, making the house all the more unique in these parts. An elevated walkway meanders out into the oxbow lake and affords a view of what remains of the canal. One mile farther north on Hwy 65 is the **Louisiana Cotton Museum** (☎ 318-559-2041), open Tuesday to Friday 9 am to 4 pm. Local civic boosters have great hopes for this museum, which is currently housed in an early-1900s farmhouse, but eventually will move into a 3600-sq-ft structure to be built on the site. A church and plantation commissary share the grounds with a working 1920s electric-powered cotton gin – the first in the state. Admission is free.

Eight miles farther north on Hwy 65 is the **Panola Pepper Sauce Co** (☎ 318-559-1774), maker of less well-known but, to this jaded palate, better sauces than Tabasco in New Iberia. The company brews a wide variety of pepper sauces, including a zippy Worcestershire and a blistering habañero sauce. Tours of the plant may be arranged by stopping by the visitor center weekdays from 8 am to 4 pm. A nearby gift shop sells Panola Pepper products at a deep discount.

By the way, ignore the tourist-targeted come-ons for **Transylvania**, 10 miles south of Lake Providence. There's nothing to see or do save a junk-filled general store and a water tower emblazoned with a bat.

Columbia

About 30 miles south of Monroe is the hamlet of Columbia, once a thriving steamboat landing on the Ouachita River. Today, the town's Main St is very sleepy. Stop by the **Schepis Museum** (☎ 318-649-2138, 107 Main St) and take a gander at the Italianate carved-stone structure built in 1916. The one-room museum, open 10 am to 4 pm Tuesday to Saturday, features a range of exhibits from modern art to antiques, all meant to showcase local talent.

A couple of doors down is the **Watermark Saloon** (☎ 318-649-0999, 101 Main St), named after a stain left on an interior wall by the 1927 flood. This saloon, the oldest on the Ouachita River, is a comfortable, well-worn haunt with high ceilings, wood floors and a pool table. Live music is featured on most Saturday nights. Just down the road a few blocks is the **Bayou Tavern** (☎ 318-649-7922), 415 Kentucky St. Though the inside is painted a garish pink, the exterior of this modular building is worth your attention. Assembled in 1927 as a distribution station for Standard Oil, this shiny, tin box, perched on the bank of a small waterway, is now a restaurant and bar serving good gumbo and plate lunches ($5 to $8). If you are curious about the building, seek out the owner, Mr Wayne, and he'll be happy you tell you its story. The tavern is open 10 am to midnight Monday to Saturday.

POVERTY POINT

The community at Poverty Point was once the hub of a network of more than a hundred Native American communities scattered throughout a region encompassing present-day Louisiana, Mississippi and Arkansas. Based on evidence of small groupings of settlements, it is generally assumed that the inhabitants of Poverty Point comprised a mixture of different tribes.

From 1500 to 750 BC, Poverty Point inhabitants enjoyed a particularly sophisticated lifestyle compared to what is known about other Indian groups of this time period. Anthropologists have found that most Indian tribes were migratory hunter-gatherers and did not form elaborate permanent settlements or create structures for religious purposes. But the residents of Poverty Point apparently had enough time and energy to build huge earthen mounds and live in what is considered to be an early village. How they could have afforded not to worry about finding food or fending off enemies is a debated topic and has led some researchers to conclude that the Poverty

Point residents must have been very early farmers no longer following the migrating herds. It is also postulated that large-scale construction of villages and ceremonial sites was possible because of a trading network that reached as far north as what is now Minnesota.

Today, many archaeologists consider Poverty Point culture the premier pre-Columbian civilization in the southeastern US, and they flock to this site. In fact, there are often more archaeologists milling about the place than tourists.

What both archaeologists and tourists come to see are a remarkable series of earthworks and mounds situated along what was once the Mississippi River – now known as Bayou Macon. Though somewhat eroded over time, the series of six concentric ridges that define the parameters of the village are still impressive when viewed from the two-story observation tower. Stretching over three-quarters of a mile in diameter, the ridges, thought to be originally 8 to 10 feet high, are purported to be the foundations for village dwellings. Six earthen mounds, most of which are located outside the ridges, are also scattered about the 1500-acre site. The mounds might have served as tombs, although no burials were evident within them.

With so much area to traverse, you will have to make a few choices if you want to spend only a few hours looking around. Upon arrival consider devoting a half-hour to the film, which gives a good introduction to the people of Poverty Point. (Granted, the film is a little too concerned with what grand folks archaeologists are.) Then you might spend a half-hour or so wandering around the display area. Here you'll see clay balls roughly the size of a grapefruit that were used to regulate heat in pit ovens. Also on display are molded owl and bird figures and intricate female torsos, wrought from the same clay. The molded figures of owls and birds are thought to be symbolic representations of their religion and/or representations of tribal identity.

After this introduction, board a shuttle (six-person minimum) for a tour of all the mounds or take a brief hike out to the most spectacular mound – a bird-shaped one measuring 700 by 640 feet at its base and rising 70 feet. The roundtrip hike will take you 30 to 45 minutes; visiting more remote mounds will take longer.

Located 50 miles northeast of Monroe near the town of Epps, off Hwy 577, a mile north of Hwy 134, Poverty Point (☎ 318-926-5492) is open daily 9 am to 5 pm. Admission is $2. Visit the Web site of the state's department of recreation, culture and tourism at www.crt.state.la.us.

RUSTON & AROUND
• pop 19,000

Ruston is the seat of government for the hill-country parish of Lincoln. Lincoln Parish was one of two 'Reconstruction parishes' (Grant Parish was the other) created by radical Republican politicians after the Civil War, and it has always been perceived as a bit different from its hill-country neighbors.

The town of Ruston was founded in 1884, when entrepreneur Robert Russ convinced the Vicksburg, Shreveport and Pacific Railroad to lay track through a 640-acre site that he owned. Russ's Town, later renamed Ruston, literally sprang up overnight as settlers flooded there for the steady work the railroad provided.

By 1890, with the organization of a Chautauqua Society, Lincoln Parish had become the educational capital of northern Louisiana. A 2000-seat tabernacle was built near Ruston, where society members hosted noted educators, philosophers and politicians, including populist William Jennings Bryan. Though the tabernacle no longer stands, the educational legacy endures.

Today, both Grambling State University and Louisiana Tech University are anchors of Lincoln Parish's economic, social and educational life. Those in search of a bucolic college town are forewarned: Ruston and surrounding Lincoln Parish are not places of great scenic charm. There are no green lawns shaded by live oaks here. But outdoor enthusiasts may find the town a good

jumping off point into Lincoln Parish Park, a mecca for mountain bikers.

Orientation

I-20 forms a northern border for Ruston, with most commercial activity clustered to the south along two main arteries: Tech Drive and Trenton St/Vienna St. Trenton and Vienna Sts run one-way through the middle of town (southward and northward, respectively), while Tech Drive runs through the Louisiana Tech campus on the west side of town.

Information

The visitor center (☎ 318-255-2031), 900 N Trenton St, is open weekdays from 8:30 am to 5 pm.

ATMs are easily found downtown, either on or just off Trenton St. The main post office (☎ 318-255-3791) is downtown at 501 Trenton St.

On the Avenue Books and Gifts (☎ 318-255-0845), 130 Park Ave, has a small assortment of books. The local public library (☎ 318-251-5030) is at 509 W Alabama Ave, while the Louisiana Tech library (☎ 318-257-3555) is just off Tech Drive.

Most motels lack laundry facilities. Try Soap Opera (☎ 318-251-9614), at 1612 Farmerville Hwy.

Lincoln General Hospital (☎ 318-254-2456) offers emergency services.

Things to See & Do

The **Lincoln Parish Museum** (☎ 318-251-0018), 609 Vienna St, is a comparatively conventional tourist attraction. Housed in a home built in 1886, it displays the usual assortment of treasures assembled to tell the story of the local, moneyed elite. That said, the narrative murals painted along the wainscoting bear a peek. Reminiscent of a lesser Thomas Hart Benton, the works tell the history of Lincoln Parish in a series of somber-hued vignettes. The museum is open only Tuesday to Friday 10 am to 4 pm. Admission is free.

For outdoor enthusiasts, **Lincoln Parish Park** (☎ 318-251-5156), north on Hwy 33, is heralded as one of the best locations for mountain biking anywhere. The park offers a 10-mile trail suitable for both beginners and experienced riders. As a blend of old jeep trails and fire lanes, the track has several challenging jumps including the 120-foot Tomac Hill. Each spring, the park hosts the XTERRA America Tour Race, a weekend of trail running, mountain bike races and live music, drawing cyclists and other athletes alike from around the country. In addition to the bike trails, camping, fishing and picnic facilities are available (see Places to Stay).

Louisiana Tech University is a tangle of concrete walkways and five-story buildings that hardly looks inviting. Founded in 1895 as an industrial school, the university now enrolls over 10,000 students in what many consider the state's finest school for math and science. If you're in town during fall, call campus information (☎ 318-257-0211) for a schedule of home football games. Louisiana Tech usually fields a good football team (former NFL star Terry Bradshaw is an alumnus), as does its neighbor Grambling State. Tech often has a good women's basketball team as well.

Charles P Adams, an emissary sent by Booker T Washington of Tuskegee Institute, founded **Grambling State University** in 1901. It's just 5 miles west of Ruston off Lincoln Ave in the town of Grambling. Originally conceived as an industrial school, Grambling State now offers a broad range of undergraduate and graduate degrees, including well-respected programs in sports administration and early childhood education.

Though the surrounding town of Grambling appears to be in shambles, the university bustles with over 8000 students. Unfortunately, there is little for a visitor to see, save the stadium where retired coach Eddie Robinson led the Grambling Tigers to victory. Robinson is one of the winningest football coaches (over 500 wins) in the history of college athletics. The current head coach is Doug Williams, the first African-American quarterback to lead his team (the Washington Redskins) to the Super Bowl. Call campus information (☎ 318-247-3811)

for a schedule of home football games and other campus events.

About 13 miles north of Ruston off Hwy 167 at the intersection of Hwys 151 and 152, near the hamlet of Dubach is the **Autrey House Museum** (☎ 318-251-0018). This 1849 log home, one of the oldest existing structures in the parish, is typical of planter homes in the hill country. It has an open central hall, built to catch the cooling breezes, flanked by two rooms on both the east and west sides and an ironstone chimney on the east side. Though few interior furnishings are present, the house is a

---

Bonnie & Clyde

For those who like to follow in felonious footsteps, the **Bonnie & Clyde Museum** (☎ 318-843-6141), in Gibsland, is a must-see. The town is where Bonnie Parker and Clyde Barrow met their fate in 1934 after a crime spree that lasted over two years. Bonnie, Clyde and gang headed to Acadia, Louisiana to stay at an out-of-the-way cabin that belonged to the father of one of their gang. One gang member, Henry Methvin, a con on the run, had started to get nervous about how long their luck would last. He secretly met with police to arrange for a reduced sentence if he led Bonnie and Clyde into a police ambush. The police used Methvin's father's car – which Clyde often mocked – as bait. They parked it by the side of the road while six sharpshooters waited on the other side. The ambush – which involved both Texas Rangers and Louisiana State Police – filled the couple with more than 167 bullet holes. Look for the stone marker along Hwy 154 that commemorates where they were gunned down by the feds. The weekend closest to May 23rd – the date of their deaths – hosts the annual Authentic Bonnie & Clyde Festival, when a re-enactment of the ambush takes place and residents stage mock bank robberies. Gibsland is just south of I-20, about halfway between Ruston and Shreveport.

fine example of the fast-vanishing dogtrot style and thus worth the trip for any architecturally curious traveler weary of white-columned Georgian mansions. Though hours are advertised, call in advance to schedule an appointment.

Special Events

Ruston hosts an annual peach festival during the first weekend in June to celebrate the area's acclaimed crop. Activities include a cooking contest, concerts by almost famous or once-famous country singers and an arts and crafts fair. Call the visitor center (☎ 318-255-2031) for more information.

More compelling are the annual Chuck Wagon Races held the first weekend in July in nearby Dubach. Everyone turns out to watch locals race through the Louisiana backwoods at breakneck speeds before setting up camp and cooking a frontier-style meal. Call ☎ 318-777-3955 for details.

Places to Stay

Both primitive ($6) and improved ($12) campsites are available at *Lincoln Parish Park* (☎ 318-251-5156), north on Hwy 33 (see earlier).

The cheapest motel in town is the *Lincoln Motel* (☎ 318-255-4512, 1104 Georgia Ave). The rooms are nothing special, but at least they're clean. They're also reasonably priced at $22/28 for singles/doubles. Also cheap, though not as well situated, is the *Pines Motel* (☎ 318-255-3268), 1705 California Ave, charging $25/35.

For a more pampering experience, the *Melody Hills Bed & Breakfast* (☎ 318-255-7127, 804 N Trenton St) has two cozy bedrooms with shared bathroom for $75 to $95 a night.

Places to Eat

Bee's Café (☎ 318-255-5610, 805 Larson St) serves a fine plate lunch in modest surroundings, but the real reason to go is for Bee's breakfast. For around $3 you get a belly-busting plate of eggs, grits and home-made biscuits. Bee's is open Monday to Friday 6 to 9 am and 11 am to 2 pm.

The *Trenton Street Café* (☎ 318-251-2103, 201 N Trenton St) is a mellow place with good pub grub served daily (lunch and dinner) for under $10 a plate.

Looking more like a bar than a food establishment, *Ponchatoula's New Orleans Cuisine* (☎ 318-254-8683, 109 E Park Ave), nonetheless, serves great boiled crawfish (in season), good gumbo and pleasingly sloppy roast beef po-boys to a college crowd. It is open 11 am to midnight Monday to Saturday and 11 am to 2 pm on Sunday.

Locals flock to the *Boiling Point* (☎ 318-255-8506), 2017 Farmerville Hwy, a mile north of I-20, for incendiary boiled crawfish and cold beer in a rather institutional setting. It is open weekdays 11 am to 9 pm.

In search of a little more atmosphere? Try *Monjunis Italian Café & Grocery* (☎ 318-251-2222, 101 N Trenton St). Especially good is the baked ravioli with stuffed Italian cheeses, covered in tomato basil or Alfredo sauce, or get a loaf of garlic bread to go ($4.95).

Entertainment

Ponchatoula's (see Places to Eat) offers occasional live music. If you want a little local color with your beer, *Stow's Bar* (☎ 318-255-9949, 210 W Park Ave) can't be beat. Before opening as a bar in 1975, the graceful old building served as both a hotel and hospital. Today, locals wearing cowboy hats share the scuffed old bar with frat boys out for a night on the town.

During the academic year, Louisiana Tech sponsors a variety of lectures, recitals, sporting events and plays. Call ☎ 318-257-4427 for information. For those in search of more 'down-home' entertainment, a 28-mile drive south down Hwy 146 is warranted. On Hwy 4 southeast of Chatham, the *Super Bee Speedway* (☎ 318-249-4595) hosts dirt track stock-car races every Saturday night at 8 pm.

Shopping

For life's necessities, the phalanx of strip malls along the interstate highway should suffice. Out on California Ave, Louisiana Tech Farm Sales (☎ 318-257-3550) offers farm-fresh milk, cheese, chickens, flowers

Racin' Round & Round

Today, stock-car racing is the nation's most well attended sport. From New England to California and almost everywhere in-between, hundreds of thousands of fans gather on weekends to cheer on their favorite drivers to victory. Until recently, the national media shunned the sport and its fans. Thought to be the province of the poor and uneducated, stock-car racing warranted little attention and little corporate sponsorship. Perhaps the public perception was a legacy of the early days of the sport when the great drivers were often part-time racers and full-time 'moonshiners' who learned how to take a curve at 100mph while evading government tax collectors intent upon stemming the distribution of home-made liquor.

Legend has it that the sport had its Southern beginnings one afternoon in the 1930s when a group of moonshine runners met in an old pasture to decide, once and for all, who had the fastest car. The first race – hardly an organized affair – was attended by the drivers alone, but as news spread and the races continued, spectators began to come and a sport was born. By the early 1950s, the sport began moving from dirt tracks to high-banked, paved raceways, and races began to be regulated by a governing body, NASCAR, the National Association for Stock Car Auto Racing.

In today's rural South, dirt-track ovals dot the landscape, and on Saturday evening, the tracks come alive with locals who have modified their Chevrolets, Dodges and Fords in pursuit of the cash prizes and bragging rites that are the spoils of the victor.

and other products at very reasonable prices. It is open weekdays 9 am to 5:30 pm.

Getting There & Away

Both Shreveport (45 miles west) and Monroe (30 miles east) have regional airports with fairly frequent service.

Greyhound (☎ 318-255-3505), 118 W Louisiana Ave, offers four daily eastbound buses to Jackson, Mississippi ($33/65 one-way/roundtrip), and three westbound buses to Shreveport ($15/29). Greyhound also travels daily to and from nearby Monroe ($9.50/19) and Alexandria ($18.50/37) as well as Dallas, Texas ($55/110), New Orleans ($60/120) and Baton Rouge.

Most everything is to or from Hwy 20; Monroe and Ruston are only about one hour apart; Shreveport is another 60 to 90 minutes away.

SHREVEPORT
• pop 188,000 • Bossier City 56,000

Is Shreveport a Southern or Western town? Ask that question of five locals and you're likely to get five different answers. Advocates of a Southern appellation point out that the city once served as the Louisiana state capital during the Civil War and that Shreveport residents were so fiercely loyal to the Confederacy that they held out against federal forces for nearly seven weeks after Lee's surrender at Appomattox.

Advocates of a Western heritage point to the city's origins as a frontier town founded in 1839 – four years after the land was 'purchased' from the Caddo Indians for $80,000 and just one year after Captain Henry Shreve cleared the 165-mile Red River logjam, opening the area to trade. They might also mention the aborted 1873 bid to annex Shreveport and lands west of the Red River by overzealous Texans. Or they might quote AJ Liebling, who posited that 'Shreveport is a dilution of Texas.'

More recent history is a bit less contentious. Until the discovery of oil, the Shreveport area economy depended upon farming, forestry and transportation. But by 1905, Shreveport and neighboring hamlets such as Mooringsport had become boomtowns complete with saloons, brothels and hard-drinking oilmen, intent upon making a fortune in exploration and speculation. Though much of the oil extraction has since shifted to offshore sites in the Gulf of Mexico, the area immediately surrounding Shreveport still has smaller wells.

LOUISIANA

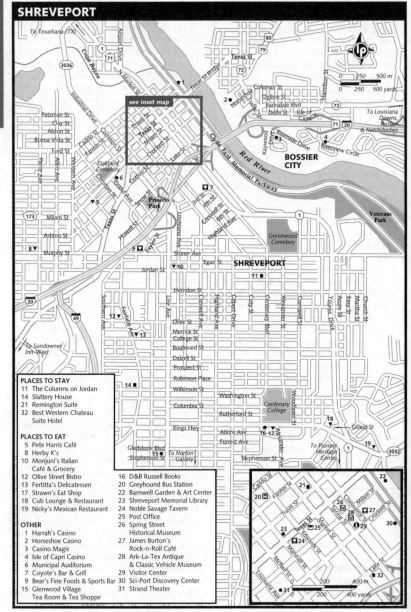

SHREVEPORT

PLACES TO STAY
11 The Columns on Jordan
14 Slattery House
21 Remington Suite
32 Best Western Chateau
   Suite Hotel

PLACES TO EAT
5 Pete Harris Café
8 Herby K's
10 Monjuni's Italian
   Café & Grocery
12 Olive Street Bistro
13 Fertitta's Delicatessen
17 Strawn's Eat Shop
18 Cub Lounge & Restaurant
19 Nicky's Mexican Restaurant

OTHER
1 Harrah's Casino
2 Horseshoe Casino
3 Casino Magic
4 Isle of Capri Casino
6 Municipal Auditorium
7 Coyote's Bar & Grill
9 Bear's Fine Foods & Sports Bar
15 Glenwood Village
   Tea Room & Tea Shoppe

16 D&B Russell Books
20 Greyhound Bus Station
22 Barnwell Garden & Art Center
23 Shreveport Memorial Library
24 Noble Savage Tavern
25 Post Office
26 Spring Street
   Historical Museum
27 James Burton's
   Rock-n-Roll Café
28 Ark-La-Tex Antique
   & Classic Vehicle Museum
29 Visitor Center
30 Sci-Port Discovery Center
31 Strand Theater

The oil boom brought more than economic wealth to the area. Though now decimated by the interstate highway system that bisects the city, there was a time when Shreveport boasted strong immigrant and African-American neighborhoods within the city.

After decades as a transportation center, Shreveport's river port went into decline following WWII. Downtown businesses were closed and boarded; riverfront warehouses stood empty. Those who were able to, left for places such as Dallas and New York in search of better opportunities. Today, downtown Shreveport is undergoing something of a renaissance. With the opening of multiple casinos, the continuing refurbishment of the old warehouses along the Red River, and an $85 million convention center under construction, local boosters are quick to proclaim the riverfront revitalization a success. Yet the first-time visitor might well wonder whether it's a bit too early to tell. Still, Shreveport is doing what it can to find new prosperity in tourism, gambling and health care, and bringing biotech companies and research institutes into the area.

Just across the Red River from Shreveport is its sister city, Bossier City, established as a trading post in the early 1840s. Home since 1933 to Barksdale Air Force Base, Bossier City retains the rough, rowdy feel of a military town. Unless you want to gamble at the city's three casinos or its thoroughbred racetrack, there's not much reason to cross the bridge.

Orientation

This city is considered part of the greater 'Ark-La-Tex' region, which comprises northwestern Louisiana, southwestern Arkansas and northeastern Texas.

On the west bank of the Red River is Shreveport. Despite its fairly compact downtown, the city is best appreciated for its suburban enclaves, fanning east and west along Line Ave, the city's tony shopping corridor. The city is bisected by I-49, running north and south, and I-20, running east and west. All is encircled by a peri-meter highway known as I-220 on the north side of town but labeled the Inner Loop on the south side.

East of the Red River, Bossier City sprawls eastward along two major corridors, Hwy 80 and I-20, with Barksdale Air Force Base accessible off I-20 via North Gate Drive.

Information

Tourist Offices The Shreveport visitor center (☎ 318-222-9391) is downtown at 629 Spring St. The Bossier City visitor center (☎ 318-226-8884) is at 100 John Wesley Blvd. Both locations have ample information on either city and are open weekdays 9 am to 5 pm.

Money ATMs are easily found in downtown Shreveport near Texas St; in suburban Shreveport along Line Ave and Ellerbee Rd; and in Bossier City along Hwy 80. With the customer always in mind, the casinos offer an abundance of ATMs.

Post Shreveport's main post office (☎ 318-677-2222) is at 2400 Texas St.

Media The *Times* newspaper covers Shreveport, Bossier City and Ark-La-Tex.

Bookstores Shreveport's best (maybe only) independent, general-interest bookstore is Tower Book Shop (☎ 318-865-7161), 724 Azalea Drive. Your best bet for new books at cheap prices is the warehouselike Books-A-Million (☎ 318-688-4488), 8932 Jewella Ave in the suburbs. For used hardbacks, D&B Russell (☎ 318-865-1685), 129 Kings Hwy near Centenary College, has a great selection of Louisiana fiction and nonfiction. It is open Monday to Friday 10 am to 6 pm, Saturday 9 am to 6 pm.

Libraries The Shreveport Memorial Library (☎ 318-226-5897) is downtown at 424 Texas St, housed in a beautiful late-19th-century building. It is open Monday through Thursday 9 am to 9 pm, and closes at 6 pm on Friday and Saturday. On Sunday, the library is open from 1 to 5 pm.

During the summer months all hours are shortened.

Laundry There are three Soap Opera Washaterias in town: 1915 Creswell Ave (☎ 318-424-8048); 3103 N Market St (☎ 318-222-6317); and 8150 Jewella Ave (☎ 318-688-6873). Super Suds (☎ 318-865-6873) is at 400 E Kings Hwy.

Medical Services The Bossier Medical Center (☎ 318-741-6000), Highland Hospital (☎ 318-798-4300) and Willis-Knighton Health Center (☎ 318-752-7500) offer emergency services.

Downtown Attractions

Flowers are the focus at the **Barnwell Garden & Art Center** (☎ 318-673-7703), 601 Clyde Fant Parkway, along the riverfront. Though the enclosed conservatory is nothing special, the adjoining park is a pleasant space for an afternoon walk or jog and affords visitors a sweeping view of the Red River. At night, the park is the best vantage point for gazing up at the neon-bathed **Texas St Bridge**, which has 3000 feet of red, pink and orange neon.

Across the street is the new 67,000-sq-foot **Sci-Port Discovery Center** (☎ 318-424-3466), a huge hands-on science museum for children. Exhibits demonstrate how wind forms dunes and drifts in the desert. The museum also houses an IMAX Dome theater. Located at 820 Clyde Fant Parkway, the museum is open Monday to Saturday 10 am to 6 pm and Sunday 1 to 6 pm. Admission is $6 for adults and $4.50 for children. If you go for the IMAX, it'll cost an extra $6 for adults, $4.50 for children (a combo deal lowers the price slightly).

The **Ark-La-Tex Antique & Classic Vehicle Museum** (☎ 318-222-0227), three blocks north of the river at 601 Spring St, is housed in a 1921 Moorish-style building with expansive tile floors and intricate woodwork. Scattered among the cars is an interesting assortment of curious objects, including antique jukeboxes and fire-fighting equipment, all on view Tuesday to Saturday

Louisiana Hayride

If you find yourself near the Municipal Auditorium in downtown Shreveport – take heart, you're in the presence of great musical ghosts. Radio producer Hoss Logan kicked off a weekly radio show here in April of 1948 to feature new country musical talent from the region. Known as the *Louisiana Hayride*, the show featured not-yet-known musical acts performing live before a 1600-strong audience. Standard enough, you might think, but the whole shebang was also broadcast across the nation to nearly 200 CBS stations (the Grand Ole Opry had a similar arrangement with NBC at the time). Those not-yet-known acts included the likes of Hank Williams, Elvis Presley, Johnny Cash and Willie Nelson – all of who went on to become very well known, thank you. The show helped launch so many careers, in fact, that people started calling it the 'cradle of the stars.' One that got away was Jerry Lee Lewis, who came calling in 1952. He showed up at Logan's office one day looking for a job playing piano. Logan apologized to the young man because he already had a piano player. A couple of years later, Jerry Lee Lewis was one of the best-selling recording artists in the country. As the story goes, whenever Lewis ran into Logan after that he would tell him, 'You son of a bitch, you wouldn't hire me,' to which Logan would respond, 'Well, you son of a bitch, you never told me you could sing!'

The Hayride is also noted for featuring Cajun acts, many of which were well known and respected in their own communities but had yet to gain a national audience.

The show ended in 1969, though two unsuccessful attempts were made to revive it to its earlier glory. Hayride albums and T-shirts are available through the official Louisiana Hayride Web site, located at www.talentondisplay.com/hayride.html.

9 am to 5 pm and Sunday 1 to 5 pm. Admission is $5 for adults and $4 for seniors and students.

Down the street is the **Spring Street Historical Museum** (☎ 318-424-0964), 525 Spring St. Originally built as a bank in 1865, the building now features a grandmother's attic-style assortment of local treasures, augmented by special exhibits. If you are interested in the history of Shreveport, this is a worthy stop. Call first for current hours of operation. Admission is $2 for adults and $1 for students and children.

Three blocks southeast along Texas St from the Spring Street Museum, look for the life-size bronze statue of Shreveport's very own Huddie 'Leadbelly' Ledbetter, famed bluesman and writer of standards such as 'Goodnight Irene.' It's near the Memorial Library. His hand points up Texas St in the direction of his old neighborhood.

Two downtown performance venues worth at least a drive-by are the art deco **Municipal Auditorium** (☎ 318-673-5100), 705 Grand Ave, original home of the *Louisiana Hayride* program where Elvis Presley made his national radio debut; and the opulent **Strand Theater** (☎ 318-226-1481), 619 Louisiana Ave, built in 1925 as the flagship for a national theater chain. The Strand was restored in the late 1980s. Both occasionally offer live performances.

Pioneer Heritage Center

This living history museum (☎ 318-797-5332) looks out of place among the 1970s architecture and flat green lawns of Louisiana State University, but it's worth a visit. It's only open Sunday from 1:30 to 4:30 pm, but if you can make it, the six late-19th-century buildings offer a great glimpse of day-to-day frontier life. The university can be reached from the freeway by taking the E 70th St exit (exit No 202).

Centenary College

Established in 1825, Centenary College is a liberal arts school with strong performing and fine arts and classics departments. The compact campus, nestled on the corner of Kings Hwy and Centenary Blvd, is home to a small but relatively progressive student body and counts Confederate president Jefferson Davis among its alumni. Originally located in Jackson, Louisiana, the college actually had to close during the Civil War due to a shortage of students. It reopened at this location in 1906. **Meadows Museum of Art** (☎ 318-869-5169), 2911 Centenary Blvd, the prime campus attraction, displays a remarkable collection of Indo-Chinese and Haitian paintings and sponsors frequent touring exhibitions. The museum is free and open to the public Tuesday to Friday noon to 4 pm. During the academic year, the university hosts a variety of lectures and performances; check out their Web site, www.centenary.edu, for a schedule of events. A student-sponsored film series is also shown while classes are in session (see Entertainment for details).

Norton Art Gallery

As you turn off Line Ave onto a meandering, suburban street, you will become quickly convinced that you've taken a wrong turn. Surely this can't be the way to the Norton Art Gallery? But there it is, in a cul-de-sac at the end of a narrow street in a thoroughly inauspicious, middle-class neighborhood. Built in 1966, the contemporary, columned building features 20 exhibition rooms, showcasing a collection that spans from European sculptures by Rodin to illustrations by American naturalist John James Audubon. Though the smaller, alcove galleries display everything from 19th-century dolls to vintage rifles, the most impressive collections are housed in the Frederic Remington Gallery, where the American artist's sculptures and paintings of the Old West are displayed alongside a collection of his personal letters and illustrations.

The gallery (☎ 318-865-4201), 4747 Creswell Ave, charges no admission and is open Tuesday to Friday 10 am to 5 pm, Saturday and Sunday 1 to 5 pm.

American Rose Center Garden

Shreveport scored a coup when the American Rose Society moved its headquarters

LOUISIANA

and gardens in 1974 from Columbus, Ohio, to a 118-acre plot on the west side of town. Today, the garden (☎ 318-938-5402) boasts over 20,000 rose bushes scattered among 64 gardens. The manicured pathways that wind through these piney hills, past burbling fountains and mountainous banks of yellow, red and white roses, are breathtakingly beautiful. Celebrity roses (the Dolly Parton, Minnie Pearl and Barbara Mandrell among them) are scattered throughout the park as are a bounty of blooming azaleas, dogwoods and other colorful flowers and trees.

The grounds are worth a good hour or two. Though spring is the best time to visit, there's always something in bloom except in December and January. For the $4 admission you are also entitled to use the playgrounds, sheltered picnic areas and barbecue pits. Open 9 am to 5 pm weekdays and 9 am to 6:30 pm weekends, the garden is just west of Shreveport off I-20/exit 5 at 8877 Jefferson Paige Rd.

Special Events
On New Year's Eve, the Independence Bowl (☎ 318-221-0712) tests the mettle of two chosen college football teams in an NCAA post-season playoff. It's held at Independence Stadium in Shreveport.

In nearby Blanchard, a Poke Salad Festival is held the Saturday before Mother's Day to celebrate this wild green that many Southerners prize. Activities include a rather campy parade as well as the usual assortment of arts and crafts booths. Call the festival organizer (☎ 337-929-2789) for more information. A little later in May, hoist a glass to honor the area's crawfish and Cajun heritage during Mudbug Madness (☎ 318-222-7403), a four-day event.

Shreveport's premier event is the Red River Revel, an eight-day street party held downtown along the river in September or October. Expect performances by well-known country and Louisiana musicians. For details call the visitor center.

Places to Stay
Camping Comfortable, clean campsites are hard to find around Shreveport. But if you're willing to drive 15 miles north, *Cypress Black Bayou Park* (☎ 318-965-0007, 135 Cypress Park Drive), off Airline Drive, has lakeside tent and RV campsites for $7.50 a night, huts for $15, and rustic cabins (with kitchen, bathroom and air-con) that sleep four for $45 a night as well as a few cottages that sleep six for $60. Visit its Web site at www.cypressblackbayou.com for more information.

Hotels, Motels & B&Bs A typical cluster of chain motels can be found at the Airline Drive exit in Bossier City and the Monkhouse Drive exit in western Shreveport. Other than that, it's slim pickings for the traveler in search of budget accommodations.

The best bet for those on a budget may be the *Sundowner Inn – West* (☎ 318-425-7467, 2134 Greenwood Rd). Located just off Texas St, the motel is convenient to downtown and the interstate. Don't expect opulence at $35/46 for singles/doubles on the weekends, $28/30 during the week.

In the downtown area, the *Best Western Chateau Suite Hotel* (☎ 318-222-7620, 800-845-9334, 201 Lake St) is well-situated, four blocks from the riverfront. Remodeled, the hotel features an outdoor pool and fitness center as well as complimentary airport and bus station transportation. Standard rooms are $80 and up, while two-room suites are $109. It's an extra $10 for each additional guest.

In the Highland historic district (an area of graceful older homes, bounded on the north by Murphy St and on the south by Kings Hwy), a number of B&Bs are worth considering. *The Columns on Jordan* (☎ 318-222-5912, 615 Jordan St) is on the fringes of the neighborhood and thus a little less expensive than many of the neighboring B&Bs. For $85 a night, guests enjoy breakfast prepared to order on the verandah beneath the looming white Doric columns.

The *Slattery House* (☎ 318-222-6577, 2401 Fairfield Ave) is a 1903 Victorian home with a wonderful back deck you might be tempted to while away the afternoon sitting on in one of their comfortable Adirondack chairs. Rooms are $99 to $195, including a full, gourmet breakfast. Reserve online at www.shreveportbedandbreakfast.com.

If you're in town on business, **Remington Suite** (☎ 318-425-5000, 220 Travis St) is a swanky, full-service retreat with all the amenities (in-room Jacuzzi bath, wet bar, laptop ports, etc). Room prices start at $95 a night during the week and $110 on the weekend.

Places to Eat

A great breakfast spot is **Strawn's Eat Shop** (☎ 318-868-0634, 125 Kings Hwy), east of Centenary Blvd. It's been in business since 1944. Though they serve a full breakfast menu, your best bet for breakfast (or an afternoon snack) is a $2 slice of one of their rich strawberry, banana or chocolate pies, topped with gravity-defying meringue. Strawn's is open Monday to Saturday 6 am to 8 pm; it opens at 7 am on Sunday.

For a quick, cheap bite on the run, try **Fertitta's Delicatessen** (☎ 318-424-5508, 1124 Fairfield Ave). Open since 1925, this ancient-looking store is one of the best places in town for lunch ($5 to $8). Famous for their Muffy sandwiches (a muffuletta-inspired deli sandwich of bologna, ham, cheese and olive salad), Fertitta's is open weekdays 9:30 am to 5:30 pm. **Fertitta's 6301 Restaurant** (☎ 318-865-6301, 6301 Line Ave), at E 72nd St, is run by the same folks but features a more upscale ambiance and choice of eats than the deli. The restaurant has received an Award for Excellence from *Wine Spectator* magazine. Entrées

Shreveport ain't exactly tofu central.

range from $10 to $25, and a piano bar enlivens the atmosphere. It is open Tuesday to Saturday from 5 pm until late and is closed the first two weeks of July.

Yearning for a taste of home cooking? Serving delicious food to a loyal clientele is **Pete Harris Café** (☎ 318-425-4277, 1335 Milam St), touted by its owners as the oldest African-American-owned restaurant in the US. The food is tasty, but the decor is a rather cavernous expanse of gray carpet and windowless walls. Best bets are the smothered chicken livers and the 'world famous' stuffed shrimp for $5 to $7. It is open seven days a week from 8 am to midnight and stays open until 3 am on Friday and Saturday.

If you're in search of a truly unique dining experience, try **Herby K's** (☎ 318-424-2724, 1833 Pierre Ave). In a derelict neighborhood where most of the other businesses have been either burned up or boarded up long ago, this Shreveport institution endures. Famous since 1936 as the home of the Shrimp Buster – four shrimp perched atop buttered French bread and served with a side of special sauce ($9) – Herby K's is as appreciated for the eccentricities of its ribald staff as for its frosty cold fishbowls of beer and delicately fried soft-shell crabs. Grab a seat at one of the shaded picnic tables in the beer garden or one of the four interior booths and relax – you've found the best seafood in Shreveport. The restaurant is open 11 am to 9 pm Monday to Thursday and 11 am to 10 pm Friday and Saturday.

Hundreds of bunches of plastic grapes hang from the ceiling at **Monjuni's Italian Café & Grocery** (☎ 318-227-0847, 1315 Louisiana Ave), a strange amalgam of dark Italian grotto and 1950s malt shop. It's open Monday to Saturday 10:30 am to 9 pm (10 pm on weekends). On Sunday brunch is served from 11 am to 2 pm. The food is great. Try the meaty lasagna ($7) or shrimp and fettuccine in cream sauce ($10) – they're made with fresh pasta. The muffulettas and po-boys are first rate as well. Another good option for Italian or Mediterranean fare is the Highland Historic district's

Olive Street Bistro *(☎ 318-221-4517, 1027 Olive St)*. The outdoor deck is a fine place to enjoy a glass of wine or cappuccino and savor some homemade bread. Try the osso buco ($11) or penne amalfi ($9), which is pasta with fresh gulf shrimp, garlic and more. The Bistro is open Monday to Thursday 11 am to 10 pm, Friday and Saturday 11 am to 11 pm.

If you're more concerned with wonderful food than a swank atmosphere, try the ***Cub Lounge & Restaurant*** *(☎ 318-861-6517, 3002 Girard St)*. Though the restaurant is an offshoot of a popular but dumpy bar, don't think for a moment that these folks aren't serious about good food. All steaks are cut to order and include a baked potato and salad for prices ranging from $13 for a rib eye to $20 for a New York strip. Nightly specials that pair a steak with quail or soft-shell crab are good bets. Reservations are suggested for Friday and Saturday nights, when the restaurant is open until 11 pm, but are not needed Monday to Thursday when it's open from 6 to 10 pm.

In the same part of town, ***Nicky's Mexican Restaurant*** *(☎ 318-868-7630, 701 E Kings Hwy)* will satisfy any craving for authentic fajitas, burritos or simple beans and rice – all of which are hard to find in these parts. Nicky's is attached to ***El Coco Loco*** *(☎ 318-868-1116)*, a bar with salsa music and enough tequila to put you under.

Entertainment

For the best independent, foreign and documentary films Shreveport has to offer, call the ***Centenary College Film Society*** *(☎ 318-869-5184)* for their current schedule.

If you're in search of live music, don't expect too much from the casinos; they tend to feature bad cover bands doing Tony Orlando and Dawn tributes. Instead, go a few blocks west of the river to the ***Noble Savage Tavern*** *(☎ 318-221-1781, 417 Texas St)*, across from the public library. Thursday to Saturday nights from 8 pm to midnight it features bluegrass, blues and other roots music in a narrow brick-walled room with high ceilings. Cover charges are usually in the $3 to $5 range.

Around a few corners in an up-and-coming part of the riverfront, ***James Burton's Rock-n-Roll Café*** *(☎ 318-424-5000, 616 Commerce St)*, between Crockett and Milam Sts, is one of a row of clubs to choose from. But this place gets the best live music acts Friday and Saturday nights on account of James Burton himself – he was Elvis' lead guitarist from 1971 until the King's death in 1977 (when the band was affectionately known as the 'Takin' Care of Business' band). Burton has also played with Merle Haggard, Buffalo Springfield and others.

Karaoke, darts and pool tables occupy a huge warehouse space known as ***Coyote's Bar & Grill*** *(☎ 318-424-0650, 1818 Market St)*. It's karaoke night every Wednesday, Friday and Saturday.

There's more singing at ***Bear's Fine Foods & Sports Bar*** *(☎ 318-425-2327, 1401 Fairfield Ave)*, where massive stuffed bears sit at a player piano that spits out show tunes. The menu is brief with Cajun appetizers and assorted sandwiches and salads for $5 and under.

Soon after it opened in 1939, the garrulous group of old codgers who gathered to drink at this local dive christened it the ***Cub Lounge*** *(☎ 318-861-6517, 3002 Girard St)*. The story goes that upon leaving home for an evening of drinking, one fellow would tell his teetotalling wife that he was headed to the Christian Union Building. After a while, everyone began to refer to the bar by the three initials. This bar is imminently comfortable and its patrons warm and welcoming. Under the same ownership (and roof) as the Cub Lounge & Restaurant (see Places to Eat), the Cub Lounge is open Monday to Saturday 7 am to 2 am.

Feeling friendly with Lady Luck? If you're intent upon gambling, you can choose from several casinos. ***Harrah's Casino*** *(☎ 318-424-7777)* is on the Shreveport riverfront, in a riverboat next to the high-rise hotel. ***Horseshoe Casino & Hotel*** *(☎ 318-742-0711, 711 Horseshoe Blvd)*, ***Isle of Capri Casino & Hotel*** *(☎ 318-678-7777, 711 Isle of Capri Drive)* and ***Casino Magic*** *(☎ 318-746-0711, 300 Riverside Drive)* are all in Bossier City. They all pack them in, and you'll notice a ton of cars with Texas plates in the parking garages. On the whole, they offer similar experiences, though Horseshoe Casino is presently the most opulent of the bunch. A newly completed $285 million *Hollywood Casino* is right next to Harrah's.

Auto (☎ 318-524-1957), 1030 E Bert Kouns Ind Loop, and drool over their selection of mint-condition classic cars and racing motorcycles. There's a 1948 Chrysler with suicide back doors and a 'big old grill' that mesmerizes visitors. Price tag: $18,500.

Spectator Sports

Shreveport is proudly home to the Shreveport Captains (☎ 318-636-5555), part of a AA league affiliated with the San Francisco Giants.

Want to watch fast cars go round and round and round? Try Boothill Speedway (☎ 318-938-5373), at 9144 Greenwood Cemetery Rd in Greenwood, 12 miles west of Shreveport. Every Saturday night at 8 pm from March through November, stock car drivers from around the country come to race at this, the South's fastest quarter-mile dirt track.

If horses are more your thing, the Louisiana Downs Racetrack (☎ 318-742-5555) is at 8000 E Texas St in Bossier City. Horses race Thursday through Sunday from late June until early November, as well as Monday during September. The rest of the time, races are simulcast from other tracks. Admission is $1 on Thursday and $3 on other days. You can visit the track's Web site at www.ladowns.com for more information.

Shopping

From fine wines to fancy duds, Line Ave is Shreveport's prime shopping street. In the 4800 block are Pierremont Mall and Uptown Shopping Center, both chock-a-block with nicer stores. Worthy of special mention is the Glenwood Village Tea Room & Tea Shoppe (☎ 318-868-3651), 3310 Line Ave, a strange hybrid of antique store, gift shop, pharmacy and English tearoom. It's open Tuesday to Saturday 10 am to 5 pm; the tearoom serves from 11 am to 3 pm.

For fantasy shopping, stop by The Big Toy Store, also known as ArkLaTex Cycle &

Getting There & Away

Greater Shreveport Regional Airport features frequent flights to hub cities. Delta offers service seven times a day to and from Atlanta, while Continental offers eight trips a day to and from Houston. American offers commuter service 10 times daily to Dallas. All the major rental-car companies are onsite. Transportation to and from downtown is best accomplished by taxi, which will cost around $25.

Greyhound (☎ 318-221-4205), 408 Fannin St near Texas St, offers 20 morning and afternoon buses to New Orleans (eight hours), Dallas (four hours) and Jackson (five hours), as well as several buses to closer cities such as Ruston, Natchitoches and Alexandria.

Sportran, the citywide bus system, is of little use in visiting the city's widely dispersed attractions. Again, it's best to have your own car.

AROUND SHREVEPORT

To get an idea of how much the area's economy owes to the oil business, take a drive up Hwy 1 toward Oil City. As you pass through Mooringsport and across Caddo Lake, the surrounding farm fields begin to feature small oil wells. By the time you reach Oil City, 30 miles or so up the highway, the roadside is dotted with pumping wells.

Just off Hwy 1, on Land Ave in tiny Oil City, is the **Caddo-Pine Island Oil and Historical Museum** (☎ 318-995-6845). Amid rusting, junked oil derricks, antique tools and tractors, sits a small-frame building that houses a collection of oil industry ephemera and Native American items. It's open on weekdays 9 am to 4 pm (with a one-hour lunch break from noon to 1 pm) and charges a $1 admission.

Better yet, stop in Mooringsport and sign up for a 90-minute cruise on Caddo Lake. Caddo Lake Adventures (☎ 318-996-7440),

7810 Sundown Drive, will guide you around the cypress trees jutting this way and that throughout the water and give you a good sense of the area's history. Reservations are required, so call ahead; tickets cost from $20 to $45.

Mississippi

Mississippi

Facts about Mississippi

Long scorned for its lamentable Civil Rights history and its low ranking on the list of nearly every national indicator of economy and education, Mississippi is a state most people feel content to malign without first-hand experience. The observable Mississippi, however, is much more complex and compelling.

Highlights

- Hwy 61, the Delta Blues Museum, juke joints and the famous crossroads along the way

- The university town of Oxford, immortalized by its beloved native son, William Faulkner

- The capital of Jackson, torched by Sherman, touched by the Civil Rights movement and kept awake by a few quirky nightspots

- A drive or bike ride along the scenic Natchez Trace Parkway – an ancient Indian footpath

- Deserted beaches, warm waters and wilderness camping on the Gulf Islands

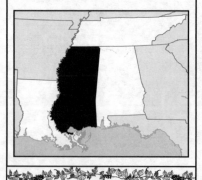

The Delta in the northwest corner of the state comes closest to what people might imagine Mississippi to be – endless miles of cotton fields and shotgun shacks. Today the landscape also includes huge Vegas-style casinos. Most travelers are drawn down Hwy 61 to discover the legendary landmarks and juke joints that have made the Delta the homeland of the blues. Blues lovers might want to schedule a trip around one of the region's major music festivals.

Central Mississippi holds the state capital at Jackson, where the old downtown commercial center remains a ghostly remnant long since forsaken for suburban sprawl along modern freeways. Some clubs, motels and hairstyles appear fixed in amber from decades back. To the east in Philadelphia, memorials remember the three Civil Rights workers killed by the Ku Klux Klan here in 1964, and nearby the Choctaw Indian nation thrives on ancestral lands.

The Gulf Coast is perhaps the most surprising part of Mississippi. Here you'll find wilderness islands with live oaks, lagoons and deserted beaches along Gulf stream waters. A ferry sails out to one of the islands; more adventurous travelers can take a sea kayak to remote and undeveloped islands for primitive camping. On the mainland, coastal towns hold a small art colony, Vietnamese markets and more casinos.

In southwest Mississippi, the Natchez Trace Parkway delivers travelers to a compact corner of the state with much dramatic history and scenery. Refined antebellum mansions in Natchez, ancient Indian mounds and leisurely bike loops make this an easy region to visit.

Northeast Mississippi holds the Magnolia State's most famous musical pilgrimage destination. Elvis Presley was born in Tupelo in 1935, and today his humble birthplace and hometown museum provides a personal glimpse into the origins of the King of Rock & Roll. Oxford, home of William Faulkner and the University of Mississippi, is the state's literary epicenter. Starkville, home to Mississippi State University, is the funkier college-town alternative.

History

The Nanih Waiya Mound at the northeastern Neshoba County line is the legendary birthplace of the Choctaw nation that dominated the Mississippi region before European settlement. The Choctaw remained on the land for more than two centuries after their first encounter with European explorers, but eventually their nation gradually lost territory to European immigration in the south. The northern part of Mississippi was the last to 'fall' to the Europeans, through questionable treaties and finally by banishment of all Indian nations in 1835 (see the Choctaw Country section, later in this chapter).

De Soto was the first European to encounter the Mississippi River in the Delta region in 1540. The first European settlement was founded on the coast in 1699 by Pierre Le Moyne, Sieur d'Iberville, in what is now Ocean Springs. France established a fort at Natchez in 1716. The territory between these original French Catholic settlements was contested by England until they finally predominated in 1763 and began moving Protestant emigrants from Atlantic colonies. Spain laid claim to French coastal lands referred to as West Florida, which stretched to the Mississippi River, until the area was overtaken by American troops in 1798.

The Mississippi Territory was created that same year, carved out of Choctaw and Chickasaw territory treaty by treaty. The territory became a state in 1817. In 1861, Mississippi was the second state to join the Confederacy, and its native son Jefferson Davis was named Confederate president. During the Civil War, the port at Vicksburg was the target of an elaborate Union campaign and siege.

Over the next century after Reconstruction, Mississippi gained an overarching reputation for repression of the civil rights of its African-American population. In the 1960s, Dr Martin Luther King Jr called Mississippi 'a desert state sweltering with the heat of injustice and oppression.' In 1963, University of Mississippi professor James Silver described it 'as near to approximating a police state as anything we have yet seen in America.' Some of the most lamentable events of the time occurred in Mississippi. Among these are the murders of Medgar Evers, Emmett Till, Earl Chaney, Andrew Goodman and Michael Schwerner (see 'A Dark Corner in Freedom Summer' boxed text, later in this chapter). On the positive side, in 1968 the Choctaws won the right to apply tribal law, and women began serving on juries.

In the decades since the dismantling of institutionalized racism, Mississippi has become a place of mostly polite, often shallow relations between the black and white communities. As in most of the US, housing, higher education and socializing occur more or less along racial lines. Encouraging signs of reconciliation include the election of the first black student president of the University of Mississippi in 2000, and the reopening of cases of racially motivated crimes going as far back as the 1960s. Some white perpetrators have already been brought to belated justice.

Geography

Mississippi occupies 47,233 sq miles (including 420 sq miles of inland water surface) and is bounded by Louisiana and Arkansas at the Mississippi River, western Tennessee to the north, Alabama to the east, and the Gulf of Mexico to the south.

The two most distinct geographical features are the Delta and the Gulf Coast. In the northwestern corner of the state, the Mississippi Delta forms a leaf-shaped alluvial basin that is around 85 miles across at its widest point and 200 miles long. The Gulf Coast stretches 44 miles from the Pearl River at the Louisiana line to the Alabama border, and includes 27 miles of white-sand beaches.

Northeastern Mississippi runs from the loess hills that form the eastern boundary of the Delta across the fertile Black Prairie

MISSISSIPPI

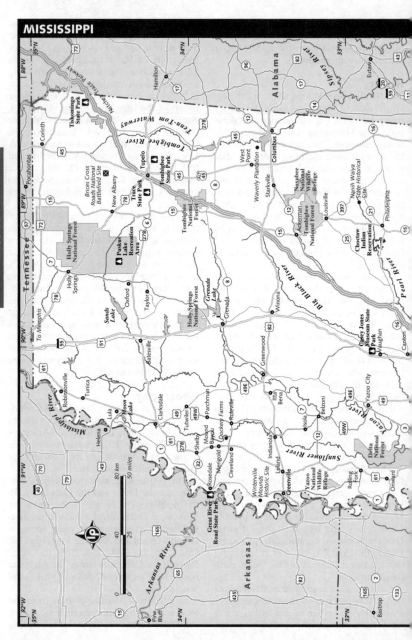

MISSISSIPPI

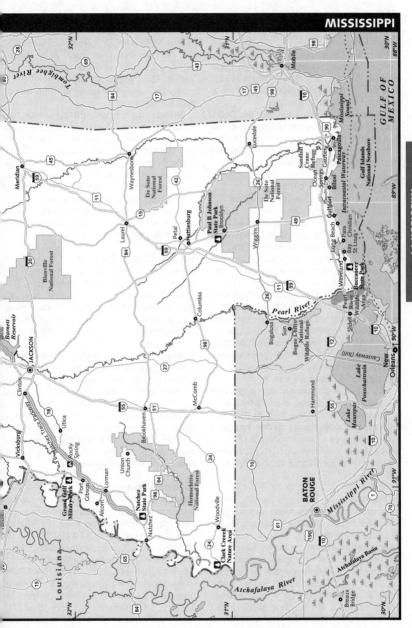

region to the uplands, which are shared with Alabama along the Tombigbee and Tennessee Rivers.

Central Mississippi, dominated by the capital, Jackson, slopes from the northern uplands through a sandier prairie region and down to the denuded Piney Woods region of southern Mississippi.

Southwestern Mississippi, like the Delta, features alluvial soils banked by loess hills in a narrow corridor along the river. To the east, these give way to a hilly farming region stretching to the Piney Woods.

Government & Politics

Perhaps no two facts about government and politics in Mississippi are more powerfully juxtaposed than these: the state legislature didn't ratify the 13th amendment outlawing slavery until 1995, and Mississippi today has a greater proportion of African-American elected officials than any other state in the nation.

Mississippi's current governor, Democrat Ronnie Musgrove, won by the narrowest of margins in early 2000. Though he had marginally more votes than his Republican opponent, Musgrove didn't have an absolute majority and the House of Representatives was required to vote for governor for the first time in Mississippi's history.

Hot topics at the moment are: improving the standard of education and whether or not to choose a state flag without the Confederate flavor of the current one. Finding a balance between conservation and commerce along the Mississippi River is a sleeping issue that periodically raises from its doze.

Economy

Mississippians have to look back to pre-Civil War days to find tasty balance sheets of statewide prosperity. Today's economic indicators find Mississippi languishing in the bottom few ranks: unemployment is high, and around 21% of the population (including a third of all children) is judged to be living in poverty. On the upside, Mississippi's situation did improve through the 1990s: the poverty rate dropped in 1990 and median household income jumped $4000 to $29,120 (75% of the national average).

The Mississippi Delta has been the recipient of Federal Empowerment Zone grants, allocated to the poorest regions in the nation. These grants attempt to build prosperity through job training and infrastructure improvement.

Primary industries still dominate the state. Mississippi is the third biggest cotton producer in the US. Catfish and soybeans are also big earners. The Mississippi Delta leads the nation in farm-raised catfish production, and Belzoni is known as the Catfish Capital of the World. Casino earnings have contributed to the state's taxation base but most of the profits go to out-of-state owners and, at a family level, slot machines help drain many household budgets.

Population & People

Mississippi's population is 2.7 million, 65% of which is living in rural communities. The most populous city is the capital, Jackson, with around 395,000 people. Of the state's 10 other cities with populations over 20,000, the largest is the coastal town of Biloxi, with 46,000 people.

Mississippi has the highest proportion of African-American residents of any state – around a third of its population. Yet this proportion is not spread evenly throughout the state; numbers may vary dramatically by region. For example, the Delta, historically a cotton-producing area, is today around 80% African-American. By contrast, the population of the Gulf Coast remains overwhelmingly white.

Information

Tourist Offices Welcome centers can be found on major interstate freeways. You can also request information from the Mississippi Division of Tourism (☎ 800-927-6378), PO Box 1705, Ocean Springs, MS 39566-1705. In the UK, you can contact the Mississippi tourist office at ☎ 1462-440787, mississippi@david-nicholson.com; there are no walk-in facilities. There are also offices in Munich, Germany (☎ 895-389-777); Garches, France (☎ 47-411-940); Zeist, the

Netherlands (☎ 30-693-3088); and Milan, Italy (☎ 2-669-9271). The official state Web site is www.visitmississippi.org.

Taxes The statewide sales tax is 7%. Hotels and other places to stay frequently carry additional lodging taxes, which vary by city.

Driving & Liquor Laws The minimum driving age is 15. Seatbelts and motorcycle helmets are required across the state. Highway speed limits reach a maximum of 70 miles per hour.

The minimum drinking age is 21 years. About a third of Mississippi's counties are dry; some wet counties limit the sale of cold beer and liquor on Sundays. Wine and spirits can be purchased from liquor stores; beer is available in grocery stores and gas stations.

State Parks & Protected Areas There are seven national forests (over 1 million acres), 29 state parks and seven national parks in Mississippi. Information about

fishing and hunting regulations and state parks is available from the Department of Wildlife, Fisheries and Parks (☎ 601-364-2163, 800-467-2757), PO Box 451, Jackson, MS 39205-0451. National forest information can be obtained from the Forest Service, 100 W Capitol St, Suite 1141, Jackson, MS 39269; call ☎ 601-965-4391 or the national toll-free camping reservations number at ☎ 800-280-2267.

Dangers & Annoyances The Delta is a very poor region so don't flaunt valuables, and lock cars and doors. Unnecessary encounters with local law enforcement are best avoided.

Interracial couples are rare and blatantly frowned upon. Most people will just encounter coldness and whispered comments; everyone is aware of the law and actual harassment is unlikely.

Mississippi Delta

The alluvial plain known as the Mississippi Delta stretches for 200 miles along the mighty river in northwestern Mississippi. The Delta is buttressed by the loess hills to the east and high river levees to the west. Yet the feeling that you're sinking down into something as you enter and climbing back out of it as you leave is only partly due to geography.

Recurrent flooding of the alluvial basin made this region sparsely populated until a levee system was built before the Civil War. With flooding controlled, the railroads moved in, providing ready access for northern hardwood industries to clear-cut and ship out millions of acres of trees. Cotton production expanded into the newly cleared land. Now more than a century later, knee-high cotton fields dominate this disturbingly flat and nearly treeless landscape, interrupted only occasionally by tin gins and pockets of cypress swamp.

In summer, the Delta sun scorches the cotton bolls till they pop open like kernels of corn on an open flame. After the harvesters tear through in October, tendrils of

---

Mississippi Radio Stations

If you're planning a blues pilgrimage, bring your own soundtrack. Mississippi's radio stations cannot be counted on. The jewels in the junk heap of vituperative talk, classic hits and bible thumping are:

Delta
KFFA 1360 AM (Helena, Arkansas) – blues show weekdays at 12:15 pm

Jackson
WMPR 90.1 FM – blues
WQJQ 105.1 FM – Motown and R&B

Oxford
WUMS 92.1 FM – eclectic mix, blues program Saturday evening

Starkville
WMSV 91.1 FM – eclectic mix

In the northwest part of the state, you can pick up some cool Memphis radio (see the Tennessee chapter).

Giving Back to the Delta

The Delta is a very poor region, and local community organizations put donations of time and money to good use.

The Clarksdale affiliate of Habitat for Humanity (☎ 662-624-8984, 201 Jefferson St) is dedicated to improving substandard housing in the region. They can always use an extra set of hands. The Care Station is grateful for any help travelers can offer in cooking and serving food to the needy. Call Verna Jones on ☎ 662-902-4066.

Blues musicians often devote their lives to their craft without the standard perks of employment such as health care. Blues Aid (☎ 870-338-3501), across the river in Arkansas, organizes concerts and other fund-raisers to provide these services to musicians and their families.

Making an offering in exchange for any impromptu concert is another way to support the community. For a front porch recital, purchase a recording if available; for a blues barber, you might request a shave and leave a big tip; and cash is rarely refused if discreetly offered.

Attending Sunday church services earns neatly dressed visitors local respect. If you decide to attend, be prepared for lengthy services (around 11 am to 1 pm) and heart-rending gospel music. It's a good idea to have something for the offering plate.

white fibers cling to barren stalks as blood red as manzanita, and 40-foot bales of cotton are stored at the side of the road.

The descendants of the cotton aristocracy remain in a clean white universe of town houses, academies, cotillions and country clubs, but this is noticeable only on a second look. At first glance, the Delta appears to be the poorest place you've ever seen – 'the South's South' – with whole families living out of tiny shotgun shacks insulated with newspaper. The Delta has the highest proportion of households without electricity or indoor plumbing in the nation. So, without air-conditioning or cool showers, most folks around here are used to working at a slower, more relaxed pace in an effort to conserve energy during the unrelenting summer heat. You might call it 'Delta time.'

It comes as no surprise that the Mississippi Delta is known throughout the world as the birthplace of the blues. Blues music, drawn from African beats, emanated from the hard living the Delta extracted from its workers. As hauntingly compelling as the Delta itself, blues musicians – from Charley Patton, WC Handy and Robert Johnson to BB King, Ike Turner and John Lee Hooker – shaped the foundation for the one of the most popular musical movements of this century. Today, visitors come from as far as Germany and Japan to make the blues pilgrimage tour – to search for Robert Johnson's alleged grave, and to pass the notorious plantations of Parchman Penitentiary and Dockery Farms. And to a blues fan, there is nothing like hearing this music in its natural context in rugged roadside juke joints, where the beer is pulled from a Coleman ice chest and late-night dancing gets down and dirty, or at a regional music festival.

Climate

The Mississippi Delta has the same subtropical climate as the rest of the region, but is perhaps more stultifying because it's unbroken by any breeze, and the treeless plain offers little relief from the sun. Consider this fact seriously if traveling from June to September. The rest of the year has mild temperatures, requiring no more than a warm sweater or light jacket in the coldest months.

HWY 61: MEMPHIS TO CLARKSDALE

As soon as you cross the state line heading south on Hwy 61 from Memphis, you'll see cotton fields stretching out to the horizon, dotted with disused gins, farm equipment, cypress swamps and a lucrative new crop: the gambling palaces of Tunica County.

Ten huge casinos are strewn west and north of Robinsonville in what has become the third biggest gambling strip in the US (after Las Vegas and Atlantic City). As well as the 'slim-as-Sally' chance of striking it rich, these always-open monoliths offer accommodations, lavish buffets and intermittently good entertainment along with the ghost of Bill Cosby and his ilk (oh, that was the *real* Bill Cosby?). Call the Tunica Convention & Visitors Bureau (☎ 888-488-6422) or check their Web site at www.tunicamiss.org to find out who's playing which casinos. The Horseshoe Casino's *Bluesville* venue *(☎ 800-303-7463, 1020 Casino Center Drive)*, in Robinsonville, books good blues acts and has a blues museum. *Sam's Town* *(☎ 800-456-0711, 1477 Casino Strip Blvd)*, in Robinsonville, has a 1600-seat concert hall that draws some big names. It's possible to pick up rooms for around $20 when it's quiet, but when there's a decent show on, the bottom line is more like $50.

At the ghost town crossroads in **Robinsonville**, the proprietor, 'Big Man,' serves generous burgers, the original fried pickles (an acquired taste) and $3 beers in a souvenir mug at the *Hollywood* *(☎ 662-363-1126)*, an old roadhouse with plank floors and high ceilings, which occasionally features live entertainment. (It's mentioned in Mark Cohn's 1977 song 'Blues Walking.')

Grabbing a bite to eat in the town of **Tunica** might prove both colorful and filling. Just behind the old gas pumps, you'll find the *Blue & White* *(☎ 662-363-1371, 1355 Highway 61 N)*, a fine coffeeshop that starts serving meals at 5 am. *Campbell's Barbecue* a few doors away also has food, and is open early for good breakfast biscuits. Time for a nap? The *Hotel Marie* *(☎ 662-357-0055, 1301 Main St)* is a surprisingly nice old-fashioned but refurbished hotel in the middle of forlorn downtown Tunica (rates start at $50 a double with breakfast).

A turn west off Hwy 61 onto Hwy 49 leads to **Lula**. Among the five or so storefronts 'downtown' is the Wash Bucket, which features a mural of blues greats as homage to Charley Patton's song 'Dry Well Blues,' which is about Lula. A quarter-mile or so south is the junction of Hwy 49 and Moon Lake Rd.

Follow Moon Lake Rd south and enter a tranquil cove of trees surrounding the misty **Moon Lake**. An old-time escape for Delta families, the lake hosts couples boating, boys fishing and lazy afternoons after Sunday dinner. The center of all this activity was the Moon Lake Club, which figures prominently in several works by Mississippi playwright Tennessee Williams, who frequented the place as a boy. Today *Uncle Henry's Place* *(☎ 662-337-2757, 5860 Moon Lake Rd)* continues to offer guest rooms ($70 double, including breakfast) and serves Southern dinners in the old lodge from Wednesday to Sunday. The casino described by Williams now resembles little more than a basement rec room, and no longer permits gambling.

The *Lady Luck Rhythm & Blues* casino *(☎ 800-789-5825, 777 Lady Luck Parkway)*, in Lula on Hwy 49 right at the Mississippi River bridge, often hires local musicians as entertainment.

Across the river in Arkansas, Helena is the home of the **King Biscuit Blues Festival** held the first weekend in October. This major regional festival is named after the radio program 'King Biscuit Time,' which used to feature Sonny Boy Williamson. These days the show is aired on KFFA 1360 AM weekdays at 12:15 pm. Visit the festival's Web site at www.kingbiscuitfest.org or call 870-338-8798, for more information. The **Delta Cultural Center** (☎ 800-358-0972, 141 Cherry St, Helena), in the rail depot downtown, is open daily till 5 pm; admission is free. The *King Biscuit Times* reports on the blues scene (for subscriptions and souvenirs call ☎ 800-637-8097).

CLARKSDALE

Clarksdale is the heart of the Delta, and its Delta Blues Museum is the major touchstone of a blues heritage tour. It's the birthplace of musical greats such as Jackie ('Rocket 88') Brenston, Sam Cooke, 'Son' House and 'Little Junior' Parker. Right on famed Hwy 61, it's also a convenient base for exploring the Delta. It evokes all of that raw anti-charm that makes the region so compelling.

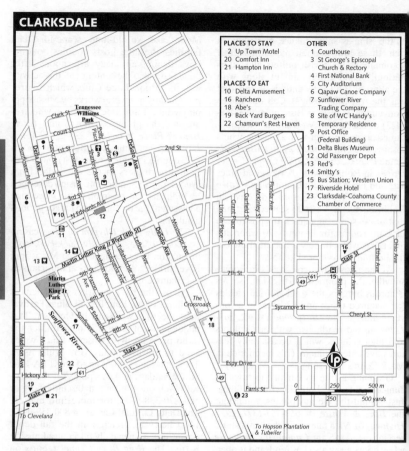

CLARKSDALE

PLACES TO STAY
2 Up Town Motel
20 Comfort Inn
21 Hampton Inn

PLACES TO EAT
10 Delta Amusement
16 Ranchero
18 Abe's
19 Back Yard Burgers
22 Chamoun's Rest Haven

OTHER
1 Courthouse
3 St George's Episcopal
   Church & Rectory
4 First National Bank
5 City Auditorium
6 Qapaw Canoe Company
7 Sunflower River
   Trading Company
8 Site of WC Handy's
   Temporary Residence
9 Post Office
   (Federal Building)
11 Delta Blues Museum
12 Old Passenger Depot
13 Red's
14 Smitty's
15 Bus Station; Western Union
17 Riverside Hotel
23 Clarksdale-Coahoma County
   Chamber of Commerce

Orientation

Hwy 61, known here as State St, skirts the old downtown area. The central business district occupies several square blocks north of the railroad tracks and east of the Sunflower River.

Across the railroad tracks is a rough-looking part of town along Martin Luther King Jr Blvd (formerly 4th St). In this area many stores are closed and boarded up, but there are still several places to eat, as well as juke joints and lots of people hanging out.

Information

The chamber of commerce (☎ 662-627-7337), 1540 DeSoto Ave (Hwy 49), can direct you to established chamber members, but they rarely can recommend what most people come to see, which is essentially what's regarded as the underbelly of their community.

You can go to First National Bank (☎ 662-627-3261), 402 E 2nd St at Leflore Ave, to cash traveler's checks. There is a Western Union office in the bus station at 1604 State St.

The main post office (☎ 662-627-7834) is in the federal building on Sharkey Ave, between 2nd and 3rd Sts.

The Northwest Mississippi Regional Medical Center (☎ 662-627-3211) is at 1970 Hospital Drive.

The local police can be reached at ☎ 662-621-8151; contact ☎ 662-627-8444 for the local fire station.

Delta Blues Museum

The blues museum (☎ 662-627-6820), 1 Blues Alley, opened in 1979 to commemorate the artists who shaped the popular music of the 20th century. In 1999, it moved to the present site in the old freight depot. The collection of artifacts – which include an effigy of Muddy Waters, photos of juke joints in action and ZZ Top's 'MuddyWood' guitar (see South of Clarksdale) – is modest, but there are detailed historical notes and temporary exhibits of Delta blues-inspired art. The library holds specialized volumes for serious researchers and there are books, tapes, CDs and souvenirs for regular fans. The museum is open Monday to Saturday; admission is free.

The Delta Blues Museum sells a small number of titles on the region, as well as on music. Look for *Living Blues* magazine, *Blues from the Delta* by William Ferris, *Lost Highway* by Peter Guralnick and *The Land Where Blues Began* by Alan Lomax.

The associated Delta Blues Education Project aims to ensure the continuance of blues music through children's education and workshops.

Other Blues Sights

The **Riverside Hotel** (☎ 662-624-9163), 615 Sunflower Ave, now a dilapidated boarding house operated by the venerable 'Rat' (a bluesy character from way back), is where Bessie Smith died in 1937 after a car accident on Hwy 61 (see the 'Empress of the Blues' boxed text). Here also in 1951, James Cotton wrote 'Rocket 88' – the song widely considered the first rock & roll release.

The **old passenger depot**, at Issaquena Ave, is where WC Handy left for Memphis

Empress of the Blues

The recording career of jazz singer Bessie Smith (1894–1937) came to an abrupt end at the Riverside Hotel in Clarksdale on September 26, 1937. Traveling from Memphis for an appearance in Clarksdale, Smith was in a car accident north of town and was brought to the black clinic, now the Riverside Hotel. A popular legend implied that she was sent here only after being refused admittance at the whites-only hospital, but this is now widely considered to be untrue.

Born in Chattanooga, Tennessee, Smith was, at her peak in the 1920s, the highest paid black entertainer of her day. She recorded 156 songs, including 'T'aint Nobody's Bizness If I Do,' 'St Louis Blues' and 'Nobody Knows You When You're Down and Out.' Her singing style influenced Billie Holiday, Mahalia Jackson and Janis Joplin.

with the seeds of the Beale St Blues in his bag. Today it's a sports bar and occasional music venue. Marked by a plaque, the site at the southwest corner of 3rd St and Issaquena Ave was Handy's home from 1903 to 1905.

Tennessee Williams Attractions

Mississippi's famous playwright Tennessee Williams, born in Columbus, spent much of his childhood here in Clarksdale at the rectory of St George's Episcopal Church at 1st St and Sharkey Ave, where his grandfather served as rector for 16 years. A tiny park in the city's affluent residential area around John and Court Sts is dedicated to the artist.

Clarksdale hosts the Tennessee Williams Festival in October. (See Special Events, below.)

Activities

Experienced river rat John Ruskey and his Qapaw Canoe Company (☎ 662-627-4070, john@island63.com), 291 Sunflower Ave, lead canoe trips along the mighty Mississippi River. Expeditions can be built to order, ranging from a local day trip to a month-long adventure from Memphis to New Orleans. Rates start around $75 a day.

Organized Tours

Ad hoc blues tours may be arranged locally through Robert Birdsong (☎ 662-624-6051, mississippimojo@yahoo.com); he's a local fireman and hardcore blues enthusiast who will adapt a tour to your interests and budget. American Dreams Safari (☎ 901-527-8870, tad@americandreamsafari.com) runs a Delta Daytrip that starts in Memphis and includes the Clarksdale area (see Organized Trips in the Memphis section of the Tennessee chapter).

Special Events

Clarksdale hosts the Delta Jubilee music festival at the end of May, the Sunflower River Blues and Gospel Festival during the second weekend in August and a Tennessee Williams Festival the second weekend in October. The festival features presentations by friends and scholars, theatrical performances, house tours and an opening dinner at Moon Lake's former casino, 20 miles north (see the Memphis to Clarksdale section). Contact the chamber of commerce for more information.

Places to Stay

The place to stay in the Clarksdale area is the **Shack Up Inn** (☎ 662-624-8329, shackup@shackupinn.com), at the Hopson Plantation, which is on the west side of Hwy 49, 2 miles south of town. This B&B (bed & beer) in a comfortably refurbished sharecropper shack costs between $35 and $50. Not your regular high-class B&B, these shacks have an altogether different and most excellent atmosphere.

The **Up Town Motel** (☎ 662-627-3251, 305 E 2nd St), at Issaquena Ave, is an acceptable cheapie (the barroom strippers have gone). Rooms start around $30 and it's right downtown. The **Comfort Inn** (☎ 662-627-5122, 818 S State St) has none of the could-be-anywhere feeling of a chain motel; the managers are enthusiastic ambassadors for their town and they make waffles from scratch every morning. Rooms are around $60, but discounts are often available. The **Hampton Inn** (☎ 662-627-9292, 710 State St) has an attractive, comfortable lobby and an inviting pool with an indoor and outdoor portion.

Though the famed Riverside Hotel (see Other Blues Sights, above) is open to overnight guests, it operates more as a rooming house. At $25/40 a night with shared facilities, you're there for the experience rather than the amenities.

Places to Eat

Abe's (☎ 662-624-9947, 616 State St) has been doing barbecue for 75 years so they've got a knack for it now. **Chamoun's Rest Haven** (☎ 662-624-8601, 419 State St) is a rare opportunity for Lebanese specialties, such as stuffed kibbie (a sort of fried meat loaf packed with roasted pine nuts), stuffed cabbage and grape leaves ($8 for a combo plate), as well as spinach pie, tabbouleh and hummus. **Back Yard Burgers** (☎ 662-624-9292, 849 State St) dishes out chili for less than $3 a bowl. **Ranchero** (☎ 662-624-9768, 1907 N State St) is a local favorite with an all-American menu and a football-hero theme.

Downtown, **Delta Amusement** (☎ 662-627-1467, 348 Delta Ave) does breakfast, plate lunches and town-renowned chili cheeseburgers. It's a battered place full of men playing cards and muttering at each other through their cigarette smoke – you could spread the character on toast. Ask around about the new location of **Hick's Superette** and the tamales that former president Bill Clinton couldn't get enough of.

Entertainment

Beyond the few major scheduled festivals, musical events are often spontaneous. Information spreads by word of mouth – ask around – and by posters that appear around town announcing a concert that very night.

On any given night, chances are that only one juke joint will feature live entertain-

Visiting Juke Joints

Most juke joints are African-American neighborhood clubs and outside visitors can be a rarity. Lots are mostly male hangouts; others are frequented by men and couples. There are very few places that local women, even in a group of two or three, would turn up without a male chaperone. The chances of women actually being assaulted are slim, but expect a *lot* of persistent, suggestive attention. For visitors of both sexes, having a friendly local with you to make some introductions can make for a much better evening. Also consider calling ahead to find out what's going on and to say you're going to stop by. If you arrive alone and unannounced, do start talking to people to break the ice, but women might want to act like they're training to be nuns.

ment, whether it's **Red's** (☎ *662-627-3166, 395 Sunflower Ave*), at Martin Luther King Jr Blvd; **Smitty's** (☎ *662-627-1525, 377 Yazoo Ave*); or other fly-by-night joints. The **Commissary** (☎ *662-624-5756*), at Hopson Plantation 2 miles south of town on Hwy 49, sometimes has music. On Friday nights in May, there's free outdoor entertainment next to the blues museum. Larger shows are held at the city's auditorium.

Shopping
Sunflower River Trading Company (☎ 662-624-9389), 252 Delta Ave, is an art gallery and store that supports local businesses and operates as an unofficial visitor welcome center. They're happy to give advice, recommend restaurants and accommodations and generally clue you in.

Getting There & Away
Bus Greyhound (☎ 662-627-7893), 1604 State St, runs buses to several cities in the region. Clarksdale has a small, clean, well-lit modern bus station right on Hwy 61. There are four buses a day between here and Memphis (two hours, $17.50), and two to

New Orleans (5½ hours, $65). Other destinations include Greenwood (1½ hours, $13.50) and Jackson (3¾ hours, $32).

There's also a Western Union office at the station.

Car Hwy 61 is memorialized in blues songs as the route that brought musicians from the Delta north to Chicago and south to New Orleans. Note that traces of 'Old Hwy 61' can be found alongside the modern highway; this was the original route 60 years ago. The 'new' highway – construction continues to make it a modern four-lane highway – bypasses the center of town.

Though it bypasses Clarksdale, the Great River Rd (Hwy 1) along the Mississippi River is another intriguing rural route through typical Delta landscapes of cotton and shantytowns. The river itself is obscured by levees.

Getting Around
Local taxi service is available from Jerry's Cab Co (☎ 662-624-9288).

SOUTH OF CLARKSDALE
Seven miles south of Clarksdale on Hwy 49 is **Stovall Farms**, once a huge plantation where Muddy Waters lived and worked. His wooden shack was cannibalized by ZZ Top guitarist Billy Gibbons for the MuddyWood

Blues legend Muddy Waters

guitar now among the collection at the Delta Blues Museum.

Fifteen miles southeast of Clarksdale on Hwy 49 is **Tutwiler**. Here, at the abandoned-looking tracks, a mural of WC Handy recounts the story of Handy's first exposure to the blues in 1903 at the train depot that was once here. Handy carried this sound to Memphis, where he popularized the Delta blues. Blues trivia: the song Handy first heard in Tutwiler made reference to 'where the Southern cross the Dog,' which was local code for the intersection of the Southern and Yazoo-Delta (also known as the 'Dog') railroads farther south in Moorhead.

The same Tutwiler mural also shows the way to the nearby grave of Sonny Boy Williamson (also known as Aleck Miller, 1908–65) adjacent to the Whitfield Church. The great harmonica player's marker (adorned with his photo, a regional custom) is often strewn with blues harps, cans of beer and other mementos.

South of Tutwiler on Hwy 49 W, **Parchman Penitentiary** has been the one-time home of many a bluesman, and has been the subject of several songs, including Bukka White's 'Parchman Farm Blues' and Miles Davis' 'Going on Down to Parchman Farms.' The 'Midnight Special' heard in many blues lyrics recalls the weekend train from New Orleans that brought visitors to the prison. Vernon Presley, father of the King, once did time here for passing a bad check. The only self-supporting penitentiary in Mississippi, Parchman used its pool of unpaid laborers (overwhelmingly African-American) to produce cotton. These days the prison is no longer self sufficient but it uses about half of the total acreage to grow vegetables. There are around 5500 inmates, most of whom are still African-American, and about 60 inmates are on death row.

Use Hwy 32 W to pick up Hwy 61 at **Shelby**, where the **Do-Drop Inn**, at 3rd and Lake Sts, is a locally famed juke joint, along with the **Windy City Blues Cafe**, across the street. Just south, you will reach the historic community of **Mound Bayou**, which was founded by freed slaves in 1887. Isaiah Montgomery, the town founder, and other former residents were once enslaved on the plantation belonging to the brother of Confederate president Jefferson Davis.

Merigold, 8 miles south of Shelby, is barely a one-horse town, but it's got three great reasons to stop. **McCarty's Pottery Store** (☎ 662-748-2293) reels in clay connoisseurs, but the real attraction is the eccentric and lovely garden out back. To reach the store, go to the bottom of 1st St, turn left and the store is on your left. It's open Tuesday to Saturday from 10 am to 4 pm. *Crawdad's* (☎ 662-748-2441) is a massive barn-like restaurant and bar with dead animals leering from the walls; the food portions are generous. It's on Park St (the wide street running parallel to the highway), near the corner of Goff and 1st Sts. If you're lucky enough to be here on a Thursday, hang around until evening and visit *Poor Monkey's Lounge* (☎ 662-748-2254), the most authentic old-time juke joint you will ever see. It's a safe and friendly place, much easier to be a stranger in than the hardcore Shelby places. To get there, turn west at South St off Hwy 61, take the next left along a road with a creek on your right and go for 1⅓ miles until you see a row of shacks on the left; Poor Monkey's has painted signs all over the front.

CLEVELAND & AROUND
• pop 15,000

Settled in 1869, Cleveland was a rough-and-tumble sawmill town and an important stop on the Vicksburg-Memphis trade route. These days, it's a pleasant and manageable place, as well as home to the Fighting Okra of Delta State University, and a source of good food and a handy music scene. It's a cool place to base yourself for a couple of days in the Delta.

The town runs off the axis of Hwys 8 and 61; the center is dotted with stores selling antiques and curios. The chamber of commerce (☎ 662-843-2712, 800-295-7473) is a good source for information on local music; it's on 3rd St, east of Hwy 61 (turn at the Kroger grocery store and it's the brick building on the right).

A few miles east on Hwy 8 between Cleveland and Ruleville is **Dockery Farms**, once a huge plantation where some music historians say the Delta blues was born. Early bluesman Charley Patton worked here, along with his teacher Henry Sloan, who was said to have been playing the blues as far back as 1897. Patton's song 'Pea Vine Blues' refers to Dockery Farms' Pea Vine railroad.

In **Ruleville** proper, a section of Front St known as Greasy St features several blues clubs.

Places to Stay & Eat

If you've ever wanted to sleep in a watermelon bed, stay at ***Molly's B&B*** *(☎ 662-843-9913, 214 S Bolivar Ave)*, at Lamar St, where Floyd Shaman's quirky wood sculptures fill the house. There's a great balcony and guests get a superb Southern breakfast. Rooms are $60 or $65.

Downtown, ***Sharpe St Station*** *(☎ 662-846-0000, 201 S Sharpe St)* is a pub-restaurant with music (often blues) a few nights a week. The elite meet to eat at ***KC's Restaurant*** *(☎ 662-843-5301)*, on the north side of Hwy 61, just north of the Hwy 8 junction. The restaurant serves Chinese-accented duck confit and wild game accompanied by a 47-page wine list. Dinners really add up but you can get away with lunch for under $15. Back down to earth, ***Airport Grocery*** *(☎ 662-843-4817)* is a casual joint with blues every so often and great food Tuesday to Saturday. It's west of town on the north side of Hwy 8 just past Bishop Rd.

ROSEDALE

Blues artists used to hop the Pea Vine train and play in juke joints along the way to the river terminus at Rosedale, 20 miles west of Cleveland at the Hwy 1 intersection. The last town in the US to have an automatic telephone exchange, Rosedale is still a sleepy place where nothing moves much faster than the river.

If you're camping, the ***Great River Rd State Park*** *(☎ 662-759-6762)* is excellent as it's one of the few parks right on the Mississippi River. There is also a lake with paddle

---

Bootlegger Etiquette

The lake in Great River Rd State Park is named after Perry Martin, a bootlegger in the 1930s who lived on a houseboat here and had a whiskey still hidden in the woods nearby. Bootleggers had to balance discretion and publicity – after all, if no one knew you were making liquor, you wouldn't sell much. Indeed, when the payoffs were going well, bootlegged whiskey jugs would be proudly stamped with the name and address of the manufacturer. Nonetheless, it was a dangerous matter to come upon a hidden still and Perry Martin was known to guard his extremely fiercely. In these lax days, there's a still (with recipe!) out in the open right by the visitor center.

---

boats for rent, a fun frisbee-golf course and bikes for rent. The visitor center has a restaurant that serves lunch only but great catfish, and there's an observation tower nearby with views of the river and hazy sunsets. Rosedale is about 5 minutes away. The park periodically floods so call ahead to check that it is open.

In Rosedale, the ***River Run Cafe*** *(☎ 662-759-6800)*, at the intersection of Hwy 8 and Hwy 1, does plate lunches and crawfish dinners. Down the main street, the ***White Front Cafe*** (plans are afoot to paint it white) has hot tamales. ***Bug's Blues Lounge*** *(☎ 662-759-0269, 515 Bruce St)* takes care of entertainment Thursday to Sunday. (Don't bother looking for non-existent street signs: Bug's is behind the courthouse.) Rosedale hosts the Crossroads Blues Festival in May.

GREENVILLE

South of Rosedale on Hwy 1, Greenville, the largest city in the Delta, has a reputation for being more liberal than its neighbors. Here in 1946, Hodding Carter won a Pulitzer Prize for editorials in his family's *Delta Democrat Times* urging racial moderation. At the time his lone voice in the staunch segregationist Delta helped set the tone for the community. Civil War chronicler Shelby Foote is also from Greenville. It was here that the levee broke in 1927, causing the catastrophic Great Flood that resulted in the building of the current – as yet unbroached – levee.

The Convention & Visitors Bureau (☎ 662-334-2711) is downtown at 410 Washington Ave. There's a state welcome center (☎ 662-332-2378) inside the *River Road Queen* paddle boat building at Hwy 82 and Reed Rd. At the river, several casinos operate around the clock. The Mississippi Delta Blues Festival, a major regional music festival, is held the third weekend in September off Hwy 454 south of town. Across the river in Arkansas, Helena's King Biscuit Blues Festival is held the second weekend in October.

Places to Stay
The best mid-price option is the *Greenville Inn & Suites* (☎ 662-332-6900, 211 Walnut St), in the old levee board building. Smart, clean rooms start around $50 and you can walk along the levee to Walnut St's restaurants and bars. Take Washington St all the way to the river and you'll hit Walnut St.

Miles of eyesore neon along Hwy 82 and the Great River Rd (Hwy 1) include every chain restaurant and hotel you've ever heard of. The no frills *Levee Inn* (☎ 662-332-1511) has rooms for around $30 and is on Hwy 82 east of Hwy 1.

Linden On The Lake (☎ 662-839-2181) is a B&B 22 miles south of Greenville on Lake Washington. The old plantation home is still owned by the original family. You can choose between rooms with antique furnishings or cabins on site. You can borrow fishing gear to hook bream, crappie and catfish. Rates are negotiable depending on length of stay and your breakfast demands. Turn west off Hwy 1 onto Hwy 436, when you get to the lake drive one-half mile north to the house.

Places to Eat
Doe's Eat (☎ 662-334-3315, 502 Nelson St), at Hinds St, has been a culinary landmark since 1941. Even Bill Clinton has sampled

---

> ## Blues Makin'
>
> When I was a boy chopping cotton, picking cotton and sharecropping, I didn't know what the blues was, I was just singing. Life was hard enough to make you sing.
>
> – Wesley 'Mississippi Junebug' Jefferson of the Wesley Jefferson Band, Clarksdale

their generous steaks and skillet-fried potatoes. There's no menu so you better be warned that a 2lb T-bone goes for an easy $34 (they don't mind if you share). It's open Monday through Saturday from 5:30 to around 10 pm; during the day they serve take-out tamales.

Entertainment
Perry's Flowing Fountain (☎ 662-335-9836, 928 Nelson St) was made famous by Little Milton in 'Annie Mae's Cafe'; Ike and Tina Turner and Howlin' Wolf have all played here. It anchors a rough strip of blues clubs that you'd think twice about strutting around solo.

There are some less edgy venues by the levee, along Walnut St. The *Walnut St Bait Shop*, at No 130, has music three or four nights a week (but it doesn't sell bait for fishing).

Getting There & Away
Greyhound (☎ 662-335-2633) stops at 3107 Hwy 82 E. The one-way fare to Jackson is $29 (five hours).

AROUND GREENVILLE
North of town on Hwy 1, **Winterville Mounds State Historic Site** (☎ 662-334-4684) preserves an ancient set of 15 Indian mounds, including one that measures six stories high. These mounds attest to the Mississippian community that thrived on the shores of the great river more than 500 years ago. Admission to the museum is $1 for adults and 50¢ for children; it's closed on Monday and Tuesday.

Got a license to sell that barbecue, miss? Pig Out Inn, Natchez, MS

Kudzu struck, and ma & pa were never seen again.

Welcome to the Blues Highway, Clarksdale, MS

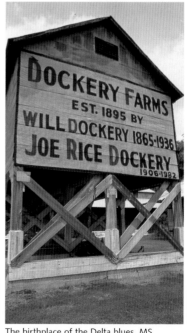

The birthplace of the Delta blues, MS

Rollin' on the wide Mississippi River adds a nice slant to dining and gambling. Natchez, MS

Gulf Coast commercial fisherman shows-and-tells his catch. MS

Old Southern recipes use muscadine grapes to make wine. MS

At **Leland**, on Hwy 82 between Hwy 61 and Greenville, visitors are greeted with the announcement that this is the birthplace of Kermit the Frog. A tiny visitor center overlooks Deer Creek and displays photographs of Jim Henson (the Muppet's creator), his Delta childhood and early Kermit and Muppet characters. At Christmas, local boy scouts and civic organizations assemble festive floats that they decorate with electric lights and plant in the water along the creek.

INDIANOLA

East on Hwy 82, Indianola and the surrounding Sunflower County have produced much of what is famous and infamous in Mississippi. The musician BB King, the chef Craig Claiborne and the Civil Rights heroine Fannie Lou Hamer all hail from here. Also the repressive Citizens Council (a white-collar version of the Klan) was born here in 1954.

In 1983, when local leaders invited both whites and blacks to a reception they sponsored for BB King, it made national news. Today the 'Beale St Blues Boy' is honored with a namesake street and a park (on Roosevelt St). His handprints and footprints are sunk unceremoniously into the sidewalk at the corner of 2nd and Church Sts (there's no street sign; it's across from Court St), a block up from the main drag on Front St.

The town hosts the BB King Homecoming on the first weekend in June, when King returns to town to play at the outdoor festival along with local musicians. Afterwards he customarily retreats to the sleek interior of *Club Ebony* (☎ 662-887-9915, *404 Hannah Ave*). To find the club from down-

town, take Second St out to Depot St, turn right and drive across the tracks – even the white folks turn up to hear him here. Live local music is featured most weekends.

GREENWOOD

The seat of Leflore County, Greenwood is named after Greenwood Le Flore, the half-Acadian, half-Choctaw negotiator of the Treaty of Dancing Rabbit Creek. This infamous treaty banished the Choctaws to Oklahoma, and enriched Le Flore with a 15,000-acre estate and hundreds of slaves. Greenwood is second only to Memphis as the largest cotton market in America.

The county came to national attention in 1955, when the white men who had confessed to the abduction and murder of 14-year-old Emmett Till (in supposed retribution for eyeing a white woman) were acquitted in about an hour. Byron de la Beckwith, convicted murderer of Medgar Evers, also hails from these parts.

The local convention and visitors bureau (☎ 800-748-9064) is at 1902 Leflore Ave. Greenwood has two mainstream attractions. **Cottonlandia** (☎ 662-453-0925), on Hwy 82 west of town, is a quirky cinderblock museum that houses not only the industry exhibits you'd expect from its name, but also a large annotated collection of Indian beadwork and projectile points, stuffed swamp critters, costumes and ankle bracelets from a celebrated local belly dancer, and Victorian furnishings belonging to the notorious Le Flore. The museum is open daily; admission is $2. Farther west on Hwy 82, the **Florewood River Plantation State Park** maintains 'living history' exhibits on this restored antebellum plantation. Admission is $3.50 for adults and $2.50 for children.

In town, Grand Blvd is an affluent residential district with circa 1890s homes. Several restaurants offer fine dining. *Yianni's* (☎ 662-455-6789, *506 Yalobusha St*) serves upscale Greek entrées for around $14 along with $5 cheeseburgers in a glamorous setting. *Lusco's* (☎ 662-453-5365, *722 Carrollton Ave*) serves steaks and seafood in private rooms that are locally legendary.

Black & Blue

If you've been singing the blues as long as I have, it's kind of like being black twice.

– Riley (BB) King

Robert Johnson at the Crossroads

Born in Hazelhurst in 1911, Robert Johnson is the most legendary of all Delta blues musicians. It's said he got his talent from having sold his soul to the devil down at the crossroads (folks here like to speculate on which crossroads it was). Tales of striking a bargain with the devil are recorded in many legends, including the following excerpt from *Folk Beliefs of the Southern Negro*, by Newbell Niles Puckett (Patterson Smith, 1968):

> If you want to make a contract with the devil…Take a black cat bone and a guitar and go to a lonely fork in the roads at midnight. Sit down there and play your best piece, thinking of and wishing for the devil all the while. By and by you will hear music, dim at first but growing louder and louder as the music approaches nearer…After a time you feel something tugging at your instrument…Let the devil take it and keep thumping along with your fingers as if you still had a guitar in your hands. Then the devil will hand you his instrument to play and will accompany you on yours. After doing this for a time he will seize your fingers and trim the nails until they bleed, finally taking his guitar back and returning your own. Keep on playing; do not look around. His music will become fainter and fainter as he moves away…You will be able to play any piece you desire on the guitar and you can do anything you want to in the world, but you have sold your eternal soul to the devil and are his in the world to come.

Johnson left only 29 songs – 'Sweet Home Chicago,' 'Me and the Devil Blues' and 'Crossroads Blues' among them – when he died outside a Greenwood bar in 1938. They say it was poison administered by a jealous husband, and that Johnson was on all fours 'baying like a hell hound' moments before he died. To this day no one can say for certain where he's buried, though a couple of memorials can be found.

The Pilgrimage
Southwest of Greenwood, two memorials to Robert Johnson can be found off Hwy 7 south of Itta Bena. Robert Johnson's gravestone (whether or not it marks his actual grave is unknown) is in

Quito, a tiny settlement that straddles Hwy 7, 5 miles south of Itta Bena (no sign identifies it as Quito). After you pass the small bridge at the start of town, turn right (west) onto the first dirt road and continue to the Payne Chapel Methodist Baptist Church. You'll find Johnson's modest marker near the swamp.

Robert Johnson's memorial is around 2 miles farther south off Hwy 7 (north of Morgan City). Turn off Hwy 7 at the sign for Mathews Brake National Wildlife Refuge and you'll find the small Mt Zion MB Church nestled in a thicket less than a quarter of a mile up the road. Johnson's memorial takes the shape of a small obelisk, inscribed with the titles of his songs and often adorned by offerings left by his fans.

Getting There & Away

The Greyhound bus station (☎ 662-453-7232) is in the center of the commercial district at Church and Main Sts and is better kept than the train station. Greenwood is an Amtrak stop on the *City of New Orleans* route; the unimpressive train station is at 506 Carrolton Ave in a run-down part of town. A one-way fare to Memphis is $20; a one-way fare to Jackson is $15.

Greenwood is 29 miles east of Indianola along Hwy 82.

BELZONI

The undisputed Catfish Capital of the World, Belzoni is surrounded by the catfish ponds that are altering the face of the Delta and, ultimately, catfish. (Belzoni is south of Greenwood on Hwy 7.)

Catfish have always been a local staple food, although they used to have a bad reputation as bottom-feeders. By feeding the farmed catfish with floating meal, the industry hopes to turn around this cultural prejudice – meanwhile, it's changing the nature of the breed itself. Besides overcoming inbred instincts to scavenge, the farmed fish are also taking on a new appearance, with the shape of their mouths becoming more fishily pointed, a departure from their pan-jawed relatives in the wild.

You can learn these and other catfish facts from the sleek, modern **Catfish Visitor Center** (☎ 800-408-4838), 111 Magnolia St, a lavishly renovated depot that's the jewel of downtown Belzoni. Beyond the video and trivia, there are catfish and industry-related paintings and sculptures inside and out – it's definitely worth a visit. Free recipe books are available upon request. Their World Catfish Festival, which features the 'world's largest fish fry,' a catfish-eating contest and the crowning of a catfish queen, attracts 20,000 fish fans on the first Saturday in April (second Saturday if Easter is the first Sunday).

You can sample the local specialty at *Alison's* (☎ 662-247-4487, 107 E Jackson St), a half-block away from the visitor center. It's a comfortable family place with booths and tables that serves plates of fried catfish,

hushpuppies, french fries and lemon cake for $10. There are also burgers and salads. On the flip side, *Little Wimp's Barbecue* (☎ 662-247-9933, 811 Hayden St), several blocks north of Jackson, is a popular barbecue joint.

Ten miles north, just south of the Isola turnoff, on the west side of Hwy 19, *Peter Bo's* (☎ 662-962-7281) serves a generous luncheon buffet for around $5.

SOUTH TO VICKSBURG

South of Hwy 82, Hwy 61 is a quiet rolling run that skirts the **Delta National Forest**. A ranger station in Rolling Fork (poorly signed – look for the green pickup trucks outside an eight-doored complex on the east side of Hwy 61, just past the Hwy 16 turnoff) distributes items such as forest maps, trail maps, and hunting, fishing and camping information.

The tiny crossroads at **Onward**, where Hwy 1 (Great River Rd) rejoins Hwy 61, is famous for its historical marker commemorating how President Theodore Roosevelt earned his famous nickname. Apparently the president was hunting nearby when an aid tried to make the task easier by capturing a cub for the President to shoot. His refusal at such easy prey earned him the nickname 'Teddy.' The Onward Store here features mechanical dancing bears (two bits a dance), bear skins and a little roadhouse saloon room with a country-music jukebox.

VICKSBURG

• pop 27,500

Vicksburg stands on a high bluff overlooking a bend in the Mississippi River. Its strategic location made it a prime target during the Civil War. As Union troops worked their way northward from the Gulf of Mexico and southward from Illinois, overpowering Confederate defenses one by one, Vicksburg came to be the final Confederate stronghold. President Lincoln considered Vicksburg the key to Union victory, declaring 'the war can never be brought to a close until that key is in our pocket.' The price of that key was one of the longest sieges in American military history.

After several unsuccessful attempts to capture the city by storm, Union General Ulysses S Grant decided to lay siege by encircling the Confederate lines of defense around the city. Federal gunboats north and south of town further cut off communications and supplies. The city held out for 47 days until its official surrender on July 4, 1863. During the siege, citizens resorted to eating rats and printing the newspaper on the back of wallpaper. The deprivation and defeat is still painfully recalled in the local collective memory; the Fourth of July wasn't celebrated in Vicksburg until the 1940s.

The national military park tells the story of the entire campaign; its cemetery contains the graves of 17,000 Civil War soldiers. The antebellum houses that survived the onslaught (one is a luxurious B&B) are best seen during the town's house tours in spring and fall; several of the mansions are open year-round as historic house museums.

Orientation & Information

Located right off I-20, Vicksburg's major sights are easily accessible from exit 4B (Clay St). The national military park makes a particularly easy detour for through-travelers as it's less than a mile from the freeway.

Vicksburg's old, slow downtown extends along several cobblestone blocks of Washington St and overlooks the river. There are several lavish casinos on the water that operate 24 hours a day. One is at the foot of Clay St; others are to the south.

There is a visitor center across from the entrance to the national park, and the offices of the local convention and visitors bureau (☎ 601-636-9421, 800-221-3536, Box 110, Vicksburg, MS 39181) are at the corner of Clay and Washington Sts, downtown by the river.

National Military Park & Cemetery

The park (☎ 601-636-0583), near I-20 on Clay St, preserves 1858 acres where the Union army laid siege to Vicksburg. From the visitor center inside the gates, a 16-mile driving tour through the rolling wooded hills leads to historic markers explaining emplacements and recounting key events in the campaign. Audio-tape tours bring the landscape to life (rentals available for $4.50). There is also an introductory film at the visitor center.

The cemetery, in which nearly 17,000 Union soldiers are buried, is in the far northern end of the park. Nearby, a museum houses the remains of the Union's iron-clad gunboat the USS *Cairo*, sunk in the Yazoo River by an electrically detonated mine (the first boat in history to be sunk in this way).

The visitor center and *Cairo* museum are open daily except Christmas. Admission is $4 per car. Inquire about guided tours (fees are extremely reasonable), Civil War reenactments in May and July, and other special events.

Historic Homes & Museums

About a dozen historic house museums in town are clustered in Vicksburg's Garden District, on Oak St south of Clay St, and also in an attractive residential district between 1st St E and Clay St (follow the signs). Admission is around $5. During the fortnight-long pilgrimages in late March, early April and mid-October – popular with lovers of interior design – multiple-house tickets are available; contact the local visitor center for exact dates and prices.

McRaven House (☎ 601-636-1663), 1445 Harrison St, served as Union headquarters for the occupation. The house is legendary as the home to the ghost of Union General McPherson; as recently as 1991 an Episcopalian priest was called in to perform a rite of exorcism – but so far, no luck. McPherson disappeared while on nightly rounds only to return the next night as a mutilated ghost. The tale he told that night, and many nights since, has been that Confederate sympathizers murdered him and dumped his body in the river. The house is closed from December through February but open daily the rest of the year.

Biedenharn's **Museum of Coca-Cola Memorabilia** (☎ 601-638-6514), 1107 Washington St, occupies the 1890 building where

Coca-Cola was first bottled. The displays include a circa 1900 soda fountain, a restored 1890 candy store and such quotes as 'Coca-Cola is a sublimated essence of all that America stands for...a decent thing honestly made.' Thirsty yet? It's open daily. Admission is $2.25 for adults and $1.75 for children.

The **Gray & Blue Naval Museum** (☎ 601-638-6500), 1102 Washington St, across the road from the Coca-Cola museum houses a diorama of the Vicksburg battlefield and a flotilla of model ships including a horse-powered ferry. Admission is $2.50 for adults and $1.50 children; it's closed on Sunday.

Other Things to See & Do
In the **Corner Drug Store** (☎ 601-662-1123), at the corner of Washington and China Sts, cannonballs, guns, moonshine jugs and other civil war paraphernalia clamor for shelf space along with regular medicinal fare.

Margaret's Grocery is also on Washington St, but it's around 3 miles north of downtown. Look for the sign: 'All is welcome – Jews and Gentiles – Here at Margaret's Gro & Mkt and Bible Class.' When the Reverend Dennis and his wife, Margaret, started the grocery, he promised to build her a castle, and he's been working on it ever since, concrete block by block, wooden spire by spire, to the extent that it's not really a grocery at all anymore. If you stop by you might be treated to one of Dennis' rambling orations.

Eight miles east in Bovina, **Earl's Art Shop** (☎ 601-636-5264), is an homage to popular advertising, including a 5-foot-high pack of Kool cigarettes and colorful cardboard jukeboxes. To get there, take the Bovina exit, pass the gas station, cross the tracks, and continue around the bend. Admission is $2. If you can't make it to Bovina, examples of Earl's art are displayed in Vicksburg at the Attic Gallery (☎ 601-638-9221) on Washington St south of Clay St.

Activities
Mississippi River Adventures (☎ 601-638-5443) runs hour-long boat cruises between

March and mid-November from the foot of Clay St ($16/8 for adults/children).

Places to Stay
Travelers may require reservations during popular pilgrimage weeks, and the lowest rates are available from November to February.

Several private campgrounds offer sites designed primarily for RV travelers. The ***Isle of Capri RV Park*** (*☎ 601-631-0402, 720 Lucy Bryson St*) is adjacent to the Isle of Capri Casino on the riverfront. ***Magnolia RV Park*** (*☎ 601-631-0388, 211 Miller St*) is clean with good facilities but the camping sites ($12) are barren. Turn west off Hwy 61, south of I-20, to get here.

At the bottom end of the price range, the ***Hillcrest Inn*** (*☎ 601-638-1491, 40 Hwy 80*) has rooms for $23/27 singles/doubles. The ***Battlefield Inn*** (*☎ 601-638-5811, 800-359-9363*), on the I-20 Frontage Rd off exit 4B, is an incongruously luxurious road motel; rates range from $40 to $75, including a breakfast buffet.

The town's grand B&B is ***Cedar Grove*** (*☎ 601-636-1000, 800-862-1300, 2300 Washington St*); enter off Oak St. It's an 1840 Greek Revival mansion on 4 acres with landscaped gardens overlooking the river. A Union cannonball is still lodged in the parlor wall, and the house retains many original antiques and gas-lit chandeliers. Their 24 guest rooms all have private bathrooms; rates range from $90 to $175 and include breakfast.

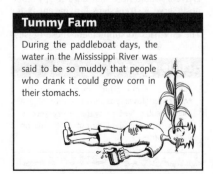

Tummy Farm

During the paddleboat days, the water in the Mississippi River was said to be so muddy that people who drank it could grow corn in their stomachs.

Places to Eat

A traditional Southern feast – pork tenderloins, fried okra, pecan pie and the like – is served at *Walnut Hills* (☎ 601-638-4910, *1214 Adams St*), at Clay St. You can have lunch daily except Saturday 'in the round' (customers sit family style at big round tables and share dishes). The soul-food equivalent is *LD's Kitchen* (☎ 601-638-9838, *1111 Mulberry St)*; go down to the bottom of Clay St and turn right, you'll see the yellow building standing alone on the right. Lunch specials are $5.25 and the bar kicks on till the early hours. *Burger Village* (☎ 601-638-0202, *1220 Washington St)*, at Clay St in downtown, is a local alternative to the many fast-food choices by the interstate; they also serve breakfast all day. Many riverfront casinos offer around-the-clock meals and ample buffets at lunch and dinner.

Getting There & Away

Greyhound (☎ 601-638-8389) operates a regional bus service from its station at 1295 S Frontage Rd. Buses run from Vicksburg to New Orleans (seven hours, $48.50), Biloxi (5½ hours, $40), Memphis, (6½ hours, $43) and Jackson (one hour, $13.50).

Vicksburg is a stop on riverboat tours along the Mississippi River conducted by the Delta Queen Steamboat Company; most originate in New Orleans (see the Riverboat section in the Getting Around chapter).

Getting Around

Drivers should note that hard-to-spy stone posts serve as street signs. Driving any faster than a crawl makes the signs easy to miss. The city tries to supplement these by sus-

Little Squirter

When it's running high in Vicksburg, the Mississippi River passes at a rate of 1.4 million cubic feet of water every second (that's the equivalent output of 60 million garden hoses).

pending intersection numbers from traffic signals in the centers of intersections but these only correspond to a publication from the convention and visitors bureau.

Central Mississippi

The rolling midlands of central Mississippi lie between the northern hills and coastal plain. Besides the sprawling state capital at Jackson and its urban attractions, the rest of the region is largely agricultural. National forests remain interspersed among croplands, woods and small rural towns.

One of the most scenic ways to see the region is along the Natchez Trace Parkway, which travels its most quiet stretch between Jackson and Tupelo. A detour along Hwys 15 and 16 to Philadelphia lands travelers in an intriguing area full of Choctaw mythology and Civil Rights history.

Most travelers only see Meridian from the frontage roads off I-20, but a few quick detours inland offer a break from the monotony of interstate travel. The midland region south of Meridian attracts the fewest visitors of any area in the state, despite the Checker Hall of Fame located outside Hattiesburg.

JACKSON
• pop 395,000

Previously known as LeFleur's Bluff (after a French-Canadian fur trader), Mississippi's capital city was renamed to honor the US national hero of the time, General Andrew Jackson. The grand Greek Revival capitol, built in 1832, remains open today as a state museum; the legislature moved into an equally grand capitol patterned after the national Capitol in 1903.

During the Civil War, Jackson was put to the torch on three separate occasions by Union troops under the direction of General William Tecumseh Sherman. The few public buildings spared by Sherman – the capitol, the governor's mansion and city hall – are treasured landmarks today. The city earned the nickname Chimneyville for what remained standing.

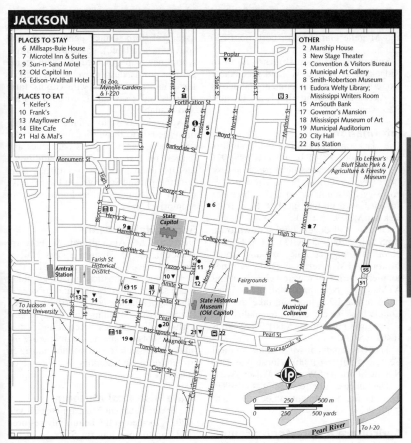

JACKSON

PLACES TO STAY
6 Millsaps-Buie House
7 Microtel Inn & Suites
9 Sun-n-Sand Motel
12 Old Capitol Inn
16 Edison-Walthall Hotel

PLACES TO EAT
1 Keifer's
10 Frank's
13 Mayflower Cafe
14 Elite Cafe
21 Hal & Mal's

OTHER
2 Manship House
3 New Stage Theater
4 Convention & Visitors Bureau
5 Municipal Art Gallery
8 Smith-Robertson Museum
11 Eudora Welty Library;
     Mississippi Writers Room
15 AmSouth Bank
17 Governor's Mansion
18 Mississippi Museum of Art
19 Municipal Auditorium
20 City Hall
22 Bus Station

MISSISSIPPI

Jackson is the home of Jackson State University, the largest historically African-American college in the state.

Although Jackson is Mississippi's largest city by far (the second-largest city, Biloxi, is nearly one-eighth its size), most modern development has eschewed the commercial center in favor of sprawling suburban areas to the north. While most of the population lives in the suburbs, they hold little appeal for travelers.

What is appealing is the ghost town that remains of downtown, which is quickened only by official state business, a few worth-

while museums, a legendary nightclub and a classic motel frozen in the 1950s.

Orientation

Jackson's downtown area consists of a short stretch of Capitol St, from the Amtrak station to the old capitol, and a few blocks to either side. Capitol St dead-ends into State St, a useful thoroughfare to more points of interest nearby.

The city's grandest attractions – the Agriculture & Forestry Museum and the Museum of Natural Science – are clustered northeast of downtown. LeFleur's Bluff

State Park nearby is nicely situated around a wooded lake. The small but inviting zoo and Mynelle Gardens are both off I-220 exit 2.

Suburban expansion stretches north to Ridgeland. Here you will find predictably modern suburban development and access to recreation around the Ross Barnett Reservoir.

Information

The Jackson Convention and Visitors Bureau (☎ 601-960-1891, 800-354-7695), 921 N President St, also has an information desk (☎ 601-960-1800) at the Agriculture & Forestry Museum; or write to them for advance information at PO Box 1450, Jackson, MS 39215-1450.

Of the half-dozen banks downtown, AmSouth (☎ 601-354-8211), 200 E Capitol St, offers foreign currency exchange and a 24-hour ATM (there's a Delta Airlines counter here). Freeway travelers can find ATMs in the Northpark Mall off I-55 just south of the I-220 junction; take the I-55 County Line Rd exit east to the mall.

Jackson's post office (☎ 601-968-0520) is at 401 E South St.

The University of Mississippi Medical Center (☎ 601-984-1000) is located at 2500 N State St north of Woodrow Wilson Ave.

The police can be reached at ☎ 601-960-0311; the fire department can be reached at ☎ 601-960-1392.

Agriculture & Forestry Museum

The 'Ag Museum' (☎ 601-713-3365, 800-844-8687) is a quarter-mile east of I-55's exit 98B, at 1150 Lakeland Drive. This complex offers thoughtful and attractive indoor and outdoor exhibits on agriculture and forestry and how they have been historically intertwined with the state's population and environment. Exhibits also reveal the state's cultural and ecological history. Kids will like it.

Enter by crossing the bridge past the crafts store to the main building: a 35,000-sq-foot hangar that houses farm machinery, including airplanes for crop-dusting and vintage cotton gins. There's a fire observa-

tion tower and Indian exhibits, too. Outside, a re-created 1920s Mississippi town features a general store (drinks, penny candy and souvenirs available), gas station, church, school, newspaper office, doctor's office, and gardens down a dusty gravel walk. An 1860s farmstead is complete with cabins, farm animals and a sawmill. Carousel rides are also available.

Admission is $4 for adults, $2 for children aged six to 18, and 50¢ for those under six. Special events such as barbecues and harvest festivals may carry an additional fee. It's open Monday to Saturday from 9 am to 5 pm and Sunday from 1 to 5 pm; it's closed on Sunday from Labor Day to Memorial Day.

Sports Hall of Fame

Next to the Agricultural & Forestry Museum, the Mississippi Sports Hall of Fame (☎ 601-982-8264) contains 21,500 sq feet of sports statistics and biographies, touch-screen video displays and tributes to Mississippi athletes such as Jerry Rice, Brett Favre, Archie Manning and Dizzy Dean. Virtual golf, fast-pitch baseball and soccer penalty shots are among the interactive exhibits. Admission is $5 for adults and $3.50 for children and seniors. It's closed on Sunday.

State Historical Museum

The State Historical Museum (☎ 601-359-6920) is located in the beautifully restored 1833 capitol building on State St at the head of Capitol St. (The current capitol is another elegant domed building several blocks west.) Unless you have a taste for political portraits, military statues and restored legislative chambers, it's worth spending all your time in the 20th-century history exhibit, packed into a small room on the 1st floor. It features careful interpretations of Mississippi's ignominious history, along with looping vintage black-and-white film footage of Civil Rights demonstrations.

The gift shop has a good selection of local-interest books, as well as magnolia-studded souvenirs. The museum is open weekdays from 8 am to 5 pm, Saturday

The Etymology of 'Redneck'

An exhibit at the State Historical Museum traces the use of the pejorative term 'redneck' to the red neckties worn in 1902 by an emergent breed of Mississippian politicians who supported the interests of small farmers and laborers. The term evolved to describe this class of working whites. Today the term has acquired a handful of unflattering characteristics, frequently stereotyped in Hollywood movies.

9:30 am to 4:30 pm, Sunday 12:30 to 4:30 pm. It's closed on major holidays. Admission is free. You can park around the back; go all the way around the hill and approach from Amite St.

Mississippi Museum of Art

The state's art museum (☎ 601-960-1515), 201 E Pascagoula St, displays a small collection of contemporary works including New Orleans surrealists, Georgia O'Keeffe and Andy Warhol. There is also photography, folk art, outdoor sculpture, rotating exhibitions from around the US and a nice gift shop and cafe. Admission is $3 for adults; the museum is closed on Monday.

The museum is part of a modern complex housing a planetarium (call ☎ 601-960-1550 for the show schedule), performing-arts organizations and the city auditorium. See Entertainment, later in this section, for more information.

Mississippi Museum of Natural Science

This impressive new museum (☎ 601-354-7303), 2148 Riverside Drive, adjoining LeFleur's Bluff State Park (follow signs from I-55), has dinosaurs to keep the school groups excited, but what's most interesting for visitors are the exhibits of local animals and plants. A 100,000-gallon network of aquariums holds 200 species of native fish, salamanders, alligators (little ones) and turtles, and there are 2.5 miles of outdoor

nature trails passing through swamp, river and bluff habitats. It's open Monday to Friday 8 am to 5 pm, Saturday 9 am to 5 pm and Sunday 1 pm to 5 pm. Admission is $4/3/2 for adults/seniors/children.

African-American Heritage Sights

The **Smith Robertson Museum** (☎ 601-960-1457), 528 Bloom St, serves as a cultural center as well as a museum for Jackson's African-American community. The 1894 building, named after a prominent city alderman, housed Jackson's first public school for African-American children. The permanent collection includes a great folk architecture exhibition which points out that not all antebellum houses were mansions, many of them were actually black-owned shacks. The galleries hold roving exhibits of contemporary artwork most dramatically displayed in the skylit atrium.

It's open weekdays from 9 am to 5 pm, Saturday mornings and Sunday afternoons. Admission is $1 for adults and 50¢ for those 18 and under. It's only a couple of blocks from the new capitol but a little tricky to find – follow signs off High St and look for the two-story building with the high-fenced parking lot in the front.

The center of the inner-city African-American community is a stretch of **Farish St**, north of Capitol St. Its heyday was in the early 1900s, when it served as the hub of black political, economic, social, religious and cultural development for the state. Today, though the district has deteriorated and is no longer a thriving commercial center, some Victorian architecture remains. The renovation of the old Alamo Theater (☎ 601-352-3365), 333 N Farish St, into an entertainment complex might spur the neighborhood's renaissance. The area's historic significance continues to be celebrated annually at the Farish St Festival on Labor Day weekend. The weekly *Jackson Advocate* (☎ 601-948-4122), headquartered one block west at 438 Mill St, carries news on the local community.

In addition, those on a black heritage tour would not want to miss the Civil Rights

And Justice Shall Prevail

A coward dies a thousand deaths, a brave man dies but once.   **– Medgar Evers**

In 1963, Medgar Evers was field secretary for the Mississippi branch of the National Association for the Advancement of Colored People (NAACP). Evers led economic boycotts of white-owned businesses that perpetuated segregation, and assembled information on the Citizens Council, a segregationist band suspected of coordinating repressive acts against blacks throughout the state. Shortly after midnight on June 12, 1963, Evers was shot with a high-powered rifle as he stepped out of his car in the driveway of his home at 2332 Margaret Walker Alexander Drive in northwest Jackson. Evers was rushed to the University of Mississippi Medical Center, where he died within the hour. He was 36 years old. Evers was buried with military honors in Arlington National Cemetery outside Washington, DC.

Byron de la Beckwith, an ardent segregationist from Greenwood, was tried twice for the murder in 1964, but both times the jury was deadlocked. In 1975 Beckwith was sentenced to five years in prison for his role in attempting to bomb the Jewish Anti-Defamation League's headquarters in New Orleans. While in Louisiana prison he boasted of killing Evers.

In the late 1980s, Evers' family pushed for the case to be reopened, and in 1991 Evers' body was exhumed in a search for new evidence. Finally, in 1994, de la Beckwith was convicted of the murder of Medgar Evers. Maryanne Vollers relates an account of the murder in her book *Ghosts of Mississippi*, and the Hollywood version of the story is based on her work.

After her husband's death, Myrlie Evers joined the sisterhood of widows whose husbands became martyrs to the cause of civil rights – a triumvirate that included Coretta Scott King and Betty Shabazz (the now-deceased widow of Malcolm X).

A life-size bronze statue of Medgar Evers stands outside the neighborhood library renamed in his honor on Medgar Evers Blvd (Hwy 49) at Sunset Drive (south of Northside Drive, accessible from I-220 or I-55). The Evars' home is a private residence but tours can be arranged by appointment only (call ☎ 601-977-7839).

exhibit at the **State Historical Museum** (see the listing earlier) or **Jackson State University**. The university (☎ 601-968-2272, 800-848-6817), 1400 John R Lynch St, a traditionally African-American institution, was founded in 1877. Today there are over 6000 students and the university is strong in marine science, early childhood studies, environmental science and meteorology.

Historic Buildings

The new capitol, designed in the image of the national Capitol in Washington, DC, and decorated with an interior nearly as lavish, has been the seat of state government since its completion in 1903. Note the monumental statue at its High St entrance dedicated to the women of the Confederacy.

The residence of Governor Ronnie Musgrove, the 1842 Greek Revival **Governor's Mansion** (☎ 601-359-6421), 300 E Capitol St, is open to visitors via a guided tour on the half-hour, Tuesday through Friday from 9:30 to 11:00 am only.

Manship House (☎ 601-961-4724), 420 E Fortification St, preserves the 1857 Gothic 'cottage villa' of ornamental painter and mayor Charles Manship. It's humble and charming compared to standard plantation house museums, and is one of the few antebellum houses that survived the war. It's closed on Sunday and Monday.

The **Municipal Art Gallery** (☎ 601-960-1582) displays contemporary works for sale by Mississippian artists in an 1860s house at 839 N State St. On the first Sunday of the month, the gallery hosts a public opening of its new exhibitions. It's closed on Monday.

Mississippi Writers Room

A small, shrinelike room in the city's Eudora Welty Library (☎ 601-968-5811), 300 N State St, is dedicated to Mississippi-born writers and poets, including heavy-hitters such as William Faulkner, Tennessee Williams, Welty herself and Richard Wright, along with authors Shelby Foote *(The Civil War: A Narrative)*, Larry Brown *(Big Bad Love)* and hundreds of others. Author portfolios are collected in notebook binders; audio and video recordings are available by request. Admission is free.

Jackson Zoo

The compact Jackson Zoo (☎ 601-352-2580), on Capitol St at Ellis Ave northwest of downtown, provides an intimate look at exotic and local species in well-designed woodland habitats that also highlight the local flora. The well-maintained facility includes an impressive barn and playground area. Admission is $4 for adults and $2 for children aged three to 12. The zoo is open daily, from 9 am to 6 pm in summer and to 5 pm the rest of the year. From I-220, take exit 2 and continue 1½ miles east to the zoo. On the opposite side of the freeway, you'll find the Mynelle Gardens.

Mynelle Gardens

Amid highway traffic a half-mile west of I-220's exit 2, is Mynelle Gardens (☎ 601-960-1894), 4736 Clinton Blvd. The garden's appeal creeps up on you as you wind into the beautifully sculpted gardens scented with magnolia and wisteria. Once inside the small refuge, all you hear are songbirds, fountains and occasional jumping fish or diving frogs. Seek out the shady swings, the small Zen sand garden and the vine-covered arched bridges. Admission is $2 for adults and 50¢ for children under 12. The gardens are wheelchair-accessible.

Outdoor Activities

Northeast of downtown off I-55, LeFleur's Bluff State Park (☎ 601-987-3923) preserves a wild little pocket of woods that is still right near the heart of the city. It supports a diverse range of activities. Many modern facilities include a swimming pool, tennis courts, a nine-hole golf course, and the woods are great for hiking nature trails and camping. There's a charge of $2 per car to enter the park; enforcement appears slack in the off-season.

Boating and **fishing** are popular activities at the 33,000-acre Ross Barnett Reservoir (☎ 601-354-3448), adjacent to the Natchez Trace Parkway north of town. Marinas, piers and picnic areas are located around its banks. Rapids (☎ 601-992-0500), a **water park** with a 215-foot twisting whip slide, wave pool and float rides, is one mile east of the spillway on Spillway Rd. Admission is $16 for anyone over 4 feet tall. Concessions and picnic tables are available.

Special Events

The biggest celebrations in Jackson are St Patrick's Day and the Jubilee Jam. Book accommodations ahead if visiting for either festival.

MISSISSIPPI

Pining for Attention

And then her mother's high-heeled slipper threw her off balance and she fell to the sidewalk in a great howling tangle of soiled white satin and torn pink net, and still nobody looked at her. I wonder if she is not, now, a Southern writer.

– Tennessee Williams

January

The Martin Luther King Jr Day celebration is held around the 15th.

February

The three-week Dixie National Rodeo & Livestock Show is held the last week in January and the first two weeks in February.

March

Mal's St Patrick's Day Festival & Parade is held around the 17th. Mal – from Hal & Mal's (see Entertainment) – is a local personality that turned this holiday into a big party.

April

Zoo Blues and the International Red Beans & Rice Festival are held the second weekend of the month.

May

Jubilee Jam Arts & Music Festival is held the third weekend of the month and carries on for three days with six music stages and many booths selling art and crafts.

June

Crawfish Festival is held mid-month.

July

Behold the Hog Wild cook-off the second weekend in July.

August

Scottish Heritage Festival is held late in the month.

September

Farish St African-American Heritage Festival occurs at the end of the month.

October

Over 10 days, the Mississippi State Fair can be counted on for fun in the early part of the month.

November

Pioneer & Indian Festival at the crafts center on the Natchez Trace (Ridgeland) is at the end of the month.

December

Chimneyville Crafts Festival is held the first weekend, while Starry Safari at the zoo and Christmas at the old capitol are celebrated throughout the month.

Places to Stay

Camping Tucked in *LeFleur's Bluff State Park* (☎ 601-987-3985), near the heart of the city at 2140 Riverside Drive, is a nicely wooded lakeside campground, right off I-55 (exit 98B) within a mile of the Agriculture & Forestry Museum and behind the Museum of Natural Science. Cozy sites are $12 for a hookup (30 RV sites). Tent camping is available for the same price; also ask about cabin rental, which costs $50 for a single.

Hotels & Motels The place to stay in Jackson is the *Sun-n-Sand Motel* (☎ 601-354-2501, 401 N Lamar St), a relic of 1950s road hotels a block from the capitol. It's all orange and turquoise, with Polynesian touches and a great trapezoidal pool with sun deck. (See Entertainment, later in this section, for details on the lounge.) Rooms are $35/40 for a single/double. *Microtel Inn & Suites* (☎ 601-352-8282, 888-771-7171, 614 Monroe St) is a good value motel that is close to downtown. The rooms are fresh and clean with microwaves and swiveling TVs; it's $45 for a single ($5 each extra person).

At the other end of the spectrum, the *Edison-Walthall Hotel* (☎ 601-948-6161, 800-932-6161, 225 E Capitol St) is the capital's preeminent hotel, with an elegant dark wood lobby, restaurant and bar, an atrium pool and less elegant but comfortable rooms (some overlooking the pool) starting at $69/79. It offers complimentary van service to/from the airport and within a three-mile radius.

Probably 95% of the people who stay in Jackson never even venture to the downtown area, staying in scores of franchise motels lining the freeway exits. All brands are represented, including the budget *Motel 6* (☎ 601-956-8848) north of town off I-55 at 6145 I-55 N. Rates are around $36 for a single.

B&Bs The *Millsaps-Buie House* (☎ 601-352-0221, 628 N State St), near the capitol, has 11 guest rooms with private bath for $90/105 for singles/doubles within a refined 1888 Victorian mansion furnished with antiques. The ***Old Capitol Inn*** (☎ *601-359-9000, 888-359-9001, 226 N State St)* is more modern with similar rates.

Places to Eat

Downtown The ***Mayflower Cafe*** (☎ *601-355-4122, 123 E Capitol St)*, behind the giant flashing neon sign, is a local institution run by Mr Mike, an aging Greek man who walks around chewing on an unlit cigar. The emphasis is on seafood but there are $5.50 weekday lunch plates, Greek salad and baklava. The ***Elite Cafe*** (☎ *601-352-5606)*, down the block at No 141, is of the same breed.

For stylized meals downtown, ***Palette Restaurant*** (☎ *601-960-2003)*, a sophisticated little alfresco cafe on the premises of the Mississippi Museum of Art, serves elegant lunches with nice wine during the week. The ***Edison-Walthall Hotel*** (see Places to Stay) caters to the power-lunch crowd with great buffets. ***Frank's*** (☎ *601-354-5357, 219 N President St)* serves good & hearty Southern fare; be prepared to queue. It's open for breakfast at 6 am and closed on Sunday.

Off the Interstate There are a couple of places easily accessible from the interstate that are nice local alternatives to freeway food. You may not need to go farther than ***Hal & Mal's*** (☎ *601-948-0888, 200 S Commerce St)*. They serve a full slate of bar food, burgers, microbrews, salads, Mississippi catfish and quiche to a mixed crowd.

Or try ***Keifers*** (☎ *601-355-6825, 705 Poplar St)* which serves inexpensive souvlaki, falafel and salads to a mixed crowd who pack into patio seats or the amply planted interior. From I-55's Fortification St exit, proceed west (toward downtown) uphill to the State St signal; turn right and continue a block or so to Poplar St and turn right again.

Entertainment

The *Clarion-Ledger*'s Weekend entertainment guide is distributed with the Thursday edition. Festivals and shows are advertised on the blues station WMPR 90.1 FM and

WQJQ 105.1 FM, which plays both Motown and R&B.

At ***Hal & Mal's***, owner and music promoter Malcolm White has covered the walls with autographed glossies of recording stars and other famous patrons (see Places to Stay for contact information). It's a great place to hear music. Hidden above the Pascagoula St underpass, it's tricky to find, but very close to the old capitol and convenient from the Pearl St freeway exit. Drive south on State St away from the capitol dome landmark and slowly bypass the Pascagoula St underpass, but turn left immediately onto the adjacent alley marked Magnolia St. At the end of the alley, you'll see Hal & Mal's to your left. Or ask anybody.

For a weirder time, you could search out the downstairs lounge at the ***Sun-n-Sand*** (see Places to Stay). The retro lounge is authentic right down to the vinyl barstools and the clientele of big-hair divorcees, off-duty cops and good old boys. It's open Monday to Friday only.

The ***Subway Lounge*** (*619 W Pearl St)*, out toward Jackson State, hosts live lowdown blues in an intimate space carved out of the basement of the old Summers Hotel. Weekend shows start at midnight. As one drummer put it in *Living Blues* magazine, the Subway is 'about the only place where middle-class whites and inner-city blacks can meet with some kind of common humanity' in Jackson.

The ***New Stage Theater*** (☎ *601-948-3531, 1100 Carlisle St)* is the state's only professional classical-arts theater company. The Museum of Art complex houses a cluster of other performing-arts organizations, including the ***Black Arts Music Society*** (☎ *601-960-2383)*, the ***Mississippi Symphony Orchestra*** (☎ *601-960-1565)*, the ***Mississippi Opera*** (☎ *601-960-1528)* and ***Ballet Mississippi*** (☎ *601-960-1560)*.

Shopping

The nonprofit Craftmen's Guild of Mississippi operates two stores in the metropolitan region selling quilts, jewelry, woodwork and a great variety of handicrafts. The guild offers an exceptional collection of traditional Choctaw arts and crafts, including baskets made of cane, white oak or pine needles; beadwork; dolls; and clothing (for adults and children). The guild also hosts crafts fairs in the fall and at Christmas, with demonstrations and Choctaw cultural arts. It's based within the Agriculture & Forestry Museum complex, where their Chimneyville Crafts Center (☎ 601-981-2499) offers retail sales (no museum admission required to shop; closed on Sunday; open Sunday afternoon in summer). The Mississippi Crafts Center (☎ 601-856-7546) is located right on the Natchez Trace Parkway in Ridgeland, north of Jackson, and is open daily.

Small selections of handcrafted souvenirs are sold in the gift shops of the State Historical Museum and the Museum of Art downtown.

Northpark Mall, off I-55 just south of the I-220 junction north of town, offers a range of stores and has ATMs.

Getting There & Away
Jackson is easily accessible by car, bus, train or plane, but for tourists it's more of a hub for through-travel than a destination in itself.

Air Jackson airport (☎ 601-939-5631), 10 miles east of downtown off I-20, is served by Delta, American, Northwest and United Airlines. Published fares hover around $500 to New York City, $200 to Chicago, $400 to Los Angeles and $350 to Miami. Most flights transit through Memphis or New Orleans so you can usually get better deals out of these larger airports.

Bus Greyhound (☎ 601-353-6342) operates many routes from a modern station at 201 S Jefferson St at Pearl St. It's conveniently downhill from the old capitol and across from the stadium in a decent area. When the Amtrak station is renovated, Greyhound will move there.

Several buses leave and arrive daily along well-traveled routes to New Orleans and Memphis. Express buses are sometimes available at no extra cost. A trip to New Orleans takes four hours and costs around $25 one way. To Memphis, the five-hour trip costs $29.

Train Amtrak's *City of New Orleans* train stops right in downtown Jackson along its route between Chicago and New Orleans (other stops include Memphis and Greenwood in the Mississippi Delta). One-way fares are comparable to buses, yet Amtrak offers discounts for roundtrip tickets.

The old, soon-to-be-renovated station (☎ 601-355-6350), on Capitol St at Mill St, is surrounded by dilapidated buildings, but it's only a long block to the edge of the commercial district (walk down Capitol St away from the railroad overpass). When will renovations be completed? Ask five different people and get five different answers.

Car South of Jackson, I-55 is a very straightforward stretch of freeway to New Orleans, well punctuated with gas stations, restaurants and chain motels. If you're looking for local color, the two-lane Hwy 51 runs a parallel route that for many years served as the thoroughfare between Memphis and New Orleans.

Natchez Trace Parkway drivers should note that it's disjunctive north of Jackson at Ridgeland to Clinton, which is west of Jackson. Posted signs divert through-travelers along I-55, I-220 and I-20. North of Ridgeland, the trace runs a scenic stretch along the Ross Barnett Reservoir before the long, quiet ride to Tupelo. South of Clinton, many attractions make this among the most interesting stretches of the trace (see the Natchez Trace section, later in this chapter).

Bicycle A resource for Natchez Trace bicyclists who need equipment or service is the Indian Cycle Shop (☎ 601-956-8383), 1060 E County Line Rd in Ridgeland. Unfortunately, they do not rent bikes.

Getting Around
If you arrive by train or bus, you could walk to several hotels, restaurants and city

sights, but to see disparate attractions you need a car. The limited bus transit is not a practical option. To procure a taxi, contact ☎ 601-355-2222.

AROUND JACKSON

From Jackson's northern suburb of Ridgeland, the interrupted **Natchez Trace Parkway** picks up again at the Mississippi Crafts

A Dark Corner in Freedom Summer

In the summer of 1964 James Earl Chaney, Andrew Goodman and Michael Schwerner were invited by churches in Philadelphia, Mississippi to help organize literacy campaigns (literacy was a prerequisite to vote) and voter-registration drives. While driving on a country road the night of June 21, the three young men – two white, one black – were arrested on a traffic violation and taken to jail. They were later released, chased through the countryside by sheriff's deputies and armed Klansmen, caught, and shot dead. Their bodies were hidden in an earthen dam outside of town.

The FBI was called in to investigate, and President Lyndon Johnson pulled in a troop of sailors to aid the search for the missing men. A local lead eventually helped authorities locate their bodies. The men accused of the murder were set free by the judge's 'not guilty' verdict in the Neshoba County Courthouse. Six of the men later faced federal charges and were imprisoned for violating the civil rights of the three activists. The maximum sentence was 10 years.

On the 25th anniversary of the killings on June 21, 1989, former Mississippi secretary of state and Philadelphia native Dick Molpus (who was 14 at the time of the murders) made an eloquent speech at an ecumenical service attended by the families of the victims:

> We deeply regret what happened here 25 years ago. We wish we could undo it. We are profoundly sorry that they are gone. We wish we could bring them back. Every decent person in Philadelphia and Neshoba County and Mississippi feels that way...We acknowledge that dark corner of our past. But we also take pride in the present, and we are hopeful about the future...If James Chaney, Andy Goodman and Mickey Schwerner were to return today, they would see a Philadelphia and a Mississippi that, while far from perfect, are closer to being the kind of place the God who put us here wants them to be. And they would find – perhaps to their surprise – that our trials and difficulties have given Mississippi a special understanding of the need for redemption and reconciliation and have empowered us to serve as a beacon for the nation...Fear has waned – fear of the unknown, fear of each other – and hope abides.

The tribute was delivered at the **Mt Zion Methodist Church**, the church whose firebombing in 1964 had prompted the three young men to come to Philadelphia, and the last church the three visited before their murder. A simple granite memorial and historical marker stands out front. The church holds a memorial service every year to educate children about the sacrifices made to obtain equal rights. Mt Zion is 10 miles east of the courthouse: travel east on Hwy 16 for 3½ miles to Hwy 482 (turn left at the sign 'Yesteryear Shack'); go north 6 miles to Hwy 747; turn right and the church is less than a mile farther on.

The **Mt Nebo Missionary Baptist Church**, which had invited the three activists, maintains a memorial out front with photos. It's downtown but tricky to find. From the courthouse, go west on Hwy 16 to Lewis Ave (see Gun 'n' Pawn at the corner); turn right on Lewis Ave and continue to Border St; turn right and go to MLK Jr Drive and turn left; go 350 yards to Adams St (see Gill's Cafe on the corner); turn right and continue 350 yards to Mt Nebo on the corner of Adams and Carver.

In both the Jewish and African traditions, it is often customary to leave small stones to remember the dead. Donations to maintain the memorial are also accepted.

MISSISSIPPI

Center. A long quiet stretch of the highway begins with a view of the Ross Barnett Reservoir and heads north to Tupelo.

Around 15 miles north near Flora, the **Petrified Forest** (☎ 601-879-8189) provides a self-guided tour past petrified logs to an earth-science museum; it is open daily. Take Hwy 80 or I-20 from Jackson to Hwy 49, turn east at Hwy 22. There are nice camping spots here too ($12).

The **Casey Jones Museum** (☎ 662-673-9864) is around 30 miles north of Jackson on I-55 in Vaughan. It occupies a restored railroad station near the site of the 1900 train crash that killed Luther 'Casey' Jones. The folk song that dramatized this event created a posthumous hero out of Jones. Exhibits detail the history of railroads in Mississippi. Admission is $1 for adults and 50¢ for children aged three to 11.

CANTON

The central Mississippi town of Canton is 25 miles north of Jackson. The exit from I-55 leading to downtown Canton goes past a row of shops so shabby it might tempt hesitant travelers to retreat.

However, further investigation of the town will uncover its tidy square, with a Greek Revival centerpiece, and residential district of Victorian homes. It is so beautiful that it looks like a movie set – which Canton was, for the film adaptation of John Grisham's *A Time to Kill* in 1995 and Willie Morris' *My Dog Skip* in 1998. Sets remain on view today; inquire about this and house tours at the visitor center (☎ 800-844-3369), in the former Trolio Hotel, west of the courthouse. Sharing space in the Trolio is **Allison's Wells School of Arts & Crafts**, a center for traditional Southern arts dating back to the late 19th century. Artisans from here and all over display their wares at the **Canton Flea Market** held only twice a year on the second Thursdays of May and October.

One of the most unusual things in town is a **monument** to black Confederates. Slave owner William Hill Howcott erected a small obelisk in the 1890s to honor his slave Willis (Howcott), 'a colored boy of rare loyalty and faithfulness whose memory I cherish with deep gratitude,' and also 'the good and loyal servants who followed the fortunes of the Harvey Scouts during the Civil War.' To find the memorial from the square, turn up N Liberty St and go two blocks to E Academy St (with the Piggly Wiggly supermarket at the corner). Turn left and go three blocks past Lyon St. The memorial is half a block past Lyon St, between two houses in a row of shotgun shacks.

PHILADELPHIA

Greek for the City of Brotherly Love, Philadelphia is notorious as the place where three Civil Rights activists were killed in 1963 during the Freedom Summer's voter registration drive. Downtown Philadelphia appears little changed since that time – the men still gather at Dot's Cafe for grits, you can sample the latest in Christian music at the River of Life bible store, the Muffler Mansion still claims there's 'No Muff Too Tough' and the local radio station announces the daily menu of school lunches. The highlight of the annual Neshoba County Fair – sometimes described as a nonstop party as it's one of the few remaining campground fairs in the US – is its horse races.

The *Stribling Drug Store* (☎ 601-656-2472, 428 Beacon St) is a good place to come for a milkshake. The *Old Benwalt Cafe (236 Byrd Ave)*, right off the square, does light meals. Philadelphia is 79 miles northeast of Jackson via Hwy 16.

CHOCTAW COUNTRY

Through a number of treaties, the Choctaw nation, which was centered around east-central Mississippi, ceded more than 63,000 sq miles of land to the US government in the early 1800s. Half-Indian, half-Acadian Greenwood LeFlore signed away the last of the Choctaw territory (an action that enriched LeFlore with a 15,000-acre estate) in the Treaty of Dancing Rabbit Creek (1830). As a result, most of the remaining Choctaw Indians were forcedly removed in 1837 and marched to reservations west of the Mississippi; this event is known as the Trail of

Tears. Only the Mississippi Band of the Choctaw avoided removal, however, most of their land was seized. It took many years of struggle with state and federal authorities before they regained control of small portions of their ancestral lands. Reservation status was granted in 1918.

Today, the industrious Choctaw reservation (population over 8300) is a major employer in the region. In fact, it's one of the five largest employers in Mississippi as a manufacturer of parts for the Ford Motor Company and also a contributor to the American Greetings card company. The reservation consists of eight communities centered west of Philadelphia, off Hwy 16. The great majority speak Choctaw as their first language.

The **Choctaw Museum of the Southern Indian** (☎ 601-650-1685), a mile or two north of Hwy 16 (follow the signs to Choctaw Industrial Park), tells the ancient story of the Choctaw. In a small room, traditional beadwork, drums and costumes are on display, along with maps that show the reduction of tribal territory. You can buy a copy of the Lord's Prayer in Choctaw, baskets, pottery and jewelry. It's free and open daily until around 4 pm and is closed Sunday morning.

The annual four-day Choctaw Indian Fair, a variation on the ancient green corn ceremony, begins in the early morning of the second Wednesday after July 4. Here at the grand gathering of *okla* (the people), you can see traditional dances, crafts and stickball competitions.

From the surrounding hardscrabble landscape of clapboard and cinder block, the **Silver Star Casino Resort** (☎ 800-656-5251), on Hwy 16, looms on the horizon like a mirage – seven stories of flashy neon and bright lights (picture an Indian reservation with valet parking). The Mississippi Band of Choctaw Indians operates the resort, which includes a high-rise hotel (with rates starting around $70). Its steak and seafood restaurant **Phillip M's** is open for dinner only and is renowned as far as Jackson, among the $50-steak crowd. On the flipside, the adjacent buffet restaurant offers all-you-can-eat for $6. The casino also hosts big-name entertainment, including performances by Loretta Lynn, Isaac Hayes, Ray Charles and Roberta Flack.

Casino revenues have enabled the reservation to buy new fire engines and police cars, and to build a new elementary school and spanking new sporting facilities.

Nanih Waiya Mound

Thirty miles northeast of the reservation's casino, in the corner of Neshoba County off Hwy 393, is Nanih Waiya Mound, the legendary birthplace of the Choctaw nation. Nanih Waiya rises about 40 feet and occupies about an acre. There are two main legends surrounding the mound's origin. One is that the Choctaws took a long journey east, led by a sacred stick and carrying their ancestors' bones. When the stick bid them stop in this area, they buried the bones. The other legend is that the Choctaws were created out of the mound. According to this creation myth, the mound was built by the Sun Father Hashtali to incubate his children. He placed seeds inside the mound and after some time, men began to emerge. The Creeks came first, then the Chickasaw, Cherokee, and last of all the Choctaw. The other tribes went away but the Choctaw decided they couldn't leave their mother (the mound) so they settled in the area.

The steep mound is across from a ranger office (☎ 601-773-7988), a cypress swamp and restrooms protected by barbed wire. Camping is not permitted. The gates are closed on Sunday.

Nearby, a historical marker at a Choctaw cemetery commemorates the Treaty of Dancing Rabbit Creek, which in 1830 forced the Choctaw to surrender the last 10 million acres of ancestral homeland. (Today's 22,000-acre reservation was later recouped.) The marker is along a gravel road that turns south off Hwy 14 at the tiny community of Mashulaville in southwestern Noxubee County.

MERIDIAN
• pop 41,036

Meridian is a common stop for I-20 through-travelers to halt, stretch their legs and grab a bite to eat at some of the mostly chain restaurants that line the freeway exits.

If you end up with more time in town, head to the far side of Meridian to Highland Park at 44th Ave and 16th St for two of the city's biggest attractions: an **antique carousel** (☎ 601-485-1801) dating to 1904, which operates March to May on weekends and June to August daily, and the **Jimmie Rodgers Museum** (☎ 601-485-1808), dedicated to the father of country music. The museum occupies an old depot with a locomotive outside. Inside, a collection includes railroad equipment from the steam-engine era and Rodgers' original guitar. Admission is $2 for adults and free for children under 10. It's open Monday to Saturday from 10 am to 4 pm and Sunday from 1 to 5 pm. There's a weeklong tribute to country music during the last week of May to honor the Singing Brakeman. Call the Lauderdale County Tourism Bureau (☎ 601-482-8001) for information.

Weidmann's (☎ *601-693-1751, 210 22nd Ave)*, is a half-mile north of I-20 exit 153, over the railroad tracks. This Meridian institution serves seafood and prime rib, in addition to simple breakfasts, sandwiches and salads. It's open daily from 6 am to 10 pm.

The Amtrak route that runs from the Atlantic Coast to New Orleans stops in Meridian (with a branch line splitting off to Dallas, Texas), but it's no city you would consider designing a stopover around. The train (☎ 601-693-6471) stops at the Greyhound station (☎ 601-693-1663), which is at 1901 Front St.

LAUREL
• pop 22,000

Probably a better leg-stretching option than Meridian or Hattiesburg, Laurel has a very pleasant downtown district with bricked-over streets and well-preserved, early-20th-century commercial buildings. The local hero is William Mason – he invented Masonite here in 1926.

The modest but pleasing **Lauren Rogers Museum of Art** (☎ 601-649-6374), at the corner of 5th Ave and 7th St, is on one of Laurel's pretty residential streets. It houses an interesting collection of Native American baskets. Admission is free; it's closed on Monday.

If you want to stay overnight, there are plenty of chain motels off I-59's exit 95B. *Cafe La Fleur* (☎ *601-426-2100, 315 Magnolia St)*, between Oak St and Central Ave, promises New Orleans-style food. The *Signature Coffee House* (☎ *601-649-3499, 520 Central Ave)*, right off the 5th Ave roundabout, is a new-style cafe (they serve panini) with a courtyard and music on Friday nights.

HATTIESBURG & AROUND
Home of the University of Southern Mississippi, Hattiesburg makes an OK stop for through-travelers on I-59.

Coney Island Café, *(400 Main St)*, is the place for a cup of joe and a slice of life. *Leatha's Bar-B-Que Inn* (☎ *601-271-6003)* is a hidden treasure with barbecued chicken, pork or beef and a miracle sauce served unceremoniously in a coffee mug with a spoon. Leatha's is 'right with God,' so no alcohol is served and the restaurant is open Monday through Friday for dinner (lunch is served Friday and Saturday only). To get there take Hardy St west of downtown to Hwy 98 W, and the restaurant is past WalMart (ask anyone if you can't spy it).

East of Hattiesburg in Petal, the **Checker Hall of Fame** (☎ 601-582-7090), 220 Lynn Ray Rd, features one of the world's largest game boards. With luck you might challenge resident expert Guichio the monkey to a game. The museum is housed in a half-brick, Tudor-style mansion complete with pool, fountains, walled garden and guard tower. International tournaments are played here occasionally. Admission is free. To find it from Hattiesburg, take Hwy 11 north to Hwy 42; go east one mile. Turn right onto Central St; turn left onto Main St and pass the shopping center. Main St turns into Leesville Rd; look for Lyn Ray Rd and turn right to Checkerland. Tours are by appointment.

Gulf Coast

The Gulf Coast is nothing like the rest of Mississippi and it never has been. The Native American nations on the coast developed their own traditions based on the area's unique coastal environment.

Its colonial history is also different. The influence of French and Spanish settlement has been retained in a character more cosmopolitan than the rough-and-ready inland country.

Just the way it's situated, the Mississippi Gulf Coast receives a breeze that the nearby city of New Orleans lacks, and for that reason it has been a popular summer resort for affluent New Orleanians since the city was founded. But the coast's primary traditional means of income has always been the seafood industry, with most schooners and canneries based in Biloxi.

In the early 1990s the coast became the target of big casino owners from Las Vegas. Since the first casino opened in 1992, a dozen huge casinos have come to dominate the sleepy fishing villages and old family resorts. At first, the casinos seemed a dismal addition, but they soon began to draw busloads of Midwesterners, conventioneers and even church groups.

And so these days the coast sports an interesting mix of people, including Southern-speaking Vietnamese, Irish (in heritage) fisherfolk who work in the fishing industry, and pant-suited gambling grandmothers just passing through with their rolls of lucky quarters.

Biloxi is the center of the vacation action. Across the bay, Ocean Springs is where you'll find the nicest residential community, with a great beach and small harbor. To the west is Gulfport, an industrial city that's being developed as a casino resort. To the east is a smaller, more low-key state park in

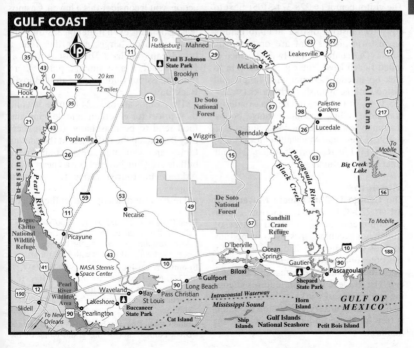

GULF COAST

Gautier (pronounced GO-shay), and the industrial city of Pascagoula, dominated by the refinery at the Alabama state line.

The Gulf shore is a long, narrow, white-sand beach that extends 26 miles and is protected by several undeveloped barrier islands. Ten miles offshore is the Gulf Islands National Seashore, which is accessible from the mainland via ferry, private charter or even sea kayak.

BILOXI
Biloxi gets its name from the Native American group that lived on these shores at the time of European contact. The French came ashore in 1699, actually landing next door in Ocean Springs but establishing settlements here and on the Gulf Islands. The town claims to be the second-oldest enduring settlement in the US, after St Augustine, Florida.

Information
The visitor center (☎ 228-374-3105), next to the town green, distributes maps of the downtown historic district and information on historic homes that are open to the public. The center is on Hwy 90, which is called Beach Blvd. You can also drop in to pick up discount coupons for hotels and casino buffets. Spanish Trail Books (☎ 228-435-1144), 781 Vieux Marché, is a wonderful bookstore selling new and vintage books. It's run by knowledgeable local guides.

Biloxi Regional Medical Center (☎ 228-432-1571), 150 Reynoir St, offers 24-hour emergency treatment.

Museums
The **George E Ohr-O'Keefe Museum of Art** (☎ 228-374-5547), 136 George E Ohr St, commemorates the 'Mad Potter of Biloxi,' an eccentric artist who named his six kids Clo, Oto, Flo, Zio, Ojo and Geo. His pots look pretty contemporary today, even though they were made a century ago. The modern museum features changing exhibitions of works by local artists as well as Ohr's pottery. Admission is $3 and is free for those under 12. It is closed on Sunday.

The **Maritime and Seafood Industry Museum** (☎ 228-435-6320) is at 115 1st St, Point Cadet. Admission to see the old photos, nets, crab pots, cannery equipment and boat parts is $3 for adults and $2 for children ages six to 16 and seniors. It's open Monday through Saturday from 9 am to 4:30 pm, and Sunday from noon to 4 pm.

There's a **Mardi Gras Museum** (☎ 228-435-6245), 119 Rue Magnolia, but visiting a museum about Mardi Gras is a lot like reading about dancing. Better to catch the celebration, or attend any local parade or festival – they all seem to include the bead-wearing and candy-throwing frenzy associated with the pre-Lenten holiday.

Casinos
The Vegas-style casinos that have grown to dominate the Mississippi coast are huge indoor theme parks on the water. There are over a million square feet of casinos here, so if you're into crawling for slot action, you'll consider this a haven. Casinos must technically be 'offshore' to permit legal gambling, even if that means they are constructed on barges no farther than a broad leap from land. The most action is at Point Cadet, a nice vantage point where the Mississippi Sound spills into Biloxi's Back Bay.

The casinos are open 24 hours a day, and their prices for entertainment, lodging and food tend to be reasonable (they expect they'll make up the difference at the gaming tables and slot machines). Their lavish buffets are your best bet for a cheap meal. Ask at the tourist office for discount coupons.

Here's a rundown of some of the casinos.

Beau Rivage (☎ 228-386-7111, 888-567-6667), 875 Beach Blvd, is the newest, fanciest casino with a dozen restaurants including the best seafood buffet in town and a hotel with 1780 rooms.

Boomtown Casino (☎ 601-435-7000, 800-627-0777), 676 Bayview Ave on Back Bay, is a Western-style casino with some Gold Rush touches. (Boomtown doesn't have an affiliated hotel.)

Grand Casino Biloxi (☎ 800-946-2946), 255 Beach Blvd, Point Cadet, is the grand dame of the

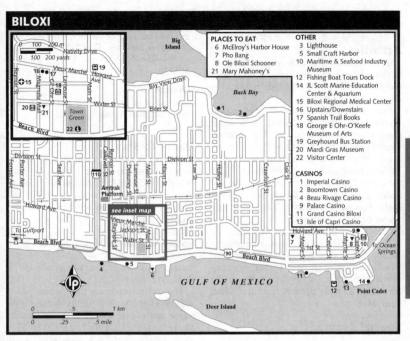

BILOXI

PLACES TO EAT
6 McElroy's Harbor House
7 Pho Bang
8 Ole Biloxi Schooner
21 Mary Mahoney's

OTHER
3 Lighthouse
5 Small Craft Harbor
10 Maritime & Seafood Industry Museum
12 Fishing Boat Tours Dock
14 JL Scott Marine Education Center & Aquarium
15 Biloxi Regional Medical Center
16 Upstairs/Downstairs
17 Spanish Trail Books
18 George E Ohr-O'Keefe Museum of Arts
19 Greyhound Bus Station
20 Mardi Gras Museum
22 Visitor Center

CASINOS
1 Imperial Casino
2 Boomtown Casino
4 Beau Rivage Casino
9 Palace Casino
11 Grand Casino Biloxi
13 Isle of Capri Casino

MISSISSIPPI

GULF OF MEXICO

Deer Island

---

coast's casinos and features a large theater as well as a posh casino and a 500-room hotel.

Isle of Capri Casino (☎ 800-843-4753), 151 Beach Blvd, Point Cadet, features jungle waterfalls, parrots, Flintstone-foam rocks and the 367-room Crowne Plaza Hotel.

Palace Casino (☎ 228-432-8888, 800-725-2239), 158 E Howard Ave, north of Point Cadet on Back Bay, was recently renovated and is a bit more low key than the others. An associated hotel opened in the summer of 2000.

Treasure Bay Casino (☎ 228-385-6000, 800-747-2839), 1980 Beach Blvd, is a massive pirate ship with an emphasis on 'merriment' appealing to slightly younger gamblers with free entertainment nightly; rates at its hotel tend to be cheaper than rates at other casino hotels.

Other Things to See & Do
The last home of Confederate president Jefferson Davis, **Beauvoir** (☎ 228-388-1313), 2244 Beach Blvd, is open for public tours. This 51-acre seaside estate includes his restored 1852 home, two museums, a cemetery and nature trails. It's open daily from 9 am to 4 pm in winter or 5 pm in summer. Admission is $7.50/6.75/4.50 for adults/seniors/children.

The **lighthouse** (☎ 228-435-6293), on Beach Blvd, was built in 1848 and remains a well-loved local landmark (it's 'the only lighthouse in the middle of a four-lane highway!'). It has a tradition of female lighthouse-keepers. There's one tour daily at 10 am, Monday through Saturday; admission is $2 for adults and $1 for seniors and children.

The **JL Scott Marine Education Center & Aquarium** (☎ 228-374-5550), at Point Cadet next to the Isle of Capri Casino, features a 44,000-gallon tank. The Gulf of Mexico tank holds indigenous species of shark, sea turtle, eel and fish. Another enclosure houses turtles and alligators. There's also a collection of seashells from around the world and part of the skeleton of a whale that beached on Ship Island. Admission is $4 for adults,

$2.50 for children under 17. It's open Monday to Saturday from 9 am to 4 pm.

Activities

The 26-mile-long beach is nice for sunbathing, sandcastle-building, wading and swimming; the gentle Mississippi Sound is clean enough and warm.

You can rent skiffs out to Deer Island, an undeveloped stretch of sand (with some shade) a half-mile from the Biloxi Small Craft Harbor (☎ 228-436-6592). Boat tours are available aboard shrimp boats and Biloxi schooners leaving from Point Cadet for about $10 for an hour-long trip; the old sailing ships were used for shrimping in the early days of the industry. Inquire at the visitor center in Biloxi.

The Biloxi Shrimping Trip (☎ 228-385-1182) is a 70-minute boat ride where shrimps and other fish are caught as they would be on a larger scale shrimping expedition. The trip costs $10 for adults and $6 for kids. The boat departs from the Small Craft Harbor.

Special Events

January

Mid-month there's a parade to celebrate Dr Martin Luther King Jr.

February

Mardi Gras festivities and parades are celebrated along the coast throughout the month. These sometimes spill over into March.

March

The Oyster Festival promises shuck & jive action.

June

The Coliseum Fair and Expo is mid-month; call ☎ 228-594-3700.

August

Get gussied up for a three-day rodeo at the Coliseum mid-month.

September

Mid-month there's a sandcastle contest on the beach in Biloxi. Nearby Pascagoula hosts the Mississippi Gulf Coast Blues Festival (☎ 228-497-5493).

October

Beauvoir's Fall Muster (☎ 228-388-9074) is held the third weekend of the month in Biloxi. The town also hosts the Ohr Fall Arts Festival (☎ 228-374-5547) on the last weekend in October.

December

Christmas on the Water boat parade can be witnessed off Biloxi's coast.

Places to Stay

Camping A private campground in the center of the action, the *Cajun RV Park* (*☎ 228-388-5590, 1860 Beach Blvd*) maintains a comfortably worn lot under tall shady trees. Tent sites are $18.50 for two people.

Hotels & Motels Motels line the coast around Biloxi. Most are modest budget motels, and nearly every possible motel chain is represented.

The casino hotels are the fanciest (some with boudoir-style red tuffets, flocked wallpaper and ornate chandeliers), and prices are reasonable, ranging from $60 to $140 for a double. There is a surprisingly small difference between the price of a room in a casino hotel and a room in a beach motel, but prices vary considerably by season. (See Casinos, earlier in this section, for contact information.)

Rates in the high summer season might be double what they are in winter, though there's less fluctuation at the casino hotels. Prices quoted here are generally for the spring and fall seasons; call the hotels for date-specific prices.

There are a few cheapies in town, but be wary of shattered windshield glass in the parking lot, decrepit Cadillacs, Confederate flag decals and the like.

Stoplights are infrequent on Beach Blvd (Hwy 90), so though summertime traffic slows to a crawl, cars may also race by at 60 mph – enough to frazzle a parent's nerves. For that reason, lodging near lit pedestrian crossings is your safest bet.

All of the following hotels are west of downtown. *Ocean Manor (☎ 228-388-2579,*

2484 Beach Blvd), just past the Holiday Inn, is a well-regarded motel with doubles for $34. The **Suntan Motel** (☎ 228-432-8641, 780 Beach Blvd), past Beau Rivage casino, is very basic, but it's within easy walking distance of downtown Biloxi and some of the casinos.

The **Biloxi Beach Resort** (☎ 228-388-3310, 800-345-1570, 2736 Beach Blvd), a few blocks west of the Holiday Inn, is a well-established 'motor hotel' that looks like it keeps the same families returning every year. Rates start at $65.

Father Ryan B&B (☎ 228-435-1189, 800-295-1189, 1196 Beach Blvd), four blocks west of the lighthouse on the corner of Caldwell St, operates out of a lovely historic house (with tours available for non-guests). It charges $80 for a double, and rates include a generous Southern breakfast.

Places to Eat

The **Ole Biloxi Schooner** (☎ 228-374-8071, 159 Howard Ave), at the foot of Myrtle St, should be your first stop. It's an old diner decorated with old black-and-white pictures of fishing schooners in their 1940s heyday, and it has a great jukebox. This is the most reliable place for fishermen's breakfasts ($4), po-boy lunches ($5) and seafood dinner plates ($13). The Biloxi Schooner is across the street from the Palace Casino on the Back Bay, and down the street from a fabulous Vietnamese market. It's closed on Sunday.

You won't find many authentic Vietnamese restaurants in the South, so it's well worth finding **Pho Bang** (☎ 228-374-7666, 295 Howard Ave), at Oak St about a half-mile west of the Ole Biloxi Schooner. Pho Bang serves good rice-noodle soups with shrimp and meat ($4.50 for a dinner bowl), along with other traditional specialties. It's open daily until 8 pm.

Locals send visitors to **Mary Mahoney's** (☎ 228-374-0163, 110 Rue Magnolia), which serves expensive seafood for lunch and dinner in butlered antebellum style within the former slave quarters of a 1737 mansion. For a more casual setting, eat in the tavern in the back. There's also a 24-hour cafe here serving café au lait and beignets around the clock.

McElroy's Harbor House (☎ 228-435-5001, 695 Beach Blvd) is a scenic seafood restaurant on the pier at the Biloxi Small Craft Harbor. Daily lunch specials start at $6; the dinner menu includes mullet and broiled shrimp for $13. It's also open for breakfast.

Casinos serve all-you-can-eat buffets at reasonable prices. The **Copa Casino** has a seafood buffet for $10, but the **Beau Rivage's** buffet ($13) is one of the best. In general, casinos offer short-order food and snacks nearly around the clock. The casinos also have big fancy restaurants, but you pay mostly for decor; service isn't appropriate for the prices. (See Casinos, earlier in this section, for other options.)

Entertainment

The casinos host plenty of entertainers, a large percentage of them being tragic has-beens like Air Supply and Herman's Hermits. Ticket prices are reasonable and many events are free. The **Coliseum** (☎ 228-594-3700, 2350 Beach Blvd) hosts big-name performers such as Merle Haggard and Pavarotti as well as the Mississippi Seawolves ice hockey team. The **Grand Casino** has a snazzy theater, and most casinos have smaller stages with comedy and cabaret-style performances.

Locals who ignore the casino scene can be found at **Upstairs/Downstairs** (☎ 228-374-5291, 785 Vieux Marché), near Rue Magnolia, which features local bands and karaoke.

Shopping

Mary Mahoney's (see Places to Eat) has a gift shop selling dainty items such as fine lace aprons and Aunt Jemima thimbles. The George E Ohr Arts & Cultural Center sells locally made crafts, Christmas ornaments and lots of pottery. The fabulously kitsch Sharksheads Souvenirs is a five-minute drive west along Beach Blvd at the bottom of Rodenberg Ave. Edgewater Mall, 2600 Beach Blvd, is between Biloxi and Gulfport.

MISSISSIPPI

Getting There & Away

Air The only airport on the coast is the Gulfport-Biloxi Regional Airport (☎ 228-863-5951), on Hwy 49 in Gulfport, a mile south of I-10 exit 34A; the airport offers nonstop flights to a limited number of cities (including Atlanta, Dallas, Tampa and Memphis).

The closest major airport is in New Orleans, which may be cheaper than flying to the regional airport, and is a drive of under two hours to Biloxi. See Local Transportation in the Getting Around chapter for shuttle information.

Bus Greyhound buses (☎ 228-436-4335) depart from 166 Main St. There are three buses a day to New Orleans (two hours, $20), six buses a day to Mobile (1¼ hours, $15) and two direct buses to Jackson, Mississippi (four hours, $31). Some indirect services to Jackson take twice as long so check the timetable before you get a ticket. Busing between Biloxi and Gulfport takes a half-hour and costs $8.50.

Train Amtrak's *Sunset Limited* runs between Los Angeles, California, and Orlando, Florida, via New Orleans and the Gulf Coast. There's a stop in Biloxi (at a somewhat forlorn outpost with a platform only).

The trip from Biloxi to New Orleans costs $23 and takes 3½ hours; to Mobile costs $15 and takes an hour. The 48-hour ride from Los Angeles to Biloxi costs just over $200 and passes through Tucson, Arizona, and Houston, Texas.

Car To get to Biloxi from Jackson take Hwy 49 south to Gulfport then turn east onto I-10. The total distance is 169 miles; allow three hours. Biloxi to New Orleans is an easy two-hour drive on I-10 but summer traffic will cause delays.

Getting Around

Cyclists should note that Biloxi is perfectly flat but the highway traffic moves at a fast clip. No rentals are available.

The Beachcomber Trolley (☎ 228-896-8080) runs between Gulfport and Point Cadet along Beach Blvd. In Biloxi, there's a stop at the lighthouse every half-hour between 6:35 am and 10:35 pm (less frequently on Sunday). Casino shuttles run between many motels and casinos. Fares are $1 to $2 depending on how far you go; $4 for all-day travel.

Grayline (☎ 228-432-2649, 800-647-3957) offers regular services to Gulfport/Biloxi Regional Airport and New Orleans International Airport.

GULFPORT

In addition to being home to casinos and an industrial port, Gulfport is the jumping-off point for ferry trips to West Ship Island, part of the Gulf Islands National Seashore. The Mississippi Gulf Coast Convention and Visitors Bureau (☎ 228-896-6699, 800-237-9493) distributes maps and information by mail (write to PO Box 6128, Gulfport, MS 39506-6128), from its offices at 135 Courthouse Rd and from its Web site at www.gulfcoast.org.

At the small craft harbor, trained bottle-nosed dolphins and sea lions perform shows at the **Marine Life Oceanarium** (☎ 228-863-0651). In a permanently docked cruise ship, **Copa Casino** (☎ 228-863-3330, 800-946-2672), 777 Copa Blvd, prides itself on having the most relaxed gaming rules.

The *Econo Lodge* (☎ 228-863-9350, 800-387-7719, 40 E Beach Blvd) offers basic motel accommodations, with beach restrooms conveniently located across the way. Rooms start at $49.

Gulfport's *Grand Casino* (☎ 800-946-2946, 3215 West Beach Blvd) is less grand than the one in Biloxi but right on the beach with a 500-room hotel. Rates range from $69 to $109 for a double.

Catfish Charlie's (☎ 228-832-9195, 11419 Canal Rd), north of Gulfport in Orange Grove, has a huge hillbilly-inspired dining hall that is decorated with old license plates and farm implements. Catfish or fried chicken plates are less than $10. It's only open Thursday to Saturday.

West Ship Island Schedule

Passenger ferries leave the Gulfport Yacht Harbor for hour-long rides to and from West Ship Island every season except winter. Roundtrip fares are $16/14/8 for adults/seniors/children ages three to 10. For information call Pan Isles (☎ 228-864-1014, 800-388-3290). Note that weather conditions may affect the schedule. No camping is permitted on the island.

Spring (first Saturday in March to second weekend in May)
Saturday and Sunday:
Departs Gulfport 9 am, 12 noon
Departs Ship Island 2:40 pm, 5:15 pm

Monday to Friday:
Departs Gulfport 9 am
Departs Ship Island 2:40 pm

Summer (second weekend in May to first Tuesday in September)
Daily: Departs Gulfport 9 am, 12 noon
Departs Ship Island 2:40 pm, 5:15 pm

Fall (first Tuesday in September to last Sunday in October)
Same as the spring schedule

Getting There & Away

Amtrak stops at a full-fledged train station in downtown Gulfport at 1419 27th Ave. The trip from Gulfport to New Orleans costs $23 and takes 3¼ hours; to Mobile the cost is $12 and it's 1½ hours. Passenger ferries to West Ship Island leave the Gulfport Yacht Harbor; see the 'West Ship Island Ferry Schedule' boxed text for more information. The Beachcomber Trolley runs frequently between Gulfport and Point Cadet along Beach Blvd. (See the Biloxi section, earlier in this chapter, for more transportation options.)

WEST OF GULFPORT

The town of **Long Beach** is home to the University of Southern Mississippi's Gulf Coast campus where the Friendship Oak stands. Legend says that folks meeting under it will be friends for life. ***Chappy's Seafood Restaurant*** (☎ 228-865-9755, 624 E Beach Blvd) has good fish and excellent fried green tomatoes; it's open daily. The Bodine Pottery & Art Studio (☎ 228-863-4734), 108 Jefferson Davis Ave, is a family business where everyone, including the kids, makes, sells and teaches clay sculpture.

In **Pass Christian** (kristi-ANN), you can see one of the Gulf of Mexico's most attractive audiences, the cluster of antebellum houses that attentively face the water. This was a favorite resort for families from New Orleans and many attractive houses and shady old oaks have survived centuries of hurricanes. Pass Christian Tour of Homes takes place the first weekend in May; call ☎ 228-452-0063, for information. In mid-July, there's a seafood festival. Wolf River Canoe & Kayak (☎ 228-452-7666), 21640 Tucker Rd, north of Pass Christian runs day or half-day trips along the Wolf River for a very reasonable $33.

In **Bay St Louis**, you can have a beer overlooking the water at ***Dock of the Bay*** (☎ 228-467-9940, 119 N Beach Blvd). ***Trapani's*** (☎ 228-467-8570, 116 N Beach Blvd) is a seafood restaurant that has diversified its menu with pasta and po-boys. Lunch is served daily; dinner is served Wednesday to Sunday only. Out of town, the NASA Stennis Space Center (☎ 228-688-2370), on I-10 exit 2, offers guided tours of the satellite facility.

From Waveland, 3 miles south of Hwy 90, follow signs to **Buccaneer State Park** (☎ 228-467-3822), 1150 S Beach Blvd, where there are water slides, a campground, a pier and nearby stretches of beach. Camping is available for $8 and $13 with hookups.

GULF ISLANDS NATIONAL SEASHORE

The national seashore preserves four barrier islands 12 miles off the eastern Mississippi coast: West Ship and East Ship, Horn and Petit Bois Islands. The national seashore also encompasses Davis Bayou on

MISSISSIPPI

the mainland in Ocean Springs (where you'll find the ranger station and a campground) and property farther east in Florida. The two most notable islands are the historic West Ship and Horn Island, a wilderness favored by adventurers and accessible only by private boat.

The narrow islands are ringed with white-sand beaches and blue-green Gulf waters. The smaller ones aren't much but dune, while the larger ones host a maritime forest of oak and pine studded with lagoons. You'll want to pack sunscreen and insect repellent when you explore these islands.

Davis Bayou

The Gulf Islands ranger station (☎ 228-875-3962) is on the mainland east of downtown Ocean Springs on Hwy 90 at a beautiful spot called Davis Bayou. The station has a nice visitor center with a film introducing barrier-island ecology; some paintings by Walter Anderson; and a deck and boardwalk overlooking the scenic marshland. The ranger station distributes comprehensive information on camping on the wilderness islands and boat charters.

On Davis Bayou, there is a pretty campground; sites aren't too private but they're well spaced and surrounded by forest. Hookup sites cost $16.

Ship Islands

What was once a single island was split in two by Hurricane Camille in 1965, becoming West Ship and East Ship Islands. In 1998, Hurricane George took another slash at East Ship, giving it a hairline fracture across the middle. Folks still expect it'll all patch itself together over time, so they tend to use the singular name Ship Island.

West Ship is the most accessible and historic of all the Gulf Islands. The island's most distinctive feature is **Fort Massachusetts**. Early in the Civil War, the Confederates seized the unfinished fort. After federal troops regained control in 1861, they finished construction and used the island as a prisoner-of-war camp and staging area for the capture of New Orleans. An African-

American Confederate troop was housed here during the war. You can take a ranger's tour or wander around on your own.

You can sunbathe, swim and hike around the island (clothing conventions become more liberal as you head east). There's a shop at the far end of the one-third-mile boardwalk running north-south between the pier and the swimming beach. The shop sells hot snacks, candy and cold drinks and supplies such as sunscreen and insect repellent. They also rent out umbrellas and beach chairs. No camping is permitted on West Ship Island but there are decent beach showers and restrooms.

An old island family runs ferry services to the island from Gulfport (see 'West Ship Island Ferry Schedule,' earlier in this chapter, for fares, times and contact information). By advance arrangement, the ferry company can provide transportation to East Ship Island (bring water and food) for $100 minimum or $50 per person during the standard ferry season. It's more expensive in winter. Camping is permitted on East Ship Island.

Horn Island

The jewel of the Gulf Islands National Seashore is Horn Island, a 3650-acre strip of pristine wilderness with pine and palmetto forests, lagoons attracting over 280 bird species and 13 miles of deserted beach – an ideal destination for hikers, sun worshipers and campers.

You can hike 30 miles around the 13-mile-long island, and there are several opportunities to cut through the half-mile-wide interior (beware of mosquitoes in forested areas). The best places to camp

Poetry of the Gulf Coast

Such a sky – such water, and Horn Island between with me walking it – the back of Moby Dick, the white whale, the magic carpet.

– Walter Anderson

are at the breezier tips of the island. No ferry serves the island, and though a ranger is stationed here, no public services are available.

To get to the island, you can either kayak or charter a boat across the Mississippi Sound. To kayak, rangers recommend starting from Shepard State Park (☎ 228-497-2244), in Gautier, east of the mainland NPS ranger station. There are several chances to quit along the way if you get into trouble. For boat charters, the park has licensed a few environmentally conscious captains who transport day-trippers and campers for around $50 per person.

Coastal painter Walter Anderson's images of Horn Island can be seen at his namesake gallery in Ocean Springs and at the ranger station just north at Davis Bayou.

OCEAN SPRINGS

Ocean Springs is a nice residential community just south of Hwy 90. Over the railroad tracks you'll find the old depot that has been converted into boutiques and shops, the compact downtown strip and renowned art museum along Washington St. It's a short drive or bike ride to the beach, which is much nicer than the Biloxi shore, or to the harbor, which is picturesque with its small fishing fleet and yacht cove.

The visitor center (☎ 228-875-4424) is at 1000 Washington Ave. It's closed on Sunday.

The **Walter Anderson Museum of Art** (☎ 228-872-3164), 510 Washington Ave, features Anderson's paintings of the Mississippi coast (particularly the Horn Island wilderness). Anderson painted in a compellingly whimsical way with a pastel palette – a style that's often been compared to Van Gogh and Picasso. It's worth a stop. Admission is $5 for adults and $2 for children (free for those under six). The museum is open daily, but closed Sunday mornings and major holidays.

Shearwater Pottery (☎ 228-875-7320, 102 Shearwater Drive) displays and sells locally crafted works; it's open weekdays only.

Spring Pilgrimage tours of homes and gardens run during the second week of

April; call ☎ 228-467-4979 for information. Fort Maurepas Living History Weekend, reenacting the arrival of Pierre Le Moyne, Sieur d'Iberville, takes place in mid-October. In early November, there's an Arts and Crafts Festival.

Places To Stay & Eat

The closest campground is near Davis Bayou (see that section, earlier in this chapter, for more information). *Shadowlawn B&B (☎ 228-875-6945, 112A Shearwater Drive)* is a lovely house right on the Gulf with a long lazy hallway leading to a massive screened porch. Rooms are $125 – ask for the front 'John & Jennie' room.

Martha's Tea Room (☎ 228-872-2554, 715 Washington Ave) makes sandwiches, salads and steamed veggies on wild rice ($5.25). It's faux flowery, and 'fresh' tuna means the can was opened this morning, but it's still a good option if you're 'po-boyed' to your eyeballs.

EAST OF OCEAN SPRINGS

The **Mississippi Sandhill Crane National Wildlife Refuge** (☎ 228-497-6322), north of Gautier off I-10 between D'Iberville and Moss Point, preserves the habitat of an unusual species of sandhill crane. While most varieties of sandhill crane are migratory birds that interbreed, the particular Mississippi sandhill crane native to this isolated habitat does not migrate nor does it interbreed. As a result, encroaching coastal development severely threatens its survival. The preserve not only protects this endangered species but also benefits the similarly endangered local red-cockaded woodpecker population. A very short nature trail stretching into the refuge allows visitors to wander in to catch a glimpse of the long-legged cranes, listen for the woodpecker cries and observe the coastal piney woods.

Shepard State Park (☎ 228-497-2244), 1024 Graveline Rd in Gautier, is nestled in a quiet corner of the coast. The 400-acre park provides hiking and biking trails and a wooded campground ($8). It's also an ideal put-in point for sea-kayak trips across the Mississippi Sound to Horn Island.

MISSISSIPPI

River of Love

The legendary Pascagoula River near the Alabama border is nicknamed the 'Singing River' for the mysterious sounds folks say emanate from its depths. The story goes that a young Biloxi Indian princess, though betrothed to a chieftain within her own warrior tribe, instead fell in love with a young man of the peace-loving Pascagoula tribe. After running off with her love, the jilted Biloxi fellow ran a raid on the Pascagoula. The Pascagoulas vowed to save the young couple or die trying. The relentless Biloxi attack pushed the community to the river and to their deaths. It's the death chant of the Pascagoula that's said to account for the strange sounds heard at the river.

At the mouth of the Pascagoula River, **La Pointe-Krebs House** (☎ 228-769-1505), 4602 Fort St in Pascagoula, is believed to be the oldest standing European structure in the Mississippi Valley. Joseph de la Pointe, who at 12 years old was a member of the original d'Iberville expedition of 1699, settled down among the Pascagoula Indians. His estate on Krebs Lake included a carpenter's shop built around 1721. This shop, which later served as a house and became fortified, was known as the Old Spanish Fort and remains standing. Its walls are whitewashed with ground oyster shells over *bousillage*, a mixture of Spanish moss and clay commonly used for insulation at the time. The house underwent extensive restoration in 1996. A nearby cemetery holds generations of residents of the historic house, and a museum on the grounds displays a mixture of pre-Columbian artifacts and memorabilia from the early 19th century and the Civil War period. Admission is $4/3/2 for adults/seniors/children. It's open daily.

DE SOTO NATIONAL FOREST

The De Soto National Forest is the largest national forest in Mississippi with over 500,000 acres of piney woods and slow moving streams stained black by the tannic acid released by decaying forest debris. It's a great place for backpacking, camping, hiking, swimming, fishing and canoeing. The ranger station (☎ 601-928-4422) is headquartered in Wiggins and distributes forest maps and information.

Black Creek is especially popular with adventurers who canoe down 21 miles of officially 'wild and scenic' river and hike along the 41-mile Black Creek Trail. The trail passes along the white sandy banks of the tannin-stained creek and under the shade of magnolias, sweet bays, sweet gums, tulip trees and oaks. It passes an ox-bow lake studded with cypress, crosses 82 bridges over streamlets and ravines, and swings off into the rolling piney woods. It is not uncommon to see deer, wild turkeys, owls, great blue herons and beavers along the stream.

A good place to pick up the trail is near Paul B Johnson State Park (☎ 228-582-7721), beside the national forest between Wiggins and Hattiesburg. You can find the entrance to the trail off Hwy 49, 4 miles south of the state park. Keep your eyes out for a service road to the east, where a small brown sign for 'Ashe Nursery and Black Creek Seed Orchard' leads a mile or so to Yeaton Spur Rd, past the nursery and orchard to the USFS-signed parking lot. Black Creek hikers may prefer to park in the secured state parking lot instead of the unsecured USFS lot, but first obtain permission for overnight parking at the desk, and be aware that not everyone around here knows about the trail.

In nearby Brooklyn, Black Creek Canoe Rentals (☎ 601-582-8817), on Carnes Rd east of Hwy 49, outfits expeditions ranging from a 5-mile day trip to a 25-mile three-day launch. (The trip will require that you bring all your own food, though a store nearby offers an opportunity for last-minute purchases.) The folks here probably know more about the creek and trail conditions than the forest service. The canoe shop has operated here since 1977 with a USFS special-use permit. A fee of $25 per day includes life vest, paddles and shuttle service (advance

Magnolia blossoms all over Mississippi.

reservations and deposits required). To get to the shop from Gulfport take Hwy 49 N to Brooklyn (about 50 miles), turn right at Brooklyn and follow the sign to the shop (about 1.5 miles on the right).

The state park makes a nice base. It offers a lake with swimming and paddle boats. The campground charges $13 for RV sites and $8 for primitive tent sites. There are also 16 cabins that are fully furnished with linens and basic cookware and dishware; make reservations for cabins well in advance around holidays.

LUCEDALE & AROUND

Around 20 miles west of the Alabama state line off Hwy 98, Lucedale evokes that small-town feel that is fast disappearing throughout the region. The famed back-scratching post downtown (on the corner of Main and Mills Sts) is rumored to have been there for at least a hundred years. But what draws most people through town is a visit to the homespun biblical shrine outside of town.

At **Palestine Gardens** (☎ 228-947-8422) visitors are guided through a scale model of the Holy Land. The Reverend Jackson (but not the Reverend *Jesse* Jackson) constructed the site, and though he passed on years ago, members of his family and con-

gregation maintain his life's work and take a good deal of pride in their knowledge of biblical history. Bring a picnic lunch; no food is available in the park. (There's a Coke machine and a grocery nearby that sells some provisions.) The gardens are open March through December, Monday to Friday from 9 am to 4 pm, Saturday from 9 am to 6 pm and Sunday from 1 to 6 pm. Admission is free.

The turnoff to Palestine Gardens is about a mile west of Lucedale, north of Hwy 98. To get to the gardens, look for Carolyn's Grocery at N Bexley Rd, turn right and drive 3½ miles to the first available right turn at a stop sign. Turn right here onto Ford James Rd, which becomes Palestine Gardens Rd.

Pilgrims might want to stop at the *Landmark Cafe* (☎ 228-766-9619), on Main St in downtown Lucedale, for breakfast or lunch. The Landmark offers alligator po-boys.

Southwestern Mississippi

The loamy brown hill region of southwestern Mississippi takes its name from the aboriginal nation – the Natchez – that flourished here. The Natchez District stretches from the Louisiana line through the city of Natchez north to Vicksburg. The Natchez civilization – distinct from the predominant Mississippian culture – reached its height in the mid-15th century. It was centered on the banks of what is today St Catherine's Creek, south of downtown Natchez. The restored Grand Village of the Natchez attests to their unique culture, one that bears striking resemblance to the Inca culture that was reaching its zenith in southern Peru around the same time. The Natchez nation was vanquished when the French retaliated to an earlier surprise attack with a devastating assault on the Grand Village in 1730.

After the coast, this region was among the first settled by Europeans. The port of Natchez grew rich on cotton exports, and large plantations flourished along the bluffs of the Mississippi River. Hwy 61 from Louisiana north through Natchez is today spotted with arcades leading to antebellum homes, many of which are open for public tours or as historic inns. The city of Natchez itself is full of historic homes. A compact downtown and residents accustomed to visitors make it an inviting, easy destination.

North of town is the Natchez Trace, an ancient Indian route that became the overland route for Mississippi River traders and a US post road. Today the trace is a streamlined national scenic parkway between Natchez and Nashville, Tennessee, and a popular bicycle-touring route that leads through forest, pasture, Indian mounds and ghost towns. Short detours lead to small towns, plantation ruins, a historic African-American college and Civil War battle sites.

During the Civil War, Natchez – a town that reportedly never flew the Confederate flag – surrendered without a fuss (which accounts in large part for the survival of many of its antebellum structures). Yet Union general Ulysses S Grant's campaign to capture the strategic port of Vicksburg farther north brought Yankee troops to the Natchez District.

The region was also distinguished during the Civil Rights era when the African-American residents of Port Gibson organized a boycott of white merchants who used discriminatory tactics.

East of the Natchez District bluffs, the land changes around the I-55 corridor. With soil too thin to support cotton cultivation, this area historically produced vegetables, fruits and nuts. Today travelers know I-55 best as the long, generally indistinct stretch endured on a trip to or from New Orleans. While facilities at highway exits are ample for through-travelers, drivers with time to kill might want to detour off onto the parallel stretch of Hwy 51. Be prepared for the typical two-lane delays, like getting stuck behind a slow-moving cabbage truck, though you're never far from meeting back up with the four-lane freeway. Before the interstate, Hwy 51 was the primary route north and south. As such, it's a stretch of road nearly as revered in local legend as Hwy 61 farther west. Towns off Hwy 51 are typical Southern hamlets. Small downtown strips are still lively for the most part.

NATCHEZ
• pop 20,000

The first capital of Mississippi, Natchez is a charming antebellum town on a high bluff overlooking the Mississippi River. But troubles lie below the sophisticated surface: the town is sharply segregated and has one of the highest murder rates in the nation.

Natchez had one of the busiest slave markets in the south and thousands of slaves worked on the local plantations, creating one of the wealthiest pre-war towns in the country. Opulent antebellum architecture and historic interior design are the town's main attractions, especially during busy pilgrimage seasons when dozens of local homes are opened to public tours. Only one plantation home – Melrose, run by the National Park Service (NPS) – has recreated slave quarters as a reminder of the source of its original affluence.

Orientation

The compact downtown area (officially a national historic district) occupies the bluff overlooking the river north of the bridge. House museums and historic inns, restaurants, shops and a bike-rental outlet are all within this attractive district. More house museums are a short drive away. The visitor center is on the edge of downtown.

Information

The impressive Natchez Visitor Reception Center (☎ 601-446-6345, 800-647-6724) is on S Canal St at Hwy 84 at the foot of the Mississippi Bridge. As well as comprehensive Natchez information, the center serves as a Mississippi Welcome Center and NPS outpost. Other facilities include an ATM and Internet access. The old depot on Canal St at State St houses the Natchez Pilgrimage Tour office (☎ 601-446-6631, 800-647-6742).

AmSouth (☎ 601-445-2600, 800-748-8501), Franklin St at Pearl St, will exchange currency and cash traveler's checks.

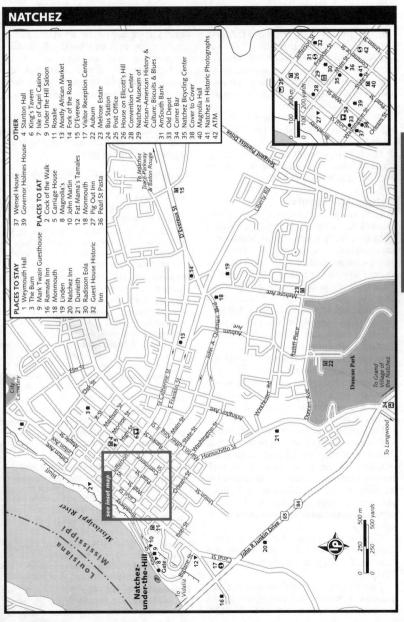

NATCHEZ

PLACES TO STAY
1 Weymouth Hall
3 The Burn
9 Mark Twain Guesthouse
16 Ramada Inn
18 Monmouth
19 Linden
20 Natchez Inn
21 Dunleith
30 Radisson Eola
32 Guest House Historic Inn
37 Wensel House
39 Governor Holmes House

PLACES TO EAT
2 Cock of the Walk
5 Carriage House
8 Magnolia's
10 John Martin
12 Fat Mama's Tamales
27 Pig Out Inn
36 Pearl St Pasta

OTHER
4 Stanton Hall
6 King's Tavern
7 Isle of Capri Casino
9 Under the Hill Saloon
11 Rosalie
13 Mostly African Market
14 Fork of the Road
15 D'Evereux
17 Visitor Reception Center
22 Auburn
23 Melrose Estate
24 Bus Station
25 Post Office
26 House on Ellicott's Hill
28 Convention Center
29 Natchez Museum of African-American History & Culture; Biscuits & Blues
31 AmSouth Bank
33 Old Depot
34 Corner Bar
35 Natchez Bicycling Center
38 Cover to Cover
40 Magnolia Hall
41 Natchez in Historic Photographs
42 ATM

MISSISSIPPI

The main post office (☎ 601-442-4361) is downtown at 214 N Canal St.

Cover to Cover (☎ 601-445-5752, 800-398-5656), 208 Washington St, operates out of a Victorian house a half-block south of the depot downtown. It has an impressive collection of books, including some on local history as well as specialty guides, biographies and cookbooks.

Natchez Community Hospital (☎ 601-445-6200) can be found at 129 Jefferson Davis Blvd.

The fire department can be reached at ☎ 601-442-3684; the police department can be reached at ☎ 601-445-5565.

Antebellum Homes

In 1899, Natchez historian Gerard Brandon IV foretold the future of the city of Natchez when he said, 'Yet hither must Mississippians ever come, as to the cradle in which the infant state was rocked. Hither will Pilgrims journey to visit our historic shrines, and to drink from the primal springs of a glorious past.' Visitors today can see antebellum style that would make Margaret Mitchell proud, thanks largely to the preservation efforts of two garden clubs – the Natchez Garden Club (now headquartered in the House on Ellicott's Hill) and the Pilgrimage Garden Club (at Stanton Hall) – and to the oil money that supported many grand restorations. The local tourist industry, worth $35 million, draws around 450,000 visitors annually.

Each pilgrimage season, around 30 historic homes are open to ticket-holders over the course of three weeks. Tour guides in antebellum costumes are stationed in each room to provide detailed descriptions of the furnishings, decor, architecture and family of residence. Other special events, including nighttime entertainment, coincide with the pilgrimage.

Pilgrimages are scheduled in spring (generally from mid-March to mid-April) and October. Tours operate daily from 8 am to 5:30 pm.

Tour passes are required and are not available at houses. You can obtain tickets in advance by phone (☎ 601-446-6631,

800-647-6742) or at the pilgrimage office in the old depot at Canal and State Sts. You can buy a morning or afternoon tour pass to see the properties open that day. It costs $24 per person for a half-day tour.

More than a dozen historic-house museums are open for public tours year-round. For visitors with the time to visit only a few, the most outstanding houses are the House on Ellicott's Hill, Longwood, Melrose, Rosalie and Stanton Hall. Most are open daily, and admission is $6. Many operate as luxurious inns.

Auburn (☎ 601-442-5981), 400 Duncan Ave at Auburn Ave, is a city-operated 1812 landmark set in the midst of the 200-acre Duncan Park (☎ 601-442-5955), which offers swimming, golfing, tennis and nature trails.

The Burn (☎ 601-442-1344), 712 N Union St, is a three-story Greek Revival mansion built in 1836; the gardens are notable for rare varieties of camellias. It's also an inn.

D'Evereux, 60 D'Evereux Drive, is a Greek Revival mansion built around 1840.

Dunleith (☎ 601-446-8500), 84 Homochitto St, is an 1856 Greek Revival 'temple' built around colonnaded galleries. Situated within a 40-acre park with many antebellum outbuildings, the house operates as an inn. John R Lynch was once a slave who fanned people in the dining room here; he went on to become a powerful post-Civil War politician, serving in both the Mississippi and the US House of Representatives.

Governor Holmes House (☎ 601-442-2366), 207 S Wall St, downtown, was the home of the last governor of the Mississippi Territory and the first governor when it became a state in 1817. It's also an inn.

House on Ellicott's Hill (☎ 601-442-2011), N Canal St at Jefferson St, a restoration project of the Natchez Garden Club, is the oldest property open for tours. Andrew Ellicott raised the American flag on this hill in 1798 in defiance of Spain, and the small two-story house was built the following year.

Linden (☎ 601-445-5472), 1 Linden Place off Melrose Ave, has been the rambling Federal-style home of the Conner family since 1849; it is now open for house tours and as an inn.

Longwood (☎ 601-442-5193), 140 Lower Woodville Rd, is an unfinished, grand, octagonal house with Oriental accents; construction was begun in 1860, disrupted by the Civil War and never completed.

Magnolia Hall (☎ 601-442-6672), 215 S Pearl St at Washington St, is a Greek Revival mansion built in 1858.

Melrose Estate (☎ 601-446-5790), 1 Melrose Ave, is a grand plantation estate operated by the National Park Service. Rangers lead tours of the plantation house ($6), and visitors can wander the grounds themselves at no charge. The slave quarters hold exhibits on the history of slavery.

Monmouth (☎ 601-442-5852), John A Quitman Parkway, is a monumental mansion; it's open to the public for tours and also has an inn and restaurant.

Rosalie (☎ 601-445-4555), S Broadway St at Canal St, is situated atop the river bluff downtown near the depot. Named after the nearby site of Fort Rosalie, the statuesque brick mansion served as Union Army headquarters during the Civil War.

Stanton Hall (☎ 601-442-6282), High St at Pearl St, is an 1857 palatial mansion and home to the Pilgrimage Garden Club. Its adjacent Cottage Restaurant offers fine dining and hosts theatrical performances.

Weymouth Hall (☎ 601-445-2304), 1 Cemetery Rd, is an 1855 Greek Revival mansion overlooking the river; it's also an inn.

Natchez-Under-the-Hill

A restored bawdytown half-hidden in a mysterious cove along the Mississippi River, Natchez-Under-the-Hill was originally the commercial center of town. Once the legitimate businesses moved higher up to the bluff, this section retained a reputation for lusty riverboat vices. Today's reconstructed version resembles an Old West frontier stage set – strangely though, it's peopled with folks that somewhat resemble the original cast of characters. Several picturesque cafes, saloons and popular family restaurants overlook the river, the bridge and the riverboat casino down the hill.

Museum of African-American History & Culture

This museum (☎ 601-445-0728), 301 Main St, recounts local African-American history from the 1880s to the 1950s in a personal way – period kitchens, costumes and ac-counts of the nightclub fire that killed dozens of community members. It's open Wednesday to Saturday from 1 to 5 pm, but hours may be extended. Donations are requested.

Fork of the Road

There's not much to see but this junction of St Catherine St, D'Evereux Drive and Liberty Rd was the site of the town's slave market. Most slaves sold here were marched from the Atlantic states to Natchez and then sold to cotton-owning landholders in the Deep South.

Grand Village of the Natchez

This archaeological park and museum (☎ 601-446-6502), 400 Jefferson Davis Blvd, contains a set of small mounds and a reconstructed hut or two in a shady glen off Hwy 61, south of town (suburban homes bank the ancient site). The museum, operated by the state's Department of Archives and History, relates how the traditions of the Natchez Indians were unique from those of neighboring nations. A trail crosses through the adjacent woods. Admission is free.

Natchez in Historic Photographs

This interesting photographic exhibition (☎ 601-442-4741) dates mostly from Victorian times and depicts locals going about daily life in town, at their homes and on the river. It's at 405 State St (between Pearl and Commerce Sts) and is open daily but closed Sunday morning. A donation of $3 is requested.

Organized Tours

Ozelle Fisher conducts Black Heritage Tours by appointment only; call ☎ 601-445-8309 or call the visitor center and ask for the Heritage Tourism Department.

Special Events

Spring pilgrimage runs for a month from the second week of March and for three weeks from mid-October. In late October, there's a hot-air balloon race, which takes off from the grounds of Rosalie.

MISSISSIPPI

Places to Stay

Natchez is an ideal place to splurge on accommodations – few cities of this size in the South offer a greater range of meticulously furnished historic houses operating as inns. Note, however, that some historic properties won't allow young children, and that some request no children of any age. Be aware that rates go up steeply during pilgrimage and accommodations are booked well ahead.

Camping Shady sites in a wooded, hilly campground are available at *Natchez State Park* (☎ 601-442-2658), 10 miles north of town at the foot of the Natchez Trace. The facilities are adequate and electricity is available. Sites cost $13.

Hotels & Motels The *Mark Twain Guesthouse* (☎ 601-446-8023, 33 Silver St) has 2nd-floor rooms in the rough-and-ready riverfront (a short hike to downtown). There are three rooms varying in size with shared bathroom that cost $55 to $75 (with balcony).

The bottom-end *Natchez Inn* (☎ 601-442-0221, 218 John R Junkin Drive), just down from the Ramada, offers basic rooms for $35. There is another couple of low-end motels across the river in Vidalia, Louisiana, within a mile of the bridge.

The *Radisson Eola* (☎ 601-445-6000, 800-333-3333, 110 Pearl St) has a graceful lobby, restaurant and courtyard that stem from its days as the town's preeminent hotel. Its six stories of guest rooms are recently renovated, kids are welcome, and it's right downtown. Standard rooms are $99, while doubles with unlovely balconies go for $125.

There are several chain motels on highway corridors north and south of town. Of these, the *Ramada Inn* (☎ 601-446-6311, 130 John R Junkin Drive), just east of the Mississippi Bridge on Hwy 84 overlooks the great river and has a pretty good pool. Rates start at $80 a double.

Historic Inns & B&Bs Natchez offers many inns and B&B lodging in grand and beautifully restored historic houses. Though they differ slightly in style, setting and perks, they are all top end (starting at around $90 for a single or double), high-quality accommodations furnished with antiques, with an emphasis on gracious Southern hospitality. Most include an elaborate breakfast; very few have pools.

The local tourist board lists over 40 inns and B&Bs in town and will help you make reservations.

The *Guest House Historic Inn* (☎ 601-442-1054, 201 N Pearl St) is nicely set between the commercial and residential districts downtown. It offers 16 rooms in a two-story 1840 house. Room rates start at $95 and include breakfast.

Five inns are landmark sights in themselves (see Antebellum Homes, earlier in this section, for descriptions): *The Burn* (☎ 601-442-1344, 712 N Union St), with seven rooms and a pool; *Dunleith* (☎ 601-446-8500, 84 Homochitto St), which has 11 rooms; *Governor Holmes House* (☎ 601-442-2366, 207 S Wall St), with four rooms in a Georgetown-style place downtown; *Linden* (☎ 601-445-5472, 1 Linden Drive), off Melrose Ave, with an animated host related to the original owners and offering seven rooms in a country setting; *Monmouth* (☎ 601-442-5852, 36 Melrose Ave), with 30 rooms in perhaps the grandest inn, is also known for its restaurant (which serves non-guests, too); and *Weymouth Hall* (☎ 601-445-2304, 1 Cemetery Rd), with five rooms.

A less expensive B&B in the center of the downtown action is *Wensel House* (☎ 601-445-8577, 206 Washington St), an 1888 two-story Victorian house. Room rates start at $85 for a double and there's a cute cottage that sleeps five for $100.

Places to Eat

Several places to eat in and around the depot offer reasonably priced, family-friendly meals. *Pulley Bones* is an open-air eatery in the old depot. *Fat Mama's Tamales* (☎ 601-442-4548, 500 S Canal St) is a log-cabin with a patio out back; great tamales are $6 a dozen. The *Pig Out Inn*

(☎ *601-442-8050, 116 N Canal St*) is a barbecue place.

At the bluff, ***Cock of the Walk*** (☎ *601-446-8920, 200 N Broadway*) is a casual Southern restaurant serving fried catfish and skillet cornbread. Downtown, ***Pearl St Pasta*** (☎ *601-442-9284, 105 S Pearl St*) serves fresh pasta and vegetables, and has a 2nd-story balcony. Tucked under the hill with an attractive river-view patio is ***Magnolia's*** (☎ *601-446-7670, 49 Silver St*), which is good for surf-and-turf.

A historic inn, ***Monmouth*** (☎ *601-442-5852*), on Melrose Ave at John A Quitman Blvd, serves a fixed-price five-course dinner with high-style plantation ambiance for $35 a person. This is a good way for budget travelers to experience Natchez without an overnight B&B stay. The ***Carriage House*** (☎ *601-445-5151*), on the grounds of Stanton Hall at 401 High St, is a lunch place.

John Martin (☎ *601-445-0605, 21 Silver St*) is an upscale restaurant popular with pilgrimaging pretties. Less frou-frou, the buffet at the casino is your best bet for late-night snacks.

Entertainment
Biscuits & Blues (☎ *601-446-9922, 315 Main St*) has music every weekend and is a good place anytime for ribs, wings and beer. The ***Corner Bar*** (☎ *601-442-2546*), on Canal St at State St, has a great jukebox. ***Under The Hill Saloon*** (☎ *601-446-8023, 25 Silver St*) has bands on weekends. ***King's Tavern*** (☎ *601-446-8845*), on Jefferson St at Rankin St, is a low-key place with acoustic music. The ***Isle of Capri Casino*** (☎ *800-722-5825*) operates around the clock on a riverboat at the bottom of Silver St below town.

Shopping
The **Mostly African Market** (☎ 601-442-5448), 125 St Catherine St, displays and sells handcrafted artwork. Purchases support a children's summer program. It's open Wednesday through Saturday (afternoons only).

The larger historic houses have gift shops selling cotton-boll wreaths, corn-husk dolls and the like.

Getting There & Away
The closest major airports are in Jackson (115 miles northeast of Natchez) and Baton Rouge, Louisiana (100 miles south of Natchez on Hwy 61). It's not advisable to use either, as you can fly into New Orleans and drive to Natchez along a scenic route through Louisiana's Plantation Country (see that chapter for more details). Without stops, this drive will take about as long as it would take to fly, and the car-rental may be less expensive. As well, the Natchez Trace Parkway, which begins here, provides further car-touring options.

Bus service is available from the Greyhound station (☎ 601-445-5291) at 103 Lower Woodville Rd. One bus daily runs between Jackson and Natchez. The bus is routed through Vicksburg; the trip takes 3 hours from Jackson to Natchez and costs $22 one-way.

The Delta Queen Steamboat Company and RiverBarge Excursion Lines (☎ 888-282-1945) run cruises up the Mississippi River that stop in Natchez; see the Riverboat section in the Getting Around chapter.

If you're driving to Jackson from Natchez, take Hwy 61 to I-20 at Vicksburg (1½ hours). You could travel the Natchez Trace Parkway but the journey – at a speed limit of 50 mph – takes two hours. Natchez is a 2½- to three-hour drive from New Orleans along Hwy 61.

Getting Around
Downtown attractions are easily seen on foot. Outlying attractions are within a short drive or comfortable bike ride away (depending on weather). Bike rentals are available from the extremely resourceful and knowledgeable folks at the Natchez Bicycle Center (☎ 601-446-7794), 334 Main St, which is closed on Sunday and Monday but will open by arrangement. The center provides maps of local and regional bike trips of varying lengths. Bike rentals cost $15 for a half day and $20 all day; no rentals to children under 15.

Trolleys run from the visitor center to downtown and Natchez-Under-the-Hill. For 45-minute whiz-by bus tours call them at

☎ 601-446-6345. Horse-drawn carriage tours leave from the depot downtown. Fares are $8 for adults and $4 for children. You can book through the visitor center.

For a cab, call ☎ 601-442-7500.

WOODVILLE & AROUND

From Natchez, Hwy 61 S finds its way to Woodville, a natural stopping point along the drive that also serves as a route to and from Louisiana's Plantation Country.

An attractive courthouse square sits at the center of little Woodville. Around the square, you'll find a free **local history museum** (☎ 601-888-3993), at the corner of Bank St and Boston Row. The museum is closed Saturday afternoon and all day Sunday. Nearby the **L&M Bakery-N-Deli** *(☎ 601-888-3600, 121 Boston Row)* has simple meat-and-three plates.

Off Hwy 24 E, the **Rosemont Plantation** (☎ 601-888-6809) gives visitors a chance to see the boyhood home of Confederate President Jefferson Davis. The plantation is open during the summer only on weekdays, except during Natchez pilgrimages in spring and fall. B&B lodgings are also offered in a cottage on the property.

West of Woodville, Pinckneyville Rd leads to one of the most beautiful natural areas in the state. Follow signs to the **Clark Creek Nature Area**, 13 miles away in the hamlet of Pond. Here winding trails traverse 1200 acres of loess bluffs and hardwood forest, past huge boulders and limestone outcroppings, and under waterfalls (one is 40 feet high). To find the trailhead, look for Pond's large white general store and turn west on the road that goes past the store to Fort Adams. The parking lot and trailhead are to the left. (Note that no restroom is available, and the store does not maintain a public restroom.)

In this corner of the state stands the linchpin of all lower Mississippi River navigation. The Old River Project here attempts to keep water channeled around Baton Rouge and New Orleans, when it would much rather run the quicker, steeper route through the Atchafalaya basin. Hydrologists fear it's just a matter of time before mother nature has her way – with dreaded consequences for communities downriver.

NATCHEZ TRACE

The Natchez Trace began centuries ago as a footpath between the homeland of the Natchez Indians and the game-rich Cumberland River valley. Roughly 440 miles in distance, the trace ran from present-day Natchez to Nashville, Tennessee. As indigenous nations established villages in the vicinity of the trace, the path became an important trade route. Early European explorers such as de Soto traveled along the trace, and French explorers set up trading posts at its northern and southern endpoints.

Use expanded tremendously with increasing European settlement in the late 18th century. Boatmen from as far north as the Ohio River valley would bring their trade down the Mississippi river to the markets of Natchez or New Orleans and return home on foot via the trace after selling the whole lot, boat lumber and all. The route became a post road in 1801 and was later widened to serve as a military road. It was along here that Major General Andrew 'Old Hickory' Jackson marched homeward after the Battle of New Orleans. Travel along the trace was quite comfortable with inns providing shelter and simple meals, but thieves, floods, occasionally unfriendly Indians and annoying insects often sabotaged homeward travelers.

With the advent of the steamboat era, the road was supplanted by river traffic. Gradually the road began to revert to nature, with a brief revival during the Civil War. Slaves were marched along the trace in chains.

A new interest in the trace began in 1909 when the Daughters of the American Revolution initiated a program to mark the old route. The Department of the Interior followed with a national historic designation in 1934. The National Park Service began paving it in the late 1930s.

Today it's a scenic stretch of meandering two-lane road through woodlands and pasture. Pull-outs and short detours lead to Indian mounds, ghost towns, plantation ruins, Civil War battle sites and snippets of the original footpath. You can see old footpaths at various mileposts: 8.7 (near Natchez), 104.5 (north of Jackson) and 221.4 (15 miles south of Tombigbee National Forest).

The parkway begins 8 miles north of downtown Natchez off Hwy 61. Mile posts at the side of the road mark distances from a planned southern terminus at Natchez. Detailed maps listing all sights along the way are available from several ranger offices along the route. The smooth wide parkway (which prohibits commercial traffic) is popular for bicycle touring. Bicyclists can request a packet of bike-touring information from Natchez Trace Parkway visitor center (☎ 800-305-7417), 2680 Natchez Trace Parkway, Tupelo, MS 38804. For local bike rentals, see Getting Around in the Natchez section, earlier in this chapter.

Natchez to Port Gibson

There is much to see within the first 20 or so miles on and around the trace. About 10 miles from Natchez at a short turnoff west is **Emerald Mound**, the second largest Indian mound in the US. It is believed that the Natchez Indians built it for ceremonial purposes and that it also might have served as a meeting and trading place. Built between 1300 and 1600 AD, the mound is interesting not only for its imposing size (35 feet high and 8 acres in area) and proximity to the trace, but it is also somewhat jarringly juxtaposed with a surrounding community of trailer beauty shops and patchwork shacks. At this same turnoff but on the other side of Hwy 61, **Natchez State Park** provides a 24-site wooded campground (less impressively maintained than NPS campgrounds) and fishing at a small lake.

Back along the parkway, the exposed **loess bluffs**, around 12 miles from Natchez, reveal the local geology of loess bluffs, dating from the Ice Age. The **Mt Locust** ranger station, a few miles on, is in a historic inn built in 1783; the inn once served the voyagers traveling the trace on foot or by horse.

A scenic 23-mile driving or biking loop starts at Mt Locust. Bicyclists can park at Mt Locust and ride north along the trace for 5 miles to Hwy 553. A turn west along Hwy 553 leads past Springfield Plantation, a general store (note the crossroads and stay left), Christ Church, Oak Grove and Cedars plantation houses (all homes are private), and through rolling countryside before winding back toward the trace. At the shack 200 yards west of the trace, a 1½-mile loop leads to Emerald Mound. Rejoining the trace after Emerald Mound is another 3 mile journey north to Mt Locust.

Another longer loop follows Hwy 552 to several attractions and the town of Port Gibson. The road leads past **Alcorn College**, founded in 1871 and considered the first land-grant college for African-Americans in the country. At **Windsor Ruins**, only the statuesque columns are left from this evidently once-grand plantation home.

In **Port Gibson**, a small exhibit in the county administration building (☎ 601-437-4994), 510 Market St, attests to the town's Civil Rights movement. (The administration building is open weekdays only.) In 1966, the local African-American community organized a grassroots voter registration drive and an economic boycott of white merchants who were reserving certain jobs and privileges for whites. Three years into the boycott, the merchants sued, and the case dragged on for 13 years until 1982, when the US Supreme Court unanimously affirmed the right of peaceful protest through economic boycott.

The exhibit was produced by Mississippi Cultural Crossroads (☎ 601-437-8905), a community organization that operates out of 507 Market St. Our Mart, next to the county building, was opened in May, 1967 by African-American townspeople to serve the people boycotting white-owned stores.

A colorful children's mural around the corner from the Cultural Crossroads celebrates multiculturalism. The 'Frishman' sign is the last relic of the Jewish-owned department store that once operated in this building; the town once housed a vibrant Jewish community that has since moved to more prosperous regions.

A parallel route to main street runs through an attractive residential district of well-tended historic homes and churches. They say General Grant thought it 'too pretty to burn' when he came through in May 1863. As a result, many antebellum structures remain standing today. ·

A detour off the trace 10 miles northwest of Port Gibson, **Grand Gulf Military Park** (☎ 601-437-5911), on Hwy 61 N, commemorates the scene of a Civil War bombardment in April 1863. The Union fleet had hoped to clear the way for a crossing here, but after five hours of battle with no relief, continued farther south to find another way across. A 42-site campground offers sites for $11; hookups are available.

Port Gibson to Rocky Springs

From Grand Gulf Military Park, north-bound travelers will find diversions at **Sunken Trace**, where you can walk through a deeply eroded stretch of the original route; the **Grindstone Ford** site, where aboriginal artifacts have been found; and a beautiful picnic spot at **Owen Creek Waterfall**. All sites are noticeably signed.

A major rest stop, about 15 miles from Port Gibson, is **Rocky Springs**. In 1860, the town was a prosperous community of more than 2500, with a church, post office and several stores. Devastated by the Civil War, yellow fever, the boll weevil and land erosion, the few survivors packed up and left, leaving behind abandoned buildings. The Methodist church, however, remains open and draws descendants out to pay respects at its cemetery. The nearby park provides a nicely wooded NPS campground (☎ 800-305-7417), which has 22 free sites available on a first-come, first-served basis. There are also hiking routes along the original trace and a ranger station.

Near Utica, the cultural heritage of Jews in the South is explored at the **Museum of the Southern Jewish Experience** (☎ 601-362-6357). To get to the museum take Hwy 18 northeast of Utica, to Morrison Rd east and follow signs to Henry Jacobs Camp. The

'Shalom Y'all' souvenirs are almost worth the trip on their own. The museum can assist travelers interested in tracing Jewish heritage in Mississippi, Memphis and Louisiana.

Northeastern Mississippi

The northeastern corner of the state contains the westernmost reaches of the southern Appalachian forest and is historically one of the least developed areas in the state. Adjacent to the west runs a sliver of the Black Belt, the fertile crescent that sweeps through the South. To the north, the hill country contains some of Mississippi's most scenic countryside – a gently rolling terrain of well-watered forests and cropland. Oxford is the state's literary and intellectual epicenter and home to the University of Mississippi campus.

Access to public land – especially national forests and state parks – is readily available throughout the region. Most locals are drawn to lakes and reservoirs that have swimming beaches; these recreation areas frequently offer trails as well. Tishomingo State Park, just outside of Tupelo, straddles the Natchez Trace Parkway just in from the Alabama line. Farther off the beaten path, the Noxubee National Wildlife Refuge south of Starkville occupies a graceful and compelling landscape of quiet woods and small lakes. Its trail network includes old plank roads that once traversed its swampy corners. In these parks, you will see the small mammals most commonly associated with the South – opossums, armadillos, squirrels, raccoons and bats, though legends of elusive panthers at large still circulate.

This region was a well-used stage for warring factions. During the French and Indian War in 1736, the English and Chickasaw fought against the French and Choctaw. The Chickasaw prevailed in what came to be called the Battle of Ackia, fought near Tupelo. Civil War battles were also fought in the region for control of strategic railroad lines that supplied Atlanta. Union general William T Sherman ordered the defeat of the commanding Confederate general Nathan B Forrest, even 'if it costs 10,000 lives and breaks the Treasury.' The two armies met in Tupelo on July 15, 1864. Though the Union held off additional Confederate attacks and temporarily secured the railroad, neither side could claim complete victory in the Battle of Tupelo. A commemorative monument on W Main St in downtown Tupelo is all that remains of the engagement.

The next major invasion of northeastern Mississippi was by the federal agencies in the first half of the 20th century. The US Army Corps of Engineers constructed the Tennessee-Tombigbee Waterway (or the 'Tenn-Tom') to direct the waters of those rivers from the state of Tennessee clear down to the Gulf of Mexico. A handful of other federal agencies, including the Tennessee Valley Authority (TVA), have had a hand in shaping the economics of the region.

TUPELO
• pop 30,685

Incorporated in 1870 and named after the native Tupelo gum tree, Tupelo is rather proud that it was the first city in the nation to provide electric power to its citizens through the TVA. It was once a railroad hub; today it supports itself through manufacturing. More upholstered furniture is manufactured in and around Tupelo's Lee County than anywhere else in the world. Yet humble Tupelo is notorious around the world as the birthplace of the King of Rock & Roll, Elvis Presley, whose dirt-poor origins here figure largely in the whole Elvis mystique.

Elvis and his family left Tupelo for Memphis when he was 13; he returned to his hometown in 1956 to play the Mississippi-Alabama Fair and Dairy Show to crowds so wild that the National Guard was called in to contain them. Elvis returned again to the fair the following year for a benefit concert with proceeds going to the city's purchase and restoration of his birth-

place, which attracts nearly 100,000 visitors each year.

Tupelo is no city you'd want to go out of your way to visit, beyond paying your respects to the King's birthplace. But because it's the largest city in these parts, and strategically positioned at several major crossroads, you might need to use its resources.

Orientation
The Natchez Trace Parkway and Hwy 78 intersect northeast of downtown Tupelo. Elvis Presley's birthplace is farther east off Hwy 78, and the short detour is well signposted.

Downtown Tupelo, however, is oddly challenging to navigate for a city this size, due to an access freeway of sorts that connects Hwy 78 with Hwy 45. You pretty much just need to stick to Gloster St to find motels, restaurants and other services along its length, with the greatest concentration around the intersection of Gloster and McCullough. The older downtown area is centered on Gloster and Main (an intersection known as 'Crosstown'), about a mile east of this intersection.

Information
The visitor center (☎ 662-841-6521, 800-533-0611) is at 399 E Main St, in front of the big Bancorp South Coliseum. There's also tourist information at the Elvis Presley Museum. There's a Natchez Trace Parkway visitor center (☎ 662-680-4025, 800-305-7417), on the parkway north of Hwy 78, that distributes maps and displays historic exhibits.

The central post office (☎ 662-841-1286) is on Main St at the corner of Church St.

In operation since 1907, Reed's (☎ 662-844-1355, 111 Spring St) hosts events by Southern writers. The Cottage Bookshop (☎ 662-844-1553, 214 N Madison St) is a used bookstore specializing in Mississippian authors and out-of-print books.

The emergency room of the Northeast Mississippi Medical Center can be reached at ☎ 662-841-4157.

Elvis Presley's Birthplace
Off Veterans Blvd in what was once the outskirts of town, the shack that was Elvis

MISSISSIPPI

Presley's birthplace now stands as a shrine to the King of Rock & Roll. The 15-acre park complex (☎ 662-841-1245), at 306 Elvis Presley Blvd, includes a museum and chapel. None of his music is played anywhere on site – this is ground too sacred for such earthly sounds.

The 450-sq-foot **shotgun shack** was built by Vernon Presley and his brother with a borrowed $180. In the front room in 1935, Elvis and his stillborn twin, Jesse, were born on January 8 at 4:35 am. A guide stationed inside collects $1 per person (50¢ for children under 12) and explains that the Presleys lived here until Elvis was three, when the house was repossessed.

The **museum** displays the private, intensely personal collection of items Elvis gave to Janelle McComb, a lifelong family friend of the Presleys. In addition to the jumpsuits and baby pictures of Lisa Marie, on display are the gifts McComb gave to Elvis, including an Elvis-tear-stained poem penned by McComb (smeared reproductions available at the gift shop). Admission $4 for adults and $2 for children.

A tiny **chapel** oriented to overlook the shack, contains Elvis' own bible, donated by his father. Admission is free.

The shack and museum are open Monday to Saturday from 9 am to 5 pm (till 5:30 pm from May through September) and Sunday from 1 to 5 pm.

Other Elvis Sights

Elvis is immortalized all around town – everyone seems to have their own story of who cut the King's hair or who taught Elvis his first chord.

Elvis bought his first guitar in 1946 for $12 at **Tupelo Hardware** (☎ 662-842-4637), 114 W Main St, downtown across from the railroad tracks. His first choice was a rifle, but his mother wouldn't go along with that. Elvis attended grades one to five at **Lawhon School**, on Elvis Presley Drive down the street from his birthplace. His fifth-grade teacher here entered Elvis in a talent contest held at the **fairgrounds** west of town (off W Main at Mulberry Alley) – the soon-to-be King won second prize for a

rendition of 'Old Shep.' Elvis earned A grades in music at **Milam Junior High School**, at Gloster and Jefferson Sts. The Presleys attended the **First Assembly of God** church at 909 Berry St at Adams St.

The only Elvis shrine that serves quarter-pounders, the Crosstown **McDonald's** (☎ 662-844-5505), 372 S Gloster St, across from the Gloster Creek Village mall, contains photo collages and descriptive captions on the life of Elvis, along with a tiny collection of memorabilia.

Tupelo Museum

'Fossilized Crocodile Found in Mississippi May Be the Lost Link' is the first exhibit to greet you at the Tupelo Museum (☎ 662-841-6438), a rambling, eclectic collection of Indian dioramas, sepia photographs of the 'tornador' that swept through town killing 210 in 1936, a Model T, a mannequin in an iron lung, a Swedish massage therapy office and homey postcards from the moon. Don't make this your first stop in Mississippi; season yourself first. The museum is a quick half-mile or so west of the Natchez Trace Parkway off Hwy 6 next to a park. Admission is $1. It's open weekdays 8 am to 4 pm, weekends 1 to 5 pm, and is closed mornings May through September.

Places to Stay

Two state parks on either side of town, *Tombigbee* (☎ 662-842-7669) to the southeast and *Trace* (☎ 662-489-2958) to the west, provide campsites for $13 ($10 for seniors) per night plus swimming and fishing. (See Around Tupelo, below.) Trace has a 600-acre lake for swimming and reportedly great bass fishing, as well as a large backcountry area with trails littered with historic debris. Horses and bikes are allowed on some trails.

The *Elvis Presley Lake & Campground* (☎ 662-841-1304) has pretty campsites by the Elvis Presley Lake. Camping is $8 a night ($13 hookups). Turn north off Hwy 78 between the two gas stations and follow the road about 2 miles.

There's a cluster of motels at the overpass rise at Gloster and McCullough Sts.

The cheapest place in town is the slightly scungy **Commodore Motel** (*☎ 662-840-0285, 1800 Main St*), about a half-mile east of Elvis' birthplace, which charges $30 (cash only) for rooms. (Main St is Business Hwy 78.) The plain **Scottish Inn** (*☎ 662-842-1961, 401 N Gloster St*) has decent small rooms for $35 (single or double); nonsmoking rooms are available.

Places to Eat

Jefferson Place (*☎ 662-844-8696, 823 Jefferson*), off Gloster St, is a Tupelo institution that is run out of a big old house. The bar-and-grill serves steaks and sandwiches 11 am to midnight; it is closed on Sunday.

Entertainment

It's a shame that in the hometown of Elvis you can't hear some good rockabilly, but Tupelo is not that kind of town – though it does host an Elvis Presley tribute week in August. Contact the visitor center for more information.

The 10,000 seat **Tupelo Coliseum** hosts major events, including concerts by nationally known performers, rodeos, the Harlem Globetrotters and Disney on Ice.

Shopping

The Elvis Presley Museum at his birthplace sells a small collection of Elvis-branded cold-drink covers, key chains and the like, but the choicest pieces are the handcrafted guitar-shaped decoupage Elvis clocks for a pricey $35. Postcards proclaiming 'From Tupelo to Graceland!' tell the whole story.

Two shopping malls – the newer one at Barnes Crossing north of town off Hwy 78, and Gloster Creek Village on Gloster St south of Crosstown – provide many department stores and specialty shops, as well as banking services, food courts and cinemas.

Getting There & Around

Greyhound (*☎ 662-842-4557, 800-231-2222*) deposits passengers at a decent bus station downtown at 201 Commerce St, directly across from the Tupelo Coliseum. Buses arrive from and depart to Memphis four times daily. The trip takes about three hours

and costs $24/22 weekends/weekdays. One bus a day travels between Oxford and Tupelo for $12 and takes 1½ hours.

Tupelo is near the junction of Hwy 78 and the Natchez Trace Parkway. Tupelo is an hour from Oxford (47 miles) and 2½ miles from Memphis (104 miles).

Taxi services are available from City Taxicab (*☎ 662-842-5277*) or Tupelo Cab Co (*☎ 662-842-1133*).

AROUND TUPELO

Two historic attractions adjacent to the Natchez Trace Parkway are within five miles north of Tupelo. The closer one is the site of a **Chickasaw village**. An information kiosk overlooking a small field tells the story of the nation that once controlled the territory from central Mississippi to central Tennessee. A **mound site**, a mile or so from the trace, reveals the earthworks constructed by Chickasaw ancestors.

For a nice selection of woodland hiking trails, visit **Tishomingo State Park** (*☎ 662-438-6914*), which straddles the Natchez Trace just in from the Alabama line. A trail network of several loop routes crosses over a swinging wooden bridge, up to rock bluffs, and to a tiny box canyon with a little waterfall. The park sponsors float trips down Bear Creek (canoe rentals available) and also offers a swimming pool, cabins, and a 62-site campground with hookups.

At **Brices Cross Roads National Battlefield**, around 12 miles northwest of Tupelo just off Hwy 45, there are exhibits, a monument, a small cemetery and an empty field commemorating the Confederate victory here in 1864. More Civil War sites – earthworks, the Battery Robinette battle site, and a historic house used as headquarters for both sides – can be found farther north on Hwy 45 in the city of **Corinth**. Historic markers are dotted along Fillmore St. Here you can stop to eat at the old drugstore lunch counter at **Borroum's** (*☎ 662-286-3361, 604 Waldron St*), downtown. Also downtown is **The General's Quarters** (*☎ 662-286-3325, 924 Fillmore St*), at Linden St, a lovely B&B in a Victorian home. Rooms start at $75. (If you're interested in more Civil War sites, you're not far from Shiloh, which is covered in the Tennessee chapter.)

About 20 miles along Hwy 78, **New Albany** is the birthplace of writer William Faulkner. The 'Faulkner Country' brochure traces the local travels of Faulkner and his family (for more information call ☎ 662-534-4354). Special remembrances are held on the late famed author's birthday (September 25).

OXFORD
• pop 10,000

Oxford feels different from the rest of Mississippi. It's bustling and prosperous without the familiar extremes of wealth and poverty. The stately courthouse square continues to be the center of community activity, keeping things to a friendly human scale – folks walk or ride bikes. Galleries, bookstores and cafes reveal the local literary bent.

Oxford is home to the University of Mississippi ('Ole Miss') and a lively intellectual community. The university's acclaimed Center for the Study of Southern Culture presides over the rumination of 'Southernalia,' from cornpone and Elvis cults to high culture. The university's blues archives hold the largest collection of blues recordings and publications in the world.

Things weren't always so pretty here. Many remember the university for some very ugly riots in 1962 that accompanied the enrollment of James Meredith, the first student to integrate the school that is widely considered 'the bastion of the Old South.' Troops were called in, and the price of the protest against Meredith's admission was the death of French journalist Paul Guihard and Oxford resident Ray Gunter. While a Confederate soldier monument occupies a prominent spot on the campus, efforts are underway to construct a Civil Rights memorial. A black student was elected student president in 2000.

The history that's easier to talk about stretches back to 1837, when the town was founded. The university opened a decade later. During the Civil War, Oxford was cap-

tured by Union soldiers and most of its buildings were burned to the ground. The few structures that remain (including from 1838 the Barksdale House, now a B&B) are treasured. But the era that's closest to the town's heart is the early 20th century, when William Faulkner mythologized the area in his famous stories of Yoknapatawpha County. Faulkner's graceful Southern home – Rowan Oak, built in 1844 – provides a personal glimpse into the life of the Bard of Mississippi. On the centenary of his birth, September 25, 1997, the city installed a statue of Faulkner on the courthouse square.

Orientation & Information

The city is centered around Courthouse Square, which is bisected by Lamar Blvd. The campus (technically in its own town of University) is a mile or so west of the town square at the head of University Ave. You can get almost everywhere on foot. There's a visitor center on the square in the yellow house next to City Hall but it's open weekends only. During the week, visit the Oxford Tourism Council (☎ 662-234-4680, 800-758-9177), 111 Courthouse Square next door. Square Books is an excellent bookstore (see Shopping, later in this section). The university radio station, WUMS 92.1 FM has some good music shows including the Hwy 61 blues program on Saturday evenings. There's free Internet access at the campus library.

University of Mississippi

From 80 students enrolled in 1848, the University of Mississippi (☎ 662-915-7211) has grown to an enrollment of 10,000 in 10 colleges and professional schools, including liberal arts, medicine and law. Today its enrollment is 12% African-American.

The university's attractive 2500-acre campus contains several 19th-century buildings shaded by magnolias and dogwood. Some of the most popular activities on campus are sporting events featuring the Ole Miss Rebels and Lady Rebels.

The university's **Center for the Study of Southern Culture** (☎ 662-915-5993) occupies

OXFORD

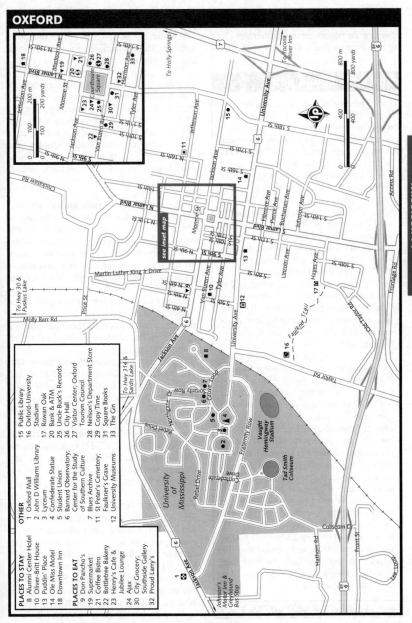

MISSISSIPPI

PLACES TO STAY
8 Alumni Center Hotel
10 Oliver-Britt House
13 Puddin' Place
14 Ole Miss Motel
18 Downtown Inn

PLACES TO EAT
9 Don Pancho's
19 Supermarket
21 Coffee Bistro
22 Bottletree Bakery
23 Henry's Cafe & Jubilee Lounge
24 Ajax
30 City Grocery; Southside Gallery
32 Proud Larry's

OTHER
1 Oxford Mall
2 John D Williams Library
3 Lyceum
4 Confederate Statue
5 Student Union
6 Barnard Observatory; Center for the Study of Southern Culture
7 Blues Archive
11 St Peter's Cemetery; Faulkner's Grave
12 University Museums
15 Public Library
16 Oxford-University Stadium
17 Rowan Oak
20 Bank & ATM
25 Uncle Buck's Records
26 City Hall
27 Visitor Center; Oxford Tourism Council
28 Neilson's Department Store
29 Copy Time
31 Square Books
33 The Gin

the 1857 Barnard Observatory building on Grove Loop. Established in 1977, the center runs degree programs in Southern studies. Its faculty members, directed by Charles

The Endangered Rebel

The University of Mississippi, whose nickname 'Ole Miss' is derived from the pet name for the mistress of a plantation, is facing an identity crisis. Its widely recognized symbols – white-haired mascot 'Colonel Reb' and its Rebels sports teams – are under attack. Like much Old South imagery, these symbols are treasured by some as sources of Southern pride, and are offensive to others because of their relationship to slavery. Yet what does the University of Mississippi stand for if not tradition? To purists, any proposed changes to the university's mascots are seen as tantamount to asking the pope to update the Church's stand on birth control.

Over the past couple of decades, Ole Miss has watered down its Confederate associations without really tackling the issue head on. Colonel Reb now looks more like a sporty Santa Claus than a bristling slave-owning soldier. 'Dixie' is no longer the Rebel's fight song but the re-orchestrated anthem still has obvious Confederate hooks. The university disassociated itself from the Confederate battle flag in the early 1980s but a sea of the flags were still waved at home football games until the late 1990s when the student union banned them. But in the skittering sideways fashion that change occurs, the ban was not because Dixie was damned, but because sticks were deemed dangerous. And the contraband still makes an appearance at pre-game picnics.

And Mississippi's government institutions aren't setting the students a great example. Debate on a new state flag stuttered in 2000 when conservatives found a loophole in Mississippi's constitution, which meant that the current flag wasn't officially the state flag. Therefore, they argued, the question of a 'new' state flag is moot.

Reagan Wilson (co-author of the *Encyclopedia of Southern Culture* and *Baptized in Blood*), are preeminent scholars in Southern lore. Its publications include the magazines *Living Blues* and *Mississippi Folklife*.

The center hosts special events to examine and celebrate Southern culture (see Special Events, later in this section). Past conferences have delved into the cult of Elvis and Southern culinary traditions. The center's welcoming offices usually have a small exhibit of some kind on display (and we're eager to see them expand their Southern kitsch collection upstairs, which presently includes vials of alleged Elvis sweat).

The university's **blues archive** (☎ 662-915-7753) contains the largest collection of blues recordings and publications in the world, including BB King's personal collection. It aims to archive and provide materials for serious researchers but anyone can go in and ask to listen to some blues recordings. For the casual visitor, there's really nothing to see but a few posters and locked stacks of tape and vinyl. Nevertheless, it remains a touchstone on the blues pilgrimage. It's in the modern Farley Hall across from the center.

The papers and mementos of native sons William Faulkner (including his Nobel citation) and James Meredith are displayed at the **John D Williams Library** (☎ 662-915-5858), behind the Greek Revival lyceum.

On University Ave at 5th, outside the campus gates, the **University Museums** building (☎ 662-915-7073) contains several collections of ancient, decorative, fine and folk arts worth a look. Admission is free; it is closed on Monday.

Faulkner's Home & Grave

The author's home of Rowan Oak (☎ 662-234-3284) is today a spiritual center for literary pilgrims and aspiring writers (its curator Cynthia Shearer is a novelist herself). The grounds and old house at Rowan Oak on Old Taylor Rd gracefully evoke the spirit of the Nobel laureate William Faulkner, who bought the property in 1930 and lived here until his death in

The Oxford of Mississippi

I discovered that my little postage stamp of native soil was worth writing about and that I would never live long enough to exhaust it. It opened up a gold mine of people, as I created a cosmos of my own.

– William Faulkner

1962. The university acquired it in 1972 from Faulkner's daughter. Built in 1840, the sparsely furnished house is set down in an arcade of oak and cedar. Here the writer produced his Snopes trilogy – *Sanctuary*, *Light in August* and *A Green Bough* – along with *Absalom, Absalom!* and *A Fable* (the story outline for which remains sketched on the wall of Faulkner's office). Rowan Oak is open Tuesday through Saturday from 10 am to noon and 2 to 4 pm, and Sunday from 2 to 4 pm only (closed on Monday and major holidays). Admission is free.

The Faulkner Trail leads through Bailey's Woods adjacent to Rowan Oak towards the university's baseball stadium (about a 10-minute walk).

Faulkner's grave is about a half-mile northeast of Rowan Oak at the cemetery on Jefferson Ave at 16th. Go down 16th St to the base of the hill; the family grave is several steps in from the worn pull-out.

Special Events

The university's Center for the Study of Southern Culture sponsors the annual Conference for the Book in April and the Faulkner Conference in August. The city hosts a Double Decker Arts Festival with plenty of local music on the last Saturday in April. Home football games are preceded by huge hobnobbing picnics in the grove – a real slice of Southern life. The season runs from late August to late November.

Places to Stay

Camping You can camp at two lake recreation areas around 10 miles outside of town;

rates are around $5 a night for primitive sites. The USFS **Puskus Lake campground** (☎ 662-252-2633) is northeast off Hwy 30, and the Army Corps of Engineers maintains several campgrounds around the **Sardis Lake reservoir** (☎ 662-487-1345), northwest off Hwy 314.

Motels & Hotels The low-end establishment downtown is the **Ole Miss Motel** (☎ 662-234-2424, 1517 University Ave), a few blocks from the square but still within easy walking distance. Modest singles/doubles are $30/35. The family who runs it say they may be able to pick folks up at the Greyhound stop. **Johnson's Motor Inn** (☎ 662-234-3611, 2305 W Jackson Ave) is friendly, clean and cheap ($32/35), but you'd need a car to stay here. Several budget motel franchises can be found around exits off the Hwy 6 Bypass.

Right on campus, the **Alumni Center Hotel** (☎ 662-232-7047, 888-486-7666, hotel@olemiss.edu, 172 Grove Loop) provides rooms with private bath for $55/63 singles/doubles.

Inns A reasonable, comfortably worn choice is **Oliver-Britt House** (☎ 662-234-8043, 512 Van Buren Ave), three blocks from the square; rates start at $45 for a single, add $10 for doubles and on weekends, when breakfast is provided. **Puddin' Place** (☎ 662-234-1250, 1008 University Ave) is a grand B&B with a lovely verandah and fireplaces in each room. It's $100 per night (single or double) including a full breakfast.

Places to Eat

Many restaurants shut down during term breaks.

The **Bottletree Bakery** (☎ 662-236-5000, 923 Van Buren Ave) serves pastries and espressos in an arty interior just off the square. **Coffee Bistro** (☎ 662-281-8188, 107 N 13th St) has entertainment some nights and is open to midnight. The cafe at **Square Books** spills out onto the balcony overlooking the square.

At **City Grocery** (☎ 662-232-8080, 152 Courthouse Square), the nouveau Southern specialties include shrimp and cheese grits and 'angels on horseback' (an elaborate smoked oyster dish) served at papered tables inside an old brick grocery. Lunch entrées are $9 to $12, dinner gets up around $20; there's a good wine list too.

For great chicken and rice or fried catfish, there's **Don Pancho's** (☎ 662-238-2736, 512 Jackson Ave), a tiny five-table place tinged with flavors from the Dominican Republic. **Proud Larry's** (☎ 662-236-0050, 211 S Lamar Blvd) serves thick burgers, pizza, calzone and pasta, and there's live entertainment on weekends.

Ajax (☎ 662-232-8880, 118 Courthouse Square) does great Southern-with-a-twist: tamale pie is $9 and the sweet potato side dish is sugary enough to save for dessert. **Henry's Cafe and Jubilee Lounge** (☎ 662-236-3757, 1006 Jackson Ave E) does wraps, po-boys and pasta in a (nearly) New York hangout.

Two far-flung restaurants are a good excuse for a drive. Eight miles east on Hwy 334, the **Yocona River Inn** (☎ 662-234-2464) serves good crawfish pie. It's open for dinner Thursday through Sunday. On Old Taylor Rd, **Taylor Grocery** (☎ 662-236-1716) is a classic catfish house open Thursday to Sunday from 5:30 to 10 pm and for Sunday lunch. A whole catfish dinner with hush puppies is $8.95. Old Taylor Rd is west on Hwy 6.

Entertainment

Thursday and Friday are the main nights for live music but you can track down sounds most nights during the academic year. The free entertainment weekly *Oxford Town* lists what's happening where; it's distributed at the tourist office and other places downtown. **Proud Larry's** (see Places to Eat) usually has the best bands. **The Gin** (☎ 662-234-0024) at the bottom of Harrison Ave near S 14th St is a rowdy college-band venue. You can catch readings at Square Books (see Shopping, below).

Shopping

More of a cultural center than a mere place to shop, Square Books (☎ 662-236-2262, 800-648-4001), 160 Courthouse Square, is the heart of Oxford's literary community, and the best bookstore in the South. Within two stories of warping plank floors that once belonged to a drugstore (the sign remains outside), Square Books packs stacks of titles and specializes in Southern writers and themes. It schedules a full calendar of author readings, and their patio cafe overlooking the courthouse is a gathering place for writers and readers. Used titles are down the street at Off Square Books. They're both open until at least 9 pm most nights.

Titles worth searching for include the Center for Southern Culture's *Living Blues* magazine, the *In Search of Elvis* conference papers, and the bimonthly *Oxford American*, published by popular novelist John Grisham, who maintains a family compound nearby.

Also around the square, Southside Gallery (☎ 662-234-9090), 150 Courthouse Square, exhibits contemporary arts, crafts and photography including folk art.

One of the oldest stores in the nation, Neilson's Department Store (☎ 662-234-1161), 119 Courthouse Square, started as a trading post out of a log cabin in 1839; nowadays it sells Villager blouses to sorority co-eds from its 1897 building on the square.

On the other side of the square, Uncle Buck's Records (☎ 662-234-7744) stocks recordings from local label Fat Possum Records (☎ 662-236-3110), which records many Delta blues musicians.

Getting There & Away

Greyhound (☎ 662-234-0094, 800-231-2222) runs a scheduled service from 2625 W Oxford Loop (off W Jackson Ave). From Oxford to downtown Memphis, the fare is $20 one-way. The fare to Tupelo (1½ hours) is $13.50; Jackson (nine hours), $59.50. Take a taxi from the bus stop to downtown Oxford.

Oxford is near the intersection of Hwys 6 and 7. The drive to Memphis is 1½ hours along Hwy 6 and I-55 N; to Tupelo is an hour along Hwy 6; and to Jackson is three hours along Hwy 6 and I-55 S.

Getting Around

There's no local bus. There are a couple of taxis; call ☎ 662-234-2250.

HOLLY SPRINGS

• pop 7261

Holly Springs' citizenry is proud of its Confederate civic organizations and the annual pilgrimage of antebellum homes. In addition, the town has found itself notorious for a very peculiar Elvis shrine. Oh, and *USA Today* named its Phillips Grocery as having the best hamburgers in the country. Holly Springs is north of Oxford on Hwy 7 near the junction of Hwy 78.

Stop at the chamber of commerce (☎ 662-252-2943), off the square at 150 S Memphis St, for information about house tours and the local history museum.

Phillips Grocery (☎ 662-252-4671, 541 Van Dorn) serves good burgers and fried okra. It's very close to the downtown square but tricky to find. To get there, follow Van Dorn a half-mile east from the square; at the lights near the gas station, you must veer left (up the hill) to continue along Van Dorn. Phillips is a block up on the right.

One of the best juke joints in the state – and that means the world – *Junior Kimbrough's*, 10 miles west of Holly Springs, burned down in April 2000. Though Junior passed on a couple of years earlier, his sons had been keeping the place jumping and its loss is a heavy blow to the blues scene. David and Kenny Kimbrough vowed to rebuild Junior's – ask around to see if they've done so.

Graceland Too

Paul MacLeod, by all evidence the world's most devoted Elvis fan, has dedicated his life to tracking the course of Elvis' live and posthumous career. Mr MacLeod has turned his house into a shrine wallpapered with Elvis posters, memorabilia and likenesses. His son, Elvis Aaron Presley MacLeod, used to live here, but is now apparently pursuing other interests in New York.

MacLeod Sr imitates Elvis with little encouragement and tells stories about the used carpet he got from the jungle room at Graceland – he sells tiny swatches of it in dime-store picture frames for around $10; folks have asked to be buried with their used Elvis carpet swatches, so he says.

This faux Graceland (☎ 662-252-7954), 200 Gholson Ave at Randolph St, will open its doors at nearly any hour of the day or night for pilgrims. It's $5 a visit – after three visits you're proclaimed a lifetime member and are entitled to have a Polaroid taken of you in a leather jacket with MacLeod standing by your side (there are walls of such snapshots). You'll find it two blocks east and one block south of Courthouse Square. (Follow Hwy 4 east; when it makes a 90-degree turn at the Christ Episcopal Church, you're a block away.)

Getting There & Away

The Greyhound (☎ 662-252-1353) bus stop is at the United Center, 1000 Craft St. It's a 40-minute trip to Oxford ($9.50).

Holly Springs is just north of the intersection of Hwys 78 and 7. Holly Springs is 29 miles north of Oxford on Hwy 7; it takes about half an hour by car.

STARKVILLE

• pop 18,458

If Oxford becomes too civilized for you, head to Starkville, the home of Mississippi State University. (In Mississippi, eldest sons attend Ole Miss; the rest go to State.) It's a laid-back town – nowhere near quaint – with a diverse population, nearby wilderness, a beatnik cafe, historic hotel, and the best public radio station in Mississippi. (Driving around the conservative heartland twisting the dial between Christian broadcasting and country-music stations, it's a shock to pick up ska on WMSV 91.1 FM.)

Orientation & Information

Signs to downtown lead drivers to the small Main St strip with shops, restaurants and the landmark State House Hotel at Jackson St. Farther east, Main St turns into University Drive, which leads to the campus.

The Starkville Visitors and Convention Council (☎ 662-323-3322, 800-649-8687) is at 322 University Drive. The wonderful Book Mart (☎ 662-323-2844) on 120 E Main stocks local-interest publications, along with the *New York Times*. There's a laundry on University Drive next to the Bulldog Deli.

Mississippi State University

Founded in 1878, Mississippi State University (☎ 662-325-2450) enrolls 14,000 students in 10 colleges and professional schools annually. Its attractive campus features several 19th-century brick buildings and is near the Noxubee Wildlife Refuge to the south. The university's home team, the Bulldogs, excels in basketball (advancing at one point to the Final Four in the NCAA tournament), and their football and baseball games are also popular. The popular novelist John Grisham is a celebrated alumnus and there's an exhibition of the page-turner's papers.

The campus also has a wine-making lab, a drive-through rose garden, an entomological collection and cheese for sale at the campus dairy. The **Templeton Music Museum** (☎ 662-325-8301) displays old Victrolas and ragtime-era antiques.

Protected Wilderness Areas

Several trails and old roads in the **Noxubee National Wildlife Refuge** (☎ 662-323-5548), south of town, attract hikers and mountain bikers, as well as naturalists for the resident bald eagles, alligators and bobcats. From the university's veterinary school, follow the country road towards Oktoc southeast for around 8 miles to Bluff Lake Rd. Trail maps are available at the headquarters in the center of the refuge, across the Noxubee River.

The rolling woods of the **Tombigbee National Forest** are 25 miles southwest of Starkville. The ranger station (☎ 662-285-3264) directly north distributes information and maps on the area's hunting, fishing, horseback riding and hiking trails.

Places to Stay

At Choctaw Lake, the USFS maintains an 18-site *campground* (☎ *800-280-2267 for*

reservations) set on a wooded hill of pine and dogwood overlooking the lake; sites cost $13 with hookups. The campground and swimming beach are both open from late spring to early fall. The *University Motel* (☎ *662-323-1421)*, on Hwy 82 W, is a rundown motel in a rundown block, but it's cheap and only a block from Main St; rates are $24/35 for a single/double.

The *State House Hotel* (☎ *662-323-2000)*, at the corner of Main and Jackson Sts, is a rare find. It's a handsomely restored 1925 hotel that caters mostly to long-term executives but they usually have rooms free for overnighters. Smart suites are $50/75, and you're right in the center of town.

For B&B lodging, *Caragen House* (☎ *662-323-0340, 1108 Hwy 82 W)* provides guest rooms in a white villa 2 miles from town. Rooms are $85 a night and $100 on weekends.

Places to Eat

Easy Street (☎ *662-324-2834, 122 N Jackson St)*, between Main St and Hwy 82, is a funky hangout that serves coffee, pastries and vegetarian stuff. The *City Bagel Cafe* (☎ *662-323-3663, 511 University Drive)*, across from the cemetery, has coffee, fresh lemonade and sandwiches; it has a nice patio. The *Bulldog Deli* (☎ *601-324-3354, 702 University Drive)* makes generous sandwiches next door to a laundry and across from *Flo & Eddie's* (☎ *601-324-6000, 801 University Drive)*, which has a long sociable bar and regular entertainment.

Rosey Baby (☎ *662-324-1949, 300 S Jackson St)* operates out of the old depot across the tracks; it serves Cajun food with a zydeco soundtrack and occasionally hosts live entertainment.

Getting There & Away

The Greyhound (☎ 662-323-3474) bus stop is at Greenoaks Superette, 570 Hwy 12 W. Tickets to Tupelo cost $19.50 (2½ hours); to Jackson, $28 (3½ hours); and to Biloxi, $60.50 (10½ hours).

If driving to Starkville, take Alt 45 S from Tupelo, turn west at Hwy 82. It's 63 miles (1¼ hours).

WEST POINT
• pop 8489

On Hwy 45 south of Tupelo, West Point has an old downtown area where the most visible industry is the manufacture of Big Yank camouflage fatigues. Along a rundown strip of abandoned storefronts, *Anthony's* (☎ *662-494-0316, 116 W Main St*) is a regional landmark mostly because of the blues nights held here on the first Saturday of every month. Folks come from as far as Memphis to hear famed Delta musicians such as Mojo Buford, RL Burnside and the Mississippi Allstars. Admission is $8, and reservations are essential.

Inside the old grocery store, fettuccine Alfredo and steaks are served at booths and red-and-white checkerboard tables while old ceiling fans overhead stir the air; there's a bar too. There's a Howlin' Wolf Blues Festival in town on Labor Day weekend.

WAVERLEY PLANTATION

Between West Point and Columbus, on the banks of the Tombigbee River, south of Hwy 50, lies an antebellum plantation house that's a legend in itself. Waverley (☎ 662-494-1399) was one of the biggest plantations in the pre–Civil War South. It was a self-contained community of 50,000 acres and hundreds of residents, 200 of whom were slaves. In its demise it was occupied by two bachelor brothers; on the death of the surviving brother in 1913 the estate was fought over by extended family members and sat vacant for 50 years. The house managed to hold on to its three floors of carved balconies, marble mantels, molten-gold leaded windows, ceiling-high mirrors, and other exquisite architectural details. In 1962, the family finally decided to sell. The current owner has stocked it with period antiques and opens it to tours. It's stunning; a highlight is the three-story-high octagonal gallery.

It's open daily from 9 am to 5 pm. Admission is $7.50 for the house tour, with reduced admission to visit the grounds only.

COLUMBUS
• pop 23,799

The town of Columbus is on Hwy 82 east of Starkville. The Victorian home and birthplace of the famous author Tennessee Williams is now the Mississippi Welcome Center (☎ 662-328-0222, 800-689-3983), 300 Main St at 3rd St.

Over a dozen of the town's many antebellum houses are opened to the public during the annual pilgrimage in early April. Another historic highlight is **Friendship Cemetery**. By marking the graves of Union soldiers (a post-war gesture of reconstruction) in this cemetery, locals inspired the national observance of Memorial Day. During the pilgrimage, a costumed Confederate officer tells tales of famous crypt residents by candlelight.

The grand old brick buildings that make up the historic campus of the **Mississippi University for Women** is also in Columbus. The college counts writer Eudora Welty among its distinguished alumnae. These days it's co-ed but still dominated by women.

Riverhill Antiques (☎ 662-329-2669), 122 3rd St S, occupies two Victorian houses side by side (near the welcome center) and is jammed with antiques from refined crystal to wooden implements.

Columbus is on the 234-mile **Tenn-Tom Waterway**, a canal system linking the Tennessee and Tombigbee Rivers to the Gulf of Mexico. The waterway is lined with recreation areas, swimming beaches, campgrounds and marinas along its length, and is popular for recreational boating. Call the Tenn-Tom Development Authority (☎ 662-327-2142), which is headquartered in Columbus, for waterway maps, recreation directories and other information.

A number of old homes operate as B&Bs. *Arbor House* (☎ *662-241-5596, 518 College St*) is one antique-filled option; rates start at $95. The welcome center can help with other bookings.

Alabama

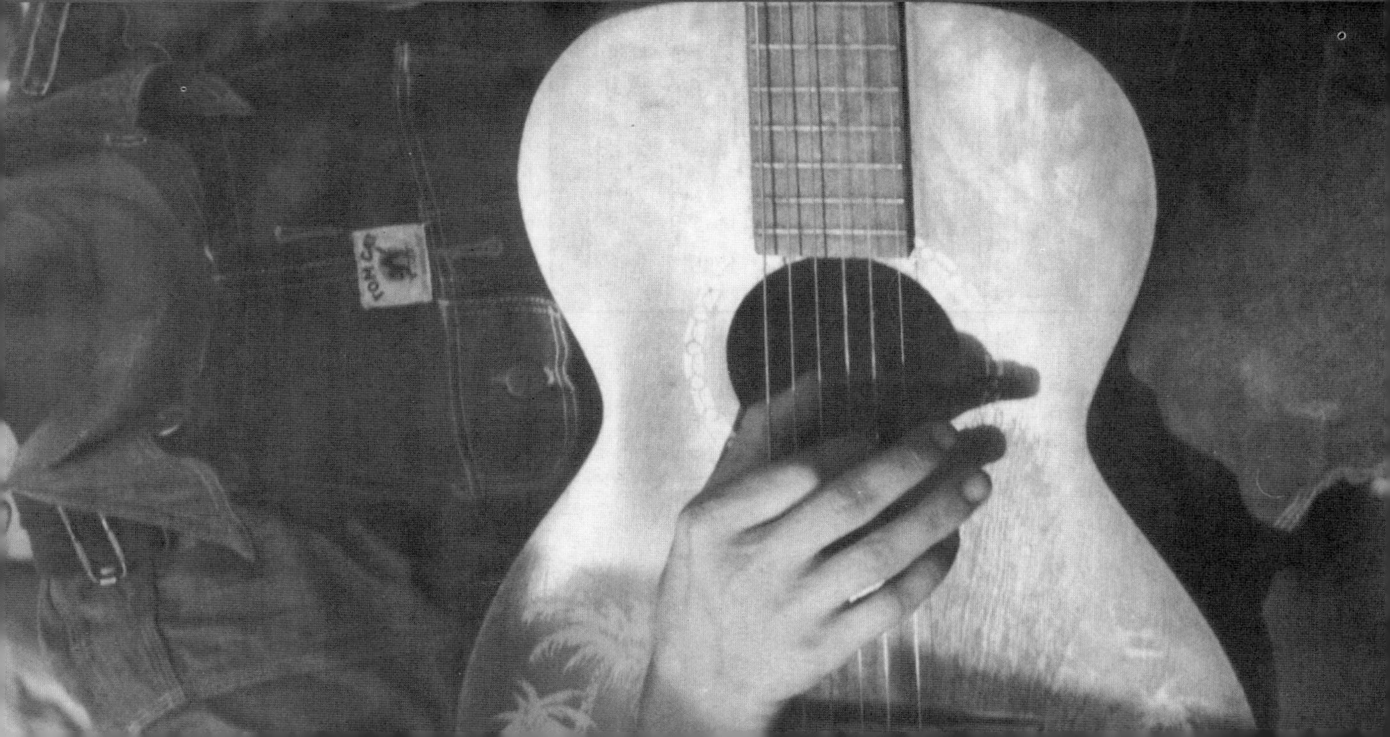

Alabama

Facts about Alabama

Alabama can't shake its reputation. It's thought of more for its past – rednecks, rebels, segregation, discrimination and public officials who made the news for all the wrong reasons – than its present. There's no denying the importance of the events of the past. Indeed, they have helped Alabamians move closer toward racial harmony. Not just by removing the 'Whites Only' and 'Colored Restrooms' signs, but by telling a

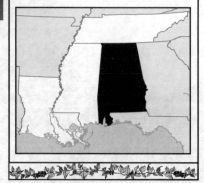

more complete history. It's impossible for visitors to miss the extra effort that is made to try to correct the wrongs of the past. Guides in most museums, historic houses and parks acknowledge the contributions made by Native Americans and African-Americans as well as European Americans. Visitors learn that before Hernando de Soto 'discovered' Alabama, there were sophisticated Native American cultures that created beautifully embellished pottery, held elaborate ceremonies, created an alphabet and constructed large earthen mounds. It's also made clear that African-Americans were not simply slaves. They built many of Alabama's historic houses, painted many of its masterpieces and fueled the cotton empire.

History

According to historians, Alabama maintained its traditional white racial and political traditions longer than any Southern state other than Mississippi, severely retarding its development. However, in the last few decades, Alabama has experienced much political and social turmoil and change.

Telling evidence of the seismic political change that Alabama has undergone is the political transformation of former governor George Wallace. Once the very symbol of the system of white supremacy, Wallace underwent an about-face from staunch segregationist in the 1960s to supporter of multiracial politics in his successful fourth-term campaign in 1982. Before his death in 1998, Wallace sought out, and usually was granted, forgiveness from a number of Civil Rights leaders, including Jesse Jackson and Coretta Scott King, Martin Luther King Jr's widow.

Long viewed condescendingly and inaccurately for its largely rural redneck population who, as the stereotype went, didn't wear shoes and ate dirt, Alabama shifted from a predominantly rural to a predominantly urban population for the first time in its history in the early 1970s. Outsiders

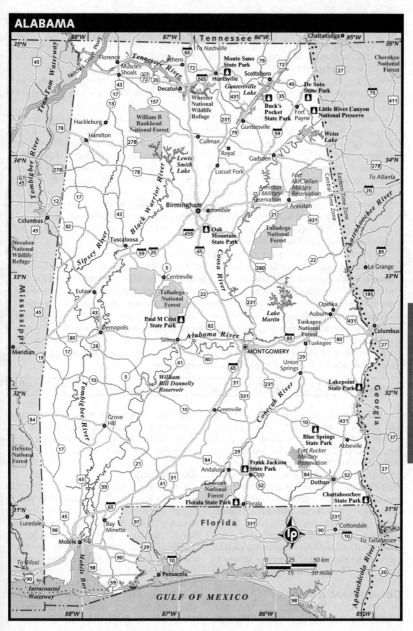

ALABAMA

Alabama's Early Residents

While the state was named after the Alibamu tribe, Alabama's most notable indigenous group were the Cherokee. In 1838, US Army outposts in northern Alabama served as staging points for the infamous forced removal of 16,000 Cherokee to Oklahoma. Along the way, 4000 of them died of exposure, starvation, and disease. They call the experience *Nunadautsun't* or 'the trail where we cried.' History would call it the Trail of Tears. The Alabama section of their route roughly parallels US Highway 72.

The Cherokee population, estimated at 50,000 before European expansion, was actually spread throughout the southern Appalachian Mountains. Following the American Revolution, the Cherokee willingly embraced European customs and culture. During the early 1800s, they adopted their government to a written constitution. They established their own courts and schools, and achieved a standard of living that was the envy of their white neighbors. Many of them owned African slaves, adopted European architecture and dress and invited Christian missionaries to establish churches. This did not impress American settlers, who wanted their land and not their friendship. President Andrew Jackson arranged for the forced removal of the Cherokee in defiance of a US Supreme Court ruling. Among those who managed to avoid removal in Alabama were a small splinter group of Cherokee whose 22,000 descendants today identify themselves as the Echota Cherokee, based in the town of Warrior.

A literally noteworthy chapter of Cherokee Indian history was the invention of a written language by Sequoyah (George Gist) in 1821 near Fort Payne. Sequoyah perfected the Cherokee alphabet, which consisted of 86 characters representing every sound in the tribe's language. His place in the international linguistic hall of fame is secured by the fact that when he began to devise the alphabet, Sequoyah was not literate in *any* language. He grasped the concept of speech-to-symbol written communication and spent several years perfecting the system. The new alphabet served the tribe well for many decades, and for a period of time there was considerable publication in the language. A Cherokee newspaper, the *Phoenix*, began publication in the native language in February, 1828. Many Cherokees still learn the syllabic writing, although several recent grammars and dictionaries have added or substituted a romanized script.

flooded in and by the early 1990s the state had grown to be the US's 22nd largest. However, the black population decreased from 40% to 25% as blacks continued to leave the state. This occurred especially in rural areas where the number of farms and factories had declined sharply. Similarly, coal and iron mining and automobile manufacturing shed workers, costing blacks thousands of high-paying union jobs. At the same time, however, the number of black elected office-holders, including judges, mayors and members of Congress, soared to more than 700, higher than ever before.

Government & Politics

In 1999, Don Siegelman, a democrat, become the state's 56th governor. The state legislature has 35 senators and 105 representatives elected for four-year terms. Alabama has two US senators, seven representatives and nine electoral votes.

Geography

At its widest point, the state measures 210 miles. Its length is 329 miles. There are 53 miles of coastline and reportedly the country's largest system of inland waterways – nearly 1000 miles in total length. Thirteen major rivers crisscross the state, carving it into seven distinct physiographic regions. These rivers helped determine the state's history. Native Americans settled fertile river valleys, giving the state one of the richest Indian histories in the country; Hernando de Soto and other Europeans explored the state by river; and the more than 1000 miles of navigable inland waterways allowed cotton to be sent to the port of Mobile, where it was shipped to markets around the world.

Recognizing the importance of navigable waterways, attempts were made as early as 1871 to improve navigation along 457 miles of the river system with the use of locks and dams, making many of them resemble long, arcing lakes. Alabama's rivers continue to influence the economy. The system moves more than 17 million tons of goods each year, including coal, iron and manganese ores, petroleum products, limestone, sand and gravel, logs, chemicals, steel products, sulfur and agricultural products.

Alabama has a geographical diversity unparalleled for a state of its size. Moving south from the rugged foothills of the Appalachians, the waterfalls, canyons and mountain lakes give way to the hilly, richly forested central highlands, before turning into the gently rolling hills of the Black Belt farm country and the lowlands that grow wiregrass and crops. These gradually yield to the marshes, bays and white-sand beaches of the Mobile and Tensaw Delta and the Gulf Coast. The highest point is Cheaha Mountain (2407 feet) in the Talladega National Forest.

As a result of its geographical variety, Alabama's ecological diversity ranks behind only California and Florida. Forests, primarily pine, cover about two-thirds of the state. More than 300 types of wildflowers are native. Azaleas, in resplendent bloom throughout the state in March and April, were brought to Alabama in the late 1700s from France. Alligators inhabit the delta swamps and wetlands north and east of Mobile and geese and ducks winter in the river wetlands of Decatur. Dauphin Island is on the migratory flyway, making it an ideal spot for watching exhausted, hungry birds returning from Central America.

Alabama and many of its rivers, counties and towns take their names from the Native Americans who lived here for thousands of years. Alabama, from the Alibamu Indians, means 'clearer of the thicket.'

Economy

As the economies of moderate neighboring states grew, Alabama suffered major economic setbacks during the racial turmoil of the 1950s and '60s.

In the 1960s, two-thirds of Alabama's rural land, mostly cotton plantations, was converted to forests for lumbering, making forest products the leading agricultural

Cotton Fever

Following the 1816 Treaty of Fort Jackson and the cession of Indian lands to the US, Alabama's cotton rush began. Like the California gold rush of 1849, tens of thousands of fortune hunters poured into the state, clearing land, planting and making fortunes selling cotton to English and American mills. By 1849 Alabama was the country's leading cotton producer, holding a 23% market share.

Indeed, cotton was king in Alabama, but the king was ruthless. Overplanting depleted nutrients from the land and it was labor intensive – between 1820 and 1860 Alabama's population rose from 127,000 to 964,000, with nearly half being slaves who worked the fields.

The Civil War was a major setback for the cotton industry. By the end of the war, the economy was a disaster. Believing cotton would pull them out of postwar economic ruin, Alabama's farmers rushed to plant more cotton and returned to a single-crop economy. Large landowners instituted sharecropping and tenant farming to replace the slave labor force. However, this new form of bondage proved no less cruel. It left the poor black and white sharecroppers and tenant farmers struggling and indebted, and made merchants, bankers and large landowners rich. For the next 45 years cotton reigned again.

It wasn't until 1911 that cotton was dethroned. It took the boll weevil less than five years to bring down the cotton industry, permanently altering the Southern economy.

product in the state. Poultry production also saw significant increases. By the 1970s Alabama was the biggest lumber producer in the South and the third-largest poultry producer in the country. In the 1980s, mills gave way to malls. The traditional textile and steel industries were eclipsed by service industries, light manufacturing, the aquaculture of catfish, construction and, in Huntsville, aerospace and high-tech industries.

The 1970s and 1980s brought roller-coaster economics to the nation as a whole and to a state whose economic ranking among the 50 states was already 47th. Alabama's per capita income was one of the lowest nationwide, a fifth of the population lived below the poverty line, infant mortality was the highest in the country and 12.5% of the people couldn't read.

Alabama's population is now 4.3 million, but the economic situation for schools, health care and the state's poor remains bleak. Many Alabamians blame politicians, whom they say have refused to pass meaningful tax and educational reforms. In turn, politicians blame the taxpayers for resolutely defeating local attempts to raise taxes for education.

Arts

Historically a state with a large rural population, it should not be surprising that much of Alabama's best art comes from the countryside. Folk artists received their greatest recognition in 1994 when Crane Hill Publishers published *Revelations: Alabama's Visionary Folk Artists*, a glossy, in-depth look at the state's distinctive culture through art.

Music Alabama boasts a long, impressive musical tradition, from Florence's WC Handy (the 'father of the blues') to the contemporary rock of Muscle Shoals' Fame Studios, from Hank Williams Sr to the group Alabama. The state's musical excellence is reflected in the Alabama Music Hall of Fame in Tuscumbia and the Alabama Jazz Hall of Fame in Birmingham.

Literature Race is a common theme in Alabamian literature for white and black writers. One of the most poignant examples is the work of novelist, critic and biographer Albert Murray, who grew up in the South during the 1920s. Murray's first book, a collection of essays called *The Omni-Americans: New Perspectives on Black Experience and American Culture* (1970), was republished as *The Omni-Americans: Some Alternatives to the Folklore of White Supremacy* in 1983. It was primarily for this work, which deals with the dilemmas of race and American identity and asserts that the similarities between American blacks and whites are more striking than their differences, that he was inducted into the American Academy of Arts and Letters in 1997.

Born in Monroeville in 1957, Mark Childress started as a journalist but turned to writing novels in 1982. *Crazy in Alabama* (1993), his most celebrated work, which has also become a movie, delivers two parallel stories set in the bitter, racially charged 1960s South.

Another Monroeville native, Harper Lee, achieved worldwide fame when her only novel, *To Kill a Mockingbird*, won the Pulitzer Prize for fiction in 1961. Set in a small Alabama town during the 1930s, the story is narrated by a six-year-old girl named Scout, who relates the events surrounding a court case in which her father, attorney Atticus Finch, defends a black man wrongly charged with raping a white woman.

Few critics took note when Winston Groom received the Southern Library Association Best Fiction Award in 1980 for *As Summers Die*, but recognition eventually came to Groom when his 1986 book, *Forrest Gump*, became a popular motion picture.

Visit the Alabama Writers' Forum's Web site at www.writersforum.org for more information on Alabama's active literary community.

Information

Tourist Offices The Alabama Bureau of Tourism & Travel (☎ 800-252-2262, www.touralabama.org), PO Box 4927, Montgomery, AL 36103-4927, runs eight welcome centers along the interstate highways just inside the state's border. They're open 24 hours a day, but they are staffed only from 8 am to 5 pm. These centers are all well signed and usually have their own on-ramps. Their main purpose is to provide a resting point for some fresh air, getting blood flowing back to your butt, grabbing brochures, using the bathroom and buying a Snickers and a Co-Coler.

The state publishes two free comprehensive guides: *Alabama: The Official Vacation Guide for the State of Alabama* and *Alabama's Black Heritage*. Local convention and visitor bureaus and chambers of commerce also dispense tourism information. The state bureau provides a list.

Time Alabama operates on Central Standard Time, with the exception of three towns – Lanett and Valley, both located at the Alabama-Georgia border on I-85, and Phenix City, also on the border on Hwys 431 and 80. They run on Eastern Standard Time.

Taxes There's a statewide sales tax of around 8%. It varies slightly by county. Hotels must collect an additional 4% occupancy tax.

Driving & Liquor Laws The legal drinking age is 21. Beverage sales stop at 2 am on Sunday – except in private clubs and the cities of Huntsville, Birmingham, Montgomery and Mobile – and restart at 12:01 am on Monday. Dry counties do not sell alcohol. There are 26 dry counties (out of 67) in Alabama. A few cities, including Clanton, Guntersville, Decatur, Enterprise, Florence, Jasper, Bridgeport and Scottsboro, are wet even though they are in dry counties. There are 22 counties that only serve draft beer. You may not transport more than one case of beer and three quarts of liquor or wine into or through a dry county. It's illegal to bring alcoholic beverages purchased outside the state into Alabama. Driving with a blood-alcohol level of 0.08% or higher is illegal. Refusal to take a breath test when stopped may result in a 90-day suspension of your driver's license.

The legal driving age is 16 years old.

State Parks & Protected Areas The Alabama Department of Conservation & Natural Resources operates 24 state parks with a wide range of facilities. Most have campsites, and many have rustic cabins and resorts or lodges. The mountain parks have hiking, biking and horseback-riding trails, including the popular, 102-mile Pinhoti Trail in northeast Alabama. Lake, river and Gulf-front parks have marinas and are great places for fishing. In addition, there are four national forests, a national monument and four national wildlife refuges.

Order the free *National Forests in Alabama Pocket Visitor Guide* by calling ☎ 334-832-4470 or writing to USDA National Forest Service, 2946 Chestnut St, Montgomery, AL 36107. The $30 annual day-use permit for all of Alabama's national forests (except the Clear Creek area of William Bankhead National Forest) will save you money if you plan to visit the forests for more than 10 days; the pass can be bought from any national forest division office and must be used within the year it is purchased. Parks have decent trail maps. If you're planning on a hiking vacation, consider Patricia S Sharpe's *Alabama Trails* and topographical maps available at ranger stations for about $4.

There are many caves in north-central and northeast Alabama. However, most are on private property and require permission to explore. Due to the high number of accidents, permission is rarely granted unless you are a member of a recognized speleological (the scientific study or exploration of caves) organization. Contact the National Speleological Society (☎ 205-852-1300), 2813 Cave Ave, Huntsville, AL 35810, for information about caving and grottos in Alabama.

The Army Corps of Engineers manages Alabama's extensive river system with locks and dams that have created numerous lakes that provide fishing, water sports, camping and hunting. Parks and a limited number of marinas rent nonmotorized aluminum boats for less than $10 a day. Motorized fishing and power-boat rentals are practically non-existent. John H Foshee's *Alabama Canoe Rides and Float Trips* is the best source book for a canoeing vacation. Rentals are limited and cost $25 to $45 a day, including shuttle. On many rivers, canoeing and rafting is dependent on adequate rainfall and dam releases. Be sure to call in advance to check water levels. For water level information on Alabama rivers, go to the Web site www.aloutdoors.com/riverlevels.html.

Despite condos and vacation homes built roof to roof in parts of Gulf Shores and Orange Beach, much of the shoreline remains natural, with white-sand beaches and sand dunes dotted with sea oats.

Northern Alabama

The northern third of Alabama, nestling in the foothills of the Appalachian Range, is covered by mountains, valleys, lakes and forests. The Tennessee River, which jogs from the northwestern corner of the state to the northeastern corner, is both scenic and an economic asset to the region. During the 1930s, the Tennessee Valley Authority brought jobs to the poorest part of the state by building dams on the river to control flooding and provide electricity. Numerous lakes surrounded by park land were created during this process and now provide unlimited outdoor opportunities. Cosmopolitan culture and nightlife can be found in Birmingham, and fantasies of space travel can be indulged in Huntsville, famous for its aerospace industry.

BIRMINGHAM
• pop 908,000

Birmingham is the largest city in Alabama. It's also the state's most cosmopolitan city, with abundant cultural and outdoor activities and a rich dining and nightlife scene. Parks and green spaces dot the urban landscape, and farms surround the suburbs that surround the city. The University of Alabama-Birmingham (UAB) is the city's largest employer.

History

When coal, iron ore and limestone – the ingredients for making pig iron and steel –

were found beneath its soil in the late 19th century, Birmingham quickly grew from a small farming town at a railroad intersection into the South's foremost industrial center, earning it the moniker, the 'Magic City.' Money flowed and thousands came to get rich. Saloons, prostitution, gambling and crime raged, and the city took on a new nickname, 'Bad Birmingham.'

Simultaneously, Jim Crow legislation began segregating the city, peaking in 1915 with zoning ordinances that restricted where blacks could live and work. A year later, it was in Birmingham that the Ku Klux Klan organized its first klavern in Alabama. Within 10 years it had 18,000 members, and by 1925 it had a stronghold on county politicians.

In the 1950s, blacks, especially returning servicemen, began verbalizing dissatisfaction with the status quo. Tension increased. Birmingham voted in 1954 to maintain segregated sports, shutting out professional teams from other cities that had white and black players. It soon became known as America's most segregated city.

White businesspeople who recognized that segregation was limiting business advocated change. Some were also worried about the impact of declining steel prices on Alabama's one-industry economy and urged diversification. Intransigent politicians refused to listen. By the 1960s race relations were smoldering and the steel industry was going into a tailspin.

Bad Birmingham

During Birmingham's wild frontier days, there were more licenses issued for 'sin' businesses – pool halls, liquor outlets and tobacco shops – than regular businesses, and those were the establishments that bothered to file. Things got so bad in 1907 that a newspaper reported that more people were murdered in this town of 30,000 residents than 'in all of Great Britain with its forty millions.' The number of arrests peaked at 11,814 that year.

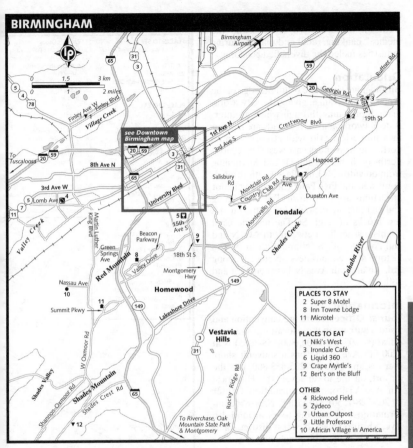

BIRMINGHAM

PLACES TO STAY
2 Super 8 Motel
8 Inn Towne Lodge
11 Microtel

PLACES TO EAT
1 Niki's West
3 Irondale Café
6 Liquid 360
9 Crape Myrtle's
12 Bert's on the Bluff

OTHER
4 Rickwood Field
5 Zydeco
7 Urban Outpost
9 Little Professor
10 African Village in America

ALABAMA

Racial tension erupted in 1963 when the commissioner of public safety, Eugene 'Bull' Connor, turned fire hoses and dogs on young students marching for civil rights near Kelly Ingram Park. Connor had actually been voted out of office a month earlier, but he refused to relinquish power. Knowing a good opponent when he saw one, the savvy Martin Luther King Jr timed the protests to confront the infamous segregationist before the courts could oust him in favor of more moderate leaders. Ironically, without Connor's fire hoses and police dogs, Birmingham would have escaped its international embarrassment and could have preserved segregation even longer. There were other, more tragic sources of shame, however. At the same time, the city endured (or perpetrated) more than 50 racially motivated bombings, including the bombing of the 16th St Baptist Church, which killed four little girls. The press renamed the city 'Bombingham' and the 'Tragic City.'

Faced with disaster, newly elected politicians forced change. Within 10 years the city council was integrated and the economy had diversified. The result was greater racial harmony and a new mayor, this time black, elected in 1979. Mayor Richard Arrington went on to serve five terms while the medical, banking, retail and manufacturing industries fueled the diversified economy.

Orientation

Birmingham sits at the southern edge of the Appalachian Range, giving the city a dramatic topography through which an interstate network weaves. It's roads are laid out in a numerical grid with streets running north-south, avenues east-west. The central north-south thoroughfare is 20th St, running from downtown's Linn Park south through Southside and Five Points South. The major attractions are downtown. The best dining and nightlife are in Southside, either on or a few blocks off 20th St. The historic Civil Rights district lies between 6th Ave N and 2nd Ave N, 15th St N and 19th St N. The historic 4th Ave business district sits along 3rd, 4th and 5th Aves N, between 15th and 18th Sts N.

Information

Tourist Offices There are convention and visitors bureaus in three locations. The main office (☎ 205-458-8000, 800-458-8085) is at 2200 9th Ave N and has a souvenir shop; there is an office (☎ 205-458-8002) at the airport, on the lower level. The Historical 4th Ave Visitors & Information Center (☎ 205-328-1850), 319 17th St N, provides information and walking tours around 4th Ave, a historic black business district. Their Web site is at www.birminghamal.org.

Money The following banks offer currency exchange: AmSouth Bank (☎ 205-326-5120), 1900 5th Ave N, and SouthTrust Bank (☎ 205-254-5230), 420 N 20th St.

Post The main post office (☎ 205-521-0302), 351 24th St N, opens Monday at 4:30 am and remains open 24 hours a day until Saturday at 4:30 am. It's closed on Saturday and Sunday.

Media Birmingham has two daily newspapers, the morning *Birmingham Post-Herald* and the afternoon and Sunday *Birmingham*

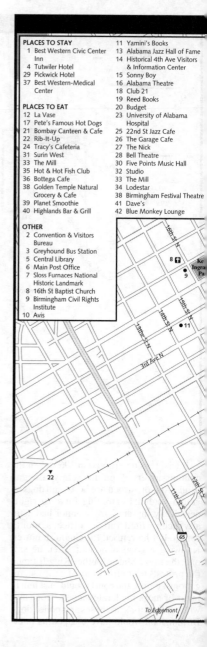

PLACES TO STAY
1 Best Western Civic Center Inn
4 Tutwiler Hotel
29 Pickwick Hotel
37 Best Western-Medical Center

PLACES TO EAT
12 La Vase
17 Pete's Famous Hot Dogs
21 Bombay Canteen & Cafe
22 Rib-It-Up
24 Tracy's Cafeteria
31 Surin West
33 The Mill
35 Hot & Hot Fish Club
36 Bottega Cafe
38 Golden Temple Natural Grocery & Cafe
39 Planet Smoothie
40 Highlands Bar & Grill

OTHER
2 Convention & Visitors Bureau
3 Greyhound Bus Station
5 Central Library
6 Main Post Office
7 Sloss Furnaces National Historic Landmark
8 16th St Baptist Church
9 Birmingham Civil Rights Institute
10 Avis
11 Yamini's Books
13 Alabama Jazz Hall of Fame
14 Historical 4th Ave Visitors & Information Center
15 Sonny Boy
16 Alabama Theatre
18 Club 21
19 Reed Books
20 Budget
23 University of Alabama Hospital
25 22nd St Jazz Cafe
26 The Garage Cafe
27 The Nick
28 Bell Theatre
30 Five Points Music Hall
32 Studio
33 The Mill
34 Lodestar
38 Birmingham Festival Theatre
41 Dave's
42 Blue Monkey Lounge

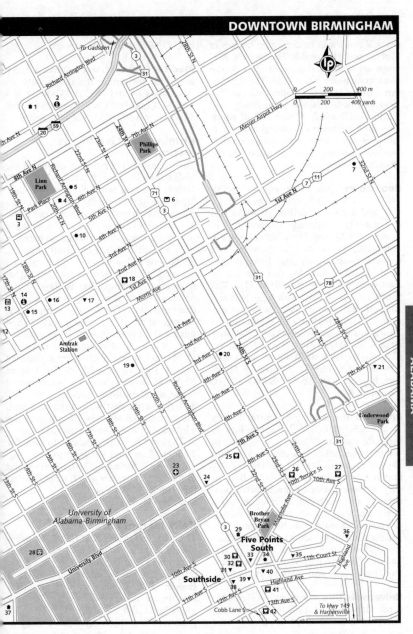

DOWNTOWN BIRMINGHAM

ALABAMA

News, which has a good entertainment supplement every Friday and shares a Web site (www.al.com) with its corporate siblings in Mobile and Huntsville. The weekly *Birmingham World* has concentrated on the black community since 1930. The city has three free alternative papers, the weekly *Creative Loafing, Birmingham Weekly* and the bi-weekly *black & white*, all of which give good coverage of cultural and entertainment happenings. *Birmingham* is a slick monthly magazine that's published by the chamber of commerce.

Bookstores Little Professor (☎ 205-870-7461), 2717 18th St S, in Homewood, has a cafe and a large selection of books and international magazines. Everything in Lodestar (☎ 205-939-3356), 2020 11th Ave S, Southside, is related to women and women's issues. Birmingham-based Books-A-Million has four locations, including Eastwood Mall (☎ 205-591-0573), 7703 Crestwood Blvd, each with large regional and periodical sections. Two bookstores specialize in the fiction and nonfiction of African-American writers: Yamini's Books (☎ 205-322-0037), 1417 4th Ave N, and the Civil Rights Institute Book Shop (☎ 205-328-9696), 520 16th St N. Smith & Hardwick Bookstore (☎ 205-591-9970) is at 3900 Clairmont Ave.

Libraries Birmingham's central library (☎ 205-226-3600), 2100 Park Place next to the Jefferson Courthouse, is comprised of two buildings linked by a crosswalk, including the exquisite South Linn-Henley Research Library (☎ 205-226-3665). Built in 1927, it houses historic maps, archival manuscripts and photographs relating to regional and state history, genealogy records and numerous collections. Its contemporary partner contains the usual books, magazines and videos. They're open Monday and Tuesday 9 am to 8 pm, Wednesday to Saturday 9 am to 6 pm, and Sunday 2 pm to 6 pm.

Universities Birmingham's biggest campus is the University of Alabama-Birmingham (UAB; ☎ 205-934-4011). It sprawls over

Southside between 11th and 20th Sts S and 5th and 10th Aves S. Campus street signs have UAB above the street name.

Medical Services There are half a dozen hospitals, including the University of Alabama Hospital (☎ 205-934-4011), 619 19th St S, and Hill Crest Hospital (☎ 205-833-9000, 800-292-8553), 6869 5th Ave S.

Birmingham Civil Rights Institute

The tribute to civil rights on display at the Civil Rights Institute (☎ 205-328-9696), 520 16th St N, downtown, will move your soul. Start with the 12-minute film introducing Birmingham from its founding to the 1920s. The Barriers Gallery shows the conditions of segregation and discrimination between 1920 and 1954 that led to confrontation. Audio, video, photography, artifacts and art are used to tell the story of the Civil Rights movement. Historic film footage shows police letting dogs loose on peaceful demonstrators. There's the reproduced, charred shell of a bus that was burned during the Freedom Rides, hundreds of photographs, the door from the Reverend Dr Martin Luther King Jr's Birmingham jail cell and vignettes of black life. The Human Rights Gallery explores the international scope of discrimination. A new research gallery is crammed with computers with access to special archives. The gift store has a broad selection of souvenirs and books.

The institute is open Tuesday to Saturday 10 am to 5 pm, and Sunday 1 to 5 pm. Admission is $3 for adults, $2 for seniors, and $1 for college students with ID; children and those under 17 years go free.
http://bcri.bham.al.us

Kelly Ingram Park

This park, on 6th Ave N at 16th St N, downtown, was the site of one of Alabama's most disturbing racial incidents. The ousted but intransigent public safety commissioner Eugene 'Bull' Connor assured himself a page in the history books when he fired water hoses and let police dogs loose on peaceful Civil Rights marchers, many of whom were children, while the international press recorded it. Bull is gone, but you're reminded of his pertinacity through sculptures of Dr Martin Luther King Jr, police dogs attacking children and children jailed with the inscription 'I am not afraid' on their cell door. It's across the street from the Civil Rights Institute and 16th St Baptist Church. Inscribed stones at the entrance to the park read, 'A Place for Revolution and Reconciliation.'

16th St Baptist Church

Long before the Civil Rights protests, this church (☎ 205-251-9402), 1530 6th Ave N, downtown, was known as 'Everybody's Church,' and served as the center of black community life. During the protests it become a gathering place for meetings and marches. When Ku Klux Klan members exploded the bomb that damaged this institution and killed four little girls on September 15, 1963, Birmingham was flung into a whirlwind of social change. The church was repaired and today serves as a house of worship and historical landmark. Of the 100,000 visitors each year, most come for the history, but the church's stained-glass windows are worth seeing (the bomb blast cleanly broke out the face of Christ, harming no other part of the stained glass). The window at the center rear of the church depicts a crucified black Christ, a gift from the people of Wales. The tragedy of the bombing has a modern postscript: two of the three suspects were arrested in May, 2000, 24 years after their presumed leader was convicted. The church is open Tuesday to Friday from 10 am to 4 pm. Tours are given on Saturday and by appointment. Services are held on Sunday at 11 am. Donations are welcome. www.16thstreet.org

Alabama Jazz Hall of Fame

This hall (☎ 205-254-2731), 1631 4th Ave N, downtown, showcases jazz musicians with ties to Alabama: Dinah Washington, Nat King Cole, Duke Ellington, Avery Parrish, James Reese Europe, Erskine Hawkins, WC Handy and even the iconoclastic Sun Ra, to name a few. Push a button and listen to Washington's velvety voice. She's one of many great jazz singers, conductors, performers and dancers you can learn about and hear in exhibits and interactive displays. Other exhibits cover the history of jazz. You'll be touched by artifacts like ticket stubs and posters from performances in the 1940s, '50s and '60s. The pink walls and art deco-patterned carpet give the place a vibrant, jazzy feel. The hall is in the historic Carver Theatre, where live performances are still held. Donations are accepted. It's open Tuesday to Saturday 10 am to 5 pm, and Sunday 1 to 5 pm. www.jazzhall.com/jazz

Sloss Furnaces National Historic Landmark

The mighty smokestacks of this massive workhorse of the 'Pittsburgh of the South' belched smoke for nearly 100 years, supplying pig iron to feed Birmingham's steel foundries until the American steel industry buckled in the 1970s. Now it serves as a museum of industry and it's also a much-favored site for concerts, festivals and special events. There is a 10-minute show on the history and technology of iron and steel in Birmingham, and tours, often led by former employees, are also available. If you feel an unexpected chill while you're there, consider yourself visited by the ghost of Theo Jowers, a former employee who died when he fell into one of the furnaces. This landmark (☎ 205-324-1911), 20 32nd St N, is just east of downtown and is open Tuesday to Saturday 10 am to 4 pm, and Sunday noon to 4 pm. Tours are given on weekends at 1 pm, 2 pm, 3 pm and by appointment at other times. Admission is free. www.ci.bham.al.us/sloss/

Five Points South

A good example of the New South's cosmopolitan urban spaces, Five Points South is *the* place to hang out in Birmingham. Think of Greenwich Village colliding with Andy Griffith's Mayberry, where artists and street characters mix, more or less, with rowdy, baseball-capped college boys. A delightful sculpture by Frank Fleming called *Cecil's*

ALABAMA

Fountain is the focal point of this popular historic area within Southside, south of downtown at the intersection of 20th St S and 11th Ave S. It depicts a ram reading a book to an audience of animals. (It's surprising that local Baptists didn't view it in an occult context and try their hands at street protesting.)

The neighborhood developed in the 1880s as one of Birmingham's first streetcar suburbs, and its heart was Five Points Circle, a major streetcar intersection. Now it has shops, restaurants, breweries and nightclubs housed in art deco buildings. The area is on the National Register of Historic Places. It has the safest ATM in town, right outside the door of the South Precinct Police Station. Take city bus No 39 (Homewood) from downtown and Homewood hotels.

African Village in America

This half-acre of yard sculpture at 912 Nassau Ave SW, 2 miles from downtown, is one of the most dramatic examples of visionary self-taught art anywhere. A pilgrimage to Alabama's Civil Rights shrines wouldn't be complete without a glimpse into this humble, private vision of peace and justice. Joe Minter, a 65-year-old carpenter, explains that he had a revelation from God in 1989. He felt led to construct a monument to African-American history rendered in found objects and house paint in his side yard. There are representations of African warriors watching their descendents' struggles in Alabama; tributes to black scientists and military leaders; re-creations of the epic Civil Rights confrontations in Birmingham, Montgomery and Selma; biblical scenes; a memorial to a little girl who was swept into a rain-swollen storm drain in 1999; and hand-lettered messages everywhere. In a piece on cultural self-criticism, Minter painted a series of street signs with names like 'Self Hate Street,' 'Gang Warfare Street,' and 'Babies Having Babies Having Babies Self-Genocide Street.' Don't worry about fear and loathing on Nassau St, though; it's a peaceful residential area. While a number of Alabama folk artists, including the visionaries, have made money from their art, Minter refuses to sell his work as he considers it a gift from God, although samples have been surfacing in museums. You should knock on Minter's front door before entering the side yard if his pickup truck is parked in the driveway; otherwise, you should view the art from the sidewalk. To get there, take I-65 south from downtown, turn right at the Green Springs Ave exit, left on Martin Luther King Drive, and a right on Nassau.

GREATER BIRMINGHAM CONVENTION AND VISITORS BUREAU

Minter uses found objects to evoke thought.

Activities

Many adventures in Alabama's backcountry are born in the map room at Urban Outpost (☎ 205-879-8850), 1105 Dunston Ave at Hagood St in the Crestline Park area, or so it seems based on all their customers' dramatic photographs that adorn the walls. The store sponsors a number of weekend guided trips throughout the region and will rent backpacks and tents. As a retailer, it is a smallish store supplying local hikers and rock climbers with mid-priced, no-nonsense gear – no $400 Patagonia or

Batter Up at Rickwood Field

What do Ty Cobb, Satchel Paige, Jackie Robinson, Willie Mays, Pie Traynor, Babe Ruth, Hank Aaron, Willie McCovey, Carl Yastrzemski, Reggie Jackson and Dizzy Dean have in common? The only ballpark in which every one of these baseball greats played at least once was Birmingham's Rickwood Field.

Opened in 1910 by railroad and mining engineer AH 'Rick' Woodward, it's America's oldest baseball park. It served as the home field for the Birmingham Barons of the Southern Association and the Black Barons of the Negro National League. Never did the two meet due to city ordinances prohibiting blacks and whites from playing together. It was also the park of the Oakland A's farm team. Professional ball left in 1989, but school and community teams still windup on the mound.

A multimillion dollar effort is underway to restore the venerable park to its glory days, and with it will come a museum commemorating the two old leagues and Southern baseball.

Rickwood Field (☎ 205-783-6333, 205-783-6332) is at 1137 2nd Ave W; its Web site is at www.rickwood.com.

North Face windbreakers here – but the selection of regional outdoor guidebooks and maps is great, and the staff will take time to give detailed advice. To check out their schedule of programs and offerings visit www.urbanoutpost.com.

Alabama Small Boats, Inc, (☎ 205-424-3634), 2370 Hwy 52, Helena, runs **canoeing** and **kayaking** trips. Most trips put in at Riverchase landing, just south of Birmingham, for the 10-mile paddle down the Cahaba River, the longest free-flowing river in Alabama. Highlights are the bluffs that climb 30 to 60 feet and the abundance of birds and other wildlife, including turtles, fish, foxes, turkeys, herons, king fishers, ducks, geese, beavers and, on rare occasions, otters and deer. Trips depart year-round

unless the water is too high or too cold, or the weather is bad. There's no white water on these peaceful nature outings. The best time to go is March to October. One-day rental is $25 for kayaks and $30 for canoes. The best deal is a three-day weekend rental for $60 (kayak or canoe). Shuttle service up the river is an additional $10 per boat, but there's a discount for three or more people. Shuttles depart Tuesday to Saturday at 8, 9 and 10 am; call a day in advance to reserve a seat. www.alsmallboats.com

Special Events

Every April, the Birmingham International Festival (☎ 205-252-7652, www.bifsalutes .org) celebrates the cuisine, entertainment and craftsmanship of a saluted country at a three-day street festival in Linn Park. Featured countries include Hungary in 2001, South Africa in 2002 and Canada in 2003.

In late January or early February the Southern Voices conference (☎ 205-444-7888) features notable regional writers and playwrights.

Father's Day weekend brings Birmingham's biggest bash with some 250,000 folks at Linn Park for the three-day City Stages music festival (☎ 205-251-1272) headed by big-name musicians and local talents. The first weekend in August has another biggie, the Heritage Festival (☎ 205-324-3333), celebrating the African-American community.

On the first weekend in October (unless, of course, a football game is scheduled), local and national jazz, blues and gospel artists turn up the heat at Sloss Furnaces during the Birmingham Jam (☎ 205-323-0569), a celebration of Southern culture and foods.

Places to Stay

Camping With 131 campsites open year-round, *Oak Mountain State Park* (☎ 205-620-2520), on Hwy 119, is 15 miles south of Birmingham off I-65 at exit 246. RV sites ($14) have electricity, water and sewer. Tent sites ($9.50) have a grill and picnic table. There's a bathhouse, laundry and store. There are 10 fully equipped two-bedroom, one-bathroom cabins surrounding a 45-acre

ALABAMA

lake that can accommodate up to eight people and cost $95 a night. Reservations are recommended on weekends, especially in summer. Go to www.bham.net/oakmtn for more information.

The new *Birmingham South KOA Kampground* (☎ 205-664-8832, 222 Hwy 33) is luxurious by most standards. It has 125 tent and RV sites with full hookups, heated pool and spa, bathhouse, camp store, grills, cabins, phones on some sites, hiking and TV in one and two-room cabins. From Birmingham take I-65 south to exit 242 (Hwy 52). Go west on Hwy 52 to the first stoplight, which is Hwy 33, and turn north. The campground is on the right.

Hotels & Motels A restaurant and pool put the *Super 8 Motel* (☎ 205-956-3650, 1813 Crestwood Blvd) a notch above your basic motel. The rooms are clean. It's east of downtown. Singles/doubles are $43/48.

The 102-room *Microtel* (☎ 205-945-5550, 251 Summit Parkway), Homewood, has queen-size beds, desks with modems and movies on cable. It's south of Southside, halfway between downtown and Oak Mountain State Park. Rooms are $42 to $46.

Inn Towne Lodge (☎ 205-942-2031, 400 Beacon Parkway W), Homewood, has weeds growing in the parking lot, but it offers daily and weekly bargain rates and lots of amenities. Rooms have a microwave, fridge, coffeemaker and fully equipped kitchen (in the higher priced rooms). There's an on-site laundry facility, a pool and complimentary continental breakfast. It's south of Southside. Ask for the corporate rate, which is $38 a night for singles or doubles, or $168 a week. Rooms 516-518 have a great view of downtown.

Best Western Civic Center Inn (☎ 205-328-6320, 2230 Richard Arrington Blvd) offers good value. It's a great location for visiting downtown attractions and has spacious rooms, modems, a swimming pool, complimentary breakfast and free parking. Singles/doubles are $69/74.

The *Tutwiler Hotel* (☎ 205-322-2100, 2021 Park Place N) is Birmingham's historic grande dame. Built in 1911, it retains much of its old-world style. The rooms are spacious, especially the corner suites, and well appointed. It has a restaurant, valet parking, morning newspapers, a pub and health club. It's situated near downtown attractions, freeways and bus routes. Rooms run from $140 to $180, however, if it isn't full, rates can go as low as $104.

The lovely art deco *Pickwick Hotel* (☎ 205-933-9555, 800-255-7304, 1023 20th St S) looms high over Five Points South, within short walking distance of some of the best restaurants, clubs and shops in the city. The rooms are bright and well appointed and the staff is cheerful. Continental breakfast is included, and so are a nightly wine and cheese reception, afternoon tea, daily newspaper and coffee. They also offer the free use of a shuttle van to points within the city. Standard rates are $89, suites are $119.

The lowest-priced hotel convenient to Five Points South is the *Best Western-Medical Center* (☎ 205-933-1900, 800 11th St S), at University Blvd – which becomes 8th Ave – on the edge of the UAB campus. Standard rates go as low as $60 for singles or doubles.

Places to Eat

Downtown Since 1915, *Pete's Famous Hot Dogs* (☎ 205-252-2905, 1925 2nd Ave N) has been feeding budget-minded customers in this tiny space. Pete is long gone, but his nephew still serves hot dogs for $1.10. Burgers and dogs with cheese cost $1.40. It's open daily 10:30 am to 7 pm.

At *Rib-It-Up* (☎ 205-328-7427, 830 1st Ave N) near Arlington mansion, diners can eat in, drive through or take out lip-smackin'-good barbecued beef, pork or chicken along with traditional Southern sides, salads and desserts. Sandwiches are $2 (regular) to $5 (jumbo). Complete dinners cost $3.50 to $7. There's no liquor. It's open Monday to Thursday 10:30 am to 9 pm, and Friday to Saturday 10:30 am to midnight.

La Vase (☎ 205-328-9327, 328 16th St N), operated by the Nation of Islam in the historic black district, serves home-style soul food that sticks to your ribs. It's a meat and vegetable place with a choice of fried or baked chicken, pot roast, meat loaf or beef ribs with two sides. Portions are very generous and inexpensive at $5 to $6. For dessert, opt for the sweet-potato pie or pound cake. Skip the cobbler. It's open Sunday to Thursday 11 am to 7 pm, and Friday and Saturday to 8 pm.

Run by a family of Greek descent, all of whom speak with pitch-perfect Alabama accents, since 1957, **Niki's West** (☎ 205-252-5751, 233 Finley Ave W) is one of Birmingham's most popular meat-and-three lunch spots. They'll also cook up a heart-attack breakfast that will make you postpone lunch until late afternoon. Breakfast and lunch cost $4 to $6. It's open Monday to Saturday 6 am to 10 pm.

Southside Pull up a stool at the juice bar at **Planet Smoothie** (☎ 205-933-7200, 1100 20th St S) for a healthy fresh fruit smoothie ($3 to $4), or natural juice and a low-fat sandwich ($3). It's open Monday to Saturday from around 10 am to 9 pm and Sunday noon to 8 pm. There's more good-for-you food around the corner at the **Golden Temple Natural Grocery & Cafe** (☎ 205-933-6333, 1901 11th Ave S). It's open weekdays 8:30 am to 7 pm, Saturday 9:30 am to 5:30 pm and Sunday noon to 5:30 pm.

Tracy's Cafeteria (☎ 205-252-7370, 729 20th St S) is another option for an inexpensive breakfast or lunch. Workers from neighboring medical facilities and from the university keep it busy, so arrive before the noon rush. Lunch with a side, dessert and beverage will set you back about $6. It's open weekdays 7 am to 2:30 pm.

Bombay Canteen & Cafe (☎ 205-322-1930, 2839 7th Ave S) is one of the best value places in town. Entrées run from $6 to $8, salads from $3.50 to $6. The 'big easy' crab cake sandwich with Louisiana lump crab meat on a toasted onion roll with roasted red pepper aioli is superb and sells out early. Veggies are cooked al dente. It's open weekdays 11 am to 2 pm.

Surin West (☎ 205-871-4531, 1918 11th Ave S), in Five Points South, is a Pacific Rim eatery that stays busy meeting Birmingham's new, but growing, demand for both sushi and Thai cuisine. The Thai side of the menu is better, especially the soups. Expect to pay up to $10 for lunch and $16 for dinner.

The Mill (☎ 205-939-3001, 1035 20th St S) is a bakery, brewery and eatery. Sit inside or take a table on the patio overlooking the Five Points South intersection. The wild mushroom and peppercorn meat loaf ($10) is a favorite. Sandwiches, served with one side, are around $6. Meals come with soup or salad and a loaf of freshly baked bread on a saucer of olive oil sprinkled with red pepper flakes and Parmesan. Draft beers come fresh from their brewery. The bakery opens at 6 am with a line waiting for 15 kinds of doughnuts and 12 kinds of big, fluffy muffins ($1.50). Food is served Sunday to Wednesday 6:30 am to 10 pm and Thursday to Saturday 6:30 am to midnight.

Included in Birmingham's upscale restaurants are the **Bottega Cafe** (☎ 205-933-2001, 2240 Highland Ave); the **Highlands Bar & Grill** (☎ 205-939-1400, 2011 11th Ave S); and the trendy **Hot & Hot Fish Club** (☎ 205-933-5474, 2180 11th Court S).

Over the Mountain You won't be considered rude if you read a book while dining at **Crape Myrtle's** (☎ 205-879-7891, 2721 18th St S), in Homewood. This small cafe in the Little Professor bookstore serves up memorable soups, salads, sandwiches and home-cooked veggies for lunch and dinner. Checks average $5.50 for lunch and $8 for dinner. It's open weekdays 11 am to 8 pm, Saturday 11 am to 3 pm, and Sunday 11 am to 2 pm.

Bert's on the Bluff (☎ 205-823-1217, 591 Shades Crest Rd), in Hoover, serves country cooking in a cafeteria-style setting. The food is good and inexpensive. A veggie sampler costs around $3. It's open weekdays 11 am to 8 pm.

Mountainbrook/Irondale Alabama's first cybercafe, **Liquid 360** (☎ 205-414-6580, 225 Country Club Rd, www.liquid360.net), at Church St behind the Piggly Wiggly grocery store in Crestline Village, serves espresso, fruit juices, pastries, sandwiches

ALABAMA

and has a full bar with microbrews, wine and cocktails. Thirty minutes of computer time is free with a $5 food or beverage purchase; without a purchase, access is $3 per half-hour.

Restaurants made famous by movies – like the *Irondale Café* (☎ 205-956-5258, *1906 1st Ave N*) – often become tourist traps. Luckily, this one escaped that fate. One reason is that Fannie Flagg renamed it in her novel, *Fried Green Tomatoes at the Whistle Stop Cafe*, and Hollywood shortened the title to the restaurant's signature dish. It is widely rumored that Flagg based the lead character, Idgie Threadgood, on her great aunt, Bess Fortenberry, who owned the diner for 50 years before selling it in 1973. The fried green tomatoes are still good, as are the rest of the homestyle meals, as the crowds of locals there attest. Lunch costs up to $8 and the cafe is closed on Saturday. Note: the 1st Ave N in Irondale is not the same 1st Ave that passes north of there from downtown Birmingham.

Entertainment

With a large population of students, Birmingham has nightlife that goes on and on and on. Check the weekly *Creative Loafing*, *Birmingham Weekly* or the bi-weekly *black & white* for listings. Many of the most popular clubs are in Southside, especially around Five Points South.

Bars & Nightclubs A local favorite is *The Garage Cafe* (☎ 205-322-3220, *2304 10th Terrace S*), which always has good music and great deli sandwiches. During the 1920s it functioned as a garage for the wealthy folks who lived in the Highlands. Out back is the courtyard shop of architect Fritz Woehly, who collects antique architectural fittings. When there's no band, there's piped music, usually about jazz. Note the beautiful wooden doors and magnificent wisteria covering the courtyard.

It's generally acknowledged that *Dave's* (☎ 205-933-4030, *1128 20th St*), at Highland Ave, serves the best martinis in town. However, if the thing with the twist isn't your drink, you can choose from 18 beers on

tap, 60 bottled imports and microbrews, premium wines by the glass and a slew of other offerings. It's one of the most popular bars in town. Just ask the folks waiting in line outside to get in.

Moving in on Dave's martini crown – having won at least one local poll – is the über-cool *Blue Monkey Lounge* (☎ 205-933-9222, *1318 Cobb Lane S*), between 13th Ave S and 14th Ave S. There's a very diverse crowd – and it *can* be a crowd – enjoying the piano jazz and smoky ambiance, but not necessarily the food. Locals boast that it's like being in New York, but Blue Monkey's Southern patrons and staff are too warm and friendly to put on that kind of act for very long.

The rock music at *The Nick* (☎ 205-252-3831, *2514 10th Ave S*) is live. The crowd is everything from creased-blue-jean chic to really hard-core bikers. It's an aural experience of the best kind. Come to hear the latest, greatest really-into-the-music-scene bands, both local and touring.

Five Points Music Hall (☎ 205-322-2263, *1016 20th St S*) books touring and local bands and can hold up to 1000 people. If you don't like crowds, you won't like it here. There's pool tables, and a dance floor that's hot on Thursday night. Enter through the back.

It's a toss-up whether people go to *Zydeco* (☎ 205-933-1032, *2001 15th Ave S*) for the 76 varieties of imported and microbrewed beers (plus 13 on tap) or for the Cajun-style crawfish or for the live music Thursday to Sunday. It's a big place with two floors and a patio. Go even if there's no live act. It claims to have the best jukebox in town.

The *22nd St Jazz Cafe* (☎ 205-252-0407, *710 22nd St S*) is *the* small, dark, intimate spot to go to when you want to grab a bite to eat and hear live jazz and blues. It occasionally has flamenco music and dancers, and has a New York jazz club ambience. It's open Wednesday to Saturday from 5 pm until it closes.

When you feel like dancing, head over to *Studio* (☎ 205-324-4500, *1036 20th St S*), where Birmingham's beautiful people go. It has a great sound system. Another favored dance spot is *Club 21 (☎ 205-322-0469, 117 Richard Arrington Blvd N)*, which has a mixed straight and gay crowd.

Cinemas The *Alabama Theatre (☎ 205-252-2262, 1817 3rd Ave N)* is a great movie house that's been completely restored to its original 1920s glamorous self. Along with concerts on its historic Wurlitzer organ, it shows first-run and art films and presents special events. It's open for tours weekdays 9 am to 4:30 pm. For a calendar of concerts and movies visit the theater's Web site at www.alabamatheatre.com.

Theater The University of Alabama's Department of Theatre performs at the *Bell Theatre (☎ 205-934-3237, 700 13th St S)*. Southern Playworks, a joint UAB and Birmingham Festival Theatre series with works by Southern playwrights, also performs at the Bell Theatre. The *Birmingham Festival Theatre (☎ 205-933-2383)* is on 19th Ave S in Five Points South and has performances of unusual works.

Shopping

Numerous antique shops are open along 7th Ave S between 29th St S and 23rd St S. The most notable antique stop is Reed Books (☎ 205-326-4460), 107 20th St S, where good stuff is stacked everywhere. Within the chaos, there is order, at least in the mind of owner Jim Reed. While most of the stuff is out-of-print books, magazines, calendars and ephemera, there are other collectibles as well.

Your best stop for fun and functional souvenirs is the Birmingham Shop (☎ 205-458-8000), 2200 9th Ave N, in the Convention & Visitors Bureau. They have pens, books, cassettes, mugs and T-shirts. The Sloss Furnaces National Historic Landmark shop (☎ 205-324-1911), 20 32nd St N, has more serious stuff to take home. Keeping with its industrial theme, it carries hand-wrought works of metal by local artists.

Sonny Boy (☎ 205-251-4209), 1715 3rd Ave N, sells religious products for people who want fast results from their prayers.

The shop offers incense, anointing oil, soaps, sprays and other items labeled under product categories such as 'Casino – Lucky Hand,' 'Cast Off Evil,' 'Concentration,' 'Pay Me Now' and 'Stay at Home.' Nothing like a Bourbon Street 'voodoo shop,' this place caters to customers who take their wares seriously.

Getting There & Away

Air Birmingham International Airport (☎ 205-595-0533), about 5 miles northeast of downtown, offers 140 flights daily, with nonstop service to 21 cities on American, Continental, Delta, Southwest, Northwest, United and US Airways Express. Southwest often has the lowest roundtrip fares (Baltimore/Washington $164, Chicago $186, Long Island, NY $204, Los Angeles $448).

Bus Greyhound (☎ 205-252-7120), 619 19th St N in downtown, serves a score of cities, including two buses daily each to Biloxi ($63, eight hours) and Gadsden ($19, one hour); three to New Orleans ($67, eight to 14 hours); four each to Huntsville ($20, two

The Highway 78 Blues

When planning an itinerary that includes the Shoals, Memphis, northern Mississippi, Birmingham or the Sipsey Wilderness, one might be tempted to use Hwy 78. On a map, it appears to be a major US highway and the shortest distance between a number of points. Maps don't show how the highway, between Hamilton and Jasper, is a patchwork of two-lane and unfinished four-lane stretches that funnels Memphis/Birmingham/Atlanta truck traffic through dangerously congested areas. Between Jasper and Birmingham, Hwy 78 is a hideous gauntlet of strip malls, inconsistent speed limits and poorly-timed traffic lights that spoil what would be a convenient and scenic country drive. Alternate east-west routes are Hwy 72 and Hwy 278 – both of these arteries connect with I-65.

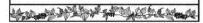

ALABAMA

hours) and Montgomery ($17, two hours); five each to Memphis ($41, five hours) and Nashville ($31, three to four hours); six to Jackson ($49, four hours); and seven to Atlanta ($29, three hours).

An Amtrak bus service connects Birmingham with Bay Minette and Mobile.

Train Amtrak (☎ 205-324-3033), 1819 Morris Ave, downtown, pulls in daily from New York ($173 one-way, 23 hours) and New Orleans ($47, seven hours), connecting Washington, DC, Atlanta, Tuscaloosa, Meridian and New Orleans.

Getting Around
Bus You can get around town, on weekdays only, on buses ($1) operated by Metro Area Express (☎ 205-521-0101), called MAX for short. Around the central business district you can take trolley-like buses (50¢) run by DART. The Ride Store (☎ 205-328-7433) ticket center serves both.

City bus (☎ 205-521-0101) No 20 (Zion City) departs 10th Ave and 50th St, about five blocks from the airport, weekdays only, between 6:10 am and 5:23 pm ($1.25).

Car Avis (☎ 205-592-8901), 2023 5th Ave N, and Budget (☎ 205-322-3596), 2301 3rd Ave S, rental-car agencies have offices in Birmingham. Hertz (☎ 205-591-6090), National (☎ 205-592-7259) and Thrifty (☎ 205-595-1900) have ticket counters at the airport; they're downstairs next to the baggage claim area.

Taxi You can call Airport Taxi Cab Company (☎ 205-833-8294, 888-712-8294), Yellow Cab (☎ 205-252-1131). Taxis to/from the airport cost about $10 for one person and $5 per additional person.

AROUND BIRMINGHAM
The section of the **Black Warrior River** known as Locust Fork, 40 miles northeast of Birmingham in Blount County, offers some of the most exciting canoeing in the South. Reminiscent of popular rivers farther up the Appalachian Range, the river's difficulty level ranges from class 3 rapids and

runnable waterfalls (for kayaks) down to easy flat-water paddling. Whitewater season runs from March through June, when water levels are higher. Morgan Outfitters (☎ 205-942-3614, 800-788-7070, morganout@aol .com), on County Road 34 in Royal, 0.4 miles north of County Road 26, rents canoes and guides trips on the easier sections and rafting/kayaking on the whitewater sections.

Morgan Outfitters will also rent canoes for the neighboring – and nearly identical – Mulberry Fork of the Black Warrior River, a good alternative when the Locust Fork is crowded. Rental prices are $32 per person for the lower two sections and $36 per canoe for the upper section. The Morgans also operate a *lodge* with rates from $75 to $100 a night. To get there, take Hwy 79 North from Birmingham for 45 miles, turn east on County Road 26, drive 3 miles and turn north on County Road 34.

ANNISTON
• pop 117, 000
Today's Anniston grew out of an industrial town with textile mills and blast furnaces laid out in the late 1800s by northern industrialists. Many of its original churches and buildings remain. An abundance of strip malls and fast-food joints mars the look of the city, but the two wonderful museums here make up for the clutter and are the main (if not the only) reason to make a stop here.

Anniston Museum of Natural History
The first thing you notice at this terrific museum (☎ 256-237-6766), 800 Museum Drive, at the junction of Hwy 21 and Hwy 431, is a prehistoric 'bird,' with a 30-foot wingspan, suspended from the ceiling. Farther inside are interesting displays of animals, plants, minerals and mummies. Good lighting and sound effects enhance the exhibits. Don't miss the bird collection with beautiful hand-painted habitats. Situated in Lagarde Park, nature continues outside in the wildlife garden and on the 'bird of prey trail,' which runs about 1½

miles through the woods. The North Route bus (see Getting Around) stops here. It's open Tuesday to Friday 9 am to 5 pm, Saturday 10 am to 5 pm, and Sunday 1 to 5 pm. Admission is $3.50 for adults, $3 for seniors and $2.50 for children.
www.annistonmuseum.org

Berman Museum of World History

This wonderful surprise of a museum (☎ 256-237-6261, 256-238-9055), at 840 Museum Drive, houses Farley and Germaine Berman's private collection of 1500 weapons and 2000 works of art. Farley was a US Army Intelligence officer in North Africa during World War II. It was there that he met Germaine, who was a French spy, and the two fell in love.

For more than 40 years the couple sought rare objects – Germaine loved art and Farley collected rare weapons. There's a Persian scimitar encrusted with 1295 rose-cut diamonds, 60 carats of rubies and a large emerald; a tea set once owned by Hitler; a plate from Napolean's field china; and real crown jewels from the Czech Republic.

It's open Tuesday to Friday 9 am to 5 pm, Saturday 10 am to 5 pm, and Sunday 1 to 5 pm. Admission is $4.50 for adults, $3.50 for seniors, military and disabled visitors, and $2.50 for children. The North Route bus stops here. www.bermanmuseum.org

Activities

Scott's Bikes (☎ 256-435-2453), 101 Ladiga St SE, in Jacksonville, just north of Anniston, rents bikes. The bikes ($15 to $20 a day) are hybrids, suitable for easy off-road trails and street riding. There's no shuttle service. Shop hours are weekdays 10 am to 6 pm, and Saturday 9 am to 5 pm.

Places to Stay

The staff at the *Lenlock Inn* (☎ 256-820-1515, 800-234-5059, 6210 McClellan Blvd) go out of their way to make guests comfortable. There's a pool, sauna, picnic area and laundry, plus free movies and coffee. Family suites have king-size or water beds. Honey-

moon suites have canopy beds. Rooms start at $36/41 for singles/doubles.

The *Victoria Inn* (☎ 256-236-0503, 1604 Quintard Drive) is part old, part new. The main house, which is more than 100 years old, has three rooms decorated with antiques ($129 to $169). The balconied annex rooms overlooking the garden and pool are $74, but rates go lower when things are slow. The rate includes a better-than-average continental breakfast Monday to Saturday and a hot country breakfast on Sunday.

Places to Eat

China Luck Restaurant (☎ 256-831-5221, 503 Quintard Drive), in Oxford (which is indiscernible from Anniston thanks to the strip mall) has tasty daily lunch specials for $4 to $5. Dinner will set you back $6 to $12. The egg rolls and fried rice are worth a try. It's open Monday to Saturday 11 am to 2:30 pm, Sunday 11:30 am to 3 pm, Sunday to Thursday 4:30 to 9:30 pm and Friday to Saturday 4:30 to 10:30 pm.

Top o' the River (☎ 256-238-0097, 3220 McClellan Blvd), in Anniston, is a family-run fish house specializing in catfish. A catfish dinner starts at $9, with sides. Chicken, steak and oysters are also available. People have been coming here from Georgia and Alabama for almost 20 years. It's open Sunday 11:30 am to 9 pm, Monday to Thursday 5 to 9 pm, and Friday and Saturday 4 to 10 pm.

The 24-hour *Alabama Show Palace* (☎ 256-831-0689, 1503 Hillyer Robinson Industrial Parkway) restaurant and bar is 'home of the $5 steak.' On Thursday night you can get all the sirloin steak you can eat for $5. It comes with a potato; add $2 for a salad. The rest of the week steaks start at $5, but you're limited to one. There's also grilled shrimp and burgers.

Getting There & Away

Greyhound (☎ 256-236-6306), 12 8th St W, has frequent service to Atlanta ($22), Chattanooga ($23), Nashville ($58) and New Orleans ($70).

Amtrak's (☎ 877-276-2767), 126 4th St W, two *Crescent* trains pass through Anniston

ALABAMA

daily, connecting it with New York and New Orleans, although one might be hard pressed to find 24 hours worth of activities between trains.

Getting Around

The local bus service, Anniston Express, operates three lines, two of which pass places of interest. All depart from Trolley Central at Gurnee Ave and 14th St E on the hour. The West/Line goes west on 14th St for several blocks, then returns and heads south on Noble St and Constantine Ave into Hobson City before returning. It passes the chamber of commerce and stops within a brisk walk of both the Greyhound station and the Amtrak stop. To get to the museums, transfer (for free) to the North Anniston Line back at Trolley Central. The fare is $1.

HUNTSVILLE
• pop 340,000

This well-to-do aerospace community in the north-central part of Alabama has the highest per capita income of any metropolitan area in the southeast. It had its high-tech beginnings in the 1950s when Senator John Sparkman brought in a group of German scientists to develop rockets for the US army. The US space program took off and attracted international aerospace-related businesses.

History

Huntsville was named after John Hunt, a pioneer who settled here in 1805 following the removal of Creek and Chickasaw Indians through forced expulsion and/or dubious land deals. By 1819, the year Alabamians met here to petition the US Congress for statehood, it was the largest town in the Alabama Territory. Wealthy merchants and planters built lavish houses in the Twickenham area, which today has the largest collection of antebellum houses in the state. During the Civil War many residents who harbored mixed feelings about secession, flew Union flags over their houses, sparing Huntsville the destruction wrought on other cities in Alabama.

Orientation

Huntsville lies in the Tennessee River Valley between Tennessee and the Tennessee River. Foothills of the Appalachian Range surround it on three sides. It lies 17 miles east of I-65. I-565 and Hwy 72 connect I-65 with Huntsville, bringing travelers from the north, south and west. Hwys 72 also draws traffic from the east while 231 and 431 connect Huntsville with rural east-central Alabama to the south.

Huntsville addresses reflect the city's layout in a quadrant: NW, SW, NE, SE. The Twickenham and Old Town historic districts lie northeast of downtown, off I-565's exit 19. A new tourist trolley provides inexpensive transportation to some major attractions.

Information

Tourist Offices The Huntsville/Madison County Convention & Visitors Bureau (☎ 256-551-2230, 800-772-2348), at 700 Monroe St, Von Braun Civic Center, is open Monday to Saturday 9 am to 5 pm and Sunday noon to 5 pm. You can find them on the Web at www.huntsville.org. The Huntsville Airport branch is open Monday to Saturday 8:30 am to 5:30 pm and Sunday 12:30 to 6 pm.

Money AmSouth Bank's downtown branch (☎ 256-535-6999), located at 200 Clinton Ave W, offers foreign currency exchange. ATMs can be found throughout the city at every branch of Compass (☎ 256-532-6269) and Colonial (☎ 256-551-4700).

Post The main post office (☎ 256-539-9686), 615 Clinton Ave, is open weekdays 8:30 am to 5 pm.

Media The *Huntsville Times* is the local daily, which shares a Web site, www.al.com, with its corporate siblings in Mobile and Birmingham. Thursday's 'Out and About' section features entertainment and events. Many newsstands carry Birmingham, Nashville and Atlanta dailies. The alternative *Rant Magazine* covers the entertainment scene for serious night owls, while

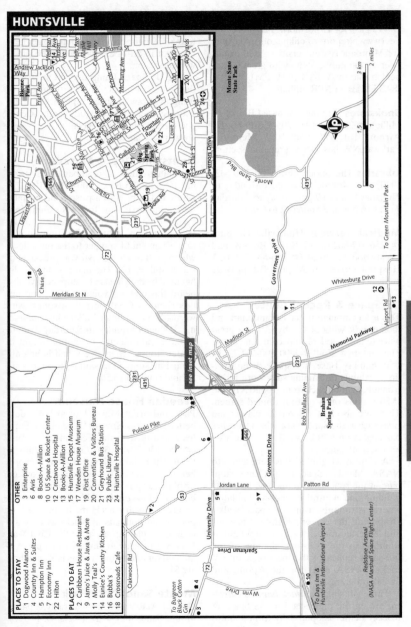

HUNTSVILLE

ALABAMA

PLACES TO STAY
1 Dogwood Manor
4 Country Inn & Suites
5 Hampton Inn
7 Economy Inn
22 Hilton

PLACES TO EAT
2 Caribbean House Restaurant
9 Jamo's Juice & Java & More
11 Molly Teal's
14 Eunice's Country Kitchen
16 Bubba's
18 Crossroads Cafe

OTHER
3 Enterprise
6 Avis
8 Books-A-Million
10 US Space & Rocket Center
12 Crestwood Hospital
13 Books-A-Million
15 Huntsville Depot Museum
17 Weeden House Museum
19 Post Office
20 Convention & Visitors Bureau
21 Greyhound Bus Station
23 Public Library
24 Huntsville Hospital

El Reportero provides coverage in Spanish and English for 17 northern Alabama counties (www.elreportero-online.com). Alabama A&M broadcasts university-related events open to the public along with great world-beat music on WJAB (90.9 FM). WLRH (89.3 FM) is an NPR affiliate.

Bookstores Birmingham-based Books-A-Million (☎ 256-883-1942, 205-536-1940), 975 Airport Rd SW, and 1001 Memorial Parkway NW, has a strong regional section.

Libraries The public library (☎ 256-532-5940), 915 Monroe St, is open Monday to Thursday 9 am to 9 pm, Friday to Saturday 9 am to 6 pm, and Sunday 2 to 6 pm.

Medical Services Huntsville Hospital (☎ 256-517-8020), 101 Sivley Rd SW, and Crestwood Hospital (☎ 256-882-3100), 1 Hospital Drive, off Airport Rd, provide medical care.

US Space & Rocket Center

This is a combination science museum and theme park without the hype. It's a great place to take a kid, or to become one again. The center (☎ 256-837-3400, 800-637-7223), 1 Tranquility Base, has space demonstrations, exhibits of training suits worn by astronauts, a moon rock from Apollo XII, and IMAX films on a 67-foot domed screen. There are also half a dozen simulators and rides such as the Space Shot, which launches passengers on a 4G, 45-mile-per-hour ride into weightlessness.

An optional guided bus tour goes to NASA's Marshall Space Flight Center, stopping at the space station module assembly building and neutral buoyancy simulator, where astronauts train for space walks. Despite all the center's high-tech exhibits and entertainment, the real highlight is standing in the awesome shadow of the full-sized replica of the massive Saturn-V rocket NASA used for the Apollo and Skylab programs.

Three gift shops, a *snack bar* and *cafeteria* are on the premises. The US Space & Rocket Center is open daily from 9 am to 5 pm (until 6 pm in summer). Admission is $14 for adults, $10 for children, including a tour, or $9/6 for the exhibit only. To get here take exit 15 off I-565, or visit its Web site at www.ussrc.com.

The **US Space Camp** opened in 1982 at the Space & Rocket Center with the goal of using the draw of space exploration to encourage youngsters to study math, science and high technology subjects. www.spacecamp.com

Huntsville Depot Museum

The state's oldest railroad passenger terminal (☎ 256-535-6565, 800-678-1819), 320 Church St, served as a prison and hospital during the Civil War. Today, it's a museum focusing on Huntsville's history and the transportation industry. The museum is rather tame until you get to the third floor, where graffiti left by Civil War prisoners of war is still legible. The place is supposedly haunted by the ghosts of – stop me if you've heard this one – a young woman and her boyfriend, a Confederate prisoner, who were killed by a single bullet while embracing. It's open Monday to Saturday 9 am to 5 pm. Hours change on holidays and in winter. Tours depart every half-hour until 4 pm. Full adult admission is $6, seniors are $5, and children $3.50.

Weeden House Museum

Poet and artist Maria Howard Weeden, better known as Howard Weeden, was born, lived and died in this Federal-style house (☎ 256-536-7718), 300 Gates Ave, downtown, which was built in 1819. The comprehensive collection of Weeden's artwork on display garners the most attention. Her book *Shadows on the Wall* appeared in 1898 to great literary acclaim. It featured 11 poems and portraits of blacks as they appeared on plantations after the Civil War. It's open Tuesday to Sunday 1 to 4 pm. Admission for adults and seniors is $2, children are $1.

Monte Sano State Park

One of Alabama's most attractive parks, Monte Sano State Park (☎ 205-534-3757),

It's Cotton Pickin' Time

Throughout the 19th and well into the 20th century, cotton was picked by hand. Then it was ginned, pressed into a bale, weighed, marked and finally sent to a port city like Decatur, Montgomery or Mobile, where it was shipped to a mill. Burgreen Black Cotton Gin, west of Huntsville, is a thriving cotton gin that allows visitors a glimpse of the modern cotton industry. You can see how cotton is processed, then go out into the field and hand-pick a boll of cotton, a step that mostly is done by machine nowadays. The gin is open for visits from September to November. Set up an appointment with Dewanda Black (☎ 256-232-2875), 29484 Huntsville Browns Ferry Rd, Madison.

From Huntsville, take Hwy 72 west to the Limestone Flea Market; turn left on Burgreen Rd and continue straight ahead for 1¼ miles. The firm runs a restaurant, *Wendells B&B* (☎ 256-232-2955) next door; note that the 'B&B' stands for Burgreen and Black, not bed and breakfast. Catfish is the favorite dish, unless it's the weekend, when the rib-eye special steals the show. Lunch costs $5.50 and dinner is $10.

5105 Nolen Ave, features more than 15 miles of trails that cover the mountain with remarkable elevation changes, lookouts, waterfalls and training walls for rock climbing. You can easily spend a day here and go back for more. It's open daily 8 am to 5 pm ($1). The setting makes it a great place to stay (see Camping, below).

Places to Stay

Camping The campground at *Monte Sano State Park* has 20 primitive tent sites and 85 improved tent and RV sites, including 20 with full hookups. Primitive sites are $6, improved sites $11 to $12, and there are 14 fully equipped rustic cabins that rent for $45 a night.

Ditto Landing (☎ 256-882-1057, 800-552-8769), on Hobbs Island Rd off Hwy 231, oc-cupies 60,000 acres along the Tennessee River. The camping area is densely wooded and there are 26 improved sites with hookups. The rate is $10 a night.

Hotels & Motels The rooms at *Economy Inn* (☎ 256-534-7061, 3772 University Drive NW), near Hwy 231/431, are furnished in somber colors, but it has free movies, a pool with patio tables and lounge chairs, and complimentary coffee in the lobby. Singles/doubles cost $30/45.

Days Inn (☎ 256-772-9550, 102 Arlington Drive), at Madison, offers complimentary continental breakfast, airport shuttle service, a free movie channel, VCR rentals and an outdoor pool. It's conveniently located between the airport and the US Space Center. Singles/doubles are $46/52 and suites cost $75.

The 164-room *Hampton Inn* (☎ 256-830-9400, 4815 University Drive NW) is within 2 miles of the US Space Center and offers complimentary continental breakfast and privileges at a nearby health club. You can relax in the whirlpool or outdoor pool in summer. Rooms have free movies and modem ports. It's $63 for a single or double.

Though it's oriented toward business travelers, the *Country Inn & Suites* (☎ 256-837-4070, 4880 University Drive NW) has an at-home feel. It's loaded with amenities, including a fitness center, pool, sauna, restaurant, lounge, mini-store, coffeemakers and hair dryers, and there's an airport shuttle. Rates are $71/83.

Rooms in one wing of the *Hilton* (☎ 256-533-1400, 401 Williams Ave) surround an attractive atrium, while others overlook a pool. It's the only hotel in downtown Huntsville. There's a restaurant, piano bar, exercise center and a popular nightclub. Room rates range from $79 to $125. Ask about off-peak discounts.

B&Bs A 10-minute drive from downtown Huntsville you'll find *Dogwood Manor* (☎ 256-859-3946, 707 Chase Rd), a restored historic home. Three guest rooms have queen-size beds and private bathrooms. Two rooms have a fireplace. There's an

ALABAMA

upstairs sun porch, a library and a new honeymoon suite. A full breakfast is included in the $75 rate (honeymoon suite $85).

Places to Eat

Only the oldest Huntsvillians can remember when *Eunice's Country Kitchen* (☎ 256-534-9550, 1006 Andrew Jackson Way) wasn't serving biscuits and gravy, country ham, and grits and eggs. It's a make-yourself-at-home place where you can pour your own coffee. Lots of celebs, politicians and families pass through these doors. Full breakfast costs $3.50 to $6, and hamburgers are $2. It's open Wednesday to Monday 5 am to noon.

The *Crossroads Cafe* (☎ 256-533-3393, 721 Clinton Ave), in the Market Square Mall, has can't-be-beat prices on hot and cold deli-style sandwiches. They even serve peanut butter and jelly ($1.50). With chips and a soft drink, a satisfying meal will cost $3.50 to $5. Food is served weekdays 11 am to midnight, and weekends 6 pm to midnight.

Molly Teal's (☎ 256-533-5988, 2003 Whitesburg Drive), at Governors Drive, combines a bakery, eatery and brewery into a popular meeting spot. Salads range from $3 for a small Caesar to $6 for southwest chicken. Soups are $1 a cup or $2.50 a bowl. They serve a good version of 'white chili,' a regional culinary oddity that's actually really good: chicken, clear chicken stock and white beans create the albino effect that distinguishes it from its tomato- and beef-based Texas cousin. Molly Teal's is open daily 6:30 am to 10 pm.

Bubba's (☎ 256-534-9888, 109 Washington St) is ostensibly your typical Southern barbecue joint that's gone a little corporate. Their menu is too long and varied to be taken seriously – the longer the menu, the more a restaurant is relying on frozen food and microwave ovens – but the sub-menu of barbecue classics is good. It's worth noting that Bubba's is probably the only barbecue joint on the planet that features an authentic sushi bar.

While not strictly vegetarian, *Jamo's Juice & Java and More* (☎ 256-837-7880, 413 Jordan Lane) is the closest you'll find in Huntsville. A bowl of Sherpa rice (red lentils, rice and barley) is served plain for $2, or with big bang vegetarian chili or vegetables for $3.50. There's live entertainment Thursday, Friday and Saturday nights. You can eat in or take out. It's open Monday to Thursday 7 am to 9 pm, Friday 7 am to midnight, Saturday 9 am to midnight, and Sunday 9 am to 9 pm.

The small, laid-back *Caribbean House Restaurant* (☎ 256-837-1474, 2612 Jordan Lane) features authentic island-style foods like jerk chicken, roti and curries. Vegetarians will feel at home as there are lots of vegetable sides and vegan dishes. Checks average $5.50 and you can eat in or take out. It's open Sunday 11:30 am to 7 pm, Monday to Thursday 11 am to 8 pm, and Friday 11 am to 3 pm.

Getting There & Away

Air Huntsville International Airport (☎ 256-772-9395), 1000 Glenn Hearn Blvd, Madison, just west of Huntsville, exit 7 on I-565, is served by American, Delta, Northwest, US Airways and several commuter lines.

Bus Greyhound (☎ 256-534-1681), 601 Monroe St NW, has two buses daily to New Orleans ($79); three each to Atlanta ($35), Birmingham ($19), Mobile ($62) and Montgomery ($43); and four to Chattanooga ($55), Decatur ($10) and Nashville ($25).

Car Taking I-65 and I-565 you can drive to Huntsville from Birmingham or Nashville in a little over two hours, or Decatur in 30 minutes. For a more scenic trip, however, slower US and state highways link Huntsville with the same cities as well as with Cullman, which is on Hwy 31 an hour south, and with the Shoals, on Hwy 72, an hour west.

Alamo, Avis, Budget, Hertz and National have rental counters at the airport. The following have offices in town: Americar (☎ 256-772-3176), 8884 B Hwy 20W, Madison; Avis (☎ 256-772-9301, 256-539-8483), 3154 University Drive; Thrifty (☎ 256-772-9653), 9300 Hwy 20W; and Enterprise (☎ 256-971-0025), 6125 University Drive.

Getting Around
Huntsville Shuttle System (☎ 256-532-7433) provides public transportation hourly on nine routes weekdays 6 am to 6 pm. The one-way fare is $1 for adults and 50¢ for seniors and students; free transfers are provided. A new tourist trolley serves downtown attractions, the Von Braun Civic Center, the botanical gardens and the US Space Center. The fare is $1 or $2 for a one-day pass.

Executive Connection (☎ 256-772-0186), a shuttle service, has a counter at the airport near baggage claim. Rates to downtown are $15 to $20. Travelers with reservations are served first.

Huntsville Cab (☎ 256-539-8288) and United Deluxe Cab (☎ 256-536-3600, 256-534-9213) offer taxi services. Taxis from the airport cost around $15 to $20.

HUNTSVILLE TO FORT PAYNE
Unclaimed Baggage Center
Ever wonder what happened to that camera or jacket that you left on the airplane? Unclaimed Baggage (☎ 256-259-1525), 509 W Willow St, Scottsboro, probably sold it. The only one of its kind in the US, this store purchases truckloads of lost and unclaimed airline passenger property and resells it. Far from being a run-down thrift store, the facility looks like a department store and even features a Starbucks Coffee stand and a 'concierge' who gives information on area attractions. There are myriad travel accessories, as well as clothing, sporting goods, electronic items and thousands of books – but no misplaced Lonely Planet guides – all at great prices. It's closed Sunday. www.unclaimedbaggage.com

Cathedral Caverns
Cathedral Caverns State Park (☎ 256-728-8193, 800-582-6282), on County Road 5 in Grant, contains one of the South's largest caverns. Upgrading public access to the cavern's depths without spoiling its natural beauty has taken years, but all the waiting has paid off for caving enthusiasts. The 160-acre cave system has 100-foot high ceilings, what may be the world's largest stalagmite, and an 80- by 120-foot mouth.

Take Jackson County Road 63 south from Hwy 72 (that junction is 16 miles west of Scottsboro and 20 miles southeast of Huntsville just east of Woodville). Cathedral Caverns Road is 3 miles south of Hwy 72 on the left. Admission is $8 and the days and hours of operation are subject to change until the park's above-ground facilities are completed.

FORT PAYNE
• pop 13,000
This small community in the valley below Lookout Mountain and Sand Mountain grew out of a stockade that held Cherokees before their forced removal to Oklahoma. Today, it's best known as the home of the country group Alabama and for its sock mills. It's proximity to the Little River Canyon and Bucks Pocket State Park makes it a convenient base for outdoor activities.

Orientation & Information
Gault Ave (Hwy 11) is the main thoroughfare. Most streets that cross it stretch numerically north and south from 1st St.

Contact the De Kalb County Visitor Association (☎ 256-845-3957), 2201 J Gault Ave N, for information; it's open weekdays 9 am to 4 pm. The post office (☎ 256-845-0434) is at 301 1st St SE. De Kalb Baptist Medical Center (☎ 256-845-3150) is at 200 Medical Center Drive.

De Kalb is a dry county. Unless otherwise posted, you may bring liquor into hotels and campgrounds. Some restaurants allow you to bring it in discreetly. Ask in advance.

Activities
For folks who want to experience nature without frills, Rebecca and Bill Adams of Adams Outdoors (☎ 256-845-2988), 6102 Mitchell Rd NE, Fort Payne, provide numerous outdoor activities, including **rafting** trips down the Little River from late winter to early June (the rest of the year the river is

too low, **rappelling** and introductory **caving** ($60 for two people). Escorted rafting trips cost $25 per person (minimum of two people) or $10 to $15 unescorted (with shuttle). They also arrange horseback riding and wagon rides. Their 70-acre spread has rustic cabins, shelters and campsites (see Places to Stay, below).

Places to Stay

For another option see De Soto State Park in the Around Fort Payne section, later in this chapter.

Tucked in the forest near De Soto State Park is 13-acre *Knotty Pine Resort* (☎ 256-845-5293, 1492 County Rd 618), which has tent ($7 to $9) and RV ($10 to $13) sites as well as cabins. Fully furnished four- and six-person cabins ($65 to $90) have fireplaces, TVs, heating systems, air-con, grills and full- and king-size beds; more rustic four-person cabins ($30 to $38) have no bathrooms, but have heat and air-con, ceiling fans, queen-size and bunk beds. There's a two-night minimum on weekends (three nights on major holidays).

Adams Outdoors (☎ 205-845-2988, 6102 Mitchell Rd NE), in the woods near De Soto State Park, rents rustic furnished two-bedroom cabins for up to eight people ($65 to $70) and secluded one-room cabins ($50 to $60). There are also screened weather-proof huts with sleeping gear, water and electricity for $20 to $30, and tent sites for $12 to $15.

The nicest feature of the *Quality Inn* (☎ 256-845-4013, 1412 Glenn Blvd), on I-59 at Hwy 35, is the kidney-shaped pool with a separate pool for kids. Singles/doubles cost $42/47.

A bit of a drive from Fort Payne is Hess and Kathy Fridley's *Ivy Creek Inn* (☎ 256-505-0722, 800-379-4711, 985 Carlton Rd), off Hwy 79 N in Guntersville just across Lake Guntersville from Buck's Pocket State Park. At $79 to $99 per night, it's far from the cheapest lodgings in the area, but the extensive hiking trails and rock formations behind the inn are gorgeous. It's also close to Cathedral Caverns. As a college student, Hess was a participant in the second Selma-to-Montgomery march in 1965, one of many stories he'll tell while leading guests on pre-breakfast nature hikes.

Places to Eat

Little River Café (☎ 256-997-0707, 4608 DeSoto Parkway NE) offers standard Southern fare with no mistakes and is a big favorite with locals. Lunch costs $5, dinner $9. It's open 10 am to 8 pm weekdays.

Peking Gourmet (☎ 256-845-1606, 2605 Gault Ave N) has a 30-item buffet including desserts that cost $5 at lunch, $7 at dinner. Very filling combination plates that include an egg roll, fried rice and wontons stuffed crabmeat and cream cheese cost around $4 at lunch and $7 to $8 at dinner.

Western Sizzlin (☎ 256-845-6111, 2200 Gault Ave N) is a regional chain that serves steaks, seafood and chicken. The buffet is the best deal. It features meat, fish, veggies and macaroni and cheese weekdays 11 am to 4 pm for $5; after 4 pm and on weekends the buffet is $7. It's open Sunday to Thursday 10:30 am to 10 pm and Friday and Saturday to 11 pm.

Getting There & Away

Located west of the Little River Canyon National Preserve and southwest of De Soto State Park, Fort Payne can be reached quickly via I-59 or by taking the scenic Lookout Mountain Parkway. You can also take Canyon Rim Drive (Hwy 176) and turn west onto Hwy 35.

AROUND FORT PAYNE
Little River Canyon National Preserve

The Little River flows through Little River Canyon, which is about 16 miles long, three-quarters of a mile at its widest and 400 to 700 feet deep, making it one of the deepest gorges east of the Mississippi River. More than 14,000 acres around the river and canyon are part of the preserve, which was established in 1992. Its headquarters (☎ 256-845-9605) are at 2141 Gault Ave N in Fort Payne. Hwy 176 (Canyon Rim Drive) follows the west rim of the canyon for 22 miles. While you're driving, the views of the waterfalls, canyon and wildflowers are the attraction. Once you're out of the car, hiking, rock climbing and white water await.

At the north end of the preserve is De Soto State Park (see later). In the middle are the dramatic 60-foot Little River Falls, accessed by an easy hike at the turnoff at Hwys 176 and 35. At the south end and on the opposite side is Canyon Mouth Park, a day-use area with a 1½-mile hiking trail, a swimming area, bathrooms, picnic tables and grills. Don't miss the lookouts on either side of Bear Creek, from where you can see Grace's High Falls, one of the highest cascades in Alabama. Trailheads are well marked along the rim road, particularly at the lookouts. Eberhardt Point – formerly Canyonland Park – has picnic tables, a great view of the canyon and a popular put-in for canoes, kayaks, rafts or inner tubes. It's a 20-minute hike down the canyon to reach the water.

To reach Canyon Mouth Park, you'll need to drive northeast along the canyon rim, then cross the canyon at Hwy 35E and turn south onto Hwy 273. Day-use hours are 7 am to sunset.
www.nps.gov/liri/

De Soto State Park

The best way to explore Lookout Mountain and Little River Canyon in depth is from this 3000-acre park, which has many facilities, including hiking trails, tennis and volleyball courts, a nature center, store (☎ 205-845-5075), restaurant, campground, lodge and chalets. The park's headquarters (☎ 256-845-0051, fax 256-845-8286) are at 13883 County Rd 89 in Fort Payne. Most of the trails pass through woodlands dotted with waterfalls and interesting rock formations. In May and June rhododendrons and mountain laurels bloom. The seasoned hiker can try the 12-mile De Soto Scout Trail, which starts at a nearby Boy Scout camp and passes through thick brush and rugged terrain. There are also some mountain biking trails. The outdoor pool is free for visitors staying in the lodge, cabins and chalets, but costs $2 for campers and day-use visitors. North of the park store is De Soto Falls, where a cascade plummets 100 feet into a rugged gorge.

Primitive sites at the **campground** (☎ 205-845-5075, 800-252-7275) are $7, $13 with water and electricity or $15 with full hookups. Sites are well spaced and shaded. The fully equipped two/four/six-person rustic cabins are $61/66/71.50. Rates at the 25-room lodge range from $54 to $57. The A-frame chalets go for $79. Call or write to the lodge office (☎ 256-845-5380, 800-568-8840, 800-252-7275), 265 County Rd 951, Fort Payne, AL 35967, for cabin, chalet and lodge reservations.

Buck's Pocket State Park

This 2000-acre jewel of a park (☎ 256-659-2000), 393 County Rd 174, is off the beaten path but close enough to De Soto State Park and Guntersville State Park to attract serious outdoor enthusiasts. Four hundred feet above the floor of the gorge, the Jim Lynn Overlook affords a stunning view of the surrounding valley. Drive up by taking the first right in the park or hike up the 2-mile Canyon Trail from the campgrounds below.

The **two campgrounds** beside Little Sauty and South Sauty Creeks are peaceful and beautiful. You will find 40 improved tent and RV sites ($12), 10 primitive sites ($8) and four backpacking sites, all wooded and spacious. There are 15½ miles of interesting trails.

To get to the park take Hwy 227 west into Grove Oak from Hwy 75. The park is well signposted from Grove Oak.

HUNTSVILLE TO THE SHOALS

The Shoals are located in the northwestern corner of Alabama 65 miles west of Huntsville. You can take the well-traveled Hwy 72, but its worth the detour to dip a little south toward Decatur on I-565 and then west on Alt Hwy 72/Hwy 20 to get there. The countryside along Alt Hwy 72 is beautiful and has historic landmarks worth visiting. In spring the landscape is limeade green with plots of deeply plowed copper-colored soil waiting to be planted with cotton. By late summer the landscape is a

ALABAMA

checkerboard of green and white, referred to as summer snow.

Mooresville

Incorporated in 1818, Mooresville, 6 miles east of Decatur and 14 miles west of Huntsville, predates Alabama's admission to the Union (1819). Disney recognized that not much had changed in Mooresville over the years; after covering the paved streets with dirt, the studio filmed the movie *Tom & Huck: The Adventures of Tom Sawyer and Huck Finn* here. Towering trees, small gardens, green lawns, picket fences and historic houses cover the town's 160 acres. The only public building is the post office, which still uses the original boxes dating from 1840.

Start at the old **Stagecoach Inn & Tavern** (1825), said to be the oldest in the state (though this is not its original location). It's the first building on your left as you enter town off I-565. Among the other notable structures are **McNiell House** (1825), on the corner of Piney and Market Sts, where President Andrew Johnson served as a tailor's apprentice when he was a young man, and the **Church of Christ**, where General James Garfield – later the 20th US president – preached sermons while the Union army was camped nearby. A tourist office brochure describes significant houses. It's available from Alabama Mountain Lakes Tourist Association (☎ 256-350-3500, 800-648-5381, fax 256-350-3519), 25062 North St, PO Box 1075, Mooresville, AL 35649. www.almtlakes.org.

Wheeler Plantation

This 50-acre plantation (☎ 256-637-8513), 12280 Hwy 20 (Hwy 72), is in Wheeler, 15 miles west of Decatur. It's the former home of General Joseph 'Fightin' Joe' Wheeler, a congressman and one of the youngest generals in the Confederate Army. The plantation is undergoing some much needed renovation, but the main house is open for tours. Operating hours are in flux due to the construction, so call before going out of your way for a visit. Admission is $4 for adults and $2 for children.

If you're heading east, grab a bite to eat at local favorite **Sonny's BBQ** (☎ 256-355-5590), on Hwy 72/Hwy 20, 4 miles east of the plantation, on the north side of the road. Wheeler is in Lawrence County, a dry county, so no alcohol is served at restaurants.

Courtland

Midway between Decatur and the Shoals, just off Hwy 72/Hwy 20, Courtland is another small town on this highway almost untouched by time. When cotton-planters from Virginia and the Carolinas arrived around 1818, they found good soil and a major waterway nearby. The planters built grand houses reflecting the style of their native states. Within a square mile, there are 27 early houses that belonged to merchants and cotton farmers, along with Victorian, colonial revival and bungalow-style houses and buildings. You can see them all on a driving tour outlined in a free brochure available from the Decatur Convention & Visitors Bureau (online at www.decaturcvb.org) and the Courtland town hall (☎ 256-637-2707, fax 256-637-9336), 361 College St. Stop to walk through the cemetery, which has intricately carved angels, Greek Revival obelisks and other unusual funerary sculptures.

The **Krout House** (☎ 256-637-6383, 551 Tennessee St), the only restaurant in town, serves a good meat-and-three at lunch 10:30 am to 1 pm weekdays.

THE SHOALS

Four cities on the Tennessee River make up the area known as the Shoals: Florence, Sheffield, Tuscumbia and Muscle Shoals. The combined population is 137,000 people. From the early days of exploration, boat pilots feared the river's treacherous 37-mile stretch of craggy rapids known as Muscle Shoals. Wilson Dam, completed in 1924, improved navigation, created recreational areas and brought inexpensive electricity to the poorest section of the US. The availability of cheap labor and power opened the door for industrialization during the 1930s and '40s.

In the late 1960s, '70s and into the '80s, the Shoals made a name for itself in the music industry. It started in 1966 when Rick Hall of Fame Recording Studios and Quin Ivy of Quinvy Studio got Atlantic Records to release Percy Sledge's hit 'When a Man Loves a Woman.' That hit was followed by hits from Wilson Picket, Aretha Franklin, the Rolling Stones, Paul Simon and many others. *Newsweek* reported that Muscle Shoals was to R&B what Nashville was to country. The local music business has slowed since its platinum days, but its studios still produce records. Fame Studios, 603 E Avalon Ave, maintains a good Web site at www.fame2 .com, but does not offer tours. The Tennessee Valley Authority and several large apparel and textile manufacturers are the biggest employers today.

The four cities are connected by Hwy 43/Hwy 72 in the west and Hwy 133, which crosses over the river on Wilson Dam, in the east.

Information

Colbert County Tourism & Convention Bureau (☎ 256-383-0783, 800-344-0783, fax 256-383-2080, www.shoals-tourism.org) is at 719 Hwy 72W, near Woodmont Drive, in Tuscumbia. It covers Muscle Shoals, Sheffield and Tuscumbia. Florence/Lauderdale Tourism (☎ 256-740-4141, 888-356-8687, fax 256-740-4142, www.flo-tour.org) is at 1 Hightower Place. It covers Florence.

The Shoals has four libraries: Florence-Lauderdale Public Library (☎ 256-764-6563), 218 N Wood Ave, Florence, which offers Internet access to its card-holding patrons, but may make exceptions for visitors; Helen Keller Public Library (☎ 256-383-7065), 511 N Main St, Tuscumbia; Muscle Shoals Public Library (☎ 256-386-9212), 1000 E Avalon Ave, Muscle Shoals; and Sheffield Public Library (☎ 256-386-5633), 316 N Montgomery Ave, Sheffield.

For medical care go to Helen Keller Hospital (☎ 256-386-4095), 1300 S Montgomery Ave, Sheffield.

WC Handy Home and Museum

WC Handy, the man known as the father of the blues for his 1912 song 'Memphis Blues,' was born (1873) and raised in this humble two-room wood cabin (☎ 256-760-6427), 620 W College St, Florence. Inside you'll see a lifetime of photos, paintings and treasures while a tape of Handy's music and a narrative plays in the background. A second building houses the Black Heritage Library, filled with journals, photos and books. Especially interesting are photos of Corporal Lawson Coffee along with his original enlistment and discharge papers from the 110th Regiment of the US Colored Infantry. The museum is open Tuesday to Saturday 10 am to 4 pm. Admission is $2 adults, 50¢ children.

Renaissance Tower

There's a splendid view of the Shoals, Wilson Dam and the Tennessee River and Valley from the top of this 300-foot observation tower (☎ 256-764-5900), 1 Hightower Place, Florence. It's open Monday to Saturday 10 to 11:30 am and 1:30 to 5 pm, and Sunday 11 to 11:30 am and 1:30 to 5 pm. Admission is $1.

The *Renaissance Grille* occupies the top floor of the tower, giving diners the best view during lunch (11:30 am to 1:30 pm) and dinner (after 5 pm), but the menu is a bit boring. The rest of the day visitors are welcome to walk around while they look.

Ivy Green

Blind and deaf since the age of 19 months, Helen Keller learned to speak, read and write with the help of a teacher named Anne

Helen Keller's home

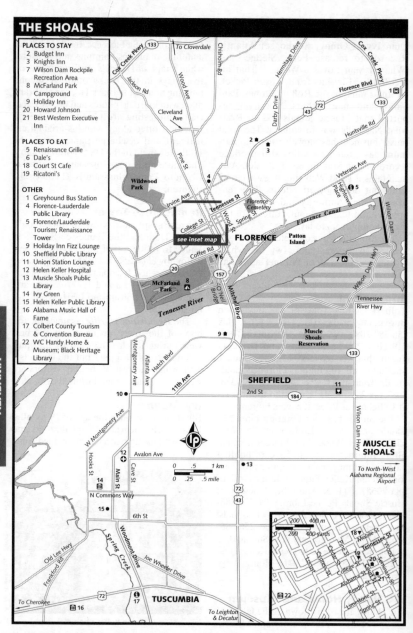

THE SHOALS

PLACES TO STAY
2 Budget Inn
3 Knights Inn
7 Wilson Dam Rockpile Recreation Area
8 McFarland Park Campground
9 Holiday Inn
20 Howard Johnson
21 Best Western Executive Inn

PLACES TO EAT
5 Renaissance Grille
6 Dale's
18 Court St Cafe
19 Ricatoni's

OTHER
1 Greyhound Bus Station
4 Florence-Lauderdale Public Library
5 Florence/Lauderdale Tourism; Renaissance Tower
9 Holiday Inn Fizz Lounge
10 Sheffield Public Library
11 Union Station Lounge
12 Helen Keller Hospital
13 Muscle Shoals Public Library
14 Ivy Green
15 Helen Keller Public Library
16 Alabama Music Hall of Fame
17 Colbert County Tourism & Convention Bureau
22 WC Handy Home & Museum; Black Heritage Library

ALABAMA

Sullivan, who was referred to Keller's parents by Alexander Graham Bell. This near-savage deaf and blind mute child grew into a woman who wrote, spoke and labored incessantly for the betterment of others and almost single-handedly destroyed age-old myths about blindness and handicapped persons.

Keller lived in this 1820s white clapboard house (☎ 256-383-4066), 300 N Commons Way, on a 640-acre wooded tract in Tuscumbia from her birth in 1880 until she left for college. Hundreds of family items, furnishings and awards for her later achievements fill the house. Out back is the original pump where Sullivan taught her to associate words with things and where Keller spoke her first words in 1887. The play *The Miracle Worker*, which chronicles her studies with Sullivan, has been performed here annually since 1961 on Friday and Saturday nights in June and July. (Fans of the play – seasoned travel writers included – often become emotional when they first see the famous water pump up close.)

Ivy Green is open Monday to Saturday 8:30 am to 4 pm, and Sunday 1 to 4 pm, except major holidays. Admission is $3 adults, $1 children.

Alabama Music Hall of Fame

Despite its rather generic locale, the Alabama Music Hall of Fame (☎ 256-381-4417, 800-239-2643, www.alamhof.org), on Hwy 72, Tuscumbia, is a grand salute to the music and artists of Alabama, most of whom left the state to seek fame and fortune. From the Ronald McDowell paintings of artists at the entrance to the actual bus the group Alabama used on tours, memories will come pouring back. It's open Monday to Saturday 9 am to 5 pm, and Sunday 1 to 5 pm, with longer hours in summer. Admission is $6 adults, $5 seniors and students, $3 children.

Places to Stay

Camping A city park, *McFarland Park Campground* (☎ 256-760-6416), off Hwy 20 just west of Hwy 157, on the Tennessee River, Florence, has a boat ramp, improved and primitive camping, picnic areas and a fishing pier. It's open for camping from April 1 to November 30. Sites cost $7 for tents, $10 for RVs.

The primitive campsites at *Wilson Dam Rockpile Recreation Area* (☎ 256-386-3451), on Rockpile Recreation Rd off Wilson Dam Hwy, Muscle Shoals, overlook the Wilson Dam from a bluff. The campground has 50 sites on gravel, 25 of which are located along the bluff over the river. Two trails provide good views of the river. The rate is $11 per night for tents and RVs. It's not staffed; you pay on the honor system.

Hotels & Motels The *Budget Inn* (☎ 256-764-7621, 1238 Florence Blvd) in Florence is really basic, but clean. There's coffee in the office and cable TV. Singles/doubles are $25.50/31.50.

Knights Inn (☎ 256-764-5421, 1241 Florence Blvd), also in Florence, has few amenities – a pool, complimentary breakfast and movie channel – but the rooms are clean and the prices reasonable. Rooms start at $33/38.50.

Microwaves and refrigerators are available on request at *Howard Johnson* (☎ 256-760-8888, 400 S Court St) in Florence. *USA Today*, a movie channel and continental breakfast are free, staff members are cheery and helpful, and rooms are $44/49.

The *Best Western Executive Inn* (☎ 256-766-2331, 504 S Court), in Florence, has a restaurant, pool and lounge. There's complimentary breakfast until 10 am and free coffee all day. Some rooms have data ports and refrigerators. Rooms are $51/56.

Service is attentive at the *Holiday Inn* (☎ 256-381-4710, 4900 Hatch Blvd) in Sheffield. The hotel is set back from the highway in the middle of a thicket of trees. There's an exercise room, outdoor pool, indoor whirlpool, lounge and restaurant. Rooms are spacious, and amenities include modem ports with surge protectors, coffee machines, irons and boards, hair dryers and showers with water massagers. Rates are $73 to $76, single or double.

ALABAMA

Places to Eat

The following restaurants are in Florence:

The large, bright *Court St Cafe* (☎ 256-767-4300, 201 N Seminary St), at Mobile St, caters to students and young professionals. It's a bit of a corporate, 'brass and glass' restaurant, but the food is good. The menu features weekday all-you-can-eat specials including chicken, ribs and linguine ($7.50 to $12.50), plus fish and steaks. It's open daily for meals 11 am to 10 pm; the popular bar is open till 11 pm.

If you're looking for a simple setting with good food, try *Dale's* (☎ 256-766-4961, 1001 Mitchell Blvd). Steaks and seafood make up the bulk of the menu. It's a casual place popular with local families, but backyard chefs all over the South use their extra-strength steak marinade. To get there cross O'Neil Bridge and take the first turn left onto the service road; Dale's is on the right. Dinner checks range from $9 to $18. It's closed Sunday.

The urbane, yet fun *Ricatoni's* (☎ 256-718-1002, 107 N Court St) keeps this city's tenuous connection with Florence, Italy, alive. In a region where many Italian restaurants fiercely compete to create the blandest of all possible red sauces, Ricatoni serves up wonderful pasta dishes and pizzas that actually contain garlic, basil and pepper. Try the smoked duck pasta. Lunch prices range from $8 to $9, dinner from $10 to $18.

Entertainment

The Shoals' cinemas include Carmike's *Capri Twin* (☎ 256-767-0211), in Regency Square Mall, and *Hickory Hills Cinema* (☎ 256-766-7700, 1946 Florence Blvd), in the Hickory Hills Shopping Center.

On Thursday night, the *Holiday Inn Fizz Lounge* (☎ 256-381-4710, 4900 Hatch Blvd), in Sheffield, hosts 'songwriter's night,' showcasing a different songwriter each week. It's a virtual who's who of music. The *Union Station Lounge* (☎ 256-383-4602, 524 E 2nd St), in Muscle Shoals, presents live rock and blues acts Tuesday and Thursday to Saturday. It has pool tables and there are pool tournaments on Monday and Friday nights.

Getting There & Away

Air Northwest Alabama Regional Airport (☎ 256-381-2869), on TE Campbell Drive in Muscle Shoals, is served by Northwest Airlink with three flights a day to and from Memphis. For service from other areas, the nearest airport in Alabama is Huntsville International Airport (☎ 256-772-9395), 1000 Glenn Hearn Blvd, 70 miles east (I-565 exit 7).

Bus Greyhound (☎ 256-764-2313), 500 E Tennessee St in Florence, runs two buses a day to the following cities: Atlanta ($51), Birmingham ($27) and Memphis ($34). Nashville ($36) and Huntsville ($14) are serviced by one daily bus.

Executive Connection provides an airport shuttle service from Huntsville (see Getting Around in the Huntsville section, earlier in this chapter) for $75.

Car There are two pleasant drives from the Shoals east to Huntsville, described in the introduction to the Huntsville to the Shoals section, earlier in this chapter. The most scenic route south to William B Bankhead National Forest is along Hwy 43, then Hwys 5 and 13 to Hwy 278 east. The route passes through Russellville, one of Alabama's best areas for canoeing; the historic town of Haleyville; and the natural wonder at Natural Bridge.

Hertz is the only car-rental agency at the Northwest Alabama Regional Airport. The major agencies have counters at the Huntsville and Memphis airports. Companies with offices in the Shoals include Enterprise Rent-A-Car (☎ 256-767-0292), 1626 Darby Drive, Florence.

Getting Around

Public transportation is provided by Dial-a-Ride (☎ 256-314-0047) with a one-way fee of $1. You need to call at least 24 hours in advance. There is no regularly scheduled service.

Express Cab Company (☎ 256-764-1010), Haney's Taxi Company (☎ 256-764-0121) and Yellow Cab of Florence (☎ 256-766-1000) provide taxi service.

THE SHOALS TO CULLMAN
Sipsey Wilderness

Operated by the United States Forest Service (USFS), this protected wilderness area within the William B Bankhead National Forest contains ancient trees, high bluffs, waterfalls, gorges, wildlife, wildflowers – in short, the best hiking trails in Alabama. The best one is Trail 200, which starts at the County Road 60 bridge. There aren't many wilderness areas in this region, and large groups have been wreaking havoc on Sipsey's fragile ecosystem, so observe leave-no-trace guidelines.

The Sipsey River system – most of it protected by Wild and Scenic designation – is canoeable from Kinlock Falls on Hubbard Creek or Forest Service Route 224 on Borden Creek to the backwaters of Smith Lake (about 30 miles). All but the last 5½ miles are rainfall dependent and usually not floatable from June through November, unless there's been a lot of rain. Canoe rentals (but not shuttle services) and water level information are available from Bear Creek Canoe Run (☎ 205-993-4459, 800-788-7070, morganout@aol.com), on Hwy 43, 2 miles north of Hackleburg.

In the Grayson area east of Bee Branch, you can also check out the historic **Pine Torch Church**, thought to be the oldest log church in the state. In the heavily trod Bee Branch area is a 500-year-old, 150-foot poplar tree purported to be the largest tree in Alabama.

The ranger station (☎ 205-489-5111) is a mile north of Double Springs on Hwy 33. It's open weekdays 7:30 am to 4 pm. At other times, check the map on the wall outside the station for directions to recreation areas elsewhere. The free *National Forests in Alabama Pocket Visitor Guide* can be ordered by calling ☎ 334-832-4470 or writing to National Forests in Alabama, 2946 Chestnut St, Montgomery, AL 36107. It has a map and gives detailed directions for reaching recreation areas in Bankhead and other national forests.

There's a $3 day-use fee in all areas of the park. Campers at Clear Creek and Corinth must pay the day-use fee in addition to camping fees. For long stays, consider the $30 annual pass valid at all Alabama national forests except for concession operated areas.

There's primitive and improved ***camping*** at Brushy Lake ($5; 13 sites), Clear Creek ($15 or $30; 102 sites), Corinth ($20; 50 sites) and Houston ($10; 86 sites). The prices are based on how modern the individual facility is. The Sipsey Wilderness area has no designated sites, so check with the ranger station before camping. Rates are the same for tents or RVs.

Double Springs

Double Springs is a speck on the map 26 miles west of Cullman on Hwy 278, but two things make it a major tourist stop: it's on

---

The Free State of Winston

History books and movies like *Gone with the Wind* give the impression that everyone in the South sided with the Confederacy. Not true. Winston County, a small county in northwest Alabama, became known as the Free State of Winston when it declared itself neutral during the Civil War. During delegate elections for the secession convention, Charles Sheats ran and won on a platform of 'vote against secession, first, last, and all of the time.' He and 22 other delegates refused to sign the secession resolutions. He returned home and held a county meeting in Looney's Tavern on July 4, 1861, with more than 2500 residents in attendance. The meeting concluded that if it were possible for states to leave the union even though they did not have the 'right' to do so, a county, by the same reasoning, could cease to be part of a state. In the end they didn't secede, but instead refused to take up arms against the Union or the Confederacy and asked to be left alone. However, when the Confederate cavalry arrived in Winston County a few months later and arrested and shot men over 18 years old for violating the Conscript Act, residents took up arms on the side of the Union.

ALABAMA

the edge of the William B Bankhead National Forest, and it's in the heart of Winston County, famous for its role during the Civil War. Playwright Lanny McAlister was taken by the way this pertinacious county fought secession and declared itself neutral, so he wrote the two-hour musical *The Incident at Looney's Tavern*, and the sequel *Aftermath & Legacy of the Incident at Looney's Tavern*. More than 20,000 visitors a year come to see the performance held in an amphitheater cut out of a hillside overlooking Bankhead National Forest. There's a raft of other distractions and attractions around the theater, but with the exception of the excursion and dinner cruises on a riverboat on Smith Lake, you can do without them.

For tickets and information call the office (☎ 205-489-5000, 800-566-6397, fax 205-489-3500) or visit the Web site at www.bham.net/looneys. Performances are held June through August, on Thursday, Friday and Saturday at 8:15 pm. Tickets cost $18 for adults, $16 for seniors, $9 for children. The boat cruise is $20/10 with/without dinner for adults, $19/9 for seniors, $15/5 for children. There's a restaurant on site, but the nearest hotels are in Cullman and Haleyville. To reach the theater, take I-65 to exit 308 (Hwy 278) at Cullman, then drive west 29 miles on Hwy 278. It's on the left.

Bear Creek Canoe Run

For fun, but easy, canoeing during summer weekends, rent a canoe from Bear Creek Canoe Run (☎ 205-993-4459, 800-788-7070, morganout@aol.com), on Hwy 43, 2 miles north of Hackleburg. Bear Creek is the only canoe stream in northern Alabama that's consistently navigable after mid-June. Each weekend, the Tennessee Valley Authority releases a zillion or so gallons of water from the Upper Bear Creek Reservoir specifically so people can paddle down the stream they dammed up. Although there are some waterfalls to portage around, this wonderfully scenic creek is beginner-safe.

CULLMAN
• pop 14,000

This town takes its name from Colonel John G Cullmann, a German refugee who founded it in 1873. You can see his likeness in a 15-foot bronze statue by contemporary Birmingham sculptor Branko Medenica; it's in front of the Cullman County Museum. You can't miss it or the church steeples – they're everywhere. Even more numerous are the chicken coops. Cullman is the top poultry producer in the country.

A highlight is the **Ave Maria Grotto** (☎ 256-734-4110), St Bernard Abbey, 1600 St Bernard Drive SE, off Hwy 278. Brother Joseph Zoettl, a Benedictine monk, may not have described himself as an artist, but clearly his work here is Southern folk art at its best. Between 1912 and 1958 he collected scrap materials from friends around the world to construct 125 well-known religious sites in miniature. The shrines are in the 3-acre garden in the abbey's grounds. Some of the shrines – Shrine of Peter, Lourdes, Noah's Ark, the Tower of Babel and Hanging Gardens of Babylon – stand alone. Others are complete towns covering a small hill. The last of the shrines on the path was made after Brother Joe died. The grotto is open daily from 7 am to dusk, except Christmas day. Admission is $4.50 adults, $3 children.

Cullman is 4 miles east of I-65 on Hwy 278, which cuts through east-west from William B Bankhead National Forest. For an alternate, more rural route to Huntsville and Birmingham, try Hwy 31, which parallels I-65.

Places to Stay & Eat

Good Hope Campground (☎ 256-739-1319, 300 Super Saver Rd), south of Cullman, is a small, basic campground with 38 primitive and improved campsites for tents and RVs. The rate is $10 a night, and it's open year-round. From Huntsville take exit 304 off I-65 and turn left. It's the first street on the left.

The *Days Inn* (☎ 256-739-3800, fax 256-739-3800, 1841 4th St SW) provides simple, clean accommodations and there's a pool and restaurant. Singles/doubles are $40/47.

The *All Steak Restaurant* (☎ 256-734-4322, 414 2nd Ave SW/Hwy 31) has been serving customers for more than 60 years. The menu includes chicken, fish and fresh vegetable dishes. Breakfast costs around $3.50, lunch specials are about $4.50, and dinner starts at $5.50. Desserts and breads are homemade. Warm, sweet orange rolls are a house specialty. It opens daily at 6:30 am and closes at 9 or 10 pm (4 pm on Sunday).

Central Alabama

Called the Black Belt, central Alabama was named for the swath of fertile soil deposited by a network of rivers. The soil is good for growing cotton, and the rivers are good for transporting it to the port of Mobile. In the 1980s, the Army Corps of Engineers created the Tennessee-Tombigbee Waterway, a 234-mile system that connects inland rivers to the Gulf of Mexico. The region has seven state parks, a national forest and numerous recreational lakes.

Football dominates the culture of central Alabama as the state's fiercest rivals, the University of Alabama at Tuscaloosa and Auburn University, sit on opposite sides of the region. Equally opposed historical forces dot this landscape: Civil War sights and antebellum mansions neighbor the important Civil Rights centers of Montgomery and Selma.

MONTGOMERY
• pop 322,000

Although Alabama's capital, Montgomery, retains a provincial feel, since the mid-19th century its primary business has been the administration of the state government. Other major employers are the cattle, dairy and lumber industries, manufacturing and a large military presence at Maxwell Air Force Base.

The small-town atmosphere belies the artistic sophistication behind two of its major attractions: the Alabama Shakespeare Festival and the Montgomery Museum of Fine Arts, both of which draw visitors from around the southeast.

History

At this bend in the Alabama River an Alibamu Indian village existed for hundreds of years. In 1817, as part of Montgomery County, which had been created by the Mississippi Territorial Legislature, the land was sold. The first two buyers were Andrew Dexter, an attorney, and a year later General John Scott. They founded Montgomery.

As the northernmost point that large boats from Mobile could travel up the river, it became an important port for shipping cotton out of the Black Belt. In 1846 the Alabama legislature moved the state capital to Montgomery. In 1861 it became the first capital of the Confederacy.

Excitement came in March 1910 when Orville and Wilbur Wright built an airfield and opened a new school of aviation. That summer, two students flew the first night flights in history. Today the field is part of Maxwell Air Force Base.

Rumblings of dissension over restrictive Jim Crow laws came from within the African-American community in the 1940s, when Edgar Nixon, a Pullman car porter, and fellow blacks asked to register to vote. But it wasn't until the mid-1950s that Montgomery's pot of discontent started to simmer. It began with Rosa Parks' arrest for not giving up her bus seat to a white man. For the next 381 days blacks boycotted city buses. On December 21, 1956, the US Supreme Court finally ordered the desegregation of Montgomery buses.

By the 1960s Montgomery was boiling. On May 20, 1961, Freedom Riders arriving at the Greyhound bus station were beaten by Ku Klux Klansmen, who were later tried and sentenced. In 1963 George Wallace was elected governor on a platform of continued segregation. He made his famous segregation speech on the capitol steps. A year later Dr Martin

ALABAMA

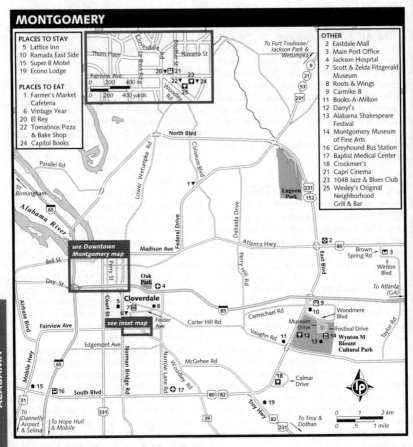

MONTGOMERY

PLACES TO STAY
5 Lattice Inn
10 Ramada East Side
15 Super 8 Motel
19 Econo Lodge

PLACES TO EAT
1 Farmer's Market Cafeteria
6 Vintage Year
20 El Rey
22 Tomatinos Pizza & Bake Shop
24 Capitol Books

OTHER
2 Eastdale Mall
3 Main Post Office
4 Jackson Hospital
7 Scott & Zelda Fitzgerald Museum
8 Roots & Wings
9 Carmike 8
11 Books-A-Million
12 Darryl's
13 Alabama Shakespeare Festival
14 Montgomery Museum of Fine Arts
16 Greyhound Bus Station
17 Baptist Medical Center
18 Crockmier's
21 Capri Cinema
23 1048 Jazz & Blues Club
25 Wesley's Original Neighborhood Grill & Bar

Luther King Jr led a march to the capitol and spoke out against segregation.

Out of Montgomery's racial strife came the Southern Poverty Law Center in 1971, headed by Civil Rights attorney Morris Dees. The center, which teaches tolerance and protects the legal rights of the poor and minorities, sponsored the Civil Rights memorial that is located outside its offices.

After surviving the Civil War and the turmoil of the Civil Rights movement, Montgomery may be successfully emerging from yet another struggle: the fight against boredom. For 22 years, conservative Mayor Emory Folmar routinely denied permits to businesspeople wanting to open nightclubs. Even pop-music concerts were banned until recently. Now, more clubs are beginning to open, and nightlife in Montgomery means more than the chirping of lonely crickets.

Orientation

Montgomery sprawls across seven hills overlooking the Alabama River. Many of its attractions are downtown and can be reached on foot. I-65 runs north-south along the western edge of town, connecting Birmingham and Mobile. I-85 starts at I-65 and splits the city in half as it heads east to Atlanta. Hwy 80 skirts the city's southwest corner, heading west to Selma. Most of downtown's north-south streets are one-way. The four-lane (sometimes six-lane) ring road around Montgomery is known as the Boulevard. Depending on where you are, it's called North, East, South or West Boulevard. Hotels, restaurants and shopping malls line it, especially between Vaughn and Woodley Rds.

Information

Tourist Offices The Convention & Visitor Center (☎ 334-262-0013, 334-240-9455), 300 Water St, downtown, is in the restored Union Station. It's open weekdays 8:30 am to 5 pm, Saturday 9 am to 4 pm, and Sunday noon to 4 pm. It has a small gift shop and puts out a comprehensive monthly events calendar and discount coupon book. On weekdays parking downtown is difficult.

Pick up a free pass that allows you to park in reserved spots marked 'Visitor Permit Parking Only' while visiting the attractions around the capitol.

Money Regions Bank (☎ 334-832-8011), 8 Commerce St, offers international currency exchange.

Post The main post office (☎ 334-244-7624), 6701 Winton Blvd, is open weekdays 7 am to 7 pm and Saturday 8 am to 4 pm. The downtown post office (☎ 334-244-7576) is at 135 Catoma St at Montgomery Ave. It's open weekdays 7:30 am to 5:30 pm, Saturday 8 am to noon.

Bookstores & Libraries Capitol Books (☎ 334-265-1473), 1140 E Fairview Ave, Cloverdale, began in 1950 as a downtown newsstand. Today it focuses on good fiction (much of it regional) and travel guides. In fact, if you're standing in Capitol Books

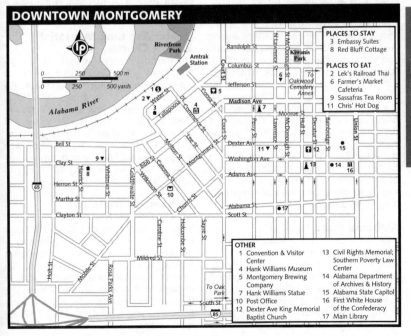

DOWNTOWN MONTGOMERY

ALABAMA

PLACES TO STAY
3 Embassy Suites
8 Red Bluff Cottage

PLACES TO EAT
2 Lek's Railroad Thai
6 Farmer's Market Cafeteria
9 Sassafras Tea Room
11 Chris' Hot Dog

OTHER
1 Convention & Visitor Center
4 Hank Williams Museum
5 Montgomery Brewing Company
7 Hank Williams Statue
10 Post Office
12 Dexter Ave King Memorial Baptist Church
13 Civil Rights Memorial; Southern Poverty Law Center
14 Alabama Department of Archives & History
15 Alabama State Capitol
16 First White House of the Confederacy
17 Main Library

right now, reading this, please proceed to the cash register.

The Birmingham-based Books-A-Million (☎ 334-272-5580), 2572 East Blvd, has lots of local-interest books as well as a large selection of international newspapers and magazines. It also has a cafe.

Roots & Wings (☎ 334-262-1700), 1345 Carter Hill Rd, is a champion of African-American culture through books, cards, calendars, magazines and recordings. There's an art gallery and a theater for readings, lectures and storytelling.

The main branch of the city's library (☎ 334-832-1394) is at 445 S Lawrence St, provides Internet access to card-holding patrons, but the administrator will make exceptions for some visitors.

Medical Services The Baptist Medical Center (☎ 334-288-2100), 2105 E South Blvd, and Jackson Hospital (☎ 334-293-8000) at 1235 Forest Ave, provide emergency and routine medical care.

Civil Rights Memorial

This stirring monument, 400 Washington Ave in the Southern Poverty Law Center, honors those who died during the Civil Rights movement. Created by artist Maya Lin, who designed the Vietnam Veterans Memorial in Washington, DC, the memorial is a circular black granite 'clock' with the names and dates of death of 40 martyrs of the movement. Water flows over it and an adjacent wall of granite is inscribed with the words that Dr Martin Luther King Jr often quoted from the Bible: 'Until justice rolls down like waters and righteousness like a mighty stream.' The memorial is open 24 hours a day and entry is free.

Alabama State Capitol

Nicknamed Goat Hill, because goats once grazed here, the capitol (☎ 334-242-3935), on Bainbridge St at Dexter Ave, is the second built on the site. The first capitol was built in 1847 but was consumed by fire two years later. The current building was erected in time for the November 1851 legislative session. The guided tour includes the three-

story spiral staircase built by Horace King, a former slave and carpenter who later served in the legislature, and the chambers where delegates voted to form the Confederate States of America.

The steps leading from Dexter Ave have witnessed some of history's big moments. Here, Jefferson Davis accepted the oath of office as president of the Confederacy in 1861. A century later, Governor George Wallace spoke the fateful words, 'Segregation now! Segregation tomorrow! Segregation forever!' in defiance of federal orders to integrate Alabama's colleges. Three years later, Dr Martin Luther King Jr delivered the speech in which he said 'Segregation is on its deathbed, and the only thing uncertain about it is how costly the segregationists and Wallace will make the funeral.'

It's open weekdays 9 am to 5 pm, and Saturday 9 am to 4 pm. Tours lasting 45 minutes are given throughout the day, except from noon to 1 pm. Admission is free.

Dexter Ave King Memorial Baptist Church

Dr Martin Luther King Jr began his involvement in the Civil Rights movement while serving as pastor at this church, 454 Dexter Ave, downtown, from 1954 to 1960. Inside, a mural depicts his life. Tours are given Monday to Thursday at 10 am and 2 pm, Friday at 10 am, and Saturday every 45 minutes from 10:30 am to 12:45 pm and by appointment. You can walk through unescorted only on Saturday from 1:30 to 2 pm. It's closed for services on Sunday.

Alabama Department of Archives & History

These are the oldest state-funded archives (☎ 334-242-4363), 624 Washington Ave, in the country. Within the walls of the elegant building is a vast storehouse that tells the story of Alabama through exhibits and art displays. The archives are open weekdays 9 am to 5 pm and Saturday 8 am to 5 pm (closed on major holidays). There's no admission charge.

First White House of the Confederacy

Jefferson Davis, president of the Confederate States of America, and his wife, Varina Anne Howell, took up residence in this house (☎ 334-242-1861) in 1861. Originally on Washington Ave, it was moved to its current location across from the capitol in 1920. It is furnished with furniture and family belongings from the Davis' home in Mississippi. There's a small Confederate museum. It's open weekdays 8 am to 4:30 pm (closed Saturday and state holidays). Entry is free.

Montgomery Museum of Fine Arts

On a sunny day it seems that all of Montgomery heads for Wynton M Blount Cultural Park, a lovely 250-acre green space on the east side of town, just off I-85. This idyllic setting serves as a backdrop for the world-class fine arts museum (☎ 334-244-5700, www.fineartsmuseum.com), 1 Museum Drive, and the Carolyn Blount Theatre, home of the Alabama Shakespeare Festival (see Entertainment, later in this section).

The permanent collection focuses on 19th- and 20th-century American art and southeast regional art. The print collection features more than a century of masters ranging from Picasso to Dürer. Kids feel right at home in ArtWorks, a hands-on interactive gallery, art studio and learning center. In addition, the museum exhibits 10 to 15 temporary shows a year. There's a museum shop and a cafe overlooking the lake. It's open Tuesday to Saturday 10 am to 5 pm (to 9 pm Thursday) and Sunday noon to 5 pm (closed major holidays). There's no admission charge. The closest bus service is the No 18, which runs from Central City and along the Boulevard and stops about a mile away.

Hank Williams Museum

Country-music fans will remember the day in 1953 when Hank Williams died in the back seat of his Cadillac at age 29. His hometown remembers him with this museum at 118 Commerce St, downtown.

The facility's holdings include the same Cadillac in which he died, his stage suits, his guitars and numerous other artifacts from the singer-songwriter's life. It's open 9 am to 6 pm Monday to Saturday and 1 pm to 4 pm Sunday. Admission is $4.

Oakwood Cemetery is the resting place of Williams and his wife, and is only five minutes away, as is the life-size statue located in Lister Hill Park across from the City Auditorium, where 20,000 mourners stood outside his funeral.

Scott & Zelda Fitzgerald Museum

The writers Zelda (née Sayre) and F Scott Fitzgerald lived at 919 Felder Ave from 1931 to 1932. They're making a big to-do about a house that the authors only spent a year in, but fans will be fans, and this place is kind of interesting. Zelda was born in Montgomery and spent most of her life here. Part of the house is a museum (☎ 334-264-4222, 334-262-1911), and a 25-minute film of the couple's life in Montgomery is

ALABAMA

Hank Williams

shown. It's open Wednesday to Friday 10 am to 2 pm, weekends 1 to 5 pm, and by appointment.

Organized Tours

Alabama Anne's Tours (☎ 334-277-2526, 800-531-0502 outside Alabama) provides sightseeing excursions for individuals and groups.

The Landmarks Foundation (☎ 334-240-4500) offers a self-driving tour with a book and cassette. The self-driving tour booklet costs $3 and the audio cassette is $7.

Special Events

The city's biggest bash is Jubilee Cityfest (☎ 334-834-7220), an arts and entertainment festival celebrated on Memorial Day weekend. Desta (☎ 334-244-5700, 334-271-5300), derived from an Ethiopian word meaning celebration, is a festival showcasing African-American arts and culture. It takes place at museums, theaters and lecture halls from January through March. National and international musicians meet in September for the annual Alabama Jazz and Blues Federation River Jam (☎ 334-240-5052) on the waterfront. The Alabama Indian Pow Wow (☎ 334-242-2831) presents Native American dancing, crafts and entertainment on the last weekend in October in Garrett Coliseum.

Places to Stay

Camping At the *Montgomery KOA* (☎ 334-288-0728, 250 Fisher Rd), in Hope Hull, there are over 100 sites. It's 4 miles south of Montgomery. Take exit 164 (Hwy 31) off I-65. For two people it's $22 for an RV site with all utilities or $17 for a tent site with electricity and water; it's $1 for each extra person.

Historic *Fort Toulouse/Jackson Park* (☎ 334-567-3002), on Fort Toulouse Rd in Wetumpka, has a 39-site campground with water and electricity. There's a bathhouse, boat launch and picnic area. Sites cost $8 for tents or $10 for RVs. Be sure to visit the fort and arboretum and to hike the nature trails. Take Hwy 231 to Fort Toulouse Rd and turn left.

Hotels & Motels The *Super 8 Motel* (☎ 334-284-1900, 1288 W South Blvd) is near I-65, Mobile Hwy and the airport road (Hwy 80). Rooms are basic but clean and have coffeemakers and free movies; some also have refrigerators. There's a pool. Singles/doubles are $35/39.

The *Econo Lodge* (☎ 334-284-3400, 800-424-4777, 4135 Troy Hwy) has 45 rooms; all have modem ports and free movies. It's close to major shopping malls, popular restaurants and the Alabama Shakespeare Theater. Rooms are $45/50.

Ramada East Side (☎ 334-277-2200, 1355 East Blvd) is within a mile of the Alabama Shakespeare Theater. There is a pool and deck, and rooms come with a complimentary continental breakfast. The popular lounge serves grilled burgers, sandwiches, fries and chicken wings. Rooms are $55/63.

Embassy Suites (☎ 334-269-5055, fax 334-269-0360, 300 Tallapoosa St), downtown on the Alabama River, in front of historic Union Station and Riverfront Park, is in one of the most attractive locations in town. Its tastefully decorated suites are frequently full. Amenities include two phones, voice mail, modem port, complimentary made-to-order breakfast and newspaper, indoor pool, fitness room, sauna, and a wine and cheese reception each evening. Locals frequent *Montgomery's*, the open-kitchen restaurant. The rate is $109 for a single or double.

Inns & B&Bs The *Lattice Inn* (☎ 334-832-9931, 1414 S Hull St) is a comfortable, cozy and professionally managed getaway, convenient to the restaurants and nightspots in Cloverdale. There are two guest rooms furnished with antiques. It also offers two modern rooms that can be made into a suite, and a pool, deck and off-street parking. The owner is renowned for his cookies, and a canister full of them is placed in each room. Room rates range from $65 to $85.

Red Bluff Cottage (☎ 334-264-0056, fax 334-262-1872, 551 Clay St), was built as an inn and has four guest rooms, all decorated with antiques. The upstairs porch affords good views of the Alabama River and capitol. Singles/doubles are $55/65, including full breakfast.

Places to Eat

There are restaurants scattered throughout the city, but three areas give you multiple options: downtown, Cloverdale and the Boulevard. See Bars & Nightclubs under Entertainment, later, for several places where you can grab a bite to eat and listen to live music.

The hot dogs at *Chris' Hot Dog* (☎ *334-265-6850, 138 Dexter Ave)* are plump and juicy. This place has been a Montgomery institution since 1917. It's open Monday to Thursday and Saturday 8:30 am to 7 pm, and Friday 8:30 am to 8 pm.

Weekday mornings the *Farmer's Market Cafeteria* (☎ *334-262-1970, 315 N McDonough St)* buzzes with customers coming for Southern breakfasts ($4). The lunch menu features country cooking, including fresh vegetables and fried chicken, catfish and barbecue. It's inexpensive and good. Expect to pay about $5.50 for lunch. It's open weekdays 5:30 am to 2 pm. There's another branch (☎ 334-271-1885) at 1659 Federal Drive.

People go to the *Sassafras Tea Room* (☎ *334-265-7277, 532 Clay St)* for the food. The atmosphere, river view and good service are just some of the extras. There's a short menu of mostly chicken and pasta dishes, and freshly made desserts such as buttermilk pie. Dinner entrées cost $8 to $15; lunch is priced at $4 to $5.50. It's open for dinner on Friday and Saturday 6 to 9 pm, and for lunch Sunday to Friday 11 am to 2 pm.

Lek's Railroad Thai (☎ *334-244-8994, 300 Water Street)*, in the Union Station, downtown, serves up good Thai dishes in an elegant, almost continental dining room. Every ingredient, from the seafood to the spices, is fresh. Lunch checks average $5, while dinner checks are around $10. It's open Monday to Thursday 11 am to 2:30 pm and 5 to 9:30 pm, Friday to 10:30 pm, and Saturday 11 am to 10:30 pm.

El Rey (☎ *334-832-9688, 1031 E Fairview Ave)*, in Cloverdale, serves up some pretty creative variations on burritos, but go there for the great atmosphere. The interior is lit mostly by self-illuminated artworks made from junk, and the sidewalk dining area is protected by small shade trees. Lunch and dinner cost $7 and $12, respectively. It's open Monday to Saturday 11 am to 10 pm and Sunday 4 to 10 pm.

Tomatinos Pizza & Bake Shop (☎ *334-264-4241, 1036 Fairview Ave)*, in Cloverdale, looks like a neighborhood pizzeria from Brooklyn, but without the framed Tony Bennett photos. Come to think of it, no one there seems particularly Italian, but the pizza is great, and the staff takes good care of you. Lunch and dinner both cost up to $9, depending on how much pizza you can hold. It's open 11 am to 10 pm Monday to Saturday. Tomatinos also serves espresso and pastries in a little shop next door 8 am to 10 pm Monday to Saturday.

The bistro-style *Vintage Year* (☎ *334-264-8463, 405 Cloverdale Rd)* has a menu that blends Southern favorites with light, fresh, trendy ingredients. There's roasted chicken with mashed potatoes and vegetables ($14) and grilled smoked double pork chop with grits and greens ($15). The salad of mixed greens, roasted tomatoes, grilled onion, Parmesan cheese and herb vinaigrette ($6) is big enough for a meal. The restaurant also has a great wine list. Reservations are suggested. It's open Tuesday to Saturday 6 to 9 pm.

Entertainment

In larger cities, the shops and cafes in a place like the center of Cloverdale – also called 'Old Cloverdale' – would simply serve the dining and entertainment needs of one neighborhood. But, this five-point intersection (Fairview Ave, Cloverdale Rd, Woodley Rd) shoulders much of the responsibility of supplying sophisticated fun to all of Montgomery.

The Thursday 'Go' section of the *Montgomery Advertiser* is a guide to local entertainment. The Alabama Jazz and Blues Federation Hot Line (☎ 334-261-0300) lists the area's jazz and blues events.

ALABAMA

Bars & Nightclubs A spot popular with a variety of ages is ***Crockmier's*** *(☎ 334-277-1840, 5620 Calmar Drive)*, off East Blvd. Some come for the food, others come to unwind in the trendy lounge where there's live music on weekends. Most acts are local or regional, but occasionally they bring in groups from elsewhere. On those nights there's a $3 to $5 cover.

There's live jazz seven nights a week at ***1048 Jazz & Blues Club*** *(☎ 334-834-1048, 1048 E Fairview Ave)*, in Cloverdale. The acts range from the Alabama Jazz Federation Jazz Jam to soloists. There's a full bar and snacks are available. When there's a cover, it's usually $3.

Darryl's *(☎ 334-277-1885, 2701 East Blvd)* has acoustic rock on Sunday and there's no cover charge. ***Wesley's Original Neighborhood Grill & Bar*** *(☎ 334-834-2500, 1061 Woodley Rd)*, in Cloverdale, showcases rock and R&B acts. Cover's $3. It's also a good place to grab a bite to eat.

The ***Montgomery Brewing Company*** *(☎ 334-834-2739, 12 Jefferson St)*, downtown, brews its own ales and lagers to wash down pasta, steaks and great gumbo. It's all served up with blues and rock on weekends. There's no cover.

Cinemas A precious rarity in the Deep South, the ***Capri Cinema*** *(☎ 334-262-4858, 1045 E Fairview Ave)*, in Cloverdale, only shows newly released independent films as well as the classics. Nonmembers pay $5.50, members pay $4 and children pay $2.

There are a few places with $3 bargain matinees: ***Eastdale 8*** *(☎ 334-277-5164, 5501 Atlanta Hwy)*, in the Eastdale Mall; and ***Carmike 8*** *(☎ 334-272-6421, 1755 Eastern Bypass)*.

Theater The ***Alabama Shakespeare Festival*** *(☎ 334-271-5353, 1 Festival Drive)* is an internationally acclaimed event. As well as Shakespeare's plays, which are performed from March through July, the company stages international classics and youth productions. There are two theaters, the 750-seat Festival Theater, where the acoustics are fabulous, and the 225-seat Octagon Theater. Don't miss the backstage tours ($5) given on weekends at 11 am, and 'Theatre in the Mind,' a free lecture on each play given by directors, actors and others involved, held on Saturday at noon. Nightly (except Sunday) performances begin at 7:30 or 8 pm; weekend matinees start at 2 pm. Tickets cost $15 to $26. Discounts are available for students, members of the military and seniors. Children's productions cost $16 for adults and $11 for children. Local hotels give theater discounts to guests.

Getting There & Away

Air Montgomery's Dannelly Airport *(☎ 334-281-5040)*, 4445 Selma Hwy (Hwy 80), is served by Delta, US Airways and Northwest Airlink. It's 15 minutes from downtown on Hwy 80 and I-65.

Bus Greyhound *(☎ 334-286-0658)*, 950 W South Blvd, has nine buses daily to Atlanta ($33, 3½ hours), six to New Orleans ($54, 6½ hours), five each to Baton Rouge ($70, seven to nine hours), Mobile ($29, 5½ hours) and Tuscaloosa ($23, three hours), four to Birmingham ($16, 1½ hours), three each to Biloxi ($53, six to seven hours), Huntsville ($39, 4½ hours) and Memphis ($59, nine hours), two to Auburn ($15, one hour) and one to Meridian ($39, four hours).

Train Amtrak *(☎ 800-872-7245)*, 335 Coosa St, downtown, has service provided by chartered bus to and from Mobile ($27 one-way) and Birmingham ($15). From there you can catch trains to Atlanta ($52) and beyond. In any case, it's faster and cheaper to take a bus to New Orleans than to connect with Amtrak trains through Mobile or Birmingham.

Car Avis, Budget, Hertz and National rental-car agencies have counters at the airport, downstairs next to the ticket counters. Enterprise *(☎ 334-277-4300)*, 137 East Blvd and 617 S Decatur St; National *(☎ 334-213-4530)*, 645 East Blvd; and Snappy Car Rental *(☎ 334-277-6600)*, 131 Eastdale Rd S, have branches in town.

Getting Around

The Montgomery Area Transit System (MATS; ☎ 334-262-7321) provides public transportation on weekdays from 6 am to 9:30 pm; there's a limited service on weekends. The fare is $1.75.

The Airport Shuttle Service (☎ 334-279-5662) runs vans between Atlanta Airport and Montgomery. The rate per person is $60 one-way or $90 roundtrip, and it's $40/60 for each additional passenger.

Checker-Deluxe Cab Company (☎ 334-263-2512), Original Queen Cab Company (☎ 334-263-7137) and Yellow Cab Company (☎ 334-262-5225) all provide taxi service. A taxi downtown from the airport is about $11 for one person, with a $1 charge for each additional passenger.

SELMA

• pop 22,000

Modern Selmians in this small city like to boast that theirs is a two-part history: part Civil War and part Civil Rights. With more than 1250 buildings, Selma's historic district is the largest and second oldest in the state. The city has 88 churches, primarily Baptist. The economy here is driven by tourism, as well as the paper and textile industrial plants of neighboring areas, and light manufacturing.

History

Located on the Alabama River, Selma's excellent transportation arteries – both rail and water, were important in moving cotton to markets. Known as the 'Queen City of the Black Belt,' its one-time wealth is evidenced by the scores of grand antebellum homes that remain even after more than 600 buildings, both industrial and residential, were burned in 1865 by federal troops following the Confederate defeat in the Battle of Selma.

The defeat was crucial for the Union. Nearly half of the munitions used by the Confederacy were manufactured at the Selma Navy Yard and Ordnance Works. Brooke cannon, the most powerful muzzle-loading cannon ever produced, and the ironclad Confederate ship *Tennessee*, which fought in the Battle of Mobile Bay, were built here.

After the Civil War, Selma quickly rebuilt, but an even bigger adversary proved to be the boll weevil. When the weevil arrived in 1914, the county produced 64,000 bales of cotton. Two years later, production had plunged nearly 80% to 14,200 bales.

The majority of Dallas County's population has historically been black due to the demand for cotton workers. As a major inland port in the Black Belt, Selma was an obvious choice for a slave-trading post. Writer John Hardy in *Selma: Her Institutions and Her Men* (1879) describes the atmosphere:

Large droves, some hundreds daily, were brought to the town by men whose business it was to trade in negroes. Several large buildings were erected in town especially for the accommodation of negro traders and their property. On the ground floor, a large sitting room was provided for the exhibition of negroes on the market, and from among them could be selected blacksmiths, carpenters, bright mulatto girls and women for seamstresses, field hands, women and children of all ages, sizes and qualities. To have seen the large droves of negroes arriving in the town every week, from about the first of September to the first of April, no one could be surprised that the black population increased in Dallas County, from 1830 to 1840, between twelve and thirteen thousand.

During Reconstruction, blacks here made many political firsts. Selma elected three black leaders to the US House of Representatives, state senate and state judicial bench.

Ironically, it was voting rights for blacks that brought Selma international infamy nearly a hundred years later on Bloody Sunday, March 7, 1965. The media captured on film state troopers and mounted deputies beating and gassing African-Americans and white sympathizers near the Edmund Pettus Bridge, who were on their way to the state capital to demonstrate for voting rights. President Lyndon Johnson intervened and the march was rescheduled to take place two weeks later under the

ALABAMA

protection of the federalized Alabama National Guard.

The marches, which had been preceded by two years of violence against blacks and white sympathizers as they held demonstrations and attempted to register voters, ended when President Johnson signed the Voting Rights Act of 1965 and sent federal registrars and observers to Alabama.

Joe Smitherman had been the pro-segregationist mayor of Selma for less than a year on Bloody Sunday. In the ensuing 35 years, he held on to his leadership despite the fact that the electorate shifted from nearly all white to 65% black. Smitherman' run for a 10th straight term ended in defea in September, 2000, when computer con sultant James Perkins became the city's firs black mayor.

Orientation

Hwy 80 enters the city from the southeast a the historic Edmund Pettus Bridge, ther runs north-south as Broad St, splitting the city. The main residential community and historic district lie west of Broad St, and the commercial and historic waterfront are to the east. At the northern end of the city

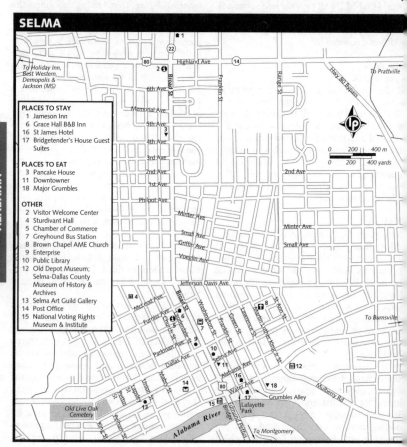

SELMA

PLACES TO STAY
1 Jameson Inn
6 Grace Hall B&B Inn
16 St James Hotel
17 Bridgetender's House Guest Suites

PLACES TO EAT
3 Pancake House
11 Downtowner
18 Major Grumbles

OTHER
2 Visitor Welcome Center
4 Sturdivant Hall
5 Chamber of Commerce
7 Greyhound Bus Station
8 Brown Chapel AME Church
9 Enterprise
10 Public Library
12 Old Depot Museum;
   Selma-Dallas County
   Museum of History &
   Archives
13 Selma Art Guild Gallery
14 Post Office
15 National Voting Rights
   Museum & Institute

Turtle cruising, Dauphin Island, AL

Goin' to sweet home Alabama

WC Handy's home in Florence, now a museum

Shimmering Gulf Shores sunset, salty sea breezes & sand between your toes, Orange Beach, AL

Brown Chapel AME Church, Selma, AL

US Space & Rocket Center, Huntsville, AL

Civil Rights Institute, Birmingham, AL

Birmingham skyline

Hwy 80 turns west as Highland Ave, which is lined with fast-food eateries, chain motels, supermarkets and shopping centers.

Information

The Selma Chamber of Commerce (☎ 334-875-7241, 800-457-3562 in Alabama) is at 513 Lauderdale St. The Visitor Welcome Center (☎ 334-875-7485), 2207 Broad St, is open daily 8 am to 8 pm and provides a wealth of information in a small gift shop with books and reprints of newspapers from the Civil War and days of the voting rights demonstrations.

The *Selma Times Journal* is the city's daily. The best calendar of events is the chamber's *In Selma*.

The public library (☎ 334-874-1720) is in the center of town at 1103 Selma Ave.

For medical help you can go to either Baptist Medical Center (☎ 334-418-4100), 1015 Medical Center Parkway, or Vaughan Regional Medical Center (☎ 334-418-6000), 1050 W Dallas Ave.

Edmund Pettus Bridge

This is the spot where marchers assembled for the Selma-to-Montgomery voting rights marches. It also was the site of Bloody Sunday. It spans the Alabama River at Water Ave and Broad St.

National Voting Rights Museum & Institute

The objects in this modest museum (☎ 334-418-0800), 1012 Water Ave, near the Edmund Pettus Bridge, make powerful statements, starting with messages on the 'I Was There Wall,' which have been left by reporters, witnesses and the men, women and children who marched on Bloody Sunday and returned three decades later to relate their experiences. Hanging on other walls are original signs reading 'We Serve Colored,' 'Colored Section in Rear,' and 'White Only.' The Footprints for Freedom room houses photos of Bloody Sunday. Other rooms cover earlier periods of history, including women's suffrage in Alabama. The institute sponsors an anniversary reenactment of the Selma-to-

Montgomery march held each year during the Bridge Crossing Jubilee (see Special Events). The museum is open Tuesday to Saturday 9 am to 5 pm. Admission is $4 for adults, $2 for children.

Old Depot Museum

If you're limited to one stop in Selma, make this it. Few museums of this size have such a rich and important collection. The reason? It serves as the Selma-Dallas County Museum of History and Archives (☎ 334-874-2197), 4 Martin Luther King Jr St. Among the artifacts are Native American arrowheads, tools, a bow-and-arrow case that belonged to Geronimo, and US army muskets that were found bent around the skulls of buried warriors. The large Civil War collection includes letters from Andrew Johnson pardoning citizens who fought for the Confederacy, musket balls weighing up to 32 pounds and made in the Selma Navy Yard, uniforms and weapons. The Work Project Administration (WPA) murals painted by Felix Gaines, one of a few African-American artists who painted for the WPA, are exceptional. The other standout is the Keipp Collection, 46 black & white photographs of African-Americans living and working on a local plantation in the late 19th century. The photographs, which were found in a bag in an old house, constitute a rare and unique collection. Curator Jean Martin is a veteran journalist and a fountain of knowledge about the county and state. The museum is open Monday to Saturday 10 am to 4 pm and by appointment on Sunday. Entry is $4 for adults, $3 for seniors and $2 for children.

Brown Chapel AME Church

This church (☎ 334-874-7897), at 410 Martin Luther King Jr St, was founded in 1866 and claims to be the first African Methodist Episcopal (AME) church in the state. It served as a meeting place throughout the Civil Rights struggle and was a starting point for the voting rights marches in 1965. Outside the red-brick building are two monuments, one honoring those who died in the struggle and one of Dr Martin Luther King Jr. Inside, the Martin Luther King Room has mementos of the movement. Tours are given by appointment.

Sturdivant Hall

This Greek Revival neoclassic antebellum mansion (☎ 334-872-5626), 713 Mabry St, is furnished with antiques donated by Robert Sturdivant, a wealthy businessman who left the city $50,000, and local residents, including Clara Weaver Parrish, an artist who designed stained glass for Louis C Tiffany. Among the museum's treasures are furnishings and personal items that belonged to the original owners and a gold clock featuring a statue of George Washington. The home, built in 1852, has numerous innovative architectural details, including jib windows that also serve as doors. It's open Tuesday to Friday 9 am to 4 pm, and Saturday 10 am to 4 pm. Admission is $5 for adults, $2 for students, children and seniors.

Old Live Oak Cemetery

'There is Glory in Graves,' reads the inscription on the Confederate Monument in the middle of this historic cemetery (☎ 334-875-7241) on Dallas Ave at King St. The cemetery derives its name from the 80 live oaks and 80 magnolias that were planted in 1879. Today, the century-old trees laced with Spanish moss shade the elaborate headstones and tombs dating back to 1829. Among the celebrated Selmians buried there are US Vice President William Rufus King. It's open weekdays from dawn to dusk and entry is free.

Organized Tours

The Chamber of Commerce offers driving- and walking-tour maps, covering ghosts, historic homes and African-American heritage and history. It also arranges for groups with an interest in the Civil Rights movement to meet people who witnessed the voting rights drives. Pick up a free copy of *Selma's Ghost Tour*. It explains the ghostly legends behind Sturdivant Hall, Grace Hall and the cemetery.

Special Events

Three of Selma's biggest events are the three-day Historic Selma Pilgrimage tours of historic homes on the third weekend of March, the four-day Civil War Reenactment of the Battle of Selma (☎ 334-875-7241) with more than 2000 participants in late April, and the Bridge Crossing Jubilee. Held the first weekend in March, the jubilee is a commemoration of the anniversary of Bloody Sunday and the Selma to Montgomery march. Activities include a pageant, a dance, women and youth conferences, a parade (in which President Clinton participated in 2000), interfaith service and inductions into the National Voting Rights Museum Hall of Fame. The Tale Tellin' Festival is held Friday and Saturday nights in October.

Places to Stay

Hotels & Motels Overlooking the Alabama River, the restored historic *St James Hotel* (☎ 334-872-3234, 1200 Water Ave) has 42 guest rooms, a good restaurant and a popular lounge whose large glass doors open onto the sidewalk, giving it a French Quarter feel. In its heyday, this was a popular first-class hotel frequented by steamboat passengers. Note the lovely grillwork around the balcony. Singles/doubles cost $85/95.

With 60 spacious rooms, a pool, movie channel and complimentary continental breakfast and newspaper, the *Jameson Inn* (☎ 334-874-8600, 2420 N Broad St/Hwy 22) offers good value. Rates are $59/63.

The two-story *Holiday Inn* (☎ 334-872-0461, 1806 W Highland Ave/Hwy 80) has a pool, complimentary continental breakfast, movie channel, restaurant and laundry service. Ask for a room off the highway. Rates are $50/58.

Best Western (☎ 334-872-1900, 1915 W Highland Ave/Hwy 80) is clean and comfortable; some of the larger rooms have kitchenettes. Rates are $48/55.

B&Bs A restored antebellum home dating from 1857, *Grace Hall Bed & Breakfast Inn* (☎ 334-875-5744, 506 Lauderdale St) has six rooms – three in the main house and three in an annex. Guests receive a tour of the mansion and full breakfast. The property has over an acre of gardens and 1000 square feet of porches. Single rooms range from $69 to $89 and double rooms from $79 to $99.

The Bridgetender's House Guest Suites *(☎ 334-875-5517, bridgtendr@aol.com, 2 Lafayette Park)*, where Washington St meets the Alabama River, sits in the shadow of the Edmund Pettis Bridge. It served as a house for, you guessed it, the bridgetender/ toll collector of an earlier bridge. Now it houses a charming pair of guest suites, with kitchens, one bedroom each, and sitting rooms overlooking the river. Suites are $65 and $74 per night, including continental breakfast.

Places to Eat

There are surprisingly few restaurants for a city this size. The real problem is on Sunday evening. A church-going town, Selma closes up on Sunday afternoon. Plan to have an early dinner, go to a fast-food eatery, or get invited to someone's house.

Many locals make the ***Pancake House*** *(☎ 334-872-2736, 1617 Broad St)* a regular morning stop. Eat in or take out breakfast or lunch. Try the fresh pies.

At ***Major Grumbles*** *(☎ 334-872-2006, 1 Grumbles Alley)*, off Water St, diners eat in what was once a cotton warehouse on the riverfront. Daily specials include red beans and rice, chicken gumbo soup, and burgers, salads and sandwiches. Lunch for two, including dessert, tax and tip costs about $14. It's open Monday to Saturday from 11 am to 11 pm.

Tally-Ho *(☎ 334-872-1390, Mangum St)* is Selma's best restaurant, serving seafood and steaks from $11 to $16. The building was originally a log cabin. It's open Monday to Saturday 5 to 10 pm. It's a bit hard to find. Take Broad St north and cross Highland Ave, after which Broad St splits. It becomes N Broad St as you veer left. Continue on N Broad St, then turn left onto Mangum St. The restaurant is on the right. You can eat in or take out.

The ***Downtowner*** *(☎ 334-875-5933, 114 Selma Ave)* serves simple but very satisfying meat-and-three lunches on weekdays. The patrons are almost all locals – you should try to sit where you can eavesdrop on all the latest gossip. Lunch costs $6, including a beverage.

Shopping

The Selma Art Guild Gallery (☎ 334-874-9017), 508 Selma Ave, offers a small but quality selection of paintings, pottery and photography by local and regional artists. People on smaller budgets can purchase beautiful note cards. The gallery holds a juried art show in March. It's open Wednesday to Saturday 10 am to 4 pm and by appointment.

Getting There & Away

Montgomery's Dannelly Airport (☎ 334-281-5040), 4445 Selma Hwy (Hwy 80), offers the closest air service. From there it's a pretty easy 40-mile drive to Selma on Hwy 80.

Greyhound (☎ 334-874-4503), 434 Broad St, makes three trips a day from Selma to Birmingham ($23, three hours), two each to Montgomery ($12, one hour) and Tuscaloosa ($17, five hours), and one a day each to Atlanta ($47, five hours) and Mobile ($33, three hours).

Enterprise (☎ 334-874-91040), at 1107 Dallas Ave, and Clean Machine Rentals (☎ 334-872-8054), 1505 W Highland Ave, provide car rentals.

Getting Around

Selma's taxi companies include Deluxe Cab (☎ 334-872-0021, 334-874-9287), at 1020 Griffin Ave, and Eastside Cab Company (☎ 334-872-4480), 103 Division St.

AROUND SELMA
Old Cahawba
Archaeological Park

It's not unheard of for a state to change its capital city, but a former capital's 'vanishing' is quite rare. From 1820 to 1826 Cahawba served as Alabama's state capital and was an important river town. Today, it has more significance to archaeologists than legislators.

Located at the confluence of the Alabama and Cahaba Rivers, it was subject to flooding, making it unsuitable as the capital. In 1826 the capital – and most of the population – moved to Tuscaloosa. Cahawba became a major railroad stop and distribution center for cotton shipped down the Alabama River. During the Civil War, the rail lines were dismantled and the town was used as a prison for Union soldiers. In 1866, floods sent the remaining population scurrying to Selma's bluffs.

The town had been abandoned for nearly 100 years when historians and archaeologists from the Alabama Historical Commission uncovered Cahawba's history and created the park. The visitor center has photos of the former capital and provides visitor maps of the old town. Signs explain the significance of different sites. There's a short nature trail, picnic tables and grills, restrooms and a boat launch on the William B Dannelly Reservoir.

The visitor center is open daily 9 am to 5 pm. The park is open daily from 9 am to dusk. From Selma, take Alabama Hwy 22 west for 8½ miles. Turn onto County Rd 9 and drive 5 miles, then turn left on County Rd 2 into Old Cahawba.

TUSCALOOSA
• pop 160,000

Choctaw and Creeks lived here until settlers displaced them in the early 1800s. The town's name comes from two Choctaw words: *tuska*, meaning 'black,' and *lusa*, meaning 'river.' Tuscaloosa was the state capital from 1826 to 1846 and has been the home of the University of Alabama (UA) since 1831. Say its name and most Alabamians will think football, specifically, UA's Crimson Tide team. While the university is a major influence economically, physically and emotionally (grown men here cry when UA loses a football game), the main sources of revenue are lumbering, paper production and light manufacturing, led by Mercedes Benz, JVC and Gulf States Paper Corporation.

Orientation

Most of the town sits on the south bank of the Black Warrior River, but part of it stretches north across the river to Lake Tuscaloosa. It's sister city, Northport, lies on the river's north bank, north and west of Tuscaloosa. UA sprawls along the river's south bank in the heart of the city.

The town is laid out in an easy-to-follow numerical grid. Numbered avenues run north-south and numbered streets run east-west. River Rd runs east-west along the south bank. University Blvd runs roughly parallel to River Rd a few miles south as it cuts through the middle of campus and ends at 28th Ave at the west end of town. On its east end it joins I-59/20, the road to Birmingham. I-359 enters the city from the south and becomes 25th (northbound) and 26th (southbound) Aves before it crosses the river to Northport. McFarland Blvd (Hwy 82) crosses I-59 and runs parallel to I-359 on the east side of town, skirting the eastern edge of the university before crossing the river.

Information

The Tuscaloosa Convention & Visitors Bureau (☎ 205-391-9200, 800-538-8696, www.tcvb.org) is located in the historic Jemison-Van de Graaf House at 1305 Greensboro Ave (24th Ave). The daily *Tuscaloosa News* has a morning and evening edition. For medical emergencies in Tuscaloosa, go to DCH Regional Medical Center (☎ 205-759-7111), 809 University Blvd E; in Northport, choose Northport/DCH (☎ 205-339-4500), 2700 Hospital Drive.

Gorgas House

Part of the sprawling Univers.ty of Alabama campus, this house (☎ 205-348-5906), on Capstone Drive at Colonial Drive, was erected in 1829 and is the oldest existing structure built by the state. Guests originally entered by climbing the paired curving stairways to the 2nd-floor balcony – the main floor was built above ground level to avoid flooding. The house has lots of family items. Free tours are given Tuesday

TUSCALOOSA

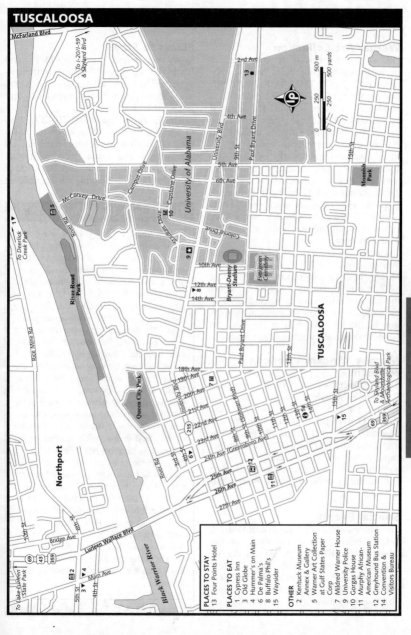

PLACES TO STAY
13 Four Points Hotel

PLACES TO EAT
1   Cypress Inn
3   Old Globe
4   Hummer's on Main
6   De Palma's
8   Buffalo Phil's
15 Waysider

OTHER
2   Kentuck Museum
    Annex & Gallery
5   Warner Art Collection
    at Gulf States Paper
    Corp
7   Mildred Warner House
9   University Police
10 Gorgas House
11 Murphy African-
    American Museum
12 Greyhound Bus Station
14 Convention &
    Visitors Bureau

ALABAMA

to Friday 10 am to 4 pm, Saturday to 3 pm, and Sunday 2 to 4 pm.

Warner Art Collection

One of the best private art collections in the world is at the Gulf States Paper Corporation (☎ 205-553-6200), 1400 River Rd NE. The corporate office, where the collection is housed, is a work of art itself. It's designed as a traditional Japanese-style temple complete with Japanese gardens in back. In essence, there are two collections of art, artifacts and sculpture: works by early and contemporary American artists and works from the Pacific Islands, Africa and Asia. The paintings of wild birds by Basil Ede are exquisite. Free tours are given weekdays at 5:30 and 6:30 pm, on Saturday hourly from 10 am to 4 pm, and on Sunday also hourly from 1 to 4 pm.

Part of the collection is at the Mildred Warner House (☎ 205-345-4062), 1925 8th St. Originally a two-room cabin built in 1822, it was expanded in the 1830s. While the house is interesting architecturally and the antiques are lovely, they pale in comparison to the art collection inside. You can view the collection weekends 1 to 5 pm.

Murphy African-American Museum

The city's first licensed black mortician, William J Murphy, lived in this 1920s cottage (☎ 205-758-2861) at 2601 Paul Bryant Drive (10th St) at Lurleen Wallace Blvd S (26th Ave). It's filled with many original pieces of furniture. Several exhibits capture how life was for middle-class and well-to-do African-Americans in the first half of the century. It's open by appointment only.

Special Events

The Moundville Native American Festival, held 15 miles south of Tuscaloosa on the Black Warrior River, in the Moundville Archaeological Park (☎ 205-371-2572), features crafts, storytellers, music and a market the last week in September. More than 30,000 visitors show up for the Kentuck Festival (☎ 205-758-1257), one of the South's premier crafts events; it's held on the third weekend in October.

Places to Stay

Many motels and hotels line McFarland Blvd (Hwy 82) from I-59 north to the university. They are also clustered along Skyland Blvd, which runs parallel to and just south of I-59.

The *Executive Inn* (☎ *205-759-2511, 1780 McFarland Blvd N*) is located on the north bank of the river and is basic, clean and inexpensive. It has a pool, free continental breakfast on weekends and free coffee daily. The staff is helpful. Singles/doubles

The Face in the Window

Henry Wells, a young black man, was accused of burning down the Pickens County Courthouse in Carrollton in 1876. Two years later he was arrested on flimsy evidence and charged with the burning and other crimes. To protect him from a lynch mob of angry townspeople, the sheriff hid him in the garret of the newly rebuilt courthouse. The mob saw him in the window and advanced toward the building. The frightened man stood looking out at the crowd. He yelled down, claiming his innocence and swore that he would haunt them if they killed him. An instant later, a flash of lightning illuminated Wells' face in a pane of the window and his anguished look was imprinted on the pane. There are two versions of the story: in one, Wells is killed by the lightning; in the other he is murdered by the mob. Whatever happened, the terrorized face remains under the eaves on the north side of the courthouse to this day, in spite of repeated scrubbing of the window, and hailstorms that have broken surrounding panes.

To get there take Hwy 82 north (northwest, actually) from Tuscaloosa for 20 miles; turn south on Hwy 86 and drive 14 miles straight to the courthouse square in Carrollton. The face in the window is waiting there for you.

are $30/$39 Monday to Thursday and $40/45 on weekends.

The *Super 8 Motel* (☎ *205-758-8878, 4125 McFarland Blvd E*) offers clean rooms with few extras other than cable movies and complimentary coffee in the lobby. Rates are $38/43.

The *Sleep Inn* (☎ *205-556-5696, 888-556-5696, 4300 Skyland Blvd*) gives you good value for your money. It's at the south end of town near I-59. The rooms have queen-size beds, hair dryers, coffeemakers, movie channels and VCRs with video rental in the lobby. Rooms are $39/51, including complimentary continental breakfast.

The *Four Points Hotel* (☎ *205-752-3200, fax 205-343-1139, 320 Paul Bryant Drive*) has an outdoor patio and a pool. It's on the university campus next to the Paul Bryant Museum. Rooms are $94/99, with a complimentary newspaper thrown in.

Terrific service earned the *Hampton Inn* (☎ *205-553-9800, 600 Harper Lee Drive*) a rating as one of the top five Hampton properties in the country. There's a pool, complimentary breakfast bar and convenience store. Rooms are clean, quiet and spacious and cost $59/65.

Best Western Park Plaza Motor Inn (☎ *205-556-9690, 3801 McFarland Blvd E*) has a pool, whirlpool and movie channel. Rate are $60/64, including breakfast.

Rooms are a bit bigger than usual at the *Courtyard by Marriott* (☎ *205-750-8384, 4115 Courtney Drive*), which has a pool, whirlpool and lounge serving drinks and appetizers. The rate is $72 for a single or double, including breakfast. It's at the intersection of I-59 and I-359.

Places to Eat
Budget & Mid-Range The small *Waysider* (☎ *205-345-8239, 1512 Greensboro Ave*), downtown, is the place for breakfast. Start with light, fluffy biscuits, add eggs or pancakes, bacon and grits. It's all good and breakfast will cost about $4. It's open Tuesday to Saturday 5 am to 1:30 pm.

Buffalo Phil's (☎ *205-758-3318*), on University Blvd at 12th Ave, is a popular student food stop for wings, burgers and pasta. Lunch costs around $6.50, and dinner ranges from $6.50 to $11. Lighted candles on the tables dress it up at night, but it has a casual, comfortable bar feel. A jazz band performs on Friday night, except in summer, and occasionally there's live entertainment on Saturday night. It opens daily at 11 am and meals are served till 11 pm. It closes at 2 or 3 am, except Sunday, when it closes at 9 pm.

At the south end of Tuscaloosa, the original *Dreamland Barbecue* (☎ *205-758-8135, 12 Jerusalem Heights Rd*), at Jug Factory Rd, off McFarland Blvd (Hwy 82), is off the beaten path, but isn't it *good*? While its branch locations in Birmingham and Mobile have all the charm of airport sports bars, this place can only be described as a *sacred* shrine for Southern barbecue pilgrims. Founder John Bishop has retired, but it's still run by his family and they still serve just pork ribs ($4.50 for a sandwich, $8 for a plate) and sliced bread. It's open Monday to Thursday 10 am to 9 pm, and Friday and Saturday to 10 pm.

Hummer's on Main (☎ *205-345-2119, 433 Main Ave*), in Northport, has yummy, healthy, fresh salads and breads. The owner, Janet Graham, bakes honey wheat, rye and sourdough breads ($5 a loaf) daily. She imports rare European cheeses and makes to-die-for pasta ($4.50) and chicken salads ($5.50). Locals come here when they want to take home something special. Her combination deli-restaurant seats 20 indoors and another dozen outdoors. It's open Tuesday to Saturday 11 am to 2 pm.

Top End The Italian fare is a little bland at *De Palma's* (☎ *205-759-1879, 2300 University Blvd*), but it's a fashionable bistro with a nice wine list and a good people-watching bar. The crowd comprises young and middle-aged professionals. Favorite dishes include pasta de Palma (an angel hair and cream creation) and pizzas. Expect to pay $10 at lunch, and $15 to $20 at dinner.

Located on a bluff overlooking the Black Warrior River, the *Cypress Inn* (☎ *205-345-6963, 501 Rice Mine Rd*), in Northport, has the best view in town for lunch and dinner.

Lunch is $5 to $6.50 and the menu includes catfish, shrimp with mushrooms and two cheeses, and vegetarian pasta. Dinner costs $11 to $17. It's open daily for dinner, and lunch is served daily except Saturday.

The **Old Globe** (☎ 205-391-0949, *430 Main Ave*), in Northport, serves spicy Cajun red beans and rice ($7) for lunch. For dinner, try the mix of seafood, vegetables and tropical fruits in the Caribbean island stew ($15). It's in a nice setting as well. Meals are served Tuesday to Thursday 11 am to 3 pm and 5 to 10 pm, and Friday and Saturday 11 am to 3 pm and 5 to 11 pm.

Spectator Sports

Tickets to watch the Crimson Tide roll over its opponents in the Bryant-Denny Stadium usually sell out to season-ticket holders. However, you can buy tickets ($26) for games at the beginning of the season. If you're in the area, call the ticket office (☎ 205-348-6111) or stop by the stadium. You might get lucky.

Shopping

The Kentuck Museum Annex & Gallery (☎ 205-758-1257), 503 Main Ave, in Northport, features changing exhibitions of fine American crafts and folk art, primarily by Southern artists. Many items for sale resemble things found in airport gift shops, but there are still a number of truly unique goods rendered in glass, textiles, wood and pottery. It's open weekdays 9 am to 5 pm, and Saturday 10 am to 4:30 pm.

Getting There & Away

The closest airport, Birmingham International (☎ 205-595-0533), is 57 miles east.

Greyhound (☎ 205-758-6651), 2520 Stillman Blvd, has six buses daily from Birmingham ($13), five daily from Jackson ($36), five from Meridian ($21), four from Atlanta ($41) and four from Selma ($17), three from Huntsville ($33), and two from New Orleans ($56).

Amtrak's *Crescent* train travels once a day each way between New Orleans ($46/92 one-way/roundtrip) and New York ($173/346), with stops including Meridian, Birmingham, Anniston and Atlanta.

Major car-rental agencies have counters at Birmingham International Airport. Rental companies with offices downtown include Budget (☎ 205-349-1300), 115 Greensboro Ave, and Enterprise (☎ 205-349-4446), 610 Skyland Blvd E.

Crown Limousine Service (☎ 205-339-5466) operates a Birmingham airport shuttle for $35 per person, one-way.

Getting Around

Tuscaloosa County Transit Authority provides public transportation weekdays from 5 am to 6 pm. Rides cost 80¢ and transfers are 20¢. Exact change is required.

Taxi companies include Deluxe Radio Cab Company (☎ 205-758-9025), Radio Cab Service (☎ 205-758-2831) and Tuscaloosa Radio Cab Service (☎ 205-349-3669).

Southwestern Alabama

The southwest corner of the state has beaches, rivers, estuaries, bays, a delta and pine-covered barrier islands. The coastline stretches 52 miles along the Gulf of Mexico, and the port town of Mobile attracted French and Spanish explorers and the ill-fated Confederate government.

MOBILE

• pop 532,000

Mobile's citizens have long since grown weary of explaining to visitors how they've been celebrating Mardi Gras since before New Orleans was founded, and few even bother to offer any other comparisons to their western neighbor. Perhaps they're trying to keep their city a secret, but in any case, Mobile is interesting and fun in the same sense as New Orleans, only with the volume and brightness turned down.

History

In 1702 Jean Baptiste Le Moyne, Sieur de Bienville, constructed Fort Louis de la

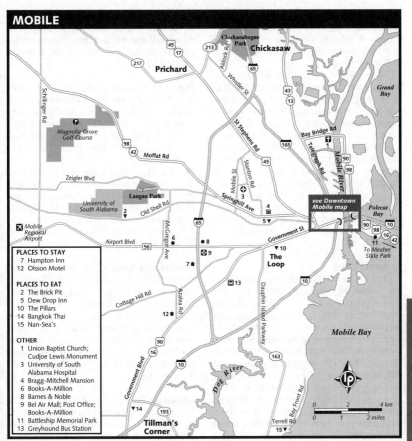

MOBILE

Chickasabogue Park

Chickasaw

Prichard

Grand Bay

Schillinger Rd

Magnolia Grove Golf Course

Whistler St

Aldock Rd

St Stephens Rd

Bay Bridge Rd

Telegraph Rd

Mobile River

Zeigler Blvd

Moffat Rd

Mobile St

Stanton Rd

Springhill Ave

see Downtown Mobile map

Polecat Bay

University of South Alabama

Langan Park

Old Shell Rd

Mobile Regional Airport

Airport Blvd

McGregor Ave

Government St

The Loop

To Meaher State Park

PLACES TO STAY
7 Hampton Inn
12 Olsson Motel

PLACES TO EAT
2 The Brick Pit
5 Dew Drop Inn
10 The Pillars
14 Bangkok Thai
15 Nan-Sea's

OTHER
1 Union Baptist Church; Cudjoe Lewis Monument
3 University of South Alabama Hospital
4 Bragg-Mitchell Mansion
6 Books-A-Million
8 Barnes & Noble
9 Bel Air Mall; Post Office; Books-A-Million
11 Battleship Memorial Park
13 Greyhound Bus Station

Cottage Hill Rd

Azalea Rd

Dauphin Island Parkway

Mobile Bay

Government Blvd

Dog River

Bay Front Rd

Tillman's Corner

Terrell Rd

0   2   4 km
0   1   2 miles

see Downtown Mobile map

ALABAMA

Mobile north of Mobile. Good-time folks that they were, the French held their first Mardi Gras celebration two years later. In 1711 Le Moyne moved the French capital of Louisiana to the site of modern-day Mobile and built Fort Condé.

Mobile scarcely had time to enjoy its status as capital of the sprawling Louisiana colony when France moved the seat of government to the newly founded (and more strategically located) New Orleans in 1722. In 1763, when Louisiana was split between Spain and England along the Mississippi River, Mobile and New Orleans were separated by political boundaries forever.

Throughout the 1800s – by then an American city – Mobile's deep bay and strategic location at the mouth of the Mobile and Tensaw Rivers ensured it a special place in Alabama's history. Cotton and, later, timber from all over the state were brought to Mobile and then shipped to ports around the world. Wealthy Mobilians built lavish homes and filled them with imported finery.

Mobile remained an important Confederate port until the last days of the Civil

War, when Admiral David Farragut defeated the Confederate ships defending it. During WWI and WWII the shipyards and port built and repaired vessels and shipped military supplies.

Today, Mobile continues its reign as a major seaport and shipbuilding center. It's a lively, elegant city with many green spaces and Spanish moss-draped 'live oaks' making canopies over wide boulevards. On many spring mornings, fog rolls in and blankets the city, but generally it lifts by midday. Dining and nightlife are upbeat and progressive. Mardi Gras continues, too, although Mobile's version is smaller, safer and saner than its New Orleans counterpart. Note that, Mardi Gras is an official holiday throughout the Mobile Bay area, and many businesses and attractions are closed.

Orientation

Called the Port City, Mobile sprawls across the northwest corner of Mobile Bay. I-10 enters the city across the 7-mile causeway over Mobile Bay. It then cuts diagonally across the city, heading southwest to Mississippi. I-65 originates in the southeast corner of the city and runs northeast to Montgomery. Hwy 193 originates on the south side at exit 17 off I-10 and continues south to Dauphin Island. A ring road encircles downtown Mobile. Government St turns into Government Blvd west of downtown. The area just west of downtown where Government St and Airport Blvd meet is called the Loop.

Information

Tourist Offices For information by mail, contact Mobile Convention & Visitors Corp (☎ 334-415-2000, 800-566-2453, fax 334-415-2060), PO Box 204, Mobile, AL 36602. Visit their Web site at www.mobile.org. To pick up information go to Fort Condé at 150 S Royal St; it's open weekdays 8 am to 5 pm.

Money Alabama-based AmSouth Bank has a number of ATMs throughout Mobile and will exchange foreign currency for US dollars. AmSouth's main branch (☎ 334-438-

8224), 31 N Royal St, will exchange US dollars for foreign currency as well as the other way around, and they offer validated parking across the street at the Republic parking lot.

Post The main post office (☎ 334-694-6108) is at 250 St Joseph St, downtown. It's open weekdays 8 am to 4:30 pm. The Bel Air Mall branch (☎ 334-478-8513), 3410 Bel Air Mall, on Airport Blvd at I-65, is open weekdays 8 am to 8 pm and Saturday 9 am to 5 pm.

Media The *Mobile Register* is the local daily. It shares a Web site, www.al.com, with its corporate siblings in Birmingham and Huntsville. The alternative *Harbinger* is published bi-weekly, while the *Inner City News* and *Mobile Beacon* are minority-focused weeklies.

Bookstores Barnes & Noble (☎ 334-450-0845), 3250 Airport Blvd, and Books-A-Million (☎ 334-471-3528), in the Bel Air Mall and at 3960 Airport Blvd, have good regional sections. Independent-bookstore fans can shop at these chains with a clear conscience; according to one resident bibliophile, the locally owned stores that were displaced by the chain giants haven't really been missed.

Libraries The central library (☎ 334-434-7073), 701 Government St, is open Monday to Thursday 9 am to 9 pm, and Friday and Saturday 9 am to 6 pm.

Medical Services The University of South Alabama Hospital (☎ 334-471-7000), 2451 Fillingim St, provides medical services and handles emergencies.

Historic House Museums

Guides in period costumes lead visitors around **Oakleigh** (☎ 334-432-1281), 350 Oakleigh Place, an 1833 Greek Revival mansion on 3½ acres. The museum is filled with fine American and European furnishings and Mardi Gras memorabilia. In contrast, Cox-Deasy House is a more modest Creole cottage built in 1850 on the grounds.

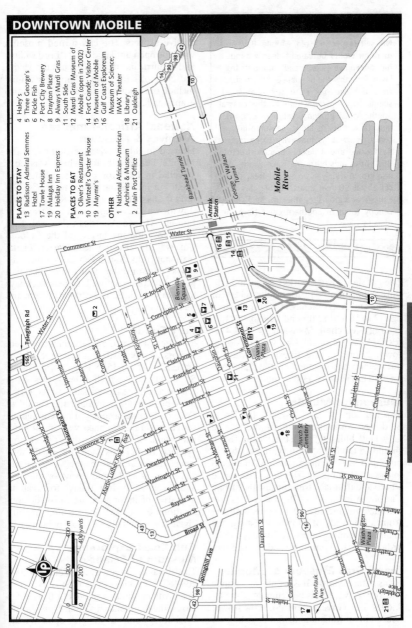

DOWNTOWN MOBILE

PLACES TO STAY
13 Radisson Admiral Semmes
   Hotel
17 Towle House
19 Malaga Inn
20 Holiday Inn Express

PLACES TO EAT
3 Oliver's Restaurant
10 Wintzell's Oyster House
19 Mayme's

OTHER
1 National African-American
  Archives & Museum
2 Main Post Office

4 Haley's
5 Three George's
6 Pickle Fish
7 Port City Brewery
8 Drayton Place
9 Always Mardi Gras
11 South Side
12 Mardi Gras Museum of
   Mobile (open in 2002)
14 Fort Condé; Visitor Center
15 Museum of Mobile
16 Gulf Coast Exploreum
   Museum of Science;
   IMAX Theater
18 Library
21 Oakleigh

ALABAMA

The Majestic Live Oak

No self-respecting old Mobile Bay area mansion would be caught dead without a half dozen live oaks spread around its front lawn. Probably the ultimate Southern shade tree, the live oak *(Quercus virginiana)*, seems to be everywhere in the coastal South. A fast-growing, yet very long-lived and stable tree, its life is measured in centuries. It owes its longevity to extremely hard wood and a flexible branch structure that withstands hurricane-force winds. It is also grown widely as an avenue tree, ideally set about 90 feet apart. It tolerates auto exhaust and grows together, forming stately canopy roads in Southern cities from Virginia to Texas.

The gift shop carries works by regional artisans. Admission is $5 for adults, $4.50 for seniors and AAA members, $3 for children age 12 to 18 and $2 for children six to 11.

Bragg-Mitchell Mansion (☎ 334-471-6365), 1906 Springhill Ave, west of downtown, is one of the finest examples of antebellum architecture on the Gulf. Admission is $5 adults, $3 students.

Museum of Mobile

This museum (☎ 334-208-7569), 111 Royal St, downtown in the Southern Market/Old City Hall building (constructed in 1857), should be the first stop for visitors – that is, once its massive renovations are completed in the spring of 2001. The building's white stucco and iron-lace trim suggest the strong Caribbean influence of its era, and its collections will include 50,000-plus artifacts from all periods of Mobile's history. It's planned operating hours are Tuesday to Saturday 10 am to 5 pm, and Sunday 1 to 5 pm.

Mardi Gras Museum of Mobile

By its nature, Mardi Gras is both very public and very private. This museum (☎ 334-208-7569), 355 Government St, downtown, housed in an Italianate town house built in

1872, will help to answer many bewildered visitors' questions about Carnival's more secretive aspects. The city-owned museum won't be open until mid-2002 ('Lord willing, and a hurricane doesn't hit us,' drawled a museum official), but planned exhibits include old costumes and historical photographs and artifacts.

National African-American Archives & Museum

Housed in the Davis Ave branch of the Mobile Public Library, which was constructed in 1930 for black residents, this small but interesting museum (☎ 334-433-8511), 564 Martin Luther King Jr Ave, downtown, has books and portraits of famous African-Americans, as well as a room covering the history of the Colored Carnival. It's also the headquarters of the National Hank Aaron Fan Club, which displays memorabilia from this baseball player, a Mobile native. It's open weekdays 8:30 am to 5 pm, Saturday noon to 4 pm and Sunday 2 to 4 pm.

Fort Condé

'Soldiers' in French military uniforms greet visitors at this partially reconstructed fort (☎ 334-208-7569), 150 S Royal St, at Church St, downtown, which now serves as a museum and the city's visitor center. Originally built in 1711 to guard the capital of France's Louisiana colony, it was completely torn down in 1820 to make way for the city's expansion. In the 1970s, when the George Wallace Tunnel was built, the small businesses that were near the fort's original site were torn down to make way for the road and to rebuild the fort. Today's fort is about a quarter of its original size. Live demonstrations of musket and cannon fire are given. It's open daily 8 am to 5 pm (free).

Gulf Coast Exploreum Museum of Science

This dynamic, interactive museum (☎ 334-208-6873), 65 Government St, was developed with children in mind, but the IMAX Dome theater makes it a great rainy-day diversion for adults as well. It's open Sunday to Thursday 9 am to 8 pm and Friday and Saturday 9 am to 9 pm during summer; the rest of the year it closes at 5 pm Sunday to Thursday. Adult admission to either the museum or the theatre is $6.50, $10 to see both. Inquire about youth, student and senior discounts.

Battleship Memorial Park

The battleship USS *Alabama* (☎ 334-433-2703, 800-426-4929), famous for escaping 9 major WWII battles unscathed, is at 2703 Battleship Parkway. Personal items and period music transport you (and the throngs of WWII veterans who visit the park) back to the 1940s before you climb aboard the USS *Drum*, a WWII submarine alongside, to explore a sailor's working life under the sea. The indoor aircraft pavilion contains historic planes and a jet simulator. There's a nice gift shop, but don't bother with the snack bar. The park is open daily from 8 am to sunset, except at Christmas. Admission is $8 adults, $4 children; there's a $2 parking fee. Take exit 27 off the I-10 causeway or from the eastern shore, exit 30.
www.ussalabama.com

Organized Tours

You might feel uneasy riding into the swamps on a 22-passenger boat named *Gator Bait* (☎ 334-460-8206) until you realize that Captain Gene Burrell has a sense of humor and is devoted to protecting wildlife. He tells amusing, informative stories on his two-hour cruise through the Mobile-Tensaw Delta, the largest inland delta in the US. You'll also see shell mounds and hear about the history of Native Americans in the delta. Don't miss this. The boat departs from Chickasaw Marina Tuesday to Saturday at 8 and 10 am and 2 pm. It's $20 for adults and $10 for children. Take I-65 north to exit 13 (Hwy 158 E), continue 2 miles to Hwy 43 and turn south. Chickasaw Marina is half a mile down the road.

Special Events

Mardi Gras, also known as Carnival, begins two weeks before Ash Wednesday, which falls 40 days before Easter. Call the visitor center (☎ 334-415-2000, 800-566-2453) for information. Throughout March there are driving tours along the streets showing the most colorful azaleas. Maps of the 'Azaela

AfricaTown

Published timelines of African-American history invariably mention that the last slave ship to bring Africans to North America was the *Clotilde*, which arrived in Mobile Bay in 1859, bearing 130 members of the Tarkar tribe (from modern-day Togo). What they never explain is how this happened 50 years after the United States banned the importation of slaves.

The explanation is both trivial and tragic. It seems that Timothy Meaher, a wealthy Mobile shipbuilder, made a wager over a few whiskies that he could elude federal agents who patrolled all major ports and smuggle Africans into the country. While his ship, the *Clotilde*, successfully returned to Mobile, the nature of its 'cargo' became known to the port authorities. The Tarkars were disbursed throughout the area, and the ship was burned and sunk by her own captain. Although most of the newly arrived Tarkars quickly assimilated within the broader African-American community, a clannish 30 remained together in the Plateau area forming the core of a community known as AfricaTown on the bank of the Mobile River on the north side of Mobile.

While descendents of the *Clotilde* captives still hold reunions in the area, there is little physical evidence of this community's origins, except for the bust of Cudjoe Lewis at the Union Baptist Church, 506 Bay Bridge Rd, and the cemetery across the street where many of the Africans are buried. Lewis (who was originally called 'Kazoola') died in 1945, possibly the last surviving slaveship captive in America.

Trail' are available at Fort Condé. The first weekend in October, BayFest features three days of big-name entertainers, food and stuff for kids. Contact the City of Mobile Special Events Office (☎ 334-470-7730) for details. For more than 45 years, the Mobile Piano Ensemble (☎ 334-645-2366) has presented a concert played by top-caliber musicians in early October. The city sponsors First Night Mobile, a nonalcoholic New Year's celebration with more than 100 musical, theatrical and dance performances outdoors on December 31. Call City of Mobile Special Events Office for information (see above).

Places to Stay

Some properties raise rates significantly during the Mardi Gras season and require minimum stays of two to three nights.

Camping In Prichard, *Chickasabogue Park* (☎ 334-452-8496, 760 Aldock Rd) is a good place to see marshland flora and fauna less than a half-hour from downtown. The 57-site campground has a bathhouse, laundry, camp store and grills. Improved sites cost $9 (water and electricity) and $12 (full utilities). Take I-65 to exit 13 (Hwy 158 W) and follow the signs.

Hotels & Motels The *Holiday Inn Express* (☎ 334-433-6923, 255 Church St) is the best buy downtown, but since it's opposite the Civic Center, you have to reserve early or get lucky. The rooms are comfortable, clean and have coffeemakers and free movies. There's an outdoor pool, free parking and complimentary continental breakfast. Singles/doubles are $54/59.

The *Hampton Inn* (☎ 334-344-4942, 930 S Beltline Hwy), off I-65 near Airport Blvd, is ideally situated for forays into both Mobile and Dauphin Island. It has an outdoor pool, free cable movies and complimentary continental breakfast. Singles range from $46 to $52, doubles range from $57 to $62.

You get far more than you'd expect for your money at *Olsson Motel* (☎ 334-661-5331, 800-351-1023 in Alabama, ☎ 800-332-

1004 elsewhere, 4137 Government Blvd), at Hwy 90 W, a 25-room, family-run operation. It's clean, the staff are courteous, and it's cheap. It's 7 miles west of downtown. Rooms cost $30/32.

The historic *Malaga Inn* (☎ 334-438-4701, 800-235-1586, 359 Church St), is *the* place to be during Mardi Gras because it's downtown on the parade route. Rooms that are nicely furnished open onto a balcony overlooking a courtyard with a fountain. There's a fine restaurant and small pool. Singles are $72, doubles are $79 and there's a corporate rate of $72. It's a bargain for its location.

The *Radisson Admiral Semmes Hotel* (☎ 334-432-8000, 800-333-3333, 251 Government St) is a renovated historic hotel. There's a restaurant, an outdoor pool and whirlpool, plus privileges at a nearby fitness center. Singles and doubles are both $119. Weekend 'super saver' discounts may drop the rate to $79.

B&Bs Felix and Carolyn Vereen run the *Towle House* (☎ 334-432-6440, 800-938-6953, fax 334-433-4381, 1104 Montauk Ave) as though they were welcoming friends. The two-story, three-bedroom historic house in the Old Dauphin historic district has one room with a private bathroom. The two rooms that share a bathroom are usually only rented to people who know each other. A full breakfast awaits guests in the morning and there are drinks in the afternoon. They charge a flat rate of $85 a night, $75 a night for two nights, or $70 for three nights or more.

Places to Eat

Seafood is a major feature of the local cuisine, and the best seafood restaurants (here and throughout the coastal South) are typified by construction that looks as though they were built in two days and weathered for 30 years. Lines form quickly.

Budget & Mid-Range In addition to its strawberry shortcake, *Oliver's Restaurant* (☎ 334-432-6142, 558 St Francis St), at

Warren Ave, is known for its incredible simmered oxtails. It's no surprise that Dauphin St bartenders and waiters love to fortify themselves at this African-American-owned, home cooking cafe before going to work. Lunch costs from $4 to $7. (This is not to be confused with the Oliver's Restaurant located in the Radisson Admiral Semmes Hotel.)

Believe it or not, the star feature at the legendary **Wintzell's Oyster House** (☎ 334-432-4605, 605 Dauphin St) is … oysters. You can order them fried, on the shell, baked, in a loaf, Bienville, Rockefeller, on a sandwich, and so on, and on; but splurge a little and try their fabulous West Indies salad. Lunch specials are $7 with fries. Dinners range from $10 to $17.

Let the Good Times Roll!

Mobile's reputation as the birthplace of Mardi Gras in North America does not rest solely on the fact that a few half-starved French colonists observed the pre-Lenten feasts here 300 years ago. Just as the French celebrations began to decline, Anglo-American residents formed parading societies in the early 1800s, including the rowdy 'Cowbellion de Rakin Society,' which was formed in 1831 after a drunken cotton broker knocked over a display of rakes and cowbells and proceeded to drag them through the streets. In 1852, a group of Mobile Cowbellians moved to New Orleans and formed the Krewe of Comus, which is now that city's oldest and most secretive Carnival society.

Modern Mardi Gras traditions unique to Mobile include the Joe Cain procession and the tossing of Moon Pies. The Joe Cain procession (held the Sunday before Fat Tuesday) features Joe Cain's Merry Widows weeping at the grave of their 'husband,' who rejuvenated Mobile's Mardi Gras after the Civil War. All of Mobile's parading societies throw Moon Pies (large chocolate-covered marshmallow cookies eaten throughout the South) along with beads and doubloons, providing sugary nourishment to the revelers lining the streets.

The crowd is very regional, mostly coastal Alabamians. Everyone seems to know each other, and they are always honored and often extra hospitable when they learn that you traveled a long way just to visit *their* Carnival. Late into the evening, having grown weary of their formal balls, silk-gowned debutantes with their white-tie-and-tail-clad escorts blend easily with the street crowds. The parades are shorter than New Orleans', but they are just as fun, and the crowds are smaller and parking is more plentiful. The city advertises its Mardi Gras as 'rated G,' like children's movies, but near the Dauphin St bars, it can get pleasantly wild at night.

There's a lot more to Mardi Gras than parades. There are balls, feasts and float parties. While most balls are private affairs, many events are open to the public – visitors included – at prices ranging from $3 to $25. Forget about getting a baby-sitter: there also are events designed expressly for young children. Check with the visitor center (☎ 334-415-2000) or go to a great unofficial Web site at www.frcr.com/mardigras for details, including parade schedules.

The Joe Cain procession is a Mobile tradition.

Mobile isn't really known for great barbecue, but don't tell that to the folks at *The Brick Pit* (☎ 334-343-0001, *5456 Old Shell Rd*), east of the University of South Alabama campus (look for the smoking grill at the roadside). Their slow-cooked 'pulled' pork, ribs and chicken are considered some of the best in the South, and rightly so. Their slogan, 'This ain't no dream, it's the real thing,' is a direct dig at the legendary, Tuscaloosa-based Dreamland Bar-B-Que, which opened a disappointingly chain-like restaurant in Mobile a few years ago. Lunch is $7 and dinner is $9.

If you instantly want to feel at home, try the *Dew Drop Inn* (☎ 334-473-7872, *1808 Old Shell Rd*). This 70-year-old diner is best known for its hot dogs with sauerkraut and onions, but it also serves tasty sandwiches and seafood loaves. You can get lunch for $6.

Top End The laid-back *Nan-Seas* (☎ 334-479-9132, *4170 Bay Front Rd*), off Hwy 163 on the southern tip of Mobile, offers a gorgeous view of Mobile Bay along with great seafood. Ask if your food can be broiled instead of fried, unless you like a lot of oily breading. Expect to pay $17 for dinner.

The food is super at *Bangkok Thai* (☎ 334-666-7788, *5345 Hwy 90*), in Tillman's Corner, and servings are generous, so make sure you're hungry. Expect to pay $7 for lunch, and up to $17 for dinner.

The *Pillars* (☎ 334-478-6341, *1757 Government St*), in the Loop, is a Mobile institution long regarded as one of the best restaurants in town. The setting, a restored historic mansion, is very elegant. The menu is continental. Breads are baked on the premises. Expect to pay $15 to $30 for dinner.

Mayme's (☎ 334-438-4701, *359 Church St*) is an elegant restaurant in the downtown Malaga Inn serving New World cuisine. The dining room opens onto a courtyard where a jazz group plays on Thursday and Friday. Dinner costs around $20 to $25.

Entertainment

Dauphin St, home of many of the city's most popular nightspots and restaurants, rarely sleeps. Instead, it takes early morning catnaps so it can start partying all over again.

The Mobile Arts Council (☎ 334-432-9796) publishes a quarterly schedule of events and answers questions about fine arts exhibits.

For the best nightlife in one area, hit the aforementioned Dauphin St, downtown, where you'll find the elegant *Drayton Place* (☎ 334-432-7438, *101 Dauphin St*), hands-down the best people-watching bar in town, located in the cavernous ground floor of the South's oldest skyscraper. *South Side* (☎ 334-438-5555, *455 Dauphin St*) is one of the street's better music halls, while *Haley's* (☎ 334-433-4970, *278 Dauphin St*), has a jukebox with good tunes. There's also *Pickle Fish* (☎ 334-434-0000, *251 Dauphin St*), which serves sandwiches and pizzas, and *Port City Brewery* (☎ 334-438-2739, *225 Dauphin St*), with a menu that features passable grazing foods: go there for the good selection of hand-crafted beers.

Catch the latest flicks at *Carmike 10* (☎ 334-660-0104, *4900 Government Blvd*), and *Dauphin Street Cinema* (☎ 334-479-0650, *3048 Dauphin St*).

Shopping

Mardi Gras favors, including balloons and beads, are popular in and out of season at Always Mardi Gras (☎ 334-433-6273), 50 S Royal St. Three George's (☎ 334-433-6725), 226 Dauphin St, has been making chocolates and candy since 1917.

Getting There & Away

Air Mobile Regional Airport (☎ 334-633-0313), 8400 Airport Blvd, is served by Continental Express, Delta, Northwest Airlink and AirTran Airlines. From the airport, it's an easy trip to downtown along Airport Blvd, which runs east-west through the middle of Mobile.

Bus Greyhound (☎ 334-478-6089), 2545 Government St, has 11 buses daily each from Baton Rouge ($51) and New Orleans ($26), eight from Pensacola ($16), five each from Atlanta ($39), Biloxi ($18), Gulfport,

Mississippi ($19) and Montgomery ($26), and three from Birmingham ($38).

Train Amtrak (☎ 334-432-4052, 800-872-7245), 11 Government St, provides services to Miami ($178/356 one-way/roundtrip) and Los Angeles ($169/338) and points in between on its *Sunset Limited* departing on Sunday, Wednesday and Friday. Amtrak also offers daily service to Chicago via Amtrak's *City of New Orleans*, changing trains in, you guessed it, New Orleans ($138/276).

Car The best way to get in and out of Mobile is on the interstates. You can drive the 169 miles to Montgomery in just under three hours. If you prefer a much more leisurely drive, take I-65 north about 20 miles north of Mobile to exit 37 (Bay Minette), where you can pick up Hwy 31. The narrow road snakes its way through scenic rural countryside and many small towns. I-10 west heads to New Orleans – a three-hour, 153-mile drive across the southwest corner of Alabama and Mississippi. Going east, I-10 crosses Mobile Bay then connects with Hwy 98 south to the eastern shore towns of Fairhope and Point Clear (one hour).

Boat The Mobile Bay ferry (☎ 334-540-7787) runs daily except for one to two weeks in December when it shuts down for maintenance. Poor weather and breakdowns also limit service. Call before making the long drive to the port. This is not only a fun sightseeing trip, but it can save a very long drive around the bay to get to the rest of Alabama's coast. From Dauphin Island, on the west side of the bay, ferries depart every 1½ hours from 8 am to 5 pm. On the east side, they leave Fort Morgan every 1½ hours from 8:45 am to 5:45 pm. One-way fares are $1 for walk-ons, $6 for motorcycles, $15 ($23 roundtrip) for cars and pickup trucks and $25 for RVs. It departs from the east end of Dauphin Island and the west end of Hwy 180, 22 miles west of Gulf Shores. The crossing takes about half an hour.

Private boats can travel the Intracoastal Waterway and the Tenn-Tom Waterway to the Gulf Coast. Alabama is said to have the most navigable inland waterways in the nation.

Getting Around

Mobile Transit Authority (MTA; ☎ 334-344-5656) provides public transportation throughout the metropolitan area Monday to Saturday 6 am to 6 pm. The fare is $1.25 plus 10¢ for transfers. Mobile Bay Transportation (☎ 334-633-5693, 800-272-6234) shuttles cost $15 from the airport to downtown, a trip for which there is no bus service.

Major car-rental agencies have counters at the airport. Avis (☎ 334-432-7766), 2241 Michigan Ave, and Enterprise (☎ 334-661-4446), 3720 Cottage Hill Rd, have offices in town.

Checker Yellow Cab Service (☎ 334-476-7711) and Mike Cab (☎ 334-457-9448) provide taxi service.

AROUND MOBILE
Meaher State Park

This overlooked state park (☎ 334-626-5529), 2 miles west of Spanish Fort on Hwy 90, covers 1327 acres in the wetlands of Mobile Bay. Most folks come to picnic, birdwatch and hike the two nature trails, one of which is a 1200-foot elevated boardwalk over the delta. This is a super spot, especially if you like waterfowl and marshes. There's also a fishing pier, a boat ramp and restrooms.

In addition there is isolated primitive *camping* ($7); choose your own site in the woods. Day use for adults is $1, for seniors and children it's 50¢.

GULF COAST

Pleasure Island stretches 32 miles along the Gulf Coast from Florida to Fort Morgan, on Mobile Bay. When the Intracoastal Waterway was created, it separated the coastal area from mainland Alabama, creating the island. There are two small towns: Orange Beach (population 3500) and Gulf Shores (population 5000). The island has several freshwater lakes and wide, white-sand beaches backed by rolling dunes dotted with sea oats.

Today, miles of the shoreline are covered with condominiums, hotels and beachfront houses with unsightly 'For Rent' signs outside. Fishing from the Gulf State Park Pier and from jetties and from charter boats is a favorite pastime here. A few companies offer sailing excursions. During the summer, traffic is heavy and restaurants are busy.

The Gulf Shore's biggest public event, the National Shrimp Festival, draws a large regional crowd in mid-October. Take in four days of arts and crafts, music and food at the Gulf Shores Public Beach (☎ 334-968-6904, festival@gulftel.com).

Orientation

From Foley, Gulf Shores Parkway (Hwy 59) runs south 12 miles before dead-ending at Hwy 182, which runs east along the shore to the Florida border and west about 6 miles to the dunes. If you're coming from the Florida Panhandle, take Hwy 292 to Hwy 182. It's a little tricky, but the scenic drive passes through the Gulf resorts in both states. Two miles north of the shore,

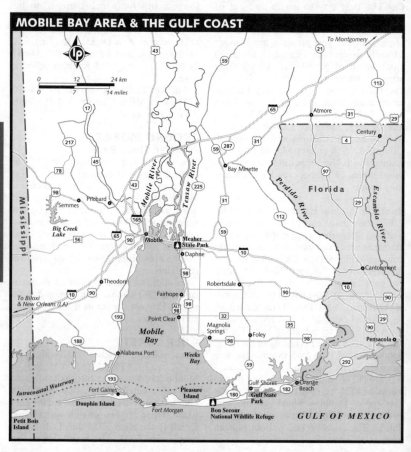

MOBILE BAY AREA & THE GULF COAST

Hwy 180 runs 22 miles west to land's end at Fort Morgan and the ferry that crosses Mobile Bay to Fort Gaines and Dauphin Island.

Information

Tourist Offices The Alabama Gulf Coast Convention & Visitors Bureau Welcome Center (☎ 334-968-7511, 800-745-7263, www.gulfshores.com), 3150 Gulf Shores Parkway/Hwy 59, is open weekdays 8 am to 6 pm. The Orange Beach Welcome Center (☎ 334-974-1510, 800-982-8562), 26650 Perdido Beach Blvd/Hwy 182, is open weekdays 8 am to 5 pm, and weekends 9 am to 5 pm.

Post The Orange Beach post office (☎ 334-981-4131), 25940 John M Snook Drive, is open weekdays 8 am to 4 pm, and Saturday 9 to 11:30 am. At Gulf Shores, the post office (☎ 334-968-7000), 2149 W First St, is open weekdays 8:30 am to 4:30 pm, and Saturday 9 am to noon.

Libraries The Gulf Shores library (☎ 334-968-1176), 221 W 19th Ave, is open Monday to Thursday 9 am to 9 pm, Friday 9 am to 5 pm, and Saturday 9 am to 1 pm. Hours at the Orange Beach library (☎ 334-981-2923), 25940 John M Snook Drive, are Monday and Tuesday 10 am to 8 pm, Wednesday, Thursday and Friday 10 am to 6 pm, Saturday 10 am to 2 pm. Internet access is available.

Medical Services The closest hospital, South Baldwin Regional Medical Center (☎ 334-952-3400), is 12 miles north in Foley at 1613 N McKenzie St (Hwy 59 N).

Gulf State Park

Look at the buildings crowding the beach nearby, and you'll be thankful that the state owns 6150 acres and 2½ miles of beach and dunes on both sides of Hwy 182. Visitors love Gulf State Park (☎ 334-948-7275), 20115 Hwy 135, and it's the state's second largest. There's an 825-foot fishing pier, beachfront resort hotel, nature center, boat launch, playground, game room, camp store,

Jubilee!

Jubilee is a rare phenomenon in which crabs, fish, shrimp, rays and other sea life swim to the shallow waters along the eastern shore of Mobile Bay. Local residents put out the call for 'jubilee!' and run to the shore with lanterns and flashlights and buckets and baskets to collect the live seafood. By morning, all the creatures have gone back to sea. The exact date is not predictable, but it generally occurs two to five times a year between June and September. An eight-page booklet called *Jubilees* explains the phenomenon. It's available at Page & Palette in Fairhope.

golf course and pool, as well as biking and hiking trails, campgrounds and cabins, tennis courts and three lakes with canoe rentals. In winter lots of retirees come in RVs. Of the four trails, the longest is 1½-mile Middle Lake, but all trails connect to form 3¾ miles of easy walking on flat, sandy-bottom paths or old pavement. As you pass the lakes, try to spot the alligators. In the stands of live oaks, saw palmettos and saw grass, look for woodpeckers, squirrels and other small animals.

The park's 2½-mile beach has lifeguards and a beach pavilion with picnic areas and restrooms. Admission is $2 per car, $1 for overnight guests and seniors, and $8 per van. The park headquarters is open weekdays 8 am to 5 pm and Saturday 8 am to 4 pm. Sunday hours vary.

The park has an enormous *campground* with 468 sites, all with water, electricity, a picnic table and grill. Most sites are shaded, and many are on the lakefront. The tent sites are $12, full hookup RV sites are $20 and RV sites with water and electricity are $17.50. Rates are lower from November to March. Nearby are 16 fully equipped rustic lakefront *cabins*. From June to August they are rented by the week only. Reservations are advised. Off-season rates start at $44 a night ($54.50 in high season) and $261 a week ($327 high season).

To get there, take Hwy 59 (also known as Gulf Shores Parkway) south from the mainland and take a left on Fort Morgan Rd, and keep an eye out for the Hwy 135 turnoff. Hwy 135 also intersects with Hwy 182 1½ miles east of where Gulf Shores Parkway reaches the Gulf of Mexico.

Bon Secour National Wildlife Refuge

This 6000-acre refuge (☎ 334-540-7720), 12295 Hwy 180, is scattered across five parcels of coastal land ranging from beach dunes to rolling pine-oak woods. Bird watchers are given a visual feast in spring and fall with the arrival of migrating birds, and wading birds can be seen the entire year. Monarch butterflies, sea turtles and wildflowers also thrive here. There are three hiking trails: Pine Beach, a 4-mile roundtrip hike; Gator Lake, also 4 miles, which leads to the beach; and Jeff Friend, a 1-mile wheel-chair accessible loop near the lagoon. The refuge office is open weekdays 7:30 am to 4 pm, trails are open dawn to dusk. There's no charge.

Fort Morgan

This brick fortress (☎ 334-540-7125) on Hwy 180 was constructed in 1834 to guard the entrance to Mobile Bay. During the Battle of Mobile Bay (see the boxed text), the fort's Confederate guns were no match for the Union fleet. You can poke around the fort, which has terrific water views, then enter the museum, which has displays containing photographs, uniforms, artifacts and

The Battle of Mobile Bay

One of the most exciting battles of the Civil War took place at Mobile Bay between Confederate admiral Franklin Buchanan, commander of the ironclad *Tennessee*, and US admiral David G Farragut, who commanded the wooden *Hartford*. On the morning of August 5, 1864, Farragut approached the mouth of the bay with 14 wooden ships, four ironclads, 2700 soldiers and 197 guns. Waiting inside the bay was an undermatched Buchanan with his ironclad, three wooden ships, 427 soldiers, 22 guns and, at the mouth of the bay, torpedoes and guns at Confederate-controlled Fort Morgan and Fort Gaines.

Federal ships, led by the ironclad *Tecumseh* charged the channel two abreast. Guns from the

ALABAMA BUREAU OF TOURISM & TRAVEL

Historic Fort Morgan

forts blazed. A torpedo immediately sunk the *Tecumseh* and smoke and fire clouded the air. The federal fleet faltered. Tied to the mainmast rigging of his ship, Farragut looked forward and shouted the order, 'Damn the torpedoes! Go ahead!' (historical accounts dispute the often quoted 'Damn the torpedoes! Full speed ahead!').

Three hours later, with the Confederate fleet all but destroyed, Farragut's fleet faced the *Tennessee* alone in the bay. Heavily damaged, unable to maneuver and surrounded, Buchanan surrendered.

weapons dating from the War of 1812 to WWII. In August a re-enactment draws crowds. The fort is open daily from 8 am to sunset, and the museum is open 9 am to 5 pm, except Thanksgiving, Christmas and New Year's Day. Admission is $3 adults, $1 students and children.

Fort Gaines

The cannons, tunnels and bastions that proved no match for Admiral Farragut during the Civil War (see the boxed text 'The Battle of Mobile Bay') still remain on this Dauphin Island landmark. Visitors can explore the entire fort, which was built out of brick. An excellent museum (☎ 334-861-6992) at the east end of Bienville Rd houses military artifacts from the mid-19th century to 1946, the period the fort was used. There's a brochure outlining a self-guided walking tour. The fort is open daily 9 am to 5 pm (except Christmas and New Year). The entrance fee is $3 adults, $1 children.

Places to Stay

Camping For camping in Gulf State Park see the park entry, earlier.

Southport Campground (☎ 334-968-6220, 26032 Hwy 182), off the Intracoastal Canal Bridge on Hwy 59 in Gulf Shores, has 113 improved and primitive sites with a bathhouse and fishing pier. Primitive tent sites are $11, or $13 with water and electricity. RV sites with sewer and cable TV cost $17.

Hotels & Motels At the *Days Inn* (☎ 334-981-9888, 800-237-6169, 21250 Hwy 182) there are rooms overlooking the Gulf and an indoor heated pool. Rates range from $45 to $250, depending on the season; continental breakfast is included.

The *Gulf State Park Resort Hotel* (☎ 334-948-4853, 21250 Hwy 182 E) is a full-service beachfront resort with a pool and restaurant. All rooms are on the beach and have a balcony. Rooms are $49 to $99, depending on the season. Suites are $99 to $199. There's a three-night minimum on holiday weekends.

Gulf Pines Motel (☎ 334-968-7911, 245 E 22nd Ave), in Gulf Shores, has a pool, and

some units have kitchenettes. Pets are allowed. Rates vary seasonally from $29 to $64 for a single or double.

Gulf Shores Plantation (☎ 334-540-5000, 800-554-0344), on Hwy 180 W and Plantation Rd 13 miles west of I-59, is typical of the oceanfront condo resorts in the area. It's loaded with activities and amenities. What sets it apart is its location about halfway between Gulf Shores and Fort Morgan, away from the beach crowds. In the low season, rates range from $79 for a studio that sleeps four to $155 for a three-bedroom suite that sleeps 10. The range is $119 to $265 in high season.

Places to Eat

Check Entertainment, later, for some additional food options.

Gulf Shores Meals at the *Gulf State Park Resort Restaurant* (☎ 334-948-4853, 21250 E Beach Blvd), off Hwy 182, are a bargain. The breakfast buffet ($5.50) features fruit, grits, biscuits and gravy, French toast, eggs, bacon, home fries and sausages. The lunch buffet ($6) changes daily, but is equally filling. Dinner buffets and specials are $7.

Gulf Shores Steamer (☎ 334-948-6344, 124 W 1st Ave), off I-59 behind Souvenir, offers nothing but steamed seafood and wins acclaim from locals as a great value. The best buys on the lunch menu are grilled red snapper at $6, and steamed shrimp at $7. Everything comes with corn, potato and coleslaw. Daily specials are $4.50 to $7. Try the turtle cheesecake. In summer, expect to wait one to two hours for dinner, or, better yet, call ahead for take-out. Its sister act, *Ribs & Reds Gulf Shores Steamer II* (☎ 334-948-3241, 128 West 1st Ave) serves steamed and fried seafood as well as ribs. Hours of operation at both are Sunday to Thursday 11 am to 9 pm, and Friday and Saturday 11 am to 10 pm.

The bohemian *Gulf Coast Coffee Merchant* (☎ 334-948-7878, 701 Bayou Village) is a cafe overlooking a bayou. Italian-style sandwiches ($5 to $6.50) made with focaccia are served Monday to Saturday 10:30 am to 4 pm. Twice a month there's entertainment

ALABAMA

($4 cover charge). They also offer beer, wine and liquor. It's open Monday to Saturday 8 am to 10 pm. In summer it's also open on Sunday from 10 am to 4 pm.

Orange Beach When locals want good seafood, a laid-back atmosphere and a good view, they go to *Zeke's Restaurant* (☎ 334-981-4001, 12887 Perdido Beach Blvd/Hwy 182). The bar's a popular meeting place. Lunch costs about $7 and dinner is around $17. It's open for lunch and dinner daily, and Sunday brunch is available from 10:30 am to 3 pm.

At the *Bayside Grill* (☎ 334-981-4899, 27842 Canal Rd/Hwy 180), in the Sportsman Marina, you can dine outdoors on a wide porch or indoors and look out picture windows. Many locals concede its one of the best restaurants in the area. The menu emphasizes seafood prepared Southern and New Orleans style. The panéed catfish ($11) is a local favorite; be prepared to pay up to $18 for other dinner entrées. Reservations are a must in summer.

Entertainment

Check Places to Eat, above, for some additional entertainment options.

Straddling the Florida and Alabama state line is the club *Florabama* (☎ 334-980-5119 in Alabama, ☎ 904-492-3048 in Florida, 17401 Perdido Key Drive), at Hwy 182. In summer and during spring break, the crowd borders on unmanageable. Since opening in 1961, the club has added patios, bar rooms, game rooms, lounges and a liquor store. As many as three bands can play at the same time on indoor and outdoor stages. It's open daily 9 am to 2:30 am.

Nolan's (☎ 334-948-2111, 508 E Beach Blvd/Hwy 182) is a popular spot for dining and dancing. It attracts a more mature audience than most beach dance halls. There's live music in the evening Tuesday to Saturday. The food selection includes Lebanese salad and Greek-style fish dishes. The kitchen is open Monday to Thursday 5 to 10 pm and Friday to Saturday 5 to 11 pm. Dancing goes on until no one is left standing.

Live Bait (☎ 334-974-1612, 24281 Perdido Beach Blvd/Hwy 182), in Orange Beach, is a fun joint that attracts a youngish crowd. It's also a decent restaurant, serving mostly seafood and popular short-order specials. The kitchen is open daily 11:30 am to 10 pm. On Thursday, Friday and Saturday the bar stays open late and there's live entertainment.

There are two cinemas in the area: *Canal St Theater* (☎ 334-981-6796, Hwy 180 E), in Orange Beach, and *Foley Cinema* (☎ 334-971-1144, Hwy 59 N).

Tennessee

Facts about Tennessee

Tennessee is like three different states in one. Memphis anchors the western Tennessee bottomland to the Mississippi Delta, with its history of cotton production, riverboat trade and blues. Tennessee's twanging capital, Nashville, is also the unofficial capital of middle Tennessee, a fertile plateau that serves as the liaison between the state's two disparate ends. Eastern Tennessee, with Knoxville as its urban center, is an Appalachian region that aligns with the Great Smoky Mountains.

The western and eastern reaches of the state are dissimilar in topography, history, racial makeup and culture. Today, Memphis and Nashville are as different from one another as blues music is from country music, and the distinct genres are apt metaphors for the individual nature of each city.

History

Fortune seekers led by Hernando de Soto in 1541 were the first Europeans to visit the area, pausing only long enough to leave firearms and disease for the Indians to mess with. Two centuries later, British traders sloped in from the east and French fur traders from the west, both groups claiming the territory, decimating wildlife and destabilizing the resident Indian tribes. Tensions erupted in the French and Indian War (1756–63), which resulted in France's ceding all land east of the Mississippi River to the British.

During the 1760s, Daniel Boone and other 'long hunters' (their hunting trips lasted up to a year) crossed the Appalachians. From 1769, the first 'overmountain' folk (those who settled over the mountains) toughed their way in, settling in defiance of British law and sometimes negotiating illegal leases with the Cherokee. One settler from North Carolina, Richard Henderson, cheekily bartered six wagonloads of goods for 20 million acres of Cherokee land, including most of middle Tennessee. There were periodic clashes between the settlers, the Cherokees and the breakaway Chickamaugas. (The Chickamaugas, under Chief Dragging Canoe, broke away from the Cherokees and settled near Chattanooga. They later sided with the Creek against white settlers.)

During the 1776 Revolution, most Native Americans sided with the British and most settlers fought against the curious British-Cherokee alliance. Postwar settlement trickled to the west, clearing the native peoples in the way by treaty and force. By the end of the century, regional identity was solid enough to agitate for admission to the

Highlights

- Elvis Presley's Graceland estate
- Shiloh's Civil War battlefield
- Great music at Nashville's cowboy dives
- Dollywood's voluptuous roller coasters
- The Tennessee portion of the Appalachian Trail
- Ocoee River, with Olympic-caliber rapids

Union. Tennessee was accepted as the 16th state in 1796.

Andrew Jackson is Tennessee's towering figure of the era. Through his efforts, the western boundary of Tennessee was extended to the Mississippi River, and British forces were defeated in the Battle of New Orleans in 1815. The charismatic Jackson was propelled all the way to the presidency in 1828. The biggest blot on his record is forced Indian removal (see the boxed text 'Trail of Tears' in the Chattanooga section, later in this chapter).

Through the 19th century, plantation society expanded as several entrepreneurial landowners established cotton plantations worked by slaves. By 1860, Tennessee's 250,000 slaves, concentrated in middle and western Tennessee, represented a quarter of the state's total population. Antislavery sentiment developed early in pro-Union eastern Tennessee, and the state's population was divided during the Civil War: 180,000 Tennesseans fought for the Confederacy and 50,000 for the Union. Around 400 battles wrought devastation upon the state's population and resources.

Tennessee actually abolished slavery on its own, by way of popular vote in 1865 (the only state to do so), and was the first Confederate state readmitted to the Union, thereby avoiding the worst of military occupation and Reconstruction. Nevertheless, there was a hostile reaction to emancipation.

The Ku Klux Klan, originally a social club, was founded in 1868 by former Confederate soldiers (led by Grand Wizard Nathan Bedford Forrest) in Pulaski in an effort to control the large numbers of freed slaves in western Tennessee. They became influential in 'protecting whites' and disenfranchising the state's blacks by restrictive poll-tax laws.

Though blacks languished under statutory and mob racism, Tennessee led the nation by introducing limited female suffrage in 1920. In a less progressive step in 1925, the state led the Bible Belt by banning the teaching of evolution in public schools. This law remained until 1967.

During the Great Depression, Tennessee began to change from a deeply rural society to a more urbanized, industrialized one. 'New South' industries begun in the early 20th century, such as timber, paper, iron and textiles, overtook agriculture, while many farmers and sharecroppers suffered badly. Drought added to the farmers' woes, and the Tennessee Valley Authority (see the boxed text 'Dam it!') was created as a New Deal project to provide flood control and hydroelectricity. It became both a symbol and an engine of Tennessee's industrial growth.

It was not until the 1960s that electoral reform and the Civil Rights movement brought representative politics to Tennessee, the home state of US vice president (at press time) Al Gore. The urban black population organized many acts of resistance during this time, including months of tense sit-ins in Nashville restaurants. Martin Luther King Jr was assassinated in Memphis in 1968, putting Tennessee firmly on the map of the Civil Rights movement

Tuning in to Tennessee

Unless you're addicted to mainstream rock or country, you'd be advised to augment your radio choices with your own tapes or CDs. The best radio in the state comes out of Memphis and Nashville.

Memphis:
WEVL 89.9 FM blues, rockabilly, bluegrass, pop and soul
WRBO 103.5 FM old-time soul
WDIA 1070 AM rhythm & blues
WAVN 1240 AM gospel
WLOK 1340 AM gospel

Nashville:
Fisk University 88.1 FM gospel, soul, eclectic
WROT 100.1 FM indie and other

Murfreesboro (Middle Tennessee):
WMTS 88.3 FM college station with eclectic playlist

TENNESSEE

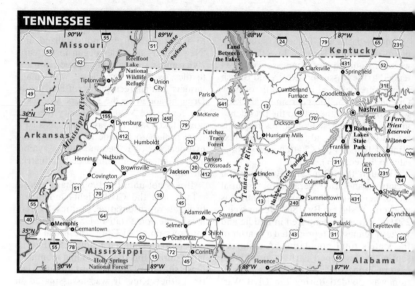

TENNESSEE

(see the Memphis section, later in this chapter).

In the last few decades, Tennessee has continued to expand its industrial base, resolving the key change from an undiversified farming state to a hearty urban economy.

Geography

Tennessee is a blue-note parallelogram, covering 44,244 sq miles (432 miles from east to west and a squat 112 miles from top to bottom). It's bordered by North Carolina over the Appalachian Mountains to the east, Kentucky and Virginia to the north, Missouri and Arkansas over the Mississippi River to the west, and Mississippi, Alabama and Georgia to the south.

The state tumbles from the Appalachian strip at its extreme east to the ridges and dips of the Great Valley. Farther west, the terrain ascends to the stony, river-slashed Cumberland Plateau before skidding into the knobbly central basin. The basin slips westward into the Tennessee River Valley, which in turn gives way to the claggy glug and rolling hill country of western Tennessee. Tennesseans divide the state strictly into East, Middle and West, though these divisions are imprinted more in regional psychology than in topography.

Government & Politics

The career of Andrew Jackson seems to have given Tennesseans a taste for politics on a national stage. As well as homegrown President James K Polk and Vice President Al Gore (presidential hopeful at press time), Tennesseans have held high ministerial and administrative office in both Republican and Democrat administrations.

The current Republican governor is Don Sundquist, who was reelected in a landslide in 1998 on an anti-crime platform; Tennessee has since reinstituted the death penalty.

Economy

Tennessee is a bridge between the often-alarming poverty of the Deep South and the spreading-belly comfort of middle America. Though unemployment is slightly lower than the US average, annual personal income in Tennessee is around $3000 below par and 13% of the state's population is judged to be below the poverty line (a

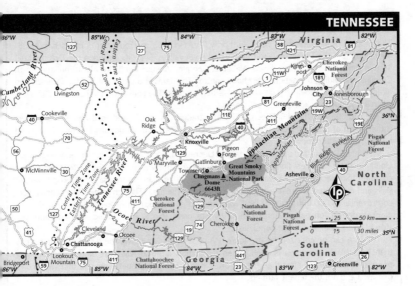

couple of points above the national average).

Significant industries include electricity (the TVA sells power to seven states) and coal mining. The $2 billion-a-year tourism industry is built on country music attractions in middle and eastern Tennessee while Graceland keeps the greenbacks flowing into Memphis. Corn, soy, tobacco, cotton and sorghum are the main agricultural products.

Population & People

Of Tennessee's population of 5.4 million, 68% live in metropolitan areas. Nashville and Memphis are the big urban kahunas with around a million residents each; Chattanooga and Knoxville are bite-sized cities in comparison.

Over 80% of Tennessee's black population lives in cities, primarily Memphis, where they make up 55% of the population, and Nashville.

Information

Tourist Offices The Tennessee Department of Tourist Development (☎ 615-741-8299, 800-836-6200 for vacation information,

TDD/TTY 615-741-0691), Rachel Jackson Bldg, 5th floor, 320 6th Ave N, Nashville, TN 37243, distributes statewide tourist information. You can find them on the Web at www.tnvacation.com.

The bicycle coordinator at the Tennessee Department of Transportation (☎ 615-741-2848), James K Polk Bldg, Suite 900, 505 Deaderick St, Nashville, TN 37243-0334, distributes state-sanctioned bike-route maps.

Taxes Sales tax is 6% in Tennessee; additional accommodations taxes vary from around 3% to 5%. Shelby County (where Memphis is located) adds a 2.25% sales tax, for a total of 8.25%; lodging taxes are added on top of this.

Driving & Liquor Laws The legal driving age is 15 years old. Children under four must ride in a car seat. Headlights must be turned on when windshield wipers are being used.

The legal drinking age is 21. No alcohol sales are permitted on Sunday morning. Tennessee has strict laws on Driving Under the Influence (DUI). A driver convicted of a

Dam it!

The creation of the Tennessee Valley Authority (TVA) in 1933 sparked a frenzy of reservoir building throughout the Tennessee and Cumberland River valleys. Since its inception the TVA has built 16 dams in seven states (Tennessee, Alabama, Georgia, Virginia, Kentucky, Mississippi and North Carolina), providing the nation's best flood control. The dams also provide water for domestic and agricultural use, hydroelectric power and leisure purposes. The constructions themselves are considered fine public buildings.

The 170,000-acre 'Land Between the Lakes,' straddling Kentucky and northwestern Tennessee, is the largest of these projects. It was built during the 1960s and is a popular boating, fishing and hunting destination today.

When the TVA started up during the Great Depression, times were hard in the Tennessee valley. Unemployment was high, flooding was a part of life, malaria was endemic and bartering was more common than cash. The TVA was a revolution: it provided work for thousands of people, taught skills and distributed affordable electricity throughout the area. Though some of its actions were controversial (1,000,000 acres of land were cleared or flooded), most agree that the delimited, planned destruction perpetrated by the TVA was preferable to the chaotic slash-and-burn destruction of a poor, desperate population.

The TVA can be criticized for its racism. White workers were given better jobs for better pay than their black counterparts. And, when population removal was part of the dam-building process, whites fared better than blacks, often because it was property owners that were compensated and not the tenant-farmers.

DUI with a child in the car may be charged with a felony offense.

Two out of Tennessee's 95 counties are dry. Ironically, one of them includes Lynchburg, producer of Jack Daniel's whiskey. In wet counties, wine and spirits can be purchased from liquor stores; beer is available in grocery stores and gas stations.

State Parks & Protected Areas The central office for Tennessee State Parks (☎ 615-532-0001, 888-867-2757) is at 401 Church St, 7th floor, Nashville, TN 37243-0446. Fishing regulations can be obtained from the Tennessee Wildlife Resources Agency (☎ 615-781-6500), PO Box 40747, Nashville, TN 37204.

Western Tennessee

For most visitors, western Tennessee means Memphis, and in many ways Memphis is more about Mississippi than it is about Tennessee: it's blacker, bluesier and better for barbecue than anywhere else in the state. If you are traveling between Memphis and Nashville, consider swinging south through Shiloh, an evocative Civil War battlefield, and Savannah, a pretty river town. If you're getting out of the Deep South altogether, you could hightail it north to Reelfoot Lake for some earthquake and eagle action before you hit Kentucky.

MEMPHIS
• pop 1,100,000

Named for the ancient Egyptian capital on the Nile, Memphis on the Mississippi is best known for the rise and fall of two men who led vastly different movements.

The King of Rock & Roll, Elvis Presley, rocketed to fame here in the late 1950s; his Graceland estate draws more than 700,000 visitors to town each year. And it was here, on April 4, 1968, that the Reverend Dr Martin Luther King Jr was assassinated on the balcony of the Lorraine Motel downtown, a sight now preserved in his honor as the National Civil Rights Museum. The sight is infused with all the solemn decorum one would expect for a fallen hero. Strangely, perhaps, so is Graceland.

But in general the city takes its cues from something that happened much earlier. In the early 1900s, WC Handy's 'Beale Street Blues' established Memphis as the home of the blues. Today, the dockside city retains a certain soulful grittiness from a history replete with cotton, riverboats and blues. The blues continue to resonate from clubs on the new and improved Beale St – the city's answer to Bourbon St – and in rugged dives around town.

Memphis-based Federal Express is the city's largest employer, with 30,000 employees. Memphis is also the home of the first supermarket (Piggly Wiggly opened here in 1916) and the original Holiday Inn, and it's the site of the first Welcome Wagon, founded here in 1928. Almost half of the US cotton crop continues to float through Memphis.

Nevertheless, for all its big-city trappings, Memphis is really more of a big town. Its major sights are easily seen in a few days, its roads are easy to navigate, and you'll probably find yourself running into the same people that you met days earlier.

History

Three thousand years ago, the loess bluffs on the eastern shore of the Mississippi River were occupied by Native American tribes (see Chucalissa Archaeological Site & Museum, later in this section, for a glimpse of what village life was like around 1500 AD).

In 1541, the locals came in contact with the troops of Hernando de Soto when he first encountered the great Mississippi River. The town was abandoned soon thereafter ('Chucalissa' is a Choctaw word for 'abandoned') and the area came under Chickasaw domination.

The earliest European settlement on the site of Memphis was the French Fort Assumption established in 1739. In 1818 a US treaty edged the Chickasaw nation out of western Tennessee, and Andrew Jackson helped found the settlement he named Memphis. The city was incorporated in 1826 and prospered on the expanding cotton trade of the fertile Mississippi Delta directly south. Early in the Civil War a Union fleet defeated Confederate naval forces at the Battle of Memphis, and federal troops occupied the city.

Though there was little physical destruction, recovery from the war was hampered by a crippling yellow-fever epidemic in 1878 that claimed more than 5000 lives. The disproportionate toll on the white population was attributed to a genetic predisposition, and surviving whites virtually abandoned the city. The following year Memphis officially declared bankruptcy, and its city charter was revoked until 1893.

The black community took over daily operations and brought the town back to its feet. A former slave named Robert Church became a prominent landowner, civic leader and millionaire by buying real estate at bargain rates. Emigrants from the Delta

---

'Boss' Crump

Born in Holly Springs in 1874, young gentleman EH Crump moved to Memphis and mixed swagger, bluff, money and sleaze to get his finger into just about every pie in town. Between 1909 and 1916 he was mayor of Memphis, but this was but the beginning of his reign of influence. Behind-the-scenes plays saw Crump-backed candidates hold office in Tennessee from the mid-1920s through to his death in 1954. His last appointee stayed in office until 1993.

His anti-union, lean-government stance kept 'Boss' Crump somewhat respectable, but a large portion of his money was channeled through shady doings and dealings. Crump had strong support in the black community of Memphis (see the boxed text 'The Memphis Bluesman,' in the Memphis section), partly through vote-buying, and Memphis was one of few Southern towns where blacks didn't have trouble voting during this era.

TENNESSEE

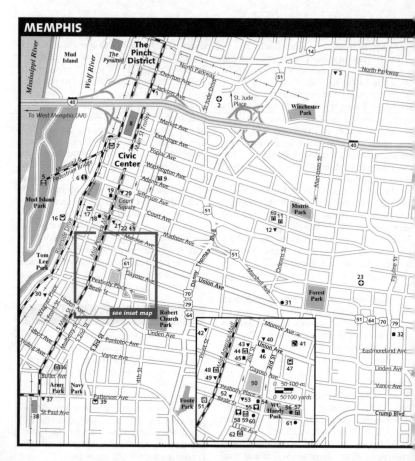

arrived in great numbers and the city thrived as the center of the cotton trade.

White citizens moved back as the cotton and logging industries rallied, attracting mostly white entrepreneurs back to the city. During the 1890s, Memphis was the world's biggest hardwood market.

In its heyday in the early 1900s, a long stretch of Beale St was the hub of social, civic and business activity for the large African-American community not only in Memphis but across the mid-South. The street gained a provocative reputation for drinking, gambling and other shady pas-

times associated with riverboat towns. The Delta cotton industry was ravaged by the boll weevil in 1914, forcing many people to look for work in Memphis. Some found their feet in the city and stayed; many others pressed farther north to Chicago.

During the Great Depression many businesses closed while others moved out to east Memphis, but industry was boosted during WWII: cotton prices were high and two military depots were built in the area. Postwar, this more prosperous Memphis constructed the speedy four-lane bridge to Arkansas and expanded the harbor.

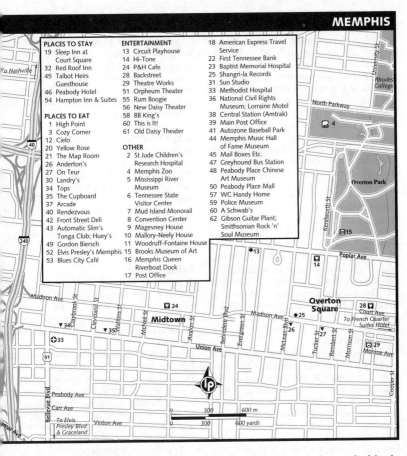

MEMPHIS

PLACES TO STAY
19 Sleep Inn at Court Square
32 Red Roof Inn
45 Talbot Heirs Guesthouse
46 Peabody Hotel
54 Hampton Inn & Suites

PLACES TO EAT
1 High Point
3 Cozy Corner
12 Cielo
20 Yellow Rose
21 The Map Room
26 Anderton's
27 On Teur
30 Landry's
34 Tops
35 The Cupboard
37 Arcade
40 Rendezvous
42 Front Street Deli
43 Automatic Slim's Tonga Club; Huey's
49 Gordon Biersch
52 Elvis Presley's Memphis
53 Blues City Café

ENTERTAINMENT
13 Circuit Playhouse
14 Hi-Tone
24 P&H Cafe
28 Backstreet
29 Theatre Works
51 Orpheum Theater
55 Rum Boogie
56 New Daisy Theater
58 BB King's
60 This is It!
61 Old Daisy Theater

OTHER
2 St Jude Children's Research Hospital
4 Memphis Zoo
5 Mississippi River Museum
6 Tennessee State Visitor Center
7 Mud Island Monorail
8 Convention Center
9 Magevney House
10 Mallory-Neely House
11 Woodruff-Fontaine House
15 Brooks Museum of Art
16 *Memphis Queen* Riverboat Dock
17 Post Office
18 American Express Travel Service
22 First Tennessee Bank
23 Baptist Memorial Hospital
25 Shangri-la Records
31 Sun Studio
33 Methodist Hospital
36 National Civil Rights Museum; Lorraine Motel
38 Central Station (Amtrak)
39 Main Post Office
41 Autozone Baseball Park
44 Memphis Music Hall of Fame Museum
45 Mail Boxes Etc.
47 Greyhound Bus Station
48 Peabody Place Chinese Art Museum
50 Peabody Place Mall
57 WC Handy Home
59 Police Museum
60 A Schwab's
62 Gibson Guitar Plant; Smithsonian Rock 'n' Soul Museum

In the early 1950s, music visionary Sam Phillips opened Sun Studio and began producing records by now-famous blues legends such as Howlin' Wolf and Rufus Thomas. This paved the way a few years later for white rockabilly artists. For Phillips to record both black and white musicians indiscriminately was a radical concept in the South at the time. Just as daring was equally renowned local WHBQ disc jockey Dewey Phillips, who had the gall to play the records cut at Sun. Following Sun's lead, more studios began springing up around Memphis, recording soul music, R&B, and rock that peaked in the 1960s and '70s.

With the Civil Rights movement of the early 1960s came racial integration. This prompted the affluent white population to move and to expand suburban development east. In 1968, city sanitation workers walked out on strike and Martin Luther King Jr came to town to lend his support. He was assassinated in Memphis on April 4 (see the boxed text 'A Conspiracy to Kill Martin Luther King Jr?').

By the 1970s the historic downtown had been largely abandoned and Beale St was in

TENNESSEE

such a state of disrepair that city planners hoped to bulldoze the whole strip. Objections by preservationists grew loud enough for the city to commit $500 million to restoration instead of complete redevelopment. A new entertainment district was sculpted out of the old commercial buildings and storefronts along the few central blocks of Beale St. Along with the new baseball stadium for the Memphis Redbirds, new retail and hotel developments are springing up nearby, and plans for more riverfront development demonstrate an ongoing commitment to the downtown Memphis area.

Orientation

Downtown Memphis runs along the east bank of the Mississippi. Riverside Dr and a promenade run parallel to the river below the bluff, with a nice view of river traffic and bridges, particularly at night, with the I-40 bridge lights making the shape of the letter 'M.' The civic and financial centers are clustered in a compact area between I-40 and Patterson St. A monorail to Mud Island River Park departs from the Civic Center, which is off Front St.

The two main east-west thoroughfares are Union Ave and Poplar Ave, which start at the river and run east through midtown where they cross and continue into East Memphis, with Union turning into Walnut Grove. Downtown, avenues generally run east-west, streets north-south.

In the northeastern area of downtown, a funky little corner around N Main St and North Parkway called the 'Pinch District' retains a few historic dives.

A short walk (or train-trolley ride) south leads to the tourist district anchored by the Peabody Hotel and centered in the Beale St strip between 2nd and 4th Sts. The compact zone around the Peabody Hotel is convenient to the Greyhound bus station, a half block east across 3rd St.

East of here there's a district of warehouses and muffler shops too long, uninteresting and suspect to walk through, but it's interrupted by a few finds such as a cafe or two and the landmark Sun Studio. A huge

medical center forms the eastern border of what's considered downtown.

Midtown runs from the medical center to East Parkway and holds Overton Square, Overton Park (including the city's zoo) and the Cooper-Young neighborhood. From here, east Memphis spreads out with miles of increasingly affluent suburban development.

Maps It's easy to get through town following major routes, but a decent map is necessary to navigate the complex freeway interchanges (see Getting Around, later in this section). Auto club members can get maps at AAA (☎ 901-761-5371), 5138 Park Ave (in East Memphis, about a mile west of I-240). Gas stations sell maps, and car-rental companies, hotels and visitor centers distribute free maps.

Information

Tourist Offices The Tennessee State Visitor Center (☎ 901-543-5333, TDD/TTY 901-521-6833) on Riverside Dr makes an easy and scenic first stop for maps, event calendars and information. It's open around the clock.

Visitors may call or write for information from the Memphis Convention and Visitors Bureau (☎ 901-543-5300, 800-863-6744), 47 Union Ave, Memphis, TN 38103.

The 24-hour Memphis information hot line can be reached at ☎ 901-753-5847. A translation service can be reached at ☎ 901-372-7373.

For visitor information online go to www.memphistravel.com or check out www.memphismojo.com.

Money There are ATMs throughout the city. Currency exchanges are available at the Memphis International Airport and in the downtown headquarters of First Tennessee Bank (☎ 901-523-4444), at 165 Madison Ave.

Post The main post office (☎ 901-521-2187) is at 555 S 3rd St. More convenient is the branch at 1 N Front St (☎ 901-576-2013), at the foot of Madison Ave downtown. There's

One skinny latte & a peanut-butter-&-banana scone, thank you very much. Java Cabana, Memphis

un Studio, Memphis

Take a loop around downtown Memphis.

iet your mojo workin' on Beale Street, Memphis.

The purple mountain majesty of Great Smoky Mountains National Park, TN

Cades Cove church, Great Smoky Mountains

Traditional mountain homes, TN

Take this Cades Cove back road and let time slip away. Great Smoky Mountains, TN

also a post office at Watkins St and Union Ave in midtown.

The Mail Center (☎ 901-725-9173), at 1910 Madison Ave in midtown, is equipped to send packages via UPS or FedEx. Downtown, try Mail Boxes Etc at 99 S 2nd St (next to the Music Hall of Fame).

Media *The Commercial Appeal* is the daily newspaper in Memphis. Expanded entertainment listings appear in the Friday and Sunday editions.

The free weekly *Memphis Flyer*, distributed at many outlets around town, covers news and entertainment from an alternative perspective. The free monthlies *Triangle Journal News* and *Family & Friends* cover news and entertainment of special interest to the gay community; they're distributed at libraries around town and in restaurants and theaters. See also www.gaymemphis .com. *Dateline Memphis* is a free weekly along the lines of the Flyer (also available at www.datelinememphis.com).

The nonprofit community radio station WEVL 89.9 FM plays a tremendous variety of local music, including blues, rockabilly, bluegrass, swamp pop and soul classics. WRBO 103.5 FM plays old time soul and R&B. Gospel can be heard on WAVN 1240 AM and WLOK 1340 AM. WDIA 1070 AM plays rhythm and blues. You'll find the local NPR affiliate at 91.1 FM.

Travel Agencies There's an American Express Travel Service (☎ 901-543-2410) downtown at 80 Monroe St, but they don't cash traveler's checks. There's a Northwest/KLM agency in the Peabody Hotel building, 149 Union Ave.

Travel services are also available at AAA (see Maps, earlier).

Bookstores Memphis has several wonderful bookstores. Davis-Kidd Booksellers (☎ 901-683-9801), 387 Perkins Rd Extended at Poplar Ave, near the Oak Court Mall, offers the most comprehensive selection, with many periodicals and out-of-town newspapers. Davis-Kidd also has a cafe and hosts author events.

Burke's Bookstore (☎ 901-278-7484), 1719 Poplar Ave, established in 1875, has rare collectibles among its new and used literary selections, and features author readings and book signings.

Xanadu Music & Books (☎ 901-274-9885), 2200 Central Ave, stocks books by local authors and out-of-print books, and you can pick up a guitar if there's nothing you want to read.

For periodicals, there's a newsstand at the corner of 2nd St and Monroe Ave, one block north of Union.

Libraries The new Memphis/Shelby County Public Library and Information Center (☎ 901-725-8895), 3030 Poplar Ave, operates 22 branch libraries around town. There is free Internet access at most libraries.

Books Look for Robert Gordon's *It Came from Memphis*, which describes the city's kookier side with a cast of midget wrestlers, wasted rock stars and grizzled bluesmen. Peter Guralnick has written a bunch of books with a Memphis focus including *Last Train to Memphis: The Rise of Elvis Presley* and *Careless Love: The Unmaking of Elvis Presley*.

Drive-in movies, cemetery stalking and the favorite local pastime – recounting what Memphis once was – are described in the *Lowlife Guide to Memphis*. It's produced and distributed by Shangri-la Records (☎ 901-274-1916), 1916 Madison Ave.

Medical & Emergency Services Call ☎ 911 in an emergency. For other police business call ☎ 901-545-2677. For the Sexual Assault Resource Center (a program so responsive it's considered a national model), call ☎ 901-272-2020.

Major city hospitals are located at Union Ave near I-240. The branches of Baptist Memorial Hospital (☎ 901-227-2727), 899 Madison Ave (Lisa Marie Presley was born on the 5th floor; the green blind in the window helps pilgrims identify the room), and Methodist Hospital (☎ 901-726-7000), 1265 Union Ave, here are two of the city's largest employers. There is also The MED (☎ 901-545-7100), 877 Jefferson Ave.

An internationally recognized center for pediatric medicine, St Jude Children's Research Hospital (☎ 901-495-3300), 332 N Lauderdale St, was established by actor Danny Thomas (note Danny Thomas Blvd).

The Memphis Center for Reproductive Health (☎ 901-274-3550), 1462 Poplar Ave at McNeil, staffs its phone lines 24 hours a day to answer medical questions.

Peabody Hotel

Not only a grand hotel, the Peabody, off Union Ave between 2nd and 3rd Sts, is the town's social hub, with its own quirky traditions. At 11 am every day, the Peabody's famous ducks descend in the elevator from their penthouse apartment and file across a red carpet to cavort in the lobby's marble fountain – the story goes that a general manager's prank in the 1930s started the tradition. (The ducks' retreat commences at 5 pm sharp – get there 15 minutes early to get a good viewing position.) The hotel complex includes a tourist information booth, pricey and formal restaurants, cafes and shops, and a travel agent; downtown tour operators park outside. See also Organized Tours, Places to Stay and Entertainment, later in this section.

Beale Street

Though only one of the original stores remains from Beale St's heyday in the early 1900s, you can still get a taste for the old commercial strip from the brick storefronts, cobblestones and, of course, its legendary blues.

The two-block strip of Beale between 2nd and 4th Sts is now the city's entertainment district. The swanky clubs, restaurants, souvenir shops and neon signs lead critics to call it a Disneyfied blues theme park. But it's hard to argue too vehemently against independent, locally owned and operated, safe, comfortable places to hear masterful live music.

The **Orpheum Theater**, at the corner of Beale and Main Sts, has been restored to its 1928 glory. A grand opera house was built here in 1895 but was later destroyed by fire.

The Elvis statue at the corner of 2nd and Beale heralds **Elvis Presley's Memphis**, a nightclub and restaurant. It's carved out of the famous clothier shop Lansky's, where Elvis bought the outfit he wore for his notorious performance on the *Ed Sullivan Show* (when the cameras showed him only from the waist up). Diagonally across the street at **BB King's**, the 'Beale St Blues Boy' himself occasionally performs at his namesake club, which was once the Colored Business Exchange building. Even if he's not there, keep your eye out for other amazing performers.

Between 2nd and 3rd Sts, the **Walk of Fame** features musical notes embedded in the sidewalk with the names of blues artists. The Beale St substation **Police Museum** (☎ 901-525-9800) exhibits criminalia such as a magnetic machine used to rig carnival games and drug paraphernalia. It's the only museum inside a working station in the US.

Owned by the same family since 1876, the landmark **A Schwab's** dry-goods store is the only original vendor still operating on Beale St. A Schwab's fills three floors with voodoo powders, thumb twiddlers, handcuffs, clerical collars, saucepans and the largest selection of hats in town. The rest of the block is filled with restaurants, shops, clubs and pubs. A ghostly façade held up on steel girders is all that remains of the Gallina Hotel.

Between 3rd and 4th Sts, the WC Handy statue overlooks **WC Handy Park**, which has an amphitheater that hosts outdoor concerts. (This is where Memphians ring in the New Year.) At the far end of the block (turn left into 4th St) is the shotgun shack where Handy raised six children.

The **New Daisy Theater** has art deco backdrops depicting the district's honky-tonk heyday, and continues to hold big-name concerts and shows. The **Old Daisy** across the road is waiting for someone with a green thumb to get her going again.

Tucked behind Beale St at 3rd St is the **Gibson Guitar plant**, where many of the models made famous by local recording stars are now manufactured. Within the plant, the Smithsonian Institution's **Rock 'n' Soul Museum** examines the social and cultural history that produced the music of the Mississippi Delta. Admission to museum is $6 for adults, $4 for children five to 17.

Memphis Music Hall of Fame Museum

The nonprofit Hall of Fame (☎ 901-525-4007), at 97 S 2nd St, illustrates popular music's roots – from African rhythms through slave chants, blues, gospel, R&B, soul and rock & roll – with 7000 sq feet of artifacts (such as bluesman Furry Lewis' shoeshine box), instruments and costumes (including Elvis' karate suit and Isaac Hayes' 10-inch platform shoes). Vintage recordings are heard through headsets, and black & white TV sets show rare film and television footage, including *St Louis Blues*, Bessie Smith's only film.

Admission seems high ($7.50 for adults), but it's a studiously researched and nicely maintained collection. Music-related books and souvenirs can be purchased at the gift shop. It's open Monday to Thursday 10 am to 6 pm, Friday and Saturday to 9 pm and Sunday noon to 6 pm.

National Civil Rights Museum

This must-see museum (☎ 901-521-9699), 450 Mulberry St five blocks south of Beale, is housed in the Lorraine Motel, where the Reverend Dr Martin Luther King Jr was fatally shot on April 4, 1968. The exterior of the turquoise 1950s motel remains much the same as it was at that time; the Cadillacs parked below the balcony were there when King was struck down.

Documentary photos and accompanying text chronicle key events in Civil Rights history. The moving, confronting and overwhelming displays culminate in the motel room maintained exactly as King left it just before he was shot.

Admission is $6, $5 for students and seniors, $4 for children six to 12. It's open Monday, Wednesday, Friday and Saturday 10 am to 5 pm, Thursday 9 am to 8 pm, Sunday 1 pm to 5 pm with extended hours in summer. It's closed Tuesday.

Mud Island Park

Above the Tennessee State Welcome Center, cross the Wolf River via a monorail and elevated walkway to 52-acre Mud Island Park (☎ 901-576-7241, 800-507-6507). The park has an impressive to-scale bas-relief reproduction of the lower Mississippi River culminating in a one-million-gallon Gulf of Mexico. You can wade in the miniature river (one step represents about a mile) and swim in the Gulf! There's a circuitous river museum that includes steamer and gunboat replicas, and music exhibits. It has a spooky ghost-train-on-foot feel. There's also a WWII bomber, an amphitheater and restaurants.

Open from mid-April through October, it's closed Monday in spring and fall, but open 10 am to 7 pm daily in summer. Adults pay $8 for all attractions; children four to 11, seniors and the disabled pay $6. You can catch the monorail on Front St between Poplar and Adams Aves.

Sun Studio

The 'most famous recording studio in the world,' Sun Studio (☎ 901-521-0664), 706 Union Ave near Marshall Ave, straddling downtown and midtown, is the nursery where rock & roll was born. Starting in the early 1950s, owner Sam Phillips recorded blues artists such as Howlin' Wolf, BB King and Ike Turner, followed by the Sun rockabilly dynasty of Jerry Lee Lewis, Carl

Site of MLK's assassination, now a museum

LEE FOSTER

TENNESSEE

A Conspiracy to Kill Martin Luther King Jr?

In the spring of 1968, Martin Luther King Jr came to Memphis to lead a march supporting striking city sanitation workers. Late in the afternoon on April 4, King was fatally shot on the balcony of the Lorraine Motel. Rioting and sporadic violence across the nation followed the murder, and the city's (as well as the nation's) recovery was slow and painful.

King's accused killer was a 40-year-old petty burglar named James Earl Ray. Ray pleaded guilty in 1969, yet three days later he recanted his guilty plea. Nevertheless, he was sentenced to 99 years in prison without a trial. Ray asserted his innocence until he died of cirrhosis in April 1998. He said that the rifle found near the murder scene was put there by conspirators who wished to frame him. Ray's father took an interesting tack, asserting that his son wasn't smart enough to have committed such a crime.

In 1978, a congressional committee doubted that Ray had acted alone, and requests from Ray's lawyers for a trial intensified. The King family also pressed for a trial. Martin Luther King's son, Dexter, met with Ray in 1997 and later said he believed Ray was a pawn in a murder conspiracy.

New ballistic tests were not conclusive and as Ray became sicker, the possibility of a trial slipped away. His death was lamented by Civil Rights activists and conspiracy theorists who now doubt that the truth will ever out.

Perkins, Johnny Cash, Roy Orbison and, of course, Elvis Presley. In 1952, Sun produced Jackie Brenston's classic 'Rocket 88' – widely regarded as the first rock & roll release. In 1955, Sun cut Elvis' first hit, 'Don't Be Cruel.'

The tiny room with its warped tiles is still active today – musicians such as U2, Def Leppard, Tom Petty and Beck have all come to Memphis to record on its hallowed ground. The 30-minute 'tour' (you stand around) goes hourly on the half-hour and includes vintage audio clips; it costs $8.50 (free for children under 12). Sun is open 10 am to 6 pm daily with extended hours in summer. A soda shop, gift shop, memorabilia exhibit and free parking are adjacent.

Graceland

The Graceland estate was home to Elvis Presley for 20 years; he died here and is buried on the grounds outside the house. Before Elvis bought the property, the estate was part of a 500-acre farm that belonged to

the Toof family; it was named Graceland after a female relative. In the spring of 1957, at age 22, Elvis purchased the house and grounds for $100,000. After Elvis' death in 1977, the estate passed to his father and grandmother (now deceased) and his daughter, Lisa Marie Presley. Priscilla Presley (who divorced Elvis in 1973) opened Graceland to tours in 1982.

Cobalt-blue drapes with gold fringe, peacock stained glass, avocado-green kitchen appliances, a 15-foot couch, yellow vinyl, a stone waterfall and green shag carpeting on the ceiling make Graceland a museum of 1970s aesthetics.

A tour of Graceland (☎ 901-332-3322, 800-238-2000, TDD/TTY 901-344-3146, www.elvis-presley.com), on Elvis Presley Blvd (Hwy 51), begins with the visitor plaza across the street. Here you'll find tour ticket sales, accessory museums, cafes, far-too-tasteful souvenir shops, and even a post office that stamps mail with a Graceland postmark. A free 22-minute film airs on the hour and half-hour in the plaza.

In busier seasons, you must wait for an assigned hour for a tour of Graceland itself, or call for reservations. From the visitor plaza, vans transport ticket holders across the street to the mansion. The tour is a narrated recording with special comments from Priscilla Presley, who was a Catholic school-girl when she first moved in with Elvis. The recording is offered in seven languages.

The mansion tour alone is $12. In the visitor plaza, the car-museum tour is $6; to view the 'Sincerely Elvis' memorabilia collection it's $5; and the aircraft collection is also $5. There are discounts for seniors and children. Admission for the whole package is $22 for adults, $20 for seniors and $11 for children seven to 12. The whole package is colossal and possibly too mind-bending for the uninitiated; the house tour alone might do it (though the cars and planes are pretty nifty).

Parking costs an additional $2, but is free for the disabled. There's a free lot next door (turn right just after the Heartbreak Hotel).

The complex is open 8 am to 6 pm daily from Memorial Day to Labor Day and 9 am to 5 pm the rest of the year. It's closed on major holidays. The mansion alone is closed Tuesday from November to February.

During candlelight vigils, which are held on the anniversary of Elvis' death (August 15), worshippers (including many impersonators) stand in line for hours for the opportunity to parade up the drive and around the King's tomb in the Meditation Garden. On or around January 8 (Elvis Presley Day in Memphis by proclamation) other special events commemorate his birthday. The mansion is specially decorated around Christmastime.

Since Graceland is a quick $8 cab ride from the airport, you could conceivably visit on a layover in winter, when it's less crowded (but not on a Tuesday – it's closed). A free shuttle runs between Elvis Presley's Memphis, downtown on Beale St, and Graceland, via Sun Studio between about 11 am and 6 pm. Inquire at any of these businesses for pickup times. Cabs from downtown to Graceland cost from $18 to $20.

Elvis the Pelvis

Born in Tupelo, Mississippi, Elvis Presley (1935-77) cut a $3 single at Memphis' Sun Studio in 1954 and rocketed from being a dirt-poor boy that was beat up at school to an international superstar.

Singer, pin-up boy, soldier, film prop, Elvis did his bit not only for crooning and swooning, but also for purple velvet, green shag pile, gold-plated phones and pharmaceutical snacking. He married Priscilla Beaulieu, a Catholic schoolgirl, and together they made Lisa Marie. Oh, he also sold over a billion records, more than any other artist, ever.

Since his death by cardiac arrest at age 42 (legend has it he died on the toilet while reading *The Scientific Search for the Face of Jesus*), Elvis has become mythologized as a cultural icon – some adherents claim to have been healed by appealing to the spirit of Elvis or by attending the shrine that his Graceland estate has become (for a house tour, it's pricey, but for spiritual healing it's a bargain).

There's no doubt that Elvis is among us: while researching this book, our trusty rental car broke down outside Graceland . . . not once, but twice! Waiting for the mechanic and eating our donuts, we know we were hanging with the King.

HLR

Historic House Tours

A fascinating place that has trapdoors and tunnels as well as exhibits of slave history is the **Slavehaven/Burkle House** (☎ 901-527-3427), 826 N 2nd St at Chelsea Ave, north of downtown. It's thought to have been a way station for runaway slaves on the Underground Railroad. Tours are given Monday to Saturday 10 am to 4 pm. Admission for adults is $5, youth (convince them!) cost $3.

Two grand turn-of-the-19th-century houses in the tiny **Victorian Village** district are open to public tours. **Woodruff-Fontaine House** (☎ 901-526-1469) at 680 Adams Ave is open 10 am to 3:30 pm Monday and Wednesday to Saturday, and 1 pm to 3:30 pm Sunday. **Mallory-Neely House** (☎ 901-523-1484), 652 Adams Ave, is open 10 am to 3:30 pm Tuesday to Saturday and 1 to 3:30 pm Sunday. Admission for either is $5; a combined ticket for both houses is $9.

Magevney House (☎ 901-526-4464), 198 Adams Ave, is smaller. It was inhabited by a middle class Irish immigrant, and the interior reflects his family's lifestyle during the mid-19th century. It's open 10 am to 2 pm Tuesday to Friday and 10 am to 4 pm Saturday with extended hours in summer (free).

Pink Palace Museum & Planetarium

The original Pink Palace (☎ 901-320-6320), 3050 Central Ave, was built here in 1923 as a residence for Piggly Wiggly founder Clarence Saunders. It reopened in 1996 as a natural and cultural history museum with a congenial mishmash of fossils, Civil War exhibits, restored WPA murals and an exact replica of the original Piggly Wiggly, the world's first self-service grocery store. The museum is open daily with extended hours Thursday to Saturday and a noon start on Sunday. Admission is $6/5.50/4.50 for adults/seniors/kids.

The planetarium has regular shows ($3.50) and features a special Elvis laser show in August. Admission to the onsite IMAX theater is $9 ($6 kids).

Brooks Museum of Art

Within Overton Park (a greenway surrounded by stately homes), the city's fine-arts museum (☎ 901-544-6200), off Poplar near Kenilworth St, fans out from its gracious central rotunda into three floors of handsome galleries. Peruvian effigy vessels from 250 BC, a gorgeous Incan poncho made from macaw and parrot feathers, a Duncan Phyfe dining table, a Picasso pitcher and spray-paint art are among its varied collection.

Admission is $5 for adults, $4 seniors, $2 students (free Wednesday). It's open daily except Monday and until 8pm the first Wednesday of each month. They have a nice gift shop and a restaurant gazing off into the park.

Peabody Place Chinese Art Museum

You didn't think you were in Tennessee to see Chinese art, but this private collection (☎ 901-523-2787), inside Pembroke Square at 119 Main St, has a caps lock 'wow' factor. The mostly Chinese items include bogglingly intricate carvings; there are also Japanese works, contemporary Eastern European glasswork and Jewish artifacts. It's closed Monday. Tickets are $5 but you can sneak a free peak from the lobby.

Dixon Gallery & Gardens

The Dixon Gallery (☎ 901-761-5250), 4339 Park Ave (between Getwell and Perkins), houses an impressive collection of impressionist and postimpressionist paintings by artists such as Monet, Degas, Renoir and Cezanne. There are 17 acres of woodland, luscious lawn and landscaped gardens. Admission Tuesday to Sunday is $5 for adults, $4 seniors, $3 students and $1 children under 12. On Monday, only the grounds are open and admission is half-price.

Memphis Botanic Gardens

Flat and featureless at first glance, these gardens (☎ 901-685-1566), 750 Cherry Rd (opposite the Dixon Gallery), become more interesting the closer you look. The Sensory Garden, a Japanese-style Garden of Tranquility and the Iris Garden are the pick of the bunch. It's open daily from March to October and admission is $4/3/2 adults/seniors/children (free Tuesday afternoon).

Chucalissa Archaeological Site & Museum

At the Chucalissa archaeological site (☎ 901-785-3160), on a remote bluff south of downtown Memphis (off Mitchell Rd, west of Hwy 61 or take the Mallory exit from I-55), the Department of Anthropology at the University of Memphis maintains a reconstructed 15th-century Native American village atop ancient moundworks unearthed during construction of the nearby state park. Around the central plaza once used for ceremonies, dances and ball games, the thatched houses belonging to the chieftain, shaman and skilled craftsmen sit on elevated earthworks that also served as burial grounds.

Museum exhibits, crafts demonstrations and a knowledgeable staff tell the story of the sophisticated Mississippian civilization that once dominated the southeastern US. Though the floodlit mannequin dioramas and red-painted concrete floors are distracting, Chucalissa nonetheless provides easy access to an authentic Mississippian sight. An archaeological highlight is an enclosed cutaway trench revealing the sequential layering of one ancient mound. Admission is $5 adults, $3 seniors and children. It's closed Monday.

A spring powwow is held on Mother's Day weekend, and a Choctaw festival featuring native dances, crafts and food is held the first weekend in August.

Other Things to See & Do

Midtown's **Overton Park** is one of the largest urban parks in the country. It features a small art museum, and concerts are held in an amphitheater. Grand Egyptian porticos decorated with colorful hieroglyphics flank the entrance to the **Memphis Zoo** (☎ 901-276-9453), at the northwest corner of the park. It's OK; come if you can't think what to do with the kids – strollers are available. Admission is $8.50

for adults, $7.50 seniors, $5.50 children two to 11. Parking costs $3 per car. The zoo is open daily.

The swank **Children's Museum** (☎ 901-320-3170), 2525 Central Ave at Hollywood (at the Mid-South Fairgrounds), entertains kids with a tree house, miniature store and bank, fire engine and performances. The price of admission is $5 for adults, $4 for seniors and children.

Also at the fairgrounds, **Libertyland** is an old-time amusement park with a huge old wooden roller coaster and dozens of other rides open seasonally. Admission is $7 ($4 after 4 pm).

At the **National Ornamental Metal Museum** (☎ 901-774-6380) an outdoor sculpture garden overlooks the Mississippi River. More metallurgical arts are on display inside – from jewelry to architectural trimmings – along with metalsmiths at work. Admission is $4 adults, $3 seniors, $2 students and children. It's closed Monday. Take I-55 from downtown and exit at Metal Museum Dr.

Two state parks offer a wide range of activities, including camping. South of town, **TO Fuller State Park** (☎ 901-543-7581), on a remote bluff off Mitchell Rd west of Hwy 61, has an 18-hole golf course and a swimming pool, and the Chucalissa archaeological site (see earlier in this section).

Thirteen miles north of town, 14,500-acre **Meeman-Shelby State Park** (☎ 901-876-5215) offers more than 20 miles of hiking and horse trails. Horse and boat rentals are available. There's also an Olympic-size pool.

Organized Tours

The best tour in town is Tad Pierson's American Dreams Safari (☎ 901-527-8870, tad@americandreamsafari.com). You drive around with Tad in his '55 Caddy and get the scoop on the real Memphis. The three-hour 'greatest hits' tour includes Sun Studio and lots of Elvis stuff and costs $50 a person. If you want to get gritty ask for a 'to hell with Elvis' backstreets tour. You don't get the official line; you do get all the gossip and a great ride. A 'Delta Blues' day tour costs $175 a person including breakfast and lunch.

Riverboat rides aboard the *Memphis Queen* (☎ 901-527-5694) depart from the foot of Monroe Ave at Riverside Dr. Sightseeing tours (1½ hours) start at $12 for adults; you'll pay more for sunset dinner, moonlight music or Sunday brunch cruises.

Gray Line (☎ 901-384-3474, 800-948-8680) offers the most foreign-language bus tours around town. It has a pickup and drop-off service from most hotels, and there are a dozen tour packages ranging from three to eight hours.

Horse-drawn carriage tours (☎ 901-527-7542) depart from outside the Peabody Hotel on Union Ave. A half-hour tour costs $30 for two passengers (kids ride free).

Outdoors Inc (☎ 901-722-8988), 1710 Union Ave, is a good resource for outdoor adventures such as canoeing, kayaking and hiking.

Special Events

Check special-events listings in the entertainment supplements in the Friday and Sunday editions of *The Commercial Appeal*. Also see listings in the free weekly *Memphis Flyer*.

January
By city proclamation, January 8 is Elvis Presley Day; the King's birthday is celebrated at his Graceland home. On or around January 15 (usually the third Monday in January), Martin Luther King Jr's Birthday is celebrated with a national holiday and a city tribute.

February
Beale St hosts a zydeco festival, and activities are scheduled to coincide with Black History Month.

March
The rowdy little Pinch District celebrates St Patrick's Day on March 17.

April
The anniversary of Martin Luther King's death is marked with a memorial march on April 4. Africa in April is a big festival. Beale St hosts a spring festival block party.

May
Memphis in May is the major citywide festival; it includes a barbecue cook-off and the Beale St Music Festival. On Mother's Day weekend (late

May or early June) the Spring Powwow is held at Chucalissa.

June
Juneteenth is celebrated on or around June 19 at Slavehaven/Burkle House and at the Freedom Festival in Douglas Park.

July
On July 4, Independence Day fireworks can be seen exploding over the Mississippi River from Mud Island Park.

August
The August 15 anniversary of the death of Elvis sparks citywide events. On the official tour, Graceland hosts a candlelight vigil to the grave. On the unofficial tour, the P&H Cafe (see Entertainment, later in this section) hosts the Dead Elvis Ball. The Memphis College of Art sponsors the annual White Trash/Black Velvet show for which 30 artists submit black velvet masterpieces; there are prizes for the culinary presentation voted 'most likely to be Elvis' favorite.'

September
The Mid-South Fair brings amusement-park rides and a carnival atmosphere to the fair-

---

The Memphis Bluesman

'The seven wonders of the world I have seen, and many are the places I have been. Take my advice, folks, and see Beale Street first.'

– WC Handy

In 1909 William Christopher Handy, a young bandleader and trumpet player from Florence, Alabama, wrote a campaign song for Memphis mayoral candidate EH Crump. 'Boss' Crump won and the song was an instant success, not so much for its lyrics as for its new sound – a tune composed of 'blue notes' that caught on with the public. The song was retitled 'Memphis Blues' and became the first blues song published. Handy followed it up with 'St Louis Blues,' which established him as the Father of the Blues. His statue stands at WC Handy Park on Beale St. The turn-of-the-19th-century shotgun shack in which he once lived is at 352 Beale St today, and can be toured ($2 adults, $1 children).

grounds for 10 days. The Cooper-Young Festival is a street party.

October

Arts in the Park runs in the latter part of the month. Visual and performing artists set up in the Botanic Gardens for three days. Native American Day at Chucalissa features children's activities.

November

Mid-month, the WC Handy Birthday Celebration pays tribute to the original Beale St bluesman (see the boxed text). At the end of the month, Starry Night, a popular drive-through extravaganza with colored lights benefits the Metropolitan Inter-Faith Association. Graceland dresses up for the holidays and stays that way till around Epiphany in early January. The Victorian Village is also specially decorated.

December

Christmas celebrations and decorations remain (see above). The traditional New Year's Eve celebration turns Beale St into a giant street party; and the Peabody hosts a gala ball.

Places to Stay

Memphis has more than a hundred hotels and motels. The most distinctive are the high-end Peabody, the Heartbreak Hotel near Graceland, and a stylish guesthouse downtown.

Camping The *KOA Kampground* (☎ 901-396-7125, 800-562-9386, 3691 Elvis Presley Blvd) is practically across the street from Graceland. Its year-round campsites cost $21, more with hookups. Cabins are $36.

South of town, *TO Fuller State Park* (☎ 901-543-7581), on a remote bluff off Mitchell Rd east of Hwy 61, has a campground, 18-hole golf course and pool. Sites cost $13 per night; hookups are available.

Thirteen miles north of town, *Meeman-Shelby State Park* (☎ 901-876-5215) offers hiking trails, a pool and boat rentals. Its 50-site campground charges $13 a site; there are hookups. Six fully equipped two-bedroom lakeside cabins (linens provided) sleep six people each and cost $60 ($70 weekends).

Motels A half-block from Graceland there's a *Days Inn* (☎ 901-346-5500, 800-329-7466, 3839 Elvis Presley Blvd). There is

nothing special about the rooms except the Elvis movies pumped into them 24 hours a day. There's a guitar-shaped swimming pool in the courtyard. Rates start at $70.

The *Red Roof Inn* (☎ 901-528-0650, 800-843-7664, 210 S Pauline St) is a plain Jane chain motel well located in the hospital district. Rooms go for around $50.

The best, most modern budget motel options are across the river in West Memphis, Arkansas. Nearly a dozen can be found in a pit-stop gulch at I-40 exit 279, including the *Motel 6* (☎ 501-735-0100, 800-466-8356); it has a pool and charges $37/43 a single/double.

With rates from $35, the tidy and small *Skyport Inn* (☎ 901-345-3220), within Memphis International Airport terminal A, is a bargain and tremendously convenient for quick layovers. It claims that its 44 rooms are soundproof. Free guest parking is included.

Hotels The landmark *Peabody Hotel* (☎ 901-529-4000, 800-732-2639, 149 Union Ave) is the most exclusive place to stay (see Peabody Hotel, earlier in this section). Rates start at $180/210 a single/double and climb from there (Romeo & Juliet suites are from $725 per night). Visit its Web site at www.peabodymemphis.com.

The *Heartbreak Hotel* (☎ 877-777-0606, 3677 Elvis Presley Blvd) offers Elvis movies and a lobby with the same faux elegance as Graceland. There are some fabulous suites here: the Hollywood Suite has a big-screen TV and oversized recliners, excellent for a group of friends; the Burning Love suite is plastered with photos of Elvis kissing a bevy of babes. The Graceland Suite includes a jungle room with working fountain. Regular rooms are $89, half-suites are $310 and full-suites are $470.

The *Sleep Inn at Court Square* (☎ 901-522-9700, 800-753-3746, 40 N Front St) is in a great location close to the river and backed by Main St. Rooms start around $80 including breakfast. *Hampton Inn & Suites* (☎ 901-260-4000, 175 Peabody Pl) has some rooms with balconies overlooking Beale St. Rooms start at $115, including a breakfast

TENNESSEE

buffet. The *French Quarter Suites Hotel* (☎ 901-728-4000, 800-843-0353, 2144 Madison Ave) is in the walkable Overton Square district – suites run from $110 (single or double) and include a breakfast buffet and airport shuttle service. There is an outdoor pool.

Talbot Heirs Guesthouse (☎ 901-527-9772, 99 S 2nd St) is a groovy apartment-hotel with nine individually decorated studio apartments ranging in price from $150 to $250.

Places to Eat

Memphis is famous for its barbecue: pork is the meat of choice, specifically chopped pork shoulder, often served as a barbecue sandwich. You can't leave Memphis without a ritual stop at the Rendezvous or Cozy Corner. Cozy Corner owner Raymond Robinson explains the subtleties of local barbecue: 'Memphis barbecue is different than any other. Hell, in Carolina, they cut it up in chunks. Here, we either slice it, chop it or pull it, and that makes all the difference.' Advice from the owner of the Rendezvous: 'Don't go into a barbecue place unless you can see the smoke.'

See also Entertainment, later, for more places to eat and be aware that many places are closed on Sunday (except on Beale St).

Downtown The *Arcade* (☎ 901-526-5757, 540 S Main St) has been around since 1919 but it's been reinvented as a new style pizza joint. It also serves breakfast. Other breakfast places include the Peabody Hotel's *Cafe Expresso* (expensive pastries and sandwiches) and the *Yellow Rose* (☎ 527-5692, 56 N Main St), a casual cafe that does cheap Southern breakfasts and lunches.

The *Rendezvous* (☎ 901-523-2746, 52 S 2nd St) – enter from an alleyway off Union Ave next to the Holiday Inn – has been in operation for 50 years. It sells five tons of barbecue ribs (a full order is $13.50) every week (and it's not even open Sunday and Monday). *Blues City Café* (☎ 901-526-3637, 138 Beale St) is an easy choice for a casual lunch or dinner on the strip, though it's often packed. It's a comfortable place to eat

alone; three tamales with a cup of chili costs $4.50.

The *Front Street Deli* (☎ 901-522-8943, 77 S Front St), at Union Ave, was featured in the movie *The Firm* and makes good sandwiches; eat in or take your food down to the water. A local favorite, *Huey's* (☎ 901-527-2700, 77 S 2nd St) at Union Ave, is a casual pub with great burgers, beer and live entertainment. The original Huey's is in midtown.

Automatic Slim's Tonga Club (☎ 901-525-7948, 83 S 2nd St) serves pan-scorched, slow-roasted and oil-drizzled entrees of yellowfin tuna, jerk duck and voodoo stew in an arty interior. Dinner is served Monday to Saturday; entrees are priced at about $15. Lunch is served weekdays for about half the price of dinner.

Elvis Presley's Memphis (☎ 901-527-6900, 126 Beale St) is the only place you can get a fried peanut-butter-and-banana sandwich (get permission from your arteries). *Gordon Biersch* (☎ 543-3330, 145 S Main St) is a handsome brewery bar with cozy booths, sports-focused TV and hearty food. They'll give you a free tasting of their German-style brews.

The Map Room (☎ 901-579-9924, 2 S Main St), at Madison, is downtown's coziest hangout, with good coffee from early in the morning, sandwiches and beer. There's live music Wednesday to Saturday. *Landry's* (☎ 901-526-1966, 263 Wagner Place), near the corner of Front and Beale Sts, is a restaurant and bar with an outdoor deck overlooking the Mississippi.

South of downtown, *Ellen's* (☎ 901-942-4888, 601 S Parkway E), at Macmillan, serves fried chicken, pork chops, great vegetables, soul food and barbecue in a well-worn corner joint with red booths.

Completely different is *Cielo* (☎ 901-524-1886, 679 Adams Ave), where creative 'new food' is served in a restored Victorian manor; entrees clock in around $20. There's a bar upstairs

In the Pinch District, north of downtown, the *High Point* (☎ 901-525-4444, 111 Jackson St) does straight up and down steaks, catfish, barbecue, burgers and homemade sausages at moderate prices. There's a big selection of local and imported beers. It's a fun place to stop for a while.

Midtown A daily slate of comfort food at *The Cupboard* (☎ *901-276-8015)*, in a shopping strip at 1400 Union Ave at Cleveland St, includes dishes such as fried catfish fillet and meatloaf with turnip greens, fried green tomatoes, corn pudding and plum cobbler for around $7. It's open 11 am to 8 pm weekdays, till 3 pm weekends. Across from Methodist Hospital, *Tops* (☎ *901-725-7527, 1286 Union Ave)*, at Claybrook St, is part of the local chain of cheap and decent barbecue joints.

In Overton Square, a drive down Madison Ave takes in all the neighborhood's offerings. *Anderton's* (☎ *901-726-4010, 1901 Madison Ave)*, at McLean Blvd, a Memphis institution since 1945, serves seafood specialties. At the ship-shaped bar, pull up a captain's chair and order a cocktail.

Eat inside or out at *On Teur* (☎ *901-725-6059, 2015 Madison Ave)*, an old favorite for vegetarian food, pecan-smoked sausages and 'jimbolaya.' The original *Huey's* (☎ *901-726-4372, 1927 Madison Ave)* serves as the neighborhood pub with great burgers and fries and occasional live music.

In the compact Cooper-Young district 4½ miles east of downtown, several restaurants, cafes and a deli are all within two blocks of the intersection of S Cooper St and Young Ave. *Java Cabana* (☎ *901-272-7210, 2170 Young Ave)* serves regular joe along with java shakes, homemade pie and entertainment that includes poetry readings and 16mm films. It opens daily at 9 am and closes at 10 pm (later on weekends). *Otherlands* (☎ *901-278-4994, 641 S Cooper St)* is a cool coffee and gift shop that does breakfast and sandwiches seven days a week, has a breezy patio out back and attracts a young crowd. *Cafe Olé* (☎ *901-274-1504, 959 S Cooper St)*, at Young, serves good Tex-Mex at tasty prices (a burrito grande is $8.25). Weekend brunches linger till 3pm. *Tsunami* (☎ *901-274-2556, 928 S Cooper St)* is a Pacific Rim fusion kinda place with entrees around $18. It's open for dinner Monday to Saturday.

The infamous *Cozy Corner* (☎ *901-527-9158, 745 North Parkway)*, near Danny Thomas Blvd (Hwy 51), in the middle of a strip mall, serves its trademark dry-rub pulled pork or barbecue Cornish game hens under multicolored fluorescent lights to a good jazz soundtrack. It's closed Sunday and Monday.

Entertainment

For entertainment listings, pick up the free *Memphis Flyer* newspaper at many outlets around town (restaurants, clubs, street corners) or the Friday and Sunday editions of *The Commercial Appeal*. Several restaurants listed above, such as Huey's, are also popular spots for live entertainment.

You can see blues on Beale St most nights, but it heats up on weekends, when the two-block strip is closed to traffic. The scene often becomes one giant block party, with streetside stands selling giant cups of beer. Since you can take your drink with you on Beale, bar-hopping is part of the scene and the modest entry charges can add up quickly. On weekends you can buy wristbands on the street ($10 to $15) that give you admission to most of the clubs. Occasional festivals (see Special Events, earlier in this section) bring free outdoor concerts to WC Handy Park.

The fancy *Elvis Presley's Memphis* (see Places to Eat, earlier) operates out of the King's old clothiers, Lansky's. At *BB King's* (☎ *901-524-5464, 800-443-8959, 143 Beale St)* the man himself performs a couple of times a year. Both places aim for a swank,

The blues King can still make Lucille cry.

Rev Green's Gospel

Some of the most soulful music in town is not heard on Beale St or at any club in town. It's at the Full Gospel Tabernacle presided over by the soul artist Rev Al Green. Rev Green's powerful oratory is backed up by electric guitar and a formidable choir. Visitors are welcome to attend the 2½-hour Sunday service at 11 am.

Etiquette tips for the uninitiated: dress neatly, place at least $1 per adult in the offering tray and don't leave early. Do not take kids who are unaccustomed to lengthy services.

To get to the church (☎ 901-396-9192), which is in Whitehaven, drive four traffic lights south of Graceland on Elvis Presley Blvd; turn right at Hale Rd and drive a half-mile west to 787 Hale Rd.

supper-club atmosphere but can end up being a bit dull. Call ahead to find out who's playing and to buy tickets. Elvis Presley's also features gospel brunches on Sunday. Otherwise, see who's playing at *This is It!* *(☎ 901-527-8200, 167 Beale St)* or *Rum Boogie Cafe (☎ 901-528-0150, 182 Beale St)*.

At the *P&H Cafe (☎ 901-726-0906, 1532 Madison Ave)*, matriarch Wanda Wilson, a colorful local character notorious for her costumes and drama, hosts the annual Dead Elvis Ball each August (closed Sunday). The hole-in-the-wall *Backstreet (☎ 901-276-5522, 2018 Court Ave)*, north of Madison at Morrison St, draws a largely gay male crowd.

Wild Bill's (☎ 901-726-5473, 1580 Vollintine Ave) is a safe and clubby juke joint with live music Friday to Sunday and guaranteed dancing (best after 1 am, when the cats finish their Beale St gigs).

Hi-Tone (☎ 901-278-8663, 1913 Poplar Ave) is an alternative music club frequented by arty types; Elvis used to learn karate at this site.

Thursday evenings through summer, Sunset Serenade at the Peabody Hotel's

Skyway is where the locals come to strut their stuff. Dress up and get ready to flutter your eyelids. There's a $6 cover. Wednesday evenings through late spring and summer, River Rendezvous on Mud Island (right by the monorail bridge) is the same kind of thing.

The *Orpheum Theatre (☎ 901-525-3000, 203 S Main St)*, at Beale St, a vaudeville palace built in 1928 and restored with a $5 million facelift, hosts Broadway shows and major concerts. The *Circuit Playhouse (☎ 901-726-4656, 1705 Poplar Ave)*, in Overton Square, and *Theatre Works (☎ 901-274-7139, 2085 Monroe)*, behind Overton Square, host most of the city's alternative theater. *Playhouse on the Square (☎ 901-726-4656, 51 S Cooper St)* has a resident company that tends more toward family entertainment.

Ballet Memphis (☎ 901-737-7322), *Memphis Symphony Orchestra (☎ 901-324-3627)* and *Opera Memphis (☎ 901-678-2706)* appeal largely to the affluent East Memphis crowd, with prices and decorum to match.

Local papers advertise shows at the casinos in Tunica, which is a half-hour south of Memphis in Mississippi.

Spectator Sports

The Memphis Redbirds (☎ 901-721-6000) play baseball at the new 15,000-capacity Autozone Park, on the corner of Union and 3rd Sts. Formed in 1998, the Redbirds are a AAA team affiliated with the St Louis Cardinals; unusually, the team is run as a non-profit organization.

The Memphis RiverKings (☎ 901-278-9009) play Central Hockey League ice hockey at the Mid-South Coliseum which is at Libertyland. The nationally ranked University of Memphis Tigers (☎ 901-678-2331) play basketball at the Pyramid, downtown near Mud Island.

The city hosts the St Jude Liberty Bowl Football Classic each year in December at the stadium at Libertyland; the Kroger-St Jude Tennis Tournament is in February and the FedEx-St Jude Golf Tournament is in June.

Shopping

Disappointingly, Graceland offers only a tasteful assortment of high-ticket Elvis-emblazoned mementos for sale (but check out the pink Cadillac phone and the Elvis-meets-Nixon postcards). Still, a comprehensive collection of Elvis tapes and videos is available here. An independent souvenir shop north of the visitor center sells float pens, customized nail clippers and Elvis clocks with swinging hips.

Sun Studio has a small but select collection of souvenirs, books and records. Music buffs will find it worth checking out.

A Schwab's (☎ 901-523-9782), 163 Beale St, is where you'll find the oddest assortment of housewares, clothing and hardware – the mezzanine is a museum of antique general-store paraphernalia. It's closed Sunday.

Flashback (☎ 901-272-2304), 2304 Central Ave, revives art deco and 1950s style with its pristine collection of vintage clothing and colorful decor – it's a combination thrift store and museum. Shangri-la Records (☎ 901-274-1916, www.shangri .com), 1916 Madison Ave, distributes its own *Lowlife Guide to Memphis*, maintains a 1970s kitsch museum and has a great selection of new and used CDs.

Look up *R Crumb Draws the Blues* and other animated classics at Memphis Comics (☎ 901-452-1304), 665 S Highland.

Wolfchase Galleria (☎ 901-372-9409), 2760 N Germantown Parkway, 30 minutes from downtown, is the nicest mall in the area. Peabody Place is the flash shopping and entertainment mall downtown.

Getting There & Away

Memphis is a hub for air (Northwest Airlines) and train travel and is also easily accessible by interstate freeway. You can even arrive by boat on a cruise from New Orleans. See the Getting There & Away chapter for more information on flights and fares.

Air Memphis International Airport (☎ 901-922-8000) is 20 minutes southeast of downtown via I-55. It is served by Northwest, American, Delta, TWA, United, US Airways and 25 regional carriers.

KLM Royal Dutch Airlines has direct nonstop flights to Amsterdam.

See Getting Around, later in this section, for airport transportation information and details.

Bus The Greyhound (☎ 901-523-1184) route between Memphis and Nashville is served by eight buses daily; the trip takes about four hours and costs $29 one-way. The route between Memphis and New Orleans is served by four buses daily. The trip takes eight to 10 hours and costs $39 one-way.

The central bus station at 203 Union Ave is downtown, next door to the Radisson Hotel and half a block away from the Peabody Hotel.

Train A sorely needed renovation of Central Station on S Main St restored the 191,000-sq-ft building to its original 1914 splendor. In addition to improving Amtrak passenger comfort and convenience, the renovated station includes retail and office space and a residential development. It connects with the Main St trolley (see Getting Around, later).

Amtrak (☎ 901-526-0052 for station information, ☎ 800-872-7245 for reservations) runs a passenger service through Memphis on the *City of New Orleans* from Chicago. See the Getting There & Away chapter for details.

Car A bank of courtesy (free) phones near baggage claim represents all the standard car-rental agencies. You can call for availability and competitive rates, and each agency will send a shuttle van to take you from the airport to their office. Agencies include Alamo, Avis, Budget, Dollar, Enterprise and National. (Book ahead if you're arriving during a special event.)

Boat There are *Delta Queen* (☎ 800-513-5028) riverboat excursions up the Mississippi that start in New Orleans and make several stops, including Memphis. See the Getting Around chapter for details.

Getting Around

To/From the Airport The airport is about 20 miles from downtown via freeways, and transportation options are limited. Taxis leave from outside baggage claim and cost around $22 to downtown. Many hotels provide free shuttle service for guests (so it may pay to add $50 to your lodging budget rather than spending it on a roundtrip taxi fare).

Public transit is cheap but extremely troublesome. Catch the No 32 bus outside baggage claim (the far island, beyond where taxis and shuttles stop). The bus first heads east then stops in midtown, necessitating a transfer to a bus that's headed downtown. Buses are infrequent. The fare is $1.10; transfers cost 10¢.

Most travelers rent cars to get to their destination. The quickest route downtown is via I-55 – but note that to travel west from the airport, you need to follow signs to I-55 north.

Bus A free shuttle runs between Heartbreak Hotel, Graceland Plaza, Sun Studio and Elvis Presley's Memphis hourly between about 11 am and 6 pm. Inquire at any of these businesses for pickup times.

Bus service around the Memphis metropolitan area is operated by Memphis Area Transit Authority (MATA; ☎ 901-722-7100) and follows a network of travel patterns and schedules of little use to visitors. The few bus shelters or benches (long waits standing exposed to the sun) are uncomfortable. That said, useful bus routes are the No 32 to/from the airport and the No 2 route, which runs between downtown and the Cooper-Young district via the Madison Ave strip of restaurants, bars and shops in Overton Square. Fares are $1.10; transfers are 10¢.

Trolley The Main St trolley (☎ 901-274-6282) runs vintage trolley cars from the Amtrak station up the pedestrian-only Main St; they then loop around the Pyramid and riverfront. It previously ran such a short distance that for the $40 million price tag it was considered a local joke, but its ex-panded service makes it a more viable form of transportation for downtown destinations. The fare is $1 (50¢ at lunchtime) and exact fare is required.

Car & Motorcycle Hwys I-40 and I-55 intersect in Memphis, though not all too cleanly, with junctions complicated by the bypass route I-240. In Memphis, I-40 goes north (while signs still direct you east), I-55 grazes downtown, and the bypass I-240 runs straight through midtown.

Memphis is a nice town to blast around on a motorcycle. (See Elvis' car and motorcycle collection at Graceland to sense the town's devotion to big wheels.)

Taxi Although relatively expensive and not widespread beyond downtown, for short, specific jaunts taxis can be a less costly alternative to renting a car. Fares from the airport to downtown are about $22; from the airport to Graceland is about $8. Downtown to Graceland it's $18 to $20. The standard fare is $2.90 for the first mile, $1.40 for each additional mile.

Call Checker Cab (☎ 901-577-7777) or City Wide Cab (☎ 901-324-4202). For those who need a cab, there are usually a few lurking at the Peabody Hotel.

Bicycle Memphis is a fairly easy city to bicycle around. Excepting the oppressive summertime heat, conditions are generally conducive to bike touring – it's a city of manageable size with streets that are wide, flat and decently maintained. But cycling is not in the local culture and there are no bike lanes or other special provisions for riders or rental bicycles.

AROUND MEMPHIS

An easy excursion from Memphis is a foray down Hwy 61 into the Mississippi Delta, particularly Clarksdale. Casinos in Tunica County, Mississippi, draw many city folk from Memphis, and both the lively college town of Oxford and Graceland Too in Holly Springs are an hour's drive away. Those on the Elvis tour will want to check out the

King's birthplace in Tupelo. For attractions and information about Clarksdale, Tupelo, Oxford and Holly Springs, see the Mississippi chapter.

The **Alex Haley House Museum** (☎ 901-738-2240) is in Henning, about 50 miles north of Memphis off Hwy 51. The Pulitzer Prize-winning author of *Roots* is buried under the front lawn.

Jackson

The only reason to hit the brakes for Jackson (85 miles northeast of Memphis) is right off I-40 at the Hwy 45 bypass: **Casey Jones Village** (☎ 901-668-1223) offers an appealing lunch and dinner buffet – if you can get by the candy store and the soda bar without filling up. It's tastefully done and makes a good break between Memphis and Nashville. The museum celebrates Casey Jones, a local hero who sacrificed his life to save the passengers on his 1900 train. Entry is $4 ($2 kids). The adjacent *Casey Jones Station Inn* (☎ 800-748-9588) offers some overnight berths in vintage cabooses.

Shiloh

Near the Mississippi border, 100 miles east of Memphis, **Shiloh National Military Park** (☎ 901-689-5275) commemorates the famous Civil War battle of Shiloh. The visitor center shows a film describing military strategy and distributes an auto-tour map of the monuments and battlefields ($2/4 per person/family). It's a beautiful and resonant site. Even if you're not a big Civil War buff, this is a good one to visit – watch the film, drive to the Hornets' Nest and soak it up.

Savannah

Nearby Savannah is a pretty river town that makes a decent lunch stop. *Savannah Cooks* (☎ 901-925-8046, 804 Main St) does sophisticated sandwiches. The highlight of the **Tennessee River Museum** (☎ 800-552-3866), 507 Main St, is a modestly lovely Indian pipe effigy that was discovered at the Indian mounds in Shiloh. The museum has walking-tour leaflets that lead you by the town's 19th-century homes – they're not breathtaking, but if it's a nice day this is a pleasant leg stretch.

If you're suddenly overstretched, one home operates as a B&B: the *White Elephant Inn* (☎ 901-925-6410, 304 Church St) is gorgeous – the Peacock Room includes a 'fainting couch' that will certainly attract travelers wearing corsets. Prices for rooms start at $80.

Adamsville

Fans of weird, kitsch minutiae won't want to miss the **Buford Pusser Home & Museum** (☎ 901-632-4080), 342 Pusser St, which celebrates the life of Sheriff Pusser, McNairy County's fighter of bootleggers in the 1960s. Some flavor: a marker excitedly notes that the laundry hamper in the bathroom came from Pusser's first home. Admission is steep at $4, but it's a classic.

Adamsville is 9 miles west of Savannah.

Reelfoot Lake National Wildlife Refuge

In the northwestern corner of the state, 110 miles north of Memphis, Reelfoot is a good place to see the bald eagles who take up winter residence here from December through mid-March. Reelfoot Lake is noted for its water lilies, large cypress trees, rampant vines and other bizarre vegetation. It was created when the 1811–12 New Madrid earthquakes lowered the ground level and the Mississippi flooded into the depression. The visitor center (☎ 901-253-7756) is a few miles east of Tiptonville, which has food and lodging.

Middle Tennessee

Fanning out from Nashville, Middle Tennessee is the place for country music, big hair and pancakes. It's also host to the super-scenic northern end of the Natchez Trace and a random spray of other attractions: a bourbon factory, high-stepping horses and one of The Farm, the world's longest-standing and best-pierced alternative communities.

NASHVILLE

• pop 1,170,000

Nashville is a great town with friendly people, cheap food, lots of wonderful music heard for next to nothing at homey country dives, and an unrivaled assortment of tacky souvenirs. Business is booming, the streets are clean and unemployment is low. Interestingly, whether it's that the US is moving toward the South or because the South is moving toward the rest of the country, Nashville seems more than ever like an all-American city – and one of the most guileless cities you're ever likely to visit.

As Country Music Capital of the World, Nashville (pronounced NASH-vul in the South) carries a certain down-home glamour. Banners and billboards announce new recording stars and record releases like accolades in a high school yearbook, and streets are named after country celebrities such as Roy Acuff and Chet Atkins. City folk wear cowboy hats and read the music industry rag *Billboard* over a short stack at the Pancake Pantry.

While famous for country music, Nashville also supports a sophisticated and diverse music scene – you can even hear soulful blues at tony cafes where discriminating patrons wear black and the men have ponytails. No one suffers a lousy sound system.

Northwest of the city off Briley Parkway is the huge Opryland complex, including a modern 4400-seat home for the Grand Ole Opry, the fantabulous Opryland Hotel and a massive new mall, Opryland Mills, which opened in early 2000 replacing the theme park. Franchises fill in the surrounding Music Valley district with motels, fast food, a KOA Kampground and cheesy nightclubs. Boats travel between Opryland and downtown to get people out on the water and to bring money and audiences to the city center, which clings to its honky-tonk character despite the best attempts of Planet Hollywood and the Hard Rock Cafe.

History

The ancient mound-builders and the wandering Shawnee of Algonquin stock occupied these Cumberland River bluffs centuries ago. Nashville was settled by Europeans in 1779 as Fort Nashborough (the name was changed to Nashville five years later). The legendary Daniel Boone had a hand in the deal, and his Wilderness Road brought immigrants over the Appalachians from Virginia, the Carolinas and northeastern states. Nashville developed rapidly as a trade and manufacturing center; it was chartered in 1806 and was named state capital in 1843.

Its vital position on the Cumberland River (linking to the Mississippi navigation system) and at the crossroads of important rail lines made it a strategic point during the Civil War. As federal troops advanced upriver, the state legislature (which held Confederate allegiances) picked up and moved to Memphis, and within the week Nashville surrendered to Union troops. Union loyalists occupied and imposed martial law on Nashville from 1862 to 1865. In 1864, as a last-ditch attempt to regain control of Nashville and cut off rail lines supplying Union General Sherman's campaign against Atlanta, Confederates attacked the occupied city. The two armies fought the bloody Battle of Nashville, and Confederate General Thomas Hood's troops were destroyed. The Union occupation was fortunate for Nashville as it saved many of the city's historic structures, a few of which are now open for tours.

The city's economic recovery after the Civil War was hampered by two major cholera epidemics that killed about a thousand people and caused thousands more to flee. The Centennial Exposition in 1897, for which the reproduction of the Greek Parthenon was built, signaled the city's eventual recovery.

Nashville's Maxwell family established the world-recognized Maxwell House coffee business here. Teddy Roosevelt himself proclaimed it 'good to the last drop' at the Maxwell House Hotel downtown. The Maxwell estate is now a fine arts center and botanical garden open to the public.

Eventually, Nashville became best known around the globe for the rocketing

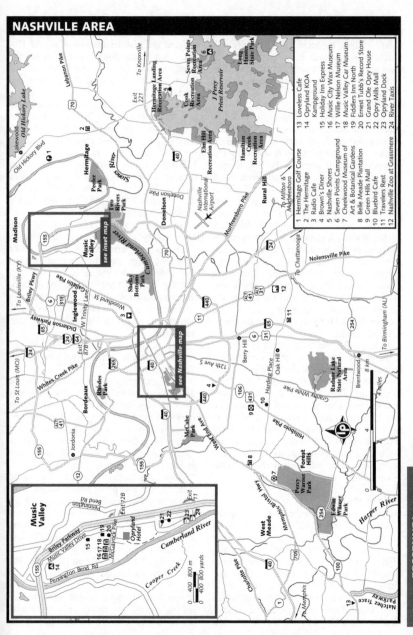

NASHVILLE AREA

1 Hermitage Golf Course
2 The Hermitage
3 Radio Cafe
4 Brown's Diner
5 Nashville Shores
6 Seven Points Campground
7 Cheekwood Museum of
   Art & Botanical Gardens
8 Belle Meade Plantation
9 Green Hills Mall
10 Green Hills Mall
11 Travelers Rest
12 Nashville Zoo at Grassmere

13 Loveless Cafe
14 Opryland KOA
   Kampground
15 Holiday Inn Express
16 Music City Wax Museum
17 Willie Nelson Museum
18 Music Valley Car Museum
19 Fiddlers Inn North
20 Ernest Tubb's Record Store
21 Grand Ole Opry House
22 Opry Mills Mall
23 Opryland Dock
24 River Taxis

TENNESSEE

popularity of its live radio broadcast 'Barn Dance' – later nicknamed the 'Grand Ole Opry' – which began in 1925. The city was quickly proclaimed the Country Music Capital of the World, and recording studios and production companies established themselves along Music Row just west of downtown.

Fisk University, established in 1885, has played a distinguished role in Nashville's African-American history. The struggling black college was partially financed by the successful benefit tours by the Fisk Jubilee Singers, who popularized traditional black spirituals in the 1870s across the US and in Europe. Today, the campus boasts the first permanent building erected for the higher education of blacks in the US, Jubilee Hall. In the 1960s, Fisk students led sit-in demonstrations at lunch counters downtown, encouraged a full economic boycott and marched on city hall to demand desegregated facilities. Their successful nonviolent protests served as a model for civil rights demonstrations throughout the South. Author WEB Du Bois is among its distinguished alumni.

In the 1970s, Nashville's patron Gaylord Enterprises invented the Oprylandia empire and shaped the city's country-music tourist business by moving the Grand Ole Opry, renovating the Ryman Auditorium, sending boats up and down the river and contributing to the economic revitalization of the downtown riverfront. Besides the entertainment business and the city's billion-dollar tourist industry, Nashville also relies on its health-care industry and Nissan plant as economic mainstays.

Orientation

Nashville is constructed on a rise along the Cumberland River. The capitol sits at its highest point; from there a busy, compact downtown of narrow one-way streets and high-rise office buildings slopes southeast to Broadway, the city's central artery. The circle of flags at the bottom of the bluff at Riverfront Park marks the head of Broadway – the directional distinction of avenues changes from north to south at this divide.

Renovation of the historic commercial buildings along 2nd Ave and Broadway has created a tourist destination called 'the District,' but locals don't seem to mind and continue to frequent favorite dives and rib joints clustered around the commercial upstarts.

Music Row is a commercial district south of I-40, less than a mile from downtown.

In the rest of sprawling Nashville, it's hard to pinpoint what constitutes a neighborhood, but a few are easily discernible. Elliston Place is a compact stretch of bohemian alternative culture about a mile west of downtown and north of West End Ave. South of West End Ave here is the Vanderbilt campus.

South of Vanderbilt, Hillsboro Village is an inner-city 'suburb' on 21st Ave S south of Blakesmore (two miles north of I-440, about 1½ miles south of downtown). After this things get vague.

'West End' is what you hear to describe the cluster of restaurants along Broadway and West End Ave on either side of the university; you might also hear simply 'around Vanderbilt.'

Across the river in East Nashville, a funky historic area called Edgefield has a tiny commercial strip.

Of course many tourists never set foot in downtown Nashville and confine their visit to the Opryland complex off Briley Parkway, out by the airport. Here the prefabricated Music Valley holds a tourist ghetto of budget motels, franchise restaurants, outlet stores and a KOA Kampground.

Most folks live in the wide reaches of the suburbs, off the pikes that fan out from downtown. The southern suburb of Green Hills, easily reached off I-440 exit 3, provides easy access south to the landmark Bluebird Cafe, or north to Hillsboro Village. The city's historic house museums – the Hermitage, Cheekwood and Belle Meade – are farther out on the pikes.

Maps A good map is indispensable to navigating around the metro area because of the complex interstate interchanges. If you

NASHVILLE

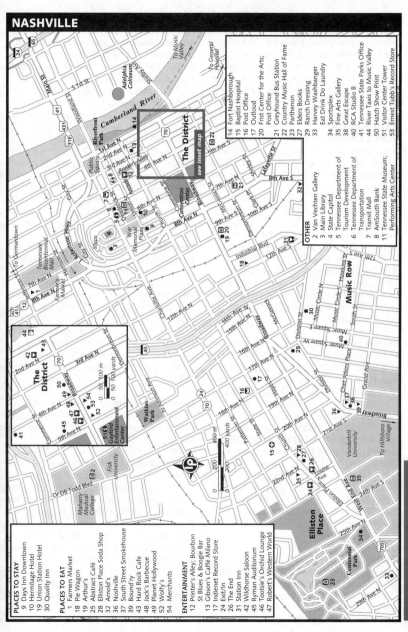

PLACES TO STAY
9 Days Inn Downtown
10 Hermitage Hotel
19 Union Station Hotel
30 Quality Inn

PLACES TO EAT
1 Farmers Market
18 Pie Wagon
19 Arthur's
25 Abstract Café
28 Elliston Place Soda Shop
32 Arnold's
36 Nashville
37 South Street Smokehouse
39 Bound'ry
43 Hard Rock Cafe
48 Jack's Barbecue
49 Planet Hollywood
52 Wolfy's
54 Merchants

ENTERTAINMENT
12 Printer's Alley; Bourbon
     St Blues & Boogie Bar
13 Gibson's Caffé Milano
17 Indienet Record Store
24 Exit/In
26 The End
31 Station Inn
42 Wildhorse Saloon
46 Ryman Auditorium
47 Robert's Western World
49 Tootsie's Orchid Lounge

OTHER
2 Van Vechten Gallery
3 Main Library
4 State Capitol
5 Tennessee Department of
     Tourism Development
6 Tennessee Department of
     Transportation
7 Transit Mall
8 AmSouth Bank
11 Tennessee State Museum;
     Performing Arts Center
14 Fort Nashborough
15 Baptist Hospital
16 Post Office
17 Outloud
20 Frist Center for the Arts;
     Post Office
21 Greyhound Bus Station
22 Country Music Hall of Fame
23 Parthenon
27 Elders Books
29 Ranch Dressing
33 Harvey Washbanger
     Eat Drink Do Laundry
34 Sportsplex
35 Fine Arts Gallery
38 Great Escape
40 RCA Studio B
41 Tennessee State Parks Office
44 River Taxis to Music Valley
50 Hatch Show Print
51 Visitor Center Tower
53 Ernest Tubb's Record Store

TENNESSEE

rent a car, ask for a complimentary map. AAA distributes maps free to members; its offices are easily found about a quarter-mile north of I-440 exit 3 at 21st Ave. Gas stations often sell comprehensive street maps. Visitor information centers distribute free maps that are less comprehensive but adequate enough.

Information

Tourist Offices The central visitor center is in the space-age tower adjacent to the arena at Broadway and 5th Ave. There's also a welcome center (☎ 615-741-2158) at the airport.

The Nashville Convention & Visitors Bureau (☎ 615-259-4730), 211 Commerce St, Suite 100, Nashville TN 37201, maintains a tourist hot line at ☎ 615-259-4700; visit its Web site at http://nashville.citysearch.com.

The *African American Guide to Cultural & Historical Sites* is available from the Tennessee Department of Tourist Development (☎ 615-741-2159) in Nashville (see Tourist Offices at the beginning of the chapter for postal address).

Money Foreign money exchanges operate at AmSouth (☎ 615-748-2000), at the corner of Union St and 4th Ave N, and at the airport (☎ 615-275-2660). American Express (☎ 615-385-3535) is at 4400 Harding Rd.

Post The main post office (☎ 800-275-8777) is at 525 Royal Parkway. The Broadway branch downtown at 901 Broadway (tucked around the side of the Frist Center for the Visual Arts) is more convenient, as is the branch in the Arcade, off 4th Ave N. Near Elliston Place, there is a branch at the corner of Church St and 18th Ave N.

Mailboxes Etc (☎ 615-846-6269), 1708 21st Ave S, packs and mails packages via US mail, UPS or FedEx.

Media *The Tennessean* is the daily newspaper with entertainment listings in its Sunday edition. The free alternative weekly *Nashville Scene* covers local entertainment and news, and is distributed at newsstands, restaurants and shops throughout the city.

Fisk University's radio station at 88.1 FM is a refreshing alternative to the many similar-sounding country stations. The local NPR affiliate is at 90.3 FM. Lightning 100 (100.1 FM) has an exciting and varied playlist of quality indie and other music.

Four times a year, country music's cable television network, the National Network (TNN; formerly the Nashville Network) films its *Wildhorse Saloon* program at the dance hall of the same name on 2nd Ave at Broadway. Call (☎ 615-883-7000) for information about this and other studio tapings.

Travel Agencies AAA (☎ 615-297-7700) provides travel planning services at 2501 Hillsboro Pike. American Express also offers travel services (see Money, above).

Bookstores Specializing in Southern history, Elders Books (☎ 615-327-1867), 2115 Elliston Place, is a great place to browse for old and new titles. The Vanderbilt University Bookstore (☎ 615-322-2994), in the university's Rand Hall, has a wide range of titles. Megastores include Davis-Kidd Booksellers (☎ 615-385-2645), 4007 Hillsboro Pike, in the Green Hills shopping complex (a mile or so south of I-440 exit 3, on the right), and Barnes & Noble at Opry Mills.

Libraries The main library (☎ 615-862-5800), at 225 Polk Ave, heads up 19 branch libraries throughout the city and Davidson County.

Universities West of downtown, Nashville is dominated by the huge central city campus of Vanderbilt University, including its large medical center. Fisk University has a humble campus northwest of downtown. Both universities have art collections worth checking out. Tennessee State University, George Peabody College and Belmont College are also in Nashville.

Gay & Lesbian Resources The Center for Lesbian and Gay Community Services (☎ 615-297-0008) is at 703 Berry Rd. Outloud (☎ 615-340-0034) is a gay bookstore at 1709 Church St; it's open daily until 10 pm.

Laundry The combination laundry-pub, Harvey Washbanger Eat Drink Do Laundry (☎ 615-322-9274), is at 106 29th Ave N, right off West End Ave. More laundromats can be easily found on 21st Ave S, around a mile north of I-440 exit 3, not far from Hillsboro Village.

Medical & Emergency Services In an emergency call ☎ 911. Otherwise, to contact the police call ☎ 615-862-8600. The Tennessee Highway Patrol can be reached at ☎ 615-741-3181.

Health care is a key industry in Nashville. Besides the county's General Hospital (☎ 615-341-4000) at 72 Hermitage Ave, major medical centers are operated by Baptist Hospital (on Church St at 20th Ave N) and Vanderbilt University.

Planned Parenthood (☎ 615-321-7216) is at 412 Dr DB Todd Blvd (which connects with 18th Ave N), north of Charlotte Ave and south of Fisk University.

Dangers & Annoyances Nonsmokers should note that Nashville is an extraordinarily smoker-friendly town.

Downtown
Walking Tour Downtown Nashville is compact and pleasant to walk around. Tall office buildings and modern halls dominate without overwhelming the city's historic structures. Pay parking is easily found in lots south of Broadway. Carry quarters for parking meters and unstaffed lots.

At downtown's western end, built on the highest point above Charlotte Ave, the 1845 Greek revival **state capitol** remains the area's principal landmark. Architect William Strickland is buried in its northeast corner, and the tomb of President James K Polk and his wife Sarah Childress Polk is outside on **Capitol Hill**. Steep stairs on its northern side lead down to the **farmers market** and the **Tennessee Bicentennial Mall** at downtown's back door. The mall begins with a massive map of Tennessee

etched into stone and then continues with an itsy-bitsy history of the state, a war memorial and a celebration of its rivers. It's not bad for getting a geographic and historical perspective of the 16th state. Beyond is Germantown (see Places to Eat, later in this section).

Facing Charlotte Ave, the capitol overlooks stately government buildings surrounding **War Memorial Plaza**. The plaza's cherry trees bloom with white blossoms in early spring. The city-block-sized **Performing Arts Center** downhill to the east also houses the **Tennessee State Museum**. The underground museum spills out onto Union St, off which you'll find the city's banks and hotels, most notably the 1910 **Hermitage Hotel** at 6th Ave N.

Union St leads east to 1st Ave N and the western end of **Riverfront Park** on the Cumberland River. The park runs between the bridges at Woodland St and Shelby Ave, providing a landscaped promenade planted with trees and busy with walkers, couples, families and horse-drawn carriages stalling car traffic along 1st Ave. In the park, just south of Church St, a stockade surrounds **Fort Nashborough**, a 1930s replica of the city's original outpost. Just north of Broadway, river taxis run from the dock out to Opryland, a scenic hour's ride away (see Getting Around, later in this section).

The historic 2nd Ave N business area was the center of the cotton trade in the 1870s and 1880s, when most of the Victorian warehouses were built (note the cast-iron and masonry façades). Today it's the heart of the area known as the District. The buildings have been renovated and now house shops, restaurants, underground saloons and nightclubs. including the Wildhorse Saloon (see Entertainment, later in this section). From 2nd Ave N, walk two blocks west on Commerce St to **Printers Alley**, a narrow cobblestone lane that's been known for its nightlife since the 1940s. Here the Bourbon St Blues & Boogie Bar anchors a cluster of nightspots that includes a showgirl showcase, a karaoke bar and a disco.

Stretching between 4th and 5th Aves and Church and Union Sts you will find the

Quick Country Music Primer

Country music is big business: it's the nation's most popular radio format – with around 2600 stations. Record sales quadrupled in the 1990s to reach $2.1 billion. Yet the sound-alike pop style that dominates radio isn't indicative of the variety of country music you can find, nor is it country music's cutting edge. In Nashville, you can hear firsthand what's new as well as a diverse range of styles. The following is the lowdown on the evolution and subgenres of country & western music.

Bluegrass This acoustic style of country music evolved out of old-time southeastern string-band music that originated in the Appalachian mountains. Bluegrass (named for the Bluegrass hills of Kentucky) makes use of the fiddle, guitar, mandolin, five-string banjo, bass and dobro guitar. Early practitioners such as Bill Monroe and his Blue Grass Boys began to define the style in the mid-1940s, leading the way for the Stanley Brothers and Flatt & Scruggs in the 1950s. Bluegrass was discovered by national audiences in the following decade's 'back-to-the-land' era and is now perpetuated at bluegrass festivals throughout the South and across the country. In Nashville you can hear it live at the Station Inn.

Cowboy The 'western' in country & western music comes from cowboy music originating in the American West. The first cowboy songs were the traditional occupational folksongs of cowboys on Western rangelands in the late 19th and early 20th century. In the 1920s, authentic cowboys such as Jules Verne Allen and Carl T Sprague made the first recordings of the style. The style exploded with the popularity of Western movies featuring singing cowboys in the '30s, including Gene Autry's *Singing Cowboy* in 1936. While the standard contemporary country & western spin has faded from popularity, twangy cowboy laments are being resurrected in new retro-style recordings.

Cajun The Acadians – Cajuns – emigrated from Canada to southern Louisiana in the late 18th century and brought with them their French folk-music heritage (see the Cajun Country chapter). Cajun folk music evolved when it was mixed with the fiddle, the guitar and the German accordion

pleasant un-mallified **Arcade**, which includes a post office and cafes. Restaurants here were the site of some of Nashville's Civil Rights sit-ins.

A walk along Broadway from Riverfront Park leads past an old feed-and-seed at 1st Ave and Broadway, the Hard Rock Cafe, an Ernest Tubb's record outlet, Planet Hollywood and the fabulous **Hatch Show Print** shop, which sells the best postcards and posters in town. On 5th Ave N (with another entrance on 4th Ave N), the Ryman Auditorium has reopened as a performance venue. A scenic, seedy cowboy ghetto along 'Lower Broad' between 4th and 5th Aves has country bars that have music from 10 am. Tootsie's Orchid Lounge on the north side is the best known of the dives. If you're so inspired that you want to join the cowboy ranks, you can buy snakeskin boots and chewing tobacco between acts at Robert's Western World next door.

West of 5th Ave, both the boxy **Convention Center** and the **Gaylord Entertainment Center** can be spotted on Broadway by the tower cone that houses a visitor center. The unmissable Country Music Hall of Fame is one block south on Demonbreun.

Country Music Hall of Fame The lavish, devotional hall of fame (☎ 615-416-2001) is a great introduction to Nashville and to the evolution of country music. It's chock full of artifacts, including Garth Brooks' trademark hat, Gene Autry's string tie and the original handwritten lyrics to 'Mamas Don't Let Your Babies Grow Up to be Cowboys.' The pièce de résistance is Elvis Presley's custom Cadillac with a convertible cover that lifts up at the press of a button to reveal

Quick Country Music Primer

encountered in Louisiana. Artists began recording as early as the 1920s, but the style had little impact until 1946, when Harry Choate's hit recording 'Jole Bon' drew wider audiences. A revival in the 1980s popularized swingier Cajun zydeco music.

Western Swing Originating in the 1930s with Texan fiddler Bob Wills and fellow bandleader Milton Brown, western swing music featured a heavily bowed fiddle with guitars, electric mandolin and big-band instruments. The dance music is a hybrid of southwestern fiddle music, big-band swing, country and blues. Its popularity peaked in the 1940s and '50s, but the style had a resurgence in the 1970s with acts such as Asleep at the Wheel and Merle Haggard.

Honky-Tonk From the roadside saloons and dance halls of the South just prior to WWII, Ernest Tubb and Hank Williams brought drinking ballads preoccupied with broken relationships and the wilder side of life. Temporarily eclipsed by rock & roll in the 1950s, the style has enjoyed a resurgence since the '60s with performers such as George Jones and Buck Owens.

Rockabilly Elvis Presley was at the forefront of this new genre with his first recordings, which combined the country music and gospel he'd grown up hearing with the blues he heard on Beale St in Memphis. Carl Perkins and Roy Orbison also wrote and recorded classic rockabilly.

Contemporary Influenced by Willie Nelson's 'outlaw' movement, Loretta Lynn and the urban-cowboy genre in the early 1980s, today's mainstream country music is dominated by Garth Brooks look-alikes and sound-alikes who suit the marketing demographics of white baby boomers outgrowing rock & roll. On the flip side is the innovative retro country-punk of Nashville's BR5-49 and artists on the Dead Reckoning label; these performers are the cutting edge of the modern Nashville sound. A good sampler of alternative country is the CD *Nashville: the Other Side of the Alley* (Bloodshot Records).

the gold-plated interior. The Hank Williams Jr room, beautiful Gibson guitars and vintage film clips and recordings are also highlights.

When the hall of fame moved to spacious new digs in 2001, interaction became a big part of the experience. As well as live music, country-karaoke and line-dancing lessons, visitors can swipe a smart card at 'automatic music tellers' stationed around the displays and pick up a personalized CD on the way out. Now that's cool.

The hall is on the corner of 5th Ave S and Demonbreun St, one long block south of Broadway on the edge of downtown. It's open 9 am to 5 pm daily year-round (8 am to 6 pm in the summer). Admission is around $15.

Inquire at the Hall of Fame about tours of **RCA Studio B**, at 27 Music Square W.

Studio B is revered in musicians' circles for producing the 'Nashville sound.' The 1950s-style studio is touted to have launched more hit records than any other recording studio in the country. When Elvis recorded a Christmas album here in the dog days of summer, they had to truck in a tinseled tree and turn up the air-con before the session would go smoothly.

Ryman Auditorium Called 'the Mother Church of Country Music,' the Ryman Auditorium (☎ 615-254-1445), 116 5th Ave N, was home to the Grand Ole Opry for 31 years. Riverboat captain Thomas Ryman built this huge gabled brick tabernacle in 1890 and dedicated it to spiritual music after he 'got the call.' At his death in 1904 the hall was named in his honor and made available for a wide variety of performances. The most famous became known as the Grand Ole Opry after a radio announcer introduced the Saturday night Barn Dance with 'For the past hour we have been listening to music taken largely from the Grand Opera, but from now on we will present the Grand Ole Opry.'

In 1974 the Opry was moved to the Opryland complex on Hwy 155. In 1994, after an $8.5 million renovation, the Ryman reopened as a performance venue.

The auditorium is best seen during performances, which vary from quaint musical theater to classical concerts. The graceful interior is evocative even when there's no show on, but admission is steep for a self-guided tour of an empty theater. Adults pay $6, and it's $2.50 for children four to 11. It's open 8:30 am to 4 pm daily.

Tennessee State Museum Housed on three floors of the Performing Arts Center building downtown on 5th Ave N and Union St, this museum (☎ 615-741-2692) traces the state's history from the effigy pots and engraved gorgets (throat-protecting armor) of ancient tribes through pioneers, pillories, daguerreotypes, sabers and Confederate dollars. Exhibits explore Tennessee's strong abolitionist movement, which began in 1797, as well as the Ku Klux Klan. It's open 10 am to 5 pm Tuesday to Saturday and 1 to 5 pm Sunday (free).

The state's **military museum**, in the classical War Memorial Building across 6th Ave, covers conflicts from the Spanish-American War to WWII (free).

Hillsboro Village

Stretching along several blocks of 21st Ave S from S Blakemore to Acklen Aves, Hillsboro Village qualifies as a neighborhood. It's home to the famed Pancake Pantry (see Places to Eat, later in this section), an unassuming breakfast spot that is an industry hangout and has been the backdrop for several music videos. Rounding out the area are upscale restaurants off Belcourt, the old Belcourt Theater (now a concert venue), the refined Provence Café (☎ 615-386-0363) at No 1705, a great used-book store,

Bookman (☎ 615-383-6555) at No 1713, funky Fido cafe and Honky Tonk Hardware (☎ 615-383-2840) at No 1818, which sell records, books, souvenirs and assorted weird stuff along with a sprinkling of hardware. At 1805 21st Ave S, there's a brewpub, Bosco's, which serves food until 3 am.

To reach this neighborhood from downtown, turn left at the Broadway split to stay on Broadway and you'll end up here. From the freeway, take I-440 exit 3 and follow 21st Ave north a mile or so.

Centennial Park

The highlight of the Centennial Exposition held here in 1897 was a chicken wire and plaster reproduction of the Greek **Parthenon**. A concrete version stands today, 'the only full-scale reproduction in the world' (one would hope). Inside is a giant 42-foot statue of the Greek goddess Athena. Admission is $2.50 for adults, $1.25 for seniors and children. Mythology books, busts and pop-up Parthenons are available in the subterranean gift shop. It's closed Monday (also closed Sunday between October and March).

Centennial Park is the city's most popular spot for urban recreation; it's off West End Ave.

University Galleries

Between Hillsboro Village and Elliston Place, Vanderbilt University maintains a fine-arts gallery (☎ 615-322-0605) on campus at 23rd and West End Aves. It's free and open afternoons only.

The small **Van Vechten Gallery** (☎ 615-329-8720), at the corner of Dr DB Todd Blvd and Jackson St at Fisk University, houses more than 100 paintings collected by Alfred Stieglitz and donated by his widow, Georgia O'Keeffe. O'Keeffe's work is displayed along with paintings by Picasso, Renoir and Cézanne. Admission is free, but donations are encouraged. It's closed Monday and on university holidays.

While you're here, visit Fisk's African art collection in the **Aaron Douglas Gallery** on campus. Visitors might also want to see Jubilee Hall on Meharry Blvd.

Music Valley

Also known as Opryland, the **Grand Ole Opry House** (☎ 619-889-3060) is the queen of this manufactured heaven 10 miles from downtown off Hwy 155 (Briley Parkway) exit 11. It seats 4400 when it hosts the Grand Ole Opry show, which moved to these digs in 1974 from its home in the Ryman Auditorium. Performances are held on Friday and Saturday nights year-round (see Entertainment, later in this section). Guided tours backstage are offered once a day by reservation for $9.

There's a museum across the plaza from the Grand Old Opry House. It tells the story of the Opry with wax characters in colorful costumes – don't miss Patsy Cline's classic 1950s rec room diorama. Admission is free.

The **Opry Mills** mall (☎ 615-514-1100), 2820 Opryland Dr, is right by the theater complex. It's got the usual suspects, including an IMAX theater, regular movie theaters, theme restaurants and shops. Prior to 2000, the Opryland USA amusement park was on this site but the Nashville number crunchers decided there were more thrills in retail than roller coasters. The mall's hours are 10 am to 9:30 pm Monday to Saturday, 11 am to 8 pm Sunday.

The legendary Patsy Cline

The **Opryland Hotel** is a sight in itself and shouldn't be missed (see Places to Stay, later in this section).

Opposite the Opryland Hotel along McGavock Pike, there are three small museums tucked out behind some souvenir shops. The **Music Valley Car Museum** (☎ 615-885-7400), 2611 McGavock Pike, displays the 1981 DeLorean owned by George Jones, Elvis' limo, and a Cadillac that once belonged to Dolly Parton. **Music City Wax Museum** (☎ 615-883-3612), 2515 McGavock Pike, features about 50 frightful wax statues of country stars in original costumes. Its Sidewalk of the Stars sports the handprints, footprints and signatures of 250 stars. The **Willie Nelson Museum** (☎ 615-885-1515), 2613A McGavock Pike, is pretty cute: as well as the artist's gold and platinum records and guitars, brace yourself for life-size cutouts of Willie and his pigtails at every turn. In the shops attached to these museums, you can browse for guitar-shaped fly swatters, hillbilly outhouse toothpick holders, Elvis cookbooks, and playing cards with 52 dated photos of big-haired country-music stars. All three museums charge $3.50 for adults, $1.50 for children six to 12.

River taxis run along the Cumberland River between downtown Nashville and the Opryland dock about 10 miles downriver (see Getting Around, later in this section). Paddleboat rides are available aboard the four-deck *General Jackson* (☎ 615-871-6100) for $22 to $52 depending on whether it's a lunch or dinner cruise.

If you're driving, take Hwy 155 (Briley Parkway) to exit 12B. It costs $6 to park at the hotel. Parking at Opry Mills might be a better option, though fees may have been introduced there too. You could also conceivably park along Music Valley Dr and walk across; it's about a 10-minute walk to the hotel and 20 minutes to Opry Mills.

Shuttle buses run between the hotel, the Grand Ole Opry, Opry Mills and the KOA Kampground at the far end of Music Valley Dr; drivers will generally drop you at any destination in between. The fare is $3 roundtrip for adults. Buses leave every 15 to 20 minutes, but schedules are uncertain. If you're in Music Valley and have a boat to catch from the Opryland dock, you may be better off walking back down rather than waiting for the shuttle. The paved, all-access, well-lit path between the dock and the Opryland Hotel is under a mile.

The Hermitage

The historic home of Andrew Jackson, the Hermitage (☎ 615-889-2941) is northeast of town off Lebanon Pike at Old Hickory Blvd. Not only is the graceful mansion one of Nashville's prized historic house museums, but the Hermitage also serves as a monument to the state's most famous political figure. Starting his national political career as Tennessee's single representative even before Tennessee had officially gained statehood, Jackson went on to become the seventh US president. The modern visitor center introduces the life of Andrew Jackson with a short film.

The 1821 mansion was built in Federal style with Grecian columns added in the 1830s. It is nicely set among gardens. The big house was once the centerpiece of a self-sufficient cotton plantation of 1500 acres worked by 150 slaves.

Admission is $9.50 for adults, $8 for seniors, $4.50 for children six to 12 (under six free). A cafeteria on the premises serves an appealing buffet for around $6.

Other Antebellum Houses

In addition to the Hermitage, three other antebellum houses are open to the public.

The **Belle Meade Plantation** (☎ 615-356-0501), 5025 Harding Place, is an 1853 Greek revival mansion that was once the centerpiece of a 5300-acre plantation and thoroughbred stud farm. Portly President Taft once got stuck in the bathtub here. Admission is $10, $4 for children six to 12 (under six free), but you can walk the grounds for free.

The **Belmont Mansion** (☎ 615-460-5459), 1900 Belmont Blvd, dates from 1850. The villa was built as a summer home for Adelicia Acklen, who was one of the wealthiest women in America at the time. Admission is $6, $2 for children six to 12 (under six free).

Travelers Rest (☎ 615-832-8197), 636 Farrell Parkway (I-65 Harding Place exit), is the restored plantation home and outbuildings constructed as early as 1799 by Andrew Jackson's presidential campaign manager. Admission is $7, $3 for children six to 11; it's closed on Monday.

Frist Center for the Visual Arts

The grand old post office has been renovated and expanded to house this new gallery at Broadway and 10th Ave S. The center concentrates on bringing modern and contemporary art from major American museums to Nashville.

Cheekwood Museum of Art & Botanical Gardens

The grand 1920s mansion of the Cheek family, heirs to the Maxwell House coffee fortune, is now open to the public as a fine-arts museum and botanical gardens. The three-story neo-Georgian home is a work in itself – the lapis lazuli mantel is a highlight. Exhibits include a collection of 600 snuff bottles and Worcester porcelain. In the nearby contemporary art gallery there are some Warhols and well-curated changing exhibits.

The lovely 55-acre gardens host classical concerts by Vanderbilt musicians in summer. A woodland sculpture trail takes an hour or so to meander – the highlight is James Turrell's *Blue Pesher*.

Cheekwood (☎ 615-356-8000) is at 1200 Forest Park Drive, 8 miles from downtown; drive south from downtown on West End Ave and follow the signs. Admission is $9 for adults, $7 for seniors and students, $5 for children (under six free). It's open daily until 4:30pm. The refined Pineapple Rooms restaurant overlooks the wooded grounds; they'll arrange picnics if you want to eat outdoors.

Nashville Zoo at Grassmere

The Nashville Zoo (☎ 615-833-1534), 3777 Nolensville Rd, is a mile from I-65 and 2 miles from I-24 on the old Grassmere estate. It's a lovely cage-free zoo with alert animals, elephant rides and a gripping 'unseen world' exhibition, which has snakes and spiders. At the Grassmere Home there are farm animals and a cottage garden. Admission is $6 for adults, $4 for seniors and children three to 12. Parking is an additional $2. From April 1 to October 31, it's open 9 am to 6 pm daily (9 am to 4 pm in winter).

Parks & Activities

Six miles of easy to moderate hiking trails are located in the 1000-acre **Radnor Lake State Natural Area** (☎ 615-373-3467). It's nestled in the steep Overton Hills six miles south of downtown (directly west of I-65). The scenic sanctuary surrounding the 85-acre lake is considered Nashville's Walden Pond.

Parkland largely surrounds **J Percy Priest Reservoir**, 10 miles east of downtown. The district manager's office (☎ 615-889-1975), on the north shore west of the dam on Bell Rd (easily accessible from I-40 exit 221, Old Hickory Blvd), distributes maps of a dozen recreation areas around the lake. There are campsites and the lake is perfect for swimming and fishing (fishing licenses are required for anyone over 12).

Nashville Shores (☎ 615-889-7050), around the dam, is a water park with slides, a beach, paddle boats and mini-golf. Admission is $14 for adults, $11 for children three to 12. Sailboats and parasails are also available (☎ 615-884-8778). For camping and cabins see Places to Stay, later in this section.

Adjacent to Hwy 100 south, **Edwin & Percy Warner Parks** (☎ 615-370-8051) offer hiking, golfing and cycle trails in the wooded hills close to the landmark Loveless Cafe and the northern terminus of the Natchez Trace Parkway. The Natchez Trace itself is one of the most popular bicycle-touring routes in the US (see the Around Nashville section, later in this chapter).

Golfing is extremely popular and there are dozens of courses in the area. Recording moguls often tee off at the Hermitage Golf Course (☎ 615-847-4001), 3939 Old Hickory Blvd.

A mile south of Opryland, east of Hwy 155, **Wave Country** (☎ 615-885-1052) water park offers a wave pool, slides and floats. It's open in summer only. Admission is $6 for adults, $5 for children (four and under free).

In town, the Centennial Park Sportsplex (☎ 615-862-8490), off West End Ave, offers a swimming pool, tennis courts and an ice skating rink.

Cumberland Transit (☎ 615-327-2453), 2807 West End Ave, rents mountain bikes for $25 a day ($140 a week) and in-line skates for $7.50 a day.

Organized Tours

The proudly trashy Jugg Sisters dish dirt and cheese snacks on their Nash Trash Tours (☎ 800-342-2132), braking only for country stars. Tours depart Thursday to Sunday from the farmers market (see Places to Eat, later in this section) and cost $22 (book ahead).

Personalized black heritage tours can be arranged by calling Bill Daniel, who you can reach at ☎ 615-890-8173.

Special Events

January
A commemoration of the Battle of New Orleans takes place at the Hermitage on January 8, with a ceremony at Andrew Jackson's tomb.

February
Mid-month the Nashville Entertainment Association Extravaganza highlights new and emerging talent at various venues around town.

March
In early March the Trail of Tears is commemorated in Red Nations Remembering.

April
In mid-April the annual Tin Pan South music festival showcases songwriters; it's held at the Ryman and other venues. The last weekend in April sees the Country Music Marathon, a running race with country acts belting it out at 28 stages along the route.

May
In early May, the Tennessee Crafts Fair brings more than 150 artisans to Centennial Park. A rite of spring for the horsey set, the Iroquois Steeplechase features races and picnics in mid-May at Percy Warner Park. On Memorial Day weekend, gospel singing groups and choirs raise the roof at Opryland for Gospel Jubilee.

June
There's an Independent Film Festival in early

TENNESSEE

June at the Green Hills cinemas in the Green Hills shopping complex. In mid-June the American Artisan Festival at Centennial Park brings craftspeople from 35 states to display their wares. The Celtic Music & Summer Solstice Celebration revels in Scottish and Irish music, dance and culture at Travelers Rest (see Other Antebellum Houses, earlier in this section), generally on Fathers Day. Mid-month, the International Country Music Fan Fair at the fairgrounds and at Opryland draws over 20,000 fans to more than 35 hours of concerts by 100 artists.

July

On July 4 the Independence Day celebration at Riverfront Park is a family event with food and fireworks (no alcohol).

August

In mid-August, the Wilson County Fair takes place in Lebanon, 30 miles east of Nashville off I-40, exit 239. It's the largest fair in Tennessee, with lots of free entertainment.

September

The Italian Street Fair kicks the month off with pasta and partying in Centennial Park. On Labor Day weekend, gospel singing groups and choirs come together at Opryland for Gospel Jubilee. The Tennessee State Fair brings livestock, midway rides and arts and crafts to the fairgrounds; price varies. In mid-September, the African Street Festival at the Tennessee State University campus features poetry, rap, reggae, blues, jazz and gospel music along with food and fashions.

October

Late September or early October an Oktoberfest is held in the tiny Germantown historic district. In late October a powwow at the Hermitage Landing Recreation Area brings Native Americans from many different nations together for traditional dances and cultural arts.

November

Starting in late November, Christmas celebrations are scheduled at the Opryland Hotel, the zoo, Belle Meade and the Belmont Mansion – most run through early January.

December

In early December, the Christmas Parade enlivens downtown and the Nashville Ballet performs the *Nutcracker* at the Tennessee Performing Arts Center.

Places to Stay

The most distinctive lodgings in Nashville are high end, including the Opryland Hotel and historic hotels downtown. There are also a handful of deluxe hotels downtown and out in West End.

Camping Occupying 27 acres, the *Opryland KOA Kampground* (☎ 615-889-0282, 800-562-7789, 2626 Music Valley Dr) is at the tail end of the commercial strip between the river and highway north of Opryland (shuttle costs $3). The campground actually trails off into the woods, providing some spacious shady sites. It has 25 cabins, country music shows, a swimming pool and weekly church services. Tent sites cost $22; sites with full hookups cost $35.

The Army Corps of Engineers maintains several campgrounds around J Percy Priest Reservoir about 12 miles east of downtown. *Seven Points* (☎ 615-889-5198, 877-444-6777), off I-40 exit 221, Old Hickory Blvd, offers swimming and is open from April to November; sites cost $17 to $21 with hookups (premium for lakeside sites).

Nashville Shores (☎ 615-889-7050), off the same exit, has 150 campsites in its extensively developed recreation area. Tent camping is $10; full hookups are $30. Rustic log cabins are available starting at $45; classier six-bed cabins with bathrooms are $95 ($125 on weekends; two-night minimum). All accommodations are closed between December and March.

Motels There's a cluster of budget motels and fast-food joints north of downtown, west of I-65 exit 87B. Note that I-65 between here and downtown is often very congested.

Two low-end, well-tended options that serve a minimal continental breakfast are the 150-room *Knights Inn* (☎ 615-226-4500, 800-843-5644, 1360 Brick Church Pike) with singles/doubles for around $25/32, and the *Hallmark Inn* (☎ 615-228-2624, 309 W Trinity Lane) with rooms for $38/48.

The *Days Inn Downtown* (☎ 615-329-7466, 711 Union St) charges $80/88 for rooms near the capitol. You could walk all over downtown from here.

The *Quality Inn* (☎ 615-242-1631, 1407 Division St) in Music Row charges $49/59. The location isn't what it was when the

Country Music Hall of Fame was next door, but it's a decent place and there's live country music in the lounge most nights.

There's a stack of motels out by Opryland including *Fiddlers Inn North* (☎ 615-885-1440, 2410 Music Valley Dr) with rooms at $39/44 a single/double, and a *Holiday Inn Express* (☎ 615-889-0086, 2516 Music Valley Dr) with rooms that start around $60.

Hotels The gargantuan *Opryland Hotel* (☎ 615-889-1000, 2800 Opryland Dr) looks like a sentimentally designed space colony – 'a cross between a Victorian hothouse and a shopping mall' according to author Bill Bryson. Covering nine acres, the self-contained Opry-sphere features cascading waterfalls, boat rides, magnolia trees three stories tall and elevated walkways above the rainforest canopy. For most of its guests, it's Eden – the hotel's wedding consultants have their own telephone exchange. Rates start at around $200. Parking costs $6. It's under a mile to the river taxi dock; shuttles are available for $3 roundtrip.

The *Union Station Hotel* (☎ 615-726-1001, 800-331-2123, 1001 Broadway) was built in 1900 and grandly restored in 1986. It's a limestone fortress with castlelike buttresses, and its exclusive restaurant is one of the city's best. Rooms start at $129. It's centrally located if you're getting around by car, but too isolated for walking.

The elegant *Hermitage Hotel* (☎ 615-244-3121, 888-888-9414, 231 6th Ave N) has housed power brokers who do business downhill from the capitol since the 1920s. Suites start at $109. Even if you don't stay overnight, have a drink in the lobby bar and soak it up. You can walk all over downtown from here.

Places to Eat

The farmers market, along 8th Ave N at Jefferson St, has the greatest variety of cheap food in one spot. Though the market here, behind Capitol Hill, dates back 30 years, it now occupies a swank modern building with lots of air and light next to the wide lawns of the Bicentennial Mall. Markets sell exotic goods such as jackfruit, curries, tomatillos

and pickled okra, along with fresh produce. Food stands offer gyros, empanadas, muffulettas, Reubens and more. A branch of the popular local *Swett's* cafeteria serves meat-and-three plates (meat with three sides).

The *Mad Platter* (☎ 615-242-2563, 1239 6th Ave N), at Monroe St two blocks north of the farmers market, is tucked away in the tiny Germantown historic district of colorful Victorians and brick walkways. It's a very pleasant place, serving upscale eclectic food; coriander-seared trout with rhubarb-apple chutney is $21.50, but you can get away with lunch under $10.

For upscale dining in downtown proper, the classic *Merchants* (☎ 615-254-1892, 401 Broadway) overlooks the lower Broad scene from the dark wooden central bar and window tables all around. Down near the Arena, *Wolfy's* (☎ 615-251-1621, 425 Broadway) does good burgers and a fine Veggie Reuben; there's also live music. In the Union Station Hotel, *Arthur's* (☎ 615-255-1494, 1001 Broadway) serves $60 fixed-price dinners to the *Southern Living* set.

The true taste of Nashville can be best found in cinder-block cabins in the industrial zone south of Broadway. Meat-and-three spots spoon out heaping portions of mashed potatoes and gravy, turnip greens and cornbread dressing along with your choice of daily specials such as roast beef, fried whole catfish, meatloaf or fried oysters for around $5. Look for the line outside *Arnold's* (☎ 615-256-4455, 605 8th Ave S), at Division, or the *Pie Wagon* (☎ 615-256-5893, 118 12th Ave S), near Demonbreun – both are open weekdays only for breakfast and lunch. *Jack's Barbecue* (☎ 615-254-5715, 416A Broadway) dishes out hole-in-the-wall barbecue. Try the turkey plate.

The *Elliston Place Soda Shop* (☎ 615-327-1090, 2111 Elliston Place) serves soda fountain treats along with meat-and-three plates; it's open 6 am to 7:45 pm daily except Sunday. The *Abstract Café* (☎ 615-321-9033, 205 22nd Ave N) calls itself 'a groovy place to chill' – it's got salads, panini, local artwork and on weekends, local musicians playing 'anything but country' on the small stage.

TENNESSEE

Farther west, the bungalow Sylvan Park neighborhood tucks away **Sylvan Park Restaurant** (☎ 615-292-9275, 4502 Murphy Rd), which serves Southern food and homemade pies.

A cluster of restaurants on Broadway beyond the West End split includes the **Bound'ry** (☎ 615-321-3043, 911 20th Ave S), which delivers fancy fare to dressed-up trendies. Much more rollicking is the **South Street Smokehouse** (☎ 615-320-5555, 907 20th Ave S), which does crabs, enchiladas, po-boys, veggie platters and late-night snacks. Open for breakfast, lunch and dinner, **Noshville** (☎ 615-329-6675, 1918 Broadway) offers New York deli specialties (lox, borscht, pickles) to eat in its crisp chrome interior or take out.

In Hillsboro Village, anchoring the neighborhood and the city's culinary scene is the classic **Pancake Pantry** (☎ 615-383-9333, 1796 21st Ave S) – look for the line down Belcourt Ave. Silver dollars, Georgia peach pancakes and blintzes are among the dozens of variations that arrive steaming and dusted with powdered sugar. It opens at 6 am daily and stays open till 3 or 4 pm for all-day breakfast or classic Southern lunches.

Fido's (☎ 615-385-7959, 1812 21st Ave S) is a Bongo Java affiliate housed in the old Jones Pet Shop. You can get cereal, coffee, bagels, chili and cakes. The world-famous 'NunBun' – a cinnamon roll that bears the likeness of Mother Theresa – is shellacked at its sister store, **Bongo Java** (☎ 615-385-5282, 2007 Belcourt Blvd).

Nearby, **Sunset Grill** (☎ 615-486-3663, 2001 Belcourt Ave) has Californian-style cuisine and an annotated wine list. It attracts customers who get whipped up into people-spotting frenzies over their teriyaki stir-fry.

Continue south on 21st Ave a half-mile beyond Hillsboro Village to **Brown's Diner** (☎ 615-269-5509, 2102 Blair Blvd), at 21st Ave S, for burgers in what appears to be a long-abandoned train car.

Entertainment

Many talented country, folk, bluegrass, Southern rock, and blues musicians and songwriters play smoky honky-tonks, blues bars, seedy storefronts and organic cafes for tips. But there are, of course, also venues such as the Ryman Auditorium. *The Tennessean* has entertainment listings in its Friday and Sunday editions. The free alternative weekly *Nashville Scene*, distributed throughout the city, covers a range of local entertainment.

For high production values, the Gaylord Opry conglomerate delivers the traditional **Grand Ole Opry** (☎ 615-889-3060) at Opryland year-round on Friday and Saturday evenings for $20.50 to $22.50 a seat. The **Wildhorse Saloon** (☎ 615-902-8200, 120 2nd Ave N) offers free dance lessons daily between 4 and 9 pm. It also has entertainment every night and hosts quarterly TNN broadcasts.

The 'lower Broad' cowboy gulch on Broadway between 4th and 5th Aves has a string of clubs that start playing music at 10 am. The crown jewel is **Robert's Western World** (☎ 615-248-4818, 416 Broadway); in fact, it's the only place you need to go. The club, with its long wooden bar and vinyl booths, has been carved out of an old western-wear clothing store. The walls are lined with cowboy boots with exotic leather and colors.

In **Tootsie's Orchid Lounge** (☎ 615-726-0463, 422 Broadway), lower Broad's most venerated dive, cowboys perform upstairs and down and, as it gets later, often out into the street as well. Hold onto your drinks tightly when the band plays 'Rocky Top, Tennessee.'

Gibson's Caffé Milano (☎ 615-255-0073, 174 3rd Ave N) is a fancy supper club for

---

Rocky Top & Roll

Tennessee may be the only member of the US to boast a state song celebrating casual sex and illegal alcohol consumption. *Rocky Top* warbles wistfully for a girl 'wild as a mink but sweet as soda pop' and folk who 'get their corn from a jar,' ie, moonshine.

big-name performers who want an intimate crowd. Chet Atkins is a regular here, and it's also hosted Peter Frampton, Mary Chapin Carpenter, Yo-Yo Ma, Johnny Cash and Emmylou Harris. You can count on entertainment Thursday to Saturday nights.

The classic down-home place to hear some of the city's most talented musicians is the small, unassuming *Bluebird Cafe* (☎ 615-383-1461, 4104 Hillsboro Pike), in a strip shopping mall in suburban Green Hills (2½ miles south of I-440 exit 3). Singer-songwriters who sell off their commercial hits to big names save their heartfelt, soulful pieces for performances here. There are often two shows on weekend nights; the early show is often free, while there's a cover charge for the later one. *Douglas Corner Café* (☎ 615-298-1688, 2106 8th Ave S) is even more low-key and has open mic nights.

The *Radio Cafe* (☎ 615-262-1766, 1313 Woodland St), at 14th St N, two miles east of downtown, 1¼ miles from the I-65 overpass, is a small club that hosts surprisingly good live entertainment nightly except Sunday.

Rock and alternative music are played at the *Exit/In* (☎ 615-321-4400) on Elliston Place and at *12th & Porter* (☎ 615-254-7236, 114 12 Ave N), over the river. *328 Performance Hall* (☎ 615-259-3288, 328 4th Ave S) hosts medium-draw touring acts. *The End* (☎ 615-321-4400, 2219 Elliston Pl), behind the row of shops, is a dive bar where you can see local bands exorcising their country demons with speed metal.

The classic venue for bluegrass is the *Station Inn* (☎ 615-255-3307, 402 12th Ave S). *Indienet Record Store* (☎ 615-321-0882, 1707 Church St) admits all ages to punk shows in the back of its storefront.

Bourbon St Blues & Boogie Bar (☎ 615-242-5837, 220 Printers Alley) is the city's premier blues venue, with live music just about every night and Cajun food. Cover runs about $5 during the week and $7 on weekends.

The *Nashville Opera* (☎ 615-292-5710) and *Nashville Symphony Orchestra* (☎ 615-255-2787) perform at the Tennessee Performing Arts Center; the orchestra also

BR5-49

As the big red boot sign outside declares, Robert's Western World is the home of BR5-49, Nashville's retro-country group that is forging new ground for old country. Named after a phone number on a skit from the old TV show *Hee Haw*, BR5-49 features Gary Bennett and Chuck Mead as lead vocalists and guitarists, Don Herron on steel guitar, mandolin, dobro guitar and fiddle, Smilin' Jay McDowell on bass and Shaw Wilson on drums. The group performs wearing string ties, neckerchiefs and shirts that snap shut. Their CD *Live from Robert's* includes their 'Hillbilly Thang' and an X-rated anthem for a lost *Andy Griffith Show* episode.

gives free concerts in Centennial Park. The *Fisk Jubilee Singers* (☎ 615-329-9528) are a gospel group from Fisk University; don't miss their summer outdoor concerts if you're in town.

Vanderbilt University's *Blair School of Music* (☎ 615-322-7651) is renowned for its concerts.

Spectator Sports

The barnstorming Tennessee Titans (☎ 615-565-4000) made it to the Super Bowl in 1999, their first season in town. They play at Adelphia Coliseum, over the river from downtown.

The Nashville Predators (☎ 615-770-2300) play professional hockey at the

Gaylord Entertainment Center. Also, the Nashville Kats (☎ 615-254-5287) play arena football here from mid-April to mid-July. The Nashville Sounds (☎ 615-242-2371), a AAA baseball team associated with the Pittsburgh Pirates, play at Greer Stadium at 534 Chestnut St.

Nashville Speedway USA (☎ 615-726-1818) auto races growl at the Tennessee State Fairgrounds.

Shopping

Sequined denim vests, American flag ties and garters emblazoned with Jack Daniel's logos can be found all over town. The nightclub Robert's Western World sells stompin' boots. A select collection of vintage western wear is sold at Ranch Dressing (☎ 615-259-4163), 113 17th Ave S at Broadway.

Ernest Tubb's (☎ 615-255-7503), 417 Broadway, has a massive range of country and bluegrass. Tubb also has an outlet in Music Valley. Shop for records of all genres, new and used CDs, comic books and videos at Great Escape (☎ 615-327-0646), 1925 Broadway at Division St.

Fusion (☎ 615-297-7977), 2108 8th Ave S, is a neat, weird vintage decor shop.

A variety of things, including cheap socks ($2 per bundle), watches, swap-meet sunglasses, low-grade and low-cost clothes and linens, is sold at the farmers market on 8th Ave N at Jefferson.

Opry Mills is the flashiest mega-mall, and it's near the Music Valley outlet stores, which, for some visitors, are the coolest thing in Nashville.

Getting There & Away

Air Nine major carriers operate out of Nashville International Airport (8 miles east of downtown off I-40), including American, Continental, Delta, Northwest, Southwest and United. Not a major hub, Nashville can be more expensive to fly into than Memphis.

Continental, Northwest and Delta have roundtrip flights to New Orleans for as low as $100, though $250 is the average fare. Delta and United have roundtrip fares to Atlanta for around $220.

Bus Greyhound (☎ 615-255-3556) operates a busy station at 200 8th Ave S, between Demonbreun St and Clark Place (a two-block walk to Broadway).

Greyhound has eight buses daily to Memphis (four hours, $29/50 one-way/roundtrip), nine to Atlanta (six hours, $37/73), and six each to Birmingham (four hours, $28/54) and New Orleans (12 to 15 hours, $42/84).

Car Major car-rental companies are represented at the airport; their courtesy phones are near baggage claim.

The most scenic way to approach Nashville is along the Natchez Trace Parkway, which begins in Natchez, Mississippi, and terminates just south of Nashville off Hwy 100; see Around Nashville, later in this chapter.

Getting Around

Downtown is easily manageable on foot, and a river taxi is the best way to get from there to Opryland. But for most other attractions and districts, it's easiest to get around by car. Bicycling is possible – the streets are wide and flat, and drivers are courteous – but bikes are not a common sight in town. See Parks & Activities, earlier in this section, for bike and in-line skate rentals.

To/From the Airport MTA bus No 18 connects the airport and the downtown transit mall (Shelter C) for $1.45. It runs roughly every hour on weekdays, but has only four departures daily on weekends. Call ☎ 615-862-5950 for exact schedules.

Many hotels have complimentary shuttles for airport service; use courtesy phones near baggage claim and wait at the island outside.

Gray Line (☎ 615-883-5555) operates an airport express to major downtown and West End hotels for $9/15 one-way/roundtrip between 6 am and 11 pm. Buy a ticket at the Gray Line counter one floor below baggage claim.

Cab fare is about $17 to downtown (flag-fall from the airport is $2.70).

Car rental is available at the airport; see Getting There & Away, earlier.

Bus The Metropolitan Transit Authority (MTA; ☎ 615-862-5950) operates city bus service. Besides the No 18 airport route, another useful route is the No 3 West End, which runs frequently from downtown out to Cheekwood and Percy Warner Park. To get out to Opryland and Opry Mills, take the No 34, the Music Valley Express, or the No 27 to the Opryland Hotel. The fare is $1.45; exact change is required unless your trip is within the downtown area (bordered by the Cumberland River, Franklin St, I-40 and Jackson St), when your trip will cost a mere 25¢.

All routes originate and terminate at the transit mall downtown at Deaderick and 4th Ave N, a block and a half from the capitol.

Trolley MTA also operates a trolley-like shuttle between major tourist sights at the riverfront and out to Music Row. The fare is $1 (no change given). In the summer season, trolleys pass every 13 minutes.

Car In town, city streets are wide and drivers are generally courteous. Downtown is tricky to navigate with all the narrow one-way streets; it's best to park the car in a lot south of Broadway or a garage north of Broadway and wander around on foot. The I-40 Broadway exit is the most direct route downtown – from I-65 take the Woodland St exit.

The three interstate freeways around Nashville – I-40, I-65 and I-24 – combined with bypass routes I-440 and I-265 and Briley Parkway, create a complicated maze of intersections. While this provides ready access to much of Nashville, it's difficult for newcomers to navigate. Note particularly that directions may be given to cities that are unfamiliar and irrelevant to your metro route (to Birmingham or Chattanooga, Memphis or Paducah), that freeways split off abruptly, and that heavy 18-wheeler traffic can block vital signs and increase anxiety on the curved highways. Map out your route carefully to avoid wrong turns.

Taxi Try Allied Taxi (☎ 615-244-7433) or Music City Taxi (☎ 615-262-0451). Fares start at $1.50; add $1.50 for each additional mile.

River Taxi The Opryland river taxi (☎ 615-883-2211) runs along the Cumberland River between downtown and Opryland. The downtown dock is south of Fort Nashborough at Riverfront Park. The service runs daily in summer (weekends only the rest of the year), departing Opryland every even hour between 10 am and 10 pm and departing downtown every odd hour between 11 am and 9 pm. Tickets are $9/13 one-way/roundtrip for adults, $7/10 for children four to 11, and can be booked ahead.

Considering how vital rivers have been to the development of Southern cities, this is one of the few opportunities to travel one. This is also a peaceful alternative to congested freeway traffic.

AROUND NASHVILLE

Surrounding Nashville beyond the broad suburban development are middle Tennessee's forested hills cut by creeks and tributaries of the Cumberland River.

Sixteen miles northeast of Nashville in Goodlettsville, the **Museum of Beverage Containers & Advertising** (☎ 615-859-5236) displays 25,000 beer and soda cans – reportedly the largest such collection in the world. It's open daily except Sunday morning; admission is $4 (children under 13 free).

About 25 miles southwest of Nashville off Hwy 100, drivers pick up the **Natchez Trace Parkway**, which leads 450 miles southwest to Natchez, Mississippi, along what was an old Indian route and later a traders' footpath. This northern section is one of the most attractive stretches of the entire route, but slow going (50 mph speed limit, many bicyclists) as the road meanders through woods and around curves overlooking beautiful Tennessee pastureland.

To find the entrance to the trace, look for the *Loveless Motel & Cafe* (☎ *615-646-9700, 8400 Hwy 100*). Still operating as a cafe (but no longer a motel), the 1940s roadhouse serves ample portions of Southern

TENNESSEE

country cooking to city folk out for a day's drive. It's open 8 am to 9 pm daily (closed 2 to 5 pm Monday to Friday). On the weekend, make reservations or endure a long wait.

Southeast of Nashville past Murfreesboro (the geographic center of the state, marked by an obelisk), in Milton off Hwy 96, **Manuel's Cajun Country Store** (☎ 615-273-2312), on Main St, features Cajun music and dancing Friday and Saturday nights from 6:30 to 9 pm. The kitchen serves up fried alligator.

Off I-40 at exit 143, 70 miles west of Nashville near Hurrican Mills, **Loretta Lynn's ranch** (☎ 931-296-7700) is a museum to the 'Coal Miner's Daughter' housed in a restored old gristmill. Visitors can tour the downstairs of Lynn's antebellum home and see a re-creation of her childhood home. In summer the ranch is crawling with country-music fans; admission is free. There are various charges for canoes and horseback riding on the property. Camping ($17 to $20) is permitted.

SHELBYVILLE

Shelbyville, 50 miles south of Nashville on Hwys 41A and 231, is the epicenter of Tennessee Walking Horse activity (see the boxed text 'Tennessee Walking Horses'). If you drive into town on the backroads, you'll see a lot of happy-looking horses grazing in the fields. The Celebration, a 10-day festival in late August, draws 200,000 breeders, trainers and enthusiasts to the Calsonic Arena on the edge of town at 721 Whitthorne St. There's also a **Walking Horse Museum** in the arena (☎ 931-684-0314). To get there head north from the square and turn right into Madison St, go over two sets of lights, then turn left into Celebration Drive. Calsonic Arena is at the end of the street and the museum is in the building on your left. It's best to call ahead to make sure it's open.

Popes Cafe (☎ *931-684-9901, 120 East Side Square*) is a good old diner for southern plates, pies and coffee.

A diesel train chugs between Shelbyville and Wartrace, another horsey town, an hour

Tennessee Walking Horses

If you didn't know they were highly trained professionals, the high-stepping, head-bobbing Tennessee walking horses might look like they're impersonating pigeons walking on hot coals. Their gaits look pretty strange to the uninitiated, but riders swear that the walking horse travels smoother than a Cadillac on fresh blacktop.

During the Civil War, Confederate Pacers bred disloyally with Union Trotters, resulting in a smooth striding neddy that was later fused with thoroughbred, standard breed, Morgan and saddle horses to come up with the Tennessee walking horse in the late 19th century.

During the annual Celebration in Shelbyville, judges look for perfect execution of the walking horse's three gaits: the flat-footed walk (pigeon on hot coals), running walk (pigeon chased by cat) and the rocking chair canter (rocking chair chased by pigeon).

to the northeast. Call ☎ 931-695-5066 for information and reservations.

LYNCHBURG

At the **Jack Daniel's Distillery** (☎ 931-759-6180) in Lynchburg, off Hwy 55, hour-long tours start between 8 am and 4 pm every day and are free. You're led around at whiskey-making pace by laconic guides with wits as dry as the county. Owing to the local liquor laws, they can't offer samples but you're encouraged to take long sniffs of the distilling whiskey.

THE FARM

You can smell the patchouli as you get near Summertown, home of The Farm. This hippie commune was started in 1971 by a tie-dyed bunch of Californians led by Stephen Gaskin. Today the village-style community is home to about 200 people. It's impressive for its longevity as well as its solar power, permaculture garden and sustainable forest. Various festivals throughout the year include drumming, dancing, DJs, workshops and general feral heaven.

Visitors are welcome if they make arrangements in advance. Get in touch by calling ☎ 931-964-3574 or writing to the Welcome Center, 34 The Farm, Summertown TN 38483 (email thfarm@usit.net). You can camp on the grounds or stay in cabins or homes for a small fee. Summertown is at the junction of Hwys 240 and 20, east of the Natchez Trace.

Eastern Tennessee

Probably the least 'Southern' place in this guide, eastern Tennessee is a mostly rural region with unhurried towns dotting the hills and river valleys. Highlights for the visitor include the Great Smoky Mountains where you can bear-spot, hike and camp; the white waters of the Ocoee River, where the rafting is great; and a portion of the Appalachian Trail, the longest footpath in the world. Tennessee's most popular attraction, Dollywood, is in Pigeon Forge, a shoppertainment paradise at the foot of the Smokies. Eastern Tennessee's main urban areas are Knoxville and Chattanooga, pleasant small riverfront cities with lively college populations and good restaurants.

Note that eastern Tennessee operates on East Coast Time (one hour forward from Nashville).

KNOXVILLE
• pop 168,000

Knoxville was once Tennessee's territorial capital and is now the seat of the state university and two strong teams, the Tennessee Volunteers (Vols) football team and the Lady Vols basketball team. It's the biggest city in eastern Tennessee and a good base for exploring the region. Its own attractions are modest but you won't care while you're sinking an ale overlooking the river.

Orientation & Information
The Gateway visitor center (☎ 865-971-4440, 800-727-8045) heads up Volunteer Landing on the riverfront. As well as local information, there are displays on the area's national parks.

A short walk along the waterfront brings you past a couple of restaurants, a marina (you can rent pedal boats) and a blink-you-missed-it locomotive trail. The restored warehouse district known as the Old City splays out from Jackson Ave and Central St. There are lots of shops, restaurants, cafes and night spots here.

Things to See & Do
The **Knoxville Museum of Art** (☎ 865-525-6101) on 10th St has a permanent collection of prints, drawings and photographs and classy rotating exhibits. Admission is $7/6/5 adults/seniors/youths (under 12 free). It's open 10 am to 5 pm Tuesday to Saturday (till 9 pm on Friday). On Sunday it opens at noon. The city's visual centerpiece is the **Sunsphere**, the main remnant of 1982's World Fair but, owing to construction of a new convention center, it's closed until the year 2002.

On the edge of downtown are two noteworthy historical sights. The 1792 **Blount Mansion** (☎ 865-525-2375), at the corner of W Hill Ave and S Gay St, was the governor's residence when Knoxville served as the capital of all US territories south of the Ohio River. It's open 9:30 am to 4:30 pm Tuesday to Friday ($5/2.50 for adults/children). A few blocks up W Hill Ave is a replica of **James White's Fort** (☎ 865-525-6514). The original, built in 1786, was the town's first house ($4/2; closed Sunday).

The swank **Women's Basketball Hall of Fame** (☎ 865-633-9000) is on Hall of Fame Drive (you can't miss the massive orange basketball). It's expensive ($8 adults, $6 kids and seniors) but it's very well done and you can shoot baskets for as long as you want in the Athletic Playground downstairs.

Neyland Coliseum seats over 100,000 fans six times a year when the **UT football** team plays – and usually crushes – opposition teams in the Southeastern Conference. Call the university's athletic department for information (☎ 865-974-1212).

Places to Stay

The *KOA* (☎ 865-933-6393) at I-40/I-75 exit 374 is your best bet for camping close to the city. You'll also find a lot of RV parks about an hour south of the city heading toward Pigeon Forge and Gatlinburg.

There are no cheap motels in the center, but east or west of downtown on I-40 at exits 378 and 398, more than a dozen chain motels vie for customers. At exit 378, try *Budget Inn of America* (☎ 800-272-6232, 323 Cedar Bluff Rd); at exit 398, there's a *Super 8* (☎ 865-524-0855, 7585 Crosswood Blvd). Note that on fall weekends, when the university's football team is playing at home, the city is very full and motels hike rates.

Places to Eat

Tomato Head (☎ 865-637-4067), on Market Square downtown, is a popular hangout with massive $5 sandwiches. Bands sometimes play here. *Calhoun's* (☎ 865-673-3355) is a Tennessee-based chain of rib and barbecue restaurants, three of which are in the Knoxville area. Its location on the river, between downtown and the UT campus, is very popular. Also on the waterfront, right by the visitor center, *Riverside Tavern by Regas* (☎ 865-637-0303) is a bar and restaurant with four patios and a good selection of salads, wood-fired pizza and steaks. *11th Street Expresso House* (☎ 865-546-3003), in the small group of Victorian homes across from the art museum, is a good spot for coffee or a snack.

Cup A Joe (☎ 865-525-0012, 132 W Jackson St), in the Old City, is a spacious cafe that serves good coffee, sandwiches and cakes. *Patrick Sullivan's Saloon* (☎ 865-637-4255, 100 N Central Ave), also in the Old City, does classic American food in a great old building.

Getting There & Away

Knoxville is one of Greyhound's smaller hubs. The station (☎ 865-522-5144), 100 Magnolia Ave, has five daily buses to Chattanooga (two hours, $13), with continuing service to Atlanta (4½ hours, $24). There is service seven times a day to Nashville (3½

hours, $22), continuing on to Memphis (eight hours, $41), and there are three direct buses daily each to Washington, DC (12 hours, $55), and Chicago (12½ hours, $60).

AROUND KNOXVILLE

Just south of the city is the **Sam Houston Schoolhouse** (☎ 865-983-1550). Its namesake taught here for five months in 1812 before joining the army. He later achieved fame as a governor of Tennessee, president of the Republic of Texas, and US senator once Texas became a state. The one-room schoolhouse was built in 1794. It is set in a beautiful rural area off Route 33 (50¢; closed Monday). Go south for 10 miles from the center of Knoxville, turn left, then left again – it's well signposted.

Just over 20 miles northwest of Knoxville, **Oak Ridge** was created in 1942 when rural families were moved out and the fledgling nuclear weapons industry moved in as part of President Roosevelt's Manhattan Project. For five years the new city was not on any map, and though 75,000 workers and their families lived within its fenced perimeter, few outsiders knew of its existence.

Two uranium enrichment plants and one plutonium-producing nuclear reactor were the hub of Oak Ridge's activity. The plutonium was taken to New Mexico to use in nuclear weapons, eventually resulting in the bombs dropped on Hiroshima and Nagasaki.

Far from turning into a radioactive ghost town, postwar Oak Ridge developed into a thriving center for research into nuclear and other energy, robotics, artificial intelligence and machining.

The **American Museum of Science and Energy** (☎ 865-576-3200), 300 S Tulane Ave, tells the Oak Ridge story. It's open daily and admission is free. Pick up a map here to get out to the graphite reactor (no longer used, but very evocative) and other sites.

All the exhibits stress the environmental consciousness of facilities past and present, but nearby lakes have signs posted warning that catfish caught here might give you cancer.

GREAT SMOKY MOUNTAINS
National Park Area

Eastern Tennessee's most famous attractions are its mountains, centered on Great Smoky Mountains National Park, the most visited park in the country. The 520,000-acre park, which spreads into North Carolina, was established in 1934 and now draws some 10 million visitors annually. The park rises from an elevation of 840 feet to over 6600 feet. This, and its position at the point where northern and southern foliage and climate patterns meet, gives the park a particularly large variety of flora and fauna. There are more than 1500 species of flowering plants inside the park and 125 tree species. Over the course of a year, about 200 kinds of birds can be seen. There are also some 60 species of mammal, including the bears for which the park is famous.

The park's best-known sights are **Clingmans Dome**, at 6643 feet the highest point in the park (you can see seven states on a clear day!), and the dramatic twin summits of **Chimney Tops**. These and the popular hiking trails around Mt LeConte are all fairly close to Gatlinburg, Tennessee. The less-visited **Cades Cove** area features an 11-mile, one-way driving loop that is very popular with cyclists.

Summer is the peak season, and you can expect the park to be extremely crowded at any time from mid-May to the end of September. The least crowded area of the park (in relative terms) is Cades Cove, which is reached via the small town of Townsend.

On the Tennessee side, the Sugarlands Visitor Center (☎ 865-436-1291) is on the main access road from Gatlinburg. This road, US 441, crosses the park for 35 scenic miles to Cherokee, North Carolina, where there is another visitor center at Oconaluftee, North Carolina. Entrance to the park is free.

Backcountry hiking and camping are your best bet for avoiding the worst of the crowds; see Places to Stay, later in this section.

Gatlinburg

There are several gateway communities providing access to the park. The best

---

Appalachian Trail

The Appalachian Trail is a 2155-mile footpath that traverses 14 states from Maine to Georgia along the ridge tops of the Appalachian Mountain Range. In Tennessee the trail passes through the Cherokee National Forest (30 miles) and Great Smoky Mountains National Park, along the North Carolina border (70 miles). This section, which passes by Clingman's Dome (6643 feet), is the highest and wildest of the entire trail.

Appalachian trampers need to bring all their own supplies including water. You don't need a permit to walk the trail but you do need a permit to backcountry camp in the National Park (see Places to Stay in the Great Smoky Mountains section).

This part of the track is covered in detail in *The Appalachian Trail Guide to Tennessee-North Carolina*, available at the Greeneville ranger station (☎ 423-638-4109), 124 Austin St. To get advice on a more extensive odyssey, contact the Appalachian Trail Conference (☎ 304-535-6331, info@atconf.org), PO Box 807, Harpers Ferry, WV 25425-0807.

---

known, and most crowded, is Gatlinburg. Because the **Ober Gatlinburg Ski Area** (☎ 865-436-5423, fun@obergatlinburg.com) is just outside town, you'll find more services here in winter, when many of the shops, restaurants and motels at other park gateways may be closed. The ski area itself is small (three lifts, eight trails), and its season is short. In summer, you can take a chairlift up the mountain and ride a simulated bobsled.

There's a visitor center (☎ 865-436-2392, 800-267-7088) on US 441 at the third stoplight in town; it is open 8 am to 6 pm daily (Friday and Saturday till 8 pm; till 10 pm in summer).

If the mood strikes you, several celebrants offer more or less instant marriages in the area – Hillbilly Weddings (☎ 865-436-3817) promises no-frills hitchings. You can get a marriage license at Pigeon Forge City Hall (☎ 865-908-6613) for around $40.

Pigeon Forge

Six miles north of Gatlinburg, Pigeon Forge is an impossibly tacky complex of motels, mini-golf, outlet malls and country music theaters/restaurants, all of which have grown up in the shadow of **Dollywood** (☎ 865-428-9488), Dolly Parton's personal theme park.

The theme park is surprisingly pleasant: there are some great rides (the Tennessee Tornado is wicked), craft demonstrations, and an eagle sanctuary – plus, the setting is beautiful. Admission is $30 for anyone 12 or over, $21 for anyone under 12. Though the park is open only from mid-April to December (call ahead for exact hours), the town operates year-round as a clean-living family destination.

Places to Stay

There are over 1000 campsites inside the national park but it can be hard to find one in summer. Sites at three of the 10 developed campgrounds may be reserved – bookings are taken five months in advance (☎ 800-365-2267). Otherwise, it's first come, first served. Camping fees are $12 to $20 per night. Of the park's 10 campgrounds only Cades Cove and Smokemont are open year-round. The rest are open from spring (usually April) through October. A permit is required for backcountry camping; call ☎ 865-436-1297 for more information or drop into Gatlinburg's Sugarlands Visitor Center (see National Park Area, earlier).

Camping outside the park is possible at, among other spots, the **KOA** (☎ 865-453-7903, 2849 Middle Creek Rd) in Pigeon Forge, open April through November. Cottage rental is available at **Wa-Floy's Mountain Village** (☎ 865-436-5575, 3610 E Parkway), about 8 miles east of Gatlinburg. Prices here start at $35.

Accommodation costs in any of the gateway towns vary greatly from season to season. Spring is the cheapest time, with motel rooms under $30 easy to find. The real cheapies have rooms for around $20 –

Tennessee Mountain Lodge (☎ 865-453-4784, 800-446-1674, 3571 Parkway) even has waterbeds. Summer and the brief fall-foliage season are the most expensive. At that time, rooms can easily go for $100. Because of the ski area, Gatlinburg is also expensive in winter, though places that remain open in other areas, such as Townsend and Cherokee, North Carolina, are likely to be fairly cheap.

Places to Eat

Just about the only pleasant place to eat is the *Old Mill* (☎ 865-429-3463, 160 Old Mill Ave), Pigeon Forge's oldest building by about 170 years. *Mel's Diner* (☎ 865-429-2184) is a fake 1950s railroad eatery, but the food's fine and it's open 24 hours – turn south at Wears Valley Rd (traffic light No 3) and you'll see it on the left.

GREENEVILLE

The pleasant town of Greeneville (about 70 miles northeast of Knoxville) is where Andrew Johnson, Abraham Lincoln's hapless successor, got his start in politics. Johnson has the dubious distinction of being the first US president ever to be impeached.

The National Park Service now preserves Johnson's tailor shop, two residences, his gravesite and a statue as historical monuments. The visitor center (☎ 423-638-3551) is adjacent to the tailor shop at the corner of Depot and College Sts. Visiting the small museum outlining Johnson's life and career is free. The homestead (one of the residences), a few blocks away, can only be seen as part of a tour ($2; purchase tickets at the visitor center). It's all open daily.

One block away on College St is a small wooden cabin. This is a reproduction of the capitol of the short-lived 'State of Franklin,' which occupied the same site from 1784 to 88. Franklin was an attempt by some of the area's early settlers to break away from North Carolina, which then claimed the region. Congress never granted it statehood, however, and the territory was included in Tennessee when that state was formed a few years later.

JONESBOROUGH

Tennessee's oldest town was also the first place in the nation to publish an anti-slavery newspaper, the *Manumission Intelligencer*, in 1819. There's a storytelling festival here the first weekend of October, but it's a cute place to visit anytime of year. The visitor center (☎ 423-753-1010) is at 117 Boone St.

There's a slew of B&Bs in the small historical district. ***Hawley House B&B*** *(☎ 423-753-9223, bandb1793@xtn.net, 114 Woodrow Ave)* has rooms from $85 in a charming log and frame house; it's an easy stroll to all the action.

Main St is full of shops and cafes. ***Dillworth Diner*** *(☎ 423-753-9009, 105 E Main St)* has Southern cooking seven days a week, storytelling Tuesdays and music Fridays. It's open daily until 8 pm for lunch and dinner (lunch only on Sunday). Next door is the slightly more gourmet ***Cornbread's Coffee House*** *(☎ 423-753-8187, 107 E Main St)*, which does all-day breakfasts and lunches, and roasts coffee out back (closed Sunday).

CHATTANOOGA

• pop 155,000

Chattanooga was born of one of the great injustices of the early USA: the removal of the Cherokee along what became known as the Trail of Tears. One of the trail's starting points was Ross's Landing in what is now downtown Chattanooga.

Once the Indians were gone, the city grew quickly. It was a key strategic point during the Civil War, and several important battles were fought nearby at Lookout Mountain and Chickamauga. After the war it became a major transportation hub, hence the term 'Chattanooga Choo-Choo' – originally a reference to the Cincinnati Southern Railroad's passenger service from Cincinnati to Chattanooga and later the title of a Glenn Miller song.

In the 1960s, Chattanooga was struggling: it was run down with a stagnant economy and so dirty that city workers brought extra shirts to work. Over the past decade the city has been spruced and sparked up by revitalized industry, the aquarium and the prettied riverfront. It's an easygoing small city and, as the home of the Moon Pie, should be viewed fondly by all sweet tooths.

Orientation & Information

Downtown Chattanooga occupies a relatively small area between the Tennessee River and Martin Luther King Jr Blvd, centering on three parallel streets: Chestnut, Broad and Market. Lookout Mountain, the site of a major Civil War battle and home to a number of the city's attractions, is a few miles southwest of the center.

Most of Chattanooga's main sights are within a few blocks of the visitor center (☎ 423-756-8687, 800-322-3344), at the corner of 2nd and Broad Sts. It sells tickets

Trail of Tears

In October 1838, 18,000 Cherokees were driven from their homes in North Carolina, Georgia and Tennessee and herded at bayonet point into wagons. The wagon train clunked west for six months, passing through Chattanooga and Nashville, Tennessee, then traversing Kentucky, Illinois, Missouri and Arkansas before halting in Oklahoma.

The prime incentive for ridding the Smoky Mountain region of Native Americans was so that white Americans could scour the hills for gold. Rumors of gold in the Smokies were longstanding, but when an Indian boy sold a nugget to a white trader in 1828, the Cherokee land was inundated with white fortune hunters, many of whom murdered natives standing in their way.

Unofficial mayhem gave way to sanctioned iniquity when President Andrew Jackson and his successor President Van Buren ordered the army to drive the Cherokee west.

Of the Cherokees who began the journey, many of them barefoot and without warm clothes or blankets, 4000 fell victim to exposure, sickness and violence along the way.

TENNESSEE

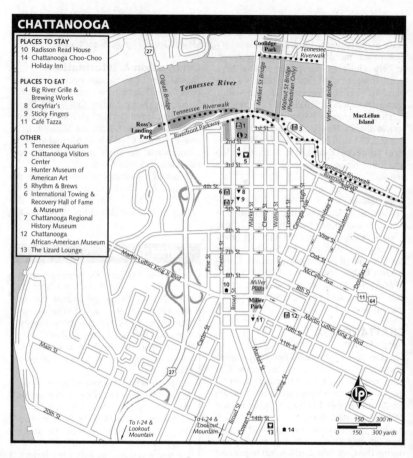

CHATTANOOGA

PLACES TO STAY
10 Radisson Read House
14 Chattanooga Choo-Choo
    Holiday Inn

PLACES TO EAT
4   Big River Grille &
    Brewing Works
8   Greyfriar's
9   Sticky Fingers
11 Café Tazza

OTHER
1   Tennessee Aquarium
2   Chattanooga Visitors
    Center
3   Hunter Museum of
    American Art
5   Rhythm & Brews
6   International Towing &
    Recovery Hall of Fame
    & Museum
7   Chattanooga Regional
    History Museum
12 Chattanooga
    African-American Museum
13 The Lizard Lounge

for most attractions, and is open 8:30 am to
5:30 pm daily.

Things to See & Do

The downtown area's architectural centerpiece is the freshwater **Tennessee Aquarium**
(☎ 800-262-0695). It's set up to mirror the
large river system running from the Appalachian Mountains to the Gulf of Mexico
and is often packed by school groups from
all over the region. Admission is $12/6.50 for
adults/children; it's open 10 am to 6 pm
daily (until 8 pm Friday to Sunday during
summer).

Nearby, Ross's Landing is a good place to
begin a riverfront stroll; you can walk right
across the Tennessee River on the
pedestrian-only Walnut Street Bridge to
Coolidge Park, where there is a climbing
wall.

Back on the south bank, the Bluff View
Art District to the east has upscale shops,
restaurants and galleries. The showpiece is
the **Hunter Museum of American Art**
(☎ 423-267-0968), which has works by Ansel
Adams and Willem de Kooning, and lovely
glass sculptures. Admission is $5/3/2.50 for
adults/students/children. It's open from

10 am to 4:30 pm Tuesday to Saturday and from 1 to 4:30 pm Sunday.

The **Chattanooga Regional History Museum** (☎ 423-265-3247), 400 Chestnut St, is well regarded. Admission is $4/3.50 for adults/children. It's open 10 am to 4:30 pm (from 11 am on weekends). Also worth a visit is the **Chattanooga African-American Museum** (☎ 423-266-8658), 200 Martin Luther King Jr Blvd, especially for the exhibit on Chattanooga native Bessie Smith. Admission is $5/3 (closed Sunday).

More bizarre is the **International Towing & Recovery Hall of Fame and Museum** (☎ 423-267-3132), 401 Broad St. It's a tow-truck museum (celebrating a Chattanoogan invention) and worth the $3.50 admission just for the curiosity value. The **National Knife Museum** (☎ 800-548-3907), 7201 Shallowford Rd, appeals to 'knife and other cutlery enthusiasts.' It's outside town near the Hamilton Place Mall, near I-75 exit 5.

Lookout Mountain

Some of Chattanooga's oldest and best-known attractions are outside the city at nearby Lookout Mountain. These include the Incline Railway (☎ 423-629-1411), a series of underground caverns called Ruby Falls (☎ 423-821-2544), and Rock City - a garden with a dramatic clifftop overlook that is just inside Georgia. All of these cost around $10 each, though combination tickets for two or more of the attractions are available. **Point Park**, at the mountain's summit, is part of the National Park Service's Chickamauga-Chattanooga National Military Park complex just over the Georgia border. The visitor center (☎ 706-866-9241) is open daily till 5:45 pm in summer. The visitor center is free, but admission to the park is $2.

Next door, **The Battles for Chattanooga Electric Map & Museum** (☎ 423-821-2812) is a private museum laying out Chattanooga's role in the Civil War. Admission is $5. The **Tennessee Civil War Museum** (☎ 423-821-4954) has an 'on-site living historian' to tell you all about it. It's right across from the Incline Railway. Admission to the museum is $6/5 for adults/children.

Places to Stay

There are many, many campgrounds around Chattanooga. The *KOA Chattanooga North* (☎ 423-472-8928) is 15 miles north of the city at I-75 exit 20. West of the city, try *Raccoon Mountain RV Park & Campground* (☎ 423-821-9403) at I-24 exit 174. It charges $20 for a full hookup and $12 for a tent site.

There are thousands of hotel rooms off Hwys I-24 and I-75 outside Chattanooga. The closest cheapies to downtown are in the less-than-wonderful area around I-24 exit 178. Your best bet here is *Comfort Suites* (☎ 423-265-0008), with singles/doubles at $69/79. The cheapest rooms at the exit are at *Motel 6* (☎ 423-265-7300), for $35/40. A bit farther out, at exit 174, you're spoiled for choice. There are eight or nine motels here, in addition to the campground mentioned above. The *Hampton Inn* (☎ 423-821-0595), at $59 in winter and $99 in summer, is probably the best value for your money. Of the real cheapies (and there are a lot of them), try the *Royal Inn* (☎ 423-821-6840), with rooms for about $45.

If you're going to splurge, there are really only two choices. The *Chattanooga Choo-Choo Holiday Inn* (☎ 423-266-5000, 1400 Market St) is in the old railway terminal. Many rooms are in converted railway carriages. Basic rates are $99 for regular rooms (nothing special) and $125 for rooms in the rail cars. Downtown, *Radisson Read House* (☎ 423-266-4121, 827 Broad St) is a meticulously restored early-20th-century hotel, parts of which date to the Civil War era. Try to get a room in the old part; they cost $110 to $120, though some discounts are often available.

Places to Eat

In the center, you can hardly do better than *Sticky Fingers* (☎ 423-265-7427, 420 Broad St). The locals agree that it has the best ribs in town. Rib dinners are $10 to $15 (try the sampler that gives you a taste of all four rib varieties). Another good bet is *Big River Grille & Brewing Works*, a brewpub on Broad St between 2nd and 3rd. The menu runs from salads and pasta to steaks and

Moon Me, Baby

The great Southern snack, the Moon Pie, consists of a dob of marshmallow sandwiched between two cookies and covered in chocolate. Its invention is attributed to an inspired traveling salesman who whispered his vision to a Chattanooga baker around 1919.

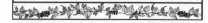

ribs. For breakfast or a quiet cup of coffee, try *Greyfriar's (406B Broad St)*. *Café Tazza (☎ 423-265-3032, 1010 Market St)* has coffee, food and poetry.

Entertainment

The place to listen to bands downtown is *Rhythm & Brews (☎ 423-267-4644, 221 Market St)*; there's usually something Wednesday through Saturday. *The Lizard Lounge (☎ 423-756-9899, 1407 Market St)* is a bit more edgy.

Getting There & Around

Chattanooga's modest airport is just east of the city. The Greyhound station (☎ 423-892-1277) is nearby at 960 Airport Rd at Shepherd St. There are eight buses daily to Atlanta (two hours, $15) and three per day to Nashville (three hours, $17). Change at

Nashville for Memphis ($37). There are also four buses per day to Knoxville (two hours, $12). From Knoxville, you can get direct buses to Washington, DC and Chicago.

Proving that it has no sense of nostalgia, Amtrak does *not* serve Chattanooga. The Tennessee Valley Railroad (☎ 423-894-8028) runs a steam train trip along some of the town's early rail lines.

For access to most downtown sights, ride the free electric shuttle buses that ply the center. The visitor center has a route map.

AROUND CHATTANOOGA

Ocoee Outdoors (☎ 800-533-7767) leads a two-hour, 5-mile rafting trip with 20 sets of rapids along the Ocoee River, the venue for the rafting events of the 1996 Olympics in Atlanta. The rapids run only when the Tennessee Valley Authority releases enough water into the river. They do this daily between Memorial Day and Labor Day and on weekends for a few weeks before and after. It's $33 Monday to Wednesday, $39 Thursday to Sunday, and you're advised to book a couple of weeks ahead. A longer trip takes in the Upper Ocoee trip (the actual Olympic course); it's recommended for experienced rafters only.

To find the rapids get off I-75 at exit 20 or 25 to Cleveland, 30 miles to the east of Chattanooga.

Glossary

AAA – American Automobile Association

antebellum – the period prior to the Civil War (Latin for 'before the war')

arpent – a French unit of land measurement equal to about 0.84 acres

Acadia – East Canadian region located between the St Lawrence River and Atlantic Ocean that included New Brunswick and part of Maine; it was settled by the French between 1632 and 1713

Acadiana – the region of southern Louisiana that was settled by the Acadian people; also known as Cajun Country

andouille – a French sausage made with tripe; the Creole version is ground pork in a casing made from smoked pig intestines; pronounced an-DOO-wee

Bama – short for Alabama and also for the University of Alabama

banquette – a diminutive form of 'banc,' meaning bench, applied to the early wooden boardwalks; it's sometimes used today to refer to sidewalks in New Orleans; pronounced BANE-kee

batture – a sedimentary deposit on the inward side of a river bend or other sluggish section on the river side of the *levee* crest; often covered with a tangled mass of trees and shrubs; pronounced BA-tur-ee

bayou – a natural canal of marshy water that is a tributary of the main river channel (from the Choctaw 'bayuk')

beignet – a deep-fried pastry that is New Orleans' version of the doughnut; typically it's sweet and covered with powdered sugar, but there are also savory versions flavored with either herbs or crab meat; pronounced ben-YEA

boudin – Cajun sausage filled with a mixture of pork, pork liver and rice; pronounced BOO-danh

bousillage – the mud and Spanish moss mixture sometimes used as a wall filler in *colombage* construction

briquette entre poteaux – the signature architectural style in New Orleans' French Quarter; similar to English half-timber construction and using bricks to fill the wall space between posts

brown and white cooking – slang for 'meat and potatoes'

café au lait – mixture of coffee and steamed milk

Cajun – a corruption of 'Acadian' referring to Louisianans descended from French-speaking colonists exiled from *Acadia* in the 18th century; may also apply to other rural settlers who live amid Cajuns

carnival – a festival held just before Lent; in New Orleans, locals often refer to Mardi Gras as 'carnival'

carpetbagger – a derogatory name given to itinerant financial or political opportunists, particularly Northerners in the reconstructed South, who carried their possessions in heavy cloth satchels; their Southern accomplices were branded as 'scalawags'

cataract – a waterfall

chantilly – a dessert topping of whipped cream with sugar and possibly a liqueur

chenier – a beach ridge formed above swamp deposits, typically covered with *live oaks* (from the French word 'chène,' oak)

chicken-fried – a breaded and deep-fried piece of meat, usually steak or pork chops, served with gravy

chicory – a relative of endive used as a coffee substitute; Creole coffee is typically a blend of coffee beans (60%) and roasted chicory root (40%)

chitlins – chitterling (pig intestine) sausages

Code Noir – the Black Code adopted by the French administration in 1724 that regulated the treatment and rights of free people of color and slaves; free people of color were accorded the rights of full citizenship except that they could not vote, hold public office or marry a white person

colombage – a type of construction using heavy timbers (horizontal, vertical and diagonal) with mortise and tenon joints

Confederacy – the 11 Southern states that seceded from the United States of America in 1860 and 1861

corvée – slave or statute labor applied to public works; plantation owners were expected to supply some slaves to maintain *levees* or public roads adjacent to their land

Courir de Mardi Gras – a horseback run through Cajun prairie country during Mardi Gras; bands of masked and costumed men ride from house to house singing and dancing in exchange for ingredients used to cook a community *gumbo*

cracklins – fried strips of pork skin and fat, considered a snack food

Creole – first coined in the early 18th century to describe children born of French immigrants in Louisiana, and, later, the children of the slaves of these immigrants; after the Civil War the term encompassed free Creoles of color; these days persons descended from any of the above cultures are considered Creole

CSA – Confederate States of America

dirty rice – white rice cooked with small quantities of chicken giblets or ground pork, along with green onions, peppers, celery and herbs and spices

dogtrot – roofed breezeway between living quarters and kitchen

dressed – a 'dressed' *po-boy* sandwich comes with lettuce, tomato and mayonnaise

entresol – the mezzanine-like area of low rooms between the ground floor and the 1st floor; in many French Quarter buildings the entresol was used for storage

étouffée – a spicy tomato-based stew that typically includes crawfish or shrimp and is served with rice; pronounced eh-too-fay

fais-do-do – a Cajun house dance

feed-and-seed – a store selling livestock feed and crop seed

filé – ground sassafras leaves used to thicken sauces

frottoir – a musical instrument, resembling a metal rubbing board, that is worn over the chest and played percussively, especially in *zydeco* music

gallery – a balcony

gens de couleur libre – literally 'free men of color,' this was the term that identified unenslaved blacks in French-speaking, antebellum Louisiana

go-cup – a plastic container provided for patrons at bars so that they can transfer their beverage from a bottle or glass as they leave; in New Orleans it is legal to drink alcoholic beverages in the street, but it's illegal to carry an open glass container

Grand Dérangement – the great dispersal of Acadians following the 18th-century colonial wars between England and France; about 10,000 Acadians were deported from Nova Scotia by the English in 1755

gris-gris – magical objects having curative, protective or evil properties; used in the Yoruba religious practice of voodoo; pronounced gree-gree

grits – coarsely ground *hominy* prepared as a mush and served with breakfast throughout the South; it picks up the flavor of whatever is ladled over it, which is often butter or gravy

gumbo – Louisiana's best loved soup; it contains seafood or chicken, and depending on whether it is made in a Creole or Cajun kitchen is thickened by either okra or *filé* powder, respectively

hominy – hulled and dried corn kernels, usually boiled and eaten as *grits*

hookup – a facility at an *RV* campsite that connects a vehicle to electricity, water, sewer and even cable TV

hushpuppy – a bread substitute served with many Southern meals; made from deep-fried balls of cornmeal and onion

jambalaya – a one-dish meal of rice cooked with onions, peppers, celery, ham, sausage and whatever else is on hand

krewe – a group whose members participate in the Mardi Gras parades

Ku Klux Klan – an organization, founded in 1866, that espouses white supremacy; although outlawed by the federal government in 1870, it has secretly conducted a campaign of violence against blacks, Jews and others whom they accuse of betraying the white race; often abbreviated to KKK

lagniappe – a small gift from a store owner or friend; literally, a 'little something extra'; pronounced LAN-yap

laissez les bons temps rouler – to have fun; literally, 'let the good times roll'

levee – a raised embankment that prevents a river from flooding

live oak – an evergreen oak indigenous to Mexico and the US

Lundi Gras – the Monday before Mardi Gras

making groceries – local parlance for the act of grocery shopping

Mardi Gras – 'Fat Tuesday,' the day before Ash Wednesday; the carnival period leading up to Lenten fasting, usually celebrated with masquerade balls and costume parades

marsh – wetland area predominantly covered with grasses rather than trees

meat-and-three – a set-price meal that includes a meat dish plus three side orders

meunière – a cooking style where food, usually fish, is seasoned, coated lightly with flour and pan-fried in butter; it's then served with a lemon-butter sauce; pronounced muhn-YAIR

mirliton – an indigenous pear-shaped vegetable with a hard shell that is cooked like squash and stuffed with either ham or shrimp and spicy dressing; also called chayote

mojo – a voodoo charm

Moon Pie – a chocolate-covered, marshmallow-filled cookie treat popular in the South

muffuletta – an enormous sandwich of ham, hard salami, provolone and olive salad piled onto a loaf of Italian bread liberally sprinkled with olive oil and vinegar

NPR – National Public Radio; a noncommercial, listener-supported broadcast organization that produces and distributes news and cultural programs via a network of loosely affiliated radio stations throughout the US

NPS – National Park Service

pain perdu – New Orleans' version of French toast; French for 'lost bread'

parish – an administrative subdivision in Louisiana that corresponds to a county in other US states

picayune – something of little value

pirogue – a dugout canoe traditionally carved by burning the center of a log and scraping out the embers; modern pirogues are shallow-draft vessels often made from plywood

po-boy – a submarine-style sandwich served on fresh French bread; fried oysters, soft-shell crabs, catfish and deli meats are offered as fillings

praline – a dessert made from caramelized sugar and nuts

R&B – abbreviation for rhythm & blues; a musical style that was developed by African-Americans that combines blues and jazz

Reconstruction – the postwar period (1865–77) during which the states of the *Confederacy* were controlled by the federal government before being readmitted into the *Union*

red beans and rice – a spicy bean stew with peppers and a hunk of salt pork or *tasso*; often served with a piece of *andouille* sausage

rémoulade – a mayonnaise-based sauce with a variety of ingredients such as pickles, herbs, capers and mustard; crawfish or shrimp rémoulade is often a cold noodle salad; pronounced ray-moo-LAHD

réveillon – a traditional Creole Christmas Eve feast

roux – a mixture of flour and butter or oil that is slowly heated and then used as a thickener in Cajun soups and sauces; pronounced roo

RV – recreational vehicle; also known as 'motor home'

second line – the partying group that follows parading musicians

swamp – a permanently waterlogged area that often supports trees

tasso – highly spiced cured pork or beef that's smoked for two days; small quantities are used to flavor many Creole and Cajun dishes

Union – of or relating to the United States of America during the Civil War

USFS – United States Forest Service

Vieux Carré – literally, 'Old Square,' this is what tourists are more likely to know as the French Quarter in New Orleans; pronounced voo car-RAY

what and what – Southern idiom meaning 'whatever' or 'it doesn't matter'; eg, 'Do you want a red cupcake, blue cupcake, or what and what?'

WPA – Works Progress (later Works Projects) Administration; a Depression-era program established to increase employment by funding public works such as roads and the beautification of public structures

y'at – an expression used by people with heavy New Orleans accents; these people say the greeting 'Where y'at?' using a very broad 'a'

zydeco – fast syncopated dance music influenced by Cajun, African-American and Afro-Caribbean cultures; it is often a combination of *R&B* and Cajun with French lyrics; bands typically feature guitar, accordion and *frottoir*

LONELY PLANET

You already know that Lonely Planet produces more than this one guidebook, but you might not be aware of the other products we have on this region. Here is a selection of titles which you may want to check out as well:

Hiking in the USA
ISBN 0 86442 600 3
US$24.99 • UK£14.99 • 179FF

Florida
ISBN 0 86442 745 X
US$19.95 • UK£13.99 • 160FF

Available wherever books are sold.

Index

Abbreviations

AL – Alabama
LA – Louisiana

MS – Mississippi

TN – Tennessee

Text

A

AAA 64-5, 74, 87
Abbeville (LA) 261-2
Abita Springs (LA) 209-10, 211
Acadian Village (LA) 272-3
Acadians. *See* Cajuns
accommodations 71, 92-6
Adamsville (TN) 495
African Village in America (AL) 416
African-Americans. *See also* Civil Rights movement; racism; slavery
history 18, 19, 26-32, 42-3, 74, 75, 237, 477-8, 498
museums 160-2, 170, 223, 307, 319, 361-2, 385, 449, 454, 460, 521
music 52, 57, 62
politics 41
population 43, 342, 475
religion 59, 60, 156-7, 449-50
tours 176
travelers 82-3
AfricaTown (AL) 461
AIDS 67, 81
air travel 102-9, 112
Alabama 404-70, **405**
economy 407-8
geography 406-7
government & politics 406
history 404, 406
state parks 409-10
Alabama Jazz Hall of Fame 415

Alabama Music Hall of Fame 435
Alabama State Capitol 442
alcohol 88, 99, 120, 199. *See also* bars
Alexandria (LA) 305-10
alligators 14, 38, 252-3, 268
American Automobile Association. *See* AAA
Amistad Research Center (LA) 170
Anderson, Walter 378, 379
Angola Prison (LA) 241
Anniston (AL) 422-4
Anniston Museum of Natural History (AL) 422-3
antiques 201-2
Appalachian Trail 517
aquariums 164, 254, 373-4, 520
architecture 48-9, 74, 384-5
armadillos 39, 316
Armstrong, Louis 50-1, 52, 76, 160, 196, 259
art galleries
LA 170-1, 201, 210, 231, 262, 274, 331
MS 363
TN 504
ATMs 70
Audubon, John James 38, 237, 238
Audubon Zoological Gardens (LA) 169
Ave Maria Grotto (AL) 438
Avery Island (LA) 260

B

Backstreet Museum (LA) 160-2

Barataria Preserve (LA) 205, 207
bars 198-200, 213, 284
baseball 100-1, 417
basketball 101
Batiste, Alvin 224, 225
Baton Rouge (LA) 227-36, **228, 230**
Bay St Louis (MS) 377
Bayou Folk Museum (LA) 303
Bayou Segnette State Park (LA) 208-9
bayous 34, 251-2
beaches 91, 374, 467
Bechet, Sidney 50, 51, 160
Belzoni (MS) 355
Berman Museum of World History (AL) 423
bicycling 91-2, 116, 117
  AL 423
  LA 174, 209, 239, 251, 283, 316
  MS 389
  TN 507, 517
Biedenharn Museum & Gardens (LA) 318-9
Bienville, Jean-Baptiste Le Moyne, Sieur de 18, 127, 171, 456-7
Biloxi (MS) 372-6, **373**
Biloxi Indians 16, 18
birds
  species 38
  watching 213, 239, 240, 255, 263, 273, 290, 468, 517
Birmingham (AL) 410-22, **411, 412-3**
Birmingham Civil Rights Institute (AL) 414

Bold indicates maps.

Bold indicates maps.

Bold indicates maps.

Boxed Text

MAP LEGEND

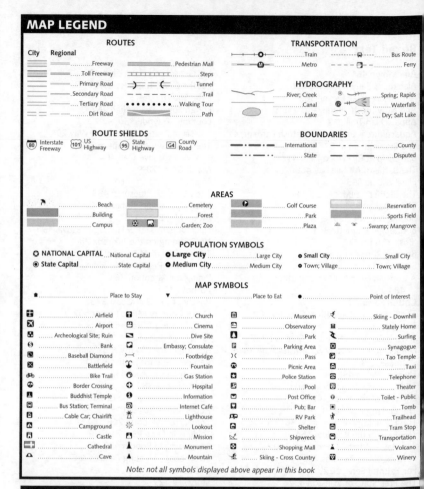

ROUTES

City	Regional	
		....Freeway
		....Toll Freeway
		....Primary Road
		....Secondary Road
		....Tertiary Road
		....Dirt Road

Pedestrian Mall
Steps
Tunnel
Trail
Walking Tour
Path

TRANSPORTATION

Train
Metro
Bus Route
Ferry

HYDROGRAPHY

River; Creek
Canal
Lake
Spring; Rapids
Waterfalls
Dry; Salt Lake

ROUTE SHIELDS

Interstate Freeway (80)
US Highway (101)
State Highway (95)
County Road (G4)

BOUNDARIES

International
State
County
Disputed

AREAS

Beach
Building
Campus
Cemetery
Forest
Garden; Zoo
Golf Course
Park
Plaza
Reservation
Sports Field
Swamp; Mangrove

POPULATION SYMBOLS

✪ NATIONAL CAPITAL ...National Capital
◉ State Capital ...State Capital
● Large City ...Large City
● Medium City ...Medium City
● Small City ...Small City
● Town; Village ...Town; Village

MAP SYMBOLS

■ ...Place to Stay
▼ ...Place to Eat
● ...Point of Interest

Airfield	Church	Museum	Skiing - Downhill
Airport	Cinema	Observatory	Stately Home
Archeological Site; Ruin	Dive Site	Park	Surfing
Bank	Embassy; Consulate	Parking Area	Synagogue
Baseball Diamond	Footbridge	Pass	Tao Temple
Battlefield	Fountain	Picnic Area	Taxi
Bike Trail	Gas Station	Police Station	Telephone
Border Crossing	Hospital	Pool	Theater
Buddhist Temple	Information	Post Office	Toilet - Public
Bus Station; Terminal	Internet Café	Pub; Bar	Tomb
Cable Car; Chairlift	Lighthouse	RV Park	Trailhead
Campground	Lookout	Shelter	Tram Stop
Castle	Mission	Shipwreck	Transportation
Cathedral	Monument	Shopping Mall	Volcano
Cave	Mountain	Skiing - Cross Country	Winery

Note: not all symbols displayed above appear in this book

LONELY PLANET OFFICES

Australia
Locked Bag 1, Footscray, Victoria 3011
☎ 03 9689 4666 fax 03 9689 6833
email talk2us@lonelyplanet.com.au

USA
150 Linden Street, Oakland, California 94607
☎ 510 893 8555, TOLL FREE 800 275 8555
fax 510 893 8572
email info@lonelyplanet.com

UK
10a Spring Place, London NW5 3BH
☎ 020 7428 4800 fax 020 7428 4828
email go@lonelyplanet.co.uk

France
1 rue du Dahomey, 75011 Paris
☎ 01 55 25 33 00 fax 01 55 25 33 01
email bip@lonelyplanet.fr
www.lonelyplanet.fr

World Wide Web: www.lonelyplanet.com *or* AOL keyword: lp
Lonely Planet Images: lpi@lonelyplanet.com.au